Decision Making:
Recent Developments and Worldwide Applications

T0189393

Applied Optimization

Volume 45

Series Editors:

Panos M. Pardalos
University of Florida, U.S.A.

Donald Hearn
University of Florida, U.S.A.

The titles published in this series are listed at the end of this volume.

Decision Making: Recent Developments and Worldwide Applications

Edited by

Stelios H. Zanakis

Florida International University,
College of Business Administration,
Decision Science & Information Systems Department,
Miami, Florida, U.S.A.

Georgios Doukidis

Athens University of Economics & Business,
Department of Management Science and Technology,
Athens, Greece

and

Constantin Zopounidis

Technical University of Crete,
Department of Production Engineering and Management,
Financial Engineering Laboratory,
University Campus, Chania, Greece

KLUWER ACADEMIC PUBLISHERS
DORDRECHT / BOSTON / LONDON

Library of Congress Cataloging-in-Publication Data

Decision making : recent developments and worldwide applications / edited by Stelios H. Zanakis, Georgios Doukidis, Constantin Zopounidis.
    p. cm. -- (Applied optimization ; v. 45)
    A selection of 31 papers representative of the 700 presented at the 5th International Conference of the Decision Sciences Institute held in Athens, Greece, July 4-7, 1999. Includes index.

    1. Decision making--Data processing--Congresses. 2. Decision support systems--Congresses. 3. Management information systems--Congresses. 4. Business--Data processing--Congresses. 5. Education--Data processing--Congresses. 6. Environmental protection--Data processing--Congresses. 7. Health services administration--Data processing--Congresses. 8. Mathematical optimization--Congresses. I. Zanakis, S. H. II. Doukidis, Georgios I., 1958- III. Zopounidis, Constantin. IV. Decision Sciences Institute. International Meeting (5th : 1999 : Athens, Greece) V. Series.

HD30.23 .D3826 2000
658.4'03--dc21

00-064701

ISBN 978-1-4419-4839-7

Published by Kluwer Academic Publishers,
P.O. Box 17, 3300 AA Dordrecht, The Netherlands.

Sold and distributed in North, Central and South America
by Kluwer Academic Publishers,
101 Philip Drive, Norwell, MA 02061, U.S.A.

In all other countries, sold and distributed
by Kluwer Academic Publishers,
P.O. Box 322, 3300 AH Dordrecht, The Netherlands.

Printed on acid-free paper

This volume is dedicated to our wives:

Eleni

Lina

Kleanthi

CONTENTS

EDITORIAL   xi

1. MANAGEMENT INFORMATION SYSTEMS

Empirical assessment of information technology chargeback systems decisions   3
D.H. Drury

Lessons learnt from the successful adoption of an ERP: The central role of trust   17
D. Gefen

Simultaneous analysis of heterogenous databases on the web: The ADDSIA project   31
J.M. Lamb, C.R. Smart

2. EDUCATION INNOVATIONS & DISTANCE LEARNING

Decision support for the management of admissions to academic programs   49
K.S. Dhir, W.H. Platt, G. Watts

The use of tacit knowledge in selection decisions in universities   65
M.A. Barrett, L.K. Hort

3. INTERNATIONAL BUSINESS

Role of political violence in foreign direct investment decisions   83
H. Singh

On the stability of countries' national technological systems   97
W. Nasierowski, F.J. Arcelus

4. MARKETING

Marketing of differentiated fresh produce   115
G. Baourakis, E. Lassithiotaki, P.M. Pardalos

A decision support system for the seller's return problem in the product line design   131
G. Alexouda, K. Paparrizos

5. FINANCE AND BANKING

Portfolio performance measures: A brief survey and hypothesis testing 143
G.L. Ghai, T.E. Pactwa, A.J. Prakash

A system dynamics model of stock price movements 157
P.L. Kunsch, M. Theys, A. Chevalier, J.-P. Iacopetta

Information effects on the accuracy of neural network financial forecasting 173
S. Walczak

Is the Taiwan stock market efficient? 183
J.P. Gupta, I.M. Pandey, Chen Chao-Fu

The dynamics of implied volatility surfaces 197
G. Skiadopoulos, S. Hodges, L. Clewlow

Application of nonstationary Markovian models to risk management in
automobile leasing 213
D.L. Smith, Y. Wu, D. Matthew

6. OPTIMIZATION & DECISION MAKING

Decision making Under Various Types of Uncertainty 233
R.R. Yager

Decision aid in the optimization of the interval objective function 251
C.A. Antunes, J. Clímaco

A fuzzy extension of a mixed integer MOLP model for solving the power
generation expansion problem 263
G. Mavrotas, D. Diakoulaki

Management science for marine petroleum logistics 279
E.D. Chajakis

7. MULTI-CRITERIA DECISION ANALYSIS, AID & PRACTICE

Dealing with missing data in rough set analysis of multi-attribute and
multi-criteria decision problems 295
S. Greco, B. Matarazzo, R. Slowinski

Cardinal value measurement with MACBETH 317
C. A. Bana e Costa, J.-C. Vansnick

Inferring a multicriteria preference model for rural development projects evaluation 331
E. Krassadaki, Y. Siskos

An adaptable framework for educational software evaluation 347
I. Stamelos, I. Refanidis, P. Katsaros, A. Tsoukias, I. Vlahavas, A. Pombortsis

Assessing country risk using a multi–group discrimination method: A comparative analysis

M. Doumpos, K. Pentaraki, C. Zopounidis, C. Agorastos

361

8. DECISION SUPPORT SYSTEMS AND INFORMATION TECHNOLOGY

RODOS: Decision support for nuclear emergencies

J. Bartzis, J. Ehrhardt, S. French, J. Lochard, M. Morrey, K.N. Papamichail, K. Sinkko, A. Sohier

381

DSS for the evaluation of national IT infrastructure investments: A study of cable television in Greece

G.M. Giaglis, K.M. Manikas, V. Pergioudakis, G.I. Doukidis, P. Miliotis

397

Global IT outsourcing decisions: Contract structure, negotiations, and global deal teams

S.T. Huhn, R.A. Holloway, B.A. Potter, R.A. Berry

413

Using Internet multimedia database information systems for decision support in conservation planning

M. Angelides, M.C. Angelides

425

An interactive workload and risk balancing model and decision support system for probationer assignment

J.R. Baker, A.C. Saydam, P.K. Lattimore

443

9. HEALTH CARE PLANNING & HOSPITAL OPERATIONS

A goal programming scheme to determine the budget assignment among the hospitals of a sanitary system

J.J. Martín, M.P. López del Amo, R. Caballero, T. Gómez, J. Molina, F. Ruiz

459

A simulation model to evaluate the interaction between acute, rehabilitation, long stay care and the community

E. El-Darzi, C. Vasilakis, T.J. Chaussalet, P.H. Millard

475

AUTHOR INDEX

487

EDITORIAL

Decision-making has become a complicated and integrated process, within a firm, an industry and globally. The continuous advances in information technology and the rapid changes in the international business environment, necessitate a change in the point of view through which decision making problems are addressed. Academic researchers and practitioners of business administration, management science and operations research are now seeking to integrate the human factor and the existing practical experiences with the sophistication achieved through the advances in research and technology, to gain managerial and decision making efficiency. The accomplishment of this integration will be a major breakthrough and thrust towards the improvement of the quality of decisions taken within the business and public administration context.

Several international scientific associations have been formed to allow the communication between academic researchers and professionals on issues relevant to the aforementioned integration. Among them, the Decision Sciences Institute is an interdisciplinary, international organization dedicated to the advancement of the science and practice of education and research about business decisions. To pursue this mission, the Institute facilitates the development and dissemination of knowledge in the diverse disciplines of the decision sciences. The Institute provides an international forum for presenting and sharing research in the study of decision processes across disciplines, in both traditional and emerging areas of study. Specifically, the Institute seeks to define the scope of quantitative methods to functional and behavioral problems of administration and the degree of sophistication that should be achieved by graduates of business schools.

The 5th International Conference of the Decision Sciences Institute with central theme "Integrating Technology and Human Decisions – Global Bridges Into the 21st Century", was held in Athens, Greece, July 4-7, 1999. The publication of this book is made on the occasion of this major international conference, and includes a representative cross section of the seven hundred papers presented by many international participants from various academic institutions and businesses around the globe.

The aim of the book is to present, in a complete edited volume, the most recent developments in the field of decision making, for addressing managerial decision problem in private and public organizations. The book covers a wide range of areas, which are essential both from an academic and practical view point, such as finance, marketing, transportation/ logistics, production/operations management, information technology, telecommunications, etc. Furthermore, the book emphasizes the presentation of methodologies that can be used to support the decision making process, and their real world applications in various settings, such as public and environmental affairs, health care planning, hospitality management, entrepreneurship, privatization in transition economies, international business, etc. These methodologies originate from the fields of operations research and management science (optimization, multiple criteria decision making, data envelopment analysis), information technology (management information and decision support systems, outsourcing, internet and electronic commerce), artificial intelligence (expert systems, neural networks, fuzzy sets) and statistics.

The proposed book has several special characteristics and features: variety of decision making fields and decision methodologies, highly recognized contributors from several countries, a variety of applications, and a considerable number of survey/expository papers. These characteristics ensure high quality and timely relevance, international/global flavor, and significant contributions in advancing the academic research and practice of decision making, through a comprehensive illustration of the current status in this field and the highlighting of possible future directions.

The present volume includes 30 papers divided in nine major parts:

1. Management information systems.
2. Education innovations and distance learning.
3. International business.
4. Marketing.
5. Finance and banking.
6. Optimization & decision making.
7. Multi-criteria decision analysis, aid & practice.
8. Decision support systems and information technology.
9. Health care planning & hospital operations.

The first part of the book refers to recent contributions and impact of management information systems in the operation of corporate entities and organizations. Drury presents and discusses the results of a survey regarding the effectiveness of chargeback systems in achieving organization goals. Gefen also conducts a survey to examine the role of trust in consultants during the adoption of enterprise resource planning (ERP) systems. The last paper of this part of the book, by Lamb and Smart reports on the development of a statistical information system which can be used to analyze heterogeneous databases on the web.

The second part of the book includes two papers related to education innovations. The first paper by Dhir et al. introduces social judgment theory as a potentially useful theoretical and methodological basis for understanding subjectivity in academic administration. Barrett and Hort report the results of a study regarding the effects of organizational culture on the selection of new members in university organizations.

The third part of the book includes two papers that deal with issues of major importance within the new globalized international business environment. Singh explores the role of political risk as a determining factor affecting foreign direct investments, while Nasierowski and Arcelus examine the impact of globalization of business practices on the policies dealing with the acquisition and development of countries' technological systems, offering a rating of 45 countries in that respect.

Marketing is the major field of interest in the fourth part of the book. The paper of Baourakis et al. presents the results of a consumer-based market survey conducted in order to identify consumer behavior regarding greenhouse vegetables. Alexouda and Paparrizos describe a decision support system that addresses the seller's return problem during product line design, using genetic algorithms.

The fifth part of the book contains a series of issues related to modern financial and banking management. Initially, Ghai et al. review the portfolio performance measures developed in the international literature, including both the well-known mean-variance measures as well as multi-factor measures. The paper of Kunsch et al. employs a systems dynamics modeling approach based on difference equations to generate behaviour patterns corresponding to different families of investors, in order to model stock price movements. Walczak investigates the effect of increasing the quantity of data used for building neural network models in forecasting currency exchange rates. The paper of Gupta et al. examines the efficiency of the Taiwan stock market, while Skiadopoulos et al. conduct an empirical study on the dynamics of volatility surfaces that are involved in arbitrage pricing. Finally, Smith et al. construct a set of integrated statistical models (nonstationary Markov processes) for credit risk management of automobile leasing.

The sixth part of the book has a more "technical" orientation compared to the previous parts; it presents some recent advances on optimization and decision making. The first paper of this part, by Yager, discusses the different structures available for the representation of partial knowledge about uncertain variables in decision making situations and suggests useful techniques for the evaluation of alternative courses of actions in the case of uncertainty. The next two papers are both related to multi-objective optimization. Antunes and Clímaco present an interactive graphical approach for linear programming problems involving an objective function with interval coefficients, while Mavrotas and Diakoulaki present a fuzzy extension of a mixed integer multi-objective programming model and its application to the power generation expansion problem. Finally, the paper of Chajakis presents a modeling approach to assist marine petroleum transporters in planning and operating their fleet, in order to achieve an optimal balance between profitability and customer service.

The seventh part of the book is devoted to the theory and practice of multi-criteria decision analysis. The first paper, by Greco et al. presents an innovative approach to address decision problems in cases of missing information, using a new extension of the rough set theory. Bana e Costa and Vansnick provide an overview of the MACBETH approach to address decision making problems using value judgments on a cardinal scale. The paper of Krassadaki and Siskos describes an application of the preference disaggregation approach of multi-criteria decision analysis in developing a model for evaluating rural development projects. The next paper, by Stamelos et al., proposes a framework for the evaluation of educational software, based on multi-criteria decision aid techniques. Finally, Doumpos et al. present a comparative study regarding the performance of a multi-criteria decision aid classification method as opposed to statistical and econometric techniques, using data regarding the country risk assessment problem.

The recent developments in decision support systems' technology and its applications in several decision-making fields is the main topic in the eighth part of the book. The first paper, by Bartzis et al. presents the development of a decision support system for managing nuclear emergencies, the outgrowth of the collaborative work of several countries following the Chernobyl disaster. Giaglis et al., report on the development of a decision support system for the evaluation of an information technology infrastructure investment of a Greek cable television network. The third paper by Huhn et al. explores the challenges of contract structuring, skill deployment, and communication methodology as they pertain to global information technology outsourcing engagements, as advocated and practiced by IBM Global Services. Angelides and Angelides illustrate the efficiency and effectiveness improvement in conversation planning through the implementation and use of Internet multimedia database information systems. Finally, Baker et al. present a model for allocating probation officer resources that combines a statistical model for probationer risk classification and an integer, nonlinear multi-criteria programming resource allocation model for workload balancing.

The book closes with two papers related to health care planning and hospital operations. The first paper, by El-Darzi et al. utilizes a queuing approach to assess the flow of patients within a geriatric department and community homes, and to allow a greater understanding of bed requirements and effective utilization of resources. In the second paper, by Martin et al., a goal programming model is developed to assign resources to public hospitals in the presence of multiple of objectives.

Sincere thanks must be expressed to the authors whose contributions have been essential in creating this volume. We are also grateful to the many referees of all papers, whose thoughtful critical reviews played a decisive role in improving the quality of this book.

Finally, we would like to thank Michael Doumpos for his administrative assistance in communicating with the authors and coordinating the material presentation of this volume.

June 2000

Stelios H. Zanakis
Florida International University, College of Business Administration,
Decision Science & Information Systems Department, Miami,
Florida 33199, USA

Georgios Doukidis
Athens University of Economics & Business,
Department of Management Science and Technology,
76 Patission Street, 10434 Athens, GREECE

Constantin Zopounidis
Technical University of Crete, Dept. of Production Engineering and Management,
Financial Engineering Laboratory, University Campus,
73100 Chania, GREECE

"It is our duty to admire acts of virtue and not words"

Democritus

1. MANAGEMENT INFORMATION SYSTEMS

EMPIRICAL ASSESSMENT OF INFORMATION TECHNOLOGY CHARGEBACK SYSTEMS DECISIONS

D.H. Drury

McGill University
Faculty of Management
1001 Sherbrooke St. West
Montreal, Quebec
Canada

Abstract: The majority of organizations either have no grasp of the value of their information technology or the measurement systems in place are considered to be inadequate. There has been a revived interest in chargeback—the policy of billing intracompany IT customers for services, to gain a firmer handle on ways to control the associated costs to overcome these deficiencies. The factors that influence the effective use of chargeback systems are investigated in organizations that currently use chargeback systems. Among these factors are the scope of applications, and rate of technological change. These have resulted in difficulties with operating cost measurement leading to the use of alternative control techniques. Organizations that are more successful using chargeback systems tended to use them as information systems to support decisionmaking rather than as strictly a cost control device. Further, the role of management as well as users is emphasized in the decisionmaking and control process.

Keywords: IT management, IT evaluation, IT cost structure, chargeback systems.

INTRODUCTION

Researchers have had difficulty in establishing a relationship between IT spending and productivity or profitability [66][73][52]. It is estimated that less than 1/5 of all corporations have a process in place by which to cost-justify IT [76]. According to a survey by CIO magazine and the Executive Insight Group Inc., CIO's are feeling widespread dissatisfaction with evaluating, monitoring, and managing systems costs. More that 2/3 of the executives surveyed expressed dismay over their companies justification system. The principle problem identified is a failure to put in place justification programs and key support mechanisms that spur greater user involvement in and ownership of information technology

3

S.H. Zanakis et al. (eds.), Decision Making: Recent Developments and Worldwide Applications, 3–16.
© 2000 *Kluwer Academic Publishers.*

systems [20]. In another survey in London, seventy-one percent of IT managers could not say whether their IT is delivering value for money, yet spending on hardware and software accounts for up to a quarter of total business costs at many firms [1]. Only 38% of top managements in textile companies believe their IT systems to be cost-effectively developed to maintain a competitive advantage or at least meet basic needs [35]. There is ample evidence that cost evaluation of IT is a universal and critical problem.

Many CEO's have tried to improve matters, perhaps by outsourcing part of the IT function or repeatedly changing the CIO [58]. The top organizations are also trying to spread IT power while bringing costs under control [12]. It is argued that the solution is for top managers to regain control of their IT departments, which often escapes the management scrutiny commonplace in the rest of the enterprise [35]. A common approach in other parts of the organization is to make departments responsible for the costs which they incur. Extensive survey evidence exists on the reasons why managers allocate other corporate and support costs to divisions and departments. A U.S. survey revealed the following ranking by frequency: 1. To remind managers that indirect costs exist and that profit must be adequate to cover some share of those costs. 2. To encourage the use of central services that would otherwise be underutilized. 3. To stimulate profit center managers to put pressure on central managers to control service costs [29]. Similar surveys were conducted among Australian and U.K. managers [64][23]. The two sets of managers gave the same ranking. Canadian executives gave similar reasons, 1. to determine costs, 2. to evaluate centers, 3. to fix accountability, 4. to allocate cost per usage, 5. to promote more effective resource usage, and 6. to foster cost awareness [6].

The extension of this approach to the control of IT has been widely advocated [68][70]. Many organizations have adopted control systems that measure usage and users are charged for IT services by means of a chargeback system. A chargeback system monitors who uses a company's IT resources and allocates the costs back to those users. Chargeback encompasses management and control of an organization's computer related assets.

Important benefits have been associated with using chargeback systems since their inception. They are expected to encourage user involvement in IT, promote awareness of costs, and supply management with cost information about IT [20][28]. More recently the objectives of chargeback systems have shifted to more economic considerations. Chargeback systems are intended to control costs, recover IT investment, assist in systems' assessments, and support restructuring and downsizing [26][27].

Other writers disagree with chargeback's aspect of control and limited scope [16]. They argue that chargeback systems are inappropriate in the current context of IT [38] and that managers are not ready to use chargeback systems [43][12]. There are many technical problems in measuring and allocating costs accurately. Further, chargeback systems are have become more complex with client/server systems, require greater record keeping and administrative costs, and difficult to measure costs are incurred outside of IT user budgets [44].

Surveys consistently show that only about 1/2 of organizations have adopted chargeback systems for IT [2][26][48][79]. Currently, the practice literature evinces a strong preference for chargeback systems as a solution to IT evaluation and control difficulties. The purpose of this paper is to investigate the effectiveness of chargeback systems. Whether organizations which use chargeback systems consider them to be successful, and the conditions for using them successfully to achieve organizational goals, is the question to be addressed. By this investigation, the research literature is extended to the empirical evaluation of chargeback systems, survey data is provided regarding the practices of organizations, and most important, evidence is presented regarding the critical issue of IT evaluation.

In the next section, prior research is used to establish the hypotheses to be tested. The development focuses on the contingency between chargeback systems evaluation, organizational, and IT properties, and management practices. Testing is from data obtained from organizations that use chargeback systems. The final section returns to the chargeback controversy and provides recommendations for practice and future research.

HYPOTHESES DEVELOPMENT

Past investigations on chargeback systems have focused more on organizational properties and context rather than on the evaluation of the chargeback approach to control [6][26][10]. These empirical studies postulated and tested conditions affecting the usage or non-usage of chargeback systems. For example, maturity of use [45][79][77] and decentralization of decisionmaking [26][36][62] have been found to affect the usage of chargeback systems. However, few studies had addressed whether positive or negative impacts actually occur or not. Those that have been completed were in the early 1980's before the technological landscape evolved [57][59]. With new technology, such as client/server systems, proliferation of applications, and a shift to more control by users, the context of IT has changed in organizations. Consequently, the hypotheses development is intended to reflect these changes in understanding organizations' assessments of chargeback systems.

Other types of systems have been evaluated in the research literature. Rainer [63] studied success of executive information systems, Yoon [83], the success of expert systems, and Raghunathan [62], the success of management planning systems. In other success studies, Venkatraman [80] examined strategic planning systems, Delone [24] small business systems, and Zahedi [85] project evaluation systems. From this background, this study focuses on the success of chargeback systems.

Delone and McLean [25] in reviewing 180 papers provided an important consolidation of past research on information systems' effectiveness. They conclude that while there are many possible constructs of effectiveness, system's success continues to capture critical evaluation dimensions. Previous studies have not examined chargeback systems success and this investigation fills this gap consistent with the prior research emphasis. There are many different dimensions of systems success. Success of a system is captured either through objective output orientated measures or through perceptual measures. The former class of studies attempts to identify the benefits of the system. However, there are no accepted methods to measure them, nor is there a consensus as to what these benefits are [22][40]. The research literature evinces a preference for perceived, rather than objectively measured effectiveness [67].

Usage as a surrogate of IT effectiveness has been employed in many studies [67][69][72]. Problems related to various types of usage, situations where usage is mandatory, and ignoring the importance or value of individual tasks have complicated this approach to effectiveness [51]. User satisfaction has also been employed. However, it has repeatedly been questioned in the literature [32][31][42][78]. Although the construct has been used by many authors, few make the argument that satisfied users alone are indicative of IT success [49]. With chargeback systems, equity or fairness [36] may be a more important consideration that isn't captured by the user satisfaction approach or the usage approach. Further, cost systems depend upon accuracy and reliability. Models of success for other types of systems do not contain many of the dimensions critical to the evaluation of chargeback systems [25]. For these reasons, the focus is on the overall evaluation of success rather than its dimensions. Success, consistent with past research, was measured in this study from the perceptions of respondents. Since each organization has its own perceptions about what it regards as success, the definition of success was left to the interpretation of the respondents. Success is measured on a seven point scale ranging from very successful to very unsuccessful in order to widely discriminate responses. Campbell [19] argues that comprehensive measures can better reflect a construct than multivariate approaches. Banker [7] found that summary judgments have higher explanatory power than combinations of the components. Chargeback success is a comprehensive measure of assessment, the purpose of which is to determine conditions that affect success.

Success depends on the objectives to be achieved. IT has evolved and yet, the objectives of chargeback systems in the literature have remained constant and their discussion leads to the first hypothesis. Associated with the use of chargeback systems is more decentralization of IT decisionmaking. Decentralization of decision making has been found to be consistent with the usage of chargeback systems [26][36][62]. Decentralization not only empowers users in the process, but also provides them with more IT alternatives than if decisions were made centrally. Thus, we would expect that the assessment of chargeback systems success and user involvement to be positively related. User involvement has been found in other systems contexts to have a significant positive impact on systems usage, satisfaction, and success [4].

Management involvement and commitment to IT has been a major area of concern. This factor has been cited in many previous studies as being a continuing issue in IT management [55][56]. Boynton [13] found that managerial IT knowledge is a dominant factor in explaining high levels of IT use. Chargeback systems should support this objective.

Many writers point to the IT cost justification objective of chargeback systems as a paramount consideration. Call [18] states that chargeback systems assure that spending on IT is not taken for granted. This puts a price on end user computer and focuses on where IT resources are needed most [15][65]. Others have focused on the process improvement objective. Ambrosia [4] argues that it puts pressure on the information center to perform better, Long [46] that it prevents unwarranted systems use, that it creates alliances among users [11], and more clearly aligns IT with business objectives [33]. These objectives are contained in the first hypothesis and should be positively related to the successful assessment of the system.

H1: Chargeback systems success is positively related to the objectives of the system: (1) user involvement and awareness, (2) management involvement, (3) cost justification, (4) and IT process improvement.

The next logical step questions what changes in the environment affect the evaluation of chargeback success. In the second hypothesis, four principal components of the IT chargeback environment are examined; (1) scale, (2) scope, (3) structure and (4) the rate of change, corresponding to the dimensions of transaction economics [81]. Empirical tests confirm the traditional importance of scale and scope as cost drivers [7][8]. A cost driver is defined to be any activity that results in costs being incurred. Because these cost drivers affect total costs and the cost structure, they are emphasized within the area of management control. The discussions by Porter [61], Williamson [81], Ouchi [60], and Yao [82], all include the dimensions of scale, scope, and change as being critical to the organization.

Within the systems literature, the principle measure of scale has been size. Nolan [57] suggested that the usage of chargeback systems as control mechanisms increase with size. Indeed, Swanson [74] argued that organizations typically could not be expected to use chargeback systems until a reasonable scale was reached. Since prior studies indicate that management control tends to increase with scale [50], it would be expected that control systems, in this case, chargeback systems, would be regarded as more successful with increases in scale. In this study, scale is measured as the number of employees in the organization.

Recently, studies have empirically examined the effect of scope through surrogate measures, principally related to complexity. Complexity has been found to be a cost driver in the systems literature, principally regarding systems projects and software development [43][71]. The importance to this study is that complexity not only increases costs, but also increases the necessity of control mechanisms to control costs. An important rationale for using chargeback systems has been found to be for controlling costs [26][48][59]. As scope increases, chargeback systems should be more successful in controlling costs [75]. In this study, the number of applications was used to measure systems scope.

The introduction of client/server and related technologies has not only had an impact on the way in which IT is used within organizations, but also on the cost structure. In a survey [3], IT budgets increased in 62% of organizations, principally expanding to newer technologies. This increases the proportion of IT costs directly controlled by users. According to a survey by Deloitte and Touche [21], more than 50% of the IT department staffers are dedicated to developing and supporting user applications. Changes in IT are increasing the labor proportion of total IT costs [53]. The newer technologies also increase indirect support and infrastructure costs which are often either hidden in various budgets or are difficult to measure [77]. These factors should make the operationalization of chargeback systems more important. In order to investigate the effect of the increase of user technologies on chargeback systems success, the proportion of non-mainframe operations costs of total operations costs is used as the measure of the cost structure.

Change in an organization engenders instability and uncertainty. In addition, switching costs and transaction costs [61][81] are incurred. Arrow [5] and Jensen [37] argue that a critical factor in achieving appropriate returns from change rests with internal coordination. Chargeback systems require communication between users and suppliers of IT services through information exchange on budgets, usages, and costs. Chargeback systems are integrating mechanisms of the organization. Consequently, chargeback systems should be more successful with rapid IT change which leads to the following hypothesis.

H2: Scale, scope, structure, and the rate of change are negatively related to chargeback system success

The first two hypotheses examine objectives and the environment. The last hypothesis follows from these since the application of chargeback systems may contain difficulties which affect its success. From the literature, scale, scope, structure, and the rate of change are expected to affect the application of chargeback systems. The issue addressed in the third hypothesis is how these dimensions have affected the application of chargeback systems. The first effect is the difficulty of measurement. Cafasso [17], Burden [14], and Molloy [54] point out that the complexity of newer systems and variety of users and applications, make cost and usage measurement more difficult. There are many hidden costs and others, such as support are difficult to measure [73]. Second, the costs of operating the chargeback system are expected to be higher [34][41[84].

These difficulties should reduce the success of chargeback systems suggesting that other control procedures, such as the IT approval process and committee structure will be more heavily relied upon in supporting the chargeback system [39][47]. These expected effects lead to the following hypothesis.

H3: Chargeback system success is negatively related to (a) system measurement difficulties (b) system costs, and positively to (c) systems alternatives.

Data were collected using questionnaires from organizations that currently use chargeback systems to test these hypotheses. The data collection procedures, sample characteristics, and tests of hypotheses are the subject matter of the next section.

EMPIRICAL ANALYSES

Data collection

The sampling methodology and sample characteristics are presented in the first part of this section. This is followed by our statistical and interpretive analysis of the results. Involvement in IT chargeback systems was initially gauged through directing a short-form questionnaire to 239 organizations. The questionnaire was sent to the Chief Information Officer since organization and technical information were required. The purpose was to identify organizations that were using any form of IT chargeback system and their characteristics. The response rate was 76%. In our initial survey, organizations were asked whether they used any form of chargeback system, 51.9% replied affirmatively and 48.1% that they did not. These general statistics do not reveal the entire story, since 15.9% of the organizations recently dropped chargeback systems in favor of other methods. In contrast, another 10.9% have adopted chargeback systems reflecting the changes which are occurring in IT.

From the responses obtained to the initial questionnaire, the sub-set of organizations which are currently using chargeback systems were then sent another, more extensive questionnaire. The questionnaire was pre-tested for wording and interpretation and adjusted accordingly. Sixty-five percent (65%) replied. Six questionnaires with incomplete data were eliminated. The non-responders were sent the questionnaires on three separate occasions. Our telephone inquiries indicated that the primary reasons for non-response were (a) companies were in the process of major systems revisions and (b) business time pressures, and not the chargeback issue. An examination of the industry, organization size, and other business variables using Chi-square tests revealed no factors that would lead to non-response bias.

The demographic data assist in putting the results into perspective. The responses were 53% manufacturing, 2% financial and 45% services. Seventy-three percent have more than 1000 employees. In addition, 33% of the organizations have more than 100 people in the IT function. The results should primarily be interpreted in the medium to large size category, although 27% of the sample has less than 1000 employees in the organization. Most of the organizations, (58.6%) are increasing IT expenditures. The minority, (17.2%) are decreasing their expenditures on IT whereas 24.2 % are maintaining the same level of expenditure. These characteristics emphasize the generalizability of the results that follow.

Results

The first hypothesis and analysis addresses the broad objectives of using chargeback systems. The evaluation of chargeback success is the dependent variable and the four objectives, the independent variables. The regression coefficients, t-values and their significance are contained in Table 1. The r-square for this regression is .648 which is significant at the .01 level. Higher levels of success are attained by organizations when the principal objectives are management involvement (.016) and IT process improvement (0.61). This result does not support much of the literature that places emphasis on users' involvement and evaluation of their systems. These were insufficient to lead to assessments of a successful system.

Table 1. Chargeback systems regression with cost process variables

H1 Variable	Coefficient	t-value	Significance
α-Coefficient	2.096	2.490	.027
User Involvement	.200	.261	.689
Management Involvement	1.374	2.97	.016**
Cost Justification	.800	1.02	.166
Process Improvement	1.1793	1.55	.061*

Significance Levels * .10   ** .05

The second hypothesis examines the effects of the IT cost environment; scale, scope, structure, and rate of change. The success measure was correlated with each of these dimensions. In Table 2, three of the Spearman correlation coefficients are positive and statistically significant. Chargeback systems are more successful in larger, more diverse IT operations where complexity becomes a problem, and where technology is changing rapidly. For the reasons stated in the hypothesis development, chargeback systems are viewed as successful in managing this set of IT environmental conditions. The exception is the cost structure.

Table 2. Correlation of chargeback systems success with cost environment variables

H2 Variable	Correlation	Significance
Scale	.274	.042**
Scope	.292	.023**
Structure	-.208	.103
Rate of Change	.284	. 037**

Significance Levels * .10   ** .05

Critics of chargeback systems argue that chargeback systems are not ready for the new environment [38] and that managers are not ready to use chargeback systems with client/server technology [16][44][17]. As the proportion of costs devoted to these IT uses increases, the hypothesis was that chargeback systems would be viewed as less successful. In fact, the Spearman correlation coefficients in Table 2 show that this does occur. But while the result is in the expected direction, the relationship is not strong as indicated by the significance level.

Hypothesis 3 extends these results to the chargeback environment. The IT dimensions of Table 2 are cross-tabulated with the chargeback environment variables; system measurement, system costs, and cost system alternatives. The results of the correlations appear in Table 3. In the first column, the correlation coefficients are in the positive expected direction for scale, cost structure, and the rate of change. However, none of these significantly create cost measurement problems. The critical issue is scope (.267) which makes cost measurement more difficult with the diversity of applications. Further, these cost measurement difficulties negatively affect the assessment of success of chargeback systems as indicated by the negative correlation coefficient (-.320).

The second column examines the relationship between the cost of operating the chargeback system and scale, scope, structure, and the rate of change. None of the correlation coefficients are significant except increasing the proportion of user costs in the cost structure does increase the costs of administering the chargeback system (.341). Further, these increasing costs are negatively associated with the success of the system. However, the result is not statistically significant.

Table 3. Correlations of cost environment variables with cost reaction variables

H3 Variable	Chargeback Measurement System Difficulties	Chargeback System Costs	Chargeback Cost System Alternatives
Scale	.034	.081	.111
Scope	.267**	.137	.278**
Structure	.146	.341**	.127
Rate of change	.022	.127	.198
Success	-.320**	-.064	.323**

Significance Levels * .10   ** .05

The third column, Systems Alternatives, is particularly revealing. With increases in scale, scope, structure and the rate of change, organizations tend to adopt other control mechanisms to supplement chargeback systems although scope is the only statistically significant variable. Chargeback systems are not viewed as standing on their own but part of a mix of control and reporting mechanisms. It is also clear from the success score (.323) that this is an important practice in using chargeback systems effectively.

These previous results bring into question the control aspect of using chargeback systems. In the final test, the sample was divided into two groups based upon the median of the success scores; 1. organizations which considered chargeback to be successful and 2. organizations whose assessment were not successful. The two groups were compared using t-tests on their responses to the success of their systems in assisting decisionmaking and providing an IT control system. The results are contained in Table 4.

Table 4. T-tests of Success and Non-success

Variable		Mean	Standard Deviation	Significance
IT Decision	U	3.00	.764	.002**
Making	S	4.66	.236	
IT Cost	U	3.89	.539	.999
Control	S	3.91	.841	

Significance Levels * .10   ** .05

In Table 4, the less successful groups appear first (U) and then the more successful group (S). IT decisionmaking is significant at the .05 level whereas there is virtually no difference for the two groups in IT cost control. While cost control is an important consideration for all organizations, organizations which use chargeback systems successfully treat them as information systems to improve decisionmaking.

CONCLUSIONS

With the pace of technological change and the accelerated growth in investment, chargeback systems have been advocated to be the solution to many difficulties in the evaluation and control of Information Technology.

Assessment of systems remains an important topic in IT research and this study extends the results of other systems studies. However, effectiveness evaluation of chargeback systems may differ from other systems because systems usage is not voluntary to users and the cost element involved requires judgments of equity, fairness, accuracy and relevancy. These issues need to be added to comprehensive models of information system success such as that developed by Delone and McLean [25]. The relative importance of these dimensions of systems effectiveness have yet to be explored and may reveal a more complex structure in the assessment of internal reporting systems. Broad measures of these concepts, such as systems complexity, were used in the absence of more refined measures in the literature requiring future research on each of the dimensions explored.

The first hypothesis addressed the determinants of successful chargeback systems. In Table 1, we find that the past objective of user involvement has given way to management involvement, cost justification and IT process improvement. The emphasis has shifted from satisfying users to utilizing IT effectively. Chargeback systems are expected to assist these objectives.

The second hypothesis linked chargeback systems to the changing IT environment. Chargeback systems are found to positively affect chargeback success with the current increasing scale, scope, and rate of IT change in Table 2. Organizations are currently using chargeback systems to manage the impact and speed of IT improvements. Where these conditions are not present, chargeback systems would be less needed and less successful. For example, a smaller operation that is stable probably could find other means of controlling IT costs rather than using chargeback systems.

The current IT environment has other impacts on using chargeback systems. The third hypothesis addressed the difficulties that organizations are encountering in using chargeback systems effectively. In Table 3, cost measurement difficulties are found to have increased, primarily due to increases in scope of applications and the diversity of systems users. This has negatively affected the success of chargeback systems. Further costs of administering the system increase with the changing cost structure. This indicates a need for more cost-effective metrics to be developed.

Organizations are found to use additional cost control and reporting practices together with chargeback systems. The relative importance of these management techniques is likely to be contingent upon the relative importance of chargeback to the organization as a prerequisite. At present, the conclusion is that chargeback systems, by themselves, are not viewed as a unique solution to IT cost control by organizations that use them.

The effect of cost structure was contrary to the expectations from the current literature. The changing IT cost structure does not seem to have affected the success of the chargeback systems in this study. There are several explanations for this result. Organizations may have simply extended chargeback systems to new IT. Chargeback systems may be so entrenched in the management philosophy such that cost structure changes are what the system is intended to control. To address this issue requires future research.

While much emphasis can be placed on technical problems in measuring costs and usages with chargeback systems, overcoming these is only the first step in using chargeback systems effectively. The second is that the cost information has an impact on the control of IT. This requires matching responsibilities of both users and management with cost incurrence. Finally, organizations which regard their chargeback systems as highly successful have taken the next step. Chargeback systems are treated as information systems to assist in the decision process and not used strictly as a control system in Table 4. This change in emphasis mirrors the changes that are occurring in IT. Distributed processing and the focus on users have given way to more standardization, centralization, and alignment of IT with organizational objectives. Thus, we see a change in objectives and problems in using chargeback systems effectively. Further, it isn't only users, but also management needs to be involved in chargeback information process. Integrating the information obtained from chargeback systems into the IT decisionmaking structure would seem to be a major challenge to future research and practice.

REFERENCES

[1] "Financial Firms Failing to Evaluate IT" (1996), *Financial Technology International Bulletin* 13(6), 4.

[2] *1978 CPU Survey* (1978), Informatics, Inc., Canogen Park, California.

[3] "Executive Stats" (1996), *PC Week* March 11, E3.

[4] Ambrosia, J.(1992), "Management by Comparison", *Computerworld* 26, 67-70.

[5] Arrow, K., (1974), *The Limits of Organization*, W.J. Norton, New York.

[6] Atkinson, A., (1987), *Intrafirm Cost and Resource Allocations: Theory and Practice*, Society of Management Accountants Research Monograph, Hamilton, Canada.

[7] Banker, R.D., S.M. Datar, S. Kekre, and T. Mukhopadhyay (1989), "Costs of Product and Process Complexity", Working Paper, Carnegie Mellon University.

[8] Banker, R.D. and H. Johnston (1993), "An Empirical Study of Cost Drivers in the U.S. Airline Industry", *The Accounting Review* 63/3, 576-601.

[9] Barki, H. and J. Hartwick (1994), "Measuring User Participation, User Involvement, and User Attitude", *MIS Quarterly* 18/1, 59-82.

[10] Bergeron, F. (1986), "Factors Influencing the Use of DP Chargeback Information", *MIS Quarterly*, 10/3, 224-237.

[11] Bergstrom, L.P. (1987), "MIS Inc: Market-Based Chargeback in the Data Center", *Business Software Review*, 6/11, 36-42.

[12] Bird, J. (1994), "The Trouble with IT", *Management Today*, 90-92.

[13] Boynton, A.C. and R.W. Zmud, and G.C. Jacobs (1994), "The Influence of IT Management Practice on IT Use in Large Organizations", *MIS Quarterly* 18/3, 299-318.

[14] Burden, K., (1994), "Client/Server Integrated Packages Face Tougher Environment", *Computerworld* 28/41, 112.

[15] Buse, J. (1988), "Chargeback Systems Come of Age", *Datamation* 34, 47-49.

[16] Butler, J. (1992), "Does Chargeback Show Where the Buck Stops?", *Software Magazine* 12/5, 48-52.

[17] Cafasso, R. (1995), "Client Server Costs Hard to Divvy Up", *Computerworld* January 23, 129.

[18] Call, B. (1987), "For Managers, Chargeback Makes Micros Count", *PC Week* March 3, 41-42.

[19] Campbell, J.P. (1997), "On the Nature of Organizational Effectiveness", in P.S. Goodman, and J.M. Pennings (Eds.), *New Perspectives of Organizational Effectiveness*, Jossey Bass, San Francisco.

[20] Cooke, D. P. and E.B. Parrish (1992), "Justifying Technology: Not Measuring Up", *CIO* 5/14 June 15, 84-85.

[21] Crowley, A. (1994), "The New Metrics", *PC Week* November 28, 26-28.

[22] Crowston, K., and M.E. Treacy (1986), "Assessing the Impact of Information Technology on Enterprise Level Performance," *Proceedings of the Seventh International Conference on Information Systems*, San Diego.

[23] Dean, G.M., and P. Blayney (1991), *Strategic Management Accounting Survey*, The University of Sydney, Sydney, Australia.

[24] DeLone, W.H. (1988), "Determinants of Success for Computer Usage in Small Business", *MIS Quarterly* 12/8, 51-61.

[25] Delone, W.H. and E.R. McLean (1992), "Information Systems Success: The Quest for the Dependent Variable", *Information Systems Research*. 3/1, 60-95.

[26] Drury, D.H. (1980), "A Survey of Data Processing Chargeback Practices", *INFOR* November, 342-353.

[27] Drury, D.H., (1997), "The Dialectic of IT Chargeback Systems", *International Journal of Technology Management* 4(5), 496-512.

[28] Elms, T. (1993), "Chargeback and the Price of Information", *Systems 3X/400* 21/12, 12-14.

[29] Fernberg, P.M. (1993), "How Safe is Your Mail Center? Are You Sure?", *Managing Office Technology* 38/9, 29-30.

[30] Fremgen, J. and S. Lia (1981), *The Allocation of Corporate Indirect Cost*, National Association of Accountants, New York.

[31] Gatian, A.H. (1994) "Is User Satisfaction a Valid Measure of System Effectiveness", *Information and Management* 26/ 3, 119-131.

[32] Hawk, S.R., and N.S. Raju (1991), "Test-Retest Reliability of User Information Satisfaction: A Comment on Galletta and Lederer's Paper", *Decision Sciences* 22, 1165-1170.

[33] Henry, B. (1990), "Measuring IS for Business Value", *Datamation* 36/7, 89-91.

[34] Hoffman, T. (1992), "Salomon Brothers Puts Chargebacks On-Line", *Computerworld* 26/42,12.

[35] Hooper, C., J. S. Hess, and C. Wielar (1994), "Info Technology: Costs Are Up, Satisfaction Down", *Textile World* 144/2, 79-80.

[36] Hufnagel, E., and J.G. Birnberg (1989), "Perceived Chargeback Systems Fairness in Decentralized Organizations: An Examination of the Issues", *MIS Quarterly* 13/4, 415-430.

[37] Jensen, M. and W. Meckling (1976), "Theory of the Firm: Managerial Behavior, Agency Costs, and Capital Structure", *Journal of Financial Economics* 3, 305-360.

[38] Karon, P. (1994), "Chargeback Not Ready for Client/Server", *Computerworld* 28/34, 106.

[39] Karten, N. (1986), "The Information Center: How to Manage User Demand", *Canadian Datasystems* 18/7, 52-56.

[40] Kauffmann, R. J., and Weill, P. (1989), "An Evaluative Framework for Research on the Performance Effects of Information Technology Investment," *Proceedings of the Tenth International Conference on Information Systems*, December 377-388.

[41] King, J. and R. Cafasso (1994), "Client/Server Trimmings", *Computerworld* 28/5, 1, 14.

[42] Klenke, K. (1992),"Construct Measurement in Management Information Systems: A Review and Critique of User Satisfaction and User Involvement Instruments", *INFOR* 30/4, 325-348.

[43] Kobielus, J. (1992), "Overcoming Net Managers' Fear of Chargeback Systems", *Network World* 9/ 7, 29.

[44] Korzeniowski, P. (1994), "Delivering Automated Operations for C/S Anything but Automatic", *Software Magazine* 14/7, 49-55.

[45] Lientz, B.P. and E.B. Swanson (1980), *Software Maintenance*, Addison-Wesley Publishing Company New York.

[46] Long, G.G. (1993), "The Next Best Thing to Being There - Video Teleconferencing", *Office Systems* 10/2, 35-39.

[47] McFarlan, G.J. (1986), "Plans and Controls for the DP Shop," *Canadian Datasystems* 18/ 9, 47-51.

[48] McGee, R.W. (1987), "Accounting for Data Processing Costs", *Journal of Accounting and EDP* 2/4, 43-49.

[49] Melone N.P. (1990), "A Theoretical Assessment of the User-Satisfaction Construct In Information Systems Research", *Management Science* January, 76-91.

[50] Miller, D. and P.H. Friesen (1984), *Organizations: A Quantum View*, Prentice-Hall, Englewood Cliffs, 1984.

[51] Miller, J. (1989), "Information System Effectiveness: The Fit between Business Needs and System Capabilities", *Proceedings of the Tenth International Conference on Information Systems*, 273-288.

[52] Mitra, S. and A. Chaya (1996), "Analyzing Cost Effectiveness of Organisations: The Impact of Information Technology Spending", *Journal of Management Information Systems* 13/2, 29-57.

[53] Moad, J. (1995), "1995 Industry Outlook", *Datamation* January 7, 16-24.

[54] Molloy, M. (1991), "Lack of Tools Hinders Usage Billing", *Network World* 8/34, 19-20.

[55] Moynihan, T. (1991), "What Chief Executives and Senior Managers Want From Their IT Departments", *MIS Quarterly* December, 475-500.

[56] Niederman, F., J. Brancheau, and J. Whetherbe (1991), "Information Systems Management Issues for the 1990's", *MIS Quarterly* December, 475-500.

[57] Nolan, R.L. (1977), "Effects of Charge-Out on User Attitudes", *Communications of the ACM* 20/3, 177-185.

[58] O'Leary, M. (1992), "Birth of a Salesman", *CIO* 5/13, 30-35.

[59] Olson, M.H. and B. Ives (1992), "Chargeback Systems and User Involvement in Information Systems: An Empirical Investigation", *MIS Quarterly* 6/2, 47-60.

[60] Ouchi, W. (1979), "A Conceptual Framework For the Design of Organizational Control Mechanisms", *Management Science* 25/9, 833-840.

[61] Porter, M. (1980), *Competitive Strategy: Techniques for Analyzing Industries and Competitors*, The Free Press, New York.

[62] Raghunathan, B. and T.S. Raghunathan (1994), "A Discriminant Analysis of the Relationship Between Charging Systems and Organizational Variables", *Omega* 22/4, 321-330.

[63] Rainer, R. Jr., and H.J.Watson (1995), "The Keys to Executive Information System Success", *Journal of Management Information Systems* 12/2, 83-98.

[64] Ramadan, S. (1989), "The Rationale for Cost Allocation: A Study of U.K. Divisionalized Companies", *Journal of Business Research* Winter, 31-37.

[65] Rappaport, D.M. (1991), "Data Network Chargeback: A Matter of Balance", *Business Communication Review* 21/12, 19-20, 24.

[66] Roach, S.S. (1991), "Services Under Siege: The Restructuring Imperative", *Harvard Business Review* 69/5, 82-91.

[67] Robey, D. (1979), "User Attitudes and MIS Use", *Academy of Management Journal* 22/3, 527-538.

[68] Rubin, D. (1992), "Getting Your Infrastructure Right: Planning for Cooperative Process", *CIO Journal* 4/3, 39-44.

[69] Schewe, C. (1976), "The Management Information Systems User: An Exploratory Behavioral Analysis", *Academy of Management Journal* 19/4, 577-590.

[70] Scott, J. (1992), "Capacity Management in the Real World", *Capacity Management Review* 20/7, 1-2, 12.

[71] Son, Y.K. (1993), "Simulation-Based Manufacturing Accounting for Modern Management", *Journal of Manufacturing Systems* 12/5, 417-427.

[72] Srinivasan, A. (1985), "Alternative Measures of Systems Effectiveness: Associations and Implications", *MIS Quarterly* 9/3, 243-253.

[73] Strassman, P. *The Squandered Computer*, Information Economics Press, 1997.

[74] Swanson, E.B. (1974), "Management Information System: Appreciation and Involvement", *Management Science* 21/2, 178-188.

[75] Tait, P. and I. Vessey (1988), "The Effect of User Involvement on System Success: A Contingency Approach", *MIS Quarterly* 12/1, 91-108.

[76] Taninecz, G. (1996), "What's the ROI?", *Industry Week* 245/18, 45-48.

16

[77] Toscano, S. (1994), "So How Much Does IT Cost?", *PC Week* July 4, 17-19.

[78] Torkzadeh, G. and W.J. Doll (1994), "The Test-Retest Reliability of User Involvement Instruments", *Information and Management* 26/1, 21-31.

[79] Van Lengen, C.A. and J.N. Morgan (1994), "Chargeback and the Maturity of MIS Use", *Capacity Management Review* 22/8, 9.

[80] Venkatraman, N. and V. Ramanujam (1987), "Planning System Success: A Conceptualization and an Operational Model", *Management Science* 33/6, 687-705.

[81] Williamson, O. (1985), *The Economic Institutions of Capitalism*, Free Press, NY.

[82] Yao, D.A. (1985), "Beyond the Reach of the Invisible Hand: Impediments of Economic Activity, Market Failures, and Profitability", *Strategic Management Journal* 9, 59-70.

[83] Yoon, Y., T. Guimaraes, and Q. O'Neal (1985), "Exploring the Factors Associated with Expert Systems Success", *MIS Quarterly* 19/2, 83-102.

[84] Young, J. (1987), "The Chargeback Process Creates a New Breed of DP Consumer", *Computerworld* 21/13A, 10-11.

[85] Zahedi, F. (1987), "Reliability of Information Systems Based on the Critical Success Factors -- Formulation", *MIS Quarterly* 11/2, 187-203.

LESSONS LEARNT FROM THE SUCCESSFUL ADOPTION OF AN ERP: THE CENTRAL ROLE OF TRUST

D. Gefen

Management Department
LeBow College of Business
Drexel University
Philadelphia, PA 19104
USA

Abstract: Enterprise Resource Planning (ERP) are large and complex software packages that integrate and manage the information needs of companies. One of the important aspects of ERP adoption is the need for extensive technical support prior to its actual use, typically by specialized consultants. This study examines the adoption of a specific ERP and analyzes the impact of users' trust in the consultants on their assessment of and self-reported use of the ERP. The study also examines antecedents of this trust. Mail survey data from 135 companies indeed shows that, as hypothesized, self-reported use was affected by perceived usefulness alone, but that trust was an influential antecedent of users' assessments of the ERP. The data also support the hypothesized role of dependability, and responsiveness regarding both software and service on trust. Implications for the ERP and software consulting industry are discussed.

Keywords: ERP, Trust, Responsiveness, Dependability, IT adoption, Perceived Usefulness, Perceived Ease of Use, TAM.

INTRODUCTION

Many companies are finding that building or buying custom made complex software packages to manage their daily operational activities is not the best way to acquire and maintain new software. Catering to this growing market are companies that create and sell "standardized" software packages that handle a variety of supply-chain management and related activities in a standardized and integrated manner. These software packages are known as Enterprise Resource Planning (ERP) software. Companies adopting an ERP as

S.H. Zanakis et al. (eds.), Decision Making: Recent Developments and Worldwide Applications, 17–30.
© 2000 *Kluwer Academic Publishers.*

their supply-chain management software package thus benefit from the adoption of an existing and properly debugged package that is updated on a regular basis. Moreover, companies adopting an ERP rather than developing the software in-house can reduce their need to employ an extensive software development and maintenance team and focus on their core business without also becoming an Information Technology (IT) company. These companies also benefit from a faster implementation of the new IT and, typically, with a reduced level of risk. Moreover, these companies can also acquire only the ERP components (known as modules) they currently need, and yet be able to add additional modules at a later date without resorting to extensive reconfiguration and rewriting of their software because of the way an ERP integrates all its software modules into one integrated database. The latter feature is another major advantage of adopting an ERP: the ability to manage all the corporate information in one integrated database, integrating all the company's processes.

As a result of these benefits, the ERP market has seen the quick rise of companies that specialize in supplying ERP and support services, such as SAP and Oracle Financials, and of companies that specialize in support activities, such as Andersen Consulting.[1] These support activities are very often a major aspect of successful ERP implementation because of the need for extensive parameter modification (though typically without the need to actually modify the software itself) and training. The latter two activities can take more than a year and cost a company implementing an ERP a considerable expense. In the USA, for example, consulting fees can cost $300 per hour.

This extensive interaction with consultants who specialize in customizing the ERP combined with user dependence upon the consultants to customize the ERP so that it will be beneficial, and the inability to properly control and monitor the consultants' activities, suggest that trust in the consultants may be a central aspect of successful ERP adoption. Trust, the belief in the moral behavior and socially acceptable conduct of others (Hosmer 1995), is typically a central aspect of any interaction with other people that is both risky and interdependent (Luhmann 1979; Fukuyama 1995). Examining the role of trust in consultants during ERP adoption is the primary research objective of this study. The role of trust is examined in the context of TAM (Davis 1989), one of the most widely used IT adoption models. No less important, is the question of how to build this trust. Examining the latter question is the second objective of this study.

The two research questions were examined using data collected from the clientele of a company that specializes in selling ERP components and the technical support that is necessary to customize them. The data support the research propositions that ERP adoption (self-reported usage) is influenced primarily by the perceived usefulness of the IT (the ERP), as implied by TAM, and that trust in the consultants plays an indirect role by affecting the perceived usefulness and ease of use of the ERP. Trust itself, in accordance with the research propositions, was positively correlated with user assessments of the consultant firm's responsiveness, good service, and confiding of sensitive information. Trust, also in accordance with the research propositions, was negatively correlated with

---

[1] Throughout the study, the term consultant relates to ERP customization experts. These consultants may be either representatives of the vendor (as is in the data surveyed here) or consultants who work in a consultant company that provides the customization service.

user assessments of the consultants' lack of dependability.

The implications of these results on the need to improve user trust in ERP consultants, and possibly software support in general, are discussed. Methods of doing so, in light of the influence of lack of dependability, responsiveness, good service, and confiding sensitive information are also discussed.

LITERATURE REVIEW

The Importance of the Customization during ERP Adoption

The successful adoption of IT, in general, and ways of facilitating it have been and remain a major topic of interest to both IT industry and academia (DeLone and McLean 1992). One of most accepted models dealing with this process is the Technology Adoption Model (TAM) (Davis 1989). The central idea behind TAM is that, when given a choice, users adopt (choose to use) a new IT because of its perceived usefulness (PU), and, to a lesser and mostly indirect degree, because of its perceived ease of use (PEOU). Davis (1989) originally examined this model on e-mail, a file-editor, and graphic packages and found that PU influenced IT adoption directly, while PEOU influenced IT adoption primarily through PU. Extensive research has since replicated this conclusion in a variety of IT types, including e-mail and gopher systems (Venkatesh and Davis 1994), spreadsheets (Mathieson 1991), DBMSs (Szajna 1994), microcomputer usage (Igbaria, et al. 1997; Karahanna et al. 1999), FAX (Straub 1994), group support systems (Chin and Gopal 1995) and expert systems (Gefen and Keil 1998). Most of these studies, with the single exception of Gefen and Keil's (1998) study of responsiveness, examined existing fully operational IT and did not therefore consider the role of technical support.

The nature of the user consultant (or any other IT technical support staff) relationship, however, should not be overlooked when dealing with the adoption of an IT that still needs considerable configuration by the technical staff before it can used appropriately (Gefen and Keil 1998). ERP are exactly that kind of IT: they are not deployed as "turn-key" projects the way word-processors are. A typical ERP, after initial installation, goes through extensive configuration without which it cannot be used successfully or be as useful and applicable as it could otherwise be. This may require setting several hundred inter-related parameters in each ERP module, and may take over a year and cost no less than the ERP package itself. Consequently, customization support is in many cases an integral part of the purchase contract itself.

This need for extensive customization adds a new dimension to IT adoption, mostly overlooked by IT adoption research: the expected benefits from this kind of a new IT do not depend on the IT alone. If the consultants do not render the customization service they are expected to provide, the company adopting the ERP is less likely to deploy the system as effectively and efficiently to support its business processes. Likewise, if the consultants do not tailor the ERP parameters appropriately, as they are contacted and expected to, the ERP will not be as easy-to-use as it should be. Indeed, research has shown that during the adoption of expert systems – also complex IT that require extensive customization to be deployed successfully – responsive technical support strongly influences the usefulness and ease-of-use of the new IT (Gefen and Keil 1998).

User Trust in the Consultants during ERP Adoption

These customization consultants define requirements, adjust the ERP parameters and/or the existing work-procedures of the users, and test the new configuration. Since most of these processes are hidden from the users until the ERP is actually deployed, the users must accept "on faith" that the consultants are doing the job properly. This is not unique to ERP; it occurs in many IT projects that require either software development or extensive customization (e.g. Shah et al 1994; Gefen and Keil 1998). Yet, the need to accept "on faith" is more pronounced in the case of ERP systems because their vast size and complexity make precise contractual legal definitions especially difficult. The immense complexity of ERP systems also means that sometimes problems are not discovered until long after implementation, sometimes years later when there is no longer a business contract with the consultants. Thus, companies adopting an ERP have little control over the consultants, yet depend on them extensively to successfully deploy it.

Trust is a central aspect of this type of relationship. Trust is a belief that other people one depends upon will fulfill their commitments in situations where one has little or no control (Deutsch 1958, Blau 1964, Rotter 1971, Schurr and Ozanne 1985) and that entail an element of risk or loss (Deutsch 1958, Giffin 1967, Hosmer 1995). It involves the anticipation that others will behave ethically (Hosmer 1995), be dependable (Kumar 1996), and take into account what is fair and acceptable (Zucker 1986). Research has narrowed this broad definition of trust to three interrelated beliefs dealing with integrity, benevolent intentions, and ability (Giffin 1967; Hosmer 1995; McKnight et al. 1998). Indeed, a company adopting a new ERP often has no choice but to trust in the integrity, benevolent (or, at least, honorable) intentions, and ability of the consultants. If the consultants lie about what they are doing or about their ability, or if they do not care about the company implementing the ERP, or are not competent, the company adopting the ERP is not likely to benefit as much from the new ERP. Consequently, the degree of trust that a company implementing a new ERP has in its consultants should influence their expectations from it.

What Builds Trust in ERP Adoption?

This leads to the second research objective: how can this trust be built? To understand what may build this trust one must take a closer look at the meaning of trust. Trust is a psychological mechanism of handling social uncertainty that results from the vast number of behaviors that other people, as independent agents, might do in the context of one's own interaction with them. To overcome this overwhelming complexity and thus allow people to interact with others in a rational manner, people must somehow presume that others will behave as they are expected to and will not suddenly behave in an unpredictable manner. This assumption is the essence of trust (Luhmann 1979). Typically, this means expecting the trusted party to fulfill commitments (Deutsch 1958, Blau 1964, Rotter 1971, Schurr and Ozanne 1985), and behave ethically (Hosmer 1995), dependably (Kumar 1996) and fairly (Zucker 1986). Behaving in this manner builds trust; not behaving in this manner ruins trust (Blau 1964; Luhmann 1979). Since a company employing ERP consultants, expects them explicitly (i.e. in a binding contract) to customize the ERP and implicitly to provide good and dependable service, behaving in this manner should build this trust.

Another related way of building trust is by explaining one's motives and objectives, thus enabling others to form appropriate expectations and not be surprised by what may seem as unpredictable behavior (Blau 1964; Luhmann 1979). Accordingly, ERP consultants may be able to build trust by confiding their goals and motives. Even if these are not exactly what the client would like, understanding what motivates the consultants could build trust in them by enabling the client to develop realistic expectations. When these expectations come true, the company is more likely to trust the consultants.

HYPOTHESES

Properly customized ERP will be configured in such a manner that will support company procedures in a more effective and efficient way, thus increasing ERP usefulness, and will avoid unneeded procedures, thus making the ERP easier to use. Trustworthy consultants will supposedly provide this service adequately, while untrustworthy vendors may not. Consequently, companies employing consultants to customize their ERP should expect a more useful and easy-to-use ERP if they can trust the consultants to customize the ERP as expected. This is especially so given that it is not practical to effectively monitor consultants and so verify that they are indeed providing the service they are expected to. Accordingly, it can hypothesized that:

H_1: *Users' trust in the ERP consultants will increase users' PU of the ERP.*
H_2: *Users' trust in the ERP consultants will increase users' PEOU of the ERP.*

In addition, in a confirmatory manner with existing TAM research cited above, the relationships between PU, PEOU and self-reported use, are hypothesized to apply also to ERP adoption. Specifically, that IT adoption depends upon PU and PEOU, and that PEOU affects PU:

H_3: *Users' PU of an ERP will affect their self-reported use of it.*
H_4: *Users' PEOU of an ERP will affect their self-reported use of it.*
H_5: *Users' PEOU of an ERP will increase users' PU of it.*

The second research objective dealt with the ERP consultants' trust building behaviors. One way of increasing trust, according to Luhmann (1979), is by behaving in accordance with the expectations others have. Companies that employ ERP consultants to customize their ERP clearly expect appropriate changes in the ERP and good service. (These details are often explicitly stated in the contract). It follows, therefore, that trust in the consultants will increase when the consultants behaves in accordance with these expectations by being responsive to requests and provide good service:

H_6: *Consultants' responsiveness to customization requests will increase trust in them.*
H_7: *Demonstrability of good service by the consultants will increase trust in them.*

The same logic also suggests that trust will be adversely influenced by behavior that demonstrates lack of dependability. When consultants, for example, promise something and do not do them later, the company deploying the ERP is less likely to trust them because of the display of untrustworthy behavior. Moreover, lack of dependability in its own right decreases trust because one cannot know what to expect of such a person and cannot expect the person, accordingly, to behave in accordance with expectations (Luhmann 1979). Another reason for this, in the case of ERP consultants, is that such behavior is clearly not the kind of service the consultants are being employed to provide.

H_8: *Lack of dependability by the consultants will decrease trust in them.*

Trust is built by behaving in accordance with other people's expectations (Luhmann 1979). Accordingly, confiding, i.e. sharing one's reasons for doing something, can increase trust by contributing to the creation of more accurate expectations. During ERP adoption, companies employing ERP consultants who confides in them about their own goals, objectives, and mistakes should be able to form more realistic expectations of what to expect from these consultants. Since realistic expectations from consultants are more likely to be fulfilled as expected, confiding by the consultants should increase trust in them. Moreover, consultants who are not afraid to reveal their own objectives and are not apprehensive about their previous mistakes demonstrate that they have nothing to hide. Such behavior, in general, builds trust (Butler 1991). Accordingly:

H_9: *Confiding by the consultants will increase trust in them.*

RESEARCH METHOD

The first step of the study included unstructured interviews with several technical (software) support managers in an attempt to define what exactly are integrity, benevolent intentions and ability in the context of adopting an ERP and other large software packages. The interviews were also designed to explicate and verify that the items reflecting good service, lack of dependability, confiding, and the three aspects of trust, adapted mainly from Crosby et al. (1990) and Gefen (1997) apply to IT adoption. The objective of these interviews was to increase the face validity and construct validity of the items.

The items dealing with integrity assess integrity, frankness, honesty, and truthfulness. The items dealing with benevolent intentions deal with consideration and caring. The items dealing with ability deal with competence, knowledge, and the use of quality control. The items dealing with good service deal with going out of one's way to be helpful. The items dealing with lack of dependability deal with not keeping promises, bending the facts, and withholding crucial information. The items dealing with confiding deal with confiding goals, objectives, and past mistakes. The questionnaire items relating to existing IS models were adapted from established scales. The scales for Perceived Usefulness (PU) and Perceived Ease of Use (PEOU) were adapted from validated TAM scales (Davis 1989). PU deals with user assessment of the efficiency and effectiveness of the IT. PEOU deals with user assessment of how easy it is to use and to learn how to use the IT. The Responsiveness scale was adapted from the perceived developer responsiveness scale (Gefen and Keil 1998). Responsiveness deals with user assessment that the consultants modify the IT as requested. The scale items used in the questionnaire all used a scale ranging from 1 ("strongly agree") to 7 ("strongly disagree"). The items are presented in Appendix 1. The company name has been changed in the Appendix to SP to protect its anonymity.

The survey was then sent out with the assistance of an ERP vendor based in the USA. The ERP vendor agreed, on condition of anonymity, to send an introductory letter and two weeks later the questionnaire itself to a random sample of its clientele. The random sample was chosen using a systematic random sample method in which every n^{th} company from an ordered list of all the ERP vendor's clientele was chosen. The introductory letter explained that the study dealt with IT adoption and was being conducted by a certain leading business school in the South. The introductory letter promised anonymity and assured the respondent that only aggregate results would be made available to the ERP vendor. The introductory letter did not explicate that the study dealt with trust or trust building. Both the introductory letter and the questionnaire packets were addressed to the ERP vendor's contact person in each firm. Each of these contact persons had worked with the ERP vendor's consultants on implementing the ERP. Each questionnaire packet contained in addition to the questionnaire a self-addressed postage-paid envelope addressed to the university. There was only one contact person in each firm. 135 complete questionnaires were returned of the 540 that were sent. All the surveyed companies used exactly the same ERP.

DATA ANALYSIS

The first step in the data analysis was to verify that the constructs displayed convergent and discriminant validity. This was done using a factor analysis with a VARIMAX rotation. After removing some of the PEOU items that loaded together with the PU items, all the items loaded highly only on the factor they were expected to, and loaded below the .40 threshold on all the other factors. The factor analysis showed eight factors with an eigenvalue above the standard threshold of 1. The 8 factors combined explained 76% of the variance. All the constructs show acceptable internal validity (Nunnally 1967), with Cronbach's α at: trust .94, PU .96, Self-reported Use .85, Confiding .84, Lack of

Dependability .76, Responsiveness .93, PEOU .91, and Good Service .84.

Appendix 2 shows the descriptive statistics and the construct correlation matrix. The data show that the ERP vendor's clientele reported that they used the ERP extensively and found it quite useful although not very easy to use. The data also show that the clients tended to show lukewarm trust toward the consultants. This may be due to client assessment that while the consultants did not show a lack of dependability, the service, responsiveness, and level of confiding provided by them was still not very good.

The next stage of the analysis examined the hypotheses using a series of stepwise linear regressions. The first stepwise regression examined Self-reported Use as the dependent variable with all the other constructs as independent variables. The stepwise linear regression included only PU as a significant independent variable (R^2=.22, β=.4669, T=5.562, p-value<.0001), supporting H_3 but not H_4. The next stepwise linear regression examined PU as the dependent variable with PEOU, Trust, Good Service, Responsiveness, Lack of Dependability, and Confiding as independent variables. The regression shows that PEOU (T=2.260, p-value =.0257, β=.1866), and more so Trust (T=5.765, p-value<.0001, β=.4759) affected PU (R^2=.33), supporting H_5 and H_1. A stepwise linear regression of PEOU with Trust, Good Service, Responsiveness, Lack of Dependability, and Confiding as independent variables showed that only Trust affected PEOU (R^2=.17, β=.4073, T= 5.006, p-value<.0001), supporting H_2. Lastly, a stepwise linear regression of Trust with Good Service, Responsiveness, Lack of Dependability, and Confiding as independent variables showed that Trust was affected (R^2=.60) by Good Service (β=.2321, T=3.190, p-value =.0018), Responsiveness (β=.3016, T=4.306, p-value<.0001), and Lack of Dependability (β=-.3965, T=-6.266, p-value<.0001), but only marginally by Confiding (β=.1035, T=1.638, p-value=.1040), supporting H_7, H_6, H_8 respectively but only marginally H_9. Nonetheless, when a linear regression of Trust with only Confiding as a sole dependent variable was run the regression was highly significant (R^2=.15, β=.3927, T= 4.832, p-value<.0001). The research model with the β values is presented in Figure 1. The two hypothesized paths that are not significant at the .05 level are shown with broken lines.

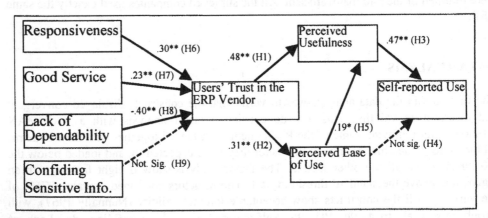

Figure 1: Research Model with Hypotheses and Beta Values

DISCUSSION AND IMPLICATIONS

Summary of Results

A central aspect of the successful deployment of ERP is customization, typically performed by specialist ERP consultants. Since the company deploying the ERP has little or no expertise in customization, it is dependent upon the consultants and cannot really monitor them. Thus, the company has little choice but to trust the consultants to customize the ERP as required. Consequently, the degree of trust that the company has in its consultants should affect their expectations of its usefulness and ease-of-use. The data analysis supports this proposition. The second objective of the study was to examine ways that consultants can increase this trust. It was hypothesized based on Luhmann's (1979) proposition that trust is built by behaving in accordance with expectations. Accordingly, it was hypothesized that when these consultants behave as they are expected to, then trust in them will increase. The data support this proposition too. When the consultants are responsive, provide good service and confide their goals, they are trusted more, while when they show a lack of dependability, trust in them decreases.

Limitations and Additional Research

The data collected and analyzed in the study was collected using a survey. This allowed for the examination of the research model in real field settings. The drawback of using a survey, however, is that surveys cannot actually show causation, although they corroborate its implied effects. Additional research using experimental designs might be necessary to establish the causation suggested in the research model.

Another problem relating to the use of surveys in field settings is the low response rate. Although the response rate in this study is in the same order of magnitude as that reported by other survey-based studies of IT adoption (e.g. Straub 1994; Igbaria et al. 1997; Gefen and Keil 1998), non-response bias cannot be ruled out. Again, additional research is necessary to show the generality of the results. Additional research is also necessary to show that trust is crucial also in other types of IT adoption. Although the finding the trust affects TAM also in freeware adoption (Gefen 1997) lends additional credibility to the generality of this proposition, studying the role of trust in other scenarios can add to the generality of the conclusions.

The mechanism Luhmann (1979) suggested for building trust, behaving in accordance with expectations, implies that many other behaviors may also build trust. These may include availability, discretion, and loyalty. Additional research is needed to study the relative importance of these and other behaviors on trust and analyze which behaviors are most effective in building trust and under what circumstances.

Implications for Practitioners

There are two major contributions of this study for practitioners: (1) the recognition that trust in the consultants customizing an ERP contributes to user assessments of how useful and easy to use the software is, and (2) that this trust can be built. These results suggest that ERP consultants and managers in charge of ERP adoption might be able to improve ERP adoption by increasing user trust in the consultants through consultant behavior that is in accordance with the users' expectations. This conclusion may also be generalize-able to other types of IT, especially given that trust has the same effect also on freeware adoption (Gefen 1997). No less important, this trust can be built, by specific behaviors, primarily by responsiveness, good service, and dependability.

It is interesting to note, in this regard, that consultants' behavior, per se, did not affected user assessments of the IT (PU and PEOU), rather this behavior affected the users' trust in the consultants, and this, in turn, affected user assessments of the IT. This seems to indicate that constructive behavior (such as responsiveness) alone does not affect software assessments. Additional research is needed to clarify this point, but if this is the case, then consultants and managers need to reason what behaviors their clients expect and behave accordingly, rather than presume that a behavior that built trust with one client might also work without change also build trust with another client.

These conclusions could be of extensive potential for the ERP industry because it shows that software adoption is not only related to software characteristics, such as PU and PEOU, but also to the trust users have in the customizing consultants and probably in the IT managers too. This implies that the job of a customization consultant and of managers in charge of ERP adoption is not just to guarantee that the software does it is job properly, though this is clearly an important aspect of it. Rather, consultants and managers in charge of ERP adoption also need to build their clients' and users' trust in them. This conclusion, research suggests, applies at least in part to freeware (Gefen 1997) and expert system (Gefen and Keil 1998), and probably applies to other types of IT, too. Consequently, consultants should make trust management an integral and central aspect of their work. The study suggested several methods of doing so: responsiveness, good service, confiding, and dependability.

In addition, since trust is built by behaving in accordance with expectations, another way of building trust could be through expectation management. Starting a project by clearly delineating user explications and discouraging unlikely expectations, and then making a point of fulfilling these expectations should build trust. Conversely, promising too much to clients or even just not discouraging unrealistic expectations may ruin trust and thus have a negative effect on ERP adoption.

Another important implication for practitioners is that the respondents when assessing their trust did not differentiate among the three belief-sets that compose trust. The items reflecting beliefs in integrity, benevolent intentions, and ability, all loaded together on one factor in the factor analysis. This implies that consultants should be aware of the intertwining nature of trust: users do not differentiate between low degrees of ability and questionable integrity or lack of benevolence. Indeed, one could hardly blame clients of suspecting the integrity and intentions of consultants who are not able to do the job.

The study also suggests that vendors should not market their ERP alone; it is marketed combined with its trustworthy configuration service. It may be advisable therefore when marketing the qualities of a new ERP system to also emphasize the trusting relationship the clients will have with the consultants. This relationship may be the make-or-break issue for many clients: a vendor can show that an ERP can do fantastic things, but getting the ERP to do it for the client at the client's site, is the real issue that interests the clients. Responsive, service-oriented, and dependable consultants can therefore give the vendor a real advantage in convincing the clients of the usefulness and ease-of-use of a specific new ERP.

Implications for Researchers

Previous research has suggested, but not actually examined, that trust might be an important aspect of IT adoption (e.g., Hard and Sanders 1997; Gefen and Keil 1998). The current study lends empirical support to this proposition and adds a theory-base to explain why trust should be so central. In doing so, the study adds several extensions to existing research on IT adoption. First, it introduces the concept of trust and its importance on ERP adoption and provides a theory-base that implies its importance beyond the realm of TAM. Second, the study, based on this theory-base, suggests and verifies several methods of building this trust. Thus, the study expands IT adoption research into a new realm that, while central to human behavior, has been mostly overlooked by IT adoption research: the way trust in other people affects human behavior and beliefs.

It is also worthy to note from a theory perspective that although the three sets of beliefs than compose trust are distinctly different concepts in daily language, they were nonetheless clustered together in the factor analysis. This implies that ability, integrity, and benevolence, at least in this case, may be so intertwined as to be indistinguishable from each other in people's minds. This result tentatively lends support to Luhmann's (1971) contention that trust is the expectation that other people will behave as one expects of them. At least in the case of ERP adoption, integrity, benevolent intentions, and ability all reflect aspects of this one generic expectation. In other words, the data suggest, in accordance with previous research (Luhmann 1971; Blau 1964; Rotter 1971), that trust is a composite belief reflected through situation-specific expectations.

Trust itself is a central aspect of socialization that indirectly influences many aspects of human behavior (Luhmann 1979; Rotter 1971; Hosmer 1995). This study suggests that trust may have the same kind of role in ERP adoption, too. ERP, and possibly also other IT, are adopted on a rational basis because they are useful, as implied by TAM, but behind this rational façade there are other social processes centered on trust. Thus, the central role of trust in forging assessments (such as PU and PEOU) and consequently behavior (such as ERP adoption) should not be overlooked during ERP adoption where customization service is essential in getting the ERP to run properly.

REFERENCES

Blau, P. (1964), *Exchange and Power in Social Life*, Wiley, NY.
Butler, J.K. Jr. (1991), "Toward Understanding and Measuring Conditions of Trust: Evolution of a

28

Conditions of Trust Inventory," *Journal of Management* 17/3, 643-663.

Chin, W.W. and Gopal, A. (1995), "Adoption Intention in GSS: Relative Importance of Beliefs," *DataBase* 26/2&3, 42-63.

Crosby, L.A., Evans, K.R. and Cowles, D. (1990), "Relationship Quality in Services Selling: An Interpersonal Influence Perspective," *Journal of Marketing* 54, 68-81.

Davis, F. D. (1989), "Perceived Usefulness, Perceived Ease of Use and User Acceptance of Information Technology," *MIS Quarterly* 13/3, 319-339.

DeLone, W.H., and McLean, E.R. (1992), "Information Systems Success: The Quest for the Dependent Variable," *Information Systems Research* 3/1, 60-95.

Deutsch, M. (1958), "Trust and Suspicion," *Conflict Resolution* 2/4, 265-279.

Fukuyama, F. (1995), *Trust: The Social Virtues & the Creation of Prosperity,* The Free Press, NY.

Gefen, D. (1997), *Building Users' Trust in Freeware Providers and the Effects of This Trust on Users' Perceptions of Usefulness, Ease of Use and Intended Use* Unpublished Doctoral Dissertation, GSU.

Gefen, D. and Keil, M. (1998), "Developer Trust-Building Behavior and User Perceptions of Perceived Usefulness: A Social-Exchange Perspective," *Database,* 29/2, pp. 35-49.

Giffin, K. (1967), "The Contribution of Studies of Source Credibility to a Theory of Interpersonal Trust in the Communication Process," *Psychological Bulletin* 68/2, 104-120.

Hart, P. and Saunders, C. (1997), "Power and Trust: Critical Factors in the Adoption and Use of Electronic Data Interchange," *Organizational Science* 8/1, 23-42.

Hosmer, L.T. (1995), "Trust: The Connecting Link Between Organizational Theory and Philosophical Ethics," *Academy of Management Review* 20/2, 379-403.

Igbaria, M., Zinatelli, N., Cragg, P. and Cavaye, A.L.M.(1997), "Personal Computing Acceptance Factors in Small Firms: A Structural Equation Model," *MIS Quarterly* 21/3, 279-305.

Karahanna, E., D.W. Straub, and N.L. Chervany (1999), "Information Technology Adoption Across Time: A Cross-Sectional Comparison of Pre-Adoption and Post-Adoption Beliefs," *MIS Quarterly* 23/2, 183-213.

Kumar, N., Scheer L .K. and Steenkamp, J. E. M. (1995), "The Effects of Supplier Fairness on Vulnerable Resellers," *Journal of Marketing Research* 17, 54-65.

Luhmann N.(1979) *Trust and Power,* John Wiley and Sons, GB (translated from German).

Mathieson K. (1991), "Predicting User Intentions: Comparing the Technology Acceptance Model with the Theory of Planned Behavior," *Information Systems Research* 2/3,173-191.

McKnight, D.H., Cummings, L.L., and Chervany, N.L. (1998), "Initial Trust Formation in New Organizational Relationships," *Academy of Management Review* 23/3, 473-490.

Nunnally, J. C. (1967), *Psychometric Theory,* McGraw-Hill, NY.

Rotter, J. B. (1971), "Generalized Expectancies for Interpersonal Trust," *American Psychologist* 26, 443-450.

Schurr, P.H. and Ozanne J.L. (1985), "Influences on Exchange Processes: Buyers' Preconceptions of a Seller's trustworthiness and Bargaining Toughness," *Journal of Consumer Research* 11, 939-953.

Shah, H.U., Dingley, S. and Golder, P.A. (1994), "Bridging the Cultural Gap Between Users and Developers," *Journal of Systems Management* 45/7, 18-21.

Straub, D.W. (1995), "The Effect of Culture on IT diffusion: E-mail and FAX in Japan and the U.S.," *Information Systems Research* 5/1, 23-47.

Szajna, B. (1994), "Software Evaluation and Choice: Predictive Validation of the Technology Acceptance Instrument," *MIS Quarterly* 18/3, 319-324.

Venkatesh, V. and Davis, F.D. (1994), "Modeling the Determinants of Perceived Ease of Use," *Proceedings of the 14th International Conf. on Information Systems,* 213-225.

Zucker, L. G. (1986), "Production of Trust: Institutional Sources of Economic Structure, 1840-1920," *Research in Organizational Behavior* 8, 53-111.

Appendix 1: Questionnaire Items:

	Ability
ab1	SP are competent in their field
ab2	SP are knowledgeable concerning their products
ab3	SP adheres to quality control standards
	Perceived Ease of Use
eo1	We find SP's software easy to use
eo2	It was easy to become skillful at using SP's software
eo3	Learning to operate SP's software was easy
eo4	SP's software is flexible to interact with
eo5	Our interaction with SP's software is clear and understandable
eo6	We find it easy to get SP's software to do what we want it to do
	Lack of Dependability
dep1	SP sometimes "bends the facts"
dep2	SP promises to do things without actually doing them later
dep3	SP withheld crucial information from us
	Integrity
in1	SP are frank when dealing with us
in2	SP are open in dealing with us
in3	SP are honest about their problems
in4	Even if explanations given by SP are rather unlikely, it is the truth
in5	When SP gives us advice they share their best judgment
in6	SP shows high integrity
	Benevolent Intentions
int1	We can count on SP to consider how their decisions will affect us
int2	SP cares for us
int3	SP puts customer's interests before their own
	Confiding
con1	SP confided in me about their own goals and objectives
con2	SP confided in me about their past mistakes
con3	SP's agent confided in me about his / her own job
	Perceived Usefulness
pu1	I find SP's software useful in my work
pu2	SP's software improves my job performance
pu3	SP's software enables me to accomplish tasks faster
pu4	SP's software enhances my effectiveness on the job
pu5	SP's software makes it easier to do my job
pu6	SP's software increases my productivity
	Responsiveness
re1	My feedback is reflected in subsequent versions.
re2	My feedback influences changes made in the software.
	Good Service
gs1	SP has gone out on a limb for us
gs2	SP has made sacrifices for us in the past
	Self-reported Use
u1	My company is a heavy user of the software provided by SP
u2	We use SP software on a daily basis
u3	We use SP software very often
u4	My company uses the software provided by SP very frequently

Appendix 2: Descriptive Statistics and Correlation among Constructs

Construct	Mean (std.) [2]	Self-report Use	PU	PEOU	Trust	Good Service	Resp.	Lack of Dep.
Self-reported Use	1.76(0.99)							
PU	3.20(1.24)	.478**						
PEOU	4.44(1.49)	.212*	.366**					
Trust	3.84(1.13)	.216*	.516**	.407**				
Good Service	4.99(1.33)	.053	.403**	.364**	.592**			
Resp.	4.35(1.36)	.065	.328**	.230*	.624**	.545**		
Lack of Dep.	4.36(1.28)	.075	-.188*	-.272**	-.552**	-.347**	-.356**	
Confiding	5.11(1.33)	.154	.373**	.271**	.393**	.413**	.308**	-.160

A double asterisks represents a significant correlation at the .01 level, and a single asterisk represents a significant correlation at the .05 level.

---

[2] Mean ranges from 1 strongly agree to 7 strongly disagree.

SIMULTANEOUS ANALYSIS OF HETEROGENOUS DATABASES ON THE WEB: THE ADDSIA PROJECT

J.M. Lamb, C.R. Smart

Centre for Educational Sociology
University of Edinburgh
7 Buccleuch Place
Edinburgh, EH8 9LW
United Kingdom

Abstract: ADDSIA (Access to Distributed Data for Statistical Information and Analysis) is a research project managed by Eurostat under the Development of Statistical Information Systems (DOSIS) initiative. It uses distributed database techniques and Web technology to facilitate more effective access to statistical data. The interface with existing systems offers the user the ability to access different sites from a single web browser, and to combine data from different sources. We describe the overall architecture of the system and identify the theoretical advances, particularly methods for documenting the data manipulation that takes place during analysis, and the development of a DTD (Document Type Description) for combining statistical data. The paper locates ADDSIA in the Decision Sciences discipline, with particular reference to information from official statistics. We review the achievements of the project, consider the impact that emerging technologies have had on it during its lifetime, and discuss the future possibilities, both theoretical and practical.

Key words: World Wide Web, Official Statistics, comparative data, metadata, XML

INTRODUCTION

Decision making depends on information, and increasingly statistical data from official sources are used for decision making. The advent of new technology, particularly the World Wide Web, has made the transfer of statistical data particularly easy. However, the interpretation of such data is not so easy. The more remote a user is from the source of the data, the easier it is for misunderstandings to creep in. Therefore, in the global context of decision making today, it is vital that as much help as possible is given to users of remote

31

S.H. Zanakis et al. (eds.), Decision Making: Recent Developments and Worldwide Applications, 31–46.
© 2000 *Kluwer Academic Publishers.*

data. This must be done in a context of increasing amounts of data and pressure on statistical offices to maintain a cost effective service. The ADDSIA system tackles this problem by offering a single browser based interface to multiple sites, each of whom can register their data, but do not need to pre-process it before entering it into the ADDSIA system. Of course this registration is not without cost, since the accompanying metadata must also be registered. However, we believe that current XML technology offers an important way forward in this area.

We shall start by giving an overview of the Decision Sciences at the end of the 20th century, and also review what is happening in the world of Official Statistics, before going on to describe the ADDSIA project in detail.

STATISTICS FOR DECISION MAKING

Any organisation is a decision making body. The use of appropriate statistics and statistical methods can provide an insight into the effect of policy [Udo99], can assess the quality and use satisfaction of a product or service [Zhu99] and ultimately help to ensure that the organisation is efficient and effective [Deming75].

The world in which we live and the society in which we operate is in a constant state of flux. To survive and prosper in such an environment, businesses must change and adapt to new markets, new products and new organisational structures while, at the same time, ensuring that they are ready to face the next set of challenges brought about by their (internal) and society's (external) development. This might take the form of looking at existing customers and trying to identify their needs, desires and expectations, both spoken and unspoken, and develop ways to ensure that their current customers remain and become their future customers [Gustafsson99].

In order to succeed in this complex environment, the business must analyse all the available data in order to make the decisions which will ensure the continued success of the organisation. However, it is often not feasible to collect the data which is needed for an analysis, either because it would be too costly to gather or because the individuals or organisations would not release such confidential or commercially sensitive information to a competitor. A substantial amount of information is available from both governmental sources such as Statbase [http1] and non-governmental sources such as the UK Data Archive [http2]. Governmental sources in particular offer a rich source of data, since organisations are often bound by a legal requirement to supply data which is both timely and accurate.

While part of the organisation-government contract is often a guarantee of anonymity, aggregated data sufficiently detailed to permit a meaningful analysis is often available. The difficulty with this "processed" data is that it will have already been manipulated to fit the concepts and terminology of the national government and these concepts may, though well defined, not be appropriate to the analysis which the organisation wishes to perform. This problem can be particularly acute when an organisation is trying to perform an analysis based on data from more than one national body as the definition of certain terms can vary, either through time or from organisation to organisation. In some cases the situation can be made more complex through regional variation. For example, within the United Kingdom, a number of legal and educational frameworks exist which have to be harmonised before a comparative analysis can be performed.

In the past, when the data was being collected and analysed by, or on behalf of, the same organisation, the documentation of the data (the metadata) was often considered to be of little importance. This was because the data was there to serve a single purpose which was known to all users, and it was then discarded. The cost of data collection is now such that organisations try to squeeze the last piece of information out of the collected data and are increasingly combining their own, collected data, with other external sources to provide sufficient data for the desired analysis. In this situation, the documentation of the data sources is of vital importance. Only by knowing exactly what it is that has been measured can an analysis have a sound base. Further, it is important that the process of the analysis be recorded and documented as any analysis places an implicit theoretical framework upon the data. Without this analysis record, the final information can be impossible to audit and may be open to multiple interpretations.

RESEARCH IN OFFICIAL STATISTICS

One of the chief sources of statistics for decision making are the data and publications of National and Regional Statistical Offices. Unlike academic or company statistics, these statistics are specifically collected and published to inform others: governments, industry, the media and the public. With each new technological advancement comes new demands for better quality, more detailed, and more timely information. In addition, businesses are resisting the demand for them to supply more information, and statistical offices therefore have to explore ways of minimising that demand. Hence, within a single organisation, they seek to co-ordinate their requests to businesses. Technology has been a factor in the increasing pressure on statistical offices, but it has also been the method by which these offices seek to meet these demands [Arondel98][Holt98].

Another significant factor in the production of official statistics has been the need for the European Union to produce EU wide statistics. Each of the 15 countries in the Union has its own statistical office, each with its own legislative foundation and institutional strategy and culture. The prime purpose of each of these institutions is to collect and publish national statistics. However, they also have a legal obligation to supply statistics to the official statistical office of the EU, Eurostat. This obligation has led to significant study of the means whereby statistical data collected from different sources and using different methodology can be reconciled. Eurostat has been a lead player in this field.

In 1987, Eurostat hosted a seminar to study 'the development of statistical expert systems'. At that time hopes of using expert systems and knowledge based databases for many information based problems were high [Barrett88]. Consequently, Eurostat funded seven research projects with topics covering automated information processing, documentation, access to statistical information, and forecasting. This active promotion of research in official statistics continued in 1995, with a larger research programme called the Development of Statistical Information Systems (DOSIS). In addition to funding 18 projects [http3], Eurostat have also supported numerous conferences. A useful forum for discussion is the annual DOSIS meeting at which project leaders present their results to fellow researchers, representatives of official statistical offices, and invited experts. These meetings offer a good opportunity for the cross-fertilisation of ideas.

At present a new round of research projects are about to be funded, and EPROS (the European Plan for Research in Official Statistics) provides a good guide to the current research topics. The advent of the World Wide Web has obviously had an impact on both the collection and dissemination of statistics, and provides a focus for research. The programme also covers advances in statistical techniques, quality assurance, the 'black economy' as well as technical issues [http4].

PUBLISHING OFFICIAL STATISTICS ON THE WEB

Official statistical offices began to take advantage of the World Wide Web in 1995/96. The first sections to take notice of the advantages the web brought were the publication and publicity departments. By 1997 over 60 references to National Statistical Institutes (NSIs) or International Agencies could be found [Lamb98], and forty-seven of these were accessed successfully. At this time most of the information to be found were reproductions of printed publications, but a year later we saw the appearance of online databases, such as Statbase [http1] and Statline [http5]. However, National Statistical Institutes still publish primarily for the national market, so, although the information can be viewed from anywhere in the world, the assumptions are that the viewer will understand the political, cultural and institutional background to the figures. Moreover, each statistical office has developed its own style of Website, which makes assembling information from different sites a major task [Kraus98].

What is needed is a unified view of different databases, so that users can concentrate on the content of the databases, and minimise the effort in combining data from different sources. The ADDSIA system aims to address this problem.

THE ADDSIA PROJECT: AIMS AND OBJECTIVES

ADDSIA (Access to Distributed Databases for Statistical Information and Analysis) is one of the DOSIS projects mentioned above. In 1995, when the project was conceived, we wrote:

> "In an ideal world statistical data would be collected using the latest technology and harmonised to exchange data via object oriented paradigms and the most advanced methods of electronic exchange. However in the present day statistical information is held in a variety of ways and it is not practical to convert existing practices of National Statistical Institutes, at least not in the short term.

Two emerging technologies can help us to utilise statistical data in an effective manner. These are Wide Area Information Systems (WAIS) and Distributed Statistical databases (DS-DBMS). This project aims to use advances in distributed databases and wide area information systems techniques to access data held in a variety of structures and make it available to users."

The technologies have advanced, but the basic needs and aims have not changed. The ADDSIA system offers a uniform interface to existing statistical data that allows the user to access both data and metadata, and construct his own queries on an integrated view of the data.

National Statistical Institutes (NSI) are committed to the collection of accurate and timely statistics, which is essential to the effective running of the state. Democratic states are also committed to open access to statistics for all social and economic actors and all citizens. However, users are becoming more sophisticated and making heavier demands on the providers of data, and at the same time, there is pressure to reduce costs. Several NSIs have developed information systems to help the process of collecting, managing and disseminating statistical information. The focus and sophistication of these systems differ, but all capture a significant amount of metadata – 'data about data' – that aids the processing of the data, and potentially leads to better understanding of the statistical output. The starting point of ADDSIA, then, was to interface with existing systems and offer the user the ability to browse metadata from different sources from a single interface, and to combine data from different sources.

THE ADDSIA ARCHITECTURE

The first premise of ADDSIA is that it is only sensible to combine data within a common *Domain*. The *Domain* is set up by an NSI on behalf of a group of *Data Providers* who wish to jointly publish their data. From the Provider's point of view datasets may be subscribed to several domains, but from the user's view the Domain is the point of entry. The Domain Server hosts access to the data, offering a User interface, and several modules for accessing data and metadata. The Domain Server is accessed via a normal web browser.

One of the most important modules in the Domain Server is the Statistical Analysis Module (SAM) which receives requests from the user interface, parses them, and sends requests to the different registered Providers. Each Provider also has a server, which acts as a buffer between the Domain and the basic data (which we call Native data). The Provider Server sends the appropriate request to the data, and passes it back to the Domain Server. Here the various responses are combined, and returned to the user interface.

Figure 1 shows the architecture of ADDSIA. It is divided into four, showing four physical locations. The User, at the top of the diagram (A) is using a standard Web browser, and links to the Domain via the Internet. The Domain (B) holds all the Domain level metadata, that is all the information that is relevant to the substantive area (for

36

example a generic definition of a school leaver, or a reference to some European wide legislation). The Domain is linked, again via the Internet, to two Data Providers (C and D). These Providers supply both the data to be linked, and the metadata relevant to their specific site.

Based on this overview, we can elaborate on the specific features of the ADDSIA system. At the outset, we took the view that the system would be an exploratory one, designed to verify particular approaches. Consequently, we have not developed the system to production standards, and we assume that the modules of ADDSIA will be embedded in the host system. Thus, for example, user registration is not handled automatically, but an e-mail is generated to the system manger to request registration.

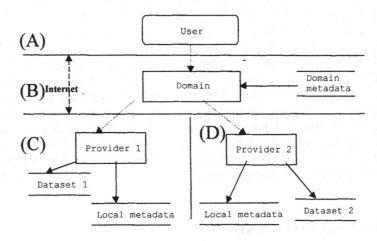

Figure 1. the architecture of ADDSIA

There are eight essential areas that the ADDSIA system has investigated. These are:

- Access to 'native' data
- Input of metadata via XML
- Use of a search engine to browse metadata
- Definition and storage of variable transformations
- A homogeneous view of heterogeneous data
- Merging of heterogeneous data
- Harmonisation under users' control, with default options supplied by Data Providers
- Production of Publication standard tables with adjustable styles and output formats

Before showing the architecture in more detail, we will identify the key terms and modules.

(1) **Native data** is data that already exists in the Data Providers' site

(2) **The SIM:** the Secure Interface Module. This module is the 'gateway' to the native data. It checks access rights, and returns summary results to the rest of the system, if appropriate

(3) **The pre-SIM:** this module is used to register a native dataset

(4) **The PARM:** Provider Access Registration Module. This module is used to register users for particular datasets and variables

(5) **The Data Provider Administration Interface:** This is the interface to the PARM, and also allows data provider metadata to be registered with the system

(6) **The PSAM:** Provider Statistical Analysis Module. This module performs statistical operations on data obtained from the SIM

(7) **The DARM:** Domain Access Registration Module: this module is used to register users to the ADDSIA system for a given domain

(8) **The Domain Administration Interface:** This is the interface to the DARM, and it also allows the domain level metadata to be registered with the system

(9) **The DSAM:** Domain Statistical Analysis Module. This module merges data supplied by one or more PSAMs

(10) **The Domain Server:** This is a webserver that allows users to access ADDSIA via their local web browser

(11) **The ADDSIA search engine:** there is a single search engine for all domains

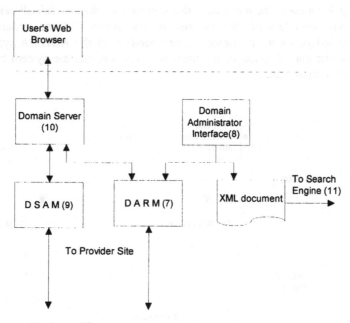

Figure 2. The modules for a single domain

38

The deployment of these modules is as follows: The SIM handles the access to native data, ensuring that only summary data is passed to the rest of the system. Metadata is input to the system either via an interactive interface, or by importing an XML file that conforms to the ADDSIA specification. In either case the XML file is made available to the search engine. The Domain Webserver handles the user interface. It also manages the user workspace. It receives requests from users for the construction of statistical tables from the available datasets and passes these requests to the DSAM. The server is also responsible for the storage of the user's transformations. The DSAM parses the requests it receives and passes them on to the appropriate PSAMs, which in turn request data from the SIM. The DSAM merges the resulting data, according to pre-defined or user-defined harmonisation rules. Finally, the Domain Server transforms the results from the DSAM into a table following the user's style specification.

Figure 2 shows the deployment of modules for a single domain, and Figure 3 shows the modules for a single provider site.

USING THE ADDSIA SYSTEM

The ADDSIA system, with the exception of the search engine, has been written entirely in Java. This provides us with the flexibility to deploy the system on a number of different operating systems. In particular, the communication facilities available with the Java language have made the implementation much easier than we initially expected. The use of appropriate middle-ware for database access means that the system is platform and database independent. In discussing the operation of the ADDSIA system we shall look firstly at the classification of the users who can operate the system before dealing with their role in more detail.

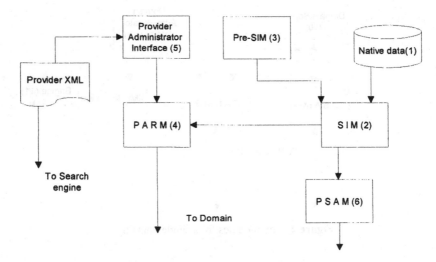

Figure 3. The modules for a single provider site

User types

The ADDSIA system has three types of operator. The distinction between the role of the operators is based on the function they perform within the system. The Domain Administrator is responsible for the existence and running of a particular domain site. The Data (Provider) Administrator is responsible for the existence and running of a Data Provider site, and also for registration with a Domain. The User accesses the domain, and thence one or more provider sites. An Administrator can of course also act as a User. The user role is further divided according to the level of access and permissions that have been granted to that user. The three levels are 'Casual', 'Normal' and 'Expert'. By 'casual' we mean a user who browses the site and has access to public information. A 'normal' user is registered with the system, and with individual sites. It is expected that he would make some commitment to learning the ADDSIA system, but would not have any detailed expertise. Many decision makers would be classed as normal users. Data for normal users is presented in a pre-defined format, as decided by the domain and data administrators. An 'expert' user is assumed to have expertise in the domain, and to have an understanding of the user and interpretation of statistical data. These users can have access to the basic data, and do not necessarily have to rely on definitions supplied by the administrators.

System set-up

Before the system can be used it needs to be configured. This is a three stage process. Firstly, a domain needs to be defined and created. Second, data providers must define their data and create provider sites. Once these two stages have been completed then the providers can register their sites with one or more domains and the system is ready for use.

The domain is defined using an interface which collects the necessary information. The information is stored in an XML document which conforms to a specific document type definition (DTD). This document stores administrative information such as the name and email address of the person responsible for the domain. It also stores information which is used in the processing of requests and, in particular, used to aid the process of harmonisation. The data provider has two different types of XML document to create: one which defines the provider themselves and one which must be completed for every dataset being registered with the domain.

XML files in ADDSIA

In ADDSIA we have defined three different types of XML files: for the domain, the provider and the dataset. In creating our own DTDs, we were conscious of two things. First, there is a need to standardise DTDs, so we were reluctant to introduce yet more. On the other hand, for the system to be used, the overhead of registering data had to be minimised for the domain manager and data provider. We looked at a number of emerging formats for dataset description, such as the DDI [http6], and felt that none met our requirements.

The final DTD [Bi99] requires only a minimum amount of information for the system to work (though there is space to include a more complete description should the provider wish). However, if the domain and data provider provide a richer set of metadata, the end user can have a better understanding of the data he is using. The domain document allows the storage of "classifications" and "concepts" which can be considered as harmonised indicators and their values. When a provider registers their data, they can, if they wish, provide a mapping from their definition of a variable to the harmonised concepts stored at the domain. The provider dataset document can describe both survey and time-series data.

This separation of data and metadata has an interesting side effect, namely that a single collection of data can be registered with more than one set of metadata. This is useful in cases where the data may have been collected, and subsequently described, in one language, say French, but is needed for a comparative analysis with another country's data, say Germany. In this case it would be possible to translate the question text and variable labels from French to German, and, for a relatively low overhead, obtain a dataset which is more readily understandable by a German speaking analyst.

It is our belief that much of the XML document creation can be performed automatically by extracting the information from other forms. As part of the support tools for ADDSIA we have created a mechanism for the extraction of much of the required information from an SPSS data dictionary. Registering a new dataset with the domain is simply a matter of telling the domain where to find the data and its XML description.

ADDSIA in operation

A full description of all the operations of ADDSIA is beyond the scope of this paper. We shall instead present a "walk through" of the main features as seen by the user and follow those operations through the system. The scenario which we present is that a user wishes to compare the attainment in mathematics of 16 year olds leaving school in Scotland in the years 1981 and 1991.

On entering the ADDSIA system their first task is to find appropriate datasets. This is performed by searching the metadata archive. The metadata interface supports both searching and browsing. Once the user is satisfied that they have found some suitable datasets then they can register for access. It is a requirement of the system that the data providers retain final control over who is able to access their data. On registration the datasets are added to the list of those available to the user. Once the registration process is complete the user is free to perform operations upon the data.

Operations are performed within the confines of a "workbook". This enables the user to be working on several analyses and to keep the data and results separate. The workbook permits the user to apply statistical or data management operations to the variables of the selected datasets. Before the user can compare the values of attainment, they need to harmonise the qualifications variable. The qualification issued in Scotland changed from O grades – which were awarded on a scale of 1-5 – to standard grades – awarded on a scale of 1-7 – during this time. The qualifications co-existed until 1996 but for simplicity we shall assume that all qualifications in 1981 were O grade and all in 1991 were standard grade. To do this they need to create some common code list and then transform the value in each variable to that common list. An example code list and the mapping for each variable is shown below.

Code list	1981	1991
High Pass	1-2	1-2
Pass	3	3-4
Low Pass	4-5	5-7
No Award	No Award	No Award

Table 1. Code list and recode for both 1981 and 1991 attainments

A transform is a combination of the **how**, the **what** and the **why** of a recode. How defines the mechanics of the recode, the what captures, in natural language, what the recode is attempting to do, the why gives the reasons or conceptual framework for the recode. In the system, the recode is only performed when the value is required and it is the definition of the recode which is stored and not the resultant variable.

Having defined the transform the user must now define the selection (age=16). Their last step is to construct a query to the system which will perform all the transforms and selections and then return the resultant table to us in a form and style of our choosing. Behind the scenes the system creates a query to be sent to the Domain Statistical Analysis Module (9). This module interprets the query and sends the constituent parts to the appropriate Provider Statistical Analysis Module (6). Each single query could contain operations for a number of different providers. Once a sub-query arrives at the provider, the Provider Access Registration Module (4) is checked to ensure that the user has the right to access the necessary datasets. Once permission has been obtained the PSAM returns the summary additive attributes for all the categories in the request. These are the sum, the sum of squares and the number of elements. From these basic components a wide range of statistical operations can be performed. It is these summary values which pass over the Internet and never any of the raw data which remains safe behind whatever security the provider deems appropriate.

Once all the sub-queries have been satisfied and the attributes returned to the domain, the system is able to satisfy the request. The sub-queries are collated into a single macro object which is then handed to the table presentation and display module for preparation into a user friendly table. The presentation module can create the table in a number of forms. For demonstration purposes we have restricted ourselves to ASCII, HTML and Excel though there is no reason why other formats could not be used. As well as being able to alter the output format, it is possible to alter the look of the table using style sheets. The order of the labels on the rows and columns is also user-defined. This table is then presented to the user.

We maintain a difference between the presentation of a table and the publication of the same table. The difference is the handling of footnotes. Often these footnotes are vital to the complete understanding of a table. In presentation mode (where the table is displayed in the web browser) most of the footnotes are not displayed, but are available through links. In publication mode, all footnotes are presented. These notes are ordered in levels of importance so that the main points are prominent and other, maybe more minor matters, are also present but further down the list.

How?

Source label fom SSLS92:DoNow Destination label from Status

Full time Student	Full Time Student ▾
Apprentice	Part Time Student ▾
Full time work	Full Time Work ▾
Part time work	Part Time Work ▾
Sandwich course	Part Time Student ▾
Nothing	Other ▾

What?

```
Assign the activity reported according
to the level of study or work required
```

Why?

```
To decide on the level of commitment to
a particular activity. For example, an
apprentice is receiving "on the job"
training and is thus focused on work.
```

[Create transform]   [Reset]

Figure 4. Defining a variable

AN EXAMPLE SESSION

Figure 4 shows how a request is built up, modifying a variable from the supplied definition to reflect the particular orientation of the inquiry. The definition captures a definition of the modification together with the reason for doing it. Figure 5 shows the graphical construction of a table, identifying the rows and columns to be constructed. The Table name and heading, and the style of the output are also selected. Figure 6 shows the resulting table.

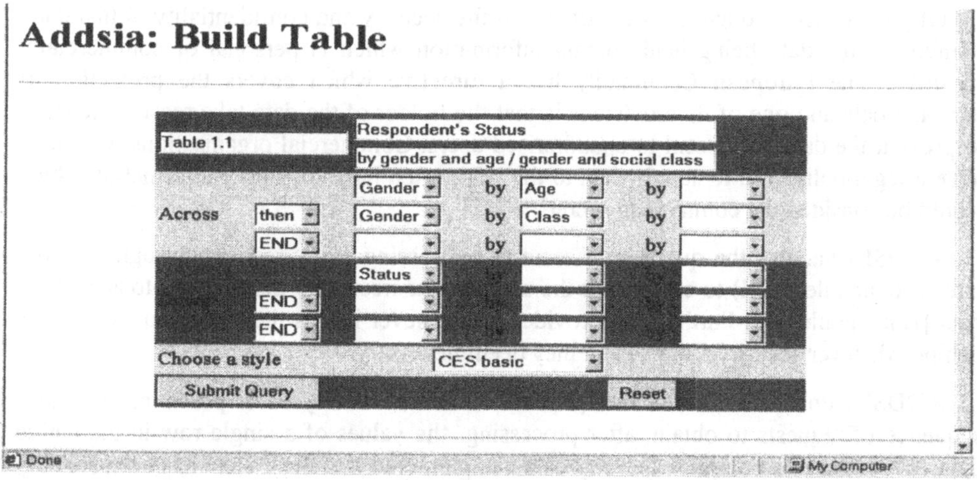

Addsia: Build Table

Figure 5. Defining a table

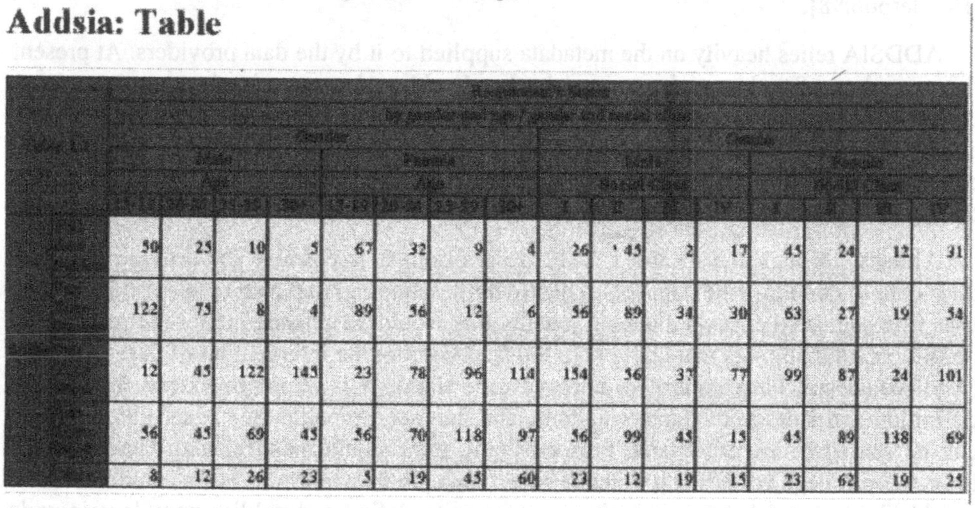

Addsia: Table

Figure 6. The resulting table

IMPLICATIONS AND ISSUES

As with any research project, a number of issues are raised during its lifetime and the system had many implications for both users and data providers. The presence in the project team of a number of NSIs meant that there was a great deal of useful discussion of how the system would work in practice and how it could be "sold" to the data provider community.

Of great concern to any provider of data is the security and confidentiality of that data. Sometimes the data being held contain information which is personal or commercially sensitive. The European Community has a directive which covers the protection of personal data and one of its provisions is that the holder of the data take reasonable steps to prevent the data being sent to unauthorised users. Commercial organisations, who may have a legal obligation to supply data to the NSI, often have to supply information which would be considered a commercial secret.

ADDSIA handles the question of security by passing every request through a secure interface module (SIM) to ensure that the user has the necessary permissions to access the data [Hatzopoulos97]. Further, the provider's data never leaves their site and can remain behind whatever security features that they deem necessary.

ADDSIA does not address the question of confidentiality. It is possible, through a sequence of requests to obtain, after processing, the values of a single row in the native data. We make an assumption that any data being entered into the system has been suitably pre-processed to remove identifying information. Tools exist to perform much of this task [Hunderpool98].

ADDSIA relies heavily on the metadata supplied to it by the data providers. At present this metadata often has to be created by hand, although some simple tools have been developed to aid the process. We see XML as a useful technology which will increase the availability and quality of metadata. We feel that we have contributed towards the definition of a XML based metadata system which can enable data providers to match their data to pre-defined domain wide concepts.

Already, through the dataset's XML description, it is possible for providers to map their data to domain-wide concepts. These default mappings can also be overridden by the user who can use their own mapping. Ideally this would be extended to let users exchange definitions of mappings that could be published without the intervention of data providers (who would still have control of access to the data). It is hoped to extend the idea of definition and storage of transformations, and can see a use for 'metadata libraries' that can be shared by users [Smart]. Presently only the domain manager and data providers have the privilege of defining domain-wide concepts that 'normal' users can access. We would like to extend this to permit expert users to define and publish new domain-wide concepts. This would be a way of adding value to the dataset in a way which would be difficult, if not impossible, with an off-line dataset. The linking of structured and unstructured metadata, and the ability to index and search files as part of an overall system is an important contribution.

The concept of ownership of data providers having full ownership of their data, while users have full freedom to define transformations and operations on that data is one that we strongly support. However, we feel that the hierarchical approach of domains and data providers could be loosened with current technology. Defining 'virtual' domain sites instead of physical domain sites would give the user more flexibility, and opens up the possibility of third parties publishing methods for dealing with data in particular areas of expertise.

In the current ADDSIA system we make the assumption that all datasets are static. That is to say that the underlying data is fixed and cannot change. We have not addressed the issue of rapidly changing datasets, or versions of datasets, and compatibility of the data over time. In addition, we would like to consider the issues of comparing time series data more fully, and to further develop the metadata definitions to cope with this type of data. The system puts a homogeneous view on the data in a number of aspects. The web browser gives a unified user interface; the SIM handles the differences of physical storage and formatting, and the metadata allows mapping between different conceptual views.

Central to the system are the statistical modules which merge not just the data, but the associated metadata, and allow the user a number of functions for controlling how data is merged. The statistical aspects of the work could also be taken forward by integrating a distributed declarative querying facility and a distributed statistical aggregation system, using distributed database and web technology.

A particular aspect of ADDSIA is its focus on presentation and publication issues. We consider two types of user: the external user who accesses the data and receives an output table on his browser, and the internal user who is producing tables for external publication. For both these types of output there are three considerations which impact on the design: output medium, appearance, and footnotes. Because of our concern with publication for third parties, we have put a good deal of emphasis on footnotes. For the final table, the footnotes come from two sources: the input metadata and the user himself. The user has the opportunity to browse the available metadata. If he uses an indicator that already exists, he can use existing metadata; if he creates a new variable, he is also required to create the accompanying metadata. We could build on work done on the model of the output table, and in formatting tables for different outputs, by defining different output channels, conforming, for example to different DTDs and style sheets.

Throughout we have referred to official statistics. The ADDSIA system is relevant to any organisation which is either producing or consuming statistical data. It has a particular relevance to any organisation which needs to combine data from different sources, perhaps held in different systems, and deliver the information in a clear, controlled and consistent manner directly to the desktop of the employee as, and when, they need it.

In conclusion, ADDSIA contributes to a debate that will be of relevance to all producers and users of statistics over the next few years. It addresses the question: "How can we publish safe, accurate, informative statistics on the Web in a global context?"

REFERENCES

Arondel, P. and Depoutot, R. (1998), "Overview of Quality Issues when dealing with socio-economic products in an international environment" XXXth ASU meeting, Rennes, May, 25–29

Barrett, M. L. and Beerel, A. C. (1988), *Expert Systems in Business a practical approach*, Ellis Hornwood Limited, Chichester

Bi, Y., Murtagh, F. and McClean, S. (1999), "Metadata and XML for Organising and Accessing Multiple Statistical Data Sources", in Proceedings of Association of Survey Computing's 3rd International Conference, Edinburgh, to appear.

Deming, W.E. (1975), "On Some Statistical aids towards Economic Production", Interfaces, Vol. 5, No. 4, August 1975, 1–15.

Gustafsson, A., Ekdahl, F. and Edvardsson B. (1999), "Developing New Services by Observing Customers", in Despotis, D. K. and Zopounidis, C. (Eds.), *Decision Sciences Institute 5th International Conference, Athens,* 1477–1479.

Hatzopoulos, M., Karali, I., Viglas, E. and Murtagh, F. (1997), ADDSIA Deliverable: 3.1, Specification of Secure Interface Module.

Holt, T (1998), "Research and Development and the Future of Official Statistics" International Seminar on New Techniques and Technologies for Statistics (Pre-Proceedings), Sorrento, 11–22.

Hunderpool, A. and Willenborg, L. (1998), "Argus, Software packages for Statistical Disclosure Control", in Payne, R and Green, P (Eds), *Proceedings in Computational Statistics 1998,* Physica-Verlag, Heidelberg, 341–345

Kraus, F. (1998), "Towards a Data Infrastructure for Socio-economic Research on Europe: Improving Access to Official Microdata at the National and European Level", Eurodata Newsletter, No. 7, 13–20.

Lamb, J. M. (1998), "National Statistical Offices and Administrations, and the Web: A Survey", Research in Official Statistics 1(1), pp.121–130

Smart, C. (1998), "Visualisation of Statistical Analysis and Processing", International Seminar on New Techniques and Technologies for Statistics (Pre-Proceedings), Sorrento, 491–496.

Udo, G. J. (1999), "Comparative Analysis of Information Technology Management Approaches", in Despotis, D. K. and Zopounidis, C. (Eds.), *Decision Sciences Institute 5th International Conference,* Athens, 1594–1595.

Zhu, F. X. and Wymer, W. W., Jnr. (1999), "Impact of Information Technology on Service Quality", in Despotis, D. K. and Zopounidis, C. (Eds.), *Decision Sciences Institute 5th International Conference,* Athens, 1795–1797.

WEB ADDRESSES

http1   http://www.ons.gov.uk/index.htm

http2   http://dawww.essex.ac.uk/

http3   http://europa.eu.int/en/comm/eurostat/research/index.htm

http4   http://europa.eu.int/en/comm/eurostat/research/fp5/documents/eprosen1.pdf

http5   http://www.cbs.nl/nl/statline/index.htm

http6   http://www.icpsr.umich.edu/DDI/codebook.html The Documentation Data Initiative: A Project to Develop an XML Document Type Definition for Data Documentation

2. EDUCATION INNOVATIONS & DISTANCE LEARNING

DECISION SUPPORT FOR THE MANAGEMENT OF ADMISSIONS TO ACADEMIC PROGRAMS

K.S. Dhir[1], W.H. Platt[2], G. Watts[2]

[1]The Pennsylvania State University at Harrisburg,
School of Business Administration
777 W. Harrisburg Pike
Middletown, PA 17057-4898, USA

[2]Swinburne University of Technology
P.O. Box 218
Hawthorne, Melbourne
Victoria, 3122, Australia

Abstract: Subjectivity plays an important role in academic assessment. Integration of information obtained by the academic administrators, no matter how objective its basic character, remains a subjective process. The limitations of human judgment have major implications for the decision making process in the academic profession. Fortunately, new tools based on theories and concepts in applied psychology, policy sciences, computer oriented data handling and graphic displays, and multiple regression analyses have made it possible to investigate the parameters of the judgment process. This enables the assessment of the role of subjectivity in decision-making. This chapter introduces social judgment theory as a potentially useful theoretical and methodical basis for understanding subjectivity in academic administration. A computerized procedure is described for identification, measurement and reporting of judgmental sources of administrative decision-making. A specific example of analysis is offered in the context of the assessment of applicants to a program of study.

Key words: Admissions, decision support, judgment analysis, social judgment theory

S.H. Zanakis et al. (eds.), Decision Making: Recent Developments and Worldwide Applications, 49–64.
© 2000 Kluwer Academic Publishers.

INTRODUCTION

This chapter describes a study conducted at the Swinburne University of Technology in Australia, in their School of Business. The study was to explore the applicability of a judgment-analytic decision support system to the assessment of the likelihood of an applicant being selected for admission to the School's Graduate Certificate in Business Administration (GCBA) program. The likelihood of a program administrator selecting a particular applicant is directly linked to the assessment of the likelihood of that applicant's success in the GCBA program. The purpose of this study, in effect, was to analyze the administrative judgment process in assessment of an applicant's likelihood of success in the program.

THE PROCESS OF HUMAN JUDGMENT

Human judgment is a process through which an individual uses social information to make decisions. The social information is obtained from an individual's environment and is interpreted through the individual's cognitive image of the environment. The cognitive image provides a representation of the environment based on past experiences and training, and essentially predisposes the person to respond to social information in predictable ways. An individual's policies or beliefs about the environment represent these patterns. Human judgments are based then upon one's interpretation of available information. They are probability statements about one's environment and how one reacts to it. This condition leads to the human judgment process being inherently limited. It is fundamentally a covert process. It is seldom possible for an individual to accurately describe his or her judgment process accurately. Ordinarily, the only means of actually explaining judgments are introspection and guessing at the reasons for the observed judgments. These explanations are generally incomplete and misleading. Subjective reporting is fallible. Judgments are thus inaccurately reported. Judgments are also generally observed to be inconsistent. Identical circumstances do not always lead to identical judgments. Observations of inconsistent judgment often lead to suspicions of hidden motives or conclusions of incompetence on the part of the decision-maker. Psychological theory of human behavior, however, finds such assumption unnecessary. Judgment is inconsistent because its process is not a fully analytical and controlled. Inconsistency is, therefore, an inherent characteristic. While covertness, inaccuracy of reporting, and inconsistency may not completely describe the human judgment process, these characteristics make clear that decision aids would prove enormously useful in overcoming the limitations of human judgment. To find means to uncover the covert process of judgment, let us examine its parameters.

PARAMETERS OF HUMAN JUDGMENT

If the parameters of one's judgmental policy orientations could be identified, then it would become possible to model the process of that person's judgment, and develop aids to assessment. This process may be explored by posing the following questions:

(a) What *factors* influence the individual's judgments? This is to identify the variables that influence the assessment of the likelihood that the participant would select a particular applicant into the GCBA program. These factors would usually have mutually exclusive characteristics or properties (Hammond *et al.,* 1975).

(b) What *relative weight* or emphasis does the individual put on each of the factors? One source of disagreement between participants arises from the fact that different weights are likely to be attached by different members to the factors (Slovic and Lichtenstein, 1973).

(c) How does the individual integrate the information regarding each factor to arrive at an overall judgment? This involves identification of the mathematical relationship that describes the dependence of the overall judgment on the factors considered. The relationship between each factor and the overall judgment may be linear or nonlinear, and the contribution of each factor to the overall judgment may be positive or negative. The nature of dependence of the overall judgment on each factor is referred to as that factor's *function-form.*

(d) What is the *consistency* with which the individual is able to make judgments? An individual may make different judgments about the same situation on different occasions. At least two characteristics of the judgment task are known to affect consistency: task complexity and task uncertainty. Studies have shown that consistency is lower when the judgment task is complex, i.e., involving more factors, rather than less; and also lower when the task requires use of nonlinear function-forms rather than linear function-forms (Hammond *et al.,* 1975; Hogarth, 1980: 56-57). Even when a decision maker intends to use a specific judgment rule as defined by specific set of factors, relative weights and function-forms, his or her judgments or assessments may deviate from those suggested by that rule. Errors may creep into the process of execution of judgment. In absence of explicit and immediate feedback on judgment, the decision maker may be unaware of the degree to which the actual judgment or assessment deviates from that intended.

The concept of consistency is different from that of accuracy. A decision-maker can be accurate but inconsistent, consistent but inaccurate, both consistent and accurate, or neither. Consistency has to do with the reliability of the decision-maker in executing the intended judgmental policy, as defined by specific set of factors, relative weights and function-forms. Lesser the deviation between the actual judgment and that intended, greater the consistency. Accuracy, however, has to do with the validity of the policy itself, i.e., whether the judgmental policy executed is indeed the one that was to be executed. Stated another way, whether the specific set of factors, relative weights and function-forms executed are indeed the ones intended for execution.

In the present case a formal application of the social judgment theory is undertaken. This theory is preferred over others (such as decision theory, goal integration theory and policy capturing) because it is not prescriptive or comparative, but simply seeks to *describe* the judgment process involved. Additionally, social judgment theory is also easy to use and the methodology involved in its application yields relatively straight forward and mathematically clean results which are easily understood by decision makers. Further, literature reports that the simple additive models of decision making based on regression analysis seem to be at least as accurate as the more complex models, and are preferred by many users with respect to most criteria of desirability (Zeleny, 1982).

THE RESEARCH METHODOLOGY

Six individuals, all members of the School of Business faculty and representing the application screening committee, participated in this study. These participants are identified in this report as Participant #1 through #6. The following steps were involved in the development of the decision support system and its application: (a) defining the problem, (b) exercise of judgment, (c) analysis of judgment, (d) feedback to the participants, and (e) the development of consensus.

(A) Defining the problem

The participants identified the factors influencing the likelihood that they would select a particular applicant into the GCBA program to be the following: (i) *Progression in Managerial Experience*: consistency of the movement of an applicant to more responsible and more senior positions, influences selection of the applicant, (ii) *Management Position*: position presently held by the applicant in the organization, from supervision of a small operational section ranging to chief executive with strategic responsibility, is deemed to influence selection, (iii) *Reason for Doing the Course*: the clarity of understanding of how the course will benefit his/her career, influences the applicant's selection, (iv) *Language Skills*: demonstrated ability to express ideas/thoughts clearly in the written application influences selection, (v) *Gender*: the gender of the applicant may be influencing selection, and (vi) *Age*: with applicants younger than 26 and older than 50 not accepted into the program, age may be a factor, too.

Each participant was asked to indicate the relative emphasis he or she places on each of the factors. To indicate this, the participant was asked to distribute 100 points among the six factors listed in such a way that the points assigned to each factor indicate the relative importance of that factor in the participant's assessment of the likelihood of and applicant being selected into the GCBA program. Each participant was also asked to indicate the functional relationship between each factor and the likelihood of being selected. The participants did this by selecting out of a menu of graph displays shown in Figure 1 one which, in his or her respective judgment, best represents the relationship between each factor (x-axis) and the assessed likelihood measure (y-axis). The options include: linear positive function, linear negative function, J-function, reverse J-function, inverted J-function, inverted reverse J-function, U-function, inverted U-function. Thus, with the relative weights for each factor described and their respective relationship with the assessment criterion indicated, we obtained the *a priori* description of each participant's policy regarding assessment of the likelihood that the participant would select a particular applicant into the GCBA program. We refer to these respective policies as the *a priori* policies of the corresponding participants.

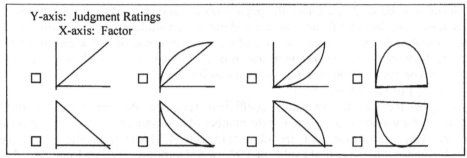

Figure 1. Menu of graph displays

(B) Exercise of judgments

A computer graphics system was used to randomly generate twenty (20) different applicant profiles, each described in terms of the six factors identified and listed earlier. To generate these, random values were assigned to each factor on the following scales: The first four factors, (i) *Progression in Managerial Experience*, (ii) *Management Positions*, (iii) *Reasons for Doing the Course*, and (iv) *Language Skills*, were each measured on a Likert scale from 1 to 10, where 1 represented a low and unfavorable level of the factor and 10 represented a high and favorable level. For *Progression in Managerial Experience*, 1 represented little progression and 10 represented a significant progression. For *Management Position*, 1 represented low level supervision duties and 10 represented chief executive position. For *Reasons for Doing the Course*, 1 shows little understanding and 10 shows a high level of understanding of course benefits. And for *Language Skills*, 1 shows little ability to express ideas/ thoughts clearly and 10 shows high ability. Of the remaining two factors, *Gender* is measured as a 1 if the applicant is male and 2 if the applicant is female, and *Age* is measured on a scale from 26 years to 50 years. A sample profile is shown in Figure 2.

Profile of Applicant 7

Gender	Female	
Age	42 yrs	On a scale from 26 to 50 years
Progression in managerial experience	10	On a scale from 1 to 10
Management position	5	On a scale from 1 to 10
Reasons for doing the course	7	On a scale from 1 to 10
Language skills	6	On a scale from 1 to 10

Rate the likelihood of the applicant's being selected in the GCBA program, on a scale from 1 to 10, where 1 would indicate that the likelihood of your selecting the candidate is *extremely low*, and 10 would indicate that this likelihood is *extremely high*.

Figure 2. Sample applicant profile

The profiles designed were tested for orthogonality to minimize the effect of intercorrelation among the factors, as follows: The objective was to establish the absence of significance among *all* correlations. The Pearson product-moment correlation coefficient may be used to estimate the population correlation coefficient. If the highest correlation coefficient thus found is established not to be significantly different from zero, then it would be fair to conclude that none of the correlation coefficients are significantly different from zero. The significance test was performed on the highest correlation coefficient observed, by computing the t-statistic as follows:

$$t = r_{ij} \cdot [\ \{\ (n - 2) / (1 - r_{ij}^2)\ \}\ ^{0.5}]$$

where r_{ij} is the sample correlation coefficient (i.e., the Pearson product-moment coefficient) for variables i and j, and n is the number of observations. In the present case, the highest correlation coefficient observed was 0.34. This corresponded to a t value of 1.53, compared to the critical t value of 1.73 for a significance level of 10 percent. The correlation coefficients of 0.34 and less were therefore deemed to be not significantly different from zero.

Each participant was then asked to assess all 20 applicant profiles for the likelihood of the participant's selecting the applicant into the GCBA program. When all profiles has been so assessed by the participants, they were given the opportunity to review the twenty profiles and make whatever revisions in the assessment ratings they deemed appropriate, until satisfied with the ratings.

(C) Analysis of Judgment

The next task was to extract from these judgments the description of the policy orientations deployed by them. This was accomplished through nonlinear multiple regression analyses. These analyses were performed with the assessment ratings given to the different profiles by the participants as dependent variable and the six relevant factors as the independent variables. These analyses yielded the parameters of the participants' respective judgmental policies. The regression model consisted of first- and second- order terms for each factor. The weights, as measures of the emphasis given to the different factors, and the function-forms for the different factors were derived from algebraic transformation of the regression model. For the mathematical details, see Hammond *et al.* (1975: 271-312, or Cooksey, 1996: 178-180). We refer to the respective policies thus obtained as the *executed* policies of the corresponding participants.

Cognitive control exercised by a participant with respect to the particular model obtained through nonlinear multiple regression analysis is measured in terms of the multiple correlation coefficient, R (Hammond and Summers, 1972). Hammond *et al.* (1975) propose that to determine whether in a specific case the multiple correlation coefficient will provide a measure of cognitive consistency, a test for lack of fit of the specific model obtained through multiple regression analysis should be performed (see Draper and Smith, 1998). If there is no evidence of lack of fit, then the multiple correlation coefficient, R, provides a measure of both consistency as well as control.

(D) Feedback to participants

The relative weights obtained from the participants are reported in Table 1. These include both, the *a priori* weights for the likelihood of the participants selecting an applicant into the GCBA program (see Table 1, Section A), and also weights obtained from the analysis of the assessment ratings of applicant profiles for likelihood of selection (see Table 1, Section B).

For each participant's policy, the function-forms for each factor were also obtained. See Figure 3 for the function-forms thus obtained, presented here collectively. These include both, the *a priori* function-forms for the likelihood of the participants selecting an applicant into the GCBA program (see Figure 3, Section A), and also function-forms obtained from the analysis of the assessment ratings of applicant profiles for likelihood of selection (see Figure 3, Section B).

Table 1. Relative weights for *a priori* and *executed* policies obtained from participants

Source	Progression	Position	Reason	Language	Gender	Age
Section A. A priori weights for likelihood of selection						
Participant #1	25.0	20.0	15.0	20.0	5.0	15.0
Participant #2	20.0	30.0	10.0	20.0	15.0	5.0
Participant #3	20.0	20.0	25.0	10.0	10.0	15.0
Participant #4	35.0	20.0	20.0	12.0	8.0	5.0
Participant #5	30.0	15.0	25.0	20.0	0.0	10.0
Participant #6	20.0	20.0	40.0	10.0	5.0	5.0
Mean	25.0	20.8	22.5	15.3	7.2	9.2
Standard Deviation	5.8	4.5	9.5	4.7	4.7	4.5
Section B. Weights obtained from executed policies						
Participant #1	11.2	26.4	14.6	19.3	9.6	18.9
Participant #2	13.0	49.3	10.9	15.4	2.2	9.2
Participant #3	16.2	29.2	41.9	3.6	1.9	7.2
Participant #4	26.0	15.6	21.6	23.1	6.2	7.5
Participant #5	27.3	14.1	32.9	16.8	2.0	6.9
Participant #6	4.8	9.5	63.9	12.0	6.5	3.2
Mean	16.4	24.0	31.0	15.0	4.7	8.8
Standard Deviation	8.0	13.2	18.1	6.1	2.9	4.9

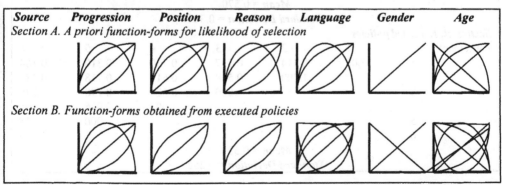

Source   *Progression*   *Position*   *Reason*   *Language*   *Gender*   *Age*

Section A. A priori function-forms for likelihood of selection

Section B. Function-forms obtained from executed policies

Figure 3. Function-forms for *a priori* and *executed* policies obtained from participants

Each participant's cognitive consistency was also measured through the multiple correlation coefficient. These are reported in Table 2.

Table 2. Participants' cognitive consistencies for *executed* policies

Participants	Consistencies
Participant #1	0.867
Participant #2	0.976
Participant #3	0.934
Participant #4	0.934
Participant #5	0.985
Participant #6	0.970
Mean	0.944
Standard Deviation	0.040

Correlations were computed between the policies of the participants. To do this, ratings were *computed* for each faculty profile presented to the participants, using the judgmental (*executed*) policies obtained through multiple regression analysis. Correlations were then computed among the sets of *computed* ratings, for two participants at a time. The use of *computed* ratings instead of the ratings actually assigned eliminated whatever effect the cognitive inconsistency might bring into the results, thus yielding a truer measure of the degree to which the policies were similar. These correlation coefficients are reported in Table 3.

Table 3. Correlations across participants' respective *a priori* and *executed* policies

Section A. A priori policies						
Participant #	1	2	3	4	5	6
1	1.000	0.818	-0.069	0.750	0.797	0.543
2		1.000	0.061	0.796	0.835	0.579
3			1.000	0.340	0.078	0.494
4				1.000	0.895	0.856
5					1.000	0.783
6						1.000

Mean = 0.570
Standard Deviation = 0.324

Section B. Executed policies						
Participant #	1	2	3	4	5	6
1	1.000	0.314	0.137	0.450	0.310	0.184
2		1.000	0.538	0.611	0.718	0.383
3			1.000	0.674	0.798	0.920
4				1.000	0.916	0.695
5					1.000	0.738
6						1.000

Mean = 0.559
Standard Deviation = 0.252

Correlations were computed between the judgments policies actually used in rating the applicant profiles and the *a priori* policies the participants had expected to use in assessing the likelihood of selection. These are reported in Table 4. To obtain these correlations, two sets of ratings were calculated for each participant, one from the *executed* policy and the other from the *a priori* policy.

Table 4. Correlations between respective participants' *a priori* and *executed* policies

Participants	Correlations
Participant #1	0.523
Participant #2	0.867
Participant #3	0.667
Participant #4	0.917
Participant #5	0.932
Participant #6	0.894
Mean	0.800
Standard Deviation	0.152

Each participant received feedback in terms of all elements of his or her own *a priori* and *executed* policies. These included the measures (shown above) of relative weights, functions forms, cognitive consistency, correlation between their own *a priori* and *executed* policies, and across other participants' *a priori* and *executed* policies, respectively. Each participant was also given the corresponding measures for all other participants, but was not told which measure came from which participant.

(E) Development of Consensus

Each participant was now asked to compare his or her *a priori* policy with the *executed* policy, and having done so, to revise the *a priori* policy to indicate what their policy ought to be when assessing the likelihood of an applicant being selected into the GCBA program. As before, each participant did this by redistributing the 100 points among the six factors indicating the relative emphasis he or she now placed on each factor. As before, each participant also selected, from the menu shown in Figure 1, that function form which best represented the relationship between each factor (x-axis) and the likelihood of being selected (y-axis). We refer to the respective policies thus obtained as the *revised* policies of the corresponding participants.

As before, a new set of twenty (20) different applicant profiles was randomly generated. However, this time, along with each profile, the participants were also shown the ratings computed for that profile from their respective *revised* policy. Further, to rate the profiles, the participants sat around a round table, and discussed each of the twenty profiles with one another. They then assigned their rating to each profile, individually, and moved on to the next one, until all twenty profiles were thus rated. As before, when all profiles had been so assessed, the participants were given the opportunity to review the twenty profiles individually and make whatever revisions in their respective assessment ratings they deemed appropriate, until satisfied with the ratings.

As before, a new set of policies was obtained through nonlinear multiple regression analyses from the ratings thus obtained. We refer to these respective policies as the *final* policies of the corresponding participants. The relative weights obtained for the *revised* and the *final* policies are shown in Table 5, in Section A and Section B respectively. The function-forms for each factor, obtained for the *revised* and the *final* policies too are shown, collectively, in Figure 4, in Section A and Section B respectively. The participants' cognitive consistencies, corresponding to the respective *final* policies are reported in Table 6. As between *a priori* and *executed* policies, correlations were again computed for each participant, between the *revised* policies and the *final* policies, respectively. These correlation coefficients are reported in Table 7. Again, as before, correlations computed between the *revised* policies and the *final* policies are reported in Table 8.

Table 5. Relative weights for *revised* and *final* policies obtained from participants

Source	Progression	Position	Reason	Language	Gender	Age
Section A. Weights obtained from revised policies						
Participant #1	20.0	20.0	25.0	20.0	5.0	10.0
Participant #2	25.0	35.0	10.0	15.0	10.0	5.0
Participant #3	20.0	20.0	30.0	5.0	10.0	15.0
Participant #4	25.0	20.0	25.0	15.0	5.0	10.0
Participant #5	25.0	15.0	30.0	15.0	5.0	10.0
Participant #6	20.0	20.0	30.0	20.0	0.0	10.0
Mean	22.5	21.7	25.0	15.0	5.8	10.0
Standard Deviation	2.5	6.2	7.1	5.0	3.4	2.9
Section B. Weights obtained from final policies						
Participant #1	10.9	25.4	34.7	22.2	2.2	4.5
Participant #2	7.0	28.2	29.7	12.5	11.8	10.8
Participant #3	13.0	16.7	49.0	11.8	4.9	4.6
Participant #4	9.9	17.5	34.3	25.4	10.5	2.3
Participant #5	13.3	18.0	31.3	29.4	4.6	3.4
Participant #6	7.0	17.1	45.8	24.2	3.3	2.7
Mean	10.2	20.5	37.5	20.9	6.2	4.7
Standard Deviation	2.5	4.6	7.3	6.6	3.6	2.9

Source	Progression	Position	Reason	Language	Gender	Age
Section A. Revised function-forms for likelihood of selection						

| Section B. Function-forms obtained from final policies | | | | | | |

Figure 4. Function-forms for *revised* and *final* policies obtained from participants

Table 6. Participants' cognitive consistencies for *final* policies

Participants	Consistencies
Participant #1	0.979
Participant #2	0.961
Participant #3	0.971
Participant #4	0.992
Participant #5	0.981
Participant #6	0.992
Mean	0.979
Standard Deviation	0.011

DISCUSSION OF THE RESULTS

Described below are the findings in terms of measures of relative weights, function-forms, cognitive consistencies, mutual consensus, and 'self-knowledge.' These are now described below:

Relative Weights and Function-forms

Taken together, the relative weights and the function-forms allow insights into a participant's policy orientations. Pair-wise comparisons between an individual's *a priori* policy and judgment policy may reveal how that individual's actual judgments may differ from his or her *a priori* expectations or assertions. For instance, as shown in Table 1, Participant #1 had expected (*a priori*) to place most emphasis on *Progression in Managerial Experience* (25.0), with both *Management Position* and *Language Skills* close behind (20.0 each). When actually rating the applicant profiles, however, Participant #1 gave most emphasis to *Management Position* (26.4), with *Language Skills* and *Age* close behind (19.3 and 18.9, respectively). This participant placed considerably less weight on *Progression in Managerial Experience* while rating the profiles than he had anticipated (11.2 vs. 25.0), and placed higher weight on *Management Position* than he had expected to (26.4 vs. 20.0). Also the function form associated with *Language* in the Participant's *a priori* policy was different from that of the judgment policy. The same was true for the function-forms associated with *Age*.

Similarly, Participant #2 had expected (*a priori*) to place most emphasis on *Management Position* (30.0), with both *Progression in Managerial Experience* and *Language Skills* being next in the order of emphasis (20.0 each). While actually rating the applicant profiles Participant #2 did give most emphasis to *Management Position* but at a level considerably higher than anticipated (49.3 vs. 30.0). *Language Skills* was next (15.4), followed by *Progression in Managerial Experience* (13.0). This participant placed considerably less weight on *Progression in Managerial Experience* (13.0 vs. 20.0) and even lesser on *Gender* (2.2 vs. 15.0) than he had anticipated. While actually rating the applicant profiles, Participant #2 emphasized *Management Position* considerably more than Participant #1 did (49.3 vs. 26.4). Participant #2 also emphasized *Gender* and *Age* considerably less than Participant #1 (2.2 vs. 9.6, and 9.2 vs. 18.9, respectively). The corresponding function-forms associated with *Progression, Position, Language, Gender,* and *Age* were different between *a priori* policy and *executed* policy. Similar variations in weights and function-forms can be discerned for all other participants.

Table 7. Correlations across participants' respective *revised* and *final* policies

Section A. Revised policies						
Participant #	1	2	3	4	5	6
1	1.000	0.913	0.006	0.422	0.957	0.849
2		1.000	-0.270	0.225	0.860	0.661
3			1.000	0.619	0.151	0.319
4				1.000	0.493	0.657
5					1.000	0.904
6						1.000
		Mean = 0.518				
		Standard Deviation = 0.358				
Section B. Final policies						
Participant #	1	2	3	4	5	6
1	1.000	0.828	0.873	0.942	0.970	0.940
2		1.000	0.702	0.868	0.826	0.753
3			1.000	0.890	0.881	0.952
4				1.000	0.971	0.958
5					1.000	0.960
6						1.000
		Mean = 0.888				
		Standard Deviation = 0.079				

Table 8. Correlations between respective participants' *revised* and *final* policies

Participants	*Correlations*
Participant #1	0.870
Participant #2	0.751
Participant #3	0.506
Participant #4	0.541
Participant #5	0.864
Participant #6	0.945
Mean	0.746
Standard Deviation	0.168

Similar comparisons can be made between *revised* and *final* policies, *a priori* and *revised* policies, and *executed* and *final* policies. While doing so, one can see the nature of compromises made by the participants in the process revising their respective policies. For instance, Participant #1 shifted from his *a priori* stand of placing most emphasis on *Progression in Managerial Experience* (see Table 1, Section A) to his *revised* stand of placing most emphasis on *Management Position* (see Table 5, Section A). Participant #6 moderated the emphasis placed on *Reason for Doing the Course* from his *executed* policy (63.9) to *final* policy (45.8). It is possible to discern corresponding shifts in function-forms as well.

In general, *Reason for Doing the Course* proved to be the most important factor in both, the participants' *executed* policies (31.0), and their *final* policies (37.5), as indicated by the corresponding means. These means were computed through regression analysis done by pooling together all the data, e.g., rating observations obtained from all the participants for each profile.

Cognitive Consistencies

A high value for multiple correlation coefficient, near 1.0, obtained from a regression analysis for a participant would indicate that the person was relatively consistent in making judgments and that the regression model used to describe the person's judgments provided a good "fit" or description of the participant's judgmental policy. The measures of cognitive consistencies with which the *executed* policies were applied in the assessment of the applicant profiles ranged from 0.867 to 0.985, with a mean of 0.944 and standard deviation of 0.040 (see Table 2). The corresponding measures for the *final* policies ranged from 0.0.961 to 0.992, with a mean of 0.979 and a standard deviation of 0.011. Not only did the mean of these measures improve from the *executed* policies to the *final* policies; the distribution of these measures became less dispersed as well.

Mutual Consensus

Consider the correlations between Participant #1 and Participant #2. The correlation between their *a priori* policies was 0.818. The corresponding measure for the two participants' *executed* policies was 0.314. Apparently, the two participants had anticipated implementing similar policies. However, due to the covert nature of the exercise of judgment, cognitive inconsistency, and inaccuracies inherent in such an exercise, the resulting *executed* policies were quite different from each other. The sources of differences in the *executed* policies are evident in Figure 3, Section B, and Table 1, Section B. The *a priori* policies indicate that differences were anticipated on the emphasis placed on *Management Position* (with differences in both relative weight and function form) and also on *Gender* and *Age* (with differences mainly in the relative weights). When actually rating the applicant profiles, the participants did place different weights on, and assign different function-forms to, the factor *Management Position*. They also placed different weights on both *Gender* and *Age*. In the case of *Age*, they also used different function-forms. There were other variations in weights and function-forms to a lesser degree.

Now consider the various correlations between Participant #1 and Participant #3's policies. The correlation for the *a priori* policies was -0.069, and that for the *executed* policies was 0.137 (see Table 3). The correlation between their *revised* policies, too, was 0.006 -- nearly no correlation at all. And yet, the compromises they made, respectively, yielded a correlation coefficient for their *final* policies as 0.873 (see Table 7). Apparently, the two participants, through the exercise of control over their policies, were able to generate a significant level of consensus.

Note that the mean of all correlations between the participants' *a priori* policies, taken two at a time, was 0.570, with a standard deviation of 0.324 (see Table 3, Section A). The mean of all correlations obtained from the *executed* policies was 0.559, with a standard deviation of 0.252 (see Table 3, Section B). The corresponding measure obtained for the *revised* policies was 0.518, with a standard deviation of 0.358 (see Table 7, Section A). However, the mean of all correlations obtained from the *final* policies was an impressive 0.888, with a standard deviation of 0.079 (see Table 7, Section B), indicating a high level of consensus attained through compromises made.

"Self-Knowledge"

Various studies have demonstrated that generally *a priori* policies differ from the policies implemented. Self-reporting of one's *executed* policy is generally faulty. This is so because, unaided, judgment is generally exercised through a covert process. In this study, for instance, in the case of Participant #1, the correlation between *a priori* and *executed* policies was 0.523 (see Table 4), and between *revised* and *final* policies was 0.870 (see Table 8). On average, the mean of the correlations between *a priori* and *executed* policies, for the six participants, was 0.800, with a standard deviation of 0.152. The corresponding correlations between *revised* and *final* policies had a mean of 0.746 and a standard deviation of 0.168.

CONCLUDING REMARKS

In this study, as in numerous others reported in the literature, participants were unable to accurately describe their own judgment process pertaining to the assessment of a criterion. As mentioned above, this has to do with the covert nature of the judgment process. However, it is possible to make the judgmental policies explicit in terms of relative weights and function-forms deployed. Once made explicit, the decision-makers can modify their policies in a controlled manner by specifying changes in weights and/or function-forms as desired, as they did in the study reported here. They could revise their respective *a priori* policies in view of the policies revealed through the analysis of their assessments, and indicate, with hind-sight, the policies that they feel *ought to be* used.

To appreciate the uniqueness of the approach presented in this report, a comparison of the procedure based on social judgment theory described here with that of the DELPHI technique (Linstone and Turoff, 1975; Rohrbaugh, 1976) would be useful. The DELPHI technique was an outgrowth of a series of studies at the RAND Corporation. By 1970 it was being widely acclaimed as a means to generate a consensus of judgment in a group. The DELPHI technique is characterized by three distinct features: (a) a *guarantee of anonymity* to the participants in the group; (b) a primarily *statistical compilation* of the group's response, and (c) a *controlled, iterative feedback* of the group's response to each member of the group prior to another set of judgments.

As in the case of the DELPHI technique, a procedure could be developed here to guarantee anonymity to the participants. The procedure described here also could compile statistics on the participants' judgmental responses. This data, however, would include information not only on the overall judgments (as in the DELPHI technique), but also on the components or parameters of the judgments (unlike the DELPHI technique). Finally, the procedure could include a controlled feedback of the participants' judgmental policies to each member of the participating group, prior to another set of judgments. In this way, not only would the overt judgment differences be made explicit (as in the DELPHI technique), but the covert policy differences, too, would become explicit (unlike the DELPHI technique). This would allow the identification of those specific parameters (i.e., factors, relative weights, and function-forms) of the individual judgmental policies which contribute to disagreements among participants (as in the case of the participants in this study). With the parameters made explicit, the decision-makers would be able to control the policy to be implemented by revising their judgmental policies in terms of factors, relative weights and function-forms. The DELPHI technique, limited to revising overt responses only, does not offer such opportunities. As in the DELPHI method, the procedure described here may be repeated until the desired degree of consensus is reached or the alternative policies considered explored.

In conclusion, the primary contribution of the approach explored in this report is that it presents an alternative approach to the assessment of applicant profiles. The description of policies, in terms of parameters of the judgment process, provides an operational definition of the decision makers' cognitive sets about the domain of applicant selectivity. Investigation of the judgment's parameters enable the development of judgmental aids to assist the decision maker in the exercise of judgment in the following manner: (a) the judgment process of the individual, though covert, internal and subjective, is clarified, externalized, and explained so that it can be examined and understood, and (b) desired changes in the judgment policy motivated by change of insights, self-understanding, group discussions, and feedback about judgment policy, can be specified and executed consistently as desired. A decision-maker may therefore define "selectivity" as well as "assess" it as defined by another. To the extent that a chosen set of trade-offs or weights are executed consistently, the policies would be implemented with improved effectiveness yielding better decisions. To the extent that a group of decision-makers agree on the policy to be specified for implementation, the decisions can be taken with a greater degree of confidence with regard to their relevancy.

REFERENCES

Cooksey, R.W. (1996). *Judgment Analysis: Theory, Methods, and Applications*, Academic Press, San Diego, California.

Draper, N. and Smith, H. (1998). *Applied Regression Analysis*, Third Edition, Wiley, New York.

Hammond, K.R. and Summers, D.A. (1972). "Cognitive control." *Psychological Review, 79*, 58-67.

Hammond, K.R., Stewart, T.R., Brehmer, B., and Steinmann, D.O. (1975). "Social judgment theory." In Kaplan, M., and Schwartz, S. (Eds.), *Human Judgment and Decision Processes*, Academic Press, New York, 271-312.

64

Linstone, H.A., and Turoff, M. (1975). *The DELPHI Method: Techniques and Applications*, Addison-Wesley, Reading, Massachusetts.

Rohrbaugh, J.W. (1976). "Conflict management in decision-making groups: A comparison of social judgment analysis and the DELPHI technique." Unpublished doctoral dissertation, University of Colorado, Boulder, Colorado.

Slovic, P., and Lichtenstein, S. (1973). "Comparison of Bayesian and regression approaches to the study of information processing in judgment." In Rappaport, L., and Summers, D.A. (Eds.) *Human Judgment and Social Interaction*, Holt, Rinehart, and Winston, New York, 16-108.

Zeleny, M. (1982). *Multiple Criteria Decision Making*. McGraw-Hill, New York.

THE USE OF TACIT KNOWLEDGE IN SELECTION DECISIONS IN UNIVERSITIES

M.A. Barrett[1], L.K. Hort[2]

[1]Sunshine Coast University
Business Faculty, Locked Bag No. 4
Maroochydore, DC Qld 4558, Australia

[2]Griffith University
School of Marketing and Management
Gold Coast Campus
Australia

Abstract: This paper reports on a study examining the effects of organisational culture - as exemplified in tacit knowledge - at the point where new organisational members are being selected. The study used an adaptation of a well tested tacit knowledge instrument administered to staff and students in two universities to examine both whether tacit knowledge with respect to specific "citizenship behaviours" is being exercised in the course of selection decisions to find a person who will "fit in", and also, if so, whether the type of tacit knowledge appeared to be conditioned by the age of the universities or the seniority of the person making the decision. Results suggested that attempts do indeed take place to make a "person-organisation" fit on the basis of tacit knowledge of specific "citizenship" issues. This happens even when information about the selection criteria indicates that these issues are not included. It also appeared that while members of both organisations preferred "citizenship" behaviours over "academic" behaviours (i.e. behaviours aimed primarily at benefiting the organisation over those primarily aimed at furthering an employee's academic career), members of the younger organisation preferred this more strongly. Contrary to much previous research, however, senior staff members of the organisations did not hold a more unified view of these issues than younger staff or students, and in fact, students were more of one mind over some issues. Also, the tacit views of members of the older organisation, while different, did not appear to be more strongly held.

Key words: Organisational culture, citizenship behaviours, decision-making, personnel selection, selection criteria, tacit knowledge.

S.H. Zanakis et al. (eds.), Decision Making: Recent Developments and Worldwide Applications, 65–80.
© 2000 *Kluwer Academic Publishers.*

BACKGROUND

Selection decisions in public sector organisations, including universities, are normally made with "selection criteria": statements of essential and desired knowledge, skills, abilities and other personal characteristics against which applicants can be measured. The decisions are meant to be "merit-based" or assessed objectively against these criteria in terms of the differential merit of each candidate. Selection criteria are thus seen as part of a process of clear and objective decision-making. This in turn corresponds to a notion of rationality seen as vital to managerial competence. Clear and objective decision-making of this kind is also seen as necessary to serve the interests of fairness in specific processes such as staff selection.

It is known, however, both from research and from everyday experience, that managerial decision-making practice regularly varies from this ideal. On the one hand, there are various forms of decision-making *failure*, arising from phenomena such as groupthink (Janis, 1982), groupshift (Wallach, Kogan and Bem, 1962), information overload (Simon, 1976; Forester, 1984), as well as a wide range of other individually-based and group-based decision-making biases and misconceptions (Bazerman, 1994). On the other hand, there are forms of non-objective decision-making which are often regarded more positively. We tend to give credit for decisions that are taken on the basis of tacit knowledge, that is, "street-smarts" rather than "book-smarts". That is, other forms of intelligence than cognitive abilities measurable on conventional academic tests are both recognised and valued in the workplace.

Sternberg *et al.* (1995) as well as numerous others over the years, have sought to define the differences between these two types of intelligence, sometimes called tacit knowledge or "street smarts", as well as study empirically its incidence in adult development. For example, Neisser (1976) was one of the first researchers to assert the distinction between "academic" and "practical" intelligence. Building on this, Wagner and Sternberg (1985) have sought to distinguish between academic and practical knowledge on the basis of the *kind of problem* that is solvable using the two types of knowledge. According to their findings, academic intelligence is good for tasks which are:

    a) formulated by others,

    b) have little or no intrinsic interest,

    c) have all needed information available from the beginning, and

    d) are disembedded from an individual's ordinary experience.

In addition, the tasks:

    e) are usually well defined,

    f) have but one correct answer and

    g) often just one method of obtaining the correct solution.

By contrast, problems people face in their daily lives, including at work, are more likely to be:

    a) unformulated or in need of reformulation,

    b) of personal interest,

    c) lacking in information necessary for solution,

    d) related to everyday experience,

    e) poorly defined,

f) characterised by multiple "correct" solutions each with liabilities as well as assets, and

g) characterised by multiple methods for picking a problem solution.

Other researchers have made the distinction between academic and practical knowledge in other ways. Examples include Williams, Denney and Schadler (1983) who found that while performance on traditional cognitive ability measures typically peaks at the end of formal schooling, 76% of the older adults in their study believed that their ability to think, reason and solve problems had actually increased over the years. Horn and Cattell (1966) had also proposed a theoretical language to describe age-related changes in intellectual ability. They distinguished between *fluid abilities*, which are required to deal with novelty in the immediate testing situation (e.g. induction of the next letter in a letter series problem) and *crystallised abilities*, which reflect acculturated knowledge (e.g. the meaning of a low-frequency vocabulary word). Fluid abilities according to several studies (Dixon and Baltes, 1986; Horn, 1982; Labouvie-Vief, 1982; Schaie, 1977/1978) appear to be vulnerable to age-related decline, but crystallised abilities appear to be maintained throughout adulthood.

Wagner and Sternberg summarise the distinction between the two types of intelligence and the parameters of their use as follows:

> Tacit knowledge refers to action-oriented knowledge, acquired without direct help from others, that allows individuals to achieve goals they personally value (Horvath *et al.*, in press). The acquisition and use of such knowledge appears to be uniquely important to competent performance in real-world endeavors. (Sternberg *et al.*, 1995, p. 916)

We examine the work of Wagner and Sternberg during the discussion of our research instrument, which is derived from the Tacit Knowledge Inventory (TKI) of these two researchers. But first, for clarity, it is necessary to distinguish some understandings of the uses of tacit knowledge which differ from the one of concern in our study, and to define the relationship of tacit knowledge to organisational citizenship.

Tacit knowledge and organisational citizenship

Recently, attention has been directed to ways tacit knowledge can be mobilised for organisational competitive advantage, organisational learning, improved product development and so on. The growth industry of knowledge management is an outcome of this interest. Its concern is to document – and hence make accessible – the kinds of knowledge individuals normally do not think to disclose. The general assumption is that tacit knowledge, derived from people's experiences and residing in their heads, is a tremendously valuable corporate asset.

In this paper, we are not concerned with the value of documenting tacit knowledge, nor with the uses to which tacit knowledge which has been documented can be put. Rather, our concern is with a specific aspect of tacit or acculturated knowledge – expectations of organisational citizenship behaviours. Organisational citizenship behaviours, according to Borman and Motowidlo (1992) and other researchers, are considerably less likely than other kinds of knowledge to be mobilised in the interests of improving organisational competitive advantage, even though they can be shown to contribute to it. They are frequently ignored in assessments of individual job performance relevant to selection criteria for jobs, even though they have been shown to have a direct positive correlation with improved organisational performance.

Studies of organisational culture (Barrett, 1995; O'Reilly, Chatman and Caldwell, 1991; Ott, 1989; Reichers and Schneider, 1990), as well as everyday experience, suggest that tacit knowledge, that is, judgements about how the person will "fit in", and especially expectations of citizenship behaviours (Borman and Motowidlo, 1992; Chatman, 1991; Rumelhart, 1983; Schneider, 1990; Wagner and Sternberg 1985), play an important role in how selection decisions are made. But first, let us discuss organisational citizenship as an issue in its own right. To do this, we need first to distinguish between task performance behaviours and contextual behaviours.

Task performance behaviours and contextual behaviours

Borman and Motowidlo (1992) use the broad domains of task performance and contextual activities to distinguish ways individuals contribute to organisational effectiveness. Task performance activities are most easily seen in work done by assembly workers in factories, doctors in hospitals, tellers in banks, etc, which involve implementing parts of the "technical core", that is, the activities in which raw materials are processed and transformed into the organisation's products. Other jobs contribute to the technical core less directly, as with jobs that replenish raw materials or distribute finished products and exchange them for necessary raw materials. Managerial work contributes to the technical core even less directly, although its value derives from servicing the technical core in various ways, e.g. by planning, organising, coordinating, supervising and performing other functions to make sure the multiple activities that do contribute directly are performed effectively and efficiently. Still other "staff" jobs, such as accounting, personnel, legal functions and public relations also do not contribute directly, but add value by providing services that enable the technical core to function well.

These activities may collectively be contrasted with another group of activities which similarly do not fall under the category of task performance but are also important for organisational effectiveness. They are referred to as "contextual activities". In the formulation of Borman and Motowidlo (1992) they include such activities as:
- Volunteering to carry out task activities that are not formally a part of the job
- Persisting with extra enthusiasm or effort when necessary to complete one's own task activities successfully
- Helping and cooperating with others
- Following organisational rules and procedures even when personally inconvenient
- Endorsing, supporting, and defending organisational objectives

(Borman and Motowidlo, 1992, p. 73)

Contextual activities differ from task performance activities in several ways. Normally, contextual activities support the organisational, social and psychological environment in which the technical core must function rather than contributing to the technical core itself. Even when this is not the case, and the activities are directed towards some function within the technical core, in contextual activities the emphasis is not on the proficiency with which those tasks are carried out, but on the initiative taken to *volunteer* to carry them out, or on the extra effort or unusual persistence shown in carrying them out. In contrast to task activities which clearly vary between jobs – indeed it is task activities which *define* jobs as different – contextual activities with the features outlined above are common to many or all jobs. In task activities the important human characteristics that covary with task proficiency are knowledge, skills and abilities. By contrast, the major sources of variation in contextual performance are volition and predisposition. Finally, task activities are role-prescribed, that is, they are formally recognised as part of the job. Contextual behaviours are much less likely to be role-prescribed.

Citizenship behaviours as a facet of contextual behaviours

As noted earlier, the work of a number of researchers demonstrates the close link between contextual behaviours and citizenship behaviours. Citizenship behaviours tend to be defined as behaviours that are extra-role, discretionary behaviours that help other organisational members perform their jobs or show support for and conscientiousness toward the organisation.

As Borman and Motowidlo (1992) point out, this conception in turn builds on earlier ideas of the informal organisation such as those set out by Barnard (1938). Similarly, Katz and Kahn (1978) distinguish between role performance and "spontaneous behaviour", which includes cooperative gestures, actions protecting the organisation, and behaviour that enhances the external image of the organisation. Organ (1988) stressed the fact that all these behaviours contribute to organisational effectiveness. Other researchers have sought to define differences *within* the organisational citizenship domain. Smith, Organ and Near (1983), for example, distinguish between "altruism": spontaneous, prosocial gestures directed towards helping others in the organisation, and "conscientiousness": generalised compliance with organisational rules and procedures. Still other researchers have sought to define different dimensions of behaviours within these two concepts, especially the first one, prosocial behaviours. Borman and Motowidlo (1992, p. 83) provide a summary of all these studies under five major headings which seem to capture the individual concepts from the domains discerned in earlier research:

BROAD RESEARCH ISSUES

There are two gaps in the literature which this study seeks to explore further: first, tacit knowledge of citizenship behaviours in relation to the organisational lifecycle; and second, tacit knowledge of citizenship behaviours in universities. These two issues are explained separately, and then examined in relation to their importance to selection decisions, including selection decisions in universities.

Tacit knowledge of citizenship behaviours and the organisational life cycle

Now we have said that the broad nature of citizenship behaviours tends to be seen as similar from job to job, and even from organisation to organisation. That is, tacit expectations of citizenship behaviours are broadly similar, in contrast to expectations of task performance behaviours. Nevertheless, it is conceivable that the different stages organisations have reached in their life cycles might lead to some specific variations in the types of citizenship behaviours tacitly expected. For example in a new university citizenship behaviours related to starting an enterprise may be expected. These may include preparedness to work outside an area of expertise, to help the university achieve a profile in the community, or to devote extra time to students. In an older, more established university other, more academically oriented behaviours may be expected, such as preparedness to perceive oneself primarily as a research academic, or preparedness to compete internationally.

Tacit knowledge of citizenship behaviours in universities

Research on citizenship behaviours in universities is limited, although other aspects of tacit knowledge in academia have been studied. Wagner and Sternberg (1985) for example, have examined those tacit knowledge strategies that are related to academic task behaviours. Some recent research on citizenship behaviours in Canadian universities shows that certain types of citizenship behaviours may actually detract from an individual's prospects for advancement, even though they enhance organisational effectiveness. For example, university staff in North America as well as other countries are evaluated with regard to a tenure decision on their research productivity and teaching effectiveness. However, given the greater emphasis on the former than the latter in most universities, a focus on organisational citizenship behaviours, which may be detrimental to a person's research productivity, may actually harm their prospects for gaining a tenured position (Skarlicki and Latham, 1995).

Tacit knowledge, citizenship behaviours and selection decisions

Given the perception that organisations and individuals may benefit – or occasionally suffer – from the exercise of extrarole or citizenship behaviours, there has been considerable interest in organisational culture and citizenship behaviours with regard to the "match" between organisations and the individuals who already work in them to determine the level of compatibility between the two. Several studies (Wagner, 1992; Wagner and Sternberg, 1985; 1987) have found that those who "fitted" the organisational culture tend to have higher job satisfaction, and intended to continue working with that organisation longer than those who were "misfits". In this study this problem of whether judgements about "fit" are being made on the basis of tacit knowledge was examined from a different point of view: that of those within the organisation *concerning those who may potentially join it.*

It has long been argued or assumed that those members who are more senior in an organisation and/or have been there longest, have the best knowledge of and access to the norms of behaviour that are determined by the organisation's culture. Indeed, to some extent this is part of the very definition of organisational culture – especially in unitarist definitions of culture – implied in expressions such as "the way we do things around here." However these assumptions raise the question of how unified senior staff really are about the value they place on citizenship behaviours as compared to other behaviours, and whether they are indeed united in their conception of the nature of such behaviours. In the university context, these issues raise the specific questions of whether senior academics and senior administrators are more united than more junior members of these organisations in how they value organisational citizenship behaviours, and the relative value of tacit assumptions about academic behaviours as compared to citizenship behaviours in universities at different stages of the life cycle. The context of selection decisions provides the framework for examining these topics.

RESEARCH HYPOTHESES

Hypotheses derived from these ideas were tested in two universities which are similar in many respects but differ in how long they have been operating: two years and 27 years respectively. Four hypotheses were tested:

Hypothesis 1

That when asked to consider a potential selection decision, individuals in both institutions will consistently favour an individual exhibiting either "academic" or "citizenship" behaviours, even when some issues within that decision are specifically excluded from the selection criteria.

Hypothesis 2

There will be a consistent difference between the two universities concerning tacit knowledge surrounding specific aspects of selection decisions, namely the relative importance of "academic" and "citizenship" behaviours.

Hypothesis 3

That senior individuals in both institutions will have the greatest degree of tacit knowledge concerning "person-organisation" fit and will hence, as a group, exhibit less variation than other groups concerning "academic" and "citizenship" behaviours.

Hypothesis 4

That individuals within the longer established university will exhibit a greater degree of shared understanding (tacit knowledge) than individuals within the more recently established university with regard to these two kinds of behaviours.

RESEARCH METHOD

Sampling groups

Three groups within each of the two institutions were used to test the four hypotheses outlined above:

A: a group of senior academic and administrative staff (in Australian terms, academics at Level B and above and administrators at level 7 and above;

B: a group of junior academic and administrative staff (in Australian terms Level A and sessional academic staff and administrative staff at level 6 or below);

C: a group of students from both Business and non-Business areas of study.

The groups sampled thus represent a continuum from the most senior to the most junior members of the two organisations of interest.

Research instrument

A modified version of the Tacit Knowledge Inventory (TKI) of Wagner and Sternberg (1991) was used to assess whether and what kinds of tacit knowledge were being applied. As noted earlier, Wagner and Sternberg have been among the most prominent of researchers into tacit knowledge. Their instrument has been constructed over many years and incorporates a number of approaches to examining the frequent finding that there are only moderate or weak correlations between measures of intelligence such as IQ tests and actual occupational performance. The approaches to measuring occupational success that have influenced the development of the TKI include:

Motivational, examining the role of motives that drive and are satisfied by intellectual behaviour, e.g. Atkinson (1958), McClelland, Atkinson, Clark and Lowell (1953);

Critical Incident, asking individuals who excel at a job to describe critical incidents which they handled particularly well or particularly poorly to analyse qualitatively the competencies demanded by a particular job, e.g. Flanagan (1954), McClelland (1976);

Simulation, the observation of individuals in situations that have been set up to simulate job performance e.g. Frederiksen (1966), Frederiksen, Saunders and Wand (1957);

Assessment Centre, which combines the first three approaches and provides summary judgements and ratings by a group of assessors, e.g. Thornton and Byham (1982); and the

Expert-Novice Differences approach, examining how experts and novices in a given domain differ in their performance on domain-relevant tasks, e.g. Chi, Glaser and Rees (1982), Chase and Simon (1973). The *Expert-Novice Differences* approach has the greatest emphasis in the instrument.

The research for the TKI began by interviewing a number of highly experienced and successful individuals in each of the domains of academic psychology and business management. They were asked to describe some typical work-related situations that might be encountered during a work week, and then provide a series of alternative actions that they might propose as possible solutions to the situation. On the basis of these interviews and an initial theoretical framework, a set of work-related scenarios and response alternatives for each career domain was assembled and administered. Item discrimination procedures were used to identify the response alternatives that differentiate between groups of individuals who differed in amounts of experience and training in each career domain.

The published TKI (from which we derived the version used in our study) uses nine scenarios and 90 response alternatives. This version was developed from 48 unique scenarios with 562 response alternatives. The instrument has been extensively tested for both reliability and validity, with satisfactory results. This is more than usually important given that the TKI has been developed for use as a diagnostic and selection instrument in organisations, and thus needs to be both professionally sound and legally defensible. More detail about the development of the TKI and its development is given in Wagner and Sternberg (1991).

The strengths of the TKI for this study thus include the fact that it is a comprehensive and soundly based instrument with which to examine the gaps in the literature discussed earlier. Its emphasis on expert-novice differences, its scenario rating approach, and its focus on organisational management issues made it appropriate at both a theoretical and an operational level for tapping into organisational citizenship and selection decision issues as facets of the management of universities.

As mentioned earlier, the published version of TKI employs nine scenarios which tap tacit knowledge of a variety of organisational management issues. Scenarios include common organisational problems such as how much consultation to undertake before ordering a semi-routine item of equipment, how to respond to an employee who breaks the chain of command to report an incidence of possible wrong-doing, how best to organise one's time when under deadline pressure, and so on. Respondents rate between eight and ten possible courses of action in response to each scenario on a scale of 1 to 7. An abbreviated example of a typical TKI scenario (slightly adapted for the Australian university setting) appears below:

> "You and a colleague are jointly responsible for completing a report on a new aspect of departmental policy or practice by the end of the week. You are uneasy about this assignment because he has a reputation for not meeting deadlines. The problem does not appear to be lack of effort. Rather, he seems to lack certain organisational skills necessary to meet a deadline and is also quite a perfectionist. As a result, too much time is wasted coming up with the "perfect" idea, policy or report.
>
> Your goal is to produce the best possible report by the deadline at the end of the week. Rate of the quality of the following strategies for meeting your goal on a 1to 7 point scale where 1 indicates an extremely bad strategy, 4 indicates a strategy which is neither good nor bad, and 7 indicates an extremely good strategy.
>
> • Divide the work to be done in half and tell him that if he does not complete his part, you obviously will have to let your immediate supervisor know it was not your fault.

- Politely tell him to be less of a perfectionist.
- Set deadlines for completing each part of the report, and accept what you have accomplished at least deadline as the final version of that part of the report.

(...)

- Ignore his organisational problem so you don't give attention to maladaptive behaviour."

Adaptation of the research instrument for the study

As mentioned earlier, the instrument was adapted to make it appropriate to the Australian university sector. For example, the original TKI had a scenario that required respondents to rate ways of acquiring a better knowledge of information technology issues for product development which would improve the company's market share. In our version this scenario was adapted to require respondents to rate ways of acquiring a better of knowledge of information technology issues for use in distance-learning programs, to improve their university's share of the education market. This was the most major adaptation of an existing scenario; other adaptations were simple changes of terminology to reflect Australian university organisational levels, occupational categories and so on.

Given our interest in examining organisational citizenship issues as a facet of tacit knowledge in the management of universities, an issue not included in the original TKI, our adaptation of the instrument included the addition of a tenth scenario we devised to test tacit knowledge of "academic" and "citizenship" behaviours in a selection decision situation in a university. An identical format to the scenarios in the original TKI was used for the new scenario. An abbreviated example of the new scenario appears below.

"You are a member of a selection panel which is selecting a new staff member at "Lecturer" level (academic level B) within your department. Rate the importance of the following strategies to ensure the best person is selected on a 1 to 7 point scale where 1 indicates an extremely bad strategy, 4 indicates a strategy which is neither good nor bad, and 7 indicates an extremely good strategy.

- Select the candidate with the highest average number of publications per year.
- Select the individual with the best quality publication(s) even if there is only one.
- Insist on seeing good teaching evaluations before making a selection decision.

(...)

- Require a doctorate qualification before considering the person for shortlisting. (Note: a doctorate is not required as part of the essential criteria for the position.)"

Four of the 10 items of the two subscales "academic behaviours" and "organisational citizenship behaviours" can be seen in the illustration. The first two and the fourth items in the illustration are "academic behaviours" items; the third represents a "citizenship behaviour". Other items from the "academic behaviours" subscale included working away from campus to develop large scale grant proposals, attending international research conferences, and so on. Other items from the "organisational citizenship behaviours" subscale included spending a lot of time with students, raising the university's profile in the local community, and so on. The development of the subscales relied on the work of Skarlicki and Latham (1995) on organisational citizenship behaviours, as well as the authors' experience of these factors. Pre-testing of the subscales on a group of about a dozen academics and students at both universities indicated adequate face validity of the concepts captured in the scenario and its possible responses.

Administration of the instrument, response rates and analytical method

With students, the instrument was administered in classes ensuring a 100% response rate. The instrument was mailed to the academic and administrative staff using the universities' internal mail service. The response rate for staff was about 60% in both institutions. The capacity of the researchers to follow up respondents within the two institutions yielded a response rate considerably higher than that usually achieved in studies of this kind. Statistical analysis was carried out using the computer analysis package SPSS.

RESULTS

Description of sample

A total of 278 usable responses were received, including 63 staff. The number of responses and their distribution across staff/student categories were approximately similar for the two universities.

Hypothesis 1

The items for "academic" and "citizenship" behaviours from the new scenario were summed to yield two subscales. T-tests and Wilcoxon Matched Pairs Signed Ranks testing of the mean responses for the subscales for all respondents were carried out. The result was a highly significant ($p<.0001$) difference between the subscales over the total group of respondents, with the preference across the entire sample being for "citizenship" over "academic" behaviours in selection decisions. Thus hypothesis 1 appears to be supported.

Hypothesis 2

The same tests on the subscales were repeated but with the total sample split between the older and the newer university. The result was a significantly stronger ($p<.01$) preference for "citizenship" behaviours over "academic" behaviours at the newer university as compared to the older one. Thus hypothesis 2 also appears to be supported. The salience of this finding was increased by the observation that mean differences between the newer and older universities in respect of other facets of tacit knowledge tested by the instrument were rarely significant.

Hypothesis 3

T-tests for equality of variances and non-parametric tests (Mann-Whitney U-Wilcoxon Rank Sum tests) were carried out on the standard deviations of the responses for the "academic" and "citizenship" subscales by senior and junior staff at the two universities. No significant difference between the two groups was found, hence hypothesis 3 is NOT supported. Senior staff do not appear more united than other groups in their tacit views of "academic" or "citizenship" behaviours. Interestingly however, *other* groups appeared more united, at least when *specific items* within the two subscales were considered. For example, students at both universities showed less variance than staff in preferring to appoint someone who was a good teacher and who would spend more time than usual with students.

Hypothesis 4

While there was a difference in the preference between the two institutions regarding "academic" and "citizenship" behaviours, T-tests of the subscales' variances for the two institutions showed no difference in the strength to which their respective preferences were held. Thus hypothesis 4 was not supported; members of the older institution do not appear to have a collectively "stronger" culture with respect to these particular tacit knowledge issues.

IMPLICATIONS AND CONCLUSIONS

Since hypotheses 1 and 2 were supported, we may tentatively conclude that attempts to make a "person-organisation" fit in organisations do indeed take place, and that "citizenship" behaviours do appear to be more highly valued in less well established organisations compared to longer established ones. Given the lack of support for hypotheses 3 and 4, however, we need to question the frequent assumption of the organisational culture literature that senior staff, "top management", will necessarily be more united concerning specific items of tacit knowledge. In fact, other groups with a specific interest in a particular aspect of organisational citizenship which affects them, may well be more in agreement. Similarly, members of an older organisation, though holding a different tacit view of a citizenship behaviour issue than a younger one, will not necessarily hold it more strongly.

The findings suggest that managers of organisations, particularly those involved in selection decisions, should not be overly confident that the use of formal selection criteria will always prevent the influence of tacit knowledge in making such decisions. They should seek ways to make more explicit the organisation's wishes with respect to issues which may influence selection behaviour.

As Borman and Motowidlo (1992) make clear, however, this is not necessarily easily done in the case of citizenship behaviours. Specifically, including contextual dimensions as performance criteria in personnel selection or merit pay situations would involve expecting and including as performance requirements such behaviours as volunteering for additional assignments, expending extra effort on job tasks, and altruistically helping co-workers and supervisors. At the least, it is paradoxical to require that that employees do more than their jobs call for. Moreover, it is difficult to imagine how sanctions might be applied to employees for not doing more than is formally expected.

A more difficult issue still, might be that introducing explicit rather than tacit expectations in these areas could upset the natural occurrence of behaviour of this kind in organisations. Drawing up detailed requirements for organisational citizenship behaviour may leave out other expressions of such behaviour. Moreover, because of the "every man for himself" aspect of merit pay and selection decision situations, it may create jealousies and competitiveness among employees in precisely those areas where cooperation is essential. Nevertheless, if the contextual dimensions of employees' contributions to organisational effectiveness are to be recognised, valued and rewarded in organisations, then organisation members need to know about them as part of the expectations relevant to their success in the organisation.

There is at least one further implication for managers. They should also not assume that senior staff will necessarily think equally strongly about certain norms of the organisation, particularly those relating to matters of organisational citizenship. In fact, our study suggests they should be aware that in fact more unified views may be encountered elsewhere in the organisation.

LIMITATIONS AND SUGGESTIONS FOR FURTHER RESEARCH

The research is necessarily limited by the nature of the organisations studied (universities). Among other issues, more research should be undertaken to understand to what extent the findings are generalisable to organisations in other industries. While previous research suggests that organisational citizenship behaviours are similar across organisations, the findings from this study suggest that tacit understandings on the part of employees about how organisational needs may best be met may vary depending on the stage reached in the organisational life cycle.

In addition, the results invite further exploration of the potential relationship between organisational citizenship and other aspects of tacit knowledge in organisations. The finding that members of newer and younger universities tended to have similar results for most items in the other (original) TKI scenarios is evidence of the robustness of the original instrument. However the fact that new and older organisations differed in the extent to which they valued organisational citizenship issues (hypothesis 2) and also that some specific interest groups rather than "top management" valued organisational citizenship behaviours more strongly (hypothesis 3) invites exploration as to whether there is an interaction between organisational citizenship and other tacit knowledge domains.

Other demographic variables such as the length of time staff had worked in an organisation and whether they had experience as supervisors may affect the ways organisational citizenship as an aspect of tacit knowledge relates to organisational decision-making. The newness of one institution compared to the other in the present study was a factor subjected to special scrutiny. However it also meant that no staff had been employed in that institution for a period longer than two years, so an investigation based on how long staff had been employed in that institution was not possible. However this could be an interesting line of inquiry given that organisational norms have been argued to become more entrenched as staff remain longer in the organisation. Similarly, greater experience as a supervisor may temper people's tacit views of how possible or desirable organisational citizenship behaviours are as management pressures increase.

Finally, organisational citizenship considered as an aspect of tacit knowledge could be explored from the perspective of gender issues in organisations. For example, tacit views of organisational citizenship could perhaps throw light on the phenomenon of the organisational "glass ceiling" - the term commonly used to describe the greater difficulty women employees experience in comparison to men in attaining positions beyond middle management level. Comparing women's and men's tacit understandings of whether and how citizenship behaviours can help them get to the top of their organisations may uncover differences between the genders. If so, and depending on the direction of the differences, we may posit that women's tacit understandings of organisational citizenship, as with some behaviours in academic settings, may actually harm their chances of advancement even though the behaviours benefit the organisation.

Many other possibilities for further investigations suggest themselves. It seems that talking about tacit things has the potential to further our understanding not just of tacit knowledge but of broader issues in how organisations work.

REFERENCES

Atkinson, J. W. (1958), *Motives in Fantasy Action and Society,* Van Nostrand, Princeton, NJ.

Barnard, C. (1938), *The functions of the executive,* Harvard University Press, Cambridge, MA.

Barrett, R. S. (1995), "Employee Selection with the Performance Priority Survey", *Personnel Psychology,* 48, pp. 653-662.

Bazerman, M. (1994), *Judgment in Managerial Decision Making,* 3rd ed, Wiley, New York.

Borman, W. C., and Motowidlo, S. I. (1992), "Expanding the Criterion Domain to Include Elements of Contextual Performance", in: Schmitt, N, Borman, W. C. and Associates (Eds.), *Personnel Selection in Organizations,* San Francisco, Jossey-Bass, pp. 71-98.

Chatman, J. A. (1991), "Organization Culture in the Service Sector: A Between Industry Comparison", *Academy of Management Proceedings,* 168-172.

Chase, W. G. and Simon, H. A. (1973), "Perception in Chess", *Cognitive Psychology,* 4, pp. 55-81.

Chi, M. T. H., Glaser, R. and Rees, E. (1982), "Expertise in Problem Solving", in: Sternberg, R. (Ed.), *Advances in the Psychology of Human Intelligence,* Erlbaum, Hillsdale, NJ, 1, pp. 7-75.

Dixon, R. A. and Baltes, P. B. (1986), "Toward life-span research on the functions and pragmatics of intelligence", in: Sternberg, R. J. and Wagner, R. K. (Eds.), *Practical intelligence: The nature and origins of competence in the everyday world,* Cambridge University Press, New York, pp. 203-235.

Flanagan, J. C. (1954), "The Critical Incident Technique", *Psychological Bulletin,* 51, pp. 327-358.

Frederiksen, N., Saunders, D. R. and Wand, B. (1957), "The In-Basket Test", *Psychological Monographs,* 71, (9, Whole No. 438).

Forester, J. (1984), "Bounded Rationality and the Politics of Muddling Through", *Public Administration Review,* January-February 1984, pp. 23-31.

Horn, J. L. (1982), "The theory of fluid and crystallized intelligence in relation to concepts of cognitive psychology and aging in adulthood", in: Craik, F. I. M. and Trehub, A. (Eds.), *Aging and Cognitive Processes,* Plenum, New York, pp. 237-278.

Horn J. L. and Cattell R. B. (1966), "Refinement and test of the theory of fluid and crystallized intelligence", *Journal of Educational Psychology,* 57, pp. 253-270.

Horvath, J. A., Forsythe, G. B., Sweeney, P. J., McNally, J. A., Wattendorf, J. M., Williams, W. M. and Sternberg, R. J. (in press), *Tacit knowledge in military leadership: Evidence from officer interviews [Technical report].* U.S. Army Research Institute for the Behavioral and Social Sciences, Alexandria, VA.

Janis, I. L. (1982), *Groupthink,* Houghton Mifflin, Boston.

Katz, D. and Kahn, R. L. (1978), *The social psychology of organizations,* Wiley, New York.

Labouvie-Vief, G. (1982), "Dynamic development and mature autonomy: A theoretical prologue", *Human Development,* 25, pp. 161-191.

McClelland, D. C. (1976), *A Guide to Job Competency Assessment.* McBer, Boston.

McClelland, D. C., Atkinson, J. W., Clark, R. A. and Lowell, E. L. (1953), *The Achievement Motive.* Appleton-Century-Crofts, NY.

Neisser, U. (1976), "General, academic and artificial intelligence", in: Resnick, L. (Ed.), *Human intelligence: Perspectives on its theory and measurement,* Ablex, Norwood, NJ., pp. 179-189.

O'Reilly, C. A., Chatman, J. A., and Caldwell, D. (1991), "People and the organizational culture: A profile comparison approach to assessing person-organisation fit", *Academy of Management Journal,* 34/3, pp. 487-516.

Organ, D. W. (1988), *Organizational Citizenship Behavior: The good soldier syndrome,* Lexington Books, Lexington, MA.

Ott, J.S. (1989), *The Organizational Culture Perspective,* San Francisco, CA., Brooks Cole Publishing Co.

Reichers, A. E., and Schneider, B. (1990), "Climate and culture: An evolution of constructs", in: Schneider B. (Ed.), *Organizational Climate and Culture,* Jossey-Bass, San Francisco.

Rumelhart, M. (1983), "The normalisation of social interaction: When shared assumptions cannot be shared", *Qualitative Sociology,* 6/2, pp. 149-162.

Schaie, K. W. (1977/78), "Toward a stage theory of adult cognitive development", *International Journal of Aging and Human Development,* 8, pp. 129-138.

Schein, E. H. (1990), "Organizational Culture", *American Psychologist,* February 1990, p. 116.

Schneider, B. (1990), "The climate for service: An application of the climate construct", in: Schneider B. (Ed.), *Organizational Climate and Culture,* Jossey-Bass, San Francisco.

Simon, H. A. (1976), *Administrative Behavior,* 3rd ed., Wiley, New York.

Skarlicki, D. P. and Latham, G. P. (1995), "Organizational Citizenship Behaviour and Performance in a University Setting", *Revue canadienne des sciences de l'administration,* 12/3, pp. 176-181.

Smith, C. A., Organ, D. W. and Near, J. P. (1983), "Organizational citizenship behavior: Its nature and antecedents", *Journal of Applied Psychology,* 68, pp. 653-663.

Thornton, G. C. and Byham, W. C. (1982), *Assessment Centers and Managerial Performance,* Academic Press, NY.

Wagner, R. (1992), "Organizational culture and employee retention", *Academy of Management Journal,* 35/5, pp. 1036-1056.

80

Wagner, R. and Sternberg, R. (1985), "Practical intelligence in real world pursuits: The role of tacit knowledge", *Journal of Personality and Social Psychology*, 49/2, pp. 436-458.

Wagner, R. and Sternberg, R. (1987), "Tacit knowledge in managerial success", *Journal of Business and Psychology*, 1/4, pp. 301-312.

Wagner, R. and Sternberg, R. (1991), *Tacit knowledge inventory for managers*, Psychological Corporation, San Antonio, TX.

Wallach, M. A., Kogan, N. and Bem, D. J. (1962), "Group influence on individual risk taking", *Journal of Abnormal and Social Psychology*, 65, pp. 75-86.

Williams, S. A., Denney, N. W. and Schadler, M. (1983), "Elderly adults' perception of their own cognitive development during the adult years", *International Journal of Aging and Human Development*, 16, pp. 147-158.

3. INTERNATIONAL BUSINESS

ROLE OF POLITICAL VIOLENCE IN FOREIGN DIRECT INVESTMENT DECISIONS

H. Singh

Department of Economics
Grand Valley State University
Allendale, MI 49401
USA

Abstract: Most developing countries are trying to attract foreign direct investment (FDI) because the traditional sources of lending such as bank loans and multilateral aid has shrunk considerably. FDI has other advantages in terms of risk sharing and technology transfers. The role of political risk as a determining factor has not been analyzed extensively. Two proxies for political risk from new data sources are analyzed along with the traditional control variables. The results of the paper indicate that besides traditional variables, two factors that influence FDI flows are: the openness of the economy and the degree of political risk.

Keywords: Foreign Direct Investment (FDI), political risk, open economy, export orientation, developing countries.

INTRODUCTION

This paper analyses the extent to which political risk influences Foreign Direct Investment(FDI) inflows to developing countries. We are interested in determining particularly what **macroeconomic factors** are conducive to decisions by multinational companies to locate their production operations (or acquire a major stake in existing operations) in developing countries. Previous research on this issue has yielded mixed results. Further work on the role of political risk is warranted for two additional reasons. First, new attempts are needed to capture political risk in developing countries by more relevant proxies. Due to the lack of pertinent data, political risk has been a difficult dimension to incorporate in empirical analysis. In this paper, we employ some new data series which have become available recently to capture different dimensions of political instability. Second, an analysis of this question is particularly relevant because of the renewed interest in FDI flows as a viable alternative for financing development. The resurgence of interest in FDI is primarily attributable to two reasons.

S.H. Zanakis et al. (eds.), Decision Making: Recent Developments and Worldwide Applications, 83–96.
© 2000 *Kluwer Academic Publishers.*

(a) Recent World Bank Reports indicate that the flow of FDI to developing countries in the late 1980s and 1990s has been increasing dramatically. These reports indicate that FDI has been harnessed by developing countries at different income levels, although middle income countries are relatively more successful than low-income countries. This is encouraging, particularly since the prospects of multilateral and commercial bank lending are limited.

(b) Decisions about FDI inflows have some inherent advantages for the development effort: risk sharing, market discipline, export orientation, technology and managerial expertise transfers etc. From these recent trends, it appears that FDI is potentially an important source of private capital for developing economies, particularly for countries which are able to create the right environment for foreign investment decisions.

Besides economic variables, the political dimensions of foreign investment should be incorporated in the analysis. An analysis of these issues will provide insights about the specific conditions that may contribute to higher FDI flows.

The paper is organized as follows: Section 2, discusses previous empirical findings and develops the background of the two hypotheses for this investigation. Section 3 presents the rationale for the control variables. Section 4, provides a description of the data set and the empirical results. The final section, follows with conclusions, policy implications and suggestions for future empirical work.

RECENT EMPIRICAL RESULTS

A comprehensive survey on the determinants of FDI based on different methodologies is provided by a recent UNCTC report by Pearce et al. (1992)

The present study approaches the issue at the aggregate country-specific level. Consequently, only broad trends about the macroeconomic determinants of gross FDI flows can be discerned. An evaluation of the empirical studies based on the aggregate econometric approach has been made by Agarwal (1980), Schneider and Frey (1985), Singh and Jung (1996).

Definition and Role of Political Risk

The definition of political risk has been controversial. Since political risk is a multidimensional researchers tend to emphasize different aspects of how the political environment can result in investment losses. Stephen Kobrin (1981) pointed out:

"What we are, or should be, concerned with is the impact of events which are political in the sense that they arise from power or authority relationships and which affect (or have the potential to effect) the firms operation. Not the events, qua events, but their potential manifestation as constraints upon foreign investors should be of concern." (p. 71).

In order to investigate how different aspects of political risk may constrain investors, researchers have employed different proxies for political risk with mixed results. Surveys by Aharoni (1966) revealed that executives rank political instability as the most important variable, apart from market potential. Conversely, Bennett and Green (1972) found that

U.S. direct investments are not affected by political instability in the recipient countries. Levis (1979) employing two proxies for political stability obtained mixed results. He found "the absence of aggressive domestic behavior within the political system against groups or officeholders" to be a significant determinant of FDI for the current period but not for the lagged period. Another variable (the legitimacy of the regime) was found to be significant for the lagged period but not significant for the current period.

Discriminant analysis of 58 developing countries by Root and Ahmed (1979) found that "the number of regular (constitutional) changes in government leadership between 1956 and 1967" was significant. However, other political variables such as number of internal armed attacks, degree of nationalism and colonial affiliation were not significant discriminators. Schneider and Frey (1985) found a negative relationship between "number of political strikes and riots in host countries" and "the inflow of foreign direct investment".

More recently, Wheeler and Mody (1992) found a broad principal component measure of administrative efficiency and political risk to be statistically insignificant. Lucas (1993) does not directly incorporate proxies for sociopolitical risk, rather he finds episodic dummies for "good events" such as the Asian and Olympic games in Korea, Acquino's accession in the Philippines and US build up in Thailand to be positively related to FDI. Conversely, "negative events" such as Sukarno's rule in Indonesia, Park's assassination in South Korea and Marcos's martial law in Philippines have a negative impact on FDI.

Singh and Jun (1996) find a broad measure of political risk significant in most specifications.

It appears that the empirical evidence about the impact of political risk is not unequivocal, partly because it is difficult to obtain reliable quantitative estimates of this qualitative phenomena for an extended period of time, particularly aspects of political risk which are viewed as a direct constraint by foreign investors. Political instability is a complex, multi-dimension phenomena. Most proxies that are available, may capture only some aspects of this complex determinant.

In this paper, we attempt to capture political risk by two ways. First, a comprehensive, qualitative measure is employed: Each country is ranked in terms of political stability by a judgmental index provided by experts in the field (PRI). This data set is obtained from Business Environmental Risk Intelligence (BERI).

Second, we utilize data about the terrorist incidents in each country: percentage of persons injured (PINJ) by terrorism as a proportion of the total injured or killed by these incidents worldwide for a specific year. The data set about terrorist incidents is obtained from Pinkerton Risk Assessment Services. Judgments made by political experts while comprehensive in nature, might not fully take into account the **sensational impact** of terrorist incidents. Terrorist incidents resulting in civilian injuries, a dramatic evidence of political risk, may tend to have wide ranging impact on FDI decisions. Consequently, the Pinkerton data set is employed to test if terrorist incidents negatively impact FDI flows by raising the perception of political risk among potential investors.

Based on this discussion, the following empirical hypotheses are tested:

Hypothesis I: Is overall political risk (measured by a qualitative, judgmental index of experts) detrimental to FDI flows in developing countries?

Hypothesis II: Do specific incidents of political risk (exhibited by violent injuries due to terrorism) reduce FDI flows?

Before testing these hypothesis, we build a rationale for control variables in the testing procedure.

RATIONALE FOR CONTROL VARIABLES

We consider which variables should be included as controls to test the two hypotheses discussed in the preceding section:

Potential Market Size: The size of the market and its growth potential appears to be an important determinant of FDI flows. Bandera and White (1968) found market size to be a significant determinant for United States FDI. Schmitz and Bieri (1972) found the one period lagged GNP of EEC to be a significant variable in a FDI demand function. Lunn (1980) also found a one period lagged GNP of EEC to be a significant explanatory variable for United States direct investment in the European market. For developing countries, Root and Ahmed (1979), Torrisi (1985), Schneider and Frey (1985), Petrochilas(1989) and Wheeler and Mody (1992) all find market size to be significant.

Since our dependent variable is FDI relative to GDP, the relationship with other GDP related variables on the right hand side of the equation may not be unequivocal. Consequently, we include the growth rate of GDP **(GDP%)** to control for actual and potential market size.

Exchange Rate: Although all the variables are converted to dollars, Lucas (1993) has contended that the exchange rate may have " a residual role with respect to exchange rate risk, for example, in determining the value of repatriated profits or in threatening restrictions on such remittances." (p. 393). In order to control for this possibility the real exchange rate is included as a control variable **(ERATE)**.

Home country factors: The inclusion of supply side factors from home countries is another possibility. Culem (1988) analyzed the **bilateral** flows of direct investment for six developed countries (United States, Germany, France, U.K., the Netherlands and Belgium). He found that the characteristics of the home country of the investing firm (such as growth rates and labor costs) did not improve the performance of the model. Since we are analyzing **global** FDI flows to developing countries, the opportunity costs of the specific host country are not directly discernible. One would expect a general increase in the opportunity costs of the home countries to influence the **size** of the **overall** flow of FDI to developing countries but not the decision by multinationals to alter its **allocation** to specific countries. Consequently, in order to control for aggregate supply side effects, we include the average industrial production index of the G-7 countries [computed from IMF's International Financial Statistics (1993)] as a control variable **(IPG7)**.

Export orientation: There are two reasons for including exports as a control variable. (1) There is a widespread perception that economies that are "open" encourage more confidence and foreign investment. One indicator of oneness is the relative size of the export sector. (2) Another reason for including exports as a control variable is the higher export propensity of foreign firms (Chen, 1994). This issue has generated considerable controversy, for instance Westphal et al. (1979) have contended that exports may be correlated with FDI not because of the higher export orientation of foreign firms but due to their disproportional representation in the main export sectors. However, as Chen (1994) correctly points out, this distinction does not negate the overall contribution of foreign firms to the export sector. Exports relative to GDP are included as a control variable **(EXPORTS)**.

Inter-regional differences: Since we are employing a pooled model, the analysis focuses on attempting to explain variations of FDI flows over time and across different countries. The time-series portion of the data encompasses the within-country variation which is captured by country-specific economic variables varying over time.

The inter-country variation presents a methodological dilemma. The interesting variation in the data across countries (which we are attempting to explain by qualitative variables), generally vary slowly over time, although the inter-country differences may be quite large. Country-specific dummy variables are not employed because they will remove this variation, leaving mostly within country variation. Nevertheless, we need to establish some form of control which will not dummy-out most of the interesting inter-country variation. We employ four dummy variables to control for region-specific factors.[1] Regional differences may exist because FDI flows are known to follow a "Triad Pattern". The regional dummies may also capture some economies of agglomeration.

Lagged Effects: Decisions about FDI flows are likely to take time to adjust to desired levels, depending upon the specific constraints faced by a transnational corporation. A simple partial adjustment process can incorporate the speed of adjustment. [see Pindyck and Rubinfeld (1991) pp. 208-209 for details]. We begin with a simple equation:

$$FDI^d_t = B_0 + B_1 PI_t + B_2 CV_t + E_t \qquad (1)$$

Where **desired** FDI stock at time t (FDI^d_t) is based on political instability (PI) at time (t), a vector of control variables (CV_t) and E_t is a random error term. Also, B_0, B_1, B_2 are coefficients of the respective variables. To see how the speed of adjustment is incorporated in this model, consider the following equation:

$$FDI_t - FDI_{t-1} = A(FDI^d_t - FDI_{t-1}) \qquad (2)$$

Equation (2) shows that changes in actual FDI will respond only partially to the difference between desired FDI and past values of FDI. In any given period, a desired level of FDI may not be completely realized (as actual FDI in the next period), because of physical and procedural constraints. The parameter "A" captures the speed of adjustment to a desired FDI level.

When we substitute FDI^d_t from (1) into (2) and rearrange, we obtain:

$$FDI_t = AB_0 + B_1 A(PI_t) + B_2 A(CV_t) + (1-A)FDI_{t-1} + AE_t \qquad (3)$$

---

[1] Wheeler and Mody (1992) have developed a similar rationale for excluding country specific dummies. Incorporating regional dummies is a traditional procedure for handling this dilemma. For instance Barro (1991) estimates a pooled model with regional dummies to analyze the determinants of economic growth.

Besides the rationale of a simple stock adjustment model, the lagged dependent variable as an explanatory variable serves two purposes. First, it reduces autocorrelation significantly. Second, the lagged dependent variable indirectly incorporates other "omitted" factors which may have influenced FDI in the previous period in a parsimonious manner. For these reasons the lagged dependent variable is employed as a control variable (**RFDI1**).

Based on the rationale discussed in this section, the fully specified (MODEL 3 in the tables) can be represented as:

$$RFDI= D_1(DASIA) + D_2(DLA) + D_3(DAFRICA) + D_4(DEUROPE) \qquad (4)$$
$$+ B_1(RFDI1) + B_2(IPG7) + B_3(GDP\%) + B_4(ERATE) +$$
$$B_5(EXPORTS) + B_6(POLITICAL\ RISK\ VARIABLE) + U_t.$$

Where **DASIA, DLA, DAFRICA** and **DEUROPE** are the intercept dummies for Asia, Latin America, Africa and Europe respectively. U_t is a random error term. All other variables have been defined in the discussion above.

EMPIRICAL RESULTS

Data Considerations

The empirical results are based on a pooled model. The period of analysis is 1978-92, for the Political Risk Index, based on 19 countries. For the Pinkerton data set, the period of analysis is 1987-92 for 21 countries.[2] The names of the countries are specified in the Tables in which the results are presented. The time period and the choice of countries is basically governed by the availability of data. Note that for each specific hypothesis, the years and the countries vary depending upon the availability of the data.[3]

Dependent Variable

A relative measure of FDI is employed to control for any large country effects. The dependent variable is FDI flows in constant dollars (normalized by the import price deflator), relative to real GDP (henceforth referred to as **RFDI**). RFDI is "net" in that it excludes repatriated profits. The fact that some developing countries have become exporters of capital is a positive sign. Consequently, outward bound FDI is not subtracted out from foreign direct investment inflows.

The definition of the variables and their sources is provided in Table 1.

---

[2] I am grateful to Pinkerton Risk Assessment Services and BERI for allowing me to use their data sets.
[3] Details of the countries included for each hypothesis are provided in the notes to the relevant tables.

Table 1. Definition and sources of variables

VARIABLE	ABBREVIATION	SOURCE
REAL FDI AS A %	RFDI	WORLD DEBT TABLES
OF GDP		WORLD BANK
ANNUAL GDP GROWTH	GDP%	WORLD TABLES
		WORLD BANK
		WORLD TABLES
REAL EXCHANGE RATE	ERATE	WORLD BANK
REAL EXPORTS AS A % OF GDP	EXPORTS	WORLD TABLES
		WORLD BANK
REAL GROWTH OF G7	IPG7	GOVT. FINANCE
COUNTRIES		STATISTICS, IMF.
POLITICAL RISK	PRI	BERI, S.A.
INDEX		
PERCENTAGE OF PERSONS		PNKERTON RISK
INJURED DUE TO TERRORISM	PINJ	ASSESSMENT SERVICES
PERCENTAGE OF PERSONS		PNKERTON RISK
KILLED DUE TO TERRORISM	PKILL	ASSESSMENT SERVICES
DUMMY VARIABLES FOR	DASIA, DLA,	CONSTRUCTED BY
DIFFERENT REGIONS	DEUROPE, DAFRICA	AUTHOR

Empirical Results

Having discussed the rationale for employing different control variables and defined the data set, we now proceed to test each hypothesis. Based on Leamer's (1985) approach, a range of specifications are estimated to assess the sensitivity of the coefficients of the hypothesized variables. The hypothesis testing can be represented by a simple equation:

$$RFDI = F(HV, CV) \qquad (5)$$

Besides the proxy for the hypothesized variable (HV), the specification of the vector of control variables (CV) is important for correctly estimating the equation. Here we have taken previous empirical work as a guide to what should be included (Section 3). The model is progressively complicated with additional control variables to analyze the robustness of the results to alternative specifications. The inclusion of additional variables can also provide insight about the degree of multicollenearity present in the estimating equation. All models are estimated with Ordinary Least Squares[4]. Since higher income countries may attract more absolute flows, all variables are in **real** and **relative** terms.

Political Risk Variables

We test the role of political risk on FDI flows by employing two proxies to capture the diverse aspects of political instability. Initially, let us consider an overall qualitative index.

Political Risk Index (PRI)

HYPOTHESIS I: Is overall political risk (measured by a qualitative, judgmental index of experts) detrimental to FDI flows in developing countries?

In the first instance, we employ a Political Risk Index (PRI) developed by Business Environment Risk Intelligence, S.A. (BERI). Approximately 60 Political Specialists from around the world, evaluate each country with respect to (1) six internal causes of political risk (fractionalization of the political spectrum, linguistic, ethnic and religious fractionalization, coercive political risk (dependence on and\or importance to a hostile power) and (2) Two symptoms of political risk (societal conflict involving demonstrations and street violence).

The qualitative index based on these criteria ranges from 0 (prohibitive risk) to 100 (complete stability). The values determined by approximately 60 political specialists are averaged for each country on a annual basis.

In order to analyze the influence of PRI on FDI flows, three specifications have been employed to test the robustness of the results. One problem with the data set is a few missing observations. As a general rule, if data is not available for a specific variable and time period, the observation is excluded from the regression estimation[5]. It is informative to assess the stability of the coffeicient of the hypothesized variable as the control variables and the sample size changes over different specifications. All results are reported after White's (1980) correction for heteroscedasticity. The results for each specification (TABLE 2) are discussed below:

MODEL 1: Initially, RFDI is regressed with Political Risk Index (PRI), GDP growth rate (GDP%), Industrial Production of the G 7 countries (IPG7), exchange rate (ERATE), and the regional dummy variables (DASIA, DLA, DAFRICA and DEUROPE). PRI is significant at the 1% level (t-value= 7.33). IPG7, ERATE and the regional dummies are significant at the 1% level.

---

[4] The economic structure of the sample countries is likely to be different and dynamic over time. Given our ignorance about the specification of this structure, a simultaneous equations model (which is more sensitive to specification errors) is considered less desirable. A simultaneous bias test is performed for each hypothesized variable.

[5] As Pindyck and Rubinfeld (1991, p. 219-20) point out, if the missing observations dropped are random, the least squares estimator is still unbiased, although there is some loss of efficiency. Since only a few observations are missing and the sample size is fairly large (ranging from 116 to 283), the loss in efficiency is not likely to be an issue.

However, there is significant autocorrelation in this specification. The low value of the Durbin Watson statistic (DW= .45) is indicative of this problem.

MODEL 2: In this specification, we introduce the lagged FDI variable to incorporate a stock adjustment model. This specification also gets rid of autocorrelation. The high t-value of RFDI1 (9.70) and the low value of the adjustment coefficient ("A" ranging from .14 to .40 in Table 2) indicates that the stock adjustment model should be employed. As one would expect, the size of the PRI coefficient is reduced drastically (from .17 to .04), but it is still significant at the 1% level.

Table 2. FDI and political risk index (PRI)

VAR.	MODEL 1	MODEL 2	MODEL 3
DEP VAR	RFDI	RFDI	RFDI
PRI	.17*	.04*	.003
	(7.33)	(3.84)	(.31)
IPG7	.11*	.029*	.018*
	(5.46)	(3.41)	(2.51)
GDP%	.0049	.0001	.015
	(.18)	(.006)	(.88)
ERATE	-.0049*	-.0002*	-.0002*
	(-2.96)	(-2.74)	(2.91)
DASIA	-16.39*	-4.42*	-2.40*
	(-6.09)	(-4.07)	(-2.81)
DLA	-17.3*	-4.61*	-2.21*
	(-6.60)	(-3.99)	(-2.47)
DAFRICA	-15.1*	-4.26*	-1.97*
	(-5.57)	(-3.73)	(-2.15)
DEUROPE	-17.70*	-4.67*	-2.03*
	(-6.05)	(-3.98)	(-2.28)
PRFDI1		.86*	-.60*
		(9.70)	(6.15)
EXPORTS			.03*
			(3.62)
F VALUE	41.25	173.41	182.1
D.W.	.45	2.63	2.37
ADJ R^2	.50	.83	.85
OBS.	283	283	281

Notes: (1) T-values are in parenthesis. * denotes significance at 95% level. The data set is from 1978-92 for the following countries Chile, Colombia, Ecuador, Egypt, Greece, India, Indonesia, Korea, Malaysia, Mexico, Nigeria, Pakistan, Philippines, Portugal, Singapore, Spain, Thailand, Turkey and Venezuela.

MODEL 3: In the third specification, we include a proxy for an "open economy," The inclusion of exports relative to GDP (EXPORTS) in the estimated equation considerably weakens the significance of the PRI coefficient (t value= .31). Since EXPORTS has the strongest correlation with RFDI out of all the explanatory variables (Correlation of .80), this result is not surprising[6]. Once the openness of the economy is taken into consideration, the qualitative proxy for political risk does not add significant explanatory power to the model.

Note that the primary focus is on the coefficients of the hypothesized variable to observe whether they are robust, as different controls are implemented. The coefficients of the control variables have not been subjected to any systematic analysis and consequently should be interpreted with caution. Some general comments about the coefficients of the control variables across various specifications are in order. In the three specifications IPG7, ERATE and the regional dummies are consistently significant.

Incidents of Terrorism

Hypothesis II: Do specific incidents of political risk (exhibited by violent injuries)reduce FDI flows?

In the second stage of the estimation process, we evaluate the significance of specific terrorist incidents on FDI flows. The three specifications discussed earlier in the context of the qualitative political risk variables have been employed again to assess whether, the percentage of persons injured in terrorist accidents (PINJ) significantly reduces FDI flows. The variable is measured as a relative proportion of all the terrorist injuries in the world for that year to mitigate any scale effects.

PINJ is significant at the 1% level in Model 1 and Model 2. However, again when Exports is introduced as a control variable, the size of the coefficient and the significant level is eroded considerably (PINJ is significant only at the 10% level). In terms of competing explanations, the openness of the economy seem to matter more than terrorist incidents, although the size of the coefficients and the significance levels for both explanatory variables are comparable.

CONCLUDING REMARKS

Are decisions about FDI inflows sensitive to political risk? The following pattern of results emerge from our analysis:
  (a) Based on two proxies we have employed to capture political risk, there is a significant impact of political instability on FDI flows to developing countries. The result holds for the qualitative overall measure of political risk, as well as, terrorists incidents reflecting injuries.
  (b) There is a caveat: once a proxy incorporating the openness of the economy is incorporated, the political risk variables are only marginally significant, at best. When, a relative measure of export orientation is introduced, the Political Risk

---

[6] There is also a high correlation (.72) between PRI and EXPORTS indicating multicollinearity as a potential cause for driving down the t-value for PRI.

Index is not statistically significant. The terrorist incident variable is significant only at the 10% level.

Table 3. FDI and percentage injured (PINJ)

VAR.	MODEL 1	MODEL 2	MODEL 3
DEP VAR	RFDI	RFDI	RFDI
PINJ	-.14* (-3.95)	-05* (-3.10)	-.03 (-1.71)
IPG7	.06* (2.31)	.008 (.34)	.003 (.14)
GDP%	.08* (3.87)	.05* (2.07)	.04 (1.45)
ERATE	-.0003* (-2.91)	-.0008* (-1.99)	-.0001* (-2.03)
DASIA	-5.40 (-1.72)	-.35 (-.15)	-.35 (-.15)
DLA	-6.25* (-1.99)	-.59 (-.26)	-.43 (-.19)
DAFRICA	-5.43 (-1.69)	-.99 (-.44)	-.61 (-.28)
DEUROPE	-5.31 (-1.70)	-.36 (-.16)	-.16 (-.07)
PRFDI1		.83* (9.11)	.75* (8.60)
EXPORTS			.02 (1.79)
F VALUE	6.68	36.49	35.11
D.W.	.63	2.47	2.44
ADJ R²	.26	.71	.73
OBS.	116	116	116

Notes:(1) T-values are in parenthesis. * denotes significance at 95% level.(2) The data set is for 1987-92 for the following countries: Argentina, Bolivia, Brazil, Chile, Colombia, Costa Rica, Ecuador, Egypt, Greece, India, Indonesia, Malaysia, Mexico, Pakistan, Panama, Peru, Philippines, Spain, Thailand, Turkey and Venezuela.

The openness of the economy appears to be a more binding constrain than political risk in FDI decisions. These results are consistent with the previous empirical work in Singh and Jung (1996). The openness of the economy may also act as a broader positive signal indicating that the government is oriented towards providing a business friendly environment[7]. The policy implication of the result is that (besides political risk), promoting exports is probably the best way to encourage mutltinationals to invest in a developing country.

A number of general caveats are in order. First, country-specific data can mask a great deal of complexity and variation within the country. As stated earlier, only broad trends can be inferred. Second, the proxies we utilize to test the hypothesis may not have captured the entire complexities of the phenomena. Because of these limitations, the results should be regarded as tentative sample evidence. One avenue for future empirical work is to investigate the dynamic influence of political risk and the openness of the economy by employing sector-specific data for FDI flows. This will enable us to track foreign investment decisions more effectively for specific industries.

REFERENCES

Agarwal, J.P., 1980, "Determinants of Foreign Direct Investments: A Survey", *Weltwirtschaftliches Archiv*, Vol. 116, pp.739-773.

Aharoni, Y.,1966, "The Foreign Investment Decision Process, Cambridge, Mass.: Harvard Graduate School of Business.

Bandera, V.N. and White, J.T., 1968, "US direct investments and domestic markets in Europe", *Economia Internazionale*, 21, pp. 117-133.

Barro, R, 1991, "Economic Growth in a Cross Section of Countries", *Quarterly Journal of Economics*, vol. CVI (2), pp. 407-444.

Bennett, P.D. and Green, R.T., 1972, "Political instability as a determinant of direct foreign investment in marketing", *Journal of Marketing Research*, 9, pp. 162-186.

Chevalier, A. and Hirsc, G., 1981, "The assessment of the political risk in the investment decision," *Journal of the Operational Research Society*, 32,7, pp. 599-610.

Chen, Edward, 1994, "Foreign Direct Investment and Trade as a vehicle for Rapid Economic Growth: The NIE Experience" Working Paper presented in Colombo, Feb. 1994.

Culem, C.G.,1988, "The Locational Determinants of Direct Investment among Industrialized Countries", *European Economic Review*, 32, pp. 885-904.

Dipak, G., 1990, "The Economics of Political Violence: The Effect of Political Instability on Economic Growth, New York: Prager.

Dollar, D.,1992, "Outward-oriented Developing Economies Really Do Grow More Rapidly: Evidence from 95 LDC's 1976-1985", *Economic Development and Cultural Change*,40,3, pp.523-544.

Gooptu, S.,1993, "Portfolio Investment Flows to Emerging Markets, Policy Research Working Papers, International Economics Division. World Bank.

---

[7] Our models do not include China due to lack of relevant data. However, anecdotal evidence of FDI flows into China is a case in point. Inspite of the fact that political risk in China is considerable, FDI flows to China have been remarkably high in the last five years. Foreign investors seem to be focusing more on the large potential market and the ability to export their products from China.

Flamm, K., 1984, "The Volatility of offshore investment, *Journal of Development Economics,* 16, pp. 231-248.

Fry, M.J., 1993, "Foreign Direct Investment in a Macroeconomic Framework: Finance, Efficiency, Incentives and Distortions." WPS 1141, International Economics Department, World Bank

Green, R., 1972, "Political Instability as a Determinant of U.S. Foreign Investment", Bureau of Business Research, University of Texas at Austin.

Helleiner, G.K., 1989, "Transnational Corporations and Direct Foreign Investment", in Handbook of Development Economics, Vol. II, Elsevier Publishers, pp. 1441-1480.

Hein, S.,1992, "Trade Strategy and the Dependency Hypothesis: A comparison of Policy, Foreign Investment, and Economic Growth in Latin America and East Asia, *Economic Development and Cultural Change,* Vol.40,3, pp. 495-521.

International Finance Corporation, May,1992, "Trends in Private Investment in Developing Countries.

Kobrin, S.,1981, "Political Risk: A Review and Reconsideration," *Journal of International Business*, Spring, pp. 67-80.

Leamer, E., 1985, "Sensitivity analysis would help", *American Economic Review*, 73, 3, pp. 308-313.

Letto-Gilles, G., 1992, "International Production, Trends, Theories and Effects", Polity Press: Cambridge, U.K..

Levis, M., 1979, "Does political instability in developing countries affect foreign investment flow? An Empirical examination," *Management International Review,* 19, pp. 59-68.

Lucas, R.,1993, "On the Determinants of Direct Foreign Investment: Evidence from East and Southeast Asia", *World Development*, Vol.21,3, pp. 391-406.

Lunn, J.L., 1980, "Determinants of US direct investment in the EEC", *European Economic Review*, 13, pp. 93-101.

Mumpower, J.L., Livingston, S. and Lee, T.J., 1987, "Expert judgments of political riskiness", *Journal of Forecasting* 6, pp. 51-65.

Nigh, D., 1985, "The effect of political events on US direct foreign investment: A pooled time-series cross-sectional analysis", *Journal of International Business Studies*, 16, p. 1-17.

Pindyck, R and Rubinfeld, D, 1991, "Econometric Models and Economic Forecasts", McGraw Hill: New York.

Pearce, R., Islam, A. and Sauvant, K., 1992, "The Determinants of Foreign Direct Investment, A Survey of empirical evidence," *United Nations Centre on Transnational Corporations*, United Nations, New York.

Petrochilas, G.A., 1989, *Foreign Direct Investment and the Development Process*, Aldershot, Avebury, 1989.

Root, F and Ahmed, A.,1979, "Empirical Determinants of Manufacturing Direct Foreign Investment in Developing Countries", *Economic Development and Cultural Change,* 27, pp. 751-767.

Schmitz, A. and Bieri, J., 1972, "EEC tariffs and US direct investments", *European Economic Review*, 3, pp. 259-270.

Schneider, F. and Frey, B.,1985, "Economic and Political Determinants of Foreign Direct Investment", *World Development*, Vol.13,2, pp. 161-175. Singh, H. and Kwang, Jun, 1995, "Some New Evidence on the Macroeconomic determinants of Foreign Direct Investment in Developing Countries" *World Bank Working Paper, International Economics Department.*

Singh, H. and Kwang, Jun, August 1996, "Determinants of Foreign Direct Investment to Developing countries," *Transnational Corporations*, U.N.C.T.D. Journal.

Singh, H, 1996, "The Role of Political Risk in Foreign Direct Investment: The Case of Six Asian Countries," in *United States-Third World, Relations in the New World Order*, Editors: Abbas Grammey and Kaye Bragg, Nova Science Publishers: New York.

Torrisi, C.R., 1985, "The determinants of direct foreign investment in a small LDC'" *Journal of Economic Development*, Vol. 10, 2, pp. 29-45.

Wheeler, D. and Mody, A., 1992, "International investment location decisions, The case of U.S. firms", *Journal of International Economics*, 33, pp. 57-76.

White, H., 1980, "A Heteroscedasticity-consistent covariance matrix and a direct test for heteroscedasticity, *Econometrica*, 48, pp. 817-838.

Westphal, L.E., et al, 1979, "Foreign Influences on Korean Industrial Development," Bulletin of the Oxford Institute of Economics and Statistics.

ON THE STABILITY OF COUNTRIES' NATIONAL TECHNOLOGICAL SYSTEMS

W. Nasierowski, F.J. Arcelus
University of New Brunswick
Faculty of Administration
Fredericton, N.B. E3B 5A3
Canada

Abstract: This paper considers the hypothesis that globalisation of business practices has led to the harmonisation of policies dealing with the acquisition and development of technology throughout the years and across countries. The data set includes the countries listed in the World Competitiveness Report (**WCR**) and covers the 1993-1997 period. The paper (i) describes the elements of a country's National Technological System (**NTS**) and of the variables used for their measurement; (ii) identifies commonalties in **NTS**s across countries, across time and across **NTS** elements; and (iii) assesses the predictive value of the model as a validation tool, by ranking countries across several dimensions related to their **NTS** and contrasting these rankings against their counterparts obtained from the **WCR**'s factor of Science and Technology.

Key words: National technological systems, national innovation systems, productivity.

INTRODUCTION

Technology, defined as any product, process or person-embodied solution (Kedia and Bhagat, 1988), is viewed as a catalyst for a firm's progress in quality and in competitive position thereby enhancing its productivity and profitability. Investment levels in technology acquisition, development, diffusion, and implementation are reaching staggering levels. As Pinsonneault (1999: E1) observes, in reference to information technology (IT) alone, "(i)t is estimated that in 1998, U.S. firms invested more than $500-billion (figures in U.S. dollars) in IT, which represents more than 50% of the annual capital spending in the U.S. Top-ranked American banks such as Chase Manhattan and Citibank as well as other companies such as Federal Express and UPS invest close to, or more than, $1-billion in IT annually. In 1998, U.S. banks spent more than $21-billion in IT, while the Canadian banks' spending was approximately $2 billion". Consequently, managerial type questions related to technological

97

S.H. Zanakis et al. (eds.), Decision Making: Recent Developments and Worldwide Applications, 97–111.
© 2000 Kluwer Academic Publishers.

change are of immediate interest to scientists, managers, and politicians. Technological progress is considered to occur when the final outcome of the application of a specific **new** technological solution leads to an increase in productivity. The incidence and degree of a country's involvement in such applications may be analysed within the context of a National Innovation System (**NIS**) (e.g. Dahlman, 1994; Dosi, et.al., 1988; Edquist, 1997; Freeman, 1995; Lundwall, 1992; Nelson, 1993).

Following Dosi, et.al. (1988) and Nelson (1993), an **NIS** may be defined as the Anetwork of agents and set policies and institutions that affect the introduction of technology that is new to the economy. The key aspects of **NIS** are the extent to which the economy acquires technology from abroad, the intensity of domestic technological effort it undertakes, and the level of technical human capital"(Dahlman, 1994, pp. 541-542). **NIS**s are formed in order to foster development, application, and diffusion of technology, thereby improving productivity.

Albeit there exists wide acceptance of the definition of **NIS** provided above, there are quite a few remaining problems related to its operationalization. Measuring some components of a country's stated technology policies, such as a desired economic specialisation pattern, is often close to impossible. Further, many past studies on **NIS** are largely based on experts' opinions, case studies, and qualitative approaches. Thus, issues of bias may become dominant, suggestions for transfer of specific solutions across countries are frequently unsubstantiated and results of studies do not pinpoint directly areas that need changes. Nevertheless, there exist several approaches designed to examine the efficiency of technology systems. Some of the early work was devoted to study the relationship between selected 'Inputs' (e.g., expenditures on R&D, quality of engineers/scientists) on selected 'Outputs' (e.g., patents and publication counts) (e.g. Pavitt, 1985; Saviotti, 1985; Soete and Wyatt, 1983; Evenson, 1991). Recently, more emphasis has been given to efficiency analyses of individual countries' systems (e.g., Reich, 1989; Dertouzos, et.al., 1989; Nelson, 1993; Georgiou and Cameron, 1995), to the identification of the fundamental factors embedded in the efficiency of technology systems (Porter, 1990), and to inter-country comparisons among national solutions (Grupp, 1992; Nelson, 1993; Maital et.al., 1994). In addition, many international studies (e.g. the Frascati Manual, 1980 and its Supplement, 1989) identify factors hypothesised as important to the management of technological development at the national level.

The point of departure of the present study is the model in Nasierowski and Arcelus (1999a), which also includes the description of the data sources, primarily the **WCR**, and of the variables used in the present study. As described below, this information has been suitably modified and updated in this paper to account for the time series nature of the current data set, which covers the 1993-1997 period and for the impossibility of obtaining time series data for some of the variables used in the earlier study. The resulting data set is detailed enough for the purpose of formulating research hypotheses.

The model used in this study is unique in several aspects. First, the interpretation of new technology is different to the traditional. By new technology we mean any solution which is new to the specific economy: it need not be the novelty in global terms. Second, the current study focuses on country related technological issues, and the importance and the impact of contextual items (e.g., existing level of technology development/adoption capability, culture characteristics, size of the country/company) on productivity and competitiveness levels. Third, our model suggests the use of three broad categories of variables, namely: Inputs

(**GERD**, employment in R&D), Moderators (country size and its culture characteristics), and Outputs (patents). Moderators are assumed to be uncontrollable elements that impact upon Inputs and Outputs, as well as at Input-Output relationships. Such an approach provides for an extension of 'classical' (Frascati Manual, 1981; Oslo Manual, 1992) views on technology management through the introduction of moderators directly into the model. A better understanding of the role of Moderators allows for a more focussed discussion on the efficiency of specific technology related policies. For these reasons, and in order to distinguish our approach from that represented by **NIS**, we have named our model as National Technology System (**NTS**).

One of the consequences of the globalisation of business practices is the tendency towards the harmonisation of the manifestations of these applications throughout the years and across countries. It is the purpose of this paper to test whether such tendency is apparent within the countries listed in the World Competitiveness Report (WCR, 1995-1999). To that effect the paper is divided into three parts, namely (i) describe the elements of a country's **NTS** and the variables used for their measurement; (ii) identify commonalties across countries, across time and across **NTS** elements; and (iii) assesses the predictive value of the model as a validation tool, by ranking countries across several dimensions related to their **NTS** and contrasting these rankings against their counterparts obtained from the **WCR**'s factor of technological advancement.

The rationale for a study of this type is threefold. First, the analysis of various **NTS** models and of its differences across countries may lead to a better understanding of the responses to technological challenges adopted in different surroundings. In addition, such an analysis may also assist in the development of new indexes (defined to be measures of intensity of groups of elements which form the **NTS**), (i) to better assess the efficiency of the various **NTS**s; (ii) to better identify countries with similar policies, as well as those nations for which changing patterns would suggest a potential technological policy shift; and (iii) to better evaluate whether potential instability in the composition of these indexes over time has implications regarding the impact of **NTS** on productivity levels. Second, typologies of technological policies can be identified (i) to improve the process of monitoring shifts from one type of a solution to another; hence (ii) to recognise more precisely areas where changes were made; thus (iii) to improve our understanding of the reasons for adopting certain solutions; and (iv) to pinpoint more accurately those specific areas that need of further analysis. This approach may prove particularly useful when examining adjustment measures. Third, the results of this study may have important implications for the crafting of technology-related policies, to the extent that they shed more light on the underlying features of specific needs for technology and its management.

ELEMENTS OF A COUNTRY'S NTS

The elements of the **I/M/O** (Inputs, Moderators and Outputs) structure of a country's **NTS** include (i) inputs, defined by Dahlman (1994, p. 452) as "the extent to which the economy acquires [new] technology from abroad, the intensity of domestic [new] technological effort it undertakes and the level of technical human capital"; (ii) outputs, resulting from this technological effort; (iii) moderators, representing the elements of the country's socio-economic structure impacting upon the inputs and the outputs, or relationship between **I** and **O**; and (iv) the **NTS'** s ultimate contribution to the national economy, namely its contribution toward technological progress via increases in productivity. Tables 2 and 3 list for each variable its symbol, type (**I**, **M** or **O**), name and assorted characteristics to be discussed below.

Inputs (I)

Inputs represent the factors directly responsible for the present and future development of technology. The following three types of inputs are identified:

- *development of technology* - This term refers to the incidence of each country's ability to develop technology by itself; and (ii) to involve private industry in this endeavour. The proxies used are: Gross Domestic Expenditure on Research and Experimental Development (**GERD**), and the degree of private business sector involvement in R&D (**BRD**);
- *acquisition of technology.* This term refers to the incidences of Foreign Direct Investment (**FDI**) and purchases of goods and commercial services (IMPO) which are assumed to bring technology from abroad (IMPO+FDI = **PUR**);
- *contribution of the human component to technology development.* The proxy for this item is reflected by employment in R&D (**EM**); and,
- *training of qualified human resources.* The assessment of this input is measured by the each country's general education expenditures (**EDU**).

Moderators (M)

Included here are those national factors hypothesised as having a direct impact upon the sector's inputs and/or outputs or upon the relationship between **I** and **O**. These include:

- *accumulated S&T capability.* It is accepted that economic prosperity depends upon innovations resulting from investments in scientific and educational advancement. Innovation reflects learning, experience, and know-how, and is firmly rooted in the prevailing economic and social structure which has been established over long periods of time (TEP, 1992). As a result, countries which have developed the needed cultural, technical, and institutional infrastructures to support S&T are expected to be more efficient in R&D. Hence, a measure of S&T stock is desirable to assess each country's past commitment to the technological development. There are no widely acceptable proxies for measurement of this phenomenon. The Purchasing Power Parity (**PPP**), a measure of a country's ability to finance technological progress, and literacy rate (LIT) are used as proxies for accumulated S&T capability.
- *cultural characteristics.* Culture has been proven to be a determinant in the adoption of management solutions. Although several works have hypothesised such a relationship (Hofstede, 1991; Kedia and Bhagat, 1988), it has remained empirically untested whether NTS can be explained on the grounds of cultural dimensions. At issue here is whether analyses of cultural underpinnings may shed more light on the reasons for specific

solutions in a technical development effort. This paper uses Hofstede's (1991) four dimensions of culture, namely Individualism (**IDV**), Masculinity (**MAS**), Power Distance (**PDI**) and Uncertainty Avoidance (**UAV**).
- *size of a country in terms of population or economic size.* At issue here is to measure a country's ability to absorb and to generate novelties. Gross Domestic Product (**GDP**), and the size of a country by population (**POPU**) are used as proxies of size.

Outputs (O)

Outputs represent the final yardstick to measure a country' s efficiency in transforming the inputs and the moderators into generators of technology. Two sets of outputs may be identified: (beyond the final outputs, which may be the contribution of **NTS** to the economy, as measured, for example, by productivity (**PROD**), increased export in high-technology sectors, or increased standard of living):
- *short-term solutions.* These are measured by counts of patents registered internally, i.e. in the country of residence (**PATR**) or externally (**PATE**). These proxies are widely used despite of their potential pitfalls (e.g. Pavitt, 1988), and despite the fact that they manifest a relatively short-term results of R&D strategies (e.g. FM, 1981).
- *final output.* It represents the NTS' s contribution to the economy, as measured by national productivity (**PROD**).

The selection of the I/M/O proxies described above represents the best effort of measuring the main variables described in the literature as components of a country's **NTS**, given the customary data restrictions. Other dimensions could have been ideally included in the study, such as those related to governmental involvement in technological development (e.g., incentive and protectionist measures), those related to patterns of R&D specialisation, to export from high-technology sectors, to increases in the standard of living and the like. The lack of relevant data, as well as unresolved dilemmas in operationalization, has resulted in dropping these concepts from this study. Certainly, there is a serious danger that some other important variables, because they cannot be quantified or data is not available, will not be examined. Thus, "the end result may be that the analysis misses important elements of what is going on" (Dahlman, 1994, p.544). This remains an unresolved issue, which requires re-evaluation as better data sources become available.

PATTERNS OF TECHNOLOGICAL BEHAVIOUR ACROSS COUNTRIES AND TIME

Even though **NTS**s are heavily dependent upon unique country-specific characteristics (e.g. Nelson, 1993), the evidence in Nasierowski and Arcelus (1999a) intimates the existence of some strategic similarities across **NTS** elements and across countries. After all, most countries generally include in their economic development plans such national priorities as the betterment of the overall (and specially technical) educational level, the increased involvement of the private sector in R&D spending, the lowering of defence-related R&D, the favouring of high-technology sectors and the like (TEP, 1991; OECD, 1989). At issue here is the likelihood that, given the globalisation of business practices, the process of operationalising these priorities has led to increases through time of the similarities in the manifestations of the resulting policies. More specifically, the question is the stability across the years of each nation' s membership in a particular group of countries with similar I/M/O structure. Special emphasis is given to potential differences in membership depending upon each country' s capability as a receptor or generator of new technology. This test is carried out through cluster analysis, with the data being weighted by size as measured in terms of either population (POPU) or wealth (GDP), respectively.

Specifically, the analysis is intended to seek answers to the following four questions: (i) are there I/M/O structures which characterise groups of countries, when the data is weighted by market size (POPU)?; (ii) are there I/M/O structures which characterise groups of countries, when the data is weighted by wealth (GDP)?; (iii) do the resulting I/M/O structures differ from each other?; and (iv) does the composition of country groupings differ on the basis of the weighting scheme utilised? To answer these questions, two cluster analyses, one per weighting scheme, were conducted. For each case, the following five-step procedure was utilised (e.g. Hair, et.al., 1995): (i) perform a hierarchical cluster analysis to identify the appropriate number of country groupings, using the cluster agglomeration coefficient as the criterion; (ii) select the number of clusters on the basis of the largest percentage increase in the agglomeration coefficient; (iii) validate the results with a non-hierarchical cluster procedure; (iv) carry out an analysis of variance (ANOVA), in order to identify the I/M/O variables primarily responsible for the resulting groupings; and (v) repeat the first four steps for variables responsible for the groupings.

In terms of country membership, the cluster analyses have consistently yielded two groups of countries for the five years under study and for the two weighting schemes, with only Taiwan and Singapore changing clusters at times. Hence, the question of stability in terms of country membership has been answered in the affirmative. As a result, a new binary variable, CT=0,1, has been created to account for each country' s membership in its respective group. Table 1 lists the countries under study and their cluster affiliation for 1997. The other measures in the Table are discussed in a subsequent section. The question as to which variables are responsible for the clusters is answered with the help of the "Cluster Tests" columns of Tables 2 and 3. They list whether (y) or not (n) each I/M/O variable contributes significantly (p-value in ANOVA under .1) to the formation of clusters. The evidence from the tables suggests that (i) most NTS elements, specially the inputs and the outputs, of the present study play important roles in the development of each country' s NTS system; (ii) there does not seem to be much difference in terms of the weights, with the exception of EM for all five years, UAV for 1996 and 1997, PATR for 1994 and 1995 and PUR for 1995 and 1996; and (iii) the generation of a new variable, CT, to account for each country's membership in its appropriate cluster. Once again, the stability of the results has been clearly established.

The results presented in this section suggest the presence of several consistent patterns of technological behaviour in the countries under study, regardless of the weighing scheme utilised. The first is characterised by two clusters with practically the same distribution of countries, irrespective whether GDP or POPU are used as weights. This justifies the addition of the new CT binary variable to the NTS data set as an indicator of cluster membership. The second pattern is derived from the similarity in the behaviour of most of the variables in the set, most with p-values under .1 and hence responsible for the groupings. Further, the clusters are not statistically significantly different in population (**POPU**) than in wealth (**GDP**), but they are with respect to other variables when weighted by **POPU** or **GDP**. Hence, the role of these moderators in terms of cluster differentiation is appropriately defined as part of a weighting scheme, rather than as an independent indicator of market size. Masculinity (**MAS**) appears to be a cultural characteristic with universal appeal, which explains why it fails to characterise either group exclusively. This is in contrast to the other three cultural variables, for which substantial differences exist among groups, with cluster-0 countries more likely to favour low power distance, high individualism, and low uncertainty avoidance. The third pattern relates to the stability cluster membership shown, over the five-year period, by the set of variables responsible for the groupings. Thus, either policies remain largely unchanged, or shifts in these policies move in a similar direction for cluster members. The final pattern deals with the substantial gap in existence between the two clusters, which cannot easily be bridged by any country. On average, Cluster-0 countries tend to enjoy higher purchasing power parity (**PPP**), are likely to be more individualistic (**IND**), more egalitarian (**PDI**), less prone towards uncertainty avoidance behaviour (**UAV**), more involved in purchases of technologies from abroad (**PUR**), exhibit a higher incidence of business involvement in R&D activities (**BRD**), have a larger commitment to employment in R&D and to the educational improvement of their people (**EDU**). Cluster-0 countries dominate the generation of outputs, especially in terms of overall quality, quantity, export potential, acceptability by others, and in terms of the ultimate economic reward, increased productivity. As a consequence of the predominance of Cluster-0 countries in new technology development and acquisition, CT may be interpreted as an index variable denoting overall commitment to technological progress.

PATTERNS OF TECHNOLOGICAL BEHAVIOUR ACROSS NTS COMPONENTS

The analysis of the previous section identified 15 **I/M/O** variables, which are hypothesised to impact upon a country's technological development. However, these **I/M/O** variables exhibit a very high degree of collinearity among them. This can be clearly shown by examining, from results not shown here, the Pearson correlation coefficients between pairs of these variables and the corresponding p-values, most of which are below .1. This renders rather futile the attempt to isolate the independent effects of individual variables. However, what remains feasible and becomes the purpose of this section is the identification of patterns of technological behaviour across **NTS** components. This suggests the need for further data reduction through the use of principal components, if any pattern of behaviour is to be established and if any changes in the pattern through time are to be identified. This search for commonalties may be carried out with the following four-step procedure of Hair, et.al. (1995). First, examine the anti-image correlation matrix to exclude from further consideration all variables with sampling adequacy below .6. Second, repeat the analysis with the remaining variables, until the Kaiser-Meyer-Olkin measure of sampling adequacy reaches the .7 (for "GDP" tests, .6) plateau was accepted. If it does not, stop: no statistically significant factor analysis is feasible. Otherwise, continue. Third, identify the number of factors to be extracted, through a selection yardstick that combines the latent-root and the percent-of-variation-explained criteria. A factor is selected if its eigenvalue exceeds 1 and it explains at least 10% of the variation. Finally, interpret the factors on the basis of those variables with factor loadings above $|.7|$. All variables and factors are expressed in standardised form, with a mean of zero and a standard deviation of 1.

The results are summarised in the second half of Tables 2 and 3, for each of the five years under consideration (1993-1997) and for the two weighing schemes (**POPU, GDP**). The principal components analysis was also carried out with three sets of variables, namely with only the inputs, only the moderators or with the entire I/M/O data set of the technological sector. As a result, National Productivity (**PROD**) was omitted, as it represents an indirect outcome rather than a direct influence on the sector. The membership variable, **CT**, has been included in all three data sets, since by its very nature it does not belong exclusively to any category but it is hypothesised to affect all. The number associated with each variable identifies the factor to which the said variable belongs, with zero indicating no membership in any factor. Observe that no variable in Tables 2 and 3 has a membership in more than one factor. This exclusive membership was determined by assigning each variable to the factor with the highest loading for that variable, provided, as stated earlier, that the loading exceeds $|.7|$. Otherwise, the variable is left unassigned. Justification for this procedure lies on the application of a VARIMAX orthogonal rotation on the factors, to minimise the value of the smaller loadings for each variable.

The evidence from the tables provide additional support to the stability patterns alluded to earlier. Both the **I only** and the **M only** factor analyses explain about 85% of the variation in the data, regardless of whether **POPU** or **GDP** are used as weights. This attests to the high explanatory power of the various summarisations and provides the first indication of stability. The second indication is revealed by the existence of a rather consistent first factor, explaining about 60% (50%) of the variation in the data with **POPU** (**GDP**) as weight. This factor identifies the cluster with the more developed countries (**CT**=0), (i) with, from the **I only** data, a higher degree of R&D culture, which leads to higher investments in education (**EDU**), in research (**GERD**) and in employment in technology (**EM**); and (ii) from the **M only** data, less egalitarian (**PDI**), more individualistic (**IDV**) and in a few cases, with higher purchasing power (**PPP**). There exists also a second factor explaining about 30% of the variation dealing with Literacy Rate (**LIT**), for the **M only** case and for **I only** with Educational Expenditures (with **GDP** as weight) and the degree of private business sector's involvement in R&D (**BRD**).

Turning to the **I/M/O** results, where the entire system is evaluated, the PVE values are lower, but still quite substantial. It indicates that, whereas the explanatory power of the summarisations is still quite high, there is a large enough residual left to suggest evidence of individualistic behaviour on the part of the various countries in their pursuit of technological improvement. With **POPU** as weight, the evidence is clear. The first factor identifies countries with the same type of characteristics as with the other two data sets, whereas the second factors emphasises the technological base, as represented by their expenditures on research (**GERD**) and the resulting patents registered therein. With **GDP** as weight, the first factor is also quite stable over time. The individual characteristics, **IDV** and **PDI**, as well as **EDU**, the education variable, are still there. However, **PPP** is included, but **CT**, only sporadically. This implies the presence of somewhat different characteristics when countries are evaluated in terms of their capabilities as generators or as consumers of technology. This can be seen by examining the **CT** values, with **GDP** as weight, where countries such as Taiwan and Korea changing cluster membership. After all, as stated earlier, what is new technology for one country may not be for another. However, the latter country could be an important producer of the said technology. This point deserves further consideration, as data sets improve in quality. There is also some evidence of instability, such as the presence of a third factor in 1994 and 1996.

ASSESSING THE PREDICTIVE VALUE OF THE MODEL AS A VALIDATION TOOL

This section is intended to form overall **NTS** rankings, per country, year and weight, on the basis of the principal components results and to test empirically whether these ranks differ from each other and from Factor 7 of the WCR (1992-1999). Factor 7's ranks are based on each country's evaluation of scientific and technical capability together with success of basic and applied research (WCR, 1992-1999, Factor 7). These tests are carried out through the use of Spearman correlation analysis (e.g. Siegel and Castellan, 1988), for the five years under consideration. These comparisons are used (i) as a validation tool of this paper's rankings, using as standard for comparison the only internationally recognised ranking procedure of a country's commitment to new technology; (ii) as a test of whether rankings produced on the basis of simple and widely available indicators can emulate the rather expensive and expert-based World Competitiveness Report counterparts; and (iii) as a test of whether the stability results of the previous sections can be extended to international comparisons of technological performance across countries. Such an approach enhances the predictive model's range of applicability in three substantial ways. First, it expands the number of countries for which rankings are produced, since, subject to availability of data, the model of this paper can now be extended to countries not in the **WCR**. Second, it generates specialised rankings obtained with different subsets of **NTS** components, which can be tailored to the user's specific concerns. Third, it identifies the biases inherent in the **WCR** rankings with respect to the various subsets of variables and weighting procedures.

The development of these rankings is based upon the computation of a **factor score** for each country/year/weight using the methodology outlined in Hair, et.al. (1995). The basic inputs are (i) the factor loadings of the previous section's principal component analysis as variable weights within each factor; (ii) the factor weights, given by 50%-50% or by the proportion of combined variation explained by each factor; and (iii) the original data of the variables listed in the Tables. With this information, the first step is to compute a combined score for each factor, as the average of the variables included in the factor, weighted by the corresponding factor loadings. This is followed by the computation of two factor scores for each country. The first is the "arithmetic" factor score for each country, obtained as the simple arithmetic average of the combined scores for each factor. Recognising the fact that each factor explains a different percentage of the total variance, the second is the "weighted" factor score for each country, computed as the weighted average of the combined scores, with the weights being the ratios of the percentage of the variance explained by that factor divided by the cumulative variance explained by the factors listed in Tables 2 and 3. As an example, the weights for 1994 *I only* (see Table 2) are 57.8/82.4 and 24.6/82.4 for factors 1 and 2, respectively. The final step is to rank the countries on the basis of the "arithmetic" and then on the basis of the "weighted" factor scores. Further details on these computations for the *1997 I only* case appear in Table 1.

The Spearman test results may be summarised as follows. The correlation coefficients between the **WCR** indexes and their counterparts from this paper are all in the high .70s and .80s., for those weighted by "POPU" and approximately 10 percentage points lower for their "GDP" counterparts. This attests to the success of the grouping techniques of this paper in reproducing rankings similar to **WCR**. It appears that the **WCR** produces rankings more in tune to those where the indexes are computed as arithmetic average of the factor loadings. However, it should be observed that both weighing techniques produced similar rankings, with Spearman correlation coefficients in the .90s. Further, there is basically no difference in the rankings throughout the years, for approximately the upper 70% of the distribution. Only at the low end of the generation and consumption of new technology, there are some changes, but they appear to be random in nature.

CONCLUSIONS

The exercise of **NTS** rankings subject of this paper has produced several useful insights. The selection of **I/M/O** variables does seem to have properly discriminated countries in terms of the degree of their technological absorptive capacity. With a few minor exceptions, the distribution of countries between the clusters conforms to what has earlier been classified as developed and developing countries. The principal components analysis has produced rather stable groupings, with high explanatory power. As receptors of technology (with **POPU** as weights), there is a solid and stable first factor, representing mostly commitment to education. Time differences are shown for the other factors, with the evidence pointing towards a second factor generally related to investment in technology. As generators of technology, the countries in the sample have shown lower degree of stability and commonality through time. These weaker results suggest the need for reconsideration of this portion of the model and especially of its explanatory variables. Whether it also implies that countries show more independence and variety of policies as generators than as consumers of new technology is an open question that only further research may be able to elucidate. Finally, the usual lags associated with the effect of investment in education and in technology on economic development in general and on productivity in particular suggests that a much longer time period may be needed to ascertain the veracity of the time patterns, or lack of thereof, found in the present study. The study of these and other issues justifies additional research.

ACKNOWLEDGEMENTS

Financial assistance to the second listed author for the completion of this research from the Natural Sciences and Engineering Research Council of Canada and from the Centre for International Business Studies at the Faculty of Administration of the University of New Brunswick is gratefully acknowledged.

REFERENCES

Dahlman Carl J. (1994), Technology strategy in East Asian developing countries, *Journal of Asian Economics*, 5, 541-572.

Dertouzos, M., Berger S., Lester, M.R.K., Solow, R.M. and Thurow, L.C (1989), *Made in America - Regaining the productive edge*, MIT Press, Cambridge Mass.

Dosi, G., Freeman, C., Nelson, R., Silverberg, G. and Soete, L. (1988), *Technical change and economic theory*, London, Pinter Publishers.

Edquist, C. (1997), Systems of innovation approaches, in C. Edquist (ed.) *Systems of innovation: technologies, institutions and organizations*, London, Pinter Publishers.

Evenson, R.E., (1991), Patent data by industry evidence for invention potential exhaustion?, *Technology and Productivity: the Challenge for Economic Policy*, OECD, Paris, 233-248.

Frascati Manual (1981), *The measurement of scientific and technical activities, proposed standard practice for surveys of research and experimental development*, OECD, Paris.

Frascati Manual Supplement (1989), *The measurement of scientific and technical activities, R&D statistics and output measurement in the higher education sector*, OECD, Paris.

Freeman, C. (1995), The "National System of Innovation" in historical perspective, *Cambridge Journal of Economics*, 19, 5-24

Georgiou, L., Dale, A. and H. Cameron (1995), "National systems for evaluation of R&D in the European Union", Special Issue of *Research Evaluation* Volume 5, April. Beech Tree Publishing, Surrey, UK.

Grupp, H., Maital, S., Frenkel, A. and Koschatzky, K. (1992), A data envelopment model to compare technological excellence and export sales in Israel and European Community countries, *Research Evaluation*, 2, 87-101.

Hair, J.F., Anderson, R.E., Tatham, R.L. and Black, W.C. (1995), *Multivariate data analysis*, 4th edition, Prentice Hall, Englewood Cliffs.

Hofstede, G.H., (1991), *Cultures and organizations: software of the mind*, McGraw Hill, London.

Kedia, B.L. and Bhagat, R.S. (1988), Cultural constraints on transfer of technology across nations: implications for research in international and comparative management, *Academy of Management Review*, 13, 559-571.

Lundwall, B-A. (Ed.) (1992), *National systems of innovation: towards a theory of innovation and interactive learning*, London, Pinter Publishers.

Maital, S., Frenkel,A., Grupp, H. and Koschatzky, K., (1994), Relation between scientific and technological excellence and export performance: theoretical model and empirical test for EC countries, *Science and Public Policy*, June, 138-146.

Nasierowski, W. and Arcelus, F.J. (1999a), Interrelationships among the elements of national innovation systems: a statistical evaluation, *European Journal of Operational Research* (forthcoming).

Nasierowski, W. and Arcelus, F.J. (1999b), Ranking countries' national innovation systems. 5th *International DSI Proceedings*, 1, 831-833.

Nelson, R.R. (ed.) (1993), *National innovation systems: a comparative analysis*, Oxford University Press, Oxford.

OECD, (1989), *R&D, production and diffusion of technology, OECD science and technology indicators report*, No.3, OECD, Paris.

Oslo Manual, (1992), *OECD proposed guidelines for collecting and interpreting technological innovation data*, OECD, Paris.

Pavitt, K. (1985), Patent statistics as indicators of innovative activities: possibilities and problems, *Scientometrics*, 7, 77-99.

Pinsonneault, A. (1999), Mythical route to ROI, *Financial Post*, September 22, E1.

Porter M. (1990), *Competitive advantage of nations*, Free Press.

Saviotti P. (1988), The measurement of changes in technological output: in van Raan (editor), *Handbook of quantitative studies of science and technology*, Elsevier, Amsterdam: 556-610.

Siegel, S. and Castellan, N.J. (1988), Nonparametric statistics for the behavioral sciences. McGraw-Hill, New York.

Soete, L.G. and Wyatt S.M.E. (1983), The use of foreign patenting as an internationally comparable science and technology output indicator, *Scientometrics*, 5, 31-54.

TEP (1992), *Technology and the economy: the key relationships*, OECD, Paris.

WCR (1992-1997), *World competitiveness report* 1992-1997, Economic Forum - IMD, Lausanne, Switzerland.

Table 1. 1997 Cluster Membership and I-only Factor Scores and Rankings: data weighed by POPU [1,2]

COUNTRY	CT	FSN	FSW	RN	RW	COUNTRY	CT	FSN	FSW	RN	RW	COUNTRY	CT	FSN	FSW	RN	RW
Argentina	1	-.76	-.90	36	40	Hong Kong	1	-.71	-.99	34	40	Philippines	1	-1.02	-1.20	45	45
Australia	0	.46	.32	17	17	Hungary	1	-.61	-.47	32	31	Poland	1	-.63	-.48	33	32
Austria	0	.49	.22	16	20	Iceland	0	.62	.32	12	16	Portugal	1	-.49	-.67	27	35
Belgium	0	.51	.48	15	15	India	1	-.94	-.99	44	42	Russia	1	-.30	.20	24	21
Brazil	1	-.78	-.75	38	36	Indonesia	1	-.77	-.49	37	33	Singapore	1	.02	.27	22	19
Canada	0	.65	.57	11	11	Ireland	0	.45	.51	18	14	South Africa	1	-.56	-.40	29	30
Chile	1	-.75	-.89	35	38	Israel	1	.73	.54	10	13	Spain	1	-.30	-.20	25	27
China	1	-.82	-.58	39	34	Italy	1	.21	.13	20	23	Sweden	0	1.25	1.22	2	1
Colombia	1	-.52	.06	28	24	Japan	0	1.01	1.07	5	3	Switzerland	0	1.29	1.19	1	2
Czech Republic	1	-.38	-.09	26	25	Korea	1	-.08	.29	23	18	Taiwan	1	.57	.55	13	12
Denmark	0	1.11	.89	3	6	Malaysia	1	-.60	-.21	31	28	Thailand	1	-.90	-1.01	42	43
Finland	0	1.07	.98	4	4	Mexico	1	-.84	-.90	40	39	Turkey	1	-.87	-.85	41	37
France	0	.89	.75	8	8	Netherlands	0	.37	.16	19	22	United Kingdom	0	.56	.58	14	10
Germany	0	.82	.82	9	7	New Zealand	0	.19	-.19	21	26	United States	0	.94	.92	6	5
Greece	1	-.60	-.35	30	29	Norway	0	.94	.72	7	9	Venezuela	1	-.92	-1.18	43	44

Notes: FSN and FSW (RN and RW) are the factor scores (rankings based on their respective factor scores) for each country, computed under the normal and the weighted procedures

[2] **Procedure to compute FSN and FSW:**

(i) Start with the factor loadings for each variable listed as significant in Tables 2 and 3. For 1997 *I only* with POPU as weight, these loadings are (.926, -.917, .826) corresponding to (EDU, CT and GERD) for the first factor and F_2 = .952 corresponding to BRD for the second factor.

(ii) Compute the combined factor scores, F_1 and F_2, for each country, as F_1 = .926EDU - .917CT + .826GERD and F_2 = .952 BRD.

(iii) Compute FSN as (F_1 + F_2)/2 and FSW as (58.6 F_1 +30.7 F_2) / 89.2. The weights for FSW are the % of variance explained by F_1, F_2 and the total, obtained from Table 2 for *I only*

Table 2. NTS Components and Assorted Characteristics: data weighted by POPU

Symbol	Type	Variable Name*	Cluster tests					I/M/O					I only					M only				
			93	94	95	96	97	93	94	95	96	97	93	94	95	96	97	93	94	95	96	97
PUR	I	Imports of Goods and Commercial Services	y	n	n	y	n	0	0	0	0	0	0	0	0	0	0					
GERD	I	Gross Domestic Expenditure on Research	y	y	y	y	y	2	2	2	1	1	1	1	1	1	1					
BRD	I	Degree of Private Business Involvement in R&D	y	y	y	y	y	0	0	0	0	0	2	2	2	2	2					
EM	I	Employment in R&D	y	y	y	y	y	0	0	0	0	0	1	1	1	1	0					
EDU	I	Total Educational Expenditures	y	n	n	n	n	1	1	1	1	1	1	1	1	1	1					
POPU	M	Country's Population	n	n	n	n	n	0	0	0	0	0						0	0	0	0	0
GDP	M	Gross Domestic Product	n	n	n	n	n	0	0	0	0	0						0	0	0	0	0
PPP	M	Purchasing Power Parity	y	y	y	y	y	1	1	1	1	1						1	0	0	0	1
PDI	M	Power Distance	y	y	y	y	y	1	1	1	1	1						1	1	1	1	1
UAV	M	Uncertainty Avoidance	n	n	n	n	n	0	0	0	0	0						0	0	0	0	0
MAS	M	Masculinity	y	y	y	y	y	0	0	0	0	0						0	0	0	0	0
IDV	M	Individualism	y	y	y	y	y	1	1	1	1	1						1	1	1	1	1
LIT	M	Literacy Rate	y	y	y	y	y	0	0	0	0	0						2	2	2	2	2
PATE	O	External Patents by Resident	y	y	y	y	y	0	0	0	0	0										
PATR	O	Patents by a Country's Residents	y	y	y	y	y	2	2	2	2	2										
PROD	O	National Productivity	y	y	y	y	y															
CT=0,1		Cluster Membership	1	1	1	1	1	1	1	1	1	1	1	1	1	1	1	1	1	1	1	1

* Notes: The (0,1,2) numbers imply membership of the variable in question in factor 1 or 2 or in neither, as indicated by the principal components analysis for I/M/O, I only or M only.

The (y,n) dichotomy indicates whether (y) or not (n) the variable in question contributes to the differences in cluster membership. That is to say, a y corresponds to a p-value under .10 for the test as to whether the variable in question is statistically different for the CT=1 countries than for their CT=0 counterparts.

			Cluster tests					I/M/O					I only					M only				
PVE		Total % of the variation in the data explained by the factors						70.5	70	67	72.7	73.2	82.4	85.1	88.9	89.1	89.2	82.9	83	83.9	82.3	83
		% explained by Factor 1						42.6	41.1	44.3	44.7	43.4	57.8	60.8	59.1	61.1	58.5	55.3	54.3	55.1	52.5	56.9
		% explained by Factor 2						27.9	29	22.7	28	29.8	24.6	24.3	29.8	28	30.7	27.6	28.7	28.8	29.8	26.1

Table 3. NTS Components and Assorted Characteristics: data weighted by GDP

Symbol	Type	Variable Name *	Cluster tests					I/M/O					I only					M only				
			93	94	95	96	97	93	94	95	96	97	93	94	95	96	97	93	94	95	96	97
PUR	I	Imports of Goods and Commercial Services	n	n	n	n	n	0	0	0	0	0	0	0	0	0	0					
GERD	I	Gross Domestic Expenditure on Research	y	y	y	y	y	2	3	2	2	2	0	1	1	1	0					
BRD	I	Degree of Private Business Involvement in R&D	y	y	y	y	y	2	3	2	2	0	2	1	1	1	1					
EM	I	Employment in R&D	n	n	n	n	n	0	0	0	0	0	0	0	0	0	0					
EDU	I	Total Educational Expenditures	y	y	y	y	y	1	1	1	1	1	1	2	2	2	2					
POPU	M	Country's Population	n	n	n	n	n	0	0	0	0	0						0	0	0	0	0
GDP	M	Gross Domestic Product	n	n	n	n	n	0	0	0	0	0						0	0	0	0	0
PPP	M	Purchasing Power Parity	y	y	y	y	y	0	2	0	0	1						0	0	0	1	1
PDI	M	Power Distance	y	y	y	y	y	1	1	1	1	1						1	1	1	1	1
UAV	M	Uncertainty Avoidance	y	y	y	y	y	0	0	0	0	0						0	0	0	0	0
MAS	M	Masculinity	n	n	n	n	n	0	0	0	0	0						0	0	0	0	0
IDV	M	Individualism	y	y	y	y	y	1	1	1	1	1						1	1	1	1	1
LIT	M	Literacy Rate	y	y	y	y	y	0	2	0	0	1						2	2	2	2	2
PATE	O	External Patents by Resident	y	y	y	y	y	0	2	0	3	2										
PATR	O	Patents by a Country's Residents	y	n	n	y	y	0	2	0	2	2										
PROD	O	National Productivity	y	y	y	y	y															
CT=0,1		Cluster Membership						1	0	1	0	1	1	0	1	1	2	1	1	1	1	1

* Notes: The (0,1,2,3) numbers imply membership of the variable in question in factor 1 or 2 or 3 or in none, as indicated by the principal components analysis for I/M/O, I only or M only. That is to say, a y corresponds to a y corresponds to
The (y,n) dichotomy indicates whether (y) or not (n) the variable in question contributes to the differences in cluster membership. That is to say, a y corresponds to a p-value under .10 to whether the variable in question is statistically different for the CT=1 countries than for their CT=0 counterparts.

			Cluster tests					I/M/O					I only					M only				
PVE		Total % of the variation in the data explained by the factors	68.6	77.5	70.3			76.3	68.6	82	81.4		83.5	86.6	86	82.7	81.4	84.1	83.9	82	81.8	
		% explained by Factor 1	40.7	28.6	38			33.2	42.5	45.3	42.1		46.6	50.1	40.7	54	42.1	55.1	55.1	51	55.7	
		% explained by Factor 2	27.9	25.3	32.3			26.8	26.1	36.7	39.3		36.9	36.5	45.3	28.7	39.3	29	28.8	31	26.1	
		% explained by Factor 3		23.4				16.3														

4. MARKETING

MARKETING OF DIFFERENTIATED FRESH PRODUCE

G. Baourakis[1], E. Lassithiotaki[1], P.M. Pardalos[2]

[1] Dept. of Economic and Management Sciences
Department at the Mediterranean Agronomic Institute of
Chania, Greece

[2] University of Florida
Dept. of Industrial and Systems Engineering
303 Weil Hall, Gainesville, FL 32611-6595
U.S.A.

Abstract: The primary objective of the present consumer-based market survey[1] was the identification of consumers' perspectives where the development of quality and environmentally friendly products is concerned. The research mainly focused on consumer behaviour with regard to fresh greenhouse vegetables produced with the restricted use of pesticides. The identification of potential new market segments and the promotion of these products, adapted to consumers' attitudes and beliefs, were set as further objectives of this field research. Personal interviews of consumers in supermarkets in the centres of three main cities of Greece were carried out for the survey. Correspondence Analysis was implemented with a view to the identification of the existing relationships among variables, and Non-Linear Principal Component Analysis for the transformation and classification of the original variables into groups. The results of the research indicated that consumers were willing to purchase the products, despite the fact that low levels of awareness and consumption were exhibited.

Key words: Greece, Vegetables, Greenhouse Crops, Quality, Consumer Behaviour, Qualitative Analytical Methods, Optimisation Methods, Market Segmentation, Consumer Surveys.

---

[1] The present survey was conducted by the Mediterranean Agronomic Institute of Chania under the EU project entitled "Development of an integrated based decision support system (KBDSS-DIMITRA) for differentiated agricultural products in Greece, Holland, the UK and Sweden".

S.H. Zanakis et al. (eds.), Decision Making: Recent Developments and Worldwide Applications, 115–130.
© 2000 Kluwer Academic Publishers.

INTRODUCTION

The goal of the current field survey was to provide a thorough insight into the behaviour, attitudes, and knowledge of consumers concerning "alternative" production methods, in particular the production of fresh greenhouse vegetables with the restricted use of pesticides.

The use of pesticides is closely related to the issue of food safety (Basiotis and Jensen, 1993). Several surveys conducted in the past, indicated the serious concern that consumers exhibited regarding the existence of chemical residues in fresh produce (Byrne, Bacon and Toensmeyer, 1994; Weaver, Evans and Luloff, 1992; Ott, 1990). First of all, due to the fact that the adoption of production techniques which deviate from the conventional is not widely implemented, awareness of their use and consequently the level of consumption among respondents was identified. In addition, other issues were elaborated, such as the intention of consumers to acquire fresh products produced with the restricted use of pesticides, their opinions concerning the use of pesticides in the various cultivation processes, as well as the importance assigned by them concerning the implementation of this particular type of production. The dietary concerns of the respondents were also examined, in order to attain a more precise understanding of their beliefs and attitudes.

The survey took place in three main cities of Greece, which were selected due to the substantial size of their populations. These cities were Athens, Thessaloniki, and Heraklion, Crete.

The issues upon which the research focused can be summarised as follows:
- Awareness and consumption of the products in question
- Factors that affect decision-making by consumers with regard to the purchasing of the products
- Consumers' attitudes towards the use of pesticides in the cultivation processes
- Consumers' dietary concerns and habits

DESIGN OF DATA COLLECTION METHOD AND DATA ANALYSIS

The research took the form of an exploratory study, the adoption of which meant that no preconceived notions were taken into account; subsequently all factors which might prove useful where included (Lehman, 1989).

The target population comprised supermarket customers of the aforementioned cities where the survey was conducted. The sample consisted of 800 randomly selected customers. Personal interviews were carried out with the respondents, following a structured questionnaire. Moreover, in order to eliminate bias, the number of questionnaires completed in each city was established in proportion to their respective populations.

Data analysis techniques employed were those of Descriptive Statistics, Cross-tabulation, Correspondence and Non-Linear Principal Component Analysis.

Cross-tabulation is a technique that identifies the relationship between two variables and provides tests and measures of association. The most widely-used measure of association is the chi-square (x^2) test, which examines the independence of the variables.

When both variables are quantitative, the Pearson correlation coefficient, which measures linear association, is the most appropriate: When the cross-tabulation uses one categorical and one quantitative data, the beta-coefficient is suitable. If ordered values are included in the tables then the Spearman correlation coefficient is indicated as a measure of association. Furthermore, Kendall's Tau-b and Kendall's Tau-c are non-parametric measures of association, ranging from –1 to +1, applied in ordinal or ranked variables. The basic difference between them is that the former takes into account the existing ties while the latter does not.

Correspondence Analysis is a technique used to interpret the relationships between variables. It permits the identification of relationships among categories within a variable or between categories of two variables. A multidimensional space is used in this analysis which depicts the correlation of the variables, determined by their distance between them as it is shown in the variable mappings.

Non-linear Principal Component Analysis is a qualitative marketing research method used for the visualisation and consequently for the interpretation of marketing data. The objective of this technique is to take a set of variables and find combinations of these for producing indices that are not correlated (Manly, 1986). These indices are called principal components. The fact that the principal components are uncorrelated means that they measure different "dimensions " in the data.

Non-Linear Principal Component analysis is considered to be effective when different types of variables are used to define a set of data, and no statistical assumptions regarding the sampling procedure or the distribution of the variables are required (Tagg, 1996). It is considered to be an extension of Principal Components Analysis since it has the ability to handle a set of not only numerical but also mixed variables (Gifi, 1985).

RESULTS OF THE RESEARCH

Awareness – Consumption

Initially, the levels of awareness and consumption of vegetables produced with the restricted use of pesticides among survey participants were identified. The findings show that approximately 31.5% of the respondents were aware of the fact that fresh greenhouse vegetables are produced with this particular method, while 6.6% alleged that they consume these products. It is appropriate here to mention the remarkable variations in awareness and consumption between the cities in which the survey was conducted.

In particular, the survey respondents of Heraklion exhibited substantially higher levels of awareness as well as consumption compared to the respondents of Athens and Thessaloniki. This can be attributed to the fact that organic agriculture, and in general methods of cultivation that deviate from the conventional, are applied more systematically around Heraklion than around the other cities where the research was carried out.

The levels of awareness and consumption of the respondents in each city, and also in total, are illustrated in the graph below.

118

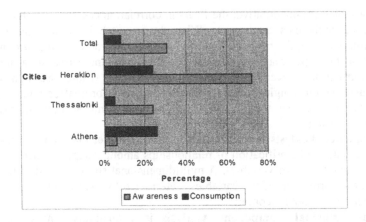

Figure 1. Levels of awareness and consumption

Moreover, the particular relationship between awareness, consumption, and the cities in which the research took place can be deduced from the high values that the chi-square test attained as well as from the significance level and the degrees of freedom[2] (see Table 1).

Table 1. Cross-tabulation of cities versus a: awareness b: consumption

	City
Awareness	X^2=86.67 P= .0000 d.f=2 Contingency Coefficient = 0.31
Consumption	X^2=55.56 P= .0000 d.f=2 Contingency Coefficient = 0.25

Taking into consideration the demographic characteristics of those included in the survey, 38.5% of the men and 23.2% of the women exhibited awareness, while the proportions in the case of consumption were 8% and 6.3% respectively. Furthermore, respondents with a high level of education (university graduates) demonstrated greater awareness and consumption of these products than respondents with a lower educational level. Where occupation was concerned, civil servants, along with housewives, were mostly familiar with the subject of the research. The demographic and socioeconomic characteristics are considered as basic determinants of consumers' perceptions regarding food quality (Van Ravenswaay, 1988; Misra et al., 1991)

In order to verify the accuracy of the replies given, a series of statements regarding the attributes of fresh greenhouse vegetables produced with the restricted use of pesticides was addressed to the respondents. The responses given exhibited a relative consistency among consumers regarding the attributes of the products and product awareness. This is derived from the high proportion of correct answers concerning the basic attributes of

---

[2] Chi-square tests the hypothesis of independence between the two variables examined. Since the level of significance is lower than .005 the hypothesis of independence is rejected. Therefore, the dependence of the variables is concluded (this is also indicated by the low degrees of freedom.

these products such as, healthiness, good flavour, being environmentally sound and having a higher price than those conventionally produced.

Another matter addressed was whether the answers given regarding the basic attributes of the specific products varied according to the city in which the survey took place. The findings show that the replies given by those in Heraklion, Crete were more consistent when compared to the others.

Consumers' inhibitions in purchasing the products

A subsequent attempt was made to identify the various factors that could operate as "inhibitors" in consumers' purchasing decisions regarding the products in question.

Initially, consumers stated the reasons why they do not consume the specific products. As shown in Table 2, the most profound reasons for non-consumption were the fact that they cannot easily be found and the lack of sufficient warranties that would certify the "alternative" production of the greenhouse vegetables.

Table 2. Reasons for not consuming fresh greenhouse vegetables produced with the restricted use of pesticides

Reasons	Answers in %
They cannot be easily found	73
They are more expensive than those that are conventionally produced	25.1
Consuming these products is not such an important issue	5.0
There is not sufficient certification about the exact method followed	51.8
The respondent was not responsible for the decisions regarding food choice	8.5
Other reasons	4.5

The probable factors that would discourage consumers from purchasing the products were then explored. That such products cannot easily be found, as well as the lack of adequate certification, were mentioned as impediments. The respondents who stated that the high price of these products in the domestic market was a feasible impediment to their purchase of them comprised (29.1%) of those surveyed. The proportion of those who would not buy these products because of their "cosmetic defects" was 21.4%, a relatively high percentage which indicates that this factor can have a serious impact on consumers' purchasing decisions.

On the other hand, respondents chose the fact that they are better for one's health than those that are produced with total use of pesticides as the main motive for their purchase. Other reasons given were the environmentally friendly nature of these products, the fact that they are safer than those that are conventionally produced, and their better flavour.

Importance attributed by consumers to the use of pesticides

Initially consumers' opinions concerning the use of pesticides in the production of fresh greenhouse vegetables were explored. The responses indicate the sensitivity of the consumers surveyed. The need for imposition of a total ban on the use of pesticides was

120

the dominant answer supported by 38% of the sample, even though some of the consumers believed that a total prohibition could not be easily attained. The necessity for strict controls on the use of pesticides was advocated by 34% of the respondents, while a call for the restricted use of pesticides was shared by 27% of the sample. Only 1% of the respondents claimed that pesticides can be safely used, a fact that indicates the familiarity of consumers with the dangers lurking behind their use.

These findings are presented in the graph below.

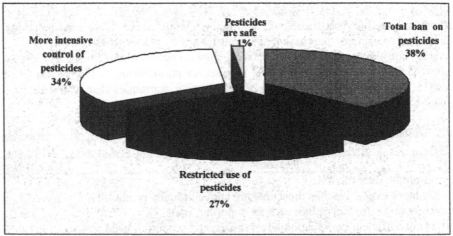

Figure 2. Consumers' opinions on the use of pesticides

The survey shows that the importance which consumers attributed to the restricted use of pesticides in the production of fresh greenhouse vegetables was treated as a very significant issue. Approximately 90% of those who participated in the survey claimed that this method of production of fresh greenhouse vegetables is an important issue. More specifically, 67.2% of those answering the question regarding the importance of this produce found it to be very significant, while 27.7% stated that it is significant. The rest of those surveyed treated the issue as not particularly significant, or even as one of indifference. Where the occupations of the respondents were concerned, civil servants and housewives assigned higher levels of importance than those in other occupations, while students were shown to exhibit the most indifference to the subject discussed.

It should be noted that the majority of those who determined this type of cultivation as an important issue suggested that the use of pesticides should be totally prohibited.

WILLINGNESS TO PURCHASE

The willingness of consumers to buy these products was examined on the basis of the following aspects:
- The willingness of consumers to buy the products, with relation to their price
- Their willingness to obtain them if the products were more readily available

• Their willingness to obtain them if they were provided with sufficient certification

The results for each case are presented below, analytically.

Price and consumers' willingness to buy the products

Two questions about price were posed to the respondents. The first one was designed to examine the intention of consumers to purchase the products if there were no substantial difference in price to those that were conventionally produced. The replies indicated the prevalent intention of those sampled to acquire these products.

More analytically, 65% of the respondents answered that they would definitely buy the products, while 23.7% were not absolutely certain. Of the rest of the respondents, 7.1% stated categorically that they would not buy them, while approximately 5% of those surveyed declined to answer.

Subsequently, the willingness of consumers to acquire the products if they were more expensive (compared to the price of the conventional products) was examined. Past surveys indicated that consumers were willing to pay premiums in order to acquire "environmentally friendly products" (Byrne et al, 1994; Lai et al., 1997).

A quite high proportion of respondents (32.3%) was reluctant to pay a higher price in order to obtain the products. The majority of consumers, nearly 40%, confirmed that they were willing to pay a premium of up to 30%, while those that would buy them even if they cost double the price of the conventional products represented almost 4% of the sample.

The various premiums on price suggested by the consumers are presented in the graph below.

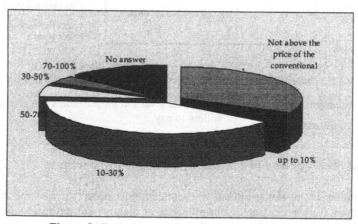

Figure 3. Consumers' willingness to pay higher prices

In order to obtain a more thorough insight into the factors that determine consumers' purchasing decisions, and in particular their willingness to pay premiums to acquire fresh greenhouse vegetables produced with the restricted use of pesticides, correspondence

122

analysis, which examined the relationship between the educational level of the respondents and the premiums they were willing to pay was carried out.

The respondents were classified, into 4 categories according to their willingness to pay premiums. The first group included those who were not willing to pay any premium above the price of the conventionally produced vegetables, while the other groups included the respondents who would readily pay a premium of up to 10%, 50% and 100% respectively.

Two-dimensional mapping was used to illustrate the relationship between the two variables. When correspondence analysis was carried out, it was shown that individuals of a higher educational level intended to pay higher premiums for purchasing the products. By contrast, respondents who had received primary or high school education related either to the category of "not willing to pay" or to the category of those who were willing to pay a premium that would not exceed 10%.

These results are shown in the figure overleaf.

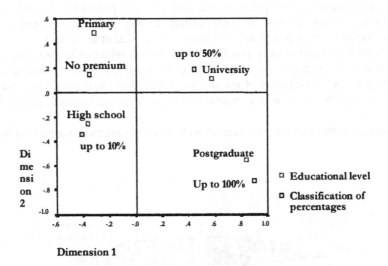

Figure 4. Correspondence analysis of the educational level and the premiums that consumers were willing to pay

Availability of the products and consumers' willingness to purchase

Where the availability of the products was concerned, almost 55% of the respondents stated that if there were no obstacles in finding them, they would definitely decide to buy the products in question rather than those that are conventionally produced.

A substantial proportion of the respondents, approximately 37%, expressed certain doubts about their willingness to purchase them, while 6% would not buy them, even if they were more readily available.

Another issue directly related to the availability of the products in question was their availability in those places where consumers usually purchase similar products.

Half of the respondents (49.0%) argued that they could not find them in the places where they usually purchase their vegetables. A significant section (32.6%) had never looked for those products in such places, while 18.5% stated that they can find them at the usual selling points.

Sufficiency of certification and consumers' willingness to buy the products

The testing of pesticides and the adequacy of certification provided regarding the cultivation processes applied are both essential (Misra et al., 1991).

According to the findings of the survey, 68% of the respondents would definitely buy fresh greenhouse vegetables produced with the restricted use of pesticides. Shoppers who were not entirely sure about their intention to buy them constituted 28% of those surveyed. A comparison of these estimates with the figures given above reveals the sensitivity of consumers and consequently their willingness to buy these products if they were provided with the necessary certification. The graph below pinpoints the willingness of consumers to buy the products in question in relation to the availability of the products and the sufficiency of the warranties which accompanies them.

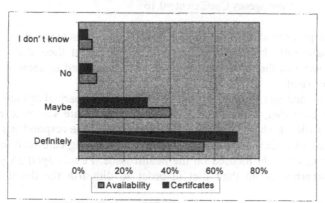

Figure 5. Consumers' willingness to buy in the case of a: greater availability, b: sufficiency of warranties

Dietary concerns

Another issue explored in the survey was the dietary habits of consumers. Firstly, the degree of concern that respondents exhibited regarding their nutrition was examined. The findings show that nearly half of those surveyed care about the way they eat, while 24% stated that they cared very much. Likewise, approximately 21% of the respondents stated that they do not particularly care about their nutrition, and finally 5% claimed that they do not care at all.

Health was indicated as the fundamental reason why respondents took care with their diet by 43% of those sampled. In addition, 25% of the respondents stated that, besides health, their appearance was a reason for following a regime of proper nutrition, while the threat of illness and the presence of children within the family were stated as reasons by

13% of the sample. Approximately 9% of the shoppers interviewed considered the matter of proper nutrition as a subject of plain preference.

Where the stability of consumers' dietary habits was concerned, almost 60% of the respondents stated that their nutritional habits have altered over recent years, while the rest have maintained the same dietary pattern (10%) and only slight changes have occurred recently. Healthier choices were being made by 38.3% of those who had altered their customary diet, 25.3% had adopted more regular eating habits, while 24.5% had turned to so-called "junk food" (mainly "fast foods").

A consideration of both the age and the occupation of the respondents revealed a dependent relationship between them and dietary concerns. These results are shown in the following table:

Table 3. Cross-tabulation of concern for diet versus a: profession b: educational level

	City
Profession	Chi Squared=77.56
	P= .0000 d.f=18 Contingency Coefficient =0.29
Educational Level	Chi-Squared=22.98
	P= .006 d.f=9
	Contingency Coefficient =0.16

Data analysis proceeded with the application of correspondence analysis in order to illustrate the relationship between consumers' concern about their diet and age. Two-dimensional mapping of the aforementioned variables was used to show the relationship, as in the graph overleaf.

It can be concluded that respondents between 18 and 24 years of age are not especially concerned about their diet, while those aged from 45 to 54 are shown to be particularly interested in their diet. It should also be noted that most of the respondents aged from 18 to 24 years of age gave their appearance as a reason for taking care with their diet, while the other age-groups merely focused on the health issue. People aged 55 years and over were mainly concerned about their diet in order to diminish the threat of a probable illness.

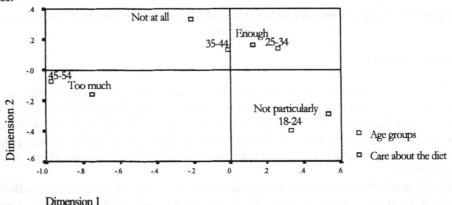

Figure 6. Correspondence Analysis between age and the significance attributed to the dietary habits of the respondents

The following table presents the definition that respondents gave in reply to an open question concerning healthy nutrition. The answers were classified into 7 categories.

Table 4. Definition of healthy nutrition

Definition of healthy nutrition	% of the sample
Pure products - No chemicals	10.9
Mainly fruit and vegetables	15.5
Properly selected/correctly cooked food	17.9
All foods in the right quantities	16.1
Traditional food	3.6
Mainly dairy products	12.8
Limited quantities of meat	11.5

IDENTIFICATION OF THE "OVERALL" CONSUMERS' ATTITUDE: NON-LINEAR PRINCIPAL COMPONENT ANALYSIS

Non-linear principal component analysis for foreground variables

In the present survey, Non-Linear Principal Components Analysis (PRINCALS) was implemented in order to identify the relation between the variables assumed to describe the "overall" attitude which consumers exhibited towards the restricted use of pesticides in the production of fresh greenhouse vegetables.

This specific technique was considered appropriate because it has the ability to handle several types of variables (Gifi A. 1985), and to reduce the original variables used into a smaller group of transformed variables without losing substantial amounts of information in comparison to the initially formed group.

Firstly, a two-dimensional PRINCALS solution was obtained, in order to analyse the relation among the 10 variables that defined consumers' attitude. All the variables included at this stage were handled as ordinal and active, meaning that all of them were taken into account in the solution. Additionally, these variables can be considered as foreground variables. Eigenvalues of .32 and .14 were extracted from the PRINCALS performance. Their sum represents the "total fit", meaning the total variance explained (0.45).

A plot of component loadings for the first two dimensions is shown in the graph overleaf. This plot indicates that the original variables can be classified into two groups. The first group consists of the level of awareness and consumption of fresh greenhouse vegetables produced with the restricted use of pesticides that consumers exhibited, while the second one consists of the variables that indicate the intention of consumers to purchase the products. The variable labelled "opinion" does not correlate highly with any of the two dimensions while the variable labelled "percentage", which corresponds to the various premiums that consumers were willing to pay, is slightly related to the second dimension only.

Furthermore, the plot shows that the first dimension mostly correlates with the variables that explain the overall "intention" of the respondents. Thus all the objects that

126

have a high score in dimension 1 will have a high score in the specific set of variables, except in the case of "opinion", which will have a low score.

The second dimension depicts the contrast between the variables that compose the first set and the majority of the second group of variables. They are situated in opposing positions in relation to the vertical axis. Here the focus is on the first group and on the willingness of consumers to buy the products, taking into consideration factors such as their price, their availability and the certification that they carry.

More specifically, the objects that have high positive values in the second dimension will have a high score for the first set of variables (the second dimension especially exhibited a strong correlation with "awareness" and "consumption"), and a low score for the second group of variables[3].

On the basis of the above findings, it is possible to extrapolate that consumers' attitudes towards the restricted use of pesticides are more accurately determined by the amount of awareness they exhibit, their consumption, the degree of importance that they attribute to the issue in question, and also by their dietary concerns.

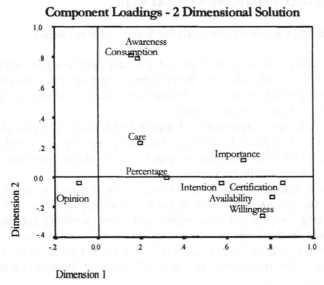

Component Loadings - 2 Dimensional Solution

Figure 7. Component loadings: two-dimensional ordinal solution (PRINCALS)

In addition, a three-dimensional ordinal solution was extracted. It accrued from the value attained by the last eigenvalue[4] in the previous two-dimensional solution. The third eigenvalue obtained (.11) was significantly high and contributed considerably to the

---

[3] Projections on the horizontal axis indicate the existing correlation among the object scores (the units of observation) in the first dimension and the quantified variables, while the projections on the vertical axis represent the correlation between the quantified variables and the object scores in the second dimension.

[4] A three-dimensional solution can be considered when 1/m, where m=the number of variables, is lower than the value of the last eigenvalue obtained in the two-dimensional solution.

acquisition of higher percentages of "explained variance" (56%), compared to the percentage of the variable explained in the case of the two-dimensional solution.

The plot in Figure 8 indicates the three-dimensional solution from the application of the PRINCALS technique. The extension into a three-dimensional solution altered the classification of the variables. More specifically, the variables labelled "awareness" and "consumption" constitute a separate group, while the other variables compose a broader set. The variables of "care" and "percentage" show the highest (positive) correlation with the third dimension, implying that objects with scores in dimension 3 will have a high score where these variables are concerned.

Component Loadings - 3 Dimensional Solution

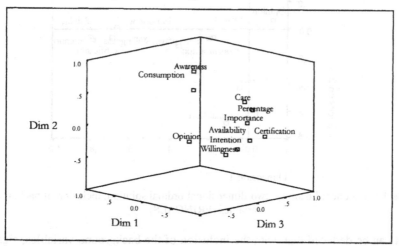

Figure 8. Component loadings: three - dimensional ordinal solution (PRINCALS)

Analysis with the addition of «background» variables

Proceeding with PRINCALS analysis, six background variables were included[5]. They were treated as active and the results depend on both categories of variables, foreground and background.

From a two-dimensional ordinal solution, the eigenvalues obtained were .19 and .15 respectively. From the component loadings values, it is clear that the first dimension is mostly correlated with the foreground variables that reflect consumers' attitudes, while the second dimension is correlated with these background variables.

The distance from the origin pinpoints the fact that importance, intention and willingness are the variables most correlated with the first dimension. There is a negative correlation between the second dimension and the variables that represent the age, marital

---

[5] As background are considered the variables that describe the demographic characteristics of consumers. The background variables included in PRINCALS were age, gender, profession, educational level, marital status and the city in which the survey took place.

128

status and profession of the respondents, indicating that objects with a large positive value for their object score will have a low value where the aforementioned variables are concerned. On the other hand, the level of education is positively related to this dimension.

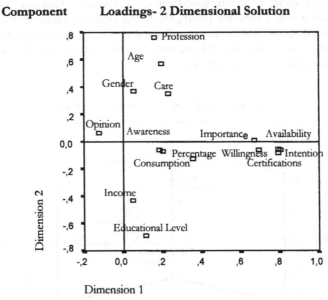

Figure 9. Component Loadings: two-dimensional ordinal solution, inclusion of background variables (PRINCALS)

Finally, it can be deduced that, with the inclusion of the background variables, significant changes did not occur in the analysis. In addition, a distinction between the "items" that underlie the attitude of the respondents and their demographic characteristics can be extracted. The variables which are positively correlated with both dimensions are those that determine the "overall" attitude of the consumer concerning the restricted use of pesticides in the production of fresh greenhouse vegetables.

Similar to the PRINCALS analysis of the foreground variables, a three-dimensional solution was extracted (this was permitted by the second eigenvalue estimated in the previous solution). The percentage of the total «explained variance» amounted to 44.9% which denotes that the inclusion of the third eigenvalue contributed substantially to the data analysis. It should be noted that the third dimension, as displayed in the corresponding graph, is mostly correlated with the variables of awareness, consumption and "city", while for the other dimensions the same is true as in the two-dimensional solution.

Component Loadings-3 Dimensional Solution

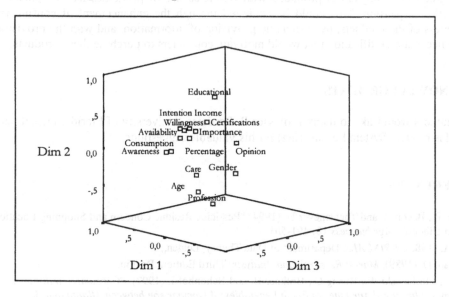

Figure 10. Component loadings: three - dimensional ordinal solution, inclusion of background variables (PRINCALS)

CONCLUSIONS

The present study focused on the identification of consumers' attitude towards fresh greenhouse vegetables produced with the restricted use of pesticides, as an "alternative" method of production. The factors that affected consumers' purchasing decisions were also explored.

The field research indicated that consumers were not particularly aware of the products in question; this lack of information has led to the limited consumption of the products. However, it should be noted that, compared to the other cities in which the survey was conducted, high levels of awareness and consumption were displayed in Heraklion, Crete.

The limited availability of the products and the absence of adequate warranties to certify the restricted use of pesticides were suggested as the basic factors that would prevent a consumer from purchasing them. "Cosmetic defects" (i.e. appearance) were also pinpointed as a possible "inhibitor" in their purchasing decisions. However, respondents showed relative willingness to purchase the products if they were more readily available, if the warranties provided were adequate, and even if they were of higher price. Here, correspondence analysis indicated that respondents with a higher level of education were more willing to pay higher premiums than the others. Consumers also seemed to be substantially concerned about their diet.

The present consumer-based market survey indicates conclusively that the market for fresh greenhouse vegetables produced with restricted use of pesticides has the potential for further expansion. This could be achieved through the enhancement of consumers' awareness of the products, by systematic provision of information, and with the provision of the necessary certification that would motivate consumers to purchase these products.

ACKNOWLEDGEMENTS

The authors would like to thank Professor P. Pardalos (University of Florida, Department of Industrial and System Engineering) for his valuable suggestions.

REFERENCES

Byrne, P., Bacon R. and Toensmeyer U. (1994),"Pesticide Residue Concern and Shopping Location Likelihood", *Agribusiness* 10: 491-501.

Gifi, A. (1985), *PRINCALS,* Department of Data Theory, Leiden,.

Lehman, D. (1989), *Market Research and Analysis,* Third Edition, Boston.

Lai, Y., Florkowski W., Huang C., Brukner B. and Schonhof I. (1997), *"Consumers Willingness to Pay for Improved Attributes of Fresh Vegetables: A Comparison between Atlanta and Berlin."* a paper submitted to the WAEA Annual Meeting, July 13-16,1997,Reno, NV.

Manly, B. (1986), *Multivariate Statistical Methods: A Primer,* Chapman and Hall Editions, London.

Misra, S., Huang G. L. and Ott S. L. (1991*), "Consumer Preferences for Certified Pesticides Residue Free Fresh Produce and Willingness to Pay for Testing and Certification"* paper presented at the 1991 Southern Agricultural Economics Association meeting, Fort Worth, TX.

Misra, S., Huang C. L. and Ott S. (1991), "Consumers' Willingness to Pay for Pesticide-Free Fresh Produce", *Western Journal of Agricultural Economics* 16: 218-227.

Ott, S. L. (1990), "Super Market Shopper's Pesticide Concerns and Willingness to Purchase Certified Pesticide Residue-Fresh Produce", *Agribusiness: An International Journal* 6:593-602.

Tagg, S. (1996), *"Breaching the Qualitative/Quantitative Divide: Repertory Grid Analysis with SPSS Princals",* MEG 96 Conference Research Methods Track Session.

Van Ravenswaay, E. (1988), "How Much Food Safety Do Consumers Want? An Analysis of Current Studies and Strategies for Future Research." *Consumers Demands in the Market Place: Public Policy in Relation to Food Safety, Quality, Human Health,* ed., C. Kathrine, pp. 89-113. Wahington DC: Resources for the Future.

Weaver, R. D., Evans D. J. and Luloff, A.E. (1992), "Pesticide Use in Tomato Production: Consumers Concern and Willingness-to-Pay", *Agribusiness* 8(2):131-142.

A DECISION SUPPORT SYSTEM FOR THE SELLER'S RETURN PROBLEM IN THE PRODUCT LINE DESIGN

G. Alexouda[*], K. Paparrizos

Department of Applied Informatics
University of Macedonia
156 Egnatia Str, POB 1591
Thessaloniki 540 06
Greece

Abstract: In this paper we present a decision support system (DSS) for the seller's return problem in the product line design. We consider that buyers choose the product that gives them maximum utility. The product line is designed so that the total marginal return from the sales of the products is maximized. The DSS we are presenting, performs "what if analysis" for a given product line profile and finds good solutions using a genetic algorithm approach. We present a genetic algorithm based heuristic for solving the product line design problem using the seller's marginal return criterion. The new approach is compared with a recently developed beam search method on randomly generated problems. Our method seems to be substantially better in terms of CPU time. Also, the solutions found by our method are better than those found by the beam search method in comparable times.

Key words: Decision Support Systems, Genetic Algorithms, Seller's Return Problem, Product Line Design, Marketing.

INTRODUCTION

New product development is an important way for a firm to gain competitive advantage. Product design is a critical success factor for product development (Kotler 1997). However, a good design alone cannot guarantee the success of a new product (Rackhan 1998).

Optimal product line design is an important managerial problem. A firm can become more competitive by offering more than a single product. However, a bad product line

[*] Corresponding author

S.H. Zanakis et al. (eds.), Decision Making: Recent Developments and Worldwide Applications, 131–140.
© 2000 Kluwer Academic Publishers.

design (or extension) can have a bad influence in the total profit of a firm (Quelch and Kenny 1994).

The significance of a computational tool that can assist a marketing manager in the product line design using the seller's return criterion is obvious. We developed a decision support system, which can perform "what-if-analysis". Because the computation time of optimization is too excessive, we use a genetic algorithm (GA) to find approximate solutions.

GAs arose with computer science. They were first invented by John Holland in the 1960s and were developed by Holland and his students and collegues at the University of Michigan in the 1960s and the 1970s. GAs are intelligent probabilistic search techniques that mimic some of the processes of natural evolution and selection (Davis 1991, Goldberg 1989, Mitchell 1996).

MARKETING DECISION SUPPORT SYSTEMS

Many researchers have dealt with the different ways of using the information technology in marketing (Decker and Gaul 1990, Talvinen 1995). Marketing decision support systems (MDSSs) are computational tools, which can help a marketing manager in the decision process. They can be defined as a coordinated collection of data, models, analytic tools and computing power by which an organization gathers information from the environment and turns into a basis for action (Little 1979).

Decision support systems (DSSs) can be classified according to the nature and scope of task to which they can be applied: specific DSSs, DSS generators and DSS tools. Specific DSSs deal with specific problems. DSS generators facilitate the development of specific DSSs. DSS tools facilitate the development of specific DSSs or DSS generators (Sprague 1989).

MDSSs show a large variety in functionality and form. They can be classified according to the questions they deal with (Wierenga, Ophuis, Huizingh and Campen 1994): What happened (level 1), Why did it happen (level 2), What will happen if (level 3), What should happen (level 4).

In this paper we present a specific MDSS for the Seller's Return Problem in Product Line Design that deals with questions of levels 3 and 4.

THE SELLER'S RETURN PROBLEM IN THE PRODUCT LINE DESIGN

By product line we mean a line of substitute products. Many researchers have dealt with the optimal product line design and proposed preference-based procedures. The conjoint analysis can be used for modelling the product line design problem. There are two different approaches to attack the problem. The first approach considers a finite set of candidate items from which a product line is selected (Green and Krieger 1985, Dobson and Kalish 1988, McBride and Zufryden 1988). The second approach constructs product lines directly from part-worths data. If the number of attributes and the numbers of attribute levels are large and the most attribute level combinations define feasible products, the computation time needed to enumerate the utilities of the candidate items can be very big. For this class of problems it is preferable to use the second approach. Kohli and Sukumar (1990) and Nair, Thakur and Wen (1995) developed the most recent heuristic methods using the second approach. Our method employs the second approach.

Because the seller's return problem of a product line design is NP-Hard, some researchers proposed heuristic methods. Kohli and Sukumar (1990) have proposed a solution procedure called dynamic-programming heuristic. It mimics a dynamic programming method using attributes as stages and attribute levels as states.

Nair, Thakur and Wen (1995) proposed a beam search (BS) heuristic for the solution of the product line design problem. Their computational study showed that the BS method finds better solutions and takes less computation time than the dynamic programming heuristic. BS methods have been developed in the 1970s for Artificial Intelligence search problems. It is a breadth-first search process with no backtracking. At any level of BS, the b most promising nodes are explored further in the search tree, where b is called the beam width. Nair, Thakur and Wen (1995) suggest a way to compute a good value of b. In our computational study we have followed this suggestion.

PROBLEM DEFINITION

We consider that buyers choose the product that gives them maximum utility and the product line is designed so that the total marginal return to the seller from the sales of the products is maximized.

The typical mathematical formulation of the product line design problem (Kohli and Sukumar 1990) considers the following sets: Let $\Omega = \{1, 2, \ldots, K\}$ denote the set of K attributes, $\Phi_k = \{1, 2, \ldots, J_k\}$ the set of J_k levels of attribute $k \in \Omega$ and $\Psi = \{1, 2, \ldots, PN\}$ the set of PN items to be selected, where the multi-attribute description of each item is to be determined by solving the seller's return problem. Also, let $\Theta = \{1, 2, \ldots, I\}$ denote the set of buyers. Let w_{ijk} denote the part worth of level $j \in \Phi_k$ of attribute $k \in \Omega$ for consumer $i \in \Theta$. The conjoint analysis can be used for the estimation of the part worths. We consider a status-quo product for each buyer. Let j^*_{ik} denote the level of attribute $k \in \Omega$ that appears in the product profile of the status-quo product for buyer $i \in \Theta$. Let v_{ijk} denote the seller's return if individual $i \in \Theta$ buys a product where level $j \in \Phi_k$ of attribute $k \in \Omega$ is used. To account for cannibalization, instead of V(k) we use D(k), the seller's marginal return matrices, as follows:

$d_{ijk} = v_{ijk} - v_{i(j^*ik)k}$, if the buyers switches from a status – quo product offered by the seller.

v_{ijk}, if the buyers switches from a status – quo product offered by a competitor.

Let x_{ijkm} be a 0-1 variable which indicates whether level $j \in \Phi_k$ of attribute $k \in \Omega$ is assigned to product $m \in \Psi$ and consumer $i \in \Theta$. In particular it is set

$x_{ijkm} = 1$, if level $j \in \Phi_k$ of attribute $k \in \Omega$ is assigned to product $m \in \Psi$ and consumer $i \in \Theta$.

    0, otherwise.

The Seller's Return Problem can be formulated as the following 0-1 integer program:

$$\max \sum_{i\in\Theta} \sum_{m\in\Psi} \sum_{k\in\Omega} \sum_{j\in\Phi_k} d_{ijk} x_{ijkm} y_i \tag{1}$$

$$\text{s.t.} \sum_{j\in\Phi_k} \sum_{m\in\Psi} x_{ijkm} = 1, \quad i\in\Theta, \ k\in\Omega \tag{2}$$

$$\sum_{j\in\Phi_k} x_{ijkm} - \sum_{j\in\Phi_{k'}} x_{ijk'm} = 0, \quad k'>k, \ k, k'\in\Omega, \ i\in\Theta, \ m\in\Psi \tag{3}$$

$$x_{ijkm} + x_{i'j'km} \leq 1, \quad i'>i, \ j'>j, \ i, i'\in\Theta, \ j, j'\in\Phi_k, \ k\in\Omega, \ m\in\Psi \tag{4}$$

$$\sum_{m\in\Psi} \sum_{k\in\Omega} \sum_{j\in\Phi_k} w_{ijk}(x_{ijkm} - x_{i'jkm}) \geq 0 \quad i'\neq i, \ i, i'\in\Theta \tag{5}$$

$$y_i \sum_{m\in\Psi} \sum_{k\in\Omega} \sum_{j\in\Phi_k} w_{ijk} x_{ijkm} \geq y_i u_i^*, \quad i\in\Theta \tag{6}$$

$$x_{ijkm} = 0,1 \text{ integer}, \quad i\in\Theta, \ j\in\Phi_k, \ k\in\Omega, \ m\in\Psi \tag{7}$$

$$y_i = 0,1 \text{ integer} \tag{8}$$

The objective function (1) selects PN products to maximize the seller's return, subject to the choice constraint for each buyer. The meaning of the constraints is as follows: Constraint (2) assures that, across products, only one level of an attribute is associated to an individual. Constraint (3) requires that across attributes, the level assigned to an individual must correspond to the same product. Constraint (4) imposes the same level of an attribute to be specified for all individuals assigned to a product. Together, constraints (2) - (4) guarantee that each individual is assigned to one item, and that each item is described in terms of one level of each attribute. Constraint (5) forces each individual to be assigned to the product which offers him the highest utility. Constraint (6) assures that the seller obtains a return from individual $i\in\Theta$ only if the new product assigned to the individual has higher utility than the utility u^*_i of his status quo product.

GENETIC ALGORITHMS

GAs work with a population of chromosomes. Each chromosome represents a candidate solution. A chromosome is a string of genes, which can take on some value from a specific finite range or alphabet. The initial population can be created randomly or using problem specific information.

A fitness function is used for the evaluation of the chromosomes. A selection method uses the fitness evaluations to choose the chromosomes, which will survive in the next population. Crossover is considered as the most important operator of GAs. It mimics biological recombination by exchanging genetic material between two chromosomes to create two offspring. There are different versions of crossover, like one-point crossover, two-point crossover and uniform crossover.Mutation is the occasional random alteration of the value at a string position (Davis 1991, Goldberg 1989, Mitchell 1996).

A brief description of GAs is as follows:

Initial population generation

Repeat

    Fitness evaluation

    Selection

    Crossover

    Mutation

Until the stopping condition is satisfied.

There are some differences between GAs and the traditional algorithms (Goldberg 1989). GAs work with an encoding of the parameter set, not the parameters themselves. They work with a population of candidate solutions rather than a single solution. Also, GAs use only payoff information, not derivatives or other auxiliary knowledge. They use probabilistic transition rules, not deterministic.

Many integer programming problems are difficult to solve and heuristic methods are used to solve them. In the last years many researchers suggested GAs for difficult integer programming problems. Correctly applied GAs seem to provide good heuristic solution procedures for these problems (Chatterjee, Carrera and Lynch 1996, Chu and Beasley 1997, Hadj-Alouane and Bean 1997, Malmborg 1996).

Many GAs have been applied in management science with a focus on production problems (Nissen 1995). In the last years some researchers have dealt with solving marketing optimization problems using GAs. Balakrishnan and Jacob (1996) developed a GA for the single product design problem. The GA approach presented in this paper deals with the product line design problem.

THE MAIN OPERATIONS OF THE DSS

We developed a user friendly DSS for the seller's return problem in the product line design using the Borland C++ Builder 3. The user interface of the DSS is menu driven. The Menu Bar includes the following menus: File, What-If-Analysis, Solver and Help.

The File menu provides familiar choices such as New, Open, Save, Save As, Close and Exit. The DSS takes as input the necessary estimated values mentioned in section 2. To insert a new problem the user has to provide the attributes and the attribute levels of the products. Also, he has to insert the elements of the buyers' part worth and the seller's return matrices. He is asked to provide the level of each attribute that appears in the status-quo product of each buyer. After the insertion the DSS computes for each buyer the utility of each status-quo product. Also, it computes the seller's marginal return matrix.

The "what-if-analysis" choice allows the user to examine different scenarios. He can insert the selected level of each attribute for each item of a product line profile and the DSS computes the total seller's return for the given product line profile.

Because the seller's return problem in product line design is NP-Hard, we are forced to use heuristic methods to solve it. We suggest a solver, which uses a GA approach. The Solver choice prompts the user to insert the number of items of the product line and then computes a good solution. The solution computed by the GA is not guaranteed to be the optimal one. The suggested product line profile and it's total seller's marginal return are displayed.

The familiar Help choice provides to the user helpful instructions.

The DSS can be improved by using constraints and other or more than one optimization objectives. Also, other heuristics can be included to find good solutions or generate the initial population of the GA. Furthermore the GA can be improved. We are going to develop such an improved DSS.

THE GENETIC ALGORITHM USED IN THE DECISION SUPPORT SYSTEM

We present the GA, which is used in the DSS. The initial population of the suggested GA is randomly generated. We have used the seller's return criterion for the fitness evaluation of each population. In each iteration 40% of the new population is produced using the reproduction operator, another 40% using the uniform crossover operator and 20% using the mutation operator. If the best candidate solution does not improve in the last 10 iterations, the GA terminates.

The GA can formally be described as follows. In this description L is the set of the candidate product lines and $M=|L|$ is the population size. The population is maintained in a matrix POP. The elements POP_{lmk}, where $l \in L$, $m \in \Psi$ and $k \in \Omega$, denote the selected level of each attribute, that is, if level $j \in \Phi_k$ of attribute $k \in \Omega$ is assigned to product $m \in \Psi$ of product line $l \in L$, then $POP_{lmk}=j$.

For the fitness evaluation of the population we have to compute the total marginal return to the seller from each product line. For this reason we compute matrices PRODUTIL, RETURN and TOTAL_RETURN. Let w_{ijk} denote the part worth of level $j \in \Phi_k$ of attribute $k \in \Omega$ for consumer $i \in \Theta$. The utility of product $m \in \Psi$ of product line $l \in L$ which is obtained by buyer $i \in \Theta$ is denoted by $PRODUTIL_{lim}$. Let m' denote the index m such as $PRODUTIL_{lim'}= \max_{m \in \Psi} PRODUTIL_{lim}$, where $l \in L$ and $i \in \Theta$. The utility of the status-quo product of individual $i \in \Theta$ is denoted by $STATUTIL_i$. Let d_{ijk} denote the seller's marginal return if individual $i \in \Theta$ buys a product where level $j \in \Phi_k$ of attribute $k \in \Omega$ is used. The marginal return to the seller from individual $i \in \Theta$ of product line $l \in L$ is denoted by $RETURN_{li}$. The total marginal return to the seller from product line $l \in L$ is denoted by $TOTAL\_RETURN_l$.

The description of the suggested GA is as follows:

STEP 1: (*Initialization*) Generate randomly an initial population of candidate product lines. Store the population in matrix POP.

STEP 2: (*Fitness Evaluation*). Compute matrices PRODUTIL, RETURN and TOTAL_RETURN, as follows:

$$\text{set } PRODUTIL_{lim} = \sum_{k \in \Omega} w_i (POP_{lmk})k \quad l \in L,\ i \in \Theta,\ m \in \Psi$$

if PRODUTIL$_{lim'}$ > STATUTIL$_i$

set RETURN$_{li}$ = $\sum_{k \in \Omega}$ d$_{i(POP_{im'k})k}$

else set RETURN$_{li}$ =0,   l ∈ L,   i ∈ Θ

set TOTAL_RETURN$_l$ = $\sum_{i \in \Theta}$ RETURN$_{li}$,   l ∈ L.

STEP 3:(Selection) Choose the (2/5)M best product lines.

STEP 4:(Crossover) Create randomly M/5 pairs of product lines chosen among the ones created in step 3. Perform the uniform crossover operator on these pairs to generate (2/5)M new candidate product lines.

STEP 5:(Mutation) Pick randomly M/5 product lines from the set of the (4/5)M product lines which were created in step 3 and 4. Alternate randomly the value at a random string position of each product line.

STEP 6:(Stopping Rule) If the best candidate solution does not improve in the last 10 iterations STOP. Otherwise, go to STEP 2.

COMPUTATIONAL RESULTS

We now report the results of a computational study performed to compare the suggested GA to the BS method. Our intention is to compare the CPU time needed by each method and the quality of the solutions.

We set the number of consumers equal to 100 and generated 180 different random problems. We considered 18 different problem sizes. For each different problem size 10 problems were randomly generated. The number of attributes ranges from five to seven and the number of attribute levels from four to six. The number of products takes the values two and three. The part-worths were generated randomly from a uniform distribution and normalized within respondent. The normalized part worths are assumed interpersonally comparable. We consider that before the introduction of our new product line, three products are available in the market, one of which is offered by our company.

The population size was set equal to 150 and the GA terminates, when in 10 consecutive iterations the best candidate solution doesn't improve. In some cases the results of the GA can be improved, if we increase the population size or if we set a more strict stopping condition. However, the population size and the stopping condition we used in our implementation perform well for the problem sizes we studied.

For each class of 10 problems we computed the mean CPU time of the GA and the BS method. Also, for the GA we computed the mean number of iterations. For the cases where the GA does better or ties the solution of the BS method, we computed the mean CPU time and the mean number of iterations needed by the GA to find or to overcome the solution found by the BS method. These computational results are presented in Table 1. In all cases the GA requires less CPU time than the BS method. For the cases, where the GA does better or ties the solution of the BS method, the GA needs only few iterations and little CPU time to find or to overcome the solution found by the BS method.

It is very important to compare the solutions of the GA and the BS method. As shown in Table 2, in the 93.88 % of the cases we have examined, the GA finds a better solution than that found by the BS method, while only in the 6.11% the BS method finds a better solution.

Table 1. Computational results of the GA and the BS method

PN	K	J	GA CPU time (secs)	CPU time* (secs)	Iterations	Iterations*	BS CPU time (secs)
2	5	4	7.18	1.66	19.30	4.20	31.24
2	5	5	8.44	2.21	22.50	5.60	31.72
2	5	6	9.62	2.12	25.60	5.33	32.19
2	6	4	9.61	3.82	24.30	9.40	32.47
2	6	5	11.98	3.79	29.70	9.14	32.74
2	6	6	14.23	4.03	34.20	9.56	33.52
2	7	4	11.87	2.87	27.60	6.30	33.68
2	7	5	12.84	4.73	29.00	10.50	34.84
2	7	6	14.54	3.80	32.60	8.20	36.20
3	5	4	14.89	4.08	31.20	8.20	59.97
3	5	5	14.36	5.36	29.20	10.60	61.31
3	5	6	17.92	5.38	36.40	10.60	61.86
3	6	4	18.21	8.38	34.90	15.78	61.87
3	6	5	20.27	11.27	37.20	20.71	62.94
3	6	6	19.47	8.41	35.20	13.44	63.80
3	7	4	21.99	9.18	38.70	15.90	64.76
3	7	5	25.81	7.80	44.00	13.00	67.48
3	7	6	30.19	7.65	50.90	12.60	70.82

*needed by the GA to find or to improve the solution of the Beam Search heuristic only for the cases, where the GA finds a better or an equivalent solution than those found by the BS method.

Table 2. Comparative results of the solutions of GA and BS for N=100

PN	K	J	GA better than BS	BS better than GA
2	5	4	10	0
2	5	5	10	0
2	5	6	9	1
2	6	4	10	0
2	6	5	7	3
2	6	6	9	1
2	7	4	10	0
2	7	5	10	0
2	7	6	10	0
3	5	4	10	0
3	5	5	10	0
3	5	6	10	0
3	6	4	9	1
3	6	5	7	3
3	6	6	9	1
3	7	4	10	0
3	7	5	9	1
3	7	6	10	0
%	93.88 %	6.11%		

The suggested GA and the BS method were implemented in the programming language Borland C++ 4.5. The computational study was performed on a PC with a Pentium Processor (16 MB RAM, 150 MHz, using Windows 95).

CONCLUSIONS

We have presented a decision support system for the seller's return problem in product line design. It has a user friendly menu driven interface and performs "what if analysis" for a given product line profile. A Genetic Algorithm is employed to find good solutions. The GA and a recently developed beam search method were compared on 18 different classes of problems each one containing 10 randomly generated problems. The proposed algorithm seems to be superior in terms of CPU time and the quality of the solutions.

REFERENCES

Balakrishnan, P. and Jacob, V. (1996), "Genetic Algorithms for Product Design", *Management Science* 42, 1105-1117.

Chatterjee, S., Carrera, C. and Lynch, L. (1996), "Genetic algorithms and traveling salesman problems", *European Journal of Operational Research* 93/3, 490-510.

Chu, P. and Beasley, J. (1997), "A Genetic Algorithm for the Generalised Assignment Problem", *Computers and Operations Research* 24/1, 17-23.

Decker, R. and Gaul, W. (1990), "Einige Bemerkungen ueber Expertensysteme fuer Marketing und Marktforschung", *Marketing ZFP* 4, 257-271.

Davis, L. (1991), *Handbook of Genetic Algorithms*, Van Nostrand Reinhold, New York.

Dobson, G. and Kalish, S. (1988), "Positioning and Pricing a Product Line", *Marketing Science* 7, 107-125.

Goldberg, D. (1989), *Genetic Algorithms in Search Optimization & Learning*, Addison-Wesley, USA.

Green, P. and Krieger, A. (1985), "Models and Heuristics for Product Line Selection", *Marketing Science* 4, 1-19.

Hadj-Alouane, A. and Bean, J. (1997), "A Genetic Algorithm for the Multiple-Choice Integer Program", *Operations Research* 45/1, 92-101.

Hurley, S., Moutinho, L., and Stephens, N. (1995), "Solving marketing optimization problems using genetic algorithms", *European Journal of Marketing* 29, 39-56.

Kohli, R., and Sukumar, R. (1990), "Heuristics for Product-Line Design using Conjoint Analysis", *Management Science* 36, 1464-1478.

Kotler, P. (1997), *Marketing Management: Analysis, Planning, Implementation and Control*, 9th ed., Prentice-Hall International, New Jersey.

Little, J. (1979), "Decision Support Systems for Marketing Managers", *Journal of Marketing* 43, 9-26.

Malmborg, C. (1996), "A genetic algorithm for service level based vehicle scheduling", *European Journal of Operational Research* 93/1, 121-134.

McBride, R. and Zufryden, F. (1988), "An Integer Programming Approach to the Optimal Product Line Selection Problem", *Marketing Science* 7, 126-140.

Mitchell, M. (1996), *An Introduction to Genetic Algorithms*, MA: MIT Press, Cambridge.

140

Nair, S., Thakur, L., and Wen, K. (1995), "Near Optimal Solutions for Product Line Design and Selection: Beam Search Heuristics", *Management Science* 41, 767-785.

Nissen, V. (1995), "An Overview of Evolutionary Algorithms in Management Applications", in: Biethahn, J. and Nissen V. (Ed.), *Evolutionaly Algorithms in Managemenent Applications*, Springer Verlag, Berlin, 43-97.

Quelch, J. and Kenny, D. (1994), "Extend Profits, Not Product Lines", *Harvard Business Review*, 75/5, 153-160.

Rackhan, N. (1998), "From Experience: Why Bad Things Happen to Good New Products", *Journal of Product Innovation Management* 15/3, 201-207.

Sprague, R. (1989), 'A framework for the development of Decision Support Systems', in: Sprague, R. and Watson, H. (Ed.), *Decision Support Systems. Putting Theory into Practice*, Prentice-Hall, USA, 9-35.

Talvinen, J. (1995), "Information systems in marketing. Identifying opportunities for new applications", *European Journal of Marketing* 29, 8-26.

Wierenga, B., Ophuis, P., Huizingh, E., and Campen, P. (1994), "Hierarchical scaling of marketing decision support systems", *Decision Support Systems* 12, North-Holland.

5. FINANCE AND BANKING

PORTFOLIO PERFORMANCE MEASURES: A BRIEF SURVEY AND HYPOTHESIS TESTING

G.L. Ghai, T.E. Pactwa, A.J. Prakash

Florida International University
College of Business Administartion
Finance Department
Miami, FL 33199, USA

Abstract:
In this paper, we explore the theoretical aspects of portfolio performance measures. First, we survey the available portfolio performance evaluation techniques, starting with the two-parameter mean-variance based measures. Then, we look at the multi-factor APT-based measures. This leads us into the higher-moments based measures, which incorporate asymmetrical returns and investors' preference for skewness. We also include some nonparametric techniques, which are popular in the evaluation of mutual funds. Next, we define the reward-to-variability ratio. As others have reported, the reward-to-variability ratio computed on the basis of sample data is not an unbiased estimator. In addition, intervaling may bias the value of the estimator. So, we obtain an exact probability distribution for one of the performance measures. This exact probability distribution should help in obtaining a better estimator of the reward-to-variability statistic and in hypothesis testing pertaining to the portfolio performance measures.

Key words:
Performance, Mutual funds, Reward-to-variability statistic, Parametric, nonparametric

INTRODUCTION

Upon endeavoring in this research, we set our sights on two main goals. First of all, we wanted to survey the current literature for the theoretical (and not empirical) aspects of various portfolio performance measures. We start with the mean-variance based measures, move to the APT-based measures, and then on to those based on higher-moments. We also discuss some nonparametric techniques, which are popular in measuring the performance of mutual funds. The second, and main, purpose of this research is to obtain an exact probability distribution for one of these performance measures. This will facilitate in obtaining the exact tests of the statistical hypotheses concerning the performance of portfolios.

143

S.H. Zanakis et al. (eds.), Decision Making: Recent Developments and Worldwide Applications, 143–155.

Since the seminal work of Sharpe (1966), the portfolio performance measure, defined as the ratio of asset's excess return over the risk-free rate of return to its standard deviation, has been used either to rank portfolios [Sharpe (1966), Smith and Tito (1969), Jensen (1968), *etc.*] or to measure whether the performance of a particular portfolio is better than the market [Jensen (1968), Ang and Chua (1979)]. In the former case, the reward-to-variability ratios are computed for various portfolios and then ranked according to the magnitude of the computed value with the highest value being considered the best. In the latter case, either the obtained reward-to-variability ratio is evaluated against a benchmark (market) reward-to-variability ratio defined as the ratio of the excess market rate of return to the standard deviation of the market's rate of return (like Ang and Chua), or Jensen's differential return measure. Usually, the Student's *t*-test is used to infer whether a particular portfolio has performed "better" than the market.

There is nothing wrong if the purpose of the performance index is to just rank the performance of various portfolios.[1] But to use this index to ascertain whether the portfolio's performance is better than the market may not be a statistically correct procedure.[2] In fact, there are two problems. First, as Miller and Gehr (1978) report, the reward-to-variability ratio computed on the basis of sample data is not an unbiased estimator of the population counterpart. Second, Jobson and Korkie (1981) show that intervaling may also bias the value of the estimator. Therefore, knowledge of the exact probability distribution may help us in obtaining a better estimator of the reward-to-variability distribution. Jobson and Korkie (1981) made the first attempt in obtaining the probability distribution of the performance index. But their result is asymptotic, and thus, may be only valid for large samples.

In this paper, we derive the exact probability distribution of Sharpe's measure, and we suggest areas of future research. In this first section, we survey the available portfolio performance measures. In the next section, we define the reward-to-variability ratio and state the hypotheses to be tested. Following that, we obtain the exact probability distribution of the reward-to-variability ratio. The next section explores the special conditions under which the reward-to-variability ratio will admit to some known conventional probability distributions, and provides the tests of statistical hypotheses concerning the performance of portfolios. The final section provides concluding remarks.

Mean-Variance Based Measures

The evaluation of the performance of professionally managed investment portfolios has been a major empirical topic in the literature. Since the pioneering works in portfolio theory of Markowitz (1952), Sharpe (1964) and Lintner (1965), investment performance has usually been evaluated utilizing the performance measures based on the one parameter, two-moment CAPM. These mean-variance composite performance measures include Treynor's (1965) reward-to-volatility index, Sharpe's (1966) reward-to-variability index, and Jensen's (1968)

---

[1] Though Roll (1978) argues that ambiguities result when the underlying generating process is taken as the market model, Peterson and Rice (1980) empirically show that ambiguities are not statistically significant when Sharpe's or Jensen's performance measures are used to rank portfolios.

[2] Note that this procedure may not be erroneous if the comparisons are made exclusively on an ad-hoc basis. However, to infer that performance is statistically significant may not be appropriate.

alpha measure. Friend and Blume (1970) describe each of these tests in detail. They report what might be the first pricing anomaly in the literature. Unexplained by the CAPM, Jensen's alpha (which is supposedly a "risk-adjusted" performance measure) is strongly inversely related to the level of beta risk. They criticize the CAPM single parameter measure, as risk-adjusted performance is dependent upon risk. They advise particular care especially when appraising individual portfolios, or when the average risk of these portfolios differs from that of the market as a whole. Most of the early evidence derived from the two parameter CAPM performance tests of Sharpe, Treynor, and Jensen suggests that (1) the rankings are similar whichever test is used [Smith and Tito (1969); Ward and Saunders (1976)]; (2) funds generally do not outperform a market index, and (3) past performance of funds is not generally a good indicator of future likely performance.

Utilizing Sharpe's, Treynor's and Jensen's methods, Ang and Chua (1979) evaluate the performance of mutual funds in the U.S. during the years 1955 to 1974. Since the composite measures have been found to exhibit systematic biases, Ang and Chua examined if the biases could be caused by the deficiency of not considering asymmetry of return distributions and the inability to specify the correct holding period. Results showed that the performance measurements that also considered the asymmetry of return distributions, in addition to the mean and variance, were better. They observed that the systematic biases could be removed through changing the holding period length for their proposed excess return index and reward-to-semivariance index, while they could not be removed for the mean-variance composite measures.

To explicitly recognize that not all assets are in equilibrium: $[E(\tilde{R}_m) - R_f] = \eta_i + \beta_i [E(\tilde{R}_m) - R_f]$. For Jensen's measure, η_i is a measure of disequilibrium. If $\eta_i = 0$, the portfolio or asset is in equilibrium. If $\eta_i > 0$, the expected return is larger than one would anticipate on the basis of the equilibrium relationship (an undervalued security). If $\eta_i < 0$, the security is overvalued.

For Treynor's, $[E(R_i) - R_f]/\beta_i = \{\eta_i/\beta_i\} + [E(R_m) - R_f]$. The left-hand side of the above equality is Treynor's measure. It is simply a translation of Jensen's measure divided by the systematic risk. In Sharpe's measure, by replacing β_i by its definition and noting that market line theory implies that the correlation between the expected return on an asset and the expected return on the market, one obtains $[E(R_i) - R_f]/\sigma(R_i) = \eta_i/\sigma(R_i) + [E(R_m) - R_f]/\sigma(R_m)$. The left-hand side is Sharpe's measure. It is simply a translation of Jensen's measure divided by the standard deviation of return. An important distinction is that Sharpe's measure can only be applied to "efficient" portfolios, whereas Jensen's and Treynor's measures can be used for any portfolio as well as individual securities.

Cumby and Glen (1990) utilize the Jensen measure to evaluate the performance of a sample of fifteen U.S.-based, internationally diversified mutual funds between 1982 and 1988. They point out that the Jensen measure is subject to some limitations, mainly errors in performance measures may arise if the fund manager possesses and utilizes superior timing information. Cumby and Glen find that the hypothesis that the Jensen measures are jointly zero is rejected at significance levels just above five percent. They state that this rejection is probably due to the preponderance of negative estimates. While positive Jensen measures are not reliable evidence of superior performance, negative Jensen measures are reliable that the manager of the fund does not provide superior performance [from Dybvig and Ross (1985)]. The authors attempt to explain why so many of the Jensen measures are negative. They put forth the possibility that the negative Jensen measures arise due to market timing ability on the part of the fund managers. Unlike the Jensen measure, the positive period weighting measure proposed by Grinblatt and Titman (1989) will provide a valid estimate when the fund manager is a market timer. So, Cumby and Glen employ this method.

Grinblatt and Titman examine a class of performance measures that includes the Jensen measure and show that certain members of the class do not suffer from the superior timing problems that arise with the Jensen measure (namely, a negative measure). This is because there is no requirement that the composition of the manager portfolio be observed. The class of measures, called period weighting measures, is defined for a sample of T observations by $\alpha = \Sigma^T_{t=1} w_t r_{pt}$, $\Sigma^T_{t=1} w_t = 1$, $\Sigma^T_{t=1} w_t r_{et} = 0$, where the weights, w_t, are functions of the return on the benchmark portfolio, and r_{pt} is the excess return on the portfolio which is to be evaluated. This portfolio is chosen from N assets with excess returns $r_{jt}, j = 1, ..., N$. In addition, r_{et} is the excess return on the portfolio that, from the view of the uninformed investor, is mean-variance efficient within the set of N tradable risky assets and whose orthogonal portfolio is used to compute excess returns. Their main result is that, if $w_t > 0$ for all t, the performance measure, denoted α^* when $w_t > 0$, converges in probability to zero for an uninformed investor and to a positive number for an investor with selectivity information and no timing information, or selectivity information and independently distributed timing information.

Cumby and Glen find that the period weighting measures are remarkably similar to the Jensen measures, both in magnitude and statistical significance. In no instance did a fund with a negative Jensen measure have a period weighting measure of the opposite sign. This suggests that negative Jensen measures are not due to the market timing ability of fund managers. Thus, they find no evidence that the funds, either individually, or as a whole, provide investors with performance that surpasses that of a broad international equity index over 1982 to 1988. Cumby and Glen also examined the performance of the funds to the Morgan Stanley index for the U.S. and find some evidence that the funds out perform the U.S. index. When compared to the results of other tests, it appeared to be that the performance relative to the U.S. index is most likely due to the benefits of international diversification, rather than superior performance by fund managers.

APT-Based Measures

Peasnell, Skerratt and Taylor (1979) suggested that Jensen's measure of portfolio performance, though invalid in terms of the Sharpe-Lintner-Black CAPM, could be justified within the framework of Ross's APT. Morris and Pope (1981) utilized this approach and calculated rankings on a subset of Jensen's original population of mutual funds under various assumptions. Their results showed that the performance rankings were altered by changes in the basis of calculating returns, the betas, and the risk-free rate of interest. As a result, it was concluded that the Jensen measure is an inadequate indicator, on its own, of managerial performance. Connor and Korajczyk (1986) also show that, in their model, the Jensen coefficient is an appropriate indicator of superior performance. They develop performance measures in an APT framework by extending Connor's (1984) equilibrium version of the APT to include a small set of investors with superior information.

Chang and Lewellen (1985) provide a one-parameter, risk-adjusted performance appraisal methodology in the multi-factor APT framework. They include statistical procedures designed to provide a set of efficient estimates of the factor portfolios that capture the systematic components of asset returns and, thereby, their risk premia. This allows separating the non-systematic components that may imply superior or inferior managed portfolio security selection performance. Their main results for a sample of mutual funds over the period 1971-1979 are, first, that more than one factor appears to have been present during the period as a systematic influence on securities' returns, and, second that the APT approach explains the observed pattern of such returns somewhat better. They conclude that mutual funds collectively have not attained superior performance.

Several researchers, most notably Levhari and Levy (1977), Ang and Chua (1979) and Levy (1981), have shown that in testing the performance measures of a security or portfolio using the CAPM, the arbitrarily chosen investment horizon affects the resultant estimates. Parhizgari, Dandapani and Prakash (1993) extend the prior research on the investment horizon to the APT. They show that, due to serial correlation, the estimates obtained for the multi-index return generating process and the arbitrage pricing model are interval dependent.

Higher-Moments Based Measures

Arditti (1967, 1971 and 1975), Bower and Wippern (1969), and Jean (1971 and 1973) all argue that two-moment performance measures may not be adequate if return distributions are asymmetrical and investors value skewness. In an attempt to alleviate the problems that may be associated with nonsymmetric rates of return, several researchers have developed other performance measures based on higher moments. For example, Ang and Chua (1979) constructed an excess return index using the three-moment CAPM developed by Kraus and Litzenberger (1976). This index incorporates investors' preference for positive skewness of returns. Prakash and Bear (1986) develop a composite performance measure incorporating skewness. In the absence of skewness, the Prakash and Bear measure reduces to the Treynor reward-to-volatility index.

Employing the above Prakash and Bear technique to evaluate the performance of 27 internationally diversified mutual funds, Stephens and Proffitt (1991) point out that a higher moment performance measure appears to be the appropriate measure for evaluating international mutual fund portfolios. This is because the rates of return distributions on these types of assets are not symmetrical. Utilizing Rubinstein's (1973) n-parameter pricing model, Stephens and Proffitt generalize the Prakash and Bear performance measure to account for any number of moments. In the absence of moments beyond the third, the Stephens and Proffitt measure reduces to the Prakash and Bear measure, while reducing to the Treynor measure in the two moment case.

Chunhachinda, Dandapani, Hamid and Prakash (1994) evaluate the performance of fourteen international stock markets utilizing two types of performance measures: first, the two moment measures of Treynor (1965) and Sharpe (1966) and second, the higher moment measures of Prakash and Bear (1986) and Stephens and Proffitt (1991). They derive the following relations: Treynor: $(\bar{R}_j - R_f)/\bar{z}_{j2}$; Sharpe: $(\bar{R}_j - R_f)/\sigma_j$; Prakash and Bear: $(\bar{R}_j -$

$R_f)/(\mu_1 \bar{z}_{j2} + \bar{z}_{j3})$; Stephens and Proffitt: $(\bar{R}_j - R_f)/(\mu_2 \bar{z}_{j2} + \mu_3 \bar{z}_{j3} + \bar{z}_{j4})$; where $\bar{R}_j = 1/N \Sigma^N_{t=1}$ R_{jt}; $\bar{z}_{ji} = 1/N \Sigma^N_{t=1} z_{jt}$; z_{jl} = covariance (for I=2), coskewness (for I=3), and cokurtosis (for I=4); μ_1 = (coskewness parameter) ÷ (covariance parameter); μ_2 = (cokurtosis parameter) ÷ (covariance parameter); and μ_3 = (cokurtosis parameter) ÷ (coskewness parameter).

Their results show statistically significant coefficients for coskewness and cokurtosis for both weekly and monthly rates of return. Thus, they also agree that an equilibrium pricing model seems to be more appropriate for evaluating the performance of international stock markets. While comparing the measures, the authors find that the rankings of seven stock markets change when higher moments are used. Their evidence suggests that the measures based on higher moments rank the portfolios closer than those based on two moments in the presence of asymmetric return distributions. Chunhachinda *et alia* also noted that the effect of intervaling was more pronounced in the higher moments-based performance measures -- correlation coefficients between rankings based on weekly and monthly data were lower for these types of tests than for Sharpe's and Treynor's measures.

Nonparametric Based Measures

Many traditional evaluation techniques generally measure performance as deviations of returns on actively managed funds from those predicted by some parametric asset pricing model employed. Mutual fund performance is positive, zero, or negative depending on whether their returns are greater, equal to, or less than, the risk-adjusted return determined by a specific parametric model used. Thus, the accuracy of performance measurement relies on the empirical plausibility of that parametric model employed. Utilizing Hansen and Jagannathan (1991), Chen and Knez (1994) developed a nonparametric approach to performance measurement. The approach basically stems from valuation functionals in which asset prices can be characterized by a minimum-variance stochastic discount factor (or pricing kernel), which is a projection of any admissible pricing kernel on the payoff space and is a linear combination of all payoffs. However, the precision of their performance measures depends on the discount factor proxy.

Theoretically, there always exists a stochastic discount factor that is linear function of returns on all assets and that correctly prices all assets. But, it is pragmatically impossible to compute such a discount factor. As long as a proxy is used in place of a true discount factor, there is bound to be some pricing error. Utilizing specification error-based measures, He, Ng and Zhang (1996) developed a new nonparametric approach that takes into account that the absolute pricing error associated with a discount factor proxy, or with an inefficient benchmark, is strictly positive. They claim that their approach imposes little structure or sensitivity to a particular model parameterization, and more importantly, it can detect superiorly informed investors.

THE REWARD-TO-VARIABILITY RATIO

Sharpe's reward-to-variability index, V_i for the ith asset is defined as $V_i = [\bar{R}_i - R_f]/s_i$ [EQ.(1)], where $\bar{R}_i$ and s_i are the mean and the standard deviation, respectively, of the rate of return of the ith asset. The reward-to-variability ratio is used either to rank a set of portfolios [Sharpe (1966), for example] or to determine whether a particular portfolio has "beaten the market" [e.g., Ang and Chua (1979)]. After computation of the ratio V_i, the usual null hypothesis that is tested is H_0: $v_i = v$ versus H_1: $v_i > v$ [EQ.(2)], where v is the benchmark index usually computed as $(\bar{R}_m - R_f)/\sigma_m$ where $\bar{R}_m$ and σ_m are, respectively, the population mean and standard deviation of the market's rates of return and v_i is the unknown population reward-to-variability ratio. The statistics used to test this null hypothesis are either the Student's t-statistic; or in the case of large samples, the standard normal z-statistic.[3]

Note, however, that the Student's t-statistic is meant to test null hypotheses about the means from normal populations. Specifically, the Student's t-statistic computed to test the null hypothesis H_0: $\mu = \mu_0$ is given by $t = (\bar{X} - \mu_0)/[SE(\bar{X} - \mu_0)]$ [EQ.(3)], where $\bar{X}$ is the sample mean. If the null hypothesis is true, then t will be distributed as a Student's t-distribution, with the appropriate degrees of freedom. Comparing (1) and (2), we can recognize two problems. First, it is clear that the Student's t-test is valid for this hypothesis purporting to the mean; but not the ratio of the mean to the standard deviation of observations, unless the sample reward-to-variability ratio V_i in the t-statistic, i.e., $t = (V_i - v)/[SE(V_i)]$ [EQ. (3′)] is normally distributed, with mean v. Second, in expression (3), μ_0 is the expectation, or the mean of $\bar{X}$; whereas in the numerator of (3′), v is the market reward-to-variability ratio, and not the expectation of V_i. In view of this, the main purpose of the paper is twofold. First, we will obtain the exact probability distribution of V_i. If this probability distribution is a mixture of probability distributions and does not readily admit to any known conventional probability distributions, then we will explore the conditions under which the null hypothesis can be tested using known statistical tests.

THE EXACT PROBABILITY DISTRIBUTION OF REWARD-TO-VARIABILITY RATIO

The denominator in expression (1) is $SD(R_i)$ and not $SD(\bar{R}_i)$. We can rewrite (1) as $\sqrt{n} \, V_i = [\bar{R}_i - R_f]/[s_i \sqrt{n}] = [\bar{R}_i - R_f]/[SD(\bar{R}_i)]$ [EQ.(4)]. If the numerator in (4) had been $[\bar{R}_i - E(\bar{R}_i)]$ instead of $[\bar{R}_i - R_f]$ $\sqrt{n} \, V_i$ would have had a Student's t-distribution with $(n - 1)$ degrees of freedom. In the absence of this, we obtain the exact sampling distribution of V_i as follows. We first assume that the parent population is normal and $\bar{R}_i$ and s_i are the sample mean and standard deviation, computed as $\bar{R}_i = \Sigma^n_{t=1} R_{it}/n$ and $s_i = [1/(n-1)] \Sigma^n_{t=1}(R_{it} - \bar{R}_i)^2]^{\frac{1}{2}}$ for a sample of size n. Since s_i, the standard deviation, cannot be zero, we assume its lower bound to be s_L;

---

[3] See Jobson and Korkie (1981).

i.e., s_L, $s_i < \infty$. According to Kendall and Stuart (1963), the sampling distribution of s_i^2 is $dF(s_i^2) = v_i^{(n-1)/2}/\Gamma[(n-1)/2] \cdot e^{-v_i s_i^2} \cdot (s_i^2)^{2(n-3)} d(s_i^2)$; $0 < s_i^2 < \infty$; where $v_i = (n-1)/(2\sigma_i^2)$, and σ_i^2 is the variance of R_i. Therefore, the sampling distribution of s_i will be $dF(s_i) = [2(v_i)^{(n-1)/2}]/\{\Gamma[(n-1)/2]\} \cdot e^{-v_i s_i^2} \cdot s_i^{n-2} ds_i$; $0 < s_i < \infty$ [EQ.(5)].

Since, in our case, we have assumed the lower bound to be s_L, we replace s_i by $(s_i - s_L)$ and get the sampling distribution of s_i as $dF(s_i) = [2(v_i)^{(n-1)/2}]/\{\Gamma[(n-1)/2]\} \cdot e^{-v_i(s_i-s_L)^2} \cdot (s_i - s_L)^{n-2} ds_i$; $0 < s_L s_i < \infty$; [EQ.(6)]. Since the population is normal, the sampling distribution of $\bar{R}_i$ will be $dF(\bar{R}_i) = 1/[\theta_i \sqrt{2\Pi}] \cdot e^{-1/2(\bar{R}_i - \mu_i)^2/\theta_i^2} \cdot d\bar{R}_i$; $-\infty < \bar{R}_i < \infty$ [EQ.(7)], where $\theta_i^2 = V(\bar{R}_i) = V(R_i)/n$ and $\mu_i = E(\bar{R}_i)$. Now letting $V_i = \bar{r}_i/s_i$, where $\bar{r}_i = \bar{R}_i - R_f$, and $U_i = s_i$. It can be easily shown (see Appendix A) that the probability density function of V_i, say $h(V_i)$, is

$$h(V_i) = \frac{v_i^{1/2(n-1)} \exp\{-\frac{1}{2}\frac{\xi_i^2}{\theta_i^2}\}}{\theta_i \sqrt{2}\,\Gamma(\frac{n-1}{2})\Gamma(1/2)} \cdot \sum_{j=0}^{\infty} [\frac{V_i \xi_i}{\theta_i^2}]^j \frac{1}{j!}\{\frac{\Gamma(\frac{n+j}{2})}{(v_i + \frac{V_i^2}{2\theta_i^2})^{\frac{n+j}{2}}} + S_L \frac{\Gamma(\frac{n-1+j}{2})}{(v_i + \frac{V_i^2}{2\theta_i^2})^{\frac{n-1+j}{2}}}\}$$

[(EQ.8)] where $\xi_i = m_i - s_L V_i$ and $m_i = E(\bar{r}_i) = \mu_i - R_f$. It is clear from (8) that the exact probability distribution of V_i, Sharpe's reward-to-variability ratio, is a complex mixture of beta distributions of the second kind.

CONDITIONS UNDER WHICH V_i WILL ADMIT TO A KNOWN PROBABILITY DISTRIBUTION

We defined $\xi_i = m_i - s_L V_i$. Assume that $m_i = 0$ and $s_L = 0$, so that $\xi_i = 0$. If we substitute $\xi_i = 0$ in (8), all of the terms except for $j = 0$ vanish, and we are left with

$$h(V_i) = \frac{1}{\theta_i \sqrt{2\pi}\,\Gamma(\frac{n-1}{2})} \cdot \frac{\Gamma(\frac{n}{2})}{(v_i + \frac{V_i^2}{2\theta_i^2})^{\frac{n}{2}}} = \frac{1}{\sqrt{2\pi\theta_i^2}\,\Gamma(\frac{n-1}{2})} \cdot \frac{\Gamma(\frac{n}{2})}{(v_i)^{1/2}(1 + \frac{V_i^2}{2v_i\theta_i^2})^{\frac{n}{2}}}$$

$$= \frac{1}{\sqrt{2v_i\pi\theta_i^2}\,\Gamma(\frac{n-1}{2})} \cdot \frac{\Gamma(\frac{n}{2})}{(1 + \frac{V_i^2}{2v_i\theta_i^2})^{\frac{n}{2}}} \tag{9}$$

But, since $v_i = (n-1)/(2\sigma_i^2)$ and $\theta_i^2 = \sigma_i^2/n$, we have $2v_i\theta_i^2 = 2(n-1)/(2\sigma_i^2) \cdot (\sigma_i/n) = (n-1)/n$ [Eq.(10)]. Substituting (10) into expression (9), we have

$$h(V_i) = \frac{1}{\sqrt{\frac{(n-1)\pi}{n}} \; \Gamma(\frac{n-1}{2})} \cdot \frac{\Gamma(\frac{n}{2})}{(1+\frac{nV_i^2}{n-1})^{\frac{n}{2}}} = \frac{1}{\sqrt{\frac{n-1}{n}} \; \Gamma(\frac{1}{2})\Gamma(\frac{n-1}{2})} \cdot \frac{\Gamma(\frac{n}{2})}{(1+\frac{nV_i^2}{n-1})^{\frac{n}{2}}}$$

$$= \frac{1}{\sqrt{\frac{n-1}{n}} \cdot \beta(\frac{1}{2},\frac{n-1}{2})} \cdot \frac{\Gamma(\frac{n}{2})}{(1+\frac{nV_i^2}{n-1})^{\frac{n}{2}}} \tag{11}$$

From (11), we can easily derive the density function of the random variable $\sqrt{n}\, V_i$, which is the density function of a Student's t-distribution with $(n-1)$ degrees of freedom, and will approach a z-distribution for large n.

CONCLUSION AND AREAS OF FUTURE RESEARCH

In this analytic paper, we demonstrated that Sharpe's reward-to-variability ratio will admit to a standard normal distribution under an extremely stringent condition. That is, in $\xi_i = m_i - s_L V_i$, m_i and s_L are both zero, which is unlikely to be satisfied in practical applications. Our next effort will be to explore and compute the theoretical values of (8), against which an exact test to test the significance of Sharpe's reward-to-variability ratio may be obtained. Specifically, after calculating the exact probability distribution of Treynor's performance measure, the null hypothesis to be tested would be $H_{01}: v_1 = v_2 = v_3 = ... = v_p$ against H_{11}: at least one pair is not equal, where v_i ($i = 1, 2, ..., p$) is the performance measure (either Sharpe's or Treynor's) of the ith portfolio. It is obvious from the exact probability distribution of Sharpe's measure that the probability distributions of the other performance measures will contain very complicated mathematical expressions; that is, if they can be obtained at all. This is an area for future research.

REFERENCES

Ang, J.S., and J.H. Chua (1979), "Composite Measures for the Evaluation of Investment Performance", *Journal of Financial and Quantitative Analysis*, 14/2, 361-384.

Arditti, F.D. (1967), "Risk and the Required Return on Equity", *The Journal of Finance*, 22/1, 19-36.

_____. (1971), "Another Look at Mutual Fund Performance", *Journal of Financial and Quantitative Analysis*, 6/3, 909-912.

_____. (1975), "Skewness and Investors' Decisions: A Reply", *Journal of Financial and Quantitative Analysis*, 10/1, 173-176.

Bower, R.S., and R. F. Wippern (1969)",Risk-Return Measurement in Portfolio Selection and Performance Appraisal Models: Progress Report", *Journal of Financial and Quantitative Analysis*, 4/4, 417-447.

Chang, E.C., and W.G. Lewellen (1985), "An Arbitrage Pricing Approach to Evaluating Mutual Fund Performance", *The Journal of Financial Research*, 8/1, 15-30.

152

Chen, Z., and P.J. Knez (1994), "Foundation for a Class of Factor Pricing Models", *Mathematical Finance*, 4/2, 121-141.

Chunhachinda, P., K. Dandapani, S. Hamid, and A.J. Prakash (1994), "Efficacy of Portfolio Performance Measures: An Evaluation", *Quarterly Journal of Business and Economics*, 33/4, 74-87.

Connor, G. (1984), "A Unified Beta Pricing Theory", *Journal of Economic Theory*, 34, 13-34.

Connor, G., and R.A. Korajczyk (1986), "Performance Measurement with the Arbitrage Pricing Theory: A New Framework for Analysis", *Journal of Financial Economics*, 15/3, 373-394.

Cumby, R.E., and J.D. Glen (1990), "Evaluating the Performance of International Mutual Funds", *The Journal of Finance*, 45/2, 497-521.

Dybvig, P.H., and S.A. Ross (1985), "The Analytics of Performance Measurement Using a Security Market Line", *The Journal of Finance*, 40/2, 401-416.

Friend, I., and M. Blume (1970), "Measurement of Portfolio Performance Under Uncertainty", *The American Economic Review*, 60, 561-575.

Grinblatt, M., and S. Titman (1989), "Portfolio Performance Evaluation: Old Issues and New Insights", *Review of Financial Studies*, 2/3, 393-421.

Hansen, L.P., and R. Jagannathan (1991), "Implications of Security Market Data for Models of Dynamic Economies", *Journal of Political Economy*, 99/2, 225-262.

He, J., L. Ng, and C. Zhang (1996), "Asset Pricing Specification Errors and Performance Evaluation", Manuscript; Financial Management Association's Competitive Paper Award - Investments.

Jean, W. H. (1971), "The Extension of Portfolio Analysis to Three or More Parameters", *Journal of Financial and Quantitative Analysis*, 6/1, 505-515.

_____. (1973), "More on Multidimensional Portfolio Pricing", *Journal of Financial and Quantitative Analysis*, 8/3, 475-490.

Jensen, M. C. (1968), "The Performance of Mutual Funds in the Period 1945-1964", *The Journal of Finance*, 23/2, 389-416.

Jobson, J.D., and B. M. Korkie (1981), "Performance Hypothesis Testing with the Sharpe and Treynor Measures", *The Journal of Finance*, 36/4, 889-908.

Kendall, M.G., and A. Stuart (1963), *The Advanced Theory of Statistics*, Charles Griffin and Company Ltd., London.

Kraus, A., and R.H. Litzenberger (1976), "Skewness Preference and the Valuation of Risk Assets", *The Journal of Finance*, 31/4, 1085-1100.

Levhari, D., and H. Levy (1977), "The Capital Asset Pricing Model and the Investment Horizon", *Review of Economics and Statistics*, 59/1, 92-104.

Levy, H. (1981), "The CAPM and the Investment Horizon", *Journal of Portfolio Management*, 7/2, 32-40.

Lintner, J. (1965), "The Valuation of Risk Assets and the Selection of Risky Investments in Stock Portfolios and Capital Budgets", *Review of Economics and Statistics*, 47, 13-37.

Markowitz, H. (1952), "Portfolio Selection", *The Journal of Finance*, 7/1, 77-91.

Miller, R.E., and A.K. Gehr (1978), "Sample Size Bias and Sharpe's Performance Measure: A Note", *Journal of Financial and Quantitative Analysis*, 13/5, 943-946.

Morris, R.C., and P.F. Pope (1981), "The Jensen Measure of Portfolio Performance in an Arbitrage Pricing Theory Context", *Journal of Business Finance & Accounting*, 8/2, 203-220.

Parhizgari, A.M., K. Dandapani, and A.J. Prakash (1993), "Arbitrage Pricing Theory and the Investment Horizon", *Journal of Business Finance & Accounting*, 20/1, 27-40.

Peasnell, K.V., L.C.L. Skerratt, and P.A. Taylor (1979), "An Arbitrage Rationale for Tests of Mutual Fund Performance", *Journal of Business Finance and Accounting*, 6/3, 373-400.

Peterson, D., and M.L. Rice (1980), "A Note on the Ambiguity in Portfolio Performance Measures", *The Journal of Finance*, 35/5, 1251-1256.

Prakash, A.J., and R.M. Bear (1986), "A Simplifying Performance Measure Recognizing Skewness", *The Financial Review*, 21/1, 135-144.

Roll, R. (1978), "Ambiguity when Performance Is Measured by the Securities Market Line", *The Journal of Finance*, 33/4, 1051-1069.

Rubinstein, M.E. (1973), "The Fundamental Theorem of Parameter-Preference Security Valuation", *Journal of Financial and Quantitative Analysis*, 8/1, 61-69.

Sharpe, W.F. (1964), "Capital Asset Prices: A Theory of Market Equilibrium under Conditions of Risk", *The Journal of Finance*, 19/3, 425-442.

_____. (1966), "Mutual Fund Performance", *Journal of Business*, 39/1, Part II, 119-138.

Smith, K.V., and D.A. Tito (1969), "Risk-Return Measures of Ex Post Portfolio Performance", *Journal of Financial and Quantitative Analysis*, 4/4, 449-471.

Stephens, A., and D. Proffitt (1991), "Performance Measurement When Return Distributions Are Nonsymmetric", *Quarterly Journal of Business and Economics*, 30, 23-41.

Treynor, J.L. (1965), "How to Rate Management of Investment Funds", *Harvard Business Review*, 43, 63-75.

Ward, C.W.R, and A. Saunders (1976), "U.K. Unit Trust Performance 1964-74", *Journal of Business Finance & Accounting*, 3/4, 83-100.

154

Appendix A. Derivation of Probability Density of V_i

Let $V_i = \overline{r_i} / s_i$, where $\overline{r_i} = \overline{R_i} - R_f$ and $U_i = s_i$, so that $\overline{r_i} = U_i V_i$ and $s_i = U_i$. Since in a normal population $\overline{r_i}$ and s_i are independently distributed, their joint probability differential by the compound probability theorem is given as $dG(\overline{r_i}, s_i) = g_1(\overline{r_i}) g_2(s_i) d\overline{r_i} ds_i$. Hence, the joint probability distribution of V_i and s_i will be $dF(V_i, U_i) = f(V_i, U_i) dV_i dU_i = g_1(V_i, U_i) g_2(U_i) J dV_i dU_i$ [EQ.(1A)] where J is the Jacobian of the transformation and equals U_i.

To obtain the probability density of V_i, we integrate out $U_i (= s_i)$ from expression (1A).

That is, $h(V_i) = \displaystyle\int_{s_L}^{\infty} g_1(V_i, U_i) g_2(U_i) J dU_i$

$$= \frac{K}{\theta_i \sqrt{2\pi}} \int_{s_L}^{\infty} e^{\frac{1}{2\theta_i^2}(V_i U_i - m_i)^2} \bullet e^{-v_i(U_i - s_L)^2} (U_i - s_L)^{(n-1)-1} U_i dU_i \qquad (2A)$$

where $K = [2v_i^{(n-1)/2}] / \{\Gamma[(n-1)/2]\}$ from (6). Substituting $y_i = U_i - s_L$ in (2A), we get

$$h(V_i) = \left[K / \left(\theta_i \sqrt{2\pi}\right)\right] \int_0^{\infty} e^{\frac{1}{2\theta_i^2}(V_i y_i - \xi_i)^2} \bullet e^{-v_i y_i^2} y_i^{n-2}(y_i + s_L) d y_i$$

$$= \left[K / \left(\theta_i \sqrt{2\pi}\right)\right][I(n-1) + s_L I(n-2)] \qquad (3A)$$

where

$$I(n-1) = \int_0^{\infty} e^{-\frac{1}{2\theta_i^2}(V_i y_i - \xi_i)^2} \bullet e^{-v_i y_i^2} \bullet y_i^{n-1} dy_i$$

and similarly $I(n-2)$; and $\xi_i = m_i - s_L V_i = (\mu_i - R_f) - s_L V_i$. Now, consider $I(n-1)$

$$I(n-1) = \int_0^{\infty} e^{-\frac{1}{2\theta_i^2}(V_i^2 y_i^2 - 2V_i y_i \xi_i + \xi_i^2)} \bullet e^{-v_i y_i^2} \bullet y_i^{n-1} dy_i = e^{-\frac{\xi_i^2}{2\theta_i^2}} \int_0^{\infty} e^{-y_i^2(v_i + \frac{V_i^2}{2\theta_i^2})} \bullet e^{\frac{V_i y_i \xi_i}{\theta_i^2}} \bullet y_i^{n-1} dy_i$$

$$= e^{-\frac{\xi_i^2}{2\theta_i^2}} \int_0^{\infty} e^{-y_i^2(v_i + \frac{V_i^2}{2\theta_i^2})} \sum_{j=0}^{\infty} [\frac{V_i \xi_i}{\theta_i^2}]^j \frac{y_i^j}{j!} \bullet y_i^{n-1} dy_i$$

$$= e^{-\frac{\xi_i^2}{2\theta_i^2}} \sum_{j=0}^{\infty} [\frac{V_i \xi_i}{\theta_i^2}]^j \frac{1}{j!} \int_0^{\infty} e^{-y_i^2(v_i + \frac{V_i^2}{2\theta_i^2})} \bullet y_i^{n+j-1} dy_i$$

Letting $(v_i + \dfrac{V_i^2}{2\theta_i^2}) y_i^2 = x_i$, so that $y_i = [x_i(v_i + \dfrac{V_i^2}{2\theta_i^2})^{-1}]^{1/2}$, we have

$$I(n-1) = e^{-\frac{\xi_i^2}{2\theta_i^2}} \sum_{j=0}^{\infty} [\frac{V_i \xi_i}{\theta_i^2}]^j \bullet \frac{1}{j!} \frac{\Gamma(\frac{n+j}{2})}{2[v_i + V_i^2/(2\theta_i^2)]^{\frac{n+j}{2}}} \qquad (4A)$$

A similar expression can be obtained for $I(n-2)$ by substituting $(n-2)$ for $(n-1)$ in (4A). Thus, substituting for $I(n-1)$ and $I(n-2)$ in (3A), expression (8) can be easily obtained.

A SYSTEM DYNAMICS MODEL OF STOCK PRICE MOVEMENTS

P.L. Kunsch[1], M. Theys[2], A. Chevalier[3], J.-P. Iacopetta[4]

[1] Universities of Brussels
Avenue A. Buyl BE-1050 Brussels, Belgium

[2] SEMA Group
Rue de Stalle 96 BE-1180, Brussels, Belgium

[3] Ecole Supérieure de Commerce de Paris
79 Avenue de la République
FR-75543 Paris Cedex 11, France

[4] CNP, Rue de la Blanche Borne 12,
BE-6280 Loverval, Belgium

Abstract: Stock prices are known to exhibit strongly non-linear behaviours, e.g. apparent random volatility, bullish or bearish trends, crashes etc. Using finite difference equations it is easy to generate pseudo-random behaviour patterns. The hope is that richer patterns can be generated in the continuous case using System Dynamics (SD). In the paper we test this possibility. Three basic behavioural attitudes are described by introducing three corresponding families of investors. α-investors are rational fundamentalists striving to stabilise the stock price toward a goal value. *Short-term βS-investors* are traders destabilising the market as they follow immediate movements and fads. *Long-term βL-investors* use arbitrage by comparing returns on stock and on risk-free assets. Although they are partly rational they provoke important departures from the fundamentals in an expanding market. It is shown that the behaviour of βL-investors is an important explicative factor of instability on the stock market.

Keywords: System Dynamics modelling, stock price, behavioural finance, fundamentalists, traders

INTRODUCTION AND PURPOSE

The pseudo-chaotic character of financial time series has been an object of fascination to economists for several decades at least. The observed fluctuations evidence a clear

S.H. Zanakis et al. (eds.), Decision Making: Recent Developments and Worldwide Applications, 157–171.
© 2000 Kluwer Academic Publishers.

departure from the traditional equilibrium models of neo-classical theory. An abundant literature is today available on this topic (see for example a compilation of papers and references in Creedy and Martin (Eds.) 1994; Heij et al. (Eds.) 1997). Many authors have explored the statistical properties of the observed non-linear and often chaotic dynamics on the financial markets. It is clear from this literature that behavioural attitudes and bounded rationality are here at work, beyond the efficient market hypothesis founded on rational expectations of the neo-classical view. The Keynesian theme of "animal spirits" has surfaced in the efforts to reconstruct a "market psychology". The present paper tries to go in the same direction for what regards the price evolution of equities on the stock market (SM).

The two next sections describe the elaboration of an original model using the System Dynamics (SD) technique to provide a causal explanation of the investor's behaviour. This point of view is rather different from most financial models based on chaos theory.

The proposed approach belongs to the class of "agent-based model" in the sense defined by Axelrod (1997). Most financial models either use inductive approach to apprehend observed price patterns, or set up deductive models to derive properties of such patterns. Agent-based modelling starts from the assumption of sets of rules to simulate agent behaviours on the market. The interaction of different rules generates data "ab initio", i.e. from first principles. In this sense the present approach is related to "popular models" of finance. However, investors as described in our model are not entirely irrational, or driven by animal spirits. Some rules also relate to the efficient market hypothesis. To our knowledge only few genuinely "ab initio" models have been developed before. The model by R.H. Day (1994) and the recent approach of "artificial stock exchange" (Arthur et al., 1997) have the suitable characteristics in our opinion. They are briefly described in the second section. These models do however not have the same transparency given by simple causal explanations of behaviour like proposed in the present paper. An additional difference of the approach is the use of continuous time by contrast with the most common discrete approach of chaos theory. The basics of our SD-modelling are presented in the third section.

In the fourth section, some typical time series generated by the model are discussed. The simulation show that the model, although it is entirely deterministic, has the capacity of generating volatile evolution patterns. For each situation, reference is made to historical patterns, using the Standard and Poor (S&P) 500 composite index. In the fifth and last section, conclusions are enounced on the usefulness of "ab initio" modelling using SD. While the predictive capabilities are limited, the essentials of a typology of characteristic price patterns are laid bare. This can help investors in staying closer to the rationality ideal or, at least, in providing a better perspective to anticipate the "market psychology". Also prospects for future development are discussed.

"AB INITIO" MODELLING OF THE STOCK MARKET (SM)

To our knowledge the first model drawing from the representation of simple investors' attitude dates back to a classical paper of the former "catastrophe theory" (Zeeman, 1977). By defining basic behaviour rules for investors, Zeeman identified an equilibrium surface of the stock return folded into a cusp catastrophe. The two control parameters of the surface were chosen to be the strength of respectively chartists and fundamentalists investing in the SM. The explicative power of this approach is in the tradition of catastrophe theory strictly limited to discontinuous changes in the evolution of prices: crashes or price upsurges. The qualitative model is still interesting for the psychology of the market. It gives a striking interpretation of common-sense rules expressed in "popular models" applicable to the SM.

R.H. Day was one of the first authors who intensively worked in non-equilibrium models inspired from chaos theory in discrete non-linear systems. Two families of investors are postulated. The first ones, called α-investors, are supposed to behave rationally. Using quantitative valuations, they are basically goal-seekers. Their quest for fundamental values ends up stabilising the market. It is why their investment profile as a function of the price has a reverse shape as it should be. On the contrary the second type, called β-investors, is in phase with the price trend. Combining the two profiles to define an iterative 1-D map of the type $p(t+1) = f[p(t)]$ one can achieve different price evolution patterns depending on the proportion of the two types of investors. Bullish or bearish patterns are generated whenever the 1-D mapping has a stable fixed point. It is a trivial result that the stability in some fixed point requires a slope in the investment profile in the plane $[p(t), p(t+1)]$ smaller than one in absolute value. Under the conditions of unstable fixed points, stable cycles or even pseudo-random behaviour, known as chaos, can be observed. This is well known in the discrete logistic equation. The conditions of chaos are fulfilled in the Day's combined profile shown in Figure 1. The proportion of β-investors is sufficient to position the profile in the right way to achieve the slope properties in the fixed points.

This model is interesting from the methodological point of view. It is today widely accepted that financial time series have a strong non-linear signature, the GARCH behaviour being an example. Unstable phases of high volatility are observed, betraying the existence of chaotic attractors. Models in Day's fashion will exhibit a complex behaviour whenever the suitable mixture of α- or β-investors has been used. Unfortunately, a discrete 1-D model will only generate chaos and nothing else. Random volatility, bullish or bearish trends, crashes etc. are beyond the potentialities. The reduction of two different behaviours to a simple iterative 1-D map does not permit to reproduce more realistic SM signatures. It is why higher dimensional models are needed. Only recently higher dimensional discrete models have been developed (see Brock and Hommes, 1997). For the sake of convenience, continuous models can be used, though it is more difficult to generate chaos (a minimum of 3-D is needed for continuous autonomous systems of ordinary differential equations). The wide recognition of a non-efficient SM comes in support for the idea of accepting Day's approach. Economists in their majority today accept that stock returns cannot be predicted. The departure from efficient market is caused by the existence of drivers outside the rational response to available information coming from fundamental analysis. As Shiller (1989) states it, smart-money investors, i.e. α-investors, who are responding to rationally expected returns are not alone to drive the market. Ordinary investors, who have many if not all features of β investors, overreact to sudden price moves or to fads. This explains why price patterns look quite random.

160

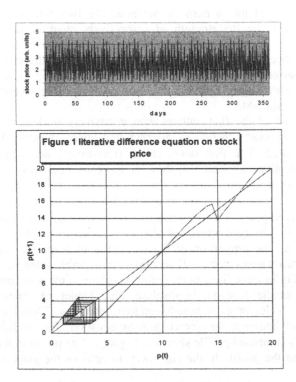

Figure 1. Iterative difference equation on stock price

Before proceeding to elaborate on the continuous simulation model proposed by the authors, it is worthwhile mentioning the recent development towards "artificial stock markets". The latter are located in the realm of artificial life with adaptive and learning capabilities (see for example Marengo and Torjman, 1996; Beltrametti et al., 1997; Arthur et al., 1997). In Arthur et al. (1997) investors are forming expectations by inductive reasoning rather that by deductive reasoning. The latter is shown by the authors to suffer from the indeterminacy characterising the celebrated Keynesian "beauty contest". The learning process initiated by the inhomogeneous set of investors consists in using genetic algorithms to continuously select and update investment rules best suited to maximise the portfolio performances. The market consists of many agents trading in a universe of stochastic dividends. It is clearly an "ab initio" approach of the type we have described above. But the aim of the present paper is not the use of classifier techniques to make stock price predictions in a turbulent environment. It is rather to distil some very basic "psychological behaviour rules" which help understand the complexity of the SM. In fact, we like to show in the following that complexity can also arise in completely frozen universes. It is why we work with a deterministic model in which economic parameter values are kept constant in each scenario. Even then unpredictability and randomness are shown to emerge. At the same time, it is hoped to gain a clear causal insight into the basic cogwheels of the SM. This is particularly useful at the time of writing: the stock prices in the Western world are apparently well above fundamentals.

SYSTEM DYNAMICS MODELLING OF THE STOCK MARKET (SM)

System Dynamics (SD) is a simulation technique using ordinary differential equations for approaching complex systems. As Richardon and Pugh III (1981) put it: "The system dynamics approach to complex problems focuses on feedback processes. It takes the philosophical position that feedback structures are responsible for the changes we experience over time". This whole approach identifies intrinsic and structural explanations of systems rather than exogenous causes. The first stage of the approach is to set up a still qualitative mental model to gain insight into causes and structures within the system. A mental model is obviously akin to the mental frame of "popular models" in behavioural finance. The influence diagram details the mental model by providing the main elements of the feedback dynamics. Typically this conceptualisation, prior to quantitative modelling, evolves through experience gathering during a typical learning-by-doing process conducted in many steps. This is not unlike the way investment strategies develop in the minds of investors. Quantitative modelling comes later. It consists in translating the influence diagram into a system of non-linear ordinary differential equations (ODE) to be solved numerically. The outputs are the time paths of the model variables: stocks, flows and auxiliaries. VENSIM 3.0 developed by Ventana Systems (1997) has been used in the present case for computing the stock price evolution in different scenarios.

For reasons of clarity the influence diagram of the stock price model has been split into three figures, 2 to 4. Each figure describes one out of three homogeneous families of investors to be detailed in the next section: α-, βS-, and βL-investors. They are extending the discrete Day's model, which had only two such families. Several important feedback loops are visible. They assist the understanding of basic behavioural rules developed in the investors' minds. Let us note some characteristics. Negative loops assist the goal-seeking approach of fundamentalists. They therefore help stabilising the stock prices. By contrast positive loops, often activated by short-term traders, are responsible for amplifying perturbation or rumours. Sometimes such a loop can act as a virtuous circle, in case it triggers a desired growth effect in prices. Sometimes it will act as a vicious circle, because the loop amplifies the market volatility or it triggers crashes. In the SM model, the two roles will be played in turn.

The universe in the SM model is very simple. There are only two assets: a risky asset at a variable homogeneous price P and a risk-free asset represented by a constant interest rate. This universe is frozen for a given simulation run. This means first that the total number of equity shares is fixed in all scenarios. Second, all economic parameters of the model are constant, including the growth rate of the fundamental value and the risk-free rate. Some fixed constraints are imposed on the available budget of the investors and their borrowing capacity.

Before we start presenting several main quantitative results, obtained with VENSIM, we now define the three families of investors and we discuss their respective behaviours.

Family of α- investors (Figure 2)

α-investors are "smart investors" as the rational goal-seekers in Day's model. Their aim is to achieve convergence towards the current goal price for the stock, minimising herewith the price discrepancy. It is why the unique feedback loop visible in figure 2 is negative. Note that in general overshooting above the equilibrium price will cause damped oscillations. The alpha goal price is the sum of two terms: fundamental value and arbitrage value:

- The fundamental value results from fundamental analysis, for example Dividend Discount Model (DDM). In our model dividends are deterministic. They could easily be made stochastic, but this would not be essential for understanding causal mechanisms in the model. They are growing with the given constant growth rate of the industry, assumed to be 7% per year in the model.
- The arbitrage value builds up as money flows to the SM away from risk-free assets. This appears as βL-investors (see below) observe a stock return above the risk-free rate (see below). In this case α-investors will adjust their long-term expectation above the fundamental value to follow the positive trend. In practice arbitrage value is incorporated into the goal price by α-investors only up to a certain point. In the model it is assumed that in a bullish market mainly driven by the arbitrage term, α-investors will cap their goal price by a maximum arbitrage value. The latter corresponds to their expectation of a reasonably high premium added to the fundamental value.

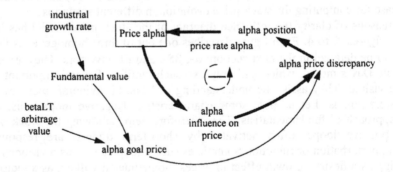

Figure 2. Negative Feedback loop of α-investors (tracking behaviour)

In the model α-investors do not experience any liquidity constraints. This is a reasonable assumption, as they stop anticipating further price growth, as the gap with the fundamental value becomes exceedingly large.

Families of β- investors

The β-investors introduced by Day are ordinary investors in Shiller's sense. They are not entirely rational with respect to the use of information coming from the market. They use different approaches for processing information, from rules of thumb to advanced technical analysis. An important aspect is the time horizon of anticipation covering a continuum between short- to long-term. The authors have extended Day's approach by considering two extremes in this continuum: βS-investors have a short-time horizon (S) while βL-investors have a long-term horizon (L).

Family of βS- investors (Figure 3)

βS-investors are myopic traders. They follow immediate price movements, ups and downs. In the model they change their stock position in proportion of the first derivative of the price. Therefore they destabilise the goal-seeking efforts of α-investors, causing permanent noise. To confirm this, a positive feedback loop is visible in the right part of figure 3. It manifests the destabilising investment approach. The driver in this loop is the first derivative of the price, initiating a vicious circle of growth or decay. A negative loop is visible in the left part of the diagram. It becomes active as the available budget drops to zero, forcing βS- investors to limit their stock position or even to liquidate part of their portfolio.

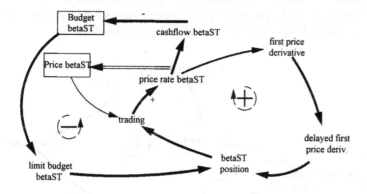

Figure 3. Feedback structure of short-term βS-investors

Family of βL- investors (Figure 4)

βL-investors have a more sophisticated approach to the market than βS-investors. Contrary to the latter, they have a long-term perspective. They permanently make arbitrage between the long-term stock return and the risk-free rate (called irate in the diagram). Their strategy is adaptive, i.e. updated at each change in the spread between the two rates. Note that the risk-free rate is fixed in each simulation run of the model. In case of a positive spread, in favour of risky asset positions, additional money is invested, curbing on the growth of the stock price. Therefore a positive feedback loop is visible in the upper part of the diagram in figure 4. It is driven by the return spread between risky

164

and risk-free assets. In case of a positive spread, this loop drives the positive loop discussed in the α-diagram. As said above, α-investors will adjust in part their goal price to follow the growing price trend caused by βL-investors' virtuous circle. In contrast to βS- investors, βL- investors have some financial robustness. They are ready to borrow money up to a certain extend anticipating further price increases. Doing so, they reinforce the growing trend by transforming it into a vicious circle. In the model as in the real world, it is therefore important, in case of a positive spread, to impose limits on an otherwise boundless growing stock price. Negative feedback loops have to be awakening in order to keep the price explosion within bounds. The main control loop is visible in the lower part of the diagram in figure 4. βL-investors have an initial budget and some important borrowing capacity up to a given limit of permissible debt level. In any case, their willingness to reimburse their loans will grow with the relative level of their debt expressed as a percentage of their stock position. This willingness is represented in the model as a barrier hindering further investment. Below a given debt threshold, βL-investors continue strengthening their stock position. Above the threshold, they experience an incentive to liquidate at least part of their stock position for limiting their debt. How much and how fast they sell depend in the model on the parameters of the debt barrier i.e. the threshold, the importance and rate of the reimbursement. In addition to this negative loop, another control is not visible in figure 4. It finds its origin in the cap imposed by α-investors on the permitted price growth above fundamentals. Beyond this point α-investors will no longer follow the trend set by βL-investors.

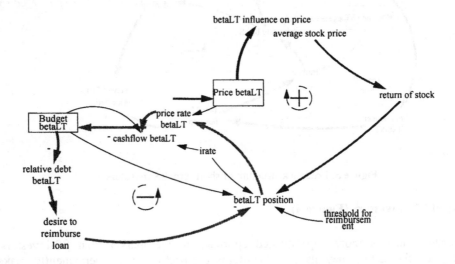

Figure 4. Feedback structure of long-term βL- investors

MAIN SIMULATION RESULTS

All following figures 5 to 9 show different conditions of the stock market over a time horizon of 1,000 days. The numerical integration brings some challenge, as the stock price evolution is all too often chaotic. Robustness in details seems, therefore, to be out of reach. A Runge-Kutta 4th order-integration scheme and a fixed time step of 0.0625 days have been adopted as giving sensible results. Deriving general patterns in several situations has deemed to the authors to be more important than achieving numerical perfection, which is anyway outside of reach in the actual chaotic conditions of the stock market.

The total stock price in Belgian francs (BEF) appears at the top of each time-diagram. The choice of absolute price values is arbitrary. This price appears in the diagrams as the sum of the three basic components attributed to the positions of the three families, i.e. of α-, βS-, and βL-investors. The different conditions in each figure correspond to varying parameters in the model, i.e. for the figure 5 to 9 the risk-free rate, the initial price, and the characteristic parameters of the debt barrier of βL-investors which appears to be the main drivers for many price patterns.

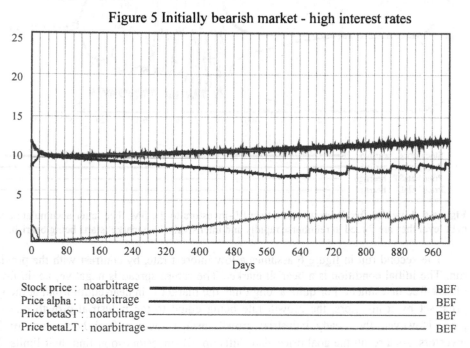

Figure 5 Initially bearish market - high interest rates

Stock price :	noarbitrage	BEF
Price alpha :	noarbitrage	BEF
Price betaST :	noarbitrage	BEF
Price betaLT :	noarbitrage	BEF

Figure 5. Test run assuming a very high risk-free rate and therefore no βL-investors

A first run shown in <u>figure 5</u> is used as a test of validity. The βL-investors are absent as arbitrage investment is completely switched off. This is achieved by keeping the risk-free rate very high. In this way, the stock market is very unattractive for long-term investors. The game is then entirely fought between the goal-seeking α-investors and the destabilising β noise-traders. The result is a regular wavy price evolution with a trend equal to the long-term industrial growth assumed to be 7% per annum (p.a.). This evolution is roughly comparable to the situation at European SM for some years after the 1987 crash. Long-term interest rates were high; growth rates were rather low, which made stock investment less attractive than conservative bond portfolios or even cash-accounts.

For the following simulation runs, the authors have looked in historical time series for rough points of comparison. The reference is the S&P 500 composite price index. Further finer calibration work could be done on the parameters of the model. This has not been attempted so far.

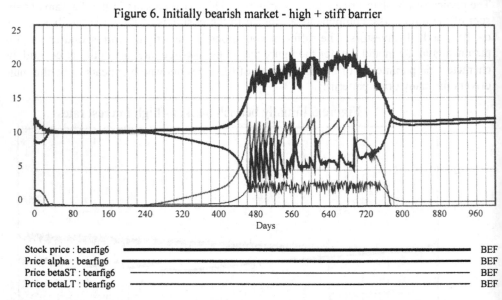

Figure 6. Initially bearish market - high + stiff barrier

Stock price : bearfig6	BEF
Price alpha : bearfig6	BEF
Price betaST : bearfig6	BEF
Price betaLT : bearfig6	BEF

Figure 6. Low risk-free interest rates attract βL-investors to the SM. The latter accumulate a high debt level they are forced to reimburse rapidly and intensively. The market starts being bearish.

The second run in <u>figure 6</u> assumes a low interest rate, by contrast with the previous run. The initial condition is a bearish market. The return spread is negative, i.e. in favour of risk-free investment. For quite a long time, the market is in near-equilibrium at the goal price set by α-investors, the growth rate being equal to the industrial growth rate (7% p.a.). However, the steady industrial growth brings about a fresh-born wave of βL-investors. As a result the goal price also shifts up. βL-investors soon find their limits. The debt barrier is reached. In this run, the threshold for maximum acceptable debt is set at 40% of the total current value of the stock position, a quite important value. In addition, it is assumed that the "debt barrier" is rather stiff and also high. This means that βL-investors have to rapidly liquidate the largest part of their stock portfolio in order to bring down their loan debt to a much lower level. This reimbursement constraint has the same effect as a reflecting barrier on the price. The price bounces back creating chaotic ups and downs of the price in search for a new equilibrium value. The larger the debt threshold, the larger will be the bouncing back of the price. The stiffness of the barrier is another element amplifying the plunge. βS-investors amplify the appeared volatility. The price volatility becomes so large that at some point the long-term return drops below the risk-free rate. βL-investors disappear from the scene after a crash of limited amplitude. The market moves to a new equilibrium following the natural trend of fundamental values.

A roughly comparable type of evolution in the S&P 500 composite price index has been observed in the period 1974 to 1977. As a consequence of the first oil crisis and the resulting inflation, the nominal interest rates were particularly high, the real rates being negative. The spread between governmental and corporate bonds was widening. As a consequence, the supply rate of money was largely declining, imposing new strains on the borrowing barrier.

In figure 7 the same assumptions are used for simulating an initially bullish market. The same assumptions on the debt barrier are used as in the previous case. A burst in price, accompanied by high volatility, sets up immediately. It manifests the same type of behaviour as GARCH in the stochastic theory. The bouncing back of the price against the debt barrier induces more volatility than in the previous case. This turbulent behaviour cannot maintain itself very long. The market moves to its fundamental equilibrium as in figure 6. After a while, a new price upsurge is observed with still more volatility than previously in the growing phase. It lasts for quite some time, exhibiting swings of considerable amplitude. As before, a crash brings back the price to its natural equilibrium. When pursuing the computation regular replica with similar shapes are periodically observed.

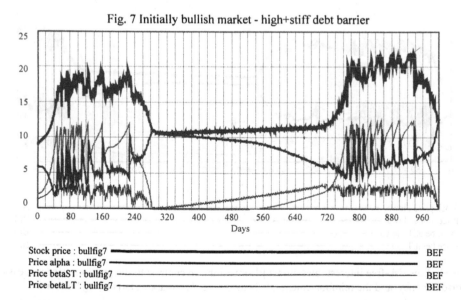

Fig. 7 Initially bullish market - high+stiff debt barrier

Stock price : bullfig7		BEF
Price alpha : bullfig7		BEF
Price betaST : bullfig7		BEF
Price betaLT : bullfig7		BEF

Figure 7. Low risk-free interest rates attract βL-investors to the SM. The latter are accumulating a high debt level. They are forced to reimburse rapidly and intensively their loans. The market starts being bullish.

Each replica in its growing phase has a similar shape to the evolution of the S&P 500 composite price index in the period starting at mid-1978 till end 1981. Following the previous period, the inflation rate had dropped from 12% to 4% p.a. The real interest rate was again positive and the prospects were therefore better. At start, the market was bullish. However the second oil crisis caused a new burst in inflation bringing down the real rates to negative values. The spread between governmental and corporate bonds widened again, slowing down the supply rate of money. A borrowing constraint appeared as in the previous period.

These two last simulations are not entirely convincing as they show an excessive volatility and too rapid crash conditions after the growth period. Adjustments in the basic parameters of the debt barrier of βL-investors, i.e. threshold, height and stiffness, are giving additional degrees of freedom as now illustrated. As an example, reducing the threshold reduces the volatility, because there is less reflection on the debt barrier.

The next run, illustrated in figure 8, is obtained from the previous one by lowering the debt threshold to 10% of the total current value of the stock position. As a result, the debt barrier is rather low, compared to the previous case. In addition the barrier is made softer by decreasing the slope in the willingness function triggering the reimbursement of loans. As a result less volatility is observed in the high price phase. The latter becomes also more sustainable and extends for a longer period than in the two previous phases.

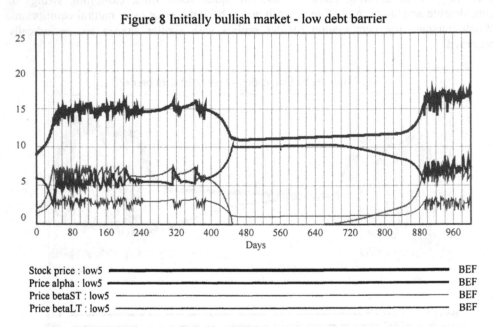

Figure 8 Initially bullish market - low debt barrier

Stock price : low5	BEF
Price alpha : low5	BEF
Price betaST : low5	BEF
Price betaLT : low5	BEF

Figure 8. Low risk-free interest rates attract βL-investors. In contrast to the previous case it is easier to borrow money, and the reimbursement rate is moderate. The market starts being bullish

A comparable evolution of the S&P 500 composite price index was observed in the period mid-1991 to end 1993. The US economy was just leaving a period of recession. The growth rate of the supply of money was close to vanishing. By contrast, the spread between governmental and corporate bonds was small. This did indicate that the obstacles to money borrowing were not structural and did not really create a barrier for money supply.

The next and last run, illustrated in figure 9, still goes a step further in achieving a sustainable price increase. The debt threshold is lowered to zero value, giving a zero height to the barrier. At the same time the barrier is kept soft, i.e. the reimbursement rate is slow. As result, a much lower volatility is achieved as the evolution sticks at the edge of the zero-barrier in a sustainable way. The stock price now incorporates the arbitrage value created by the positive spread in returns. The trend is given by the growth rate of fundamentals. The only permanent instability is caused by small βS-movements. The price is maintained at its upper level and it continues to grow at the industrial growth rate of 7% p.a.

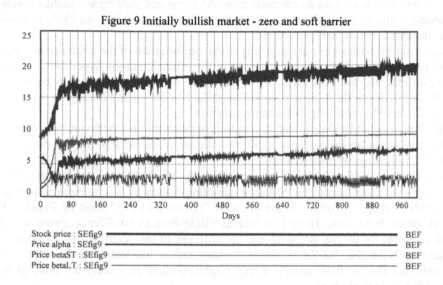

Figure 9 Initially bullish market - zero and soft barrier

Stock price : SEfig9	BEF
Price alpha : SEfig9	BEF
Price betaST : SEfig9	BEF
Price betaLT : SEfig9	BEF

Figure 9. Low risk-free interest rates attract βL-investors to the SM. It is easy to borrow money and the reimbursement rate is slow. The market starts being bullish

This situation of long-term sustainable growth with limited volatility in the price is also roughly comparable to the situation in the Western SM described by the S&P 500 composite price index for the period mid-1995 to mid-1998, before the limited crash in the second half of 1998. During that period, a continuous growth of the stock price has been recorded. As assumed in the present simulation, a sustainable flow of liquidity has been invested in the SM for arbitrage reasons by "ordinary investors". As an example, U.S. pensioners facing low risk-free interest rates have been moving to the SM. In Europe the "European Monetary Unit" convergence criteria leading to a common currency unit

(EURO) has imposed low interest rates, limited public deficits, and reduced public debts. High-rate governmental bonds have been called back, while saving accounts became unattractive. A lot of money has been flowing to the stock market heating up the prices.

CONCLUSIONS AND FURTHER WORK

The main objective of the proposed "ab initio" approach is to provide a causal model in behavioural finance. In the opinion of the authors the applied SD-methodology departs from the usual interpretations using discrete chaos theory. The latter are far from transparent (see for recent surveys of the literature Heij and al. (Eds.) 1997; Creedy et al. (Eds.) 1994). By contrast the present analysis stresses causal interpretations. It therefore provides straightforward explanations by identifying simple feedback structures created by few investors' attitudes. Though the proposed model is completely deterministic, it is able to portray several complex patterns of real stock markets. Refined SD models of this type are thinkable to capture and to anticipate SM dynamics. Adding stochastic aspects to the models would be a trivial think to do. In the author's opinion it is not likely to provide deeper insights into fast market dynamics.

The main by-product of our modelling is the confirmation of the existence of "animal spirits" next to rational behaviours supposed in the efficient market hypothesis. At a time of volatile markets, the analysis of the behavioural price drivers seems to be of some interest. In particular the increased volatility of the SM due to day trading on the Internet suggests further SD-modelling in the same direction.

As a main result of the present approach it appears that the behaviour of "ordinary" βL-investors could be an important explicative factor of the volatile price pattern on the SM for the following two main reasons:

- The psychological willingness to contract loans to chase the growing price trends appears as a key factor (the SM as a gambling casino as it is sometimes popularly stated). Perhaps the origin of the ominous "financial bubble" must be found in this risk prone behaviour. There is a vicious circle here as confidence grows with the stock price. So do the threshold and the stiffness of the "debt barrier" causing hard landing. Note also that the barrier is dynamic rather than static. As the recent Asian crisis has shown, fresh money supply might continue to sustain the price growth, moving aside the barrier.

- At the same time, the fear of the bubble by anticipation is growing, another psychological and perhaps irrational attitude. In our model, α-investors stop incorporating additional arbitrage growth into their goal prices. While this helps bringing down the price closer to fundamentals, there is an additional risk here. Massive sales of α-stock to β-investors further drive the debt spiral and enhance the ruin-provoking mechanisms.

Of course, one drawback in the model is the clear-cut definition of the group of investors. In the real world, neither institutional investors nor traders are definitely respectively α- or β-investors. Each investor has features of each elementary type, acting alternately as a fundamentalist, technical analyst or noise trader (see Brock and Hommes, 1997). The main difficulty is that the proportion of each type depends on the market conditions. There are additional feedback loops to be drawn in the model inducing these changes in attitudes. The same applies to the parameters of the frozen universe. In the real world, influence links exist between industry growth and stock price. More elaborate model could focus on these weak spots in modelling. Also, in the real world, the availability of liquidity for investment is not fixed. For example, in the first part of 1998, additional monies were flowing to Western markets away from the Asian markets as the latter were caught in turmoil. Herewith the sustainability of the growth is maintained for a longer period, or a later "hard landing" is somewhat softened.

The relative strength of each group of investors must be handled as an additional parameter to be calibrated under the given economic conditions. This is part of the improvements and tuning of the model. Other possibilities not yet explored are the definition of softer debt barriers and the role of α-investors in caring for a damping in the anticipated price crash.

In conclusion we feel that a refined SD modelling of basic investors' attitudes is a rewarding task for future development. Though it is probably illusory to expect some forecasting from such rough models, the causal interpretation has a great value per se. In particular it can deliver a warning signal to ordinary investors driven by unbounded Keynesian "animal spirits". Unlimited growth is impossible on earth and, by consequence, on the stock market.

REFERENCES

Arthur, W.B., Holland, J.H., LeBaron, B., Palmer, R. and P. Tayler (1997) Asset Pricing Under Exogeneous Expectations in an Artificial Stock Market in Arthur, W.B., Durlauf, S.N., and Lane D.A. (Eds.) *The Economy as an Evolving Complex System II*. Proceedings Vol. XXVII, Santa Fe Institute Studies in the Sciences of Complexity. Reading MA: Addison Wesley.

Axelrod, R. (1997) *The Complexity of Cooperation, Agent-Based Models of Competition and Cooperation*, Princeton: University Press.

Beltrametti, L., Fiorentini, R., Marengo, L. and R. Tamborini (1997) A learning-to-forecast experiment on the foreign exchange market with a classifier system. *Journal of Economic Dynamics and Control* (21): 1543-1575.

Brock, W.A., and C.H. Hommes (1997) Models of Complexity in Economics and Finance" in C. Heij et al. (Eds.) op. cit.: 3-44. Chichester, England: John Wiley & Sons, Ltd.

Creedy, J., and V.L. Martin (Eds., 1994) *Chaos and Non-Linear Models in Economics- Theory and Applications*. Brookfield, Vermont: Edward Elgar Publ. Co.

Day, R.H. (1994) *Complex Economic Dynamics, Vol. I An Introduction to Dynamical Systems and Market Mechanisms*. Cambridge, MA: MIT Press,

Heij, Ch., Schumacher, H., Hanzon B., and K. Praagman (Eds., 1997) *System Dynamics in Economic and Financial Models*. Chichester, England:John Wiley & Sons, Ltd.

Marengo, L. and H. Tordjman (1996) Speculation, Heterogeneity and Learning: A Simulation Model of Exchange Rates Dynamics. *Kyklos*, 49(3): 407-438.

Richardson, G.P., and A.L. Pugh III (1981) *Introduction to System Dynamics Modeling*. Productivity Press, Portland, Oregon.

Shiller, R.J. (1989) *Market volatility*. Cambridge, MA & London, England: The MIT Press.

Ventana Systems, Inc. (1997) *VENSIM 3.0 software*, Harvard, MA.

Zeeman, E.C. (1977) *Catastrophe Theory – Selected Papers 1972-1977*. Reading, MA: Addison-Wesley Publ. Co.

INFORMATION EFFECTS ON THE ACCURACY OF NEURAL NETWORK FINANCIAL FORECASTING

S. Walczak

University of Colorado at Denver
College of Business & Administration
Campus Box 165, PO Box 173364
Denver, CO 80217-3364
USA

Abstract: When data quantities are fixed, as they are for most financial modeling techniques at the time of model construction, a problematic issue in developing optimal models including neural network models is the selection of training and validation sets within the data. A general heuristic used with time-series models and especially with neural network time-series forecasting models is that as the size of the training data set increases, then the accuracy of the time-series model also increases. However, acquiring additional model building data increases the time and financial costs of a model. This chapter investigates the effect of increasing the quantity of data used for training/building neural network forecasting models in the domain of currency exchange. Results indicate that a minimum of one to four years of data is capable of producing maximum performance neural network forecasting models, achieving forecasting accuracy of sixty percent or greater for many currency exchange rates.

Key words: Neural networks, backpropagation, currency exchange, training set size, time-series, forecasting.

INTRODUCTION

Neural networks are increasingly being used to solve financial forecasting problems (Hammerstrom 1993, Ruggiero 1994, Widrow et al. 1994, Wong & Selvi 1998, Zahedi 1996). However, financial time-series and foreign exchange rate forecasts are difficult to model (Zhang & Hu 1998). Hsieh (1989) and others (Cornell & Dietrich 1978, Diebold & Nason 1990) have demonstrated that foreign exchange and other financial time series follow a random walk. Neural networks provide a valuable tool for building non-linear

S.H. Zanakis et al. (eds.), Decision Making: Recent Developments and Worldwide Applications, 173–182.

models of data, especially when the underlying laws governing the system are unknown (Zhang & Hu 1998). Neural network forecasting models have outperformed both statistical and other machine learning models of financial time series, achieving forecast accuracy of up to 58 percent (Refenes 1993, Steurer 1993), thus making them an opportune method for performing financial time-series modeling.

When data quantities are fixed, as they typically are for any financial modeling technique at the time of model construction, a problematic issue in developing optimal models including neural network models is the selection of training and validation sets within the existing data sample. A general heuristic that is used with time-series models of any kind (Box et al. 1994, Gately 1996) and especially with neural network time-series forecasting models is that as the size of the training data set increases, then the accuracy or quality of the time-series model also increases. Non-time-series neural network applications have also followed this training data maximizing schema, employing such techniques as bootstrap and jackknife to increase the quantity of training data available for building neural network categorization models. However, the bootstrap and jackknife techniques are not applicable to time-series data, as these techniques ignore the time-dependent nature of the data.

Furthermore, Bansal et al. (1993) have noted that data (training, test, and standard use) represents an important and recurring cost for information systems in general and neural networks in particular. In this chapter, empirical analysis is used to evaluate the contribution of information to neural network financial time-series forecasting models for various foreign exchange rates. Initially, a minimal data set of one year's worth of data is used for training the foreign exchange forecasting models. Additional years of training data are then added to the initial training data set and the neural network model is retrained on the larger data set. Training data are the closing daily spot values from the New York market for six different foreign currency exchange rates against the US dollar from 1973 until 1994, representing the largest training sets ever used to build neural network foreign exchange forecasting models. Evaluation data are the corresponding daily spot rate values for the first two quarters of 1995.

Forecasting accuracy with respect to the direction of change in the exchange rate is used to measure the effect of the larger data sets on the neural network model's performance. Various researchers (Green & Pearson 1994, Levich 1981, Taylor 1988) have argued that evaluating time-series forecasting models using the direction of change is the optimal analysis method and that using other techniques such as Root Mean Square Error (RMSE) or other similar measures (e.g., MAE, MAPE, etc.) may produce misleading results.

Foreign exchange rates, though only one of many financial time-series, form an invaluable test domain. Diebold and Nason (1990) have concluded that non-linearities of exchange rates cannot be exploited to improve out-of-sample forecasts and Lequarré (1993) has set a glass ceiling of 60 percent as the maximum attainable forecasting performance by foreign exchange forecasting neural networks. Therefore, if the quantity of training data does have any significant effect on forecasting performance, the results should be readily seen. In addition to using foreign exchange options as an investment strategy, Walczak et al. (1998) have noted that multi-national firms can realize significant capital gain by knowing when to instantiate necessary currency trades.

RELATIONSHIP OF THE NEURAL NETWORK FOREIGN EXCHANGE
MODELS TO PREVIOUS RESEARCH

The neural network models described in the next section all use the backpropagation training method on homogeneous input data sets. Hornik et al. (1989) and White (1990) have demonstrated that the backpropagation training algorithm is capable of learning arbitrary mappings and thus serving as universal approximators. Additionally, the backpropagation algorithm is commonly available and frequently used in research (Fu 1994, Widrow et al. 1994), thus producing benchmarks and other comparative studies. Finally, various researchers have indicated that backpropagation trained neural networks produce superior performance to neural networks trained with various other training paradigms (Barnard & Wessels 1992, Benjamin et al. 1995, Walczak 1998). Readers interested in the algorithmic details of backpropagation are referred to the references (Fu 1994, Gately 1996, Hertz et al. 1991, Hornik et al. 1989, Smith 1993, White 1990).

Previous research has indicated that both homogeneous (Hu et al. 1999, Mehta 1995, Refenes 1993, Ruggerio 1994, Steurer 1993, Zhang & Hu 1998) and heterogeneous (Walczak et al. 1998) input models may work for foreign exchange forecasting, with the majority of attempted models being homogeneous. Homogeneous models utilize data from the specific time series being forecast or directly obtainable from that time series (e.g., a k-day trend or moving average), while heterogeneous models utilize information from outside the time series (e.g., using the S&P 500 or Hang Seng index) in addition to the time series itself. Homogeneous models rely on the predictive capabilities of the time series itself, corresponding to a technical analysis as opposed to a fundamental analysis. Homogeneous models only are used in the empirical analysis so that the only change to all models will be the impact of additional data from the time-series being forecast.

Input variable selection is not the primary topic of this chapter and has been discussed elsewhere (Smith 1993, Tahai et al. 1998, Walczak & Cerpa 1999, Zhang & Hu 1998). The homogeneous input variables used in the foreign exchange empirical evaluations follow the design utilized by Walczak et al. (1998) in their heterogeneous foreign exchange neural network models (that were trained on only a single year of data). Autocorrelation coefficients for the lag values of the foreign currencies tested in the current research are used to select significant lags. The one-day lag value of the daily spot rate is always used as an input value. Additional lags (e.g., two-day, three-day, or five-day lags) are used as input values to the neural network if a statistically significant autocorrelation coefficient was previously reported in the research of either Cornell and Dietrich (1978) or Levich and Thomas (1993). As an example, the input values for the dollar/pound foreign exchange forecasting neural network are the one-, two-, and five-day New York closing spot rate lags and the dollar/mark model uses a one-, two-, and three-day lag input vector.

RESULTS OF USING DIFFERENT TRAINING SET SIZES

As stated in the previous sections, neural network models trained using the backpropagation learning algorithm and utilizing homogeneous input variables of multiple time lags are constructed to forecast the one-day future directional change to various foreign currency exchange rates. While both one and two hidden layer neural network architectures are trained and tested for each currency to enable the best fit to an arbitrarily complex function (Fu 1994), the single hidden layer neural networks consistently outperform their two hidden layer counterparts and as such, only the single hidden layer neural network results are reported. Additionally, multiple hidden node quantities for the single hidden layer are also evaluated in order to solve any potential problems with over-fitting and under-fitting the training data set (Barnard & Wessels 1992), with the best performing architecture normally having five hidden nodes, as shown in Figure 1.

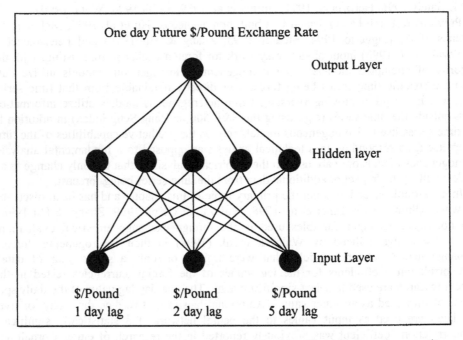

Figure 1: Sample neural network model used to test the effect of information quantity.

Again, the purpose of the research reported in this chapter is to provide empirical evidence on the effect of increasing training set sizes and does not analyze other neural network design variables. Similar to the Occam's razor heuristic for selecting between alternative scientific explanations, a heuristic used in neural network development is to use the minimum size network capable of learning the desired pattern (Hertz et al. 1991, Mehra & Wah 1992) and hence the use of several different hidden node architectures to approximate an optimal solution. The design of hidden layers and quantities of hidden nodes per layer is discussed extensively in Walczak and Cerpa (1999).

The first currency exchange rates to be evaluated for training set size effects are the US dollar/British pound, US dollar/German mark, and US dollar/Japanese yen daily spot rate values. These currencies represent four of the five most frequently traded currencies around the world (Federal Reserve Bank of New York 1995). Training sets for each of the three major currencies are produced as shown in Table 1. All of the training sets have an ending date of 31 December 1994. The out-of-sample evaluation data set is the 125 sample data set from 2 January 1995 through 30 June 1995. The division of data sets in this manner simulates the prospective use of the trained neural networks on future (unforeseen) data.

Table 1. Neural network training sets.

Training Set	Years of data	Start Date
1	1	3 January 1994
2	2	4 January 1993
3	3	2 January 1992
4	4	2 January 1991
5	5	2 January 1990
6	7	4 January 1988
7	9	2 January 1986
8	11	3 January 1984
9	13	4 January 1982
10	15	2 January 1980
11	21.75	3 March 1973

The 33 individual neural networks for each training set and for each currency (11 * 3) are trained for 20000 iterations on the training data and then tested a single time on the evaluation data set. Results for neural network forecasting accuracy for these three primary currencies are displayed in Table 2.

Table 2. Neural network forecasting results for $/pound, $/mark, and $/yen exchange rate changes.

Training Set	$/pound	$/mark	$/yen
1 (1 year)	61.6 %	60.0 %	59.2 %
2 (2 years)	**62.4 %**	**61.6 %**	59.2 %
3 (3 years)	53.6 %	56.8 %	56.0 %
4 (4 years)	52.8 %	55.2 %	59.2 %
5 (5 years)	54.2 %	60.8 %	59.2 %
6 (7 years)	51.2 %	58.4 %	59.2 %
7 (9 years)	52.8 %	59.2 %	59.2 %
8 (11 years)	**62.4 %**	58.4 %	40.8 %
9 (13 years)	57.6 %	56.8 %	59.2 %
10 (15 years)	56.0 %	60.0 %	59.2 %
11 (22 years)	57.6 %	59.2 %	59.2 %

From Table 2, it can be seen that for the $/pound and $/mark neural network forecasting models, the neural networks achieve a very good forecasting accuracy and then as additional years of training data are added to the initial training set, performance increases and then declines. The maximum forecasting performance for both the $/pound and the $/mark neural networks occurs with two years of training data. All three neural network models outperform or equal the performance of the full 21.75 years training set with just one or two years of data. For the $/pound neural network with two-years of training data, the result is 78 winning trades versus 47 losing trades. Following the law of large numbers (Hogg & Craig 1978), this would result in 24.8 percent clear wins (wins minus losses), producing a net increase in the currency portion of an investment portfolio.

A further examination of the net portfolio gain achievable using the minimal training set neural networks is provided by a simulation of $/pound currency trades during the test (hold-out) sample period. The simulation assumes that a single pound contract (Walczak 1995) is purchased or sold on each trading day based on the forecast of the neural network. The net gain to the trader during the 6 months of the simulation is $1418.75 per contract.

The $/yen neural network shows an unusual behavior in that almost all of the training sets produce identical results (with the exception of the 11 years training set, which may have contained some inadvertent noise). While the $/yen neural network forecasts using only one or two years of data do not exceed the performance of larger training sets, the fact that additional data does not improve the forecasting accuracy and the additional data incurs time and monetary costs (Bansal et al. 1993) implies that the smaller training data set sizes should be used.

Next, to verify that the results obtained for the pound, mark, and yen are extensible to other currencies, an abbreviated evaluation is performed for the $/Swiss franc, $/French franc, and $/Italian lira daily exchange rates. The neural network models for each of the three new foreign exchange rates is constructed using the exact same methodology as described for the original three neural network forecasting models, with the exception that only training sets 1-5 and 11 are used to evaluate the effect of larger training set sizes. Forecasting accuracy results for the new foreign exchange rate neural network forecasts are displayed in Table 3.

Table 3. Neural network forecasting results for three additional exchange rate changes.

Training Set	$/French franc	$/Swiss franc	$/lira
1 (1 year)	59.2 %	55.2 %	57.6 %
2 (2 years)	57.6 %	56.8 %	52.8 %
3 (3 years)	59.2 %	56.8 %	48.8 %
4 (4 years)	44.8 %	57.6 %	49.6 %
5 (5 years)	57.6 %	50.4 %	53.6 %
11 (22 years)	59.2 %	54.4 %	56.0 %

Similar to the previous results, the three new neural network foreign exchange forecasting models show an initial increase to a maximum forecasting accuracy and then subsequent declines and all of the neural network models outperform or match the performance of the largest possible training set size with just one or two years of training data. The French franc, similar to the yen matches the full 21.75 year training set performance with just a single year of training data. Both the Swiss franc and lira neural network models behave similar to the pound and mark neural network models with the one or two year training data set models outperforming the full 21.75 year training set model. The Swiss franc also indicates that a training set size greater than two years of training data may be required to obtain optimal neural network forecasting performance.

DISCUSSION

Very few attempts have been made by neural network researchers or developers to analyze the effect of training set size on time-series neural network forecasting performance. Zhang and Hu (1998) use a single comparison of a sixteen year training set size to a six year training set size for forecasting the $/pound exchange rate. Their results support Box et al. (1994) and others (Gately 1996) who claim that larger training sets produce better forecasting models with the sixteen year model outperforming the six year model. More recent research by Hu et al. (1999) attempts to compare a five year training set size to multiple other training set sizes up to 17 years of training data. As seen in Table 2, the five year training set size for the $/British pound exchange rate produces sub-optimal results. Additionally, the Hu et al. (1999) research is seriously flawed as they utilize RMSE, MAE, and MAPE values to evaluate the performance of the resulting neural networks and as stated earlier, this produces potentially misleading results. Other than these two efforts, no other research has been performed until now, that evaluates the effect of training set size on neural network financial time-series forecasting.

From Tables 2 and 3, it can be seen than more recent data is better at forecasting future data than larger collections of training set data that contain data further away in time. The idea that more recent data is better at predicting future data is intuitively appealing and is similar to the idea of a random walk model (in which only the previous time period has any relation to the next time period). Unlike a random walk model though, the neural network time-series forecasting models are able to incorporate knowledge that is still recent, although further removed from the present time (by one to four years).

The results displayed in Tables 2 and 3 also help to explain why previous neural network foreign exchange forecasting models have failed to break through Lequarré's 60 percent accuracy ceiling. Previous research has tended to utilize too much training data, typically four years of data or more (Hu et al. 1999, Jamal & Sundar 1998, Refenes 1993, Steurer 1993, Tenti 1996, Zhang & Hu 1998), which produces sub-optimal results. For example, Steurer (1993) achieves a forecast accuracy for the $/mark exchange rate of just under 57 percent, which is identical to the current results obtained using three years or thirteen years of training data. Steurer indicates that sixteen years of data were used in training his model, thus if the training set size is reduced to the two most recent years of data, an increase in the forecasting performance of the developed neural network model would be expected.

The results displayed for the $/Swiss franc neural network forecasting model indicate that occasionally, a training set size of greater than two years may be needed. A generalized method for obtaining maximum performance with minimal data costs for neural network financial time-series forecasting models would be:

1. Identify relevant input variable set (outside of the scope of this paper).

2. Train the resultant neural network architecture on a single year of training data. (Note that multiple hidden node architectures should be evaluated simultaneously.)
3. Increment the training data set by one year. Re-train the one-year training data set neural network model and evaluate on the same test data set.
4. Compare the larger training set size neural network's forecasting performance to the previous neural network model's performance.
5. If the most recent (largest) training set size neural network's forecasts exceeds the performance of the previous training set size neural network's forecasts, repeat process from step 3, otherwise retain the previous neural network as the optimal model and record the training set size.

This method is tested by evaluating the daily closing values for the CAC-40 French stock market index. Training data for the CAC is available from 1988 through 1999, enabling training set sizes up to 10.33 years. The neural network models forecasting the CAC-40 index peaked at two years of training data and declined when additional years of training data were used to develop neural network forecasting models. In order to thoroughly evaluate the generalized method, additional neural network models past three years of training data were built up to six years of training data and one neural network model using the full 10.33 years of training data available. The two year training data set neural network model identified by the generalized method outperformed all other neural network models built using larger training sets. The results presented here are similar and in accordance with other research applied on financial time-series in other capital markets (Siriopoulos et al. 1996).

CONCLUSIONS

Empirical evidence has been produced and shown that contradicts current neural network time-series development methodology. Current methodology states that larger training set sizes will produce better performing forecasting models. The results of the study reported in this chapter indicate that generally a maximum of two years of data is all that is required to develop optimal neural network time-series forecasting models. This result immediately imparts both a time and financial savings when developing neural network financial time-series forecasting models, by reducing the quantity of data required to train the neural network (Bansal et al. 1993).

A generalized methodology for identifying the minimum training set size that will produce the best performance in neural network time-series forecasting models was presented. This generalized methodology was then evaluated against a non-foreign exchange time-series (the CAC-40 stock index) to demonstrate the robustness of the methodology for developing neural network financial time-series forecasting models.

REFERENCES

Bansal, A., Kauffman, R.J. and Weitz, R.R. (1993), "Comparing the Modeling Performance of Regression and Neural Networks as Data Quality Varies: A Business Value Approach", *Journal of Management Information Systems* 10(1), 11-32.

Barnard, E. and Wessels, L. (1992), "Extrapolation and Interpolation in Neural Network Classifiers", *IEEE Control Systems* 12(5), 50-53.

Benjamin, C. O., Chi, S., Gaber, T. and Riordan, C.A. (1995), "Comparing BP and ART II Neural Network Classifiers for Facility Location", *Computers and Industrial Engineering* 28(1), 43-50.

Box, G.E.P., Jenkins, G.M. and Reinsel, G.C. (1994), *Time Series Analysis*, 3rd Edition, Prentice Hall, Englewood Cliffs, NJ.

Cornell, W.B. and Dietrich, J.K. (1978), "The Efficiency of the Market for Foreign Exchange Under Floating Exchange Rates", *The Review of Economics and Statistics* 60, 111-120.

Diebold, F.X. and Nason, J.A. (1990), "Nonparametric Exchange Rate Prediction?", *Journal of International Economics* 28, 315-332.

Federal Reserve Bank of New York (1995), *April 1995 Survey of Foreign Exchange Market Activity in the United States*, Federal Reserve Bank, New York.

Fu, L. (1994), *Neural Networks in Computer Intelligence*, McGraw-Hill, New York.

Gately, E. (1996), *Neural Networks for Financial Forecasting*, Wiley, New York.

Green, H. and Pearson, M. (1994). "Neural Nets for Foreign Exchange Trading", in: Deboeck, G.J. (Ed.), *Trading on the Edge*, Wiley, New York, 123-129.

Hammerstrom, D. (1993), "Neural networks at work," *IEEE Spectrum* 30(6), 26-32.

Hertz, J., Krogh, A., and Palmer, R. (1991), *Introduction To The Theory of Neural Computation*, Addison-Wesley, Reading, MA.

Hogg, R.V. and Craig, A.T. (1978), *Introduction to Mathematical Statistics, Fourth Edition*, Macmillan, New York.

Hornik, K., Stinchcombe, M. and White, H. (1989), "Multilayer Feedforward Networks Are Universal Approximators", *Neural Networks* 2(5), 359-366.

Hsieh, D.A. (1989), "Testing for Nonlinear Dependence in Daily Foreign Exchange Rates", *Journal of Business* 62(3), 339-368.

Hu, M.Y., Zhang, G., Jiang, C.X. and Patuwo, B.E. (1999), "A Cross-Validation Analysis of Neural Network Out-of-Sample Performance in Exchange Rate Forecasting", *Decision Sciences* 30(1), 197-215.

Jamal, A. M. and Sundar, C. (1998), "Modeling Exchange Rates With Neural Networks", *Journal of Applied Business Research* 14(1), 1-5.

Lequarré, J.Y. (1993). "Foreign Currency Dealing: A Brief Introduction", in: Gershenfeld, N.A. and Weigend, A.S. (Eds.), *Time Series Prediction: Forecasting the Future and Understanding the Past*, Addison-Wesley, Reading, MA, 131-137.

Levich, R.M. (1981), "How to Compare Chance with Forecasting Expertise", *Euromoney* (August), 61-78.

_____ and Thomas, L.R. (1993), "The significance of technical trading-rule profits in the foreign exchange market: a bootstrap approach", *Journal of International Money and Finance* 12, 451-474.

Mehra, P. and Wah, B. W. (1992), *Artificial Neural Networks: Concepts and Theory*, IEEE Press, New York.

Mehta, M. (1995), "Foreign Exchange Markets", in: Refenes A. (Ed.), *Neural Networks in the Capital Markets*, Wiley, New York, 177-198.

Refenes, A.N. (1993), "Constructive Learning and Its Application to Currency Exchange Rate Forecasting", in: Trippi, R. and Turban, E. (Eds.), *Neural Networks in Finance and Investing*, Irwin, New York, 465-493.

Ruggiero, M.A. (1994), "Getting the lag out", *Futures* 23(4), 46-48.

Siriopoulos, C., Markellos, R.N. and Sirlantiz, K. (1996), "Applications of artificial neural networks in emerging financial markets", in: Refenes, A.,Mostafa, Y. and Moody, J. (Eds.), *Neural Networks in Financial Engineering*, World Scientific, Singapore, 284-303.

Smith, M. (1993), *Neural Networks for Statistical Modeling*, Van Nostrand Reinhold, New York.

Steurer, E. (1993), "Nonlinear Modelling of the DEM/USD Exchange Rate", in: Refenes, A. (Ed.), *Neural Networks in the Capital Markets*, Wiley, New York, 199-211.

Tahai, A., Walczak, S. and Rigsby, J.T. (1998), "Improving Artificial Neural Network Performance Through Input Variable Selection", in: Siegel, P., Omer, K., deKorvin, A., and Zebda, A. (Eds.), *Applications of Fuzzy Sets and The Theory of Evidence to Accounting II*, JAI Press, Stamford, Connecticut, 277-292.

Tenti, P. (1996), "Forecasting Foreign Exchange Rates Using Recurrent Neural Networks", *Applied Artificial Intelligence* 10, 567-581.

Taylor, S.J. (1988), *Modelling Financial Time Series*, Wiley, New York.

Walczak, S. (1995), "Developing Neural Nets for Currency Trading", *Artificial Intelligence in Finance* 2 (1), 27-34.

Walczak, S. (1998), "Neural Network Models for A Resource Allocation Problem", *Transactions on Systems, Man and Cybernetics* 28 B(2), 276-284.

_____ and Cerpa, N. (1999), "Heuristic Principles For The Design Of Artificial Neural Networks", *Information and Software Technology* 41(2), 107-117.

_____, Tahai, A. and Karim, K. (1998), "Improved Cash Flows Using Neural Network Models for Forecasting Foreign Exchange Rates", in: Siegel, P., Omer, K., deKorvin, A., and Zebda, A. (Eds.), *Applications of Fuzzy Sets and The Theory of Evidence to Accounting II*, JAI Press, Stamford, Connecticut, 293-310.

Widrow, B., Rumelhart, D.E. and Lehr, M.A. (1994), "Neural Networks: Applications in Industry, Business and Science," *Communications of the ACM* 37(3), 93-105.

White, H. (1990), "Connectionist Nonparametric Regression: Multilayer Feedforward Networks Can Learn Arbitrary Mappings," *Neural Networks* 3(5), 535-549.

Wong, B.K. and Selvi, Y. (1998), "Neural network applications in finance: A review and analysis of literature (1990-1996)", *Information and Management* 34, 129-139.

Zahedi, F. (1996), "A Meta-Analysis of Financial Applications of Neural Networks," *International Journal of Computational Intelligence and Organizations* 1(3), 164-178.

Zhang, G. and Hu, M.Y. (1998), "Neural Network Forecasting of the British Pound/US Dollar Exchange Rate," *Omega, International Journal of Management Science* 26(4), 495-506.

IS THE TAIWAN STOCK MARKET EFFICIENT?

J.P. Gupta[1†], I.M. Pandey[2], Chen Chao-Fu[3]

[1] Groupe Ecole Supérieure de Commerce de Paris
79, avenue de la République
75543 Paris Cedex 11, France

[2] Indian Institute of Management
Ahmedabad, India

[3] School of Management
Asian Institute of Technology
P.O. Box 4, Klong Luang
Pathumthani 12120, Thailand

Abstract: The main objective of the Taiwan Government in reforming the Taiwan Stock Exchange (TSE) has been to establish Taiwan as an Asia-Pacific financial centre. A number of policies to liberalise and internationalise the market have been promulgated and implemented after the Security Exchange Law Amendment (SELA). The liberalisation and internationalisation of TSE is expected to make it informationally efficient. Theoretically, the technical analysis should lose its effectiveness if a market is efficient. This study, using the serial correlation test, the run test and the normality test and simulation on mechanical rules that adopted stochastic and moving average convergence and divergence, examines the efficiency of the TSE in the period after financial deregulation and liberalisation.

Key Words: Filter rule, Market efficiency, Run tests, Serial correlation tests, Taiwan Stock Exchange, Technical analysis, Technical indicators tests

[†] Corresponding author: Jyoti Gupta, Professor, Groupe Ecole Supérieure de Commerce de Paris, 79 avenue de la république, 75011 Paris, France. Tel. 01 49 23 22 94- Fax. 01 49 23 20 80- E-mail: gupta@escp.fr

S.H. Zanakis et al. (eds.), Decision Making: Recent Developments and Worldwide Applications, 183–196.

INTRODUCTION

A number of empirical studies have tested the efficient market hypothesis (EMH) in the case of developed countries. In recent years, one could also witness the interest of researchers in understanding the capital markets in emerging economies. The Majority of these studies indicate that capital markets are efficient, at least, in the sense that the share price patterns can not be predicted on the basis of the past information. This is referred to as the weak-form efficiency. The empirical tests used to verify the weak form of efficiency can be divided into two types: (1) statistical tests of price series over time, and (2) the use of various mechanical trading rules or other factors that are considered "technical" in nature. The first type of tests provide support for the hypothesis that stock price changes are independently distributed random variables. In other words, the intrinsic value of a stock price series fluctuates in a random manner as new information enters the market. The second type of tests try to obtain abnormal profits in a simulation to test the EMH which implies that the future price can not be predicted by using past information.

While most of the research studies found evidences that support EMH, however, in many emerging markets like Taiwan, the technical and fundamental analysts still continue to flourish, commanding sizeable quantities of investors' capital in the process. If EMH do stand well in the emerging Taiwan stock market, then it means investors who believe in those technical analysts are wasting their money and those specialists have to start to worry about their future. Is the Taiwan stock market efficient? The objective of this paper is to attempt an answer to this question.

THE TAIWAN STOCK EXCHANGE[*]

The development of Taiwan stock market may be divided into three phases: (1) before 1962, (2) between 1962 and 1987, and (3) after 1987. Before 1963, there was no centralised trading place for securities transactions, and the trading was done through the over-the-counter market (OTC). The establishment of the Taiwan Stock Exchange (TSE) in 1962 laid the foundation for the later activities in the Taiwan capital market. Taiwan's securities market thus has a relatively short history when compared with those of other countries. In January 1988, the government promulgated the Securities Exchange Law Amendment (SELA) to improve the functioning and scope of the domestic stock market. Since then, the market is much more liberalised and internationalised.

The TSE reform has been a dynamic and complex process as the regulatory authorities, in particular the Ministry of Finance (MoF) and the Securities Exchange Commission (SEC), have attempted to liberalise and internationalise the TSE to improve its efficacy for both the users and suppliers of capital. Many substantial reforms have been implemented since the 1988 SELA. For instance, the reforms include the permission for the new entry

---

[*] For more details, please refer to publications of Taiwan Stock Exchange Corporation (1994 & 1997) and Taiwan Stock Exchange (1997).

of securities firms, securities investment trust enterprises (SITEs), securities investment consulting enterprises (SICEs), and securities finance companies; the relaxation of investment by foreign individual and institutions; the raising of ceilings of foreign investment; deregulation of investment by financial institutions; and the deregulation of share issuing. All these reforms are intended to make the TSE much deeper and broader. At present, the Taiwan Stock Exchange (TAIEX) has been added to the MSCI Emerging Markets Indices (EMI) and this is expected to draw significant buying interest from foreign investors.

In 1967, there were two stock indices published by the Taiwan SEC; that is, the TAIEX and the Non-Financial. Since 1981, two more indices, stock category A and stock category B, are available. Moreover, eight industrial sector indices were also introduced by using the prices of December 29, 1986 as the base day. These eight indices include: cement and ceramics; foods, plastics and chemical; textiles, electrical, paper and pulp; construction; and banking and insurance. After 1994, fourteen more sector indices were published by the TSEC where some of them were split from the original indices.

EMPIRICAL STUDIES OF WEAK-FORM EFFICIENCY

Fama (1970; 1976) defined the efficient market as a market in which firms can make production-investment decisions, and investors can choose among the securities that represent ownership of firms' activities under the assumption that security prices at any time "fully reflect" all available information; a market in which prices always fully reflect available information is called "efficient."

Some empirical tests do show that it is possible to devise trading schemes based on very short term price swings that will on average out perform buy-and-hold (B&H) strategy. However, when one takes account of the minimum trading costs that would be generated by small filters, their advantage over B&H strategy disappears. (Alexander, 1964 ; Fama, 1976). Radcliffe (1994) draws a distinction between a perfectly efficient and an economically efficient market. According to him, a perfectly efficient market is one in which prices always reflect all known information, prices adjust instantaneously to new information, and speculative profits are simply a matter of luck. In an economically efficient market, prices might not adjust instantaneously to information, but, over the long run, speculative profits can not be earned after transaction costs such as brokerage commissions and taxes are paid.

Researchers have used four methods to test the EMH (Efficient Market Hypothesis) in the weak form:

- Serial correlation test
- Run test
- Filter rule tests
- Technical indicators tests

Serial Correlation Test

A serial correlation or auto-correlation is a test of the correlation between the return on a stock in a given time period with its return in a subsequent time period. In an efficient market, the serial correlation coefficients should not be significantly different from zero. Trading decisions based on past returns are possible if the auto-correlation is significantly large.

By far the most comprehensive test has been conducted by Fama (1965) who examined daily returns for each of the 30 stocks in the Dow Jones Industrial Average between the years 1957 to 1962. He found that the auto-correlation was generally positive, but statistically very close to zero. He also calculated correlations for returns using lags of time intervals greater than a day, i.e. over four-, nine-, and sixteen-day intervals and then correlated with prior four-, nine-, and sixteen-day returns. Again, a few correlations were statistically different from zero and, the correlations were too small to be useful to traders.

The subsequent studies by Kendall (1953), Cootner (1962), and Moor (1964) are noteworthy. These studies and many others including tests that were carried out on the Taiwan Stock Exchange (Table 1) generally arrived at the same conclusions as Fama (1965). Radcliffe (1994) has summarised the findings of these studies.

Table 1. Summary of serial correlation test in Taiwan

Researcher	Data	Results
Lin Yi Chung (1978)	Monthly close price of 11 stocks from 1971 to 1977	Not correlated
Huang Shr Lu (1978)	Half-monthly price of 23 stocks from Feb. 1973 to Feb. 1978	Not correlated
Chang Jin Kue (1980)	Weekly price of 20 stocks from 1973 to 1978 (1 − 4 lags)	Independent between lags.
Lee Hue Hong (1986)	Daily, weekly and monthly price of 33 stocks from 1976 to 1984	Not correlated

Run Test

A run is a sequence of successive days/weeks/months in which the price moves in the same direction. Each day/week/month is classified as being a day/week/month of price rise or price fall, and the lengths of the runs are tallied. If this series of observations was random, the index of one sector traded on one day would be independent of that on any other. Then, a high index would be no more likely to be followed by another high index than by a low index.

In Taiwan, Kue (1980) tested the weekly price of 20 stocks listed on the TSE and found that their changes of returns were randomly distributed. Further, Hong (1985) tested the daily, weekly and monthly prices of 33 listed stocks from 1976 to 1984, and concluded that the TSE conformed to the weak form of the EMH.

Tests of Technical Analysis

The Dow theory, formulated by Charles H. Dow, is the foundation of much of the technical analysis. William P. Hamilton and Robert Rhea modified and polished the theory later on. The modern Dow theory is an integration of the ideas of Dow, Hamilton and Rhea.

Magee (1966) has provided a comprehensive definition of technical analysis. He states: "Technical analysis is the science of recording, usually in graphic form, the actual history of trading (price changes, volume of transactions, etc.) in a certain stock or in 'the averages' and then deducing from that pictured history the probable future trend". The basic premise of technical analysis is that the demand-supply forces determine the security prices. According to the protagonists of Random Walk Hypothesis (RWH), this is not at all possible because price movements are seemingly display of a totally random process. Thus, there is no way to predict the future price movements. Although a great number of empirical studies on the effectiveness of technical analysis have been conducted during this century, the issue still remain disputable. Two important tests of technical analysis include filter tests and technical indicators tests.

Filter tests. Some well-known studies using the filter rule tests are those carried out by Alexander (1961), Fama & Blume (1966) and Sweeney (1988). In Taiwan, the similar tests were carried out by several researchers. The findings of some of the studies are given in Table 2.

Table 2. Summary of studies of filter rule tests

Researcher	Data	Results
Hsu Shr Hau (1979)	27 stocks which have largest trading value in 1973 from 1974 to 1977	Performance of Filter Rule is better than B & H. The market is not efficient.
Lee Huei Hung (1985)	Randomly select 33 stocks	Filter of 1% to 10% not valid. Filter of 11% valid.
Chen Shen (1985)	Stocks that with largest trading value in 15 sectors from 1975 to 1982	Valid
Lin Chung Yong (1989)	32 stocks which have the highest turnover during the period of 1986 to 1989 and studied during 1987 to 1988	With transaction cost, filter of 6% to 30% can obtain excess return.
Alexander (1964)	Dow Jones Industrials from 1897 to 1927 and S&P Industrials from 1929 to 1959	Invalid
Fama and Blume (1966)	30 stocks listed in the New York Stock Exchange form 1957 to 1962	Invalid
Sweeney (1988)	Same as above mentioned 30 stocks from 1970-1982	Valid

Test on other technical indicators. Several technical indicators are also used in practice in predicting the share price changes. Researchers have carried out tests of the effectiveness of these indicators. Results of some of these studies in Taiwan, are shown in Table 3.

Table 3. Studies of technical indicators in Taiwan

Researcher	Data	MA	RSI	BIAS	KD	R%	MACD
Lee Huei Hung (1985)	Randomly select 33 stocks	X					
Yie Jr Wu (1986)	Weighted Index	O					
Lin Chung Yong (1989)	32 stocks which have the highest turnover during the period of 1986-1988 and studied during 1987-1988	X	X				
Hsu Jue Long (1989)	50 blue chips in Category A from 1975 to 1982	X	X	X			
Yo Kuo Gee (1990)	147 stocks randomly selected		O				
Chen Hsin Chiang (1990)	22 stocks randomly selected which were listed before 1989 for 1 year (1989)	X	X	X	X		
Lai Sheng Chang	32 stocks which were selected from different sectors and listed before 1983 from 1984 to 1989	O	X			X	
Chan Yi Ching (1990)	166 stocks from 1980 to 1989	O					
Tsai Yi Long (1990)	110 stocks listed before Aug. 1986 from 1986 to 1989	O	X	X	X	X	O
Fang Kuo Jung (1991)	Weighted Index and 7 Sector Index from 1987 to 1990	O	X	O	O	O	X
Su Jr Long (1992)	Weighted Index from 1987 to 1991			X		X	
Kuang Yin Lin (1993)	Weighted Index from 1967 to 1991	O	X	X	X	X	

O *represents the way is valid,* X *represents the way is not valid*

METHODOLOGY AND DATA

Most studies of the EMH in Taiwan relate to pre-reform period when the Taiwan stock market was narrow and highly restricted. The present study uses the TSE data of the post-liberalisation period. The sector indices, tested in this study, included the TAIEX and the eight industrial sector indices published after 1986. Since most policies to improve the market were promulgated after 1990, the study, therefore, tested the efficiency of the market over a 7-year period from 1990 to 1997 which was further broken into two periods: October 1990 to October 1993 and October 1993 to October 1997.

The weekly data of each sector from October 13, 1990 to October 13, 1997 were collected from the TSE. The data included weekly open and close indices and return in percentage points. Nine indices studied are: TAIEX; Cement and Ceramics; Food, Plastics and Chemical; Textiles; Electrical; Paper and Pulp; Construction; and Banking. In order to compare the level of efficiency in two periods, the tests were conducted for the period of October 13, 1990 to October 12, 1993 and October 13, 1993 to October 13, 1997, respectively.

In the study, the simulation and statistical tests were used with the objective of testing the weak form efficiency of the TSE and thus, examining the effectiveness of technical analysis in the TSE. The following hypotheses were tested:

H1 the population correlation coefficient of successive price changes in different lags are zero.

H2 the changes in stock prices are randomly distributed.

H3 the changes in stock prices follow a normal distribution.

The first hypothesis would test the efficiency of the market. In this case, the correlation coefficients of returns between different lags should be zero, or just slightly different from zero; the absolute t-value should not be larger than $t_{n-2, a/2}$.

The second hypothesis would test the randomness of the series of prices changes. It would detect whether trends exist in price changes. If a series of price changes is random, the changes of prices of shares traded on one day will be independent of that on any other day, and there will be no abnormal profit that can be obtained from the trading rules.

The third hypothesis would test whether the random variables in this study follow a normal distribution. If it is a normal distribution, the skewness will be zero or close to zero. In addition, for the normal distribution, the population kurtosis should be 3. The Bowman-Shelton test for normality is, therefore, based on the closeness to 0 of the sample skewness and the closeness to 3 of the sample kurtosis. The significance at 5% and 10% significance level will be tested.

In the case of simulation on mechanical trading rule, the decision rules to judge whether the market is efficient in its weak form or not is that: (i) whether or not the performance of mechanical trading rule (technical analysis) is better than that of the buy-and-hold (B&H) strategy; and (ii) whether or not the first condition can be sustained in different time periods. The rates of return under technical analysis and B&H strategy in different periods are compared and tested by using t-test in order to detect if their performances are significantly different from each other. It is believed that if the market is efficient in its weak form, the expected value of excess rate of return is zero. In other words, one technical indicator is effective only if there is positive excess rate of return obtained, and it is consistently positive in two consecutive periods as well as the whole study period under 5% and 10% significant level.

As for the simulation, the technical indicators, stochastic K%D and moving average convergence and divergence (MACD), are employed.

While studies in the past have generally used daily data to carry out simulation, we have used weekly and monthly data in order to test its effectiveness in longer time intervals. By comparing the performance of mechanical rules and that of B&H strategy, it is expected to test the effectiveness of individual technical indicator as well as the weak form of the EMH.

RESULTS

Serial Correlation Test

The sample serial correlation coefficients of return were computed for TAIEX and eight sectors for lag of one week to lag of ten weeks. Most of the sample serial correlation coefficients (see Table 4) are quite small and some of them are negative. There is no significant difference between the correlation coefficients of periods I, II and III. Most of the serial correlation coefficients within lags 3, 5, 6, and 9 are larger than that in the other lags and lag 3 is the most significant. The results are similar for the sectorial indicies.

Run Test

The results of the run test are given in Table 5. The results show that the null hypothesis is rejected only in the second period for food sector under 10% significance level as well as in the first period of plastics and chemical sector under 5% significance level. In case of other sectors, z-values are quite small and the null hypothesis can not be rejected. In period III, all the series of prices changes are found to be random.

Normality Test

The results of the normality test are shown in Table 6. In the first period, all the prices have positive skewness while in the second period some of them have negative skewness. However, for the entire period of the study, the skewness coefficients for the TAIEX and all the eight sectors are all positive. Further, the range of the coefficients of kurtosis spreads from 0.30 to 6.66. Most of them are around 2.00-3.00. However, the results of the test show that only the TAIEX in the second period is inconsistent with the null hypothesis, the others, no matter in which period, all reject the null hypothesis. In all, the price changes of the TAIEX are close to the normal distribution, but not exactly. For the other sectors, the results show that they do not conform to the normal distribution. Furthermore, the results do not indicate that the price changes are closer to normal distribution in the second period.

Simulation on Mechanical Trading Rules

Our results show that most of the time K%D has performed poorer than B&H strategy except in paper and pulp sector. Also, its performance in the second period is much worse than in the first period and that causes its performance in the whole study period to be worse than B&H strategy.

By adopting MACD in the simulation, the results show that the performance of MACD is much better than K%D. The performance of MACD in the first period is better than B&H strategy. However, in the second period, only the performance in two sectors: cement and ceramics and food is better than B&H strategy. The performance in the other sectors, which is similar in the case of K%D, are much worse than in the first period. The detailed results are shown in Table 7.

Table 4. The results of serial correlation test – TAIEX

| Lag | Period I | | | | | Period II | | | | | Period III | | | | |
| | | | | t-statistic | | | | | t-statistic | | | | | t-statistic | |
	n	r	t-value	5%	10%	n	r	t-value	5%	10%	n	r	t-value	5%	10%
1	157	0.0568	0.7078	1.9754	1.6547	206	0.0228	0.3263	1.9717	1.6524	364	0.0443	0.8445	1.9665	1.6491
2	156	0.0775	0.9643	1.9755	1.6548	205	0.0761	1.0881	1.9717	1.6524	363	0.0770	1.4665	1.9666	1.6491
3	155	0.1052	1.3085	1.9756	1.6549	204	0.1853	**2.6796	1.9718	1.6524	362	0.1370	**2.6251	1.9666	1.6491
4	154	0.0320	0.3946	1.9757	1.6549	203	0.0179	0.2543	1.9718	1.6525	361	0.0276	0.5230	1.9666	1.6491
5	153	0.1128	1.3952	1.9758	1.6550	202	-0.0400	-0.5668	1.9719	1.6525	360	0.0524	0.9925	1.9666	1.6491
6	152	-0.0153	-0.1875	1.9759	1.6551	201	-0.1009	-1.4308	1.9720	1.6525	359	-0.0528	-0.9988	1.9666	1.6491
7	151	-0.0570	-0.6966	1.9760	1.6551	200	-0.0375	-0.5286	1.9720	1.6526	358	-0.0429	-0.8105	1.9667	1.6491
8	150	-0.0750	-0.9153	1.9761	1.6552	199	0.0844	1.1892	1.9721	1.6526	357	-0.0047	-0.0886	1.9667	1.6492
9	149	-0.0187	-0.2265	1.9762	1.6553	198	-0.1483	**-2.0993	1.9721	1.6527	356	-0.0660	-1.2437	1.9667	1.6492
10	148	0.0295	0.3565	1.9763	1.6554	197	-0.0995	-1.3968	1.9722	1.6527	355	-0.0252	-0.4728	1.9667	1.6492

* The null hypothesis is rejected under 10% significance level.
** The null hypothesis is rejected under 5 % significance level.
Period I: 13 Oct. 1990 to 13 Oct. 1993, Period II: 13 Oct. 1993 to 13 Oct. 1997, Period III: 13 Oct. 1990 to 13 Oct 1997

Table 5. The results of run test

| | Period I (Oct. 13, 90–Oct. 9, 93) | | | | Period II (Oct. 16, 93– Oct. 11, 97) | | | | Period III (Oct. 13, 90–Oct. 11, 97) | | | |
	Sample Size	No. of Runs	Median	Z-value	Sample Size	No. of Runs	Median	Z-value	Sample Size	No. of Runs	Median	Z-value
1 TAIEX	156	81	0.0019	0.3212	208	103	0.0061	-0.2780	364	183	0.0048	0.0000
2 Cement & Ceramics		85	-0.0001	0.9639		109	0.0016	0.5560		193	0.0011	1.0497
3 Food		87	0.0034	1.2010		93	0.0030	*-1.6681		176	0.0031	-0.7348
4 Plastics & Chemical		91	0.0022	**1.9278		105	0.0035	0.0000		191	0.0034	0.8398
5 Textile		85	-0.0014	0.9639		95	0.0030	-1.3901		182	0.0040	-0.1050
6 Electrical		79	0.0056	0.0000		100	0.0084	-0.6951		178	0.0081	-0.5249
7 Paper & Pulp		84	-0.0024	0.8032		94	0.0009	-1.5291		173	-0.0001	-1.0497
8 Construction		77	0.0000	-0.3213		103	0.0018	-0.2780		169	0.0011	-1.4696
9 Banking		81	-0.0050	0.3213		115	0.0028	1.3901		184	0.0012	0.1050

* The null hypothesis is rejected under 10% significance level
** The null hypothesis is rejected under 5% significance level
\# Z-statistics: 5% significant = 1.96, 10% significant = 1.645

Table 6. The result of normality test

	Period I (Oct. 13, 90–Oct. 9, 93)				Period II (Oct. 16, 93– Oct. 11, 97)				Period III (Oct. 13, 90–Oct. 11, 97)			
	Sample Size	Skewness	Kurtosis	B-Value	Sample Size	Skewness	Kurtosis	B-Value	Sample Size	Skewness	Kurtosis	B-Value
1 TAIEX	157	0.3981	3.02	*4.1237	208	0.1029	2.41	3.3894	365	0.3161	3.65	**12.5657
2 Cement & Ceramics		0.2701	2.53	3.3727		0.0376	1.20	**28.0893		0.2258	2.60	**5.5025
3 Food		0.4376	2.67	**5.7756		-0.0596	2.13	**6.5899		0.3614	3.74	**16.2638
4 Plastics & Chemical		0.6564	2.87	**11.4553		0.4716	2.78	**8.1346		0.5953	3.17	**22.0455
5 Textile		0.6473	2.92	**11.4064		-0.2719	1.90	**13.0557		0.2977	2.79	**6.0867
6 Electrical		0.4712	2.90	**5.8803		0.1967	0.30	**64.3539		0.3255	1.71	**31.7082
7 Paper & Pulp		0.6075	1.00	**35.7917		-0.0129	1.51	**19.3175		0.3252	1.28	**51.4290
8 Construc.		0.2587	1.49	**16.6560		0.0615	1.93	**29.4842		0.2182	1.97	**18.8801
9 Banking		0.4177	2.43	**6.7085		1.2652	6.66	**171.8275		0.7367	4.16	**53.5398

1 Bowman-Shelton Statistic

Sample Size n	10% Significant	5% Significant
150	3.43	4.39
200	3.48	4.43
300	3.68	4.60
400	3.76	4.74

Table 7. Comparison on the performance of K%D and B&H

Sector		B & H Profit	K%D Profit	Excess Return	Standard Deviation	t-Value	t-Statistics 5%	10%
TAIEX	Period I	478.91	915.75	0.0004	0.0029	**4.2464	1.6462	1.2823
	Period II	1141.44	29.87	-0.0006	0.0025	-9.5845	1.6459	1.2821
	Period III	2183.21	984.57	-0.0004	0.0027	-7.7634	1.6454	1.2819
Cement &	Period I	399.93	158.11	-0.0001	0.0020	-2.1984		
Ceramics	Period II	63.06	-289.80	-0.0002	0.0018	-5.2493		
	Period III	496.95	-172.68	-0.0002	0.0018	-5.7547		
Food	Period I	620.38	1101.48	0.0030	0.0025	**4.0343		
	Period II	812.53	296.35	-0.0007	0.0027	-10.3686		
	Period III	1954.26	487.40	-0.0005	0.0027	-9.3208		
Plastics &	Period I	441.43	71.15	-0.0012	0.0034	-11.7897		
Chemical	Period II	846.40	470.26	-0.0002	0.0025	-2.4577		
	Period III	1677.08	639.50	-0.0003	0.0026	-6.1981		
Textile	Period I	446.42	1131.01	0.0006	0.0038	**5.4604		
	Period II	503.10	72.76	-0.0002	0.0029	-2.3075		
	Period III	1186.89	1252.53	0.0000	0.0031	0.7734		
Electrical	Period I	837.96	624.51	0.0000	0.0027	-0.5917		
	Period II	3506.89	543.06	-0.0019	0.0036	-20.5185		
	Period III	7332.15	1506.72	-0.0023	0.0032	-35.7906		
Paper &	Period I	288.44	1669.90	0.0010	0.0040	**8.6671		
Pulp	Period II	270.81	1689.22	0.0005	0.0027	**7.2624		
	Period III	646.99	4797.65	0.0007	0.0033	**10.7341		
Construction	Period I	640.37	1013.97	0.0003	0.0030	**3.7883		
	Period II	613.65	579.87	-0.0001	0.0018	-1.0850		
	Period III	1662.52	2094.05	0.0000	0.0024	-0.8549		
Banking	Period I	438.37	363.65	0.0002	0.0043	1.3729		
	Period II	959.05	-402.04	-0.0007	0.0033	-7.7937		
	Period III	1834.40	-184.59	-0.0005	0.0037	-6.7139		

Period I: 13 Oct. 1990 to 13 Oct. 1993
Period II: 13 Oct. 1993 to 13 Oct. 1997
Period III: 13 Oct. 1990 to 13 Oct 1997
** The null hypothesis is not accepted under 5% significance level

Although K%D failed in some sectors in the first period and most of the sectors in the second period, it still performed very well in the paper and pulp sector. MACD failed in the second period in most of the sectors but still performed better than B&H in cement and ceramics sector and food sector. These evidences indicate that, for every individual technical indicator, it can obtain excess return in one stock but might not perform in the same in other stocks. The movement pattern of one stock price is directly influenced by different conditions and circumstances in that period of time. One should choose the technical indicator that can better predict the movement pattern of the stock. However, it is very difficult to foresee the movement pattern of one stock price and investors may lose money if they adopt a wrong technical indicator.

Our results indicate that the longer interval can stop creating disguising signals of a technical indicator. However, it makes the indicator slow in generating signals. Hence, the performance of adopting indicators of longer intervals might not be better than that of indicators of shorter intervals. It is also revealed that even though, in all the sectors except electrical, the weekly MACD obtained excess return in the first period, it could not consistently beat B&H strategy in the second period. Therefore, one technical indicator that was effective in one period of time might not be effective in the other period of time.

It is shown from our results that by adopting weekly K%D or MACD, investors are not able to obtain excess return in the second period. Meanwhile, the performance of both K%D and MACD in the second period is much poorer than in the first period. However, in some sectors such as electrical in the first period and construction and banking in the second period, the total amount of profit obtained from simulation is larger than under B&H strategy, but their excess rates of return are very close to zero and their t-values are not big enough to reject the null hypothesis. Thus, the null hypothesis can not be rejected and the market is efficient in its weak form in the second period. It is believed that the market has improved after the introduction of policies of internationalisation and liberalisation by the Taiwan government.

CONCLUSIONS

The results of the serial correlation test show that there is no significant correlation between stock price changes and lags. The successive price changes are independent with each other; this implies that it is very difficult to find variables which are useful in predicting future share prices and returns. Further, the results of the run test indicate that the series of price changes are randomly distributed. No trend is observable in the series of price changes and consequently, no abnormal profit can be obtained from carrying out trading rules. The results of normality test show that the series of variables do not conform to normal distribution. The results of the run test are quite consistent with the serial correlation test. Being a non-parametric test, the run test makes no assumption about the distribution from which the observations are drawn. Thus, the Taiwan stock market conforms to the weak form of efficiency.

The results of simulation on mechanical trading rules (K%D and MACD) show that the market do generally conform to the weak form efficiency. The weekly K%D can not obtain excess return in the first period and it is even worse in the second period. The weekly MACD can obtain abnormal profit in the first period but it can not consistently do so in the next period. The performance of both weekly K%D and MACD in the second are much worse than that in the first period.

In view of the simulation results, we can not completely neglect the worth of technical analysis. Generally, one experienced technician or analyst would not simply adopt one technical indicator, but he is likely to consider several indicators and methods in the investment appraisal process and finally make a decision. Therefore, it is quite difficult to test whether technical indicators are effective or not.

The results of statistical tests and simulation are generally consistent with each other and basically conform to the weak form of EMH. However, the results of statistical tests do not completely match with the results of simulation, especially in the first period. The results of serial correlation test and run test show that the series of price changes and successive prices changes are independent and randomly distributed in the first period. However, the results of simulation show that K%D can obtain excess return in some sectors and so does MACD in most of the sectors in the same period. Similar inconsistencies also exist in the second period. The main reason for concluding that both methods conform to EMH is that, in most cases, they are not able to consistently obtain excess return in the second period. Besides, the results of statistical tests do not show any significant difference between two periods.

REFERENCES

Alexander, S.S. (1964), "Price movement in speculation sarkets: Trends or random walks, No. 2", in: Cootner, P.H (ed.), *The Random Character of Stock Market Prices*, MIT Press, Cambridge, 338-372.

Anderson, S.C. (1989), "Evidence on the reflecting barriers model: New opportunities for technical analysis?", *Financial Analysts Journal*, May-June.

Bishop, III E.L. and Rollins, J.R. (1977), "Lowry's reports: A denial of market efficiency?", *Journal of Portfolio Management*, Fall, 21-27.

Bohan, J. (1981), "Relative strength: Further positive evidence", *Journal of Portfolio Management*, Fall, 36-39.

Semkow, B.W. (1994), *Taiwan's Capital Market Reform: The Financial and Legal Issues*, Oxford University Press, New York.

Cheng, C.W. (1989), *Investment Technical Analysis*, 5th Ed., Taipei.

Chi, S. (1996), *Taiwan as an Asian Financial Centre*, Industry of Free China, 37-46

Chou, S.-R. (1989), *An Empirical Analysis of Stock Market Anomalies: Evidence From the Republic of China in Taiwan*, University of Kentucky.

Cootner P.H. (1962), "Stock prices: Random vs. systematic changes", *Industrial Management Review* 3/2, 24-45.

Curtis M.A. and Rahfeldt, D. (1986), *Timing the Market - How to Profit in Bull and Bear Markets with Technical Analysis*, Probus Publishing Co., Chicago.

Edwards, R.D. and Magee, J. (1992), *Technical Analysis of Stock Trends*, 6th Ed., John Magee Inc., Boston.

Fama, E.F. (1965), "The behaviour of stock market prices", *Journal of Business* XXXII, 34-105

Fama, E.F. (1970), "Efficient capital markets: A review of theory and empirical works", *Journal of Finance*, May, 383-417.

Fama, E.F. (1976), *Foundation of Finance*, Chapter 5, Basic Books, New York.

Fama, E.F. (1991), "Efficient capital market: II", *Journal of Finance* XLVI/5, 1575-1613

Fisher, L. and Lorie, J. (1964), "Rates of return on investments in common stock: The year-by-year record, 1926-1964", *Journal of Business* XXXVII, January.

Francis, J.C. (1986), *Investment: Analysis and Management*, 4th Ed., McGraw-Hill, New York.

Jensen, M.C. and Benington, G.A. (1970), "Random walks and technical theories: Some additional evidence", *Journal of Finance* XXV/1, 469-481.

Levy, R.A. (1967), "Relative strength as a criterion for investment selection", *Journal of Finance* XXII/4, 595-610.

Li-Teh Hsu, (1996), *Developing Taipei as a Regional Financial Center and Taiwan's Equity Market*, Industry of Free China, 75-82

Murphy, J.J. (1986), *Technical Analysis of the Futures Markets: A Comprehensive Guide to Trading Methods and Applications*, New York Institute of Finance, New York.

Pinches, G.E. (1970), "Random walk hypothesis and rechnical analysis", *Financial Analysts Journal*, March-April, 104-110.

Pin-Kung Chiang, (1996), *The APROC Plan: Into the Asia-Pacific Century as a Regional Hub*, Industry of Free China, 47-53

Pruitt, S.W., Maurice Tse, K.S. and White, R.E. (1992), "The CRISMA trading system: The next five years", *Journal of Portfolio Management*, Spring, 22-25.

Radcliffe, R.C. (1994), *Investment: Concepts, Analysis, Strategy*, 4th Ed., HarperCollins College Publishers, New York.

Schultz H.D. and Coslow S. (1966), *A Treasury of Wall Street Wisdom*, Investors Press, 250.

Securities & Exchange Commission (1997), *1996 SEC Statistics*, Vol. 27, Taipei.

Securities & Futures Institute (1997), *The Securities Market in the Republic of China*, Taipei.

Schwager, J.D. (1996), *Technical Analysis*, John Wiley & Sons, New York.

Sweeny, R.J., "Evidence on short-term trading strategies: Here is a reinvestigation of the evidence", *Journal of Portfolio Management*, Fall, 20-26.

Sweeney R.J., "Some new filter rule tests: Methods and results", *Journal of Finance and Quantitative Analysis* 23/3, 291-300.

Shen, T.T. (1996), *Sustainable Development: The Role of Bankers and Investors*, Industry of Free China, 55-61

Sheu, Y.D. (1996), *Developing Taipei into a Regional Financial Center*, Industry of Free China, 41-45.

Wang, K-Y. (1996), *The Development and Prospect of the Taiwan Stock Market*, Asian Institute of Technology, Bangkok.

Ying, C.C. (1966), "Stock market prices and volume of sales", *Econometrica* 34, 676-685.

THE DYNAMICS OF IMPLIED VOLATILITY SURFACES[*]

G. Skiadopoulos[1,2], S. Hodges[2], L. Clewlow[2]

[1] Athens Derivatives Exchange
Lekka 23-25, Athens, Greece

[2] Financial Options Research Centre
University of Warwick
Coventry CV4 7AL, United Kingdom

Abstract: This empirical study is motivated by the literature on "smile-consistent" arbitrage pricing with stochastic volatility. We investigate the number and shape of shocks that move the implied volatility surface by applying Principal Components Analysis. Our methodology differs from the one followed by Skiadopoulos, Hodges and Clewlow (1998) who looked at the dynamics of implied volatility smiles for a given expiry bucket. We examine the dynamics of implied volatility surfaces under two different metrics: the strike metric and the moneyness metric. We find similar results for both metrics. Using a variety of criteria, we conclude that two shocks explain the movements of the volatility surface. The first shock is interpreted as a shift, while the second one has a Z-shape. The results have implications for both option pricing and hedging and for the economics of option pricing.

Keywords: Implied Volatility Smile, Implied Volatility Surface, Implied Volatility, Principal Components Analysis.

INTRODUCTION

The need to price and hedge exotic options consistently with the prices of standard European options has motivated the growing literature on "smile-consistent" no-arbitrage

[*] We would like to thank participants at the 1998 FORC Conference and at the 1999 Decision Science Institute Conference. We would also like to thank Russell Grimwood, Jens Jackwerth, Wojtek Krzanowski, Joao Pedro Nunes, Juan Carlos Mejia Perez and Chris Strickland for helpful discussions and comments. Part of this paper was written while the first author benefited from the Human Capital & Mobility Programme of the European Commission. Financial support from the Corporate Members of FORC is also gratefully acknowledged. Any remaining errors are our responsibility alone.

S.H. Zanakis et al. (eds.), Decision Making: Recent Developments and Worldwide Applications, 197–211.
© 2000 *Kluwer Academic Publishers.*

stochastic volatility models (Dupire (1992), Derman and Kani (1998) and Ledoit and Santa-Clara (1998)). The aim of this paper is to investigate the dynamics of implied volatilities since this is a prerequisite for the implementation of these models.

The Black-Scholes model (B-S 1973) is widely used to price and hedge standard and exotic options. Its popularity among practitioners arises from its tractability. However, the empirical evidence (see among others Derman and Kani (1998), Heynen (1994), and Rubinstein (1985)) contradicts its prediction of a constant implied volatility[1]. Implied volatilities strongly depend on the maturity (term structure) and strike (smiles or skews) of the option under scrutiny. Moreover, implied volatilities vary in a stochastic way, across different points in time for a given option (Gemmill 1996). These results suggest that the implied volatilities of options with different strikes and expirations, form a two-dimensional surface which has certain dynamics.

The evolution of the implied volatility surface undermines the use of the B-S formula as a model for the correct pricing and hedging of standard, and especially, of exotic options (Davydov and Linetsky 1999). In order to cope with this issue, a number of option pricing models have been proposed which give rise to smiles or skews, and to a term structure of implied volatilities, roughly similar to what is observed empirically. These models provide for stochastic volatility (see for example Hull and White (1987), or jump processes (see for example Merton (1976)), or both (Scott 1997). However, none of these models fit observed implied volatility patterns well (see Das and Sundaram (1998), Taylor and Xu (1994)).

These problems have led to the recent literature on "smile consistent" no-arbitrage stochastic volatility models. This approach is similar to the Heath, Jarrow, Morton (HJM, 1992) methodology for stochastic interest rates. Rather than specifying the underlying asset's process in advance, the models use the European market option prices to infer information about the underlying asset process. They do this by taking today's standard option prices as given, and letting them evolve stochastically in such a way as to preclude arbitrage. This ensures the correct pricing of standard options, and is relevant to the pricing of exotic options. For example, Derman and Kani (1998) start from today's option prices and assume a stochastic process for the forward volatility. They then find the no-arbitrage condition that its drift must satisfy. Ledoit and Santa-Clara (1998) propose a model where the implied rather than the local volatilities are used to obtain a simple no-arbitrage condition that the drift of the implied volatility process must satisfy.

In order to implement this type of models, we need to understand the dynamics of the implied volatility surface. We answer the three questions related to this: (1) how many factors are needed to explain the dynamics of the implied volatility surfaces?, (2) what do these factors look like?, and (3) how are these factors correlated with the innovation in the underlying asset's process[2]?

The technique that we use in order to answer the three questions is Principal Components Analysis (PCA). It is applied to the changes in implied volatilities over time. The changes in implied volatilities are indexed in two different ways (metrics): the strike

---

[1] The implied volatility is the volatility value which equates the market option price to the option price given by a B-S type model.

[2] This also parallels work on implementing the HJM term structure model where Litterman and Scheinkman (1988) and others, have applied Principal Components Analysis to analyze innovations in the yield curve.

level, and the moneyness level. Our methodology differs from the one followed in Skiadopoulos, Hodges and Clewlow (S-H-C,1998) where they examined the dynamics of implied volatilities for individual expiry buckets (hereafter, we will refer to this paper as the smile analysis). On the contrary, in this paper we look at the dynamics of implied volatilities across *both* the strike (moneyness) metric and the ranges of days to maturity. By doing so, we incorporate the effect of the term-structure on the dynamics of implied volatilities. It may be the case that short and long-term implieds are driven by different shocks (see Xu and Taylor (1994)). This could result in a different number (and possibly shape) of shocks driving the whole implied volatility surface from those driving individual smiles. The practical importance of our results is that we can cope with the vega risk of portfolios containing options with different expiries and strikes which are subject to the same volatility shock (rather than being subject to different shocks for the different expiries, as it was the case in S-H-C).

We are able to identify two factors which explain about 53% (60%) of the variance in the strike (moneyness) metric. The first factor is interpreted as an essentially parallel shift and the second as a Z-shaped twist. Our results are remarkably consistent across years. To implement a "smile-consistent" no-arbitrage stochastic volatility model for the pricing and hedging of futures options we need three factors. One is required for the underlying asset, and the other two for the implied volatility. A related paper by Kamal and Derman (1997) has also investigated the same issue. They have used a different data set and a somewhat different methodology; their results are markedly different from ours. We comment further on the differences between the two studies in the concluding section of the paper.

The paper is organized as follows. First, we describe the data set used and how we have screened it. In the third section we describe the PCA technique; we explain why it was chosen and how it will be applied to analyze the data. In the fourth and fifth sections we analyze the dynamics of the implied volatility surface under the strike and moneyness metric, respectively. Next, we calculate the correlations between the changes of the principal components and the underlying asset price. Finally, we discuss the implications of our results.

THE DATA SET

Source Data

We use daily data on futures options on the Standard and Poor 500 index (S&P 500) from the Chicago Mercantile Exchange (CME) for the years 1992-95. The futures contracts have maturities every March, June, September and December and their last trading day is the business day prior to the third Friday of the contract month. The options have maturities March, June, September, December and serial months. For the serial months expiry options, the underlying instrument is the future with the nearest expiry. The last day of trading for March, June, September, December expiring options, is the same day as the underlying futures contract.

The primary data for this study are the transaction report "Stats Database", compiled daily by CME. We extract from this, for the purposes of our study, the closing options and futures prices. In addition, we use London Euro-Currency interest rates (middle-rates) on the US dollar, obtained from Datastream, to proxy for the riskfree rate. Daily interest rates for 7-days, one-month, three months, six months and one year were used, while those for other maturities were obtained by linear interpolation.

Since the S&P500 options futures are American-style options, implied volatilities were calculated using the algorithm of Barone-Adesi and Whaley (1987), so as to capture the early exercise premium.

Screening the Data

In the first stage, the raw data are screened for data errors. Observations which violate the arbitrage boundary conditions are excluded. We eliminate data where the option price is less than, or equal to, its intrinsic value. We also exclude options having a price of less than 10 cents, and we eliminate short-term options with less than 10 days to expiry because they are very sensitive to small errors in the option price.

In a second stage, we exclude data likely to introduce errors into our volatility estimates. We construct our smiles by using out-of-the-money (OTM) puts for low strikes, and OTM calls for the high ones. The data on in-the-money (ITM) calls and puts are not used because they have high deltas; their prices and their implied volatilities are therefore very sensitive to the non-synchroneity problem (see Harvey and Whaley (1991)). Provided the put-call parity relationship holds (there is a simple arbitrage if it does not), puts and calls must have identical implied volatilities (in the absence of measurement error problems). Our procedure reduces the effects of errors due to non-synchronous data, without introducing any sources of bias.

We also decided to exclude implied volatilities calculated from options having a vega less than eight on the grounds of the probable magnitude of their measurement error[3]. For a given measurement error ΔC in the option price (e.g. arising from the bid-ask spread) the resulting error in the implied volatility $\Delta\sigma_{imp}$, is (approximately) ΔC/vega. There is a trade-off between accuracy and number of observations that we exclude. The choice of eight for the vega cutoff was made following a preliminary examination of the data (see S-H-C). As a result we are able to eliminate most of the noise and to retain about 40% of the observations for calls and 70% of the observations for puts.

PRINCIPAL COMPONENTS ANALYSIS AND THE IMPLIED VOLATILITY SURFACE

In this section, we outline the Principal Components Analysis (PCA) methodology used in this paper. PCA is used to explain the systematic behavior of observed variables, by

---

[3] Vega is defined as $vega = \frac{\partial C}{\partial \sigma_{imp}}$, where C is the call option value and σ_{imp} its implied volatility.

means of a smaller set of unobserved latent random variables. Its purpose is to transform p correlated variables to an orthogonal set which reproduces the original variance-covariance structure.

We apply PCA to decompose the variance-covariance structure of first differences of implied volatilities. To achieve this, we measure the daily differences of implied volatilities ($\sigma_{imp,t+1} - \sigma_{imp,t}$) across different levels of strikes (or moneyness) and different ranges of days to expiry (expiry buckets). For example, one of our variables provides a time series of the first differences of implied volatilities which correspond to a strike level of 360 and expiry range 90-10. Typically, for each expiry bucket we have 7-10 levels of strikes (moneyness) in each year, with 100-225 observations for each level.

In general, denote time by $t=1,...,T$ and let p be the number of variables. Such a variable is a (T×1) vector $\mathbf{x}$. The purpose of the PCA is to construct *Principal Components* (PCs hereafter) as linear combinations of the vectors $\mathbf{x}$, orthogonal to each other, which reproduce the original variance-covariance structure. The first PC is constructed to explain as much of the variance of the original p variables, as possible (maximization problem). The second PC is constructed to explain as much of the remaining variance as possible, and so on. The coefficients with which these linear combinations are formed are called the *loadings*. In matrix notation

$$Z = XA \tag{1}$$

where $\mathbf{X}$ is a (T×p) matrix, $\mathbf{Z}$ is a (T×p) matrix of PCs, and $\mathbf{A}$ is a (p×p) matrix of loadings. The first order condition of this maximization problem results to

$$(X'X - lI)A = 0 \tag{2}$$

where l_i are the Lagrange multipliers and I is a (p×p) identity matrix. From equation (2) it is evident that the PCA is simply the calculation of the eigenvalues l_i and the eigenvectors of the variance-covariance matrix $S=X'X$. Furthermore, the variance of the ith PC is given by the ith eigenvalue, and the sum of the variances of the PCs equals the sum of the variances of the $\mathbf{X}$ variables.

When both variables and components are standardized to unit length, the elements of A' are correlations between the variables and PCs and they are called *correlation loadings* (see Basilevsky (1994) for more details). If we retain $r<p$ PCs then

$$X = Z_{(r)}A'_{(r)} + \varepsilon_{(r)} \tag{3}$$

where $\varepsilon_{(r)}$ is a (T×p) matrix of residuals and the other matrices are defined as before having r rather than p columns. The percentage of variance of $\mathbf{x}$ which is explained by the retained PCs (*communality* of $\mathbf{x}$) is calculated from the correlation loadings. After retaining $r<p$ components, we look at equation (3) to examine the size of the communalities, and the meaning of the retained components.

PCA is a natural and parsimonious technique to identify the number and the interpretation of stochastic shocks that move the implied volatilities. It enables us to simplify the complex dynamics of the volatility surface, by identifying its most important components, without imposing any prior structure. This contrasts, for example, with the alternative regression analysis approach of estimating a specific function of time and moneyness (see Taylor and Xu (1994)). PCA is preferred to factor analysis, for our analysis, because of its variance maximization property

We investigate the dynamics of implied volatilities by performing PCA on the first differences of implied volatilities, so as to avoid any problems arising due to non-stationarity. The variables x of changes of implied volatilities to which we apply the PCA will be indexed in two different ways (metrics): (a) the strike level (strike metric), and (b) the moneyness level (K-F)/F*100 (moneyness metric). For a fixed day, the smiles (or skews) are going to look the same in both the strike and moneyness metric. However, the dynamics of implied volatilities will be different across the two metrics (see Section 6).

The strike metric is chosen because the arguments of Derman, Kani and Zou (1996) imply that it is a natural metric to examine the dynamics of deterministic volatility models. The moneyness metric is chosen because there are theoretical reasons (see Heynen (1994), Taylor and Xu (1994)) suggesting that the dynamics of smiles are a function of moneyness in a stochastic volatility model. If a deterministic volatility model is the true model, then implieds should have a "small" variation in the strike metric, and a "large" variation in the moneyness metric. The reverse will happen if a stochastic volatility model is the correct description of the world.

In order to look into the dynamics of implied volatilities as a surface for a given year, first we group the data into different buckets for distinct ranges of days to expiry. Then, we choose the strike (moneyness) levels for each expiry bucket. Finally, all the variables are brought together to perform the PCA.

The expiry buckets were chosen, so as to cope with the missing observations that occur due to the screening criteria that we have applied. We are not going to replace our missing values, because we do not know how this will bias our results (see Anderson et al. (1983)). Instead, we are going to apply *listwise deletion* i.e. we will delete the whole day for which at least the observation for one variable is missing. Listwise deletion is applied after taking the first differences, so as differences in implieds are 1-day differences.

Pooling the ranges and applying listwise deletion will decrease considerably the number of observations if the expiry ranges are too fine. It turns out that the intervals of days to maturity that give us a satisfactory number of observations (not less than 100) and permit us to measure smiles across a wide range (not less than 20 variables) once they are pooled together, are 90-10, 180-90 and 270-90.

PCA ON THE STRIKE METRIC

In this section, we investigate the dynamics of the implied volatility surface when the differences in the implieds are indexed with the strike level.

Number of Retained Principal Components and a First Interpretation

We now decide on the number of components to be retained and we look at their interpretation. Earlier researchers have used a variety of rules of thumb to determine the number of components to be retained. For example, they keep the components corresponding to eigenvalues larger than the mean of all the eigenvalues (mean eigenvalue rule of thumb), or they keep the components which explain 90% of the total variance. As Basilevsky notes "such practice is statistically arbitrary, and seems to be prompted more by intuitive concepts of practicality and "parsimony", than by probabilistic requirements of sample-population inference."

We determine the number of components to be retained by looking at a range of criteria in an evenhanded way. First, we apply Velicer's (1976) non-parametric criterion[4]. Next, working with components retained under this criterion, we look at the communalities. Finally, we look at the interpretation of the PCs.

Velicer proposes a non-parametric method for selecting nontrivial PCs, i.e. components which have not arisen as a result of random sampling, measurement error, or individual variation. His method is based on the partial correlations of the residuals of the PCs model, after $r<p$ components have been extracted. The criterion can be described as follows: The variance-covariance matrix of the residuals $\varepsilon_{(r)}$ in equation (3) is given by

$$\varepsilon_{(r)}'\varepsilon_{(r)} = X'X - A_{(r)}'A_{(r)} \tag{4}$$

Let $D = \mathrm{diag}(\varepsilon_{(r)}'\varepsilon_{(r)})$ Then, $R^* = D^{-\frac{1}{2}}\varepsilon_{(r)}'\varepsilon_{(r)}D^{-\frac{1}{2}}$ is the matrix of partial correlations of the residuals. If r_{ij}^* represents the ith row, jth column element of R^*, then the Velicer statistic is given by

$$f_r = \sum_{i \neq j}\sum \frac{r_{ij}^{2*}}{p(p-1)} = \sum_{i=j}\sum \frac{r_{ij}^{2*}-p}{p(p-1)} \tag{5}$$

and lies in the interval 0 to 1. The behavior of f_r is that it is decreasing until a number r^* and then it increases again. Velicer suggests that $r=r^*$ should be the number of components to be retained.

In Table 1 we show the results from applying Velicer's criterion and the mean eigenvalue rule of thumb. We also show the percentage of the variance explained by each one of the first three PCs. We can see that Velicer's criterion keeps one PC in year 1994, and two PCs in the other years. The reduction in the dimensionality of the variables is legitimate, since $f_0 > f_1$. The mean eigenvalue rule of thumb retains too many PCs. This is a commonly encountered characteristic of this criterion and it shows why we should not rely on such ad-hoc rules (see Jackson 1991). The average, across the years, explained by the two components variance is 52.5%.

---

[4] Most of the tests used for determining the number of PCs to be retained, are parametric based on the assumption of multivariate normality (For a review of these tests, see Basilevsky (1994)). However, application of the Bera-Jarque test showed that the null-hypothesis of univariate, and hence of multivariate normality, was rejected. Therefore, we decided to use a non-parametric method.

Table 1. Principal Components in the Strike Metric: r^*= the number of components retained under Velicer's criterion (minimum of $f_0,...,f_3$), 1 = the number of components retained under rule of thumb, with percentage of variance explained by components 1-3.

Year	f_0	f_1	f_2	f_3	r^*	1	1st PC	2nd PC	3rd PC
92	0.1814	0.1807	0.1807	0.1808	2	6	42.5	12.9	6.8
93	0.1415	0.1410	0.1409	0.1410	2	5	37.5	12.7	7.2
94	0.0513	0.0511	0.0512	0.0512	1	6	40.8	9.8	7.2
95	0.1235	0.1229	0.1226	0.1227	2	5	29.9	23.7	9.3

Next, we look at the interpretation of the first three PCs[5]. If any PC appears to be mostly noise, then we will prefer to reject it. The first PC has a Z-shape in all the ranges, apart from 90-10 in the years 1994, and 1995. The second PC, in the range 90-10, has a shift interpretation. In the longer expiry ranges, it has a triangular shape for the years 1992, 1993 and 1994, and a Z-shape in the year 1995. Finally, graphs for the third PC suggested strongly that it was just noise, confirming the interpretation from Velicer's procedure. Therefore, under the variety of criteria that we applied, we judge that we can only identify two shocks driving the implied volatility smiles of the S&P 500 futures options in the strike metric. However, the shapes of the retained two PCs are not consistent across years and expiries. This is exhibited by Figure 1 which shows the correlation loadings of the first and second PCs in the strike metric for the ranges 90-10 and 180-90, respectively. (for the sake of clarity, we have interpolated across the missing variables in these graphs). In order to obtain a better interpretation, we will utilize a rotation method, explained in the next section.

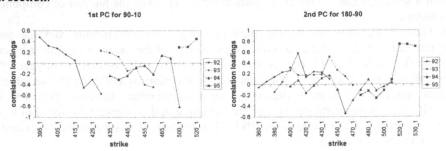

Figure 1. First and Second PCs in the Strike Metric for the 90-10 and 180-90 Expiries.

Interpretation of the Rotated PCs

We would like the first PC to be as close to a parallel shift, as possible (this would also be consistent with the Taylor series expansion intuition). We use a rotation technique to achieve this. We form new rotated loadings from the original ones **A**, by multiplying them by the rotation matrix

---

[5] We also looked at the communalities explained by one, two, and three PCs. The communalities criterion suggests that we should retain two PCs, since the third PC did not increase the explained communalities significantly.

$$T = \begin{bmatrix} \cos\theta & -\sin\theta \\ \sin\theta & \cos\theta \end{bmatrix}$$

where θ is the angle of rotation. The rotated components still explain the same total amount of variance, as the unrotated ones, but the total variance may have been re-distributed between the two (see Basilevsky (1994) for the properties of orthogonal rotations). For the purposes of our study, we choose T, so as the loadings on the first rotated PC are as flat, as possible[6]. We accomplish this by using a regression to find the orthogonal rotation which minimizes the least squares distance between the loadings of the first PC and a vector of constants.

After performing the rotation, the first PC in the range 90-10, has a shift interpretation in the years 1992, 1993 and 1995. In the year 1994 it has a shift interpretation for all, but the extreme strikes. In the other two ranges, the first PC has a triangular shape in every year. In general, the shape of the first rotated PC is very similar to that of the second unrotated PC. The size of its effect is bigger for the shorter expiries. The second rotated PC in the range 90-10, has a Z-shape in 1992, and it is a shift in the other years. In the other two ranges it has a Z-shape. The magnitude of the second PC is greatest for the longer expiries. Figure 2 shows the first and second rotated PC in the strike metric for the ranges 90-10 and 180-90, respectively, across the years.

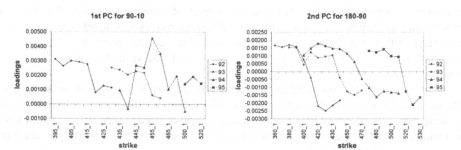

Figure 2. First and Second Rotated PCs in the Strike Metric for the 90-10 and 180-90 Expiries.

In Table 2 we show the percentage of the variance explained by each one of the two rotated PCs, and the cumulative explained variance (as well as the percentage for the original first component). We can see that the first rotated PC explains less amount of variance than the second rotated one.

---

[6] A rotation which tries to reveal a "targeted" interpretation is called a "Procrustes" rotation (see Jackson (1991)). Our choice of targeting on a flat "shift" loading seems to be novel. We checked that the most popular rotation methods, such as the varimax, the quartimax and the oblique method could not produce the desired interpetation. This is due to the way that they are constructed (for more details about these rotation methods see Basilevsky (1994)).

Table 2. Percentage of Variance Explained by the Unrotated First PC and by the Rotated PCs on the Strike Metric.

Year	Unrot. 1st PC	1st PC	2nd PC	Cumulative
92	42.5%	13.4%	42.0%	55.4%
93	37.5%	17.3%	33.0%	50.3%
94	40.8%	11.5%	39.0%	50.5%
95	29.9%	28.4%	25.2%	53.6%
Average	37.7%	17.6%	34.8%	52.5%

It is worth noting that the number and, the interpretation of the rotated PCs in the strike metric is the same as the one that S-H-C found in the smile analysis.

PCA ON THE MONEYNESS METRIC

Construction of the Moneyness Metric

To construct our variables, we first choose a grid of moneyness points for them. We measure implied volatilities at a number of different moneyness levels chosen as fixed percentage difference between the strike and the futures price F_t. This involves interpolation across the implied volatilities for these fixed variables, since F_t is always changing.

In choosing this grid we need to be careful not to make it too fine. If we allowed two different grid points to fall between adjacent strikes, they would both be interpolated from the same two data points. This would produce spurious dependence which would distort our results. We have therefore chosen moneyness levels which are slightly coarser than the coarsest spacing of the strikes.

Number of Retained Principal Components and a First Interpretation

We investigate the dynamics of the volatility surface in the moneyness metric just as we did for the strike metric. In other words, we apply three criteria to decide how many components to retain, and then we use a rotation in order to obtain a clean interpretation.

In Table 3, we show the results from applying Velicer's criterion and the mean eigenvalue rule of thumb. We also show the percentage of the variance explained by each one of the first three PCs. We can see that in every year the test keeps two PCs, while the reduction in the dimensionality of the variables is legitimate, since $f_0 > f_1$. The mean eigenvalue rule of thumb retains too many PCs. This shows why we should not rely on such ad-hoc rules (see Jackson (1991)).

Table 3. Principal Components in the Moneyness Metric: r^*= the number of components retained under Velicer's criterion (minimum of $f_0,...,f_3$), l = the number of components retained under rule of thumb, with percentage of variance explained by components 1-3.

Year	f_0	f_1	f_2	f_3	r^*	l	1st PC	2nd PC	3rd PC
92	0.1847	0.1838	0.1836	0.1838	2	4	38.6	22.7	10.7
93	0.1722	0.1714	0.1711	0.1713	2	4	34.5	26.7	10.2
94	0.1894	0.1884	0.1884	0.1885	2	6	40.6	19.2	10.2
95	0.1726	0.1713	0.1712	0.1714	2	4	39.2	18.3	9.4

The graphs for the first two PCs showed that they do not have a consistent shape across years and expiries[7]. For example, the first PC has a Z-shape in the range 90-10 for the years 1992 and 1993. However, in the same range it has a shift interpretation for the years 1994 and 1995. The second PC has a shift interpretation in the range 180-90 for the year 1992. On the other hand, in the same range, it has a mixture of positive and negative correlation loadings for the year 1992. The graphs for the third PC showed that it is noise.

Hence, all the criteria that we applied, suggest that two PCs are adequate in explaining the implied volatility surface dynamics. The two PCs explain on average, across the years, 60% of the total variance. Compared to the strike metric (see Table 1), the cumulative variance is bigger in the moneyness metric with the difference ranging from 4% up to 10%. This difference is stemming from the higher amount of variance explained by the second PC in the moneyness metric.

Interpretation of the Rotated PCs

As with the analysis in the strike metric, we will apply a rotation to our original PCs.

The first PC moves the implied volatility surface consistently across ranges and across years and its shape "approaches" the shift interpretation. The effect of the shift component attenuates with expiry. The second PC, in general, has a Z-shape across years, even though it has a shift interpretation in the range 90-10 in the years 1994 and 1995. There is not much sign of attenuation with expiry (we do not report any figures because of space limitations). More important, the number of shocks and their interpretation is the same for both the smiles and the surfaces.

Our analysis shows that the implementation of a "smile consistent" no-arbitrage stochastic volatility model suggests the need for three factors. One is required for the underlying asset and two more for the implied volatility. The loadings of the two PCs may be useful for volatility risk management, even though we do not know whether they will be stable (in fact, they exhibit some variability over the years). With this type of factor model, the definition of vega can be generalized to the sensitivities to each of the volatility shocks.

In Table 4 we show the percentage of the variance explained by the first and second rotated PCs (as well as the percentage for the original first component). We find that it is

---

[7] The communalities criterion suggests that we should keep two PCs in the surface analysis in the moneyness metric, just as it was the case in the strike metric.

not the shift which has the dominant effect on the implied volatility surface, but the second PC.

Table 4. Percentage of Variance Explained by the Unrotated First PC and by the Rotated PCs on the Moneyness Metric.

Year	Unrot. 1st PC	1st PC	2nd PC	Cumulative
92	38.6%	22.7%	38.6%	61.4%
93	34.5%	26.9%	34.3%	61.2%
94	40.6%	19.5%	40.4%	59.5%
95	39.2%	18.4%	39.2%	57.5%
Average	38.2%	21.8%	38.1%	60.0%

CORRELATIONS BETWEEN THE FUTURES PRICE AND THE PRINCIPAL COMPONENTS

We calculate the correlations between the proportional changes of the futures price and the changes of the rotated PCs, by using the futures price from each expiry range and the common "pooled" PC. Knowledge of these is necessary in order to complete the specification of the process for the evolution of implied volatilities.

In Table 5 we show the correlations ($\frac{F_{t+1}-F_t}{F_t}$) between the proportional changes of the futures price and the changes of each one of the first two rotated PCs for both the strike and the moneyness metric. The correlations are calculated with the Pearson coefficient. One asterisk is displayed when the coefficient is significant at 5% significance level, and two asterisks are displayed when the coefficient is significant at 10% significance level. In the strike metric, the correlation is positive for both the PCs (even though the correlation for the first PC is insignificant for year 1992). In the moneyness metric, the correlation for the first PC is negative , while for the second PC is positive, apart from year 1993[8]. The negative correlation can be thought of as a leverage effect (Christie (1982)). The positive sign of correlation for the second PC implies that when the asset price falls (rises), the twist in the volatility smile decreases (increases), i.e. the high strike implieds increase less (more) than the low strikes ones. We investigated the scatterplots in order to explain the change of sign in the calculated correlations for year 1993. Although there were some outliers, removing them did not affect the sign of the correlation (apart from the 90-10 range, where the correlation became insignificant). The sign of the correlations in the moneyness metric, is the same for both the smile and the surface analysis. This shows that

---

[8] The dependence of the sign of correlation on the metric, shows the dependence of the dynamics of implied volatilities on the metric. Since the correlation has the same sign as the covariance, we show that the correlation depends on the metric by looking at the covariance between $\Delta\sigma_t=\sigma(t+1)-\sigma(t)$ and ΔF under both metrics. Let the covariance in the strike metric be $Cov_{strike}=Cov(\Delta\sigma_t(K),\Delta F)$. Then, in the moneyness metric, for a given moneyness level we have $Cov_{mon}=Cov[\sigma_{t+1}(K+\Delta F)-\sigma_t(K),\Delta F]$. Expanding $\sigma_{t+1}(K+\Delta F)$ as a Taylor series of order one around a point K we get: $Cov_{mon}=Cov[\sigma_{t+1}(K)+ \Delta F\sigma_{t+1}'-\sigma_t(K), \Delta F]= Cov_{strike}+ \sigma_{t+1}'Var(\Delta F)$. Therefore, whether or not the correlation sign is going to alter as we change metrics, depends on the slope of the skew, the point around which we do the expansion and the variance of ΔF.

the sign of the correlation is not affected by whether we examine the whole implied volatility surface, or just the individual smiles.

Table 5. Correlations between Percentage Changes of the Futures Price with Changes of the Rotated PCs on the Strike and Moneyness Metrics.

Range			1992	1993	1994	1995
90-10	**Strike**	ΔPC1	0.12	0.09	-0.11	0.26**
		ΔPC2	0.40**	0.33**	0.06	0.24*
	Moneyness	ΔPC1	-0.28**	-0.36**	-0.56**	-0.29**
		ΔPC2	0.35**	-0.32**	0.16	0.26*
180-90	**Strike**	ΔPC1	0.11	0.14	0.25**	0.26*
		ΔPC2	0.41**	0.36**	0.38**	0.26*
	Moneyness	ΔPC1	-0.29**	-0.27**	0.03	-0.29**
		ΔPC2	0.35**	-0.43**	0.27**	0.26*
270-180	**Strike**	ΔPC1	0.11	0.15*	0.26**	0.23*
		ΔPC2	0.41**	0.37**	0.36**	0.26**
	Moneyness	ΔPC1	-0.27**	-0.28**	0.06	-0.31**
		ΔPC2	0.35**	-0.44**	0.27**	0.27**

Regarding the size of the correlation, it seems that it changes stochastically over the years, as expected. This may pose problems for the implementation of models such as Ledoit and Santa-Clara's (1998).

CONCLUSIONS AND IMPLICATIONS OF THE RESEARCH

In this paper, we investigated the dynamics of implied volatilities surfaces by applying Principal Components Analysis (PCA). This is a first step towards the implementation of "smile-consistent" stochastic-volatility models for the pricing and hedging of standard and exotic options. In particular, we answered three questions; the number of shocks that appear in the volatility process, their interpretation, and their correlation with proportional changes in the underlying asset.

The PCA was performed on the first differences of implied volatilities measured under the strike and the moneyness metric. After considering three criteria (Velicer's criterion, communalities, interpretation), we found that two components could be reliably extracted. Next, we obtained a clear interpretation for them by constructing and applying a "Procrustes" rotation to the retained components. The first component can be interpreted as a parallel shift, and the second as a Z-shaped twist. These results were in most cases very consistent for the four separate years 1992, 1993, 1994 and 1995. On average, the two factors explained 53% and 60% of the surface variation in the strike and moneyness metric, respectively. The correlations between the proportional changes in the futures price with the changes in the rotated PCs were positive for both PCs in the strike metric.

In the moneyness metric, they were negative for the first PC and either positive or negative for the second PC.

Our results have further implications. First, applying PCA both to individual volatility smiles (see S-H-C) and to the whole volatility surface gave consistent results on both the number of factors (two) and their interpretation. In this respect, the term structure of implied volatilities does not affect the dynamics of implieds. However, the magnitude of the shocks may differ between the individual smiles and the surface.

Second, the results from the application of the PCA under the strike and moneyness metrics, can be used to assess whether either the deterministic, or the stochastic volatility models (or both), are mis-specified. Simulating implied volatilities from such models and performing PCA on them, will provide a yardstick to measure how small or large, the variation of the empirical implieds is in both metrics.

Third, our results are in contrast with Kamal and Derman's (1997). They analyze the dynamics of implied volatilities of over the counter (OTC) S&P 500 and Nikkei 225 Index options. They find that three PCs explain about 95% of the variance of the volatility surface. Their interpretation is a level of volatilities for the first PC, a term structure of volatilities for the second PC and a skew for the third. Their results suggest that a four factor model for pricing and hedging options under a stochastic volatility "smile consistent no-arbitrage pricing" type model is an appropriate one. Our work, identifies a model with one less factor, but cautions that the factor structure has higher dimensionality since it explains only 53% and 60% of the surface variation[9]. These differences could be attributed to either one (or all) of the following: (a) the market futures option data have a noisier volatility structure than that estimated from the quotations for OTC index options, (b) the dynamics of the volatility surface may simply depend on the choice of the underlying asset. This is analogous to the documented fact that the magnitude of observed implied volatility smiles, depends on the underlying asset (Fung and Hsieh 1991). Future research should apply PCA to different data sets, so as to solve these issues.

REFERENCES

Anderson, A., Basilevsky, A., and Hum A. (1983), "Missing Data : A Review of the Literature" in Rossi, P., Wright, J., and Anderson, A., *Handbook of Survey Research*, Academic Press.

Basilevsky, A. (1994), *Statistical Factor Analysis and Related Methods Theory and Applications*, Wiley Series in Probability and Mathematical Statistics.

Barone-Adesi, G., and Whaley, R. (1987), "Efficient Analytic Approximation of American Option Values", *Journal of Finance* 42, 301-320.

Black, F., and Scholes, M. (1973), "The Pricing of Options and Corporate Liabilities", *Journal of Political Economy* 81, 637-654.

Christie, A. (1982), "The Stochastic Behavior of Common Stock Variances, Value, Leverage and Interest Rate Effects", *Journal of Financial Economics* 10, 407-432.

---

[9]It is worth noting that our model has similarities to that used recently in a time series analysis of index returns by Gallant, Chien and Tauchen (1998). Using daily data on close-to-close price movements and the high/low spread, they find that a model with two stochastic volatility shocks plus the underlying asset component, fits the data very well, and in particular it mimics the long-memory feature of volatility.

Das, S., and R. Sundaram. (1998), "Of Smiles and Smirks: A Term-Structure Perspective", *Journal of Financial and Quantitative Analysis*, forthcoming.

Davydov, D., and Linetsky, V. (1999), "Pricing Options on One-Dimensional Diffusions: A Unified Approach", Working Paper, University of Michigan.

Derman, E., Kani, I., and Zou, J. (1996): "The Local Volatility Surface: Unlocking the Information in Index Option Prices", *Financial Analysts Journal* 52, 25-36.

Derman, E., and Kani, I. (1998), "Stochastic Implied Trees: Arbitrage Pricing with Stochastic Term and Strike Structure of Volatility" *International Journal of Theoretical and Applied Finance* 1, 61-110.

Dupire, B. (1992), "Arbitrage Pricing with Stochastic Volatility", Working Paper, Societe Generale Division Options, Paris.

Fung, K., and Hsieh, D. (1991), "Empirical Analysis of Implied Volatility: Stocks, Bonds and Currencies", Working Paper, Fuqua School of Business, Duke University.

Gallant, A., Chien, H., and Tauchen, G. (1998), "Calibrating Volatility Diffusions and Extracting Integrated Volatility", Working Paper, Duke University.

Gemmill, G. (1996), "Did Option Traders Anticipate the Crash? Evidence from Volatility Smiles in the U.K., with U.S. Comparisons", *Journal of Futures Markets* 16, 881-897.

Harvey, C., and Whaley, R. (1991), "S&P 100 Index Option Volatility", *Journal of Finance* 46, 1551-1561.

Heath, D., Jarrow, R., and Morton, A. (1992), "Bond Pricing and the Term Structure of Interest Rates: A New Methodology For Contingent Claims Valuation", *Econometrica* 60, 77-105.

Heynen, R. (1994), "An Empirical Investigation of Observed Smile Patterns", *Review of Futures Markets* 13, 317-354.

Hull, J., and White, A. (1987), "The Pricing of Options on Assets with Stochastic Volatilities", *Journal of Finance* 42, 281-300.

Jackson, E. (1991), *A User's Guide to Principal Components*, Wiley Series in Probability and Mathematical Statistics.

Kamal, M., and Derman, E. (1997), "The Patterns of Change in Implied Index Volatilities", Goldman Sachs, Quantitative Strategies Notes.

Ledoit, O., and P. Santa-Clara. (1998), "Relative Pricing of Options with Stochastic Volatility", Working Paper, University of California, Los Angeles.

Litterman, R., and Scheinkman, J. (1988), "Common Factors Affecting Bond Returns", Goldman Sachs, Financial Strategies Group.

Merton, R. (1976), "Option Pricing when Underlying Stock Returns are Discontinuous", *Journal of Financial Economics* 3, 125-144.

Rubinstein, M. (1985), "Non-Parametric Tests of Alternative Option Pricing Models", *Journal of Finance* 40, 455-480.

Scott, L. (1997), "Pricing Stock Options in a Jump-Diffusion Model with Stochastic Volatility and Interest Rates: Applications of Fourier Inversion Methods", *Mathematical Finance* 7, 413-426.

Skiadopoulos, G., Hodges, S., and Clewlow, L. (1998), "The Dynamics of Smiles", French Finance Association Meetings Proceedings, Lille.

Taylor, S., and Xu, X. (1994), "The Magnitude of Implied Volatility Smiles: Theory and Empirical Evidence for Exchange Rates", *Review of Futures Markets* 13, 355-380.

Velicer, W. (1976), "Determining the Number of Components from the Matrix of Partial Correlations", *Psychometrica* 41, 321-327.

Xu, X., and Taylor, S. (1994), "The Term Structure of Volatility Implied by Foreign Exchange Options", *Journal of Financial and Quantitative Analysis* 29, 57-74.

APPLICATION OF NONSTATIONARY MARKOVIAN MODELS TO RISK MANAGEMENT IN AUTOMOBILE LEASING

D.L. Smith, Y. Wu, D. Matthew

University of Missouri-St. Louis
School of Business Administration
8001 Natural Bridge Rd.
St. Louis, MO 63121
USA

Abstract: Automobile leasing is a growing and competitive business in which the lessor absorbs the risk of fluctuations in used-car prices, in addition to normal credit risks. To explore the various dimensions of risk in automobile leasing, we construct a set of integrated statistical models using account-level data from a major U.S. financial institution. Nonstationary Markovian models represent the life of a lease. A dozen logistic and regression models represent alternative paths on termination. We describe the comprehensive model and its validation, demonstrate its utility for management of credit risk, and provide new understanding about the character of the credit instrument.

Key words: Risk management, Forecasting, Credit, Leasing, Nonstationary Markov chains

INTRODUCTION

In 1995, approximately 31% of new-car financial transactions at the retail level in the United States occurred with a leasing contract. This represents a phenomenal growth from 13% of transactions in 1990, and the percentage is projected to grow further through the year 2000 (ABA, 1997). The most common form of lease is "closed-ended", allowing the lessee, upon termination, to turn in the vehicle or alternatively to acquire the automobile for the "residual value" specified in the leasing contract. Ideally, the residual value would be equivalent to the market value of the vehicle at the maturation date for the lease, and the terms of the lease (monthly payment including interest expense and service charges)

S.H. Zanakis et al. (eds.), Decision Making: Recent Developments and Worldwide Applications, 213–230.
© 2000 *Kluwer Academic Publishers*.

would provide an appropriate risk-adjusted return to the lessor.

Competing for business in the mid 1990's, financial institutions wrote leases for tens of billions of dollars in aggregate, expecting a continuation of buoyant markets for used cars to secure their financial interest as leases matured. As waves of vehicles reached the used car market when leases did mature, downward pressures on used car prices, combined with high residual values in the leasing contracts, resulted in unexpected financial losses in several market segments. Credit managers must continually confront the following questions in an uncertain business environment:

1. What magnitude of financial reserves is required to cover credit losses on repossessions?
2. What reserves are required to cover losses incurred on disposing of vehicles turned in at termination of their leases?
3. How many vehicles will have to be handled and disposed of?
4. How does the propensity to turn in vehicles on the termination of a lease depend upon used-car prices and residual values in leasing contracts?
5. If residual values in new contracts are adjusted downward to protect against losses on disposing of vehicles turned in at maturation (resulting in higher monthly payments), will the reduction in expected losses be sufficient to compensate for the potential loss of business to competitors?
6. How do risks compare in different geographical areas, where climate and usage patterns can affect the general condition and markets for used vehicles?
7. How do risks compare for leases of different duration?

In this paper, we describe a comprehensive model developed for a major U.S. financial institution to assist in addressing these questions. We illustrate the structure of the model, present the results of validating tests, and demonstrate the model's use for management of credit risk. With tools of this type, managers can identify troublesome market segments and produce information helpful for pricing financial products commensurately withrisk.

RELATED RESEARCH

Zanakis et al. (1986) have summarized applications of management science to banking, noted the relationship of profitability to the provision for loan loss reserves, and asserted the need for new analytical tools in an increasingly competitive business environment.Cyert et al. (1962) were early users of stationary Markov chains to project default rates and losses associated with revolving trade credit. Altman (1989) and Asquith et al. (1989) in a study of bond portfolios, showed, however, that rates of transition to default differ significantly according to the age of the assets.Kang and Zenios (1992) cast the issue of age-dependent rates of loan prepayment for mortgages in terms of "seasoning" and "burnout" phenomena. Campbell and Dietrich (1983) showed that the age of a mortgage, ratio of outstanding principal to the property's market value, interest rates, and unemployment rates were all significant in explaining mortgage prepayments, delinquencies and defaults.Cunningham and Capone (1990) showed different determinants of delinquency, prepayment and default for fixed-rate versus adjustable-rate mortgages.Zipkin(1993) proposed an analytical approach using Markov chains as an efficient alternative to "elaborate stochastic simulation" in evaluating mortgage-backed securities.Lawrence, Smith and Rhoades (1992) found that borrower delinquency patterns were dominant indicators of default risk and that information obtained with the loan application diminished in relative value as the credit aged. Concerned with predicting lifetime performance of individual accounts, Smith and Lawrence (1995) showed how multinomial logit models or, alternatively, normalized probabilities from nonlinear regression models could be used to create nonstationary Markov chains that capture systematic changes in transition probabilities as credits mature.Smith, Sanchez and Lawrence (1996) have reported the construction of a comprehensive model for home mortgages that predicts incidence of prepayment, delinquency, default, and losses on defaulted loans. Rosenberg and Gleit (1994) have summarized quantitative methods used in credit management, with particular attention on the development of credit scores, based on borrower characteristics and credit history. Credit scores, which essentially predict the likelihood of default, are used to support the decision whether to extend credit, and in choosing intervention strategies where evidence of distress arises for the holder of an active account. Curnow et al. (1997) describe credit-scoring applications to the equipment leasing business.In this paper, we adapt and integrate these various concepts to accommodate a complicated credit instrument of medium duration (the automotive lease).

STRUCTURE OF THE MODEL

The model for automobile leases is constructed with account-level data to represent the alternative states of individual accounts at monthly intervals.It allows the probabilities of transitions among states to vary with account characteristics and market conditions, and to change as the lease ages.We aggregate the state probabilities for individual leases to compute the expected number of leases in each of the alternative states at the beginning of each month in the forecasting horizon.We recognize all losses net of recoveries on the date of termination.The expected loss on termination, multiplied by the probability of termination, is aggregated to producethe expected loss associated with leases that are terminated in a period.That way, the expected loss on a lease is distributed over its scheduled life (and beyond) in accordance with the likelihoods that termination will occur each month.The advantage of this disaggregated approach is that it accommodates changes in characteristics of the portfolio and market conditions.It also allows the analysis of risk for portfolio segments on numerous dimensions.

Estimation of Transition Probabilities

Setting the stage for a Markovian structure with monthly state transitions, a lease is defined as being in one of the seven states on its monthly date: (1) Current, (2) Delinquent 30-59 days, (3) Delinquent 60-89 days, (4) Delinquent 90-119 days, (5) Delinquent 120+ days, (6) Terminated without repossession of the vehicle,(7) Terminated with repossession of the vehicle. The last two states are terminal (absorbing) states.Probabilities of transition to each of the seven states (from each of the five non-terminal states) are recomputed as part of the monthly forecasting recursion for each individual lease as it is projected to mature. The decision-support system, as implemented, allows any of three basic alternatives for the construction and calibration of equations for the transition probabilities.

The first alternative uses ordinary least squares (OLS) regression models with a 0-1 dependent variable for the probability of transition into a specified state.The seven equations for transition probabilities from each state are estimated individually, with truncation of probabilities that are beyond the zero-one range and proportional rescaling to ensure that the probabilities add to one.This efficient alternative is usually preferred by corporate analysts because of its simplicity.It has provision for automatic step-wise addition and deletion of variables in search of best model, allows different variables to be used in estimating the likelihood of transition into different states, and results in model coefficients that are most directly translated into differences in actual probabilities -- particularly for 0-1 independent variables.

The second alternative uses logistic regression models with individual estimation of transition probabilities and proportional re-scaling of probabilities to ensure they add to one.This approach is less efficient computationally but it avoids the need to truncate probabilities.It has a provision for automatic step-wise addition and deletion of variables in search of best model and allows different variables to be used in estimating the likelihood of transition into different states, but the coefficients of the model pertain to ratios of logarithms of probabilities and are less convenient to interpret.

The third alternative usesmultinomial logistic models.This technique is the most cumbersome, most computationally demanding, and least flexible alternative, but guaranteed to produce nonnegative probabilities that sum to one without truncation and re-scaling, as all transition probabilities out of a state are estimated simultaneously.The same variables must be used to predict the likelihood of transition into different states from a given state. The technique has no provision for automatic stepwise addition and deletion of variables in search of the best model, but the analyst may start with selection from stepwise OLS or stepwise logistic analyses and test for the significance of individual variables in the multinomial model.In past experimentation with other portfolios, the estimates for aggregate reserve requirements and projected distributions of accounts among alternative states each period have been shown to be almost identical for the three techniques (Smith and Lawrence, 1995).

The aforementioned research has demonstrated the importance of incorporating variables to account for the seasoning (age) effects of a financial asset. Related to age of the lease are both the borrower's net equity in the asset and his apparent ability to meet the obligation.If the borrower's equity is low or negative, there is a much greater risk that the lessor will have to take possession of the physical asset and incur the costs of disposal. An automobile lease is generally structured so that the nominal equity in the vehicle begins near zero, becomes negative as the vehicle changes from new car to used car and enters the steep part of the depreciation curve, and approaches zero again as market depreciation eases and the linear drop in book equity continues toward the residual value.We incorporate direct evidence of ability to pay in three ways: (1) by the age of the credit itself (i.e., the length of time for which the borrower has managed to avoid default), (2) by a credit score computed from information in the loan application and credit bureau histories, and (3) by the current state of delinquency. Indirect evidence of ability to pay is also found in variables related to the equity position. Borrowers who furnish large down payments, who choose shorter leasing terms (duration's) with higher payments, and who qualify for leases under a regular credit review rather than an easy credit promotion, generally tend to be in better financial positions.

Historical transitions from each of the five active (nonterminal) states to each of the seven financial states revealed sharp shifts in transition probabilities during the last few months in the scheduled life of the lease.This is natural, as decisions to replace or to keep the vehicle are motivated by the scheduled termination of the lease.We therefore added three indicator variables to allow step shifts in probabilities each month as two, one, and zero months remain.Additional indicator variables were defined for anniversary dates of the lease, to allow for the relatively minor (but statistically significant) phenomenon of reconsideration by borrowers as the same stage in the automobile model cycle is reached and perhaps as licensing and insurance renewals occur.

In summary, the variables used in computing the transition probabilities are:

1. Stage in maturation of the lease as represented by the proportion of term expired (age of lease in mos. / term in mos.) and by five indicator (0-1) variables telling whether the lease is approaching maturation (zero, one or two months remaining), beyond the contracted maturation date, orat an anniversary date (24 or 36-month stage)
2. Financial terms of the lease as represented by percent down payment, compound rate of depreciation that produces the residual value from the initial capitalization over the term of the lease (expressed as an annual rate), capital formation rate (ratio of monthly depreciation to total monthly payment), length of the lease (24 mo. or less, 25-36 mo., 37-48 mo., 49-60 mo., over 60 mo.), original loan to value of the vehicle, and whether the lease was written under an easy credit promotion
3. Credit Score for the applicant at origination of the lease (estimated likelihood of repossession within two years)
4. Automobile characteristics as represented by whether vehicle is new or used, the value of "hard add-ons" as percentage of the manufacturer's suggested retail price (MSRP), capitalization range (using categories with $15k, $18k, $22k, and $26k break points), and whether the vehicle is imported or domestic
5. Cohort credit score (average credit score of all applicants for whom leases originated in that year)
6. Whether origination occurred on or after Jan 1, 1995, a time after which cohort credit scores are unavailable
7. Marketing Region (Northeast, Southeast, West, and Central)
8. Monthly seasonal variables are allowed but repressed in the current form because only 11 months of transitionswere used in calibration(They may be activated at will.)
9. Market value estimates based on published "black-book" pricesfor the year-make-model-series-body
10. Interaction variable between the proportion of lease expired and the indicator

(dummy) variables for new-used, to allow the effect of maturation to be different for leases on new versus used cars

11. Interaction variable between proportion of lease expired and loan-to-value, to allow the effect of loan-to-value ratio to depend on the proportion of lease expired

12. Interaction variable to allow the impact of market value to residual value to depend upon the proportion of lease expired.

A 50% sample of all accounts active during the most recent year was used to construct the transition probability curves (292,508 accounts).Eleven months of transitions were analyzed using the status of accounts at the twelve most recent billing dates (generating a total of 2.4 million account transitions).Variables were retained if they were statistically significant at the 0.1 level (and with correct sign for relevant variables).Each of the listed variables met that test in at least one of the transition equations.

In Table 1 we present OLS coefficients attached to variables in the selected equations that give relative rates of transition among states. (Intercepts of the equations are ignored in the table.)To illustrate how the risk profile of a lease changes over its life, we created a series of plots that showed how the likelihoods of various events change through time for a typical lease.The plots (available by request from the authors) showed a decline in the likelihood that the vehicle will be repossessed when payments are overdue as the vehicle ages, and sharp increases in the likelihood that the lease will be terminated (without repossession) in the few months just before maturation. One could thus see from the relative magnitudes of coefficients, and shapes of the transition curves, some dominant patterns.

Ceteris paribus, leases are more likely to change from a current state this month to a delinquent state next month if they have a higher credit score (estimated risk of default) at the time of the application for the lease, if the original loan-to-value ratio is high, if the lease is for longer duration, if the lease was issued after year 1995, if the lease was written under an easy credit promotion, if there is a low rate of capital formation, andif the down payment is a lower percentage of the original capital value of the lease.The likelihood of transition from current to delinquency increases in the last few months of the scheduled life of the lease and as the lease extends beyond the scheduled maturity.(Some of the phenomenon at maturity is dueto the timing in processing contracts on termination.)The various terms involving current loan amount in comparison to market value (ESTLV, ESTMVRES, MATLVAL, and MATMVRES) appear in the model as moderating variables related to age of the lease. The influence of those variables is felt more strongly (in the expected direction) in the illustrated equation for the complementary probability that a lease in the current state will remain current rather than become delinquent.

Table 1. Model Coefficients for Selected Transition Probabilities *

Variable	Current to Current	Current to 30 days	30 days to Current	60 days to Current	90 days to Current	90 days to Repo
MATPRP	-0.0894 [d]		-0.1174 [d]			
LOGAGE	-0.0088 [d]	0.0081 [d]				-0.0819 [d]
AGE24	0.0098 [d]	-0.0014 [b]				
AGE36	-0.0029 [b]					
TWOMOS	-0.0299 [d]	0.0037 [d]			-0.0834 [a]	
ONEMO	-0.0770 [d]	0.0018 [a]				-0.1154 [a]
ZROMOS	-0.3311 [d]	0.0177 [d]	-0.1744 [d]	-0.0911 [b]	-0.0780 [a]	-0.1237 [a]
OVERTERM	-0.7906 [d]	0.1179 [d]	-0.4976 [d]	-0.2359 [d]	-0.1322 [d]	-0.1211 [d]
DEPRRATE	0.2569 [d]	-0.1582 [d]	1.0041 [d]	0.6981 [d]		
TR25TO36	-0.0045 [d]					
TR37TO48	-0.0122 [d]	0.0011 [b]		-0.0189 [a]		
TR49TO60	-0.0146 [d]	-0.0021 [d]				
TR61PL	-0.0227 [d]	0.0044 [d]	-0.0279 [b]		0.0285 [a]	
PCTDOWN		-0.0001 [b]	0.0023 [d]			
CAPFORM	0.0604 [d]	-0.0429 [d]	0.2004 [d]	0.2068 [b]		
ORIGLV2	-0.0373 [d]	0.0229 [d]	-0.1502 [d]	-0.1423 [b]	-0.2217 [d]	
CREDEASE	-0.0143 [d]	0.0163 [d]	-0.0454 [d]			
PCTADD	0.0002 [d]	0.0001 [c]	-0.0008 [a]			
USEDCAR	-0.0054 [d]		-0.0386 [d]	-0.0352 [a]	-0.0631 [c]	
USEDPRP	0.0097 [c]					0.2076 [d]
IMPORT	-0.0021 [d]	0.0011 [c]	-0.0148 [b]	-0.0207 [a]		
P15TO18			-0.0105 [a]			
P18TO22		0.0014 [d]	-0.0157 [b]			
P22TO26	-0.0017 [c]	0.0031 [d]	-0.0238 [d]			
P26		0.0038 [d]			-0.0271 [a]	
NTHEAST		0.0046 [d]				
STHEAST	-0.0031 [d]		-0.0503 [d]	-0.0459 [d]		0.0342 [a]
WEST	0.0035 [d]	-0.0036 [d]		-0.0243 [a]		
SCORE2	-0.0051 [d]	0.0059 [d]	-0.0416 [c]			
SCORE3	-0.0098 [d]	0.0105 [d]	-0.0619 [d]			
SCORE4	-0.0125 [d]	0.0149 [d]	-0.1096 [d]			
SCORE5	-0.0180 [d]	0.0193 [d]	-0.1498 [d]			
CR SCORE	-3×10^{-5} [d]	3×10^{-5} [d]		-4×10^{-5} [c]		
COSCORE	0.0018 [d]		-0.0176 [d]		-0.0093 [b]	
AFT95	-0.0030 [c]	0.0023 [d]			-0.0198 [a]	-0.0690 [d]
ESTLV		-0.0043 [d]	0.0594 [b]	0.0613 [a]		
MCUSHION	9×10^{-7} [d]	-9×10^{-7} [d]	8×10^{-6} [d]	1×10^{-5} [b]		-7×10^{-6} [a]

* two-tailed levels of statistical significance: a=.1, b=.01, c=.001, d=.0001.

Table 1. Model Coefficients for Selected Transition Probabilities (continued)

Variable	Current to Current	Current to 30 days	30 days to Current	60 days to Current	90 days to Current	90 days to Repo
ESTMVRES	0.0194 [d]	-0.0088 [d]	0.0717 [d]			
MATLVAL	0.0689 [d]	-0.0117 [d]				
MATMVRES	0.0091 [a]					
N	1,438,764	1,438,764	52,976	9,309	3,151	3,151
R^2	0.2371	0.0160	0.0882	0.0377	0.0336	0.0533

Next consider the likelihood of transition from a state of 30-days delinquent back to current, in comparison with 30-days delinquent to 60-days delinquent.The higher the credit score (risk of default as estimated at origination), the more likely that delinquency will increase rather than disappear.The higher the market value of the automobile relative to the residual value or outstanding balance on the lease, the more likely that delinquency will disappear, rather than increase.Delinquency on used cars has a higher likelihood of increasing rather than disappearing, in comparison to delinquency on new cars.The importance of current loan-to-value seems to increase as a lease becomes delinquent.

Comparing the coefficients in the equations for transitions from the 60-to-89 days delinquent state, leases with a high rate of capital formation, *ceteris paribus*, are less likely to advance to a higher state of delinquency; leases written under an easy credit promotion are more likely to advance in delinquency; leases on imported vehicles are morelikely to advance in delinquency than are leases on domestic vehicles; and leases with a greater equity cushion (market value less book value) are more likely to revert to a current state than leases with smaller equity cushions.

Relative magnitudes of the coefficients for the equations giving transition probabilities for accounts 90-119 days delinquent (not shown because of space limitations) suggest that repossession of the vehicle is less likely to occur in the following month if the lease is nearing or past scheduled maturation, if the vehicle is located in the southeast,and if there is a more substantial equity cushion (market value less book value).Delinquency is more likely to diminish if there is ahigher equity cushion.For advanced states of delinquency, there are fewer statistically significant coefficients and much lower values for R^2. This is consistent with results in other studies. Credits in advanced stages of delinquency are in a separate risk class that is most profoundly conveyed by the state itself and by new credit-bureau information.Also, because relatively few accounts reach the highly delinquent states, there are fewer observations available for refining the estimating equations for the relevant transition probabilities.Models that contain current credit bureau information and other variables that describe historical payment behavior can be constructed for predicting which of the delinquent accounts are most likely to default.They are impracticable, however, for a lifetime recursion model because the information is not available for future time periods.

Role of Credit Scores

An important variable in determining the risk associated with the lease is the creditworthiness of the borrower.Determination of the creditworthiness by some methodology is taken for granted in this paper.We should, however, acknowledge the process by which this was done. Using data at the time of the loan application, a credit score is computed which represents the likelihood that the lease will terminate with repossession within the first 24 months of its life. It was produced using neural network models calibrated from applications to new-car leases issued in 1990-94 considering the borrower's income, employment history, family size, outstanding credit, and payment history on previous loans.The credit score for individual leases was unavailable for many of the older leases, but for those leases we were able to compute the over-all percentage of leases that terminated within the first 24 months.We call this empirical percentage the "cohort score".In constructing our models for the state transition probabilities, we include both the cohort score, to reflect the general risk of repossession for leases written under similar competitive and economic conditions, and the individual credit score to reflect the additional risk assessment for the individual lease.A separate cohort score is determined for each year of origination and for different groupings of leases by term (less than 24 months, 25 to 36 months, 37 to 48 months, 49 to 60 months, and over 60 months). It allows us to provide some information about credit score for the older leases with missing individual scores and to estimate the additional informational content in the variation of individual credit scores for the newer leases.

The forecasting model itself uses actual cohort scores where available (i.e., for periods with leases more than 24 months old) and projected cohort scores for leases originated in recent periods.We can therefore use the projected cohort scores for new leases to moderate forecasts, reflecting the company's expectations of the gross impact of recent changes in economic conditions and recent changes in general quality of the lessee pool."Behavioral" scores may also be derived to incorporate additional information about current payment history on the lease and on other outstanding credit. In the Markovian structure presented, all such "behavioral" information is embedded in the current state of the lease.Alternatively, it could be included to create separate equations for the transition probabilities applied to the first period of the planning horizon.Experimentation with such a two-stage approach for home-equity lines of credit (Smith et al., 1997) did produce better success in identifying specific accounts that are likely to default.In that study, however, the two-stage approach produced similar estimates of the total number of accounts that would default.

Development of Depreciation Curves for Market Segments

The market value of the vehicle must be projected as part of the forecasting recursion. Depreciation curves were developed to express the ratio of current market value to original manufacturer's suggested retail price (MSRP) as a function of the model age of the vehicle. We define the model age of the vehicle as the number of months since October 1 of the year preceding the nominal model year of a vehicle.Constructing the curves in this manner, we weight the data for a market segment according to the number of cars of a given year-make-model-series-body that have been in the portfolio during the recent year.Because the market-price data are for the 1994-1997 period, the ratios of market price to MSRP in the first year of the depreciation curve, for example, were derived from data for 1994-1997 cars.The ratios for the fifth year, in contrast, were derived from data for 1990-1993 models.

The model is structured to provide depreciation curves of the form

$$Log(estmv/msrp) = \beta_0 + \beta_1 \text{ (model age)} + \beta_2 \text{ (model age)}^2 + \Sigma \, S_i.$$

A log-quadratic equation of this type allows for initial depreciation at the time of purchase, further depreciation at a percentage rate that changes at a constant rate through time, and seasonal effects.Eleven monthly seasonal indicator (0-1) variables (S_i, $i = 1,2,3,...,11$) allow for seasonal behavior in used-car prices. It is noteworthy that historical depreciation patterns have differed substantially among the market segments. Forecasting the future values of car prices is accomplished by applying the standard depreciation curve for a general model segment to the most recent black-book market price for the year-make-model-series-body.The disposition of vehicles upon termination is highly related to the ratio of market-to-book value of the vehicle.We recommend, therefore, that "stress testing" be performed with different assumptions about future prices in different market segments.

Models for Estimating the Severity of Loss on Termination of the Lease

The risk of loss on termination of a lease is highly dependent upon the nature of the termination.Vehicles may be repossessed when payments are seriously in arrears.Termination may occur as a result of an insurance settlement from an accident or theft.The lessee may voluntarily terminate the lease prior to the scheduled maturity date, terminate the lease on the scheduled maturity date, or extend the lease on a monthly basis.In each of these voluntary terminations, the lessee may retain the vehicle or turn it in for disposal by the lessor.Different charges and collection procedures apply in each case.We therefore employ a dozen logistic and regression models in an hierarchical fashion to account for the various alternatives:

1. A regression model for the percentage of book value lost on repossessions.
2. A logistic model for the likelihood that a termination without repossession occurs with insurance settlement.
3. A regression model for percentage of book value lost on insurance settlement.
4. Alogistic model for the likelihood that vehicle is kept when lease is terminated early by the lessee.
5. A regression model for percentage of book value lost on vehicle turned in after early voluntary maturation.
6. A regression model for percentage of book value lost on vehicle kept after early voluntary termination.
7. A logistic model for likelihood that the vehicle is kept when lease is terminated at the normal maturation time by lessee.

8. A regression model for percentage of book value lost on vehicle turned in after normal maturation.

9. A regression model for percentage of book value lost on vehicle kept after normal termination.

10. A logistic model for likelihood that vehicle is kept when lease is terminated late by the lessee.

11. A regression model for percentage of book value lost on vehicle turned in after late maturation.

12. A regression model for percentage of book value lost on vehicle kept after late termination.

To construct these models, we used data for 8,633 accounts terminated with repossession and 247,201 accounts terminated without repossession between January, 1995 and May, 1997.Variables used in the construction of the models for termination were: (1) stage in maturation of lease (months expired, proportion of term expired, whether in last month, next to last month or past scheduled maturity), (2) contractual depreciation rate((cap-residual)/term), (3) percentage down payment, (4) proportion of monthly payment contributing to equity (contractual depreciation rate / total monthly pmt), (5) original loan-to-value (original capitalization / [manuf. suggested retail price + cost of hardadds]), (6) ratio of current book value to current market value, (7) whether the contract includes an early termination charge, (8) marketing region (Northeast, Southeast, West, and Central), (9) whether the lease was issued under an easy credit promotion, (10) whether the lease was on a new or used car, (11) whether vehicle was an import or domestic make, (12) geographic region, (13) capitalization range (defined by $15k, $18k, $22k, and $26k break points), (14) duration of the lease (24 mo. or less, 25-36 mo., 37-48 mo., 49-60 mo., over 60 mo.), (15) monthly seasonal indicator variables, (16) an interaction variable for proportion of term expired and new-used, to allow the impact of the age of the lease to depend on whether the lease is on a new or used car, (17) an interaction variable for proportion of term expired and loan-to-value, to allow the impact of the loan-to-value ratio to depend upon the age of the lease.Again, we retained variables in the individual models only if they were statistically significant at the 0.1 level (effectively .05 for one-tailed tests).

To show the dominant variables in determining the fate of a lease on termination, in Table 2 we provide coefficients attached to the explanatory variables of several equations in the termination hierarchy(with constant terms ignored). The first column pertains to the percentage of book value lost on a repossessed vehicle.Coefficients in that equation reveal, as expected; a higher expected loss when book values are high relative to market value of the vehicle, and a lower percentage loss on leases for which the rate of capital formation is high.In addition, they reveal a lower percentage loss on more expensive vehicles, a higher percentage loss on new cars than on used cars if they are repossessed early in the lease,but a higher percentage losses on used cards than on used cars if they are repossessed late in the lease (revealed bythe coefficient for the interaction variable USEDPRP=usedcar*matprp). The seasonal variables show higher percentage losses on repossessions that occur in October and November.

Table 2. Coefficients in Selected Models for Termination Experience [*]

Variable	PCT BV Lost on Repossession	Likelihood that Normal Termis Turned In	PCT BV Lost on Normal Term. Turned-In	PCT BV Lost on Normal Term. Kept
VINTAGE		N/A	0.0969 [d]	0.2000 [d]
MATPRP	-11.0103 [a]			
LOGAGE	-4.5401 [c]			
AGE24		0.1387 [d]	5.0310 [d]	-1.8953 [d]
AGE36		-0.1118 [d]	-4.2036 [d]	-1.5951 [d]
TMODAGE	0.4081 [d]	-0.0028 [d]	-0.1689 [d]	-0.0392 [d]
TWOMOS				
ONEMO				
ZROMOS				
OVERTERM	7.3769 [b]			
TR25TO36		0.1901 [d]	5.3203 [d]	-3.2978 [d]
TR37TO48		0.0940 [d]	-0.4888 [a]	-6.2285 [d]
TR49TO60	-1.2300 [a]	0.0779 [d]		-7.8150 [d]
TR61PL		0.0469 [b]	1.3714 [b]	-8.1724 [d]
PCTDOWN		-0.0065 [d]	N/A	-0.0371 [d]
CAPFORM	-9.3399 [c]	-0.3445 [d]	-8.9709 [d]	0.4765 [a]
ORIGLV2	22.3641 [d]	0.1768 [d]	N/A	N/A
CREDEASE	3.2279 [c]			1.1471 [a]
BOOK			N/A	N/A
USEDCAR	-6.6746 [d]	-0.0273 [a]	3.7010 [d]	2.2886 [d]
USEDPRP	9.1646 [a]			
IMPORT		0.0357 [d]	5.0317 [d]	-0.7785 [d]
P15TO18		-0.0343 [d]	-0.5599 [d]	-0.7454 [d]
P18TO22	-2.6561 [d]	-0.0423 [d]		-0.8970 [d]
P22TO26	-4.1475 [d]	-0.0406 [d]	1.2677 [d]	-1.4267 [d]
P26	-4.2764 [d]	-0.0219 [d]	1.7953 [d]	-2.3383 [d]
NTHEAST	5.6985 [d]	0.0677 [d]	2.8117 [d]	0.8042 [d]
STHEAST	2.8243 [d]	0.0171 [d]	3.0467 [d]	0.4475 [d]
WEST	2.2344 [c]	-0.1022 [d]	-2.2285 [d]	0.2299 [c]
FEB		-0.0165 [c]		-0.2950 [c]
MAR	-1.2364 [a]	0.0320 [d]	-1.4548 [d]	-0.4895 [d]
APR		0.0118 [a]	-2.0306 [d]	-0.3058 [c]
MAY		-0.0238 [d]	-2.3548 [d]	0.2083 [a]
JUN			-2.6364 [d]	
JUL			-2.1726 [d]	0.2274 [b]
AUG		-0.0216 [d]	-2.2502 [d]	
SEP		-0.0235 [d]	0.7009 [a]	
OCT	2.1364 [b]		1.9025 [d]	
NOV	3.1462 [d]		2.5398 [d]	
DEC		0.0221 [d]	1.1919 [d]	
ESTLV	28.8796 [d]	0.8897 [d]	66.0483 [d]	5.2321 [d]
MATLVAL	14.3261 [c]			
N	8,633	113,826	53,957	59,869
R²	0.1727	0.1945	0.5226	0.0414

The next column in Table 2 pertains to the likelihood that a vehicle will be turned in rather than kept if termination occurs as scheduled in the leasing contract. Again, as

---

[*] Two-tailed level of statistical significance: a = .1, b = .01, c = .001, d = .0001

expected, the automobile is more likely to be turned in if the book value (which would equal the residual value at maturation of the lease) is high relative to the market value.Vehicles in the mid-price range, *ceteris paribus*, are more likely to be kept by lessees than are very expensive or very economical vehicles.Vehicles on short-term leases are more likely to be turned in at maturation than are vehicles on long-term leases.

Considering the coefficients for the percentage of book value lost on a vehicle turned at maturation date, it is obvious that the impact of the current book-to-market value is most profound.There are regional differences (with higher percentage losses in the northeast and southeast) and seasonal effects (with lower percentage losses in spring and summer months and higher expected losses late in the calendar year).Higher percentage losses occurred on used cars rather than new cars and on imports rather than domestic models. Vehicles kept by the lessee at normal maturation of the lease can have associated losses if the lessor, seeing a poor market for the used vehicle, offers a financial incentive to the lessee.The last column pertains to the model for percentage loss net of such incentives.The effects of various variables are relatively muted, in comparison with effects in the model for vehicles turned in.

The influence of book-to-market value (estlv) is again the most significant.The R^2 coefficient for the model giving percentage of book value lost on vehicles turned in at maturation is .52, but for the model giving percentage of book value lost on vehicles kept at normal maturation the R^2 coefficient (although significantly significant at the .0001 level) is only .04.In the latter case, the magnitude of loss is quite small and subject to much random variation.

As with the transition probabilities, the risk associated with termination changes throughout the life of a lease. Plots were produced to show of the likelihood that a simulated lease will be active each month, the likelihood that an active lease will result in repossession in the current month (peaking mid-life), the expected loss if repossession occurs (gradually decreasing), and net expected risk of loss (expected loss as a percent of book value) in the current year (increasing from zero to a local maximum mid-life, and with a final up-tick after maturation).Other plots revealed comparable information for terminations that occur without repossession. Figure 1, for example, illustrates the likelihood that a hypothetical 42-month lease remains active at different stages of its scheduled life. Figure 2 illustrates the change in likelihood that a termination occurs with an insurance settlement, with vehicle turned in, or with vehicle kept as the lease ages.It also shows the loss as a percentage of outstanding book value that is expected to accrue in conjunction with different types of termination as the lease matures.

226

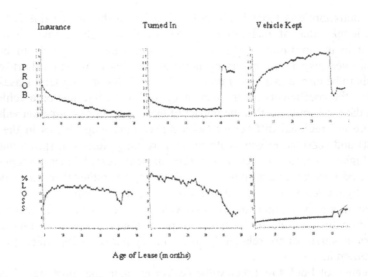

Age of Lease (months)

Figure1. Likelihood that a Lease Remains Active

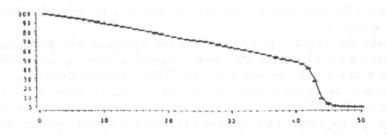

Figure 2. Likelihood a Termination Occurs in Different Ways (with Assoc. Loss)

The over-all risk of loss with insurance settlement reaches a peak at about 15 months and then declines. The expected loss on vehicles turned in drops steadily, but the risk increases near maturation as the likelihood of the vehicle's being turned in increases sharply.The expected loss on vehicles kept after voluntary termination increases over the life of the lease, with an up-tick at maturation as the likelihood of a negotiated closure to the lease increases.The over-all risk (not plotted here) is the result of the compound effects of these phenomena.

STRUCTURAL VALIDATION

The model was calibrated using a cross-sectional sample of accounts that had been established at different times (to provide variation in the stage of the lease), with leases of varying durations, on cars with different characteristics, and with some leases written under an easy-credit promotion. Instead of developing separate models for different market segments (an impractical task), we relied on combinations of indicator (0-1) and continuous variables with selected interaction terms to incorporate this information into the model. To test for possible bias in major market segments, the model was applied to a 10% sample of the accounts that were held out from the calibration exercise for validation purposes. We comparedthe predicted and actual numbers of accounts current, delinquent, terminated without repossession, and terminated with repossession after the passage of eight months (the latest date for which actual results were available for the study). Table 3 illustrates the degree of agreement between predicted and actual percentages of accounts in each state for different financial products and for leases that originated in different years. Differences in risks attributable to stage in life of a lease and to customer market segment are apparently quite well represented in the forecasts generated by the model.

INFORMATION GENERATED FOR RISK MANAGEMENT

With the comprehensive model, a number of important questions may be addressed objectively. We investigated how the risk profile in the portfolio would change under different assumptions about the rates of depreciation on used cars henceforth. This scenario was imposed by altering the projected depreciation rates over the remaining lives of leases on automobiles in the portfolio as of September 1997, while running the portfolio through the comprehensive model. Market values as of that date were derived from current black-book prices (or estimated from historical curves for cars without published black-book prices). Remaining depreciation for the first scenario (base run) was derived from the historical depreciation curves as described earlier. For other scenarios, we adjustedeach month's depreciation by equivalent compound annual rates ranging between −3% and +5%. The percentages of cars projected to terminate in different ways were altered substantially; so were the average losses on termination. The impact was greatest on the number ofvehicles projected to be turned in at the end of the lease, and on the aggregate expected losses incurred on those leases (relative to the contractual return). The impact was less profound but still significant on repossessions. The projected impact was minor on losses associated with vehicles kept (as slightly higher average losses were offset by lower frequencies), and minor on terminations with insurance settlements.

Some interesting cross-sectional differences emerged when the portfolio was segmented according to credit score on the loan application. As expected, the projected repossession rates were systematically higher as the credit scores (which measure credit risk) increased. It appeared that risk of loss associated with insurance settlements also increased with the credit score. People with higher credit scores were, however, predicted to be less likely to turn in the vehicles on termination of the lease. This would have an offsetting effect on the risk of repossession in the event of higher rates of depreciation in used car prices. This may reflect greater difficulty for people in this class to undertake the financial obligations associated with a replacement vehicle, and a greater likelihood of keeping the used vehicle longer. There were also some regional differences in the risk

228

profiles.Repossession rates were projected to be greater in western markets (dominated by California), but severity of loss on termination was projected to be lower there.Risk of loss on vehicles turned in at the end of the lease is projected to be greatest in the northeast where salt and winter driving hazards are great. Management has used the model to examine projected risk along other dimensions (such as for specific market segments or make-model designations) and found that deviations from projections are generally consistent with deviations of actual depreciation (as revealed in current black-book prices) from historical depreciation patterns.In projecting risk for a specific market segment, therefore, it is important to analyze whether leases on an unusual number of vehicles of a particular make-model are scheduled to mature together, thus altering supply-demand relationships in the marketplace

Table 3. Results of 8-Month Projection on Hold-Out Sample for Different Financial Products and Origination Years

Portfolio Segment (sample size)	Current	Delin-quent	Termi-nated	Repos-sessed
All leases projected(42,519 accounts)	73.16	4.26	21.50	1.07
All leases actual (43,286 accounts)	72.26	4.38	22.34	1.03
New cars projected(38,420 accounts)	72.56	3.99	22.51	0.95
New cars actual(38,670 accounts)	71.45	4.03	23.60	0.93
Used cars projected(2,573 accounts)	79.54	4.97	13.61	1.89
Used cars actual(3,075 accounts)	81.17	5.30	12.07	1.46
Easy Credit projected(1,527 accounts)	79.39	10.10	9.43	2.89
Easy Credit actual(1,542 accounts)	74.90	11.29	11.15	2.66
1996 leases projected(14,780 accounts)	90.96	4.29	3.66	1.08
1996 leases actual(15,175 accounts)	90.19	4.40	4.42	1.00
1995 leases projected (14,282 accounts)	73.61	4.65	20.53	1.20
1995 leases actual (14,591 accounts)	71.95	4.65	22.19	1.21
1994 leases projected(7,362 accounts)	58.47	4.19	36.31	1.03
1994 leases actual(7,406 accounts)	57.68	4.35	36.92	1.05
1993 leases projected(3,732 accounts)	49.36	3.46	46.37	0.82
1993 leases actual(3,762 accounts)	48.66	3.92	46.66	0.75
Pre1993 leases projected(1,760 accts.)	25.35	3.02	70.75	0.87
Pre1993 leasesactual(1,763 accounts)	24.33	3.07	72.09	0.51

CONCLUSION

The comprehensive model described in this paper has provided valuable insights regarding the risk associated with the automobile lease, a credit instrument that has experienced rapid growth worldwide.It has proved to be accurate in predicting financial performance of leases at different stages of maturation and for different financial products (for new cars, used cars, and easy-credit promotions) when applied to a hold-out sample for testing structural validity of the model.Application of the model in a corporate environment has enabled the objective assessment of financial risk, identification of financial reserves appropriate to cover potential losses, study of the potential financial consequences of changing terms of the lease (duration, down payments, residual values), and review of pricing of financial products in light of the attendant risk.

The Markovian structure with nonstationary transition probabilities to project the condition of a portfolio at monthly interviews has been demonstrated in previous work to be quite robust under different estimating techniques.We have applied the technique successfully in three different large financial institutions on secured portfolios ranging from mobile homes to first mortgages, to second mortgages, to home equity lines of credit, and finally to automobile leases.The use of OLS models with 0-1 dependent variables and nonlinear independent variables (with truncation of probabilities near or below zero and near or above 1.0) seems justified (with very large sample sizes) in light of the results of structural validation on hold-out samples. Nevertheless, further research should be performed to compare the forecasting performance of alternative OLS, logistic and multinomial logistic models. Considering the high degree of accuracy achieved here and findings from similar research on the other portfolios, it is questionable, however,whether significant improvement in forecasting accuracy results from the more cumbersome estimation approaches.More important seem to be the influence of changes in risk characteristics of accounts that compose portfolios as blocks of securities are bought or sold andas changes occur in economic and competitive circumstances.

The hierarchical structure used for analyzing the consequences on termination of leases is very useful in depicting risk in consonance with managerial concepts and industry practice. There are, however, alternative Markovian structures that might be employed.We handled leases that terminated without repossession (state 6) by employing the logistic estimators hierarchically for insurance settlement and then for keep versus turn-in decisions. This was to avoid proliferation of states and thus simplify the computation of transition probabilities. Insurance settlements, however, are more directly related to the number of vehicles on the road under lease by the company than to the number of terminated leases (which, of course, is also related to number of vehicles under lease).A better estimate of the number of vehicles terminated with insurance settlements might thus occur by treating terminations of that type as a separate terminal (absorbing) state in the transition equations, instead of treating them as a subset of terminations without repossession. Further experimentation with alternative structures of this nature, with two-stage models mentioned earlier (that could incorporate additional variables for the first period of the planning horizon), and with different forms of survival models (that may ignore intervening states of delinquency on the path to termination) are in order.Considering the importance of used-vehicle prices in the final outcome, researchers might also concentrate on identifying key factors that determine market prices of used vehicles, and experiment with different ways to incorporate them into forecasting models of this type.

Note: An unabridged version of this paper with extensive tables and charts may be obtained from the authors.

REFERENCES

ABA Banking Journal, 1997, 89 (2), 34-37

Altman, E.I.Measuring Corporate Bond Mortality and Performance,*Journal of Finance*, 1989, 44, 909-922.

Asquith, P,D.W. Mullins Jr. and E.D.Wolff.Original Issue High Yield Bonds: Aging Analysis of Defaults, Exchanges, and Calls, *Journal of Finance*, 1989, 44, 923-953.

Campbell, T.S., and J.K. Dietrich.The Determinants of Default on Insured Conventional Residential Mortgage Loans, *Journal of Finance*, 1983, 38, 1569-1581.

Cunningham, D.F. and C.A. Capone Jr.The Relative Termination Experience of Adjustable to Fixed Rate Mortgages,*Journal of Finance* 1990, 5, 1687-1703

Curnow, G., G. Kochman, S. Meester,D. Sarkar, andK. Wilton. Automating Credit and CollectionsDecisions at AT&T Capital Corporation, *Interfaces*, 1997, 27(1), 29-52

Cyert, R.M., H.J. Davidson and G.L. Thompson.Estimation of the Allowance for Doubtful AccountsbyMarkov Chains,*ManagementScience* , 1962, 8, 287-303.

Kang, P. and S. Zenios.Complete Prepayment Models for Mortgage-Backed Securities, *Management Science* 1992, 38, 1665-1685.

Lawrence, E.C., L.D. Smith and M. Rhoades.An Analysis of Default Risk in Mobile Home Credit, *Journal of Banking and Finance* ,1992, 16, 299-312.

Rosenberg, E. and A. Gleit.Quantitative Methods in Credit Management: A Survey, *Operations Research*, 1994, 42(4), 589-613.

Smith, L.D., and E.C. Lawrence.Forecasting Losses on Liquidating Long-Term Loan Portfolio, *Journal of Banking and Finance*, 1995, 19, 959-985.

Smith, L.D., S.M. Sanchez, and E.C. Lawrence.A Comprehensive Model for Managing Risk on Home Mortgage Portfolios, *Decision Sciences*, 1996, 27(2), 291-317.

Smith, L.D., D. Mathew, Ya-Yung Wu, Disaggregation Strategies in Building Forecasting Models for Portfolios of Secured Loans", *Decision Sciences Institute Proceedings*, San Diego, CA 1997.

Zanakis, S.H., L.P. Mavrides and E.N. Roussakis.Applications of Management Science in Banking, *Decision Sciences*, 1986, 17, 114-128.

Zipkin, P. Mortgages and Markov Chains: A Simplified Valuation Model, *Management Science*, 1993, 39, 683-691.

6. OPTIMIZATION & DECISION MAKING

DECISION MAKING UNDER VARIOUS TYPES OF UNCERTAINTY

R. R. Yager
Iona College
New Rochelle, NY 10801

Abstract: We focus on the problem of decision making in the face of uncertainty The issue of the representation of uncertain information is considered and a number of different frameworks are described: possibilistic, probabilistic, belief structures and graded possibilistic. We suggest methodologies for decision making in these different environments. The importance of decision attitude in the construction of decision functions is strongly emphasized.

Keywords: Uncertainty, Possibility Distribution, Dempster-Shafer, Interval Probability

INTRODUCTION

The basic issues involved in decision making under incertitude can best be understood using the decision matrix shown in figure 1.

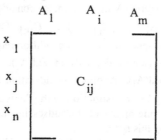

Figure 1. Decision Matrix

In this matrix the A_i correspond to a collection of alternative courses of action open to the decision maker, one of these actions must be selected by the decision maker. The elements x_j are possible values associated with a relevant variable V; here one and only one of these values must be assumed by V. Generally the value of V is unknown before the decision maker must make a selection from among the alternative courses of action. Finally C_{ij} is the payoff to the decision maker if he selects alternative A_i and V assumes the value X_j.

While we implicitly implied that V is a single variable, more generally V can be indicative of a collection of variables, a joint variable $V \equiv (V_1, V_2, ...V_q)$ In this case each x_i is a q-tuple of values, one for each of the variables, that is $x_i = (x_{i1} , x_{i2} , x_{i3} ,....., x_{iq})$. In the following, unless indicated, we shall assume V to be a single variable. However, most comments we make regarding this assumed single variable can be

S.H. Zanakis et al. (eds.), Decision Making: Recent Developments and Worldwide Applications, 233–250.
© 2000 Kluwer Academic Publishers.

attributed to any of the individual components making up V in the case when V is a joint variable.

A variable can be described as being a particular type depending on the mode used for the selection of its value from its solution space $X = \{x_1, x_2, ..., x_n\}$. Two types can be readily identified, although more may exist. The first type of variable we shall denote as *sentient*, and the second as *capricious*. We shall say a variable is a sentient variable if its value is selected by some agent who has understandable goals in selecting this value, typically a human being, although it can be an organization. We shall refer to the object selecting the value of V in this case as a sentient agent. We should note that the sentient agent's selection goals may be based on considerations related only to this decision, or based on considerations external to the decision at hand, or based upon a combination. We shall say that a variable is a capricious variable if its value is selected by some agent whose goals are incomprehensible in selecting the value. Variables selected by chance under random experiments are examples of of this type. We shall refer to the agent doing the selection in this caprious case as nature. Classically, these two environments have been referred to as game theory and decision making under uncertainty. In cases in which V is a joint variable some component variables may be sentient and others capricious.

A general framework for selecting the best alternative in this decision problem can be described. For each alternative A_i we calculate a value $Val(A_i)$ and then select as the best the alternative the one that has the largest of these values. A number of considerations should go into the formulation of this function. Some of these simply enter as parameters; others effect the structure of the function Val. Let us briefly comment on some of these considerations. In calculating $Val(A_i)$, a major consideration should be the collection of payoffs associated with A_i, $C_i = [C_{i1}, C_{i2}, ..., C_{in}]$. One required property here is the monotonicity of Val with respect to C_i. This condition requires that increasing the value of any of the C_{ij}.should not cause a decrease in $Val(A_i)$. More specifically, if $C_{jk} \geq C_{ik}$ for all k, then $Val(A_j) \geq Val(A_i)$. Another consideration is the "worth" of the payoffs. In some situations there may be no distinction to the decision maker in a payoff of \$100 or \$110. Utility theory is one approach to addressing this issue, fuzzy sets provide another approach to addressing this issue.

As noted in decision making under uncertainty it is assumed that the value of the variable V is selected by some capricious agent called nature. While here we don't know the exact mechanism used to select the value of V, we often have some information which biases our belief about which element in X will be selected as the value of V. Classically two different situations have been considered regarding our information about the value of variable V. The first case is one in which we assume the existence of a probability distribution over the set X of possible values in which p_i is the probability associated with x_i. The second case is one in which we only assume knowledge of the set of possible outcomes that V can assume.

The assumption of only two situations regarding our information about the value of the uncertain variable is very limiting with respect to the wide spectrum of knowledge that we can have and the many different types of statements human beings use to express knowledge about unknown variables.

Our focus in this work is on the problem of decision making uncertainty. Our goal here is to discuss a number of different structures available for the representation of partial knowledge about uncertain variables and to suggest techniques useful for the valuation of alternative courses of action in the presence of these different kinds of uncertainties.

DECISION ATTITUDE IN POSSIBILISTIC DECISION MAKING

We shall first consider the classic case of possibilistic uncertainty and discuss the role of decision attitude. With possibilistic uncertainty as noted above we have a situation in which all we know about the variable of interest, V, is that it must take its value in the set $X = \{x_1, x_2, \ldots x_n\}$, called the feasible or possible set of values for V. Possibilistic information can be obtained in a number of different ways. One way partial information which is possibilistic in nature is obtained is from linguistic data supplied by experts. For example, if V is a variable corresponding to interest rates at some time in the future, the statement that "interest rates will be less then 6%" would generate a set of possible values corresponding to the subset of interest rates considered as being less then 6%. Possibilistic information can also be obtained by physical limitations associated with the variable of interest.

From a decision making point of view for each alternative A_i, possibilistic information induces a bag of possible payoffs under the selection of A_i, $[C_{i1}, C_{i2}, \ldots, C_{in}]$. A number of different approaches have been suggested for evaluating alternatives in this environment. Among these are: **Pessimistic**: $Val(Ai) = Min_j[C_{ij}]$, **Optimistic**: $Val(Ai) = Max_j[C_{ij}]$, **Average/neutral**: $Val(A_i) = \frac{1}{n} \sum_{j=1}^{n} C_{ij}$, **Arrow-Hurwicz Criteria**: $Val(A_i) = \alpha\, Max_i[C_{ij}] + (1 - \alpha)\, Min_i[C_{ij}]$ (for $\alpha[0, 1]$)

Each one of these approaches can be seen as reflecting a particular attitude on the part of the decision maker. For example, in the first one, as the name indicates, the decision maker is essentially displaying a pessimistic attitude, one in which he is assuming that the worst of the possible outcomes will occur. Thus we see that a significant aspect of these methods is the centrality of the choice of decision attitude in the process of valuating alternatives. Also, quite clear in this situation is the subjectiveness of the choice.

In Yager (1992) we provided for a unification and generalization of these approaches to decision making when we only have a set of possible outcomes. The approach is based upon the OWA operator which was originally introduced in Yager (1988). A collection of papers on this operator can be found in Yager and Kacprzyk (1997). We first describe the OWA operator.

An **Ordered Weighted Averaging (OWA)** operator of degree n is a mapping $F_W: R^n \rightarrow R$ which has an associated vector weighting vector W, whose components satisfy **W–1:** $w_j \in [0,1]$ for $j = 1$ to n and **W–2:** $\sum_{j=1}^{n} w_j = 1$ and where $F_w(a_1, a_2, \ldots, a_n) = \sum_{j=1}^{n} w_j b_j$, with b_j being the jth largest of the a_i.

Essentially, the OWA operator involves a reordering of the arguments, then a linear aggregation. Thus if B is the vector of reordered arguments then we can express this as

$$F_W(a_1, a_2, \ldots, a_n) = W^T B,$$

it is the inner product of the weighting vector and the vector of ordered arguments.

In Yager (1992) we suggested the use of the OWA operator as a structure for providing a unification and generalization of the decision making formalism used in decision making under possibilistic uncertainty. Assume A_i is a decision alternative with payoff bag $[C_{i1}, C_{i2}, ..., C_{in}]$. Then Yager suggested using $Val(A_i) = F_W(C_{i1}, C_{i2}, ..., C_{in})$ as the valuation of the alternative. First, it is noted that by appropriately selecting W, we can obtain any of the previously introduced evaluation functions.

1). If $W = W_*$ where $w_j = 0$ for $j = 1$ to $n - 1$ and $w_n = 1$, we get

$Val(A_i) = Min_j[C_{ij}]$, the pessimistic decision maker.

2) If $W = W^*$, where $w_1 = 1$ and $w_j = 0$ for $j = 2$ to n, we get $Val(A_i) = Max_j[C_{ij}]$, the optimistic decision maker..

3).If $W = W_A$, where $w_j = \frac{1}{n}$ for all j, $Val(A_i) = \frac{1}{n}\sum_{j=1}^{n} C_{ij}$, the neutral decision maker

4) If $W = W_H$, where $w_1 = \alpha$, $w_n = 1 - \alpha$ and $w_j = 0$ for $j = 2$ to $n - 1$
we get $Val(A_i) = \alpha Max_j[C_{ij}] + (1 - \alpha) Min_j[C_{ij}]$, the Arrow-Hurwicz criteria.

In this framework Yager (1992) referred to W as the attitudinal vector and introduced a measure of optimism associated with a given vector: $\alpha(W) = \frac{1}{n-1} \sum_{j=1}^{n} w_j (n - j)$. We note that $\alpha(W_*) = 0$, $\alpha(W^*) = 1$, $\alpha(W_A) = 0.5$ and $\alpha(W_H) = \alpha$

In addition to unifying the existing decision making techniques, the introduction of the OWA formalism provides for a generalization of the potential means we have for evaluating alternatives. The generalization introduced here is one in which by selecting any W meeting the two conditions, W-1 and W-2 specified above, we get a valuation function. This of course provides us with an infinite family of possible valuation functions. It would be useful here to address the issue of providing some direction for the process of selecting an attitudinal vector W. The more deep our understanding of the valuation methodology, the more intelligently we can select the attitudinal vector W.

Yager (1997) suggested an interesting interpretation of the valuation process. Noting that the elements in the attitudinal vector W, as required by W-1 and W-2, satisfy the properties of a probability distribution, they lie in the unit interval and sum to one, he suggested that the components in W can be interpreted as a kind of subjective probabilities. In particular, he suggested that w_j can be interpreted as the decision maker's subjective probability that the jth best outcome will occur. With this interpretation, the pessimist is saying, since in this case $w_n = 1$, that the probability that the worst thing will happen is one while the optimist is saying that the probability that the best thing will happen is one. Under this interpretation of the w_j's, as these type of probabilities and with b_j being the jth best payoff, we see then the evaluation $Val(A_i) = \sum_{j=1}^{n} b_j w_j$ is a kind of expected value.

In order to use this OWA approach for valuating alternatives, we need select an attitudinal vector W. A number of approaches have be suggested for the determination of the attitudinal vector W. One approach is a direct approach in which a decision maker directly provides information about the attitudinal vector. Here a decision maker directly provides the w_j values to be used here the interpretation of w_j as the probability that the jth best outcome will occur may be of use in eliciting these weights. In this same spirit of direct elicitation one may consider use of a technique based upon Saaty's (1980) comparison matrix. Another approach can be based upon a learning of the attitudinal vector. Here we would look at the performance of the decision maker in real or artificial situations and use these examples to learn his attitudinal vector. A very useful tool for this approach is the learning algorithm developed by Filev and Yager (1998) which allows the learning of the weights in OWA operators.

Another approach is to specify a particular "type" of decision maker: optimistic, pessimistic, neutral, etc. More generally we envision the selection of an attitudinal vector W from a small class of preselected vectors.

Another approach in this spirit of selecting the attitudinal vector from prescribed of class of vectors, one that is very undemanding in its requirements on the decision maker and yet allows selection from an infinite class of possible attitudinal vectors, is based upon the work O'Hagan (1990) did on ME-OWA operators. In this approach, all that is required of the decision maker is that they provide a value $\alpha \in [0, 1]$ indicating their desired degree of optimism. Using this value the weights for the appropriate attitudinal vector can be obtained by solving the following mathematical programming problem.

$$\textbf{Maximize: } \sum_{j=1}^{n} w_j \ln(w_j)$$

$$\textbf{Subject to:} 1.\ w_j \in [0, 1],\ 2.\ \sum_{j=1}^{n} w_j = 1,\ 3.\ \frac{1}{n-1} \sum_{j=1}^{n} w_j (n-j) = \alpha$$

In the above we see that constraints 1 and 2 are the basic constraints for the OWA vector. Constraint 3 assures us that the degree of optimism of the determined vector satisfies our desired condition of α. The objective function can be seen as one of maximizing the entropy of the determined weights. This approach can be seen as a generalization of the Arrow-Hurwicz (1972) criteria. In both approaches the decision maker supplies a degree of optimism. In the Arrow-Hurwicz criteria, we only allocate weight to the maximal and minimal payoffs associated with an alternative. In this approach the weight is distributed to all the payoffs associated with the alternative being evaluated.

The following example illustrates the use of the OWA operator.

Example:

	x_1	x_2	x_3	x_4
A_1	100	30	60	50
A_2	70	60	50	80

Here $B_1 = \begin{bmatrix} 100 \\ 60 \\ 50 \\ 30 \end{bmatrix}$ and $B_2 = \begin{bmatrix} 80 \\ 70 \\ 60 \\ 50 \end{bmatrix}$ are the ordered payoffs for alternatives A_1 and A_2. Let us look at different kinds of decision makers.

(1) $W^T = \begin{bmatrix} \frac{1}{2} & \frac{1}{2} & 0 & 0 \end{bmatrix}$, this is a strongly optimistic decision maker. Here Val(A_1) =

$\frac{1}{2}$ (100 + 60) = 80 and Val(A$_2$) = $\frac{1}{2}$ (80 + 70) = 75, A$_1$ is preferred.

(2) $W^T = \begin{bmatrix} 0 & 0 & \frac{1}{2} & \frac{1}{2} \end{bmatrix}$, strongly pessimistic decision maker. In this case Val(A$_1$) = $\frac{1}{2}$(50 + 30) = 40 and Val(A$_2$) = $\frac{1}{2}$(60 + 55) = 55, A$_2$ is preferred.

(3) For the neutral decision maker, $W^T = \begin{bmatrix} \frac{1}{4} & \frac{1}{4} & \frac{1}{4} & \frac{1}{4} \end{bmatrix}$ we get Val(A$_1$) = $\frac{1}{4}$(100 + 60 + 50 + 30) = 60 and Val(A$_2$) = $\frac{1}{4}$(80 + 70 + 60 + 50) = 65. Here A$_2$ is preferred.

(4) If we consider a decision maker with α = 0.65 and use the weights obtained by solving the preceding mathematical programming problem, we have

$$W^T = \begin{bmatrix} 0.4 & 0.28 & 0.19 & 0.13 \end{bmatrix}$$

In this case Val(A$_1$) = (4)100 + (0.28)(60) + (0.19))50 + (13)50 = 70.2

Val(A$_2$) = (0.4)80 + (28)(70) + (0.19))60 + (13)50 = 69.5

DECISION MAKING WITH PROBABILISTIC INFORMATION

An often used conjecture regarding the information available about the state of nature is that it is of a probabilistic type. Implicit in this is the assumption that the process used to determine the state of nature is a biased random experiment. The information about this bias is carried by a probability distribution $P = (p_1, p_2, ..., p_n)$, here p_j is the probability that x_j will be the value of the state of nature, V, Prob(V = x_j) = p_j. In this situation the commonly accepted approach to evaluating the different alternatives is to use the expected value, Val(A$_i$) = $\sum_{j=1}^{n} C_{ij} p_j$

Yager (1999) questioned the unexamined use of the expected value as the appropriate valuation procedure. There he raises the issue that the concept of decision attitude must also be included in the formulation of the valuation function in this probabilistic environment as it was in the possibilistic one. It is noted that the use of the expected value, often a very good choice, implies a particular decision attitude, a neutral one, and may not, in some cases, truely reflect the attitude of the decision maker who may indeed be more optimistic or pessimistic. Withstanding the preceding comment in the following we assume the expected value as the appropriate valuation function and concern ourselves more with questions related to our knowledge about the probabilities associated with the outcomes.

In many decision making problems the assumption of precise probabilistic information is a requirement that is not justified by available information. The information available is less precise. We shall here describe some techniques available to address this issue.

Consider the situation which we shall call an Interval Probability Assessment (IPA). In an IPA rather than having some precise value p_j for Prob(V = x_j), we have a range of possible values, $[B_j, T_j]$, such that $p_j \in [B_j, T_j]$. Here we don't know the exact probability distribution P associated with the random experiment. As a matter of fact, any triple $(p_1, p_2, ..., p_n)$ such that $p_j \in [B_j, T_j]$ and $\sum_{j=1}^{n} p_j = 1$ is a valid probability distribution. We note that the required condition for the existence of at least one valid

probability is within this IPA is that $\sum_{j=1}^{n} B_j \leq 1 \leq \sum_{j=1}^{n} T_j$

We shall say that the IPA is consistent if the above condition holds. Generally, under the assumption of a consistent IPA, there exists many possible probability distributions. Given a consistent IPA, $[B_j, T_j]$, as a first step in using this a refinement can be made with respect to ranges associated with the probabilities. Consider the simple case in which we have only two elements and a IPA in which $p_1 \in [0.5, 1]$ and $p_2 \in [0.2, 0.7]$. What should be clear here is that while p_1 can go anywhere up to 1 since the minimal value for p_2 is 0.2 and the total of p_1 and p_2 must be one, p_1 will never exceed 0.8 for any valid probability distribution. In a similar way since the minimal value for p_1 is 0.5 we see that the value for p_2 will never exceed 0.5 in any valid probability distribution generated from this IPA. As another example consider the case where we have three elements and an IPA in which $p_1 \in [0, 1]$, $p_2 \in [0, 0.3]$ and $p_3 \in [0.4, 0.5]$. Here we see that this is a consistent IPA. However here we note that that while p_1 has a range that goes down to zero because of the upper bounds associated with p_2 and p_3 it will never go below 0.2 in any valid probability distribution. The implication of the above examples is that we can often refine a consistent IPA to provide tighter bounds of the interval without losing any information about possible probability distributions. Assume $p_j \in [B_j, T_j]$ is a consistent IPA an associated refined IPA is a set of bounds $p_j \in [L_j, U_j]$ such that (Klir, 1998)

$$\textbf{R-1: } L_j = Max(B_j, 1 - \sum_{i \neq j} T_i) \text{ and } \textbf{R-2: } U_j = Min(T_j, 1 - \sum_{i \neq j} B_i)$$

We see the refined IPA (RIPA) has the properties: **1.** $[L_j, U_j] \subseteq [B_j, T_j]$ for all j, **2.** Any probability distribution $\mathbf{P} = (p_1, p_2, \ldots, p_n)$ obtained by selecting $p_j \in [B_j, T_j]$ is also satisfies $p_j \in [L_j, U_j]$.

Thus we see that starting with a consistent IPA provided by the decision maker we can apply R-1 and R-2 to obtain a RIPA. In the following we shall work with the RIPA.

In order to provide a solution to this problem of decision making with IPA's, we must look at the problem in a slightly different framework. Figure #2, given below, will be of assistance here.

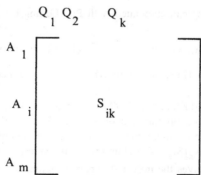

Figure #2. Alternative View of Decision Making with IPA's

Here again the A_i correspond to our alternative actions. However in this case our uncertainty corresponds to our knowledge about which is the correct probability distribution. Here Q_k corresponds to a possible probability distribution valid under the assumed IPA. Thus, $Q_k = [p_{k1}, p_{k2}, \ldots, p_{kn}]$ where p_{kj} is the probability of x_j under probability distribution Q_k. In this framework S_{ik} is the valuation of A_i under the assumption of probability distribution Q_k. Since the valuation function used is the expected value we get that $S_{ik} = \sum_{j=1}^{n} C_{ij} \, p_{kj}$.

It should be strongly emphasized that the interval uncertainty associated with IPA manifests itself in an uncertainty with respect to the value of the probability distribution and the set of Q_k are those probability distributions possible under the IPA. Furthermore these available probability distributions are those available under the RIPA.

We see that this decision problem is essentially the same type as in the preceding section, possibilistic decision making: we have a set of alternatives, a set possible values for our uncertain value, the effective possibility distribution, and a payoff for each pair. With this understanding then we see that we can use any of the techniques suggested in the previous section to evaluate Val(A_i). However, the problem is complicated by the fact that the collection of the possible states of nature, the set of Q of valid probability distribution, is continuously infinite. Because of the complexity of the space Q, it is difficult to evaluate Val(A_i) in a general way as was done in the preceding using OWA operators. However, Val(A_i) can be obtained for some particular types of decision attitude, among these is the neutral decision maker. Yager and Kreinovich (1999) solved this problem for the case of a neutral decision maker. We recall a neutral decision maker is one who evaluates an alternative A_i by taking the average of the S_{ik} across all k. It was shown that the valuation of A_i can be expressed as $\text{Val}(A_i) = \sum_{j=1}^{n} C_{ij} \, \widehat{P}_j$ where C_{ij} is the under A_i if x_j is the value of V and where $\widehat{P}_j$ is a probability defined such that

$$\widehat{P}_j = L_j + \frac{\Delta_j}{\sum_{i=1}^{n} \Delta_i} \left(1 - \sum_{i=1}^{n} L_i\right)$$

where $\Delta_j = U_j - L_j$, the spread associated with P_j. Letting $L = \sum_{i=1}^{n} L_i$, the total lower probability, and $\Delta = \sum_{i=1}^{n} \Delta_i$, we get $\widehat{P}_j = L_j + \frac{\Delta_j}{\Delta} (1 - L)$. It can be shown that the $\widehat{P}_j$ is a probability distribution. Thus, here Val(A_i) is a kind of expected value or weighted average.

The result of Yager and Kreinovich (1999) as noted corresponds to the case of a neutral decision maker. The decision function of an optimistic decision maker can also be obtained even in this infinite environment. In the case of the optimistic decision maker, we have $\text{Val}_{op}(A_i) = \text{Max}_k[S_{ik}]$. To obtain this value we must find the valid probability distribution Q_k^* which gives the maximal expected value. Essentially, this becomes a problem of finding the valid probability distribution generated by the RIPA that assigns as much as possible of the probabilities to x_j's that have high payoffs.

In the following we shall, without loss of generality, assume the C_{ij} for A_i have been indexed in descending order, $C_{ir} \geq C_{is}$ if $r < s$. In this case $Val_{op}(A_i) = \sum_{j=1}^{n} C_{ij}\tilde{P}_j$ where $\tilde{P}_j = L_j + \beta_j$. The β_j are determined as follows: **0.** Let $L = \sum_{j=1}^{n} L_j$, **1.** If $L = 1$, set all $\beta_j = 0$ and exit, **2.** Calculate $Sum(j) = L + \sum_{i=1}^{j} \Delta i$ and let j^* be the minimal j such that $sum(j) \geq 1$. Then

$\qquad$ i. $\beta_j = \Delta_j$ for $j < j^*$
$\qquad$ ii. $\beta_j = 0$ $\quad$ for $j > j^*$
$\qquad$ iii. $\beta_j = 1 - Sum(j^* - 1)$ for $j = j^*$.

The decision function of a pessimistic decision maker can also be obtained in this environment. Here $Val_{pes}(A_i) = Min_k[S_{ik}]$. In this case our requirement becomes that of finding the valid probability distribution which has as much of the probabilities assigned to x_j's that have low payoffs.

Again, we shall assume that the C_{ij} for A_i have been indexed in descending order. In this case $Val_{pes}(A_i) = \sum_{j=1}^{n} C_{ij} \ddot{P}_j$ where $\ddot{P}_j = L_j + \alpha_j$. The α_j are determined as follows:

0. Let $L = \sum_{j=1}^{n} L_j$, **1.** If $L = 1$, set all $\alpha_j = 0$ and exit, **2.** Calculate $Sum(j) = L + \sum_{i=j}^{n} \Delta i$ and let j^* be the maximal j such that $sum(j) \geq 1$. Then

$\qquad$ i. $\delta_j = \Delta_j$ for $j > j^*$
$\qquad$ ii. $\delta_j = 0$ $\quad$ for $j < j^*$
$\qquad$ iii. $\delta_j = 1 - Sum(j^* + 1)$ for $j = j^*$.

Example: The following example illustrates the situation. Again we consider the payoff structure of the preceding example.

	x_1	x_2	x_3	x_4
A_1	100	30	60	50
A_2	70	60	50	80

Here we assume that the value of V is selected by some probabilistic mechanism where

$\qquad$ $p_1 \in [0, 0.5]$ "not more than half", $p_2 \in [0.4, 0.6]$ "about 50%",

$\qquad$ $p_3 \in [0, 1]$ "unknown", $p_4 \in [0.1, 1]$ "at least 0.1

From this we can induce the following refined probabilities

$\qquad\qquad$ $p_1 \in [0, 0.5]$, $p_2 \in [0.4, 0.6]$, $p_3 \in [0, 0.5]$, $p_4 \in [0.1, 0.5]$

Here $L_1 = 0$ & $\Delta_1 = 0.5$, $L_2 = 0.4$ & $\Delta_2 = 0.2$, $L_3 = 0$ & $\Delta_3 = 0.5$, $L_4 = 0.1$ & $\Delta_4 = 0.4$

In this case $L = 0.5$ and $\Delta = 1.6$, since $\hat{P}_j = L_j + \dfrac{\Delta_j}{\Delta}(1 - L)$ we have $\hat{P}_j = L_j + \dfrac{\Delta_j}{1.6}(0.5) =$

$L_j + 0.625\Delta_j$, hence the Yager-Kreinovich probabilities are $\widehat{P}_1 = 0.16$, $\widehat{P}_2 = 0.45$, $\widehat{P}_3 = 0.16$, $\widehat{P}_4 = 0.23$ using these probabilities we get A_2 as the best choice since .

$$\text{Val}(A_1) = (0.16)100 + (0.45)30 + (0.16)60 + (0.23)50 = 50.6$$
$$\text{Val}(A_2) = (0.16)70 + (0.45)60 + (0.16)50 + (0.23)80 = 64.6$$

Asume an optimistic decision. Consider alternative A_1; here the ordered payoffs are

$$B_1 = \begin{bmatrix} 100 \\ 60 \\ 50 \\ 30 \end{bmatrix}. \text{ The associated probability vector is } P = \begin{bmatrix} L_1 + \beta_1 \\ L_3 + \beta_3 \\ L_4 + \beta_4 \\ L_2 + \beta_2 \end{bmatrix} = \begin{bmatrix} 0 + \beta_1 \\ 0 + \beta_3 \\ 0.1 + \beta_4 \\ 0.4 + \beta_2 \end{bmatrix}$$

Since the sum of L_j is 0.5 we have $1 - 0.5 = 0.5$ to allocate to the β_j values. Since this is an optimistic decision maker, we start at the top. Since $\Delta_1 = 0.5$, we allocate this to β_1 and this uses up all our available weight. Hence, $p_1 = 0.5$, $p_2 = 0$, $p_3 = 0.1$, $p_4 = 0.4$. Using this we get $\text{Val}(A_1) = (0.5)100 + 0(60) + (0.1)(50 + (0.4)(30) = 0.67$.

$$\text{For } A_2 \text{ the ordered payoff vector is } B_2 = \begin{bmatrix} 80 \\ 70 \\ 60 \\ 50 \end{bmatrix} \text{ and thus } P = \begin{bmatrix} L_4 + \beta_4 \\ L_1 + \beta_1 \\ L_2 + \beta_2 \\ L_3 + \beta_3 \end{bmatrix} = \begin{bmatrix} 0.1 + \beta_4 \\ 0.0 + \beta_1 \\ 0.4 + \beta_2 \\ 0.0 + \beta_3 \end{bmatrix}$$

Here again we have 0.5 to allocate to the B_j. Because of the optimistic value we start at the top, since $\Delta_4 = 0.4$ we can make $\beta_4 = 0.4$ and the remaining 0.1 we allocate to β_1 Thus, $p_1 = 0.5$, $p_2 = 0.1$, $p_3 = 0.4$, $p_4 = 0$. In this case $\text{Val}(A_2) = (0.5)80 + (0.1)(70) + (0.4)60 + (0)50 = 71$ Thus, A_2 is the choice.

Let us consider a pessimistic decision maker. Ordering the payoffs for A_1 we get B_1 and

$$\text{therefore } P = \begin{bmatrix} L_1 + \delta_1 \\ L_3 + \delta_3 \\ L_4 + \delta_4 \\ L_2 + \delta_2 \end{bmatrix} = \begin{bmatrix} 0 + \delta_1 \\ 0 + \delta_3 \\ 0.1 + \delta_4 \\ 0.4 + \delta_2 \end{bmatrix}. \text{ Here we start allocating the available probability}$$

weight of 0.5 from the bottom upward and obtain $p_1 = 0$, $p_2 = 0$, $p_3 = 0.4$, $p_4 = 0.6$. In this case the valuation is $\text{Val}(A_1) = (0.6) 30 + (0.4) 50 = 38$

$$\text{For } A_2 \text{ we get } B_2 = \begin{bmatrix} 80 \\ 70 \\ 60 \\ 50 \end{bmatrix} \text{ and therefore } P = \begin{bmatrix} 0.1 + \delta_4 \\ 0 + \delta_1 \\ 0.4 + \delta_2 \\ 0 + \delta_3 \end{bmatrix} = \begin{bmatrix} 0.1 \\ 0.0 \\ 0.4 \\ 0.5 \end{bmatrix}. \text{ For the pessimistic}$$

case $\text{Val}(A_2) = (0.1) 80 + (0)(70) + (0.4) 60 + (0.5) 50 = 57$, A_2 is clearly the choice.

A unification and generalization of the above procedures can be obtained. Assume b_j is the jth largest payoff associated with an alternative A. Let L_j and Δ_j be the lower bound and range of the associated probabilities obtained from the RIPA. Here $\text{Val}(A) = \sum_{j=1}^{n} b_j\, p_j$ where $p_j = L_j + w_j$ and the w_j are such that $0 \le w_j \le \Delta_j$ and $\sum_{j=1}^{n} w_j = 1 - L$

$$(L = \sum_{j=1}^{n} L_j).$$

The procedure used for determining the w_j distinguishes the various decision making attitudes. In the case of a neutral decision making we use $w_j = \frac{\Delta_j}{\Delta} (1 - L)$, the $(1 - L)$ is allocated proportionally to the spreads. For the optimistic decision maker we sequentially allocate the available weight $(1 - L)$. We start by making w_1 as big as possible, then we proceed to make w_2 as big as possible, etc. We continue until we use up all $(1 - L)$. For the pessimist we also allocate the available weight sequentially. However here we start from the bottom, we try to make w_n as big as possible and then go to w_{n-1}, etc., continuing until we finish all of the $(1 - L)$. Other imperatives can be envisioned based upon this unification. Let us consider some of these. We shall use OPT[w_j] to indicate a process of making w_j as big as possible within the constraints of 1 and 2 above. Let the **LIST** be an ordered list of the n indices, 1, 2, ...n. Let **LIST**(i) be the ith element in this list . Then a sequential process for determining the weights is: For i = 1 to n OPT($W_{LIST(i)}$). Here we first optimize, the first element is the list , then the second, etc. By using different manifestations of **LIST** we get different valuation imperatives. Here we note that if **LIST** = [n, n–1, n–2, ..., 1] we get the pessimistic attitude. On the other hand if **LIST** = [1, 2, ..., n] we the optimist. Another possibility for **LIST** is one starting from the middle values and working out, this median like.

DECISION MAKING WITH D-S BELIEF STRUCTURES

Thus far we have considered decision making in situations in which the information about the uncertain variable V is either probabilistic or possibilistic. The Dempster-Shafer belief structures (Dempster 1967, 1968; Shafer 1976, 1987) provide an uncertain knowledge representation model that provides for a generalization of these two types of representation. We first provide a formal characterization of the Dempster-Shafer belief structure.

A Dempster-Shafer belief structure defined on a set X has an associated collection of subsets of X, B_j for j = 1 to n, called focal elements and a mapping m associating values with subsets of X, $m:2^X \rightarrow [0, 1]$, such that $\sum_{j=1}^{n} m(B_j) = 1$ and $m(A) = 0$ for A not a focal element.

Two measures defined on belief structures are the measures of plausibility and belief. The plausibility measure Pl is a mapping Pl: $2^X \rightarrow [0,1]$ defined as $Pl(A) = \sum_{\substack{all\ j\ s.t. \\ A \cap B_j \neq \emptyset}} m(B_j)$. The measure of belief, Bel, is a mapping on subsets of X defined by $Bel(A) = \sum_{\substack{all\ j\ s.t. \\ A \subseteq B_j}} m(B_j)$. It can be shown that $Bel(A) = 1 - Pl(\overline{A})$.

A special case of belief structures are called consonant belief structures in this case the focal elements are nested, that is they can be indexed so that $B_1 \subset B_2 \ldots \subset B_n$. In this case the plausibility measure has the special property that $Pl(E \cup F) = Max[Pl(E), Pl(F)]$

A number of different semantics can be associated with the D-S belief structure. We shall find the following semantics, one very much in the spirit of random sets, useful for our current interest, decision making under uncertainty. Let V be a variable that takes its value in the set X, V is what we called the state of nature. Assume our knowledge about the value of this variable is that it is determined at least in part by performance of a biased random experiment. In this random experiment the outcomes, rather being elements of X are subsets of the space X. Furthermore, it is assumed that the actual value of V must be an element of the set that is determined by the random experiment. We let p_j be the probability that F_j is the outcome subset of the experiment. If we assign $F_j = B_j$ and let $m(B_j) = p_j$ then we can represent this as a D-S belief structure.

Probabilistic uncertainty is a special case of D-S structure in which the focal elements are singletons, $B_j = \{x_j\}$ and $m(B_j) = p_j$, the probability of x_j. We note that possibilistic uncertainty is a special case of a belief structure, it is one in which $B_1 = X$ and $m(B_1) = 1$.

The following example provides an illustration of a situation in which we have knowledge of an uncertain variable which is not representable by the possibilistic or probability model but is representable by the D-S belief structure.

Let V be a variable corresponding to interest rates at some future date. Assume interest rates are determined by the Federal Reserve Board. Assume that the board is considering three policies: make interest rates low, make interest rates high and not interfere with interest rates. We believe that there is a 50% chance that the first policy will be followed, 20% chance of the second and a 30% chance of the third. We can represent the information about the variable V, future interest rates, as a belief structure in which B_1 is the subset of X, the set of interest rates, consisting of low interest rates, B_2 is the subset of X consisting of high interest rates and $B_3 = X$, any interest rate.

Given a D-S belief an issue of concern is the determination of the probability that the value of V lies in some subset A of X, Prob(A). Generally, because of the type of uncertainty modeled by the D-S this value can't be precisely obtained. The best we can do is to find upper and lower bounds, $Prob^+(A)$ and $Prob^-(A)$ such that

$$Prob^-(A) \leq Prob(A) \leq Prob^+(A)$$

It can be shown that these bounds are related to the measures of of plausibility and belief introduced earlier, in particular $Prob^+(A) = Pl(A)$ and $Prob^-(B) = Bel(A)$.

Using this D-S representation various types of the knowledge can be represented for example the knowledge that that $Prob(A) \geq \alpha$ is representable by a belief structure in which $B_1 = A$ and $B_2 = X$ and $m(B_1) = \alpha$ and $m(B_2) = 1 - \alpha$. The knowledge that $Prob(A) = \alpha$ is representable in this structure by a belief structure in which $B_1 = A$ and $B_2 = \overline{A}$ and where $m(B_1) = \alpha$ and $m(B_2) = 1 - \alpha$.

We shall now turn to the issue of decision making in situations in which our knowledge about the uncertain variable is represented by a D-S belief structure.

Assume we have a decision problem of the type shown in figure #1 where our knowledge about the uncertain variable is represented by a belief structure with focal elements $F_1, \ldots, F_q$ with weighting function m. Yager (1992) suggested a general approach to this decision problem based upon a determination of a valuation $Val(A_i)$ for each alternative and the selection of the alternative with the largest valuation. The procedure used for the valuation of an alternative suggested in Yager (1992) is given in the following. In order to use this approach the decision maker must provide a value $\alpha \in [0, 1]$ corresponding to the degree of optimism he wants to use in the decision problem. This degree of optimist will be used to generate attitudinal weighting vectors using the O'Hagan algorithm. In the following we shall use $W_{\alpha,r}$ to indicate the attitudinal vector of dimension r generated from this algorithm based upon α degree of optimism. The procedure suggested by Yager for evaluating alternative A_i is as follows:

1). For each focal element F_j calculate $Val(A_{i/j})$ where $Val(A_{i/j}) = (W_{\alpha,n_j})^T B_j$ and n_j is the cardinality of the focal set F_j. B_j is the vector consisting of the ordered payoffs that are associated with the elements in F_j and the alternative A_i ($Val(A_{i/j})$ is an OWA aggregation with attitudinal vector W_{α,n_j} and arguments C_{ik} for all $x_k \in F_j$).

2)Calculate $Val(A_i)$ as the expected value of the $Val(A_{i/j})$ that is $Val(A_i) =$

$$\sum_{j=1}^{n} Val(A_{i/j}) \, p_j \text{ here of course } p_j = m(B_j).$$

We see we have used both of the classic types of decision making techniques. In step one we used the possibilistic technique and in step two we used the expected value characteristic of probabilistic environment. The following example illustrates the procedure just described.

Example: Again we assume the following decision matrix:

	x_1	x_2	x_3	x_4
A_1	100	60	70	50
A_2	90	80	60	100

We assume knowledge of the uncertain variable V is expressed by the following belief structure with three focal elements: $F_1 = \{x_1, x_2\}$, $F_2 = \{x_2, x_3, x_4\}$ and $F_3 = \{x_3, x_4\}$ where $m(F_1) = 0.5$, $m(F_2) = 0.3$ and $m(F_3) = 0.2$.

Here we shall assume our degree of optimism $\alpha = 0.75$. Using the O'Hagan algorithm we find the following attitudinal vectors for n = 2 and 3.

$$n = 2: \quad w_1 = 0.75 \qquad w_2 = 0.25$$
$$n = 3 \quad w_1 = 0.62 \qquad w_2 = 0.27 \qquad w_3 = 0.11$$

For F_1, F_2, and F_3 the collection of associated payoffs are [100, 60], [60, 70, 50] and [70, 50] respectively. These result in following ordered payoff vectors:.

$$B_1 = \begin{bmatrix} 100 \\ 60 \end{bmatrix} \qquad B_2 = \begin{bmatrix} 10 \\ 60 \\ 50 \end{bmatrix} \qquad B_3 = \begin{bmatrix} 70 \\ 50 \end{bmatrix}$$

Using this we get $Val(A_{1/1}) = (100)(0.75) + (60)(0.25) = 90$

$$Val(A_{1/2}) = (70)(0.62) + (60)(0.27) + 50(0.11) = 65.1$$
$$Val(A_{1/3}) = (70)(0.75) + (50)(0.25) = 65$$

Finally, $\text{Val}(A_1) = \sum_{j=1}^{3} \text{Val}(A_{1/j}) \, p_j = (90)(0.5) + (65.1)(0.3) + (65)(0.2) = 77.53$

If we used $\alpha = 0.5$ instead of 0.75 then for $n = 2$ we get $w_1 = w_2 = \frac{1}{2}$ and for $n = 3$ we get $w_1 = w_2 = w_3 = \frac{1}{3}$. In this case $\text{Val}(A_{1/1}) = \frac{1}{2}(100 + 60) = 80$, $\text{Val}(A_{1/2}) = \frac{1}{3}(60 + 70 + 50) = 60$ and $\text{Val}(A_{1/3}) = \frac{1}{2}(70 + 50) = 60$. Here $\text{Val}(A_1) = (80)(0.5) + (60)(0.3) + (60)(0.2) = 70$. Notice the valuation for $\alpha = 0.5$ is less then the case in which we used $\alpha = 0.75$ this is because it is more pessimistic.

We can calculate $\text{Val}(A_2)$ in a similar manner, however we shall not do this.

In the following we shall consider an extension of the Dempster-Shafer belief structure. In the D-S belief structure the weights $m(F_j)$, which are called the basic assignment weights, have the property of a probability distribution; they lie in the unit interval and sum to one. We shall now consider the case in which the $m(F_j)$ are expressed by an Interval Weight Assessment (IWA). In this case rather than exactly knowing the value of $m(F_j)$ we are given an interval in which it lies. In particular here we assume that we have for each focal element F_j and interval $[B_j, T_j]$ such that $m(F_j) \in [B_j, T_j]$. We shall say that the IWA is consistent if $\sum_{j=1}^{n} B_j \leq 1 \leq \sum_{j=1}^{n} T_j$. Thus in this case their exists some additional uncertainty as to what the effective basic assignment function.

Since a valid basic assignment function has the property of a probability distribution, its components lie in the interval and sum to one, we can impose some additional constraints which allows us to further refine the bounds on each of the intervals and be sure that the $m(F_j)$ lie in these refined intervals. Given an IWA, a collection of intervals $[B_j, T_j]$, we shall call the collection of intervals $[L_j, U_j]$ the Refined Interval Weight Assessment (RIWA) where $L_j = \text{Max}(B_j, 1 - \sum_{i \neq j} T_i)$ and $U_j = \text{Min}(T_j, 1 - \sum_{i \neq j} B_i)$.

The procedure for obtaining the valuation $\text{Val}(A_i)$ of an alternative in the case of a D-S structure with interval weight assessments is based upon an extension of the procedure used in the case when we know the exact basic weights combined with the technique we used for the case of interval probability assessments. Thus our procedure is again a two step procedure:

1). Calculate $\text{Val}(A_{i/j}) = (W_{\alpha,n})^T B_j$

2) Calculate $\text{Val}(A_i) = \sum_{j=1}^{n} \text{Val}(A_{i/j}) \, \widehat{P}_j$ where the $\widehat{P}_j$ are calculated using the Yager-Kreinovich formulation: $\widehat{P}_j = L_j + \frac{\Delta_j}{\Delta}(1 - \sum_{i=1}^{n} L_i)$ where $\Delta_j = U_j - L_j$ and $\Delta = \sum_{j=1}^{n} \Delta_j$.

We see that step one is unaffected by the interval weight assessment while step to must take it into account.

The following example illustrates the use of this approach.

Example: Here we consider the same problem as in the preceding example except instead of having $m(F_i)$ specified as exact values we have them specified as follows: $m(F_1)$ is *no more than 50%*, $m(F_2)$ is *at least 60%* and $m(F_3)$ is *between 20 and 30%*. In this case the IWA is expressed as: $m(F_1) \in [0,.0.5]$, $m(F_2) \in [0.6, 1]$ and $m(F_3) \in [0.2, 0.3]$. From this we obtain the associated RIWA which is: $m(F_1) \in [0,.0.2]$, $m(F_2) \in [0.6, 0.8]$ and $m(F_3) \in [0.2, 0.3]$. As in the preceding using $\alpha = 0.75$ we get $Val(A_{1/1}) = 90$, $Val(A_{1/2}) = 65.1$ and $Val(A_{1/3}) = 65$. Using the Yager-Kreinovich effective probabilities

$$\widehat{P}_j = L_j + \frac{\Delta_j}{\Delta}(1 - \sum_{i=1}^{3} L_i) = L_j + \frac{\Delta_j}{0.5}[1 - 0.8] = L_j + (0.4)\, \Delta_j$$

giving us $\widehat{P}_1 = 0.08$, $\widehat{P}_2 = 0.68$ and $\widehat{P}_3 = .24$. Thus here we get for the valuation of A_1

$$Val(A_1) = \sum_{j=1}^{q} Val(A_{1/j})\, \widehat{P}_j = (0.08)(90) + (0.68)(65.1) + (0.24)(65) = 67.$$

In this environment we are essentially using possibilistic decision making in two parts of the valuation process. First is used in the calculation of the $Val(A_{i/j})$, here we use the α value to obtain the weights of the OWA operators, the attitudinal vectors. The second occurrence of the use of possibilistic decision making is in the process of converting the RIWA into effective probabilities, here we assumed by default a neutral measure of optimism which lead to the use of Y-K formulation for the these weights, $\widehat{P}_j$. It may be interesting to consider some kind of coordinated policy here. For example, we could allow the decision maker to specify a value α this value could then be used to generate the weights in OWA vectors used in step one. This α could be used to guide the process of converting the the RIWA into effective probabilities. For example we could partition the unit interval into three ranges $[0, g_1]$, $(g_1, g_2]$ and $(g_2, 1]$ the if α falls into the first range we generate the effective probabilities by a pessimistic procedure, if α falls into the second range we generate the effective probabilities by Y-K procedure and if α falls into the third range we generate the effective probabilities by an optimistic procedure. We could of course independently indicate the attitudes to be used in each of the procedures.

GRADED POSSIBILISTIC DECISION MAKING

As we have noted possibilistic type of uncertainty is often generated from linguistic information. An example of this is the statement "interest rates will be low." Here we obtain as the set of possible interest rates all those considered as low. With the introduction of Zadeh's (1965) work on fuzzy sets we have become much more aware of the fact that concepts such as "low interest rates" rather than being crisp and well bounded are imprecise and fuzzy. In particular, the set of low interest rates rather than being a crisp set is in reality a fuzzy subset. This observation requires us to have to come to grips with graded possibilistic information. In particular, information about a variable V based on fuzzy subsets induces a possibility distribution Π (Zadeh 1978) on the domain of V where for each x in the domain $\Pi(x) \in [0, 1]$ indicates the possibility that x is the value of the variable V. We shall at this point not digress into the theory of possibility other then to say that a possibility distribution is often generated from a fuzzy subset A representing some concept by setting $\Pi(x) = A(x)$, the membership grade of the element in the fuzzy subset A. We note that Dubois and Prade (1988) provide a comprehensive introduction to

248

the field. Here we shall consider the problem of decision making with graded possibilities. Thus we shall assume for each $x \in X$ there exists a value $\Pi(x) \in [0, 1]$ indicating the possibility that x is the value of V.

As with all cases of possibilistic decision making we must provide some indication of the decision makers attitude, here we shall assume a decision maker with degree of optimism α. For notational simplicity we shall use $OWA_\alpha(G)$ to indicate the aggregation of the elements in the set G using the attitudinal vector generated by the O'Hagan algorithm for degree of optimism α and dimension equal to the cardinality of G.

In calculating $Val(A_i)$ in this case of graded possibilistic uncertainty rather then treating all outcomes similarly we need give more weight to those outcomes having larger grade of possibility. The following is a suggested procedure for evaluating $Val(A_i)$ in this environment of graded possibility

0. Determine the largest degree of possibility for any element in the domain X of the uncertain variable and denote this as U_{max}.

1. For each $u \in [0, U_{max}]$ denote F_u as the subset of X for which $\Pi(x) \geq u$. F_u are sometimes called level sets.

2). For each F_u obtain the bag of associated payoffs for the alternative being evaluated, B_u. Thus if $x_k \in F_U$ then C_{ik} is in the bag B_u.

3). Calculate $Val(A_{i/u}) = OWA_\alpha(B_u)$

4). $Val(A_i) = \dfrac{1}{U_{max}} \displaystyle\int_0^{U_{max}} OWA_\alpha \, du$

The following example illustrates this approach.

Example: Assume the payoffs for some alternative A_i is

	x_1	x_2	x_3	x_4
A_1	100	60	70	50

and we have the following information on graded possibilities: $\Pi(x_1) = 0.8$, $\Pi(x_2) = 0.3$, $\Pi(x_3) = 1$ and $\Pi(x_4) = 0.5$. In this case

$$F_u = \{x_1, x_2, x_3, x_4\} \qquad u \leq 0.3$$
$$F_u = \{x_1, x_3, x_4\} \quad 0.3 < u \leq 0.5$$
$$F_u = \{x_1, x_3\} \qquad 0.5 < u \leq 0.8$$
$$F_u = \{x_3\} \qquad 0.8 < u \leq 1$$

and therefore,

$$B_u = \{100, 60, 70, 50\} \qquad u \leq 0.3$$
$$B_u = \{100, 70, 50\} \qquad 0.3 < u \leq 0.5$$
$$B_u = \{100, 70\} \qquad 0.5 < u \leq 0.8$$
$$B_u = \{70\} \qquad 0.8 < u \leq 1$$

For simplicity we shall assume a neutral decision maker, $\alpha = 0.5$. Thus at each level we take the average.

$$Val(A_{1/u}) = 70 \qquad u \leq 0.3$$

$$Val(A_{1/u}) = 73.3 \quad 0.3 < u \le 0.5$$
$$Val(A_{1/u}) = 85 \qquad\qquad 0.5 < u \le 0.8$$
$$Val(A_{1/u}) = 70 \qquad\qquad 0.8 < u \le 1$$

$$Val(A_1) = \int_0^1 A_{1/u} \, du = (70)(0.3) + (73.3)(0.2) + (85)(0.3) + (70)(0.2) = 75.16$$

A natural extension here is to consider the cases in which we have graded possibility in Dempster-Shafer belief structures. In this case the focal elements rather then being crisp subsets of the domain would be fuzzy subsets of the domain. Here each focal element F_j would induce a graded possibility distribution Π_j on the domain of the uncertain variable in which $\Pi_j(x) = F_j(x)$, the membership grade of x in the fuzzy focal element. The valuation process in this case would require that in calculating $Val(A_{i/j})$, the valuation of the alternative with respect to the jth focal element, we use the procedure described in this section for graded possibilistic decision making.

REFERENCES

Arrow, K. J. and Hurwicz, L. (1972), "An optimality criterion for decision making under ignorance," in Uncertainty and Expectations in Economics, edited by Carter, C. F. and Ford, J. L., Kelley: New Jersey.

Dempster, A. P. (1967), "Upper and lower probabilities induced by a multi-valued mapping," Ann. of Mathematical Statistics 38, 325-339.

Dempster, A. P. (1968), "A generalization of Bayesian inference," Journal of the Royal Statistical Society, 205-247.

Dubois, D. and Prade, H. (1988), Possibility Theory : An Approach to Computerized Processing of Uncertainty, Plenum Press: New York.Filev, D. P. and Yager, R. R. (1998), "On the issue of obtaining OWA operator weights," Fuzzy Sets and Systems 94, 157-169.

Klir, G. J. (1998), "Statistical modeling with imprecise probabilities," Report # AFRL-IF-RS-TR-1998-166, Air Force Research Laboratories, Rome, NY.

O'Hagan, M. (1990), "Using maximum entropy-ordered weighted averaging to construct a fuzzy neuron," Proceedings 24th Annual IEEE Asilomar Conf. on Signals, Systems and Computers, Pacific Grove, CA, 618-623.

Saaty, T. L. (1980), The Analytical Hierarchy Process., McGraw-Hill: New York.

Shafer, G. (1976), A Mathematical Theory of Evidence, Princeton University Press: Princeton, N.J..

Shafer, G. (1987), "Belief functions and possibility measures," in Analysis of Fuzzy Information, Vol 1: Mathematics and Logic, edited by Bezdek, J. C., CRC Press: Boca Raton: Florida.

Yager, R. R. (1988), "On ordered weighted averaging aggregation operators in multi-criteria decision making," IEEE Transactions on Systems, Man and Cybernetics 18, 183-190.

Yager, R. R. (1992), "Decision making under Dempster-Shafer uncertainties," International Journal of General Systems 20, 233-245.

Yager, R. R. (1997), "On the inclusion of importances in OWA aggregations," in The Ordered Weighted Averaging Operators: Theory and Applications, edited by Yager, R. R. and Kacprzyk, J., Kluwer Academic Publishers: Norwell, MA, 41-59.

Yager, R. R. (1999), "Including decision attitude in probabilistic decision making," International Journal of Approximate Reasoning 21, 1-21, 1999.

250

Yager, R. R. and Kacprzyk, J. (1997), The Ordered Weighted Averaging Operators: Theory and Applications, Kluwer: Norwell, MA.

Yager, R. R., Kacprzyk, J. and Fedrizzi, M. (1994), Advances in the Dempster-Shafer Theory of Evidence, John Wiley & Sons: New York.

Yager, R. R. and Kreinovich, V. (1999), "Decision making under interval probabilities," International Journal of Approximate Reasoning 22, 195-215.

Yager, R. R., Ovchinnikov, S., Tong, R. and Nguyen, H. (1987), Fuzzy Sets and Applications: Selected Papers by L. A. Zadeh, John Wiley & Sons: New York.

Zadeh, L. A. (1965), "Fuzzy sets," Information and Control 8, 338-353.

Zadeh, L. A. (1978), "Fuzzy sets as a basis for a theory of possibility," Fuzzy Sets and Systems 1, 3-28.

DECISION AID IN THE OPTIMIZATION OF THE INTERVAL OBJECTIVE FUNCTION

C.A. Antunes[1], J. Clímaco[2]

[1] Dept. of Electrical Engineering, Univ. of Coimbra, 3030 Coimbra and INESC, Rua Antero de Quental, 199; 3000 Coimbra, Portugal

[2] Faculty of Economics, Univ. of Coimbra, 3000 Coimbra, and INESC, Rua Antero de Quental, 199; 3000 Coimbra, Portugal

Abstract: An interactive graphical approach is proposed to deal with linear programming problems whose objective function has interval coefficients. The interval objective function problem is converted into a three-objective problem, by filtering the directions associated with the extreme rays which generate the convex cone encompassing all objective function gradients that can be obtained within the specified intervals for the coefficients. The weight space is then used as an operational means to display useful information to the decision maker in the search for satisfactory solutions to the interval problem. Additional limitations imposed on the objective functions can be translated onto the weight space to aid reducing the scope of the search.

Key words: Interval objective function; multiple objective linear programming; weight space; interactive decision aid; nondominated solutions.

INTRODUCTION

The actual coefficients of the objective function to be optimized in linear programming models are not generally known with precision. Those numbers derive from estimates by experts, subjective judgments in complex environments, imprecise measurements, etc. However, it is possible in most situations to specify with a reasonable degree of accuracy ranges of admissible values for the coefficients, that is each coefficient is a closed interval rather than a single real value. The uncertainty and imprecision underlying the objective

S.H. Zanakis et al. (eds.), Decision Making: Recent Developments and Worldwide Applications, 251–261.

function coefficients are thus captured by means of intervals, which define a region the coefficients can possibly take.

Let us consider the single objective linear programming (SOLP) problem

$$\text{max} \quad c\,x$$
$$\text{s. t.} \quad x \in X$$
$$X = \{\, x \in R^n \mid Ax = b, x \geq 0, b \in R^m \,\}$$

The coefficients of the objective function $c=(c_1,...,c_n)$ are closed intervals defined by an ordered pair $[c_{Lj}, c_{Rj}]$, where c_{Lj} and c_{Rj} are the left and the right limit of c_j, respectively. The interval may also be denoted by its center and width as $<c_C, c_W>$, such that $c_C = \frac{1}{2}(c_L + c_R)$ and $c_W = c_R - c_L$. An interval vector is a vector whose components are interval numbers.

Let Φ be the closed and convex hyper-rectangle (with sides parallel to the coordinate axes), where any $c \in \Phi$ can be expressed as a convex combination of the elements of the set defined by the 2^n extreme points, given by $\{r^1,...,r^{2^n}\} = \{r \in R^n \mid r_j \in \{c_{Lj}, c_{Rj}\}$, $j=1,...,n\}$. Without loss of generality, it is considered that all n decision variable coefficients are expressed in terms of intervals, in order to simplify the notation (a precisely known coefficient has $c_R = c_L$).

$$\Phi = \{\, c \in R^n \mid c_j \in [c_{Lj}, c_{Rj}], j=1,...n \,\}$$

Since Φ is bounded, any $c \in \Phi$ can be written as a convex combination of the r^i $(i=1,...2^n)$. These are the extreme rays which generate the convex cone encompassing all objective function gradients that can be attained within the specified intervals for the coefficients (Steuer, 1981).

The linear programming problem with interval coefficients in the objective function has been addressed, among others, in Chanas and Kuchta (1996), Inuiguchi and Sakawa (1997), Ishibuchi and Tanaka (1990), and Steuer (1981).

Three algorithms (F-cone, E-cone and all emanating edges) are presented in Steuer (1981), which compute all extreme points and unbounded edge directions that are multiparametrically optimal with respect to the ranges specified for the objective function coefficients (that are LP optimal for at least one $c \in \Phi$), by applying vector-maximum theory. The algorithms rely on the contraction of the cone of objective function gradients.

Inuiguchi and Sakawa (1997) introduce the concept of maximin achievement rate solution. The authors also propose a solution algorithm based on a relaxation procedure, which involves solving a linear fractional programming problem.

In Ishibuchi and Tanaka (1990) it is proposed converting the interval SOLP into the bi-objective linear programming problem

$$\max \quad f_L(x) = c_L \, x$$
$$\max \quad f_C(x) = c_C \, x$$
$$\text{s. t.} \quad x \in X$$

The solution set to the interval SOLP is then obtained as the nondominated solutions (set of feasible solutions for which the improvement of an objective function value implies the worsening of at least other objective function value) to the bi-objective problem. The two objectives to be maximized are the worst case (left limit in maximization problems) and the average case, thus reflecting a conservative strategy.

A family of preference relations is introduced in Chanas and Kuchta (1996), and the solution of the interval objective function problem is determined by optimizing a parametric LP problem. This is essentially a weighted sum of the two objective functions $f_L(x) = c_L \, x$ and $f_R(x) = c_R \, x$.

The weighted-sums scalarizing function to compute the nondominated solutions, as suggested in Ishibuchi and Tanaka (1990), is

$$\max \quad \{ \lambda_1 \, f_L(x) + \lambda_2 \, f_C(x) \}$$
$$\text{s. t.} \quad x \in X$$
$$\lambda_1 + \lambda_2 = 1 \,, \lambda_1 \,, \lambda_2 \geq 0$$

As it is well known, the nondominated extreme solutions to the multiple objective linear programming (MOLP) problem can be obtained by optimizing a weighted-sums scalarizing function, and varying the weights in the interval $[0,1]$ (the sum of the weights adding-up to 1).

The operational approach used in Chanas and Kuchta (1996) is similar, but using $f_R(x)$ in the place of $f_C(x)$, which generally permits to enlarge the range of solutions thus obtained because in this latter case the whole range of coefficient values between c_L and c_R (the "pessimistic" and the "optimistic" scenarios) can be analyzed.

However, if there is a strong correlation between the directions associated with f_L and f_R, and consequently also f_C, only a small number of potential solutions to the interval problem are obtained (or even one solution only). That is, the corresponding convex cone is very "narrow". Moreover, even though c_L and c_R are quite different, the directions associated with f_L and f_R can be strongly correlated (or even the same). In the limit situation, Φ can be a hyper-cube with the same left limits and the same right limits for all coefficients (that is, the convex cone associated with f_L and f_R reduces to a half-ray).

On the other hand, the exhaustive computation of all potential solutions to the interval problem generally involves a huge computational burden and, more important than that, this effort is not worthwhile in most situations. In fact, presenting the decision maker

(DM) with a large set of solutions, in many cases with just slight differences among the objective function values, may further complicate an already complex decision problem.

In this introduction the motivation and interest of the study have been provided. An interactive approach based on the weight space for a three-objective LP problem is proposed in the next section. This approach is then illustrated by means of an example, and some conclusions are drawn in the final section.

AN INTERACTIVE APPROACH BASED ON THE WEIGHT SPACE

The approach proposed in this paper enables to analyze, in general, a larger range of solutions to the interval SOLP. This interactive graphical approach is not exhaustive, in terms of computing all parametrically optimal solutions as in Steuer (1981), but it requires a much lower computational effort. The interval objective function problem is converted into a three-objective problem, which enables to use the weight space for displaying useful information to the DM. The aim is to provide the DM information in a way that promotes comprehension and insights in the progressive search for potential solutions to the interval problem.

The approximation of Φ is based on constructing a three-objective LP problem by filtering the set of directions associated with $\{r^1,...,r^{2n}\}$. The filtering method is aimed at determining the "most distinct" directions. Anyone of the methods mentioned in Steuer (1986) can be used: furthest point outside the neighborhoods, closest point outside the neighborhoods or first point outside the neighborhoods.

The direction corresponding to $f_L(x)=c_L x$ is used as the seed point for the filtering method, and it is thus automatically retained (thus reflecting a conservative strategy). The other two objective functions are selected by the filtering method (they can even be different depending on the method) in a way they can be considered the "most distinct". This procedure may be viewed as an attempt to obtain a "good" inner approximation of Φ (the more open the convex cone defined by the objective function gradients, the higher, in general, the number of potential solution to the interval problem), whereas the enveloping cone proposed in Steuer (1981) can be viewed as an outer approximation.

Therefore the three-objective problem to be considered is

$$\max \quad f_L(x)=c_L x$$
$$\max \quad f_D(x)=c_D x$$
$$\max \quad f_E(x)=c_E x$$
$$\text{s. t.} \quad x \in X$$

where $f_L(x)$ represents the "pessimistic" scenario, with $f_D(x)$ and $f_E(x)$ corresponding to the "most distinct" directions retained by the filtering procedure (using the direction associated with $f_L(x)$ as the seed).

It can also be envisaged introducing $f_R(x)$ into the model, replacing $f_L(x)$ or any of the other functions, in order to explicitly address the "optimistic" scenario. This can be done by using the direction corresponding to $f_R(x)$ as the seed point for the filtering method.

The scalarization process to compute nondominated (extreme) solutions to the multiple objective linear programming (MOLP) consists in optimizing a weighted sum of the p objective functions:

$$\max \quad \lambda_1 f_1(x) + \lambda_2 f_2(x) + \dots + \lambda_p f_p(x) \tag{1}$$
$$\text{s. t.} \quad x \in X$$
$$\lambda \in \Lambda = \{\lambda : \lambda \in R^p, \Sigma \lambda_k = 1, \lambda_k \geq 0, k = 1, \dots, p\}$$

Nondominated solutions can be computed by considering some $\lambda_k=0$ (for instance, the cases corresponding to the optimization of each objective function individually). However, in this situation, optima of (1) which are only weakly nondominated solutions to the MOLP problem may be found. For computational purposes a small ε may be used to prevent this problem.

The decomposition of the weight space (which is a by-product of the optimization of the weighted-sum scalarizing function) is used as an meaningful operational means to convey information to the DM. The graphical display (for p=3) of the set of weights which leads to each nondominated extreme solution can be achieved through the decomposition of the weight space. From the simplex tableau corresponding to a nondominated basic solution to the weighted-sum problem, the corresponding set of weights is given by $\lambda^T W \geq 0$, where $W=C_B B^{-1} N - C_N$ is the reduced cost matrix (w_{kj} being the marginal rate of change of objective function $f_k(x)$ caused by the introduction of one unit of nonbasic variable x_j into the basis). B (C_B) and N (C_N) are the submatrices of A (C) corresponding to the basic and nonbasic variables, respectively.

The region comprising the set of weights corresponding to a nondominated extreme solution, defined by $\{\lambda^T W \geq 0, \lambda \in \Lambda\}$, is called indifference region. The DM can thus be indifferent to all the combinations of weights within this region, because they lead to the same nondominated solution. The boundaries between two contiguous indifference regions represent the nonbasic efficient variables (those which when introduced into the basis lead to an adjacent nondominated extreme point through a nondominated edge). A common boundary between two indifference regions means that the corresponding nondominated solutions are connected by a nondominated edge. If a point λ belongs to several indifference regions this means that they correspond to nondominated solutions lying on the same face.

The analysis of the weight space is thus a valuable decision aid tool in "learning" the shape of the nondominated solution set, and consequently in grasping the potential solutions to the interval problem. The decomposition of the weight space as a means to make a progressive and selective learning of the nondominated solution set and evaluate the stability of selected nondominated solutions to changes in the coefficients is exploited in Antunes and Climaco (1992), Climaco and Antunes (1987, 1989).

The weight space can also be used as a graphical means to present the DM information regarding inferior limitations he/she wants to impose on the objective functions, namely on $f_L(x)$ values (reflecting his/her preferences throughout the interactive process regarding the "conservative" strategies). These limitations can be "hard constraints" (imposed in a definitive way) or "soft constraints" (used to obtain more information and revocable thereafter). In order to compute the region of the weight space where the additional limitation $f_L(x) \geq f_L^{min}$ holds, then the auxiliary problem to be solved is

$$\text{max} \quad f_L(x) = c_L \, x \qquad\qquad (2)$$
$$\text{s. t.} \quad f_L(x) \leq f_L^{min}$$
$$x \in X$$

The nondominated extreme points of the modified feasible region which are (alternative) optimal solutions to (2) are selected and the subregions of the weight space corresponding to each of these points are computed and displayed (these are the indifference regions defined by $\lambda^T W \geq 0$, corresponding to each nondominated alternative basis). The union of all these subregions determines the region of the weight space where the additional limitation on the objective function value is satisfied. If the DM is only interested in solutions which satisfy $f_L(x) \geq f_L^{min}$ then it is sufficient, from now on, to restrict the search to sets of weights within this region.

Note that this technique can also be used to impose additional limitations on f_C, whenever f_L and f_R are considered in the three-objective model, for f_C can be written as a positive linear combination of f_L and f_R ($f_C = 0.5 \, f_L + 0.5 \, f_R$).

AN ILLUSTRATIVE EXAMPLE

The proposed approach will be illustrated using the following example:

$$\text{max} \ z = [0,3] \, x_1 + [-1,5] \, x_2 + [1,2] \, x_3 + [1,4] \, x_4$$
$$\text{s. t.} \quad 2 \, x_1 + \quad x_2 + 4 \, x_3 + 3 \, x_4 \leq 60$$
$$3 \, x_1 + 4 \, x_2 + \quad x_3 + 2 \, x_4 \leq 60$$
$$x_1 + 2 \, x_2 + 3 \, x_3 + 4 \, x_4 \leq 50$$
$$4 \, x_1 + 3 \, x_2 + 2 \, x_3 + \quad x_4 \leq 50$$
$$x_1, x_2, x_3, x_4 \geq 0$$

By filtering the directions associated with the 16 extreme rays of Φ, using the one associated with f_L as the seed point, the "most distinct" directions which are found lead to the three-objective problem:

$$\text{max} \ f_L(x) = \quad - x_2 + \quad x_3 + x_4$$
$$\text{max} \ f_D(x) = \quad 5 \, x_2 + 2 \, x_3 + x_4$$
$$\text{max} \ f_E(x) = 3 \, x_1 + 5 \, x_2 + \quad x_3 + x_4$$
$$\text{s. t.} \quad x \in X$$

The 8 nondominated extreme solutions which can be obtained are:

Table 1. Nondominated solutions for the 3-objective problem (f_L, f_D, f_E)

Solution	f_L	$x=(x_1, x_2, x_3, x_4)$	f_R	Width	Area(%)
1	15.714	(0,0,12.857,2.857)	37.143	21.429	4.71
2	-10.0	(0,14,4,0)	78.0	88.0	61.11
3	-15.0	(0,15,0,0)	75	90.0	4.17
4	10.0	(0,4,14,0)	48.0	38.0	2.12
5	0.0	(0,10,10,0)	70.0	70.0	7.06
6	-5.0	(0,12.5,5,2.5)	82.5	87.5	18.06
7	7.5	(2.5,5,12.5,0)	57.5	50.0	1.37
8	12.5	(7.5,0,7.5,5)	57.5	45.0	1.41

The corresponding decomposition of the weight space is displayed in fig. 1 (all figures are actual copies of screen displays). Two nondominated faces (defined by extreme point solutions 1-4-7-8 and 4-5-7) and 9 nondominated edges are identified. The display of the weight space also permits to identify another face (defined by extreme point solutions 8-7-5-6, for which its interior points (those not located on edges 8-7, 7-5, 5-6) are not strictly nondominated.

Although f_R is not an explicit function in this three-objective model its value for each solution can be computed to give information on the ranges of the objective function value of these potential solutions to the interval problem. Moreover, the width (f_R-f_L) can also be used as an indicator to select a final solution. The area occupied by each indifference region (corresponding to a nondominated extreme solution to the three-objective problem) is also useful as a measure of stability of the solution regarding changes in the weights (even though it must be used with precautions due to its dependence on the relative lengths of the objective function gradients).

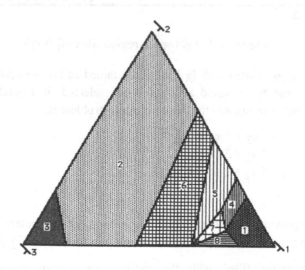

Figure 1. The weight space for the 3-objective problem (f_L, f_D, f_E)

If the DM is only interested in solutions for which $f_L(x) \geq 5$ (a conservative approach) then solving problem (2) leads to the weight space region displayed in fig. 2. The search can be restricted to this region to compute nondominated solutions satisfying that additional limitation on f_L (by comparing with fig. 1 it can be seen that only solutions 1, 4, 7 and 8 could then be reached).

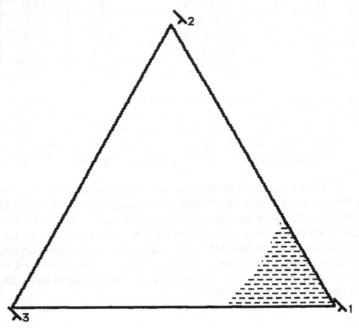

Figure 2. Weight space region where $f_L(x) \geq 5$

If the direction associated with f_R has been retained as the seed point in the filtering procedure, $f_L(x)$ and $f_D(x)$ would also have been selected (it depends on the filtering method and the metric used), and the three-objective problem is:

$$
\begin{aligned}
\max \quad f_L(x) &= \quad\quad - x_2 + \ x_3 + \ x_4 \\
\max \quad f_D(x) &= \quad\quad 5\,x_2 + 2\,x_3 + \ x_4 \\
\max \quad f_R(x) &= 3\,x_1 + 5\,x_2 + 2\,x_3 + 4\,x_4 \\
\text{s. t.} \quad & x \in X
\end{aligned}
$$

Some of the previous solutions are again obtained, but new potential solutions to the interval problem can be reached (solutions 3, 8 and 9 in table 2 and fig. 3).

The weight space filled with the indifference regions corresponding to the nondominated extreme solutions is displayed in fig. 3. It can be recognized that only solutions 1, 10, 9, 8 and 3 could be computed with the bi-objective model (f_L, f_R). By optimizing the center function $f_C = f_L + f_R$, solution 8 would be obtained as the optimal one.

Table 2. Nondominated solutions for the 3-objective problem (f_L, f_D, f_R)

Solution	f_L	f_R	$x=(x_1,x_2,x_3,x_4)$	Width	Area(%)
1	15.714	37.143	(0,0,12.857,2.857)	21.429	5.35
2	-10.0	78.0	(0,14,4,0)	88.0	15.00
3	-5.0	85.0	(0,11.667,0,6.667)	90.0	13.94
4	10.0	48.0	(0,4,14,0)	38.0	1.82
5	0.0	70.0	(0,10,10,0)	70.0	4.47
6	-5.0	82.5	(0,12.5,5,2.5)	87.5	51.87
7	7.5	57.5	(2.5,5,12.5,0)	50.0	0.26
8	0	82.5	(5, 7.5,0, 7.5)	82.5	3.14
9	10	70.0	(10,0,0,10)	60.0	3.09
10	12.5	57.5	(7.5,0,7.5,5)	45.0	1.06

The weight space is completely filled with indifference regions (that is, all nondominated extreme solutions to the three-objective problem have been computed) for the sake of illustration. The aim of the proposed approach is to provide a progressive and selective learning of the set of nondominated solutions to the three-objective problem (and thus potential solutions to the interval problem) by using the weight space as a meaningful operational means. The DM will decide upon the interest to exploit regions of the weight space not yet filled based on the information about potential solutions gathered so far.

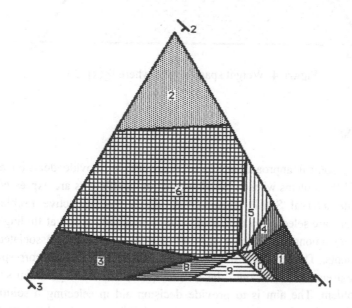

Figure 3. The weight space for the 3-objective problem (f_L, f_D, f_R)

260

If the DM is interested in proceeding the search in regions where $f_C(x) \geq 36$ is satisfied then solving problem (2) with objective function $0.5f_L + 0.5f_R$ and the additional constraint $0.5f_L + 0.5f_R \leq 36$ leads to the identification of the hatched region of the weight space (fig. 4). By comparing figures 3 and 4, it can be concluded that only solutions 3, 6, 8 and 9 satisfy the additional constraint on $f_C(x)$.

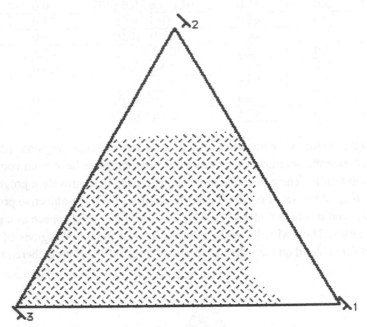

Figure 4. Weight space region where $f_C(x) \geq 36$

CONCLUSIONS

An interactive graphical approach has been presented to provide decision aid in the optimization of LP problems whose objective function coefficients are expressed in terms of intervals. The interval SOLP is converted into a three-objective problem whose objective functions are selected by means of a filtering method aimed at finding the "most distinct" directions among the extreme rays defining the convex cone associated with the interval coefficients. This enables to display the indifference regions corresponding to nondominated extreme solutions onto the weight space, which are potential solutions to the interval problem. The aim is to provide decision aid in selecting a solution to the interval SOLP by using the weight space as an insightful operational means to convey information to the DM, while avoiding the computational burden associated with the exhaustive computation of all solutions.

Investigation of the extension of this approach to MOLP with interval coefficients is currently underway. The study of the behavior of indifference regions is proposed in Antunes and Climaco (1992) to evaluate the stability of selected nondominated solutions to changes in the coefficients of the objective functions and in the right-hand sides of the constraints. The application of this approach to tackle uncertainty in models for energy (namely regarding the quantification of environmental impacts) and telecommunications (regarding issues related to costs and revenues of new services) planning is also being investigated.

ACKNOWLEDGEMENT

This work has been partially supported by FCT project PRAXIS XXI 2/2.1/MAT/465/94.

REFERENCES

Antunes, C. H., and Clímaco, J. (1992), "Sensitivity analysis in MCDM using the weight space", *Operations Research Letters* 12, 3, 187-196.

Clímaco, J., and Antunes, C. H. (1987), "TRIMAP - A tricriteria interactive linear programming package", *Foundations of Control Engineering*, 12, 3, 101-119.

Clímaco, J., and Antunes, C. H. (1989), "Implementation of a user friendly software package - a guided tour of TRIMAP", *Mathematical and Computer Modelling* 12, 1299-1309.

Chanas, S., and Kuchta, D. (1996), "Multiobjective programming in optimization of interval objective functions - A generalized approach", *European Journal of Operational Research* 94, 594-598.

Inuiguchi, M., and Sakawa, M. (1997), "An achievement rate approach to linear programming problems with an interval objective function", *Journal of the Operational Research Society* 48, 25-33.

Ishibuchi, H., and Tanaka, H. (1990), "Multiobjective programming in optimization of the interval objective function", *European Journal of Operational Research* 48, 219-225.

Steuer, R. E. (1981), "Algorithms for linear programming problems with interval objective function coefficients", *Mathematics of Operations Research* 6, 3, 333-348.

Steuer, R.E. (1986), *Multiple Criteria Optimization: Theory, Computation and Application*, Wiley.

A FUZZY EXTENSION OF A MIXED INTEGER MOLP MODEL FOR SOLVING THE POWER GENERATION EXPANSION PROBLEM

G. Mavrotas, D. Diakoulaki

National Technical University of Athens
Laboratory of Industrial and Energy Economics
Zografou Campus, Athens, GR 157 80
Greece

Abstract: This paper presents a generation approach for mixed integer multiple objective linear programming problems which is developed on the basis of a multicriteria branch and bound algorithm. The application study concerns the power generation expansion problem, which is represented by a model with discrete and continuous variables. The problem solution provides the whole set of efficient solutions along with the corresponding efficient combinations of the new power plants. In order to facilitate the decision maker in his choice each efficient combination is characterized by triangular fuzzy numbers denoting the range of values of the objective functions achieved by the associated efficient solutions.

Key words: Multiple oblective linear programming, MOLP, mixed-integer MOLP, expansion planning

INTRODUCTION

Most Multiple Ojective Linear Programming (MOLP) methods are designed to solve problems with only continuous variables. However, continuous variables are not sufficient to represent discrete phenomena encountered in many practical decision situations. These phenomena are usually incorporated into models using integer variables. When only some of the variables are integer the problem becomes Mixed-Integer MOLP (MIMOLP). The only tools available for handling MIMOLP problems are based on interactive methods, mainly because generation approaches are very demanding on computational resources (Climaco et al., 1992). The interactive methods aim at isolating the preferred solution among the efficient solutions of the problem through the interaction with the DM. The

S.H. Zanakis et al. (eds.), Decision Making: Recent Developments and Worldwide Applications, 263–277.
© 2000 Kluwer Academic Publishers.

DM drives the search expressing his/her choices in samples of efficient solutions. However, the use of the interactive methods is questionable when the frequent interaction with the DM is difficult or when multiple DMs must guide the search. Unlike the interactive approaches, generation approaches aim at producing the whole set of efficient points. The main drawback of the generation approaches is that they cannot handle large multiple objective problems. The required computational effort is prohibitive while the size of the derived efficient set causes "information overload" to the DM. However, when the size of the problem allows the use of generation approaches, they provide the DM with valuable information which can be further processed. They inform the DM about the whole context of the decision situation (efficient set), thus reinforcing his confidence on the final decision.

The method presented in this paper is a generation approach especially designed for mixed-integer problems. It exploits the discrete characteristics of the integer formulation along with the multiple objectives in order to provide the DM with all the potential actions. First, the set of the *efficient combinations* is derived. The efficient combinations are the combinations of integer variables which result in efficient solutions for the problem. They convey abundant information to the DM, since they usually represent the structure of the examined system while the corresponding efficient solutions may refer to its operation. In a second phase, the evaluation of the efficient combinations on the objective functions is performed, using triangular fuzzy numbers in order to compare them and choose the most preferred one. The efficient combinations are usually far less in number than the efficient solutions, so that the "information overload" caused to the DM by the generation approaches is avoided. If the DM wishes, he/she can proceed further to identify the preferred solution in the selected efficient combination. The method is appropriate for small and medium size MIMOLP problems, as an alternative to the only possibility so far, the interactive approaches.

The problem examined in this paper is the expansion of the Greek power generation system. The main dilemma faced is the extent by which natural gas (recently introduced in the Greek energy system), coal and hydro plants will be used for power generation by substituting for the traditionally used lignite and oil. The above problem can be adequately approximated by means of a mixed 0-1 MOLP model including integer (the number of each type of power units) and continuous (output of each type of power units) variables.

The rest of the paper is organized as follows: The methodological issues of the proposed method are described in the next section. The application study with the model formulation and some indicative results are presented in the third section. Concluding remarks are given in the last section.

MIXED INTEGER MULTIPLE OBJECTIVE PROGRAMMING

The Multicriteria Branch and Bound Algorithm

The developed method relies on a branch and bound algorithm, which is formulated so as to generate the efficient set in mixed 0-1 MOLP problems (Mavrotas and Diakoulaki, 1998). The conventional branch and bound algorithm, which is widely used to solve mixed integer and mixed 0-1 linear programming problems, is properly modified in order to handle multiple objectives and to provide the whole set of efficient solutions. Unlike the single objective case, the multicriteria branch and bound algorithm is not directly applicable with general integer variables. These have to be transformed into a sum of 0-1 variables (Williams, 1985). If y is an integer variable with upper bound UB, it can be represented as:

$$y = \delta_0 + 2\delta_1 + 4\delta_2 + 8\delta_3 + \ldots + 2^k \delta_k \qquad (1)$$

where δ_i are 0-1 variables and $2^k \leq UB \leq 2^{k+1}$.

The combinatorial tree is traversed as in the single objective case using depth first search. The procedure is modified in order to take account of the vector (instead of scalar) characteristics of the multiple objective problem. The flowchart of the Multicriteria Branch & Bound (MCB&B) algorithm is depicted in Figure 1. At each intermediate node the optimum of each objective function is calculated and the vector of the ideal point is formed. At the final nodes (where all 0-1 variables are assigned to 0 or 1) the set of the corresponding efficient extreme points is generated and stored in the list L_{ef}. This list is dynamic and is updated whenever a final node is visited: the new efficient points are compared with those already stored in the list, in order to discard the dominated ones. In accordance with the incumbent solution of the single objective case the list L_{ef} is called incumbent list. The points which remain in the incumbent list after the completion of the combinatorial tree's searching constitute the efficient solutions of the multiple objective problem.

The combinations of the binary variables which lead to the efficient solutions are called efficient combinations. A branch of the combinatorial tree can be terminated prematurely if the problem of the corresponding node becomes infeasible or if the fathoming condition is fulfiled. The fathoming condition states that if the ideal point of a node is dominated by any other point in the incumbent list then the corresponding node is fathomed and the branch is terminated.

In comparison with the single objective case the multiple objective procedure is much more computational intensive. It performs multiple optimizations at each intermediate node, the fathoming condition is harder to meet due to the vector (instead of scalar) comparisons, the updating of the incumbent list is much more complicated than the updating of the incumbent solution and finally, the generation of the efficient solutions in the final nodes (the most time consuming part of the algorithm) is a rather complicated procedure.

The computational procedure developed for the above presented Multicriteria Branch & Bound algorithm is based on the Revised Simplex with Bounded Variables (RSBV) (Murtagh, 1981).

266

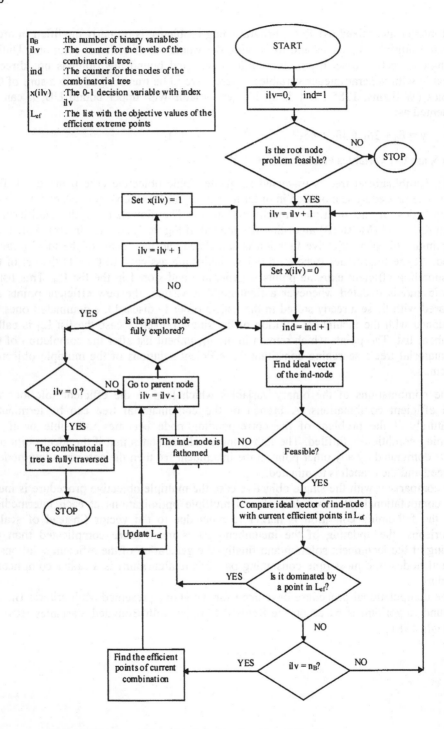

Figure 1. Flowchart of the multicriteria branch and bound algorithm

The module for the generation of efficient points in the final nodes is based on the Multicriteria Simplex Method (Zeleny, 1982) for vector maximization. The relative algorithm is based on the property of the connected efficient set (all efficient bases are connected, there are no isolated efficient extreme points) and it proceeds in three steps: In the first step, it calculates the first efficient solution from the lexicographic optimization of one objective function. In the second step, the Evans-Steuer criterion is used to identify the efficient non-basic variables, leading to adjacent efficient solutions. In the third step, the algorithm is moving to an adjacent efficient solution. Steps 2 and 3 are repeated until all adjacent efficient solutions are examined. The course of the algorithm can be represented with a tree structure where each node is an efficient extreme solution. The tree is traversed using breadth first search and a book-keeping system is used, in order to compare the currently generated efficient solutions to the one already found and to store the new ones (Steuer, 1989).

The succesive optimizations needed for the calculation of the ideal point at each node are performed using the "warm start" technique (starting from the last optimal base). The transition from one node to the other is performed by binding (or releasing) the corresponding binary variable and using the dual simplex algorithm for checking feasibility. When a binary variable is assigned to 0, it is forced to exit the basis at its lower bound while when it is assigned to 1, it is forced to exit the basis at its upper bound (predefined to be 1).

In order to deal with large sized MIMOLP problems, some accelerating options can be incorporated in the method in order to reduce solution time. The insertion of bounds in the objective functions according to the DM's preferences is used in order to reduce the search area. The filtering of the efficient points in the incumbent list is used for reducing their number. Finally, the generation of an approximation of the efficient set (using the e-constraint method or the weight method) instead of the whole set in the final nodes, reduces considerably the solution time. It is explained by the replacement of the most time-consuming part of the algorithm (the production of all the efficient extreme solutions in the final nodes) by a much faster procedure.

Representation of the Efficient Combinations

In MIMOLP problems, the efficient combinations are usually of primary importance because they provide information about the basic structure of the corresponding efficient solutions. Since each efficient combination is associated with several efficient solutions, it is difficult for the DM to perceive differences in the values of the objective functions and to compare efficient combinations to each other. It is therefore proposed to aggregate the information contained in the criteria values of the corresponding efficient solutions by means of triangular fuzzy numbers (TFN). With the TFN formulation we can handle the set of efficient solutions which belong to an efficient combination, as a single item (entity). In this way, we manage to reduce the objects which are to be compared by the DM (the efficient combinations are far less than the efficient solutions) avoiding the DM's "information overload".

Each TFN is denoted by the triplet (l, m, r) where l is the lowest possible value, m is the most possible value and r the highest possible value of the fuzzy number. In the specific case, the criterion values of each efficient combination are expressesed as TFNs (l_{ik}, m_{ik}, r_{ik}) where l_{ik} is the lowest value, m_{ik} is the average value (corresponding to the most possible value of the fuzzy number) and r_{ik} is the highest value of the k-th criterion among the efficient solutions of the i-th efficient combination. Furthermore, these values can be normalized according to the criteria's best and poorest values in order to obtain, in TFN format, the percentage of criteria achievement , for each combination. Subsequently, the importance of criteria can be expressed either as linguistic variables which are in turn transformed into the proper TFNs (Chen and Hwang, 1992), or as real numbers in [0,1]. Using the algebra of fuzzy sets we can perform the requested operations in order to calculate the overall score of each efficient combination as a fuzzy number and then compare them to each other according to the principles of fuzzy numbers' ranking (Chen and Hwang, 1992). Another possibility is to use the interactive filtering technique (Steuer, 1989) in order to isolate the preferred combination. In order to apply the interactive filtering technique with fuzzy numbers, the TFN's centroids are used as the corresponding crisp equivalents.

APPLICATION TO POWER GENERATION EXPANSION PLANNING

The Greek power generation sector heavily depends on domestic lignite resources which have been intensively exploited, especially after the two oil crisis (Mavrotas et al., 1995). The introduction of natural gas in the country's energy system as well as the environmental improvements in the technology of coal burning offer the opportunity of diversifying the electricity production mix by reducing at the same time CO_2 emissions.

The model

An MIMOLP pilot model was constructed for the description of the power generation system in year 2005. The electricity demand is described by the load duration curve (LDC) which shows the number of hours in a year that the power demand equals a specific value (Stoll, 1989). The area under the LDC represents the total demand of electricity. The LDC of 2005 is approximated with 4 orthogonal sub-sections in order to comply with the linear requirements of the model (Martins, 1996) and is depicted in Figure 2, with the relative data in Table 1. The present system includes lignite, hydro, oil and natural gas units. The candidates for addition units are lignite, oil, natural gas, coal and three hydro plants. Wind energy and imports of electricity are treated as continuous variables. The units' characteristics are shown in Tables 2and 3.

Table 1. LDC linear approximation

Subsection	Time (hours)	Cumulative Power (MW)	Subsection's power (MW)
1	8760	3400	3400
2	7000	4800	1400
3	3000	5800	1000
4	800	7100	1300

Table 2. Existing units

	Fuel	Capacity (MW)	Availability factor	CO_2 emission coefficient (tCO_2/MWh)	Variable cost (ECU/MWh)
L1	Lignite	3720	0.78	1.32	13.31
L2	Lignite south	800	0.77	1.45	19.68
G	Natural gas	1080	0.87	0.40	28.83
P	Oil	660	0.79	0.90	40.30

Table 3. Candidate units

	Fuel	Capacity (MW)	Maximum units	Availability factor	CO_2 emission coefficient (tCO_2/MWh)	Variable cost (ECU/MWh)	Fixed cost (kECU/yr)
NL	Lignite	300	4	0.78	1.32	11.26	41832
NC	Coal (IGCC)	580	2	0.80	0.20	17.52	78274
NG	Nat.gas	450	3	0.87	0.40	26.62	32845
NP	Oil	150	2	0.79	0.90	18.88	12811
W	Wind	600	Continuous	0.33	-	-	88 / MW
H1	Hydro	124	1	1	-	-	12218
H2	Hydro	180	1	1	-	-	21546
H3	Hydro	193	1	1	-	-	13375

* Wind and Hydro units have a negligible variable cost

The pilot model has 3 objective functions, 20 constraints, 48 variables including 7 upper bounded variables and 7 integer which are expressed, using equation (1), with 12 binary variables. For a more realistic approximation of the problem, some technical constraints which have resulted from a discussion with Greek Public Power Generation experts, are taken into account in constructing the model. That is, it is assumed that lignite, natural gas and coal units participate in all 4 subsections of the LDC, while oil units, new hydro units and imports may only be used in subsection 4 (peak load). Imports are restricted to no more than 160 GWh with cost 0.31 euro/kwh. Due to their operation, wind parks are considered only for base load, that is, subsection 1. Unlike the other new units, the new wind parks' size is considered to vary gradually and its representation can be made with a continuous variable. The contribution of the existent hydro units is a priori determined and they do not participate in the optimization process. It is assumed that they provide a fixed amount of energy in base load, working at their technical minimum (500 MW).

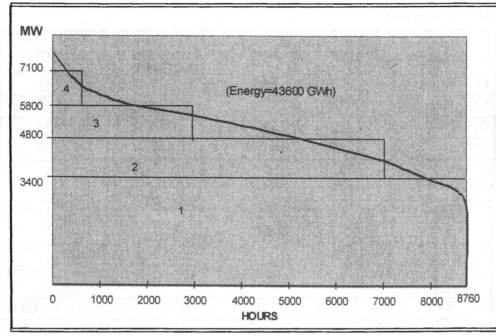

Figure 2. The estimated load duration curve (LDC) and its orthogonal approximation of the greek power system for 2005

The first objective function concerns the minimization of the annual electricity production cost (including fuel costs, O&M costs, annualized invesment costs for new units) and is expressed in thousand euros (keuro).

$$\min \ z_1 = \sum_{j=1}^{4} T_j \sum_{i=1}^{K} VC_i x_{ij} + \sum_{i=1}^{NK} FC_i n_i \tag{2}$$

Lowercase letters refer to the variables while uppercase letters refer to the parameters of the model. x_{ij} is the output in MW of the i-th type units in sub-section j of the LDC (continuous variable), K is the number of all unit types ($K=13$), NK is the number of new unit types with discrete capacities ($NK=7$, all new unit types except wind parks). n_i is the number of the new i-th type units operating in the examined year (integer variable), VC_i is the variable cost (=fuel cost+variable O&M cost in keuros/MWh), FC_i is the fixed cost (= annual investment cost + annual O&M fixed cost (keuro/year) and T_j is the number of hours in j-th sub-section (j=1,...,4).

The second objective function concerns the minimization of the total amount of CO_2 emissions (in kt) produced annually from the electricity generation sector.

$$\min \ z_2 = \sum_{j=1}^{4} T_j \sum_{i=1}^{k} EF_i x_{ij} \tag{3}$$

where EF_i is the emission factor of the i-th type of fuel.

The third objective function expresses the maximization of the demand satisfaction in an uncertain future. The function is derived by modeling the power demand of subsection

j as a fuzzy number with lowest acceptable value LD_j and upward tolerance TOL_j. This means that the corresponding inequalities are soft constraints of the form:

$$\sum_{i=1}^{K} x_{ij} - \mu \cdot TOL_j \geq LD_j \qquad j = 1..4 \tag{4}$$

The tolerances are set at 100 MW, 200 MW, 300 MW and 400 MW for j=1,2,3,4 respectively indicating the increase of uncertainty for higher loads. The above constraint implies that the power demand for subsection j must be at least LD_j and the response to a potential increased demand is shown by μ, the degree of demand satisfaction. In terms of fuzzy sets, μ is the membership function of the fuzzy number which expresses the uncertain demand and must lie between 0 and 1 (the proper constraint is added to the model). In order to maximize the demand satisfaction we must maximize μ. So, the third objective function is:

$$\max z_3 = \mu \tag{5}$$

The constraints of the described model refer to the capacity of units, the satisfaction of demand, the required reserve margin of the installed capacity, the upper limit of natural gas used for power generation, and the equations of type (1) for the transformation of integer to binary variables.

Specifically, the capacity constraints for each type of unit are expressed with the following relations.

$$\sum_{j=1}^{4} x_{ij} \leq AF_i\, C_i \qquad (for\ i = 1,..., K - NK) \qquad \text{for existing units} \tag{6}$$

$$\sum_{j=1}^{4} x_{ij} - AF_i\, C_i\, n_i \leq 0 \quad (for\ i = 1,..., NK) \qquad \text{for candidate units} \tag{7}$$

where C_i is the capacity of i-th type unit and AF_i the corresponding availability factor.

The demand satisfaction in each LDC's sub-section is expressed with relation (4). The required reserve margin (RM) which must be covered by the installed capacity of the system is set to 10% of the peak demand. This is expressed by the following constraint:

$$\sum_{i=1}^{NK} C_i\, n_i + \sum_{i=1}^{K-NK} C_i \geq (1 + RM)\sum_{j=1}^{4} (LD_j + \mu\, TOL_j) \tag{8}$$

The natural gas constraint expresses that the amount of the natural gas which feeds the power generation units, cannot exceed a certain percentage (set to 70%) of the total natural gas imported in the country (which is upper bounded by the capacity of the pipeline about $3.4 \times 10^6\, m^3$).

$$\sum_{j=1}^{4} T_j \sum_{p=natura\,\lg\,as} x_{pj} \leq E_{ng}\ NGSUP \tag{9}$$

where *NGSUP* is the maximum natural gas supply for power generation, E_{ng} is the efficiency of natural gas in power generation (E_{ng}=0.5) and p refers only to natural gas fired units.

Finally, the transformation of integer to binary variables adds 4 equality constraints of type (1) to the model.

The necessary data for the parameters were drawn from the Greek Public Power Corporation.

Results

Using the MCB&B method, 110 efficient combinations (out of 385 feasible combinations) were detected, containing 1001 efficient solutions. The computational time was 10'45" in a Pentium 333 Mhz. At the end of the solution process, the values of the objective functions as well as the values of the structural, slack and surplus variables for each efficient solution are stored in a file, to be available to the DM.

It should be noted that if a conventional MOLP model is used, with post-processing of the obtained efficient solutions (by rounding the variables which express the number of units to the closest integer (Martins, 1996)), the number of the derived efficient combinations is only 12. It is obvious that a lot of efficient combinations remain undiscovered with the continuous formulation of the examined multiple objective problem.

According to the procedure described in the previous section, the derived efficient combinations can be further processed in order to elicit the most promising ones according to the DM's preferences. In the case of the power generation expansion problem each efficient combination corresponds to a different configuration of the power generation units and specifies a different investment plan. In order to reduce the number of the examined combinations, filtering techniques (Steuer, 1989) and/or bounding of the objective functions (Mavrotas and Diakoulaki, 1998) can be implemented. For illustrative purposes, Table 4 shows three of the efficient combinations, namely, minimum cost (a), minimum CO_2 emissions (b) and maximum demand satisfaction combinations (c).

Table 4. New units from combinations (a), (b) and (c).

	NL	NC	NG	NP	H1	H2	H3
(a) minimum cost	3	0	3	0	1	1	1
(b) minimum CO_2 emissions	0	2	3	1	1	1	1
(c) maximum demand satisfaction	3	2	3	2	1	1	1

The TFNs which express the criterion performance of the above mentioned combinations are presented to the DM as shown in Table 5. It can be seen that the information so presented can be easily perceived by the DM and can greatly facilitate his search towards the final decision.

Table 5. TFN representation of the criteria values in the combinations (a), (b) and (c)

	Z_1 (Meuro)	Z_2 (Mt)	Z_3
(a) minimum cost	(856, 861, 880)	(44.0, 46.3, 46.8)	(0.00, 0.02, 0.03)
(b) minimum CO_2 emissions	(951,1037,1125)	(28.4, 33.3, 42.0)	(0.00, 0.29, 0.35)
(c) maximum demand satisfaction	(1089,1190,1287)	(32.7, 36.6, 45.0)	(0.90, 0.99, 1.00)

The above TFNs can also be transformed into the TFNs which indicate the degree of achievement for each combination at every objective function. This useful information for the DM can be extracted using the following relations: For each l_{ij}, m_{ij}, and r_{ij}, the percentage of achievement is calculated using the following relations:

$$p_{ij} = 1 - (v_{ij}-v_{minj})/(v_{maxj}-v_{minj}) \qquad \text{for minimization criteria} \qquad (10)$$

$$p_{ij} = (v_{ij}-v_{minj})/(v_{maxj}-v_{minj}) \qquad \text{for maximization criteria} \qquad (11)$$

p_{ij} is the percentage of achievement for combination i at objective function j, v_{ij} declares the corresponding values of l_{ij}, m_{ij}, and r_{ij} and v_{maxj} and v_{minj} are the maximum and minimum values of criterion j over all the efficient set. In the illustrative graph of Figure 3, the comparative effectiveness of the three combinations in the criteria can be revealed.

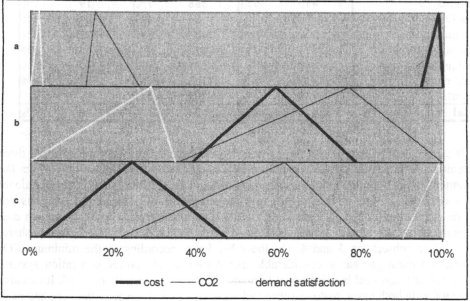

Figure 3. Percentage of criteria achievement for efficient combinations (a), (b), and (c)

With this visualization, the DM also gets critical (useful) information about the spread of the values associated with the corresponding efficient solutions. As shown in Figure 3, efficient combination (b) and to a lesser degree (c) cover a broader range than efficient combination (a), in criteria achievement. Therefore, they offer more flexibility in the selection of an appropriate operational plan (efficient solution). Each efficient combination corresponds to an investment plan (system's structure), while each efficient solution corresponds to an operation plan of the power generation system. At every efficient solution the energy production can be easily calculated with a short post processing: for each unit the value of the variable declaring the output (in MW) is multiplied by the hours of the corresponding LDC's subsection. For example, the results for three distinct efficient solutions (namely, the minimum cost, minimum CO2 emissions and one of the maximum demand satisfaction solutions) are shown in Table 6.

Table 6. Energy output for selected efficient solutions (GWh)

	Minimum cost		Minimum CO$_2$ emissions		Maximum demand satisfaction	
Existing hydro units	4380	*10%*	4380	*10%*	4380	*9%*
New hydro units	398	*1%*	398	*1%*	398	*1%*
Lignite units	23816	*54%*	16323	*37%*	22588	*48%*
Lignite south units	3840	*9%*	0		0	
New Lignite units	6150	*14%*	0		2106	*4.5%*
Oil units	410	*1%*	388	*1%*	19	*0%*
New Oil units	0		94	*0.5%*	189	*0.5%*
Nat. gas units	0		7485	*17%*	5305	*11%*
New Nat. gas units	2879	*7%*	4515	*10%*	2254	*5%*
Coal units	0		8129	*19%*	8129	*17%*
Wind parks	1752	*4%*	1752	*4%*	1752	*4%*
Imports	0		160	*0.5%*	0	
Total	**43624**	**100%**	**43624**	**100%**	**47120**	**100%**

It can be noticed that new hydro units and wind parks are fully exploited in all three extreme solutions, while lignite is replaced by coal and natural gas as we move from the minimum cost to the minimum CO$_2$ emissions solution. In Figures 4 and 5 the operational plans obtained for the minimum cost and the minimum CO$_2$ emissions solutions are shown in the form of the corresponding LDCs. It can be seen that in the minimum cost solution, lignite dominates power generation with natural gas having a small share, restricted to subsections 3 and 4. On the other hand, according to the minimum CO$_2$ emissions natural gas has a considerable distribution to the power generation system, along with the new coal burning units. Lignite's share is significantly reduced. It can also be seen that in both cases, hydro-electric and wind energy participate in the base and peak load of the system.

It is worthwhile to point out some general remarks concerning the structure of the efficient combinations as a whole. The number of new natural gas units vary between 2 and 3 (the maximum) in all the efficient combinations, indicating the potential of this energy form. Among the new hydro units H1 and H3 seem to be the most promising ones, appearing in 102 and 92 efficient combinations respectively, while H2 appears in 72. The number of new lignite, coal and oil units in the efficient combinations varies from zero to their maximum number.

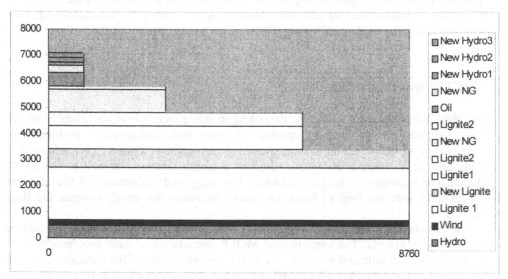

Figure 4. The participation of units in the LDC according to the minimum cost solution

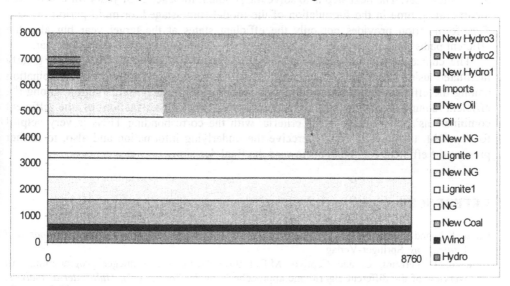

Figure 5. The participation of units in the LDC according to the minimum CO_2 emissions solution

In the power generation expansion problem, the course toward the preferred efficient solution can be performed in two steps. First, the DM has to compare the investment plans using the corresponding TFNs which represent their performance in the three criteria. Then, if the DM wishes to proceed further, he has to choose the preferred solution among the efficient solutions of the already chosen efficient combination. This solution represents the preferred operational plan for the selected investment plan. If the number of the efficient combinations or efficient solutions is too large, the interactive filtering technique (Mavrotas et al., 1995) is suggested.

CONCLUDING REMARKS

The MIMOLP generation approach, described in this paper, allows for identifying the whole efficient set and can be applied to small and medium-sized problems. In comparison with interactive approaches the developed method provides richer information to the DM as it indicates the whole range of potential solutions as well as the set of efficient combinations of integer variables. The suggested elaboration of the efficient combinations with the help of fuzzy set theory facilitates the search towards the final decision.

The proposed method can effectivelly solve the power generation expansion problem under multiple criteria. The conventional MOLP formulation of such problems fails to accuratelly find all potential solutions due to the discrete nature of the variables denoting the new units. The described pilot model is a steady-state model which solves the problem for a future year. The next step is to solve the problem for a series of years which involves incorporating time in the formulation of the model (time-staged, or multi-period model). This formulation provides not only the efficient states at the target year but also the efficient paths (how many units to install in intermediate years) toward the target year.

The course toward the preferred efficient solution in MIMOLP problems is greatly facilitated using the two-step approach: First, selection of the preferred combination among the efficient combinations and then selection of the preferred solution among the efficient solutions of the selected combination. The representation of the efficient combinations' performance in the criteria, with the corresponding TFNs is very helpful for the DM. It allows to better perceive the underlying information and also, to further process the efficient combinations toward the final decision.

REFERENCES

Chen, S.J. and Hwang, C.L. (1992), *Fuzzy Multiple Attribute Decision Making: Methods and Applications*, Springer-Verlag

Climaco, J., Ferreira, C. and Captivo, M.E (1997), "Multicriteria integer programming: An overview of the different algorithmic approaches", in: J. Climaco (ed), *Multicriteria Analysis*, Springer-Verlag, 248-258.

Martins, A. G., Coelho, D., Antunes, H. and Climaco, J. (1996), "A multiple objective linear programming approach to power generation planning with demand side management (DSM)", *International Transactions in Operational Research*, 3/4, 305-317.

Mavrotas, G. and Diakoulaki, D. (1998), "A branch and bound algorithm for mixed zero-one multiple objective linear programming", *European Journal of Operational Research,* 107, 530-541.

Mavrotas, G., Diakoulaki, D. and Papayannakis L. (1999), "An energy planning approach based on Mixed 0-1 MOLP", *International Transactions in Operational Research,* 6, 231-244.

Murtagh, B.A. (1981), *Advanced Linear Programming: Computation and Practice,* McGraw-Hill.

Steuer, R.E. (1989), *Multiple Criteria Optimization-Theory, Computation and Application,* 2nd edition, Krieger, Malabar FL.

Stoll, H.G. (1989), *Least-Cost Electricity Utility Planning,* John Wiley & Sons.

Williams, H.P. (1985), *Model Building in Mathematical Programming,* John Wiley & Sons.

Zeleny, M. (1982), *Multiple Criteria Decision Making,* Mc-Graw-Hill.

MANAGEMENT SCIENCE FOR MARINE PETROLEUM LOGISTICS

E.D. Chajakis

Princeton University
Department of Chemical Engineering
The Engineering Quadrangle, Rm. A425
Princeton, New Jersey 08544-5263
USA

Abstract: Management Science modeling can assist marine petroleum transporters in planning
              and operating their fleet. By supporting the fleet's integration into the supply chain
              of petroleum, it enables an optimal balance of profitability and customer service.
              Each of the small case studies presented here exposes an aspect of the business
              problem and shows the role of modeling in quantifying previously intuitive concepts,
              defining new performance measures and supporting routine decision making.

Key words: Logistics, Petroleum, Supply Chain, Shipping, Ship Scheduling, Fleet Scheduling,
              Crew Planning, Crude Oil Supply, Fleet Size, Mix and Deployment, Marine
              Transportation, Capacity Planning, Optimization, Simulation, Forecasting

MODELING THE PETROLEUM SUPPLY CHAIN

As each of the 75 million barrels of crude oil that surface on an average day flows from
production to final consumption, it needs transportation and storage somewhere along the
way. Both activities entail certain costs, some of which can remain "invisible" unless we
adopt a systematic way for identifying and attacking them. The petroleum cycle can be
viewed as a supply chain. It is possible to model the entire supply chain of petroleum as a
single system but this would only be potentially valuable at a strategic level. At the
tactical and operational levels, decision making concerning successive links of the chain is
spread across different departments of an integrated oil company, therefore meaningful
models must encompass only the part of the system affected by each group's decisions.
Each of the following sections describes a brief case study where the use of management
science produced benefits for the marine petroleum transporter, the oil company customer
or both. The applications span all links of the petroleum supply chain where marine
transportation is required and are presented in order from upstream to downstream.

S.H. Zanakis et al. (eds.), Decision Making: Recent Developments and Worldwide Applications, 279–292.
© 2000 *Kluwer Academic Publishers.*

CRUDE OIL SUPPLY

Oil refineries receive crude oil by tanker or pipeline and it is imperative to have an uninterrupted supply to ensure continuous operation because refinery shutdowns, such as for lack of crude oil, are costly and hazardous. Pipeline supply is relatively smooth; however, tanker deliveries tend to become irregular by factors outside the refinery manager's control, such as crude oil markets and weather. To protect themselves against a crude shortage that might lead to a shutdown, managers of refineries that rely too much on tanker deliveries tend to keep very high levels of crude inventory, incurring holding costs that can accrue to enormous proportions considering that crude stocks of refineries can reach in the millions of barrels. Irregular arrivals cause tanker queues at the refinery, which incur hefty demurrage costs. We have modeled the crude supply system of one or more refineries as a multi-period mixed integer program. Decisions include crude oil contracts to buy or sell, tankers to spot-charter, routing of time-chartered tankers and crude inventory levels to keep at the refinery to ensure production of the desired mix of products. The model, typically run on a rolling horizon basis covering 8 to 12 weeks forward, has helped reduce the total system cost of crude supply by producing schedules with regular tanker arrivals and thus reduced inventory holding and demurrage costs.

Including Crude Distribution in the Refinery System View

Refinery models typically consist of sets of linear or nonlinear equations derived from the refinery's characteristics; sets of decision variables representing modes of operation; and a set of criteria that specify optimal operating modes. Advances in computing technology have made it possible to solve refinery models faster and faster. The faster they can be solved, the more possible it becomes to represent the refinery's operation in finer and finer detail through extraordinarily complex mathematical programs consisting of tens of thousands of equations and decision variables.

Certain variables of a refinery model represent crude distribution to the refinery either via pipeline or marine vessel and take into account that crude may remain in tank storage before use. Pipeline inflows are typically smooth and predictable, while tanker deliveries account for rapid sharp increases and decreases in crude inventories. There are many crude types, classified by their gravity and sulphur content and labeled by the point of origin. Each type yields a distinct array of products for every mode of refinery operation.

In today's refinery models, all variables are continuous numbers including tanker deliveries, e.g., 0.667 tankers discharging today. That seems odd since computing and modeling technology nowadays enable the representation of tanker deliveries as integer numbers and the solution of the resulting models in reasonable times. The reason why the oil industry has yet to take advantage of the state of the art is simple: When the refining process is seen as a system unto itself, modeling so accurately is not necessary since crude inventory at the refinery acts as a smoothing buffer. However, when we view *crude supply and refining together* as a system to be optimized then we cannot accept a schedule in which fractions of tankers deliver. Such a schedule is impossible in our world.

Optimizing Crude Distribution

Transportation and crude oil logistics are the third largest cost component, behind crude purchasing and refining. With oil prices at a steep trough in late 1998, they accounted for roughly 11 percent of the total cost of every refined barrel of petroleum. In the first half of 1997, it was standing around 5 percent. Thus, optimizing transport and logistics offers substantial profit-enhancing opportunities. As a process, marine crude transportation is more complex than pipeline from a logistics point of view, so it yields more opportunities for uncovering and subsequently attacking "invisible" components of total system cost.

Table 1 shows the annual bottom line impact of a 10-cent per barrel reduction in logistics costs. Since this reduction is easily attainable through intelligent scheduling and the use of modeling tools, not capital investment, it contributes directly to the gross profit of the refinery. With the per-barrel figures used in this illustration, typical for late 1998, this 7 percent reduction translates to a 23 percent increase in profit.

Integrating Crude Distribution

In an ideal world, shipments of crude oil would arrive at the refinery in regular time intervals to supply a roughly constant daily rate of consumption. In the less-than-ideal reality, interarrival times of shipments are highly irregular. There is a steep cost and environmental risk of shutting a refinery down for lack of crude oil. Refinery managers respond to the irregularity of tanker arrivals by keeping high levels of safety stock, incurring the associated increased inventory holding cost. The price of the excessive inventory is a typical "invisible" cost.

Weather uncertainty is partly to blame for irregularity in tanker arrivals. Among the man-made culprits, fluctuations of vessel charter rates and crude oil market prices predominate. They compel crude oil traders to crowd purchases during times of "low" prices. This can save a few pennies per barrel off crude purchasing and/or chartering costs, but if the associated increase in inventory holding and possibly vessel delay (demurrage) costs is factored in it could prove to be rather myopic in the context of total system costs, which get reduced only at a good tradeoff between crude purchasing and logistics costs.

Table 1. Impact of a 7% reduction in logistics costs using estimated North American East Coast refinery figures and crude oil prices typical for late 1998.

Components of Cost (per barrel)	Before	After	Difference
Crude purchasing:	$9.67	$9.67	
Refining:	$2.72	$2.72	
Logistics:	$1.50	$1.40	-$0.10
Total:	$13.89	$13.79	-$0.10
Market price of refined products yielded by each barrel of crude:	$14.30	$14.30	
Contribution to profit per barrel:	$0.44	$0.54	$0.10
Refinery output (bbls/day):	350,000	350,000	

Total annual output (365 days):	127,750,000	127,750,000	
Total annual profit contribution:	$56,210,000	$68,985,000	$12,775,000
% change in profit contribution:			23%

Although there were articles on crude tanker scheduling, e.g., Brown, Graves and Ronen (1987), crude scheduling had not been addressed in comprehensive models encompassing the entire system from the oil field to the refinery crude storage tanks. So we developed a new model which considers these broad upstream crude supply issues (Chajakis, Welch, Andrews and Murphy 1997, Chajakis 1997, Chajakis 1999a, Welch and Chajakis 1999b). It encompasses the whole range of operational crude supply decisions, including those for purchasing, tanker chartering and inventory, and ties them to refinery production plans and market prices for products. Using Mixed Integer Programming (MIP), our model generates optimal short-term crude supply schedules on a rolling horizon basis.

Given crude oil prices and inventory holding costs, refining costs, oil product prices, freight rates as well as availability of spot and time charters, our model computes a set of optimal decisions that maximize the total profit contribution (revenue-cost) over an 8-12 week forward time horizon. Decisions include:

- Size and timing of crude oil contracts to buy or sell.
- Best spot charters to use, if any, to transport crude from the oil fields to the refineries.
- Optimal routing of time charters that supply the refineries.
- Mix of products to produce and crude types to use given refinery yields.

Extensive testing of the model has demonstrated that in an optimal crude supply schedule, lower system costs are achieved by striking a balance among crude purchasing, tanker chartering, demurrage, and crude inventory holding costs. In these optimal test schedules, the variance in the tanker interarrival times is significantly reduced over that of historic interarrival times. Applied to operational schedules, results could significantly reduce irregularity in tanker arrivals and consequently crude safety stocks and their cost.

TANKER LIGHTERING

Lightering is the transfer of crude oil from a discharging tanker to smaller vessels to enable the tanker to sail to a refinery's docks at shallow-draught ports or channels. It adds a cost component to the supply chain but, on the other hand, it can help decrease inventory holding costs and demurrage, and add flexibility to the crude supply process. The ability of a lightering fleet to smoothly integrate into the supply chain depends on sound decision making across all levels of the hierarchy. At the strategic and tactical levels, a simulation that we have developed helps us determine optimal fleet size and composition to provide an optimal tradeoff between fleet utilization and customer service, which is measured by service times (Andrews, Murphy, Wang and Welch 1996, Chajakis 1997, Chajakis 1998, Murphy and Chajakis 1999b, Welch and Chajakis 1999b). For operational level decisions, we built a scheduling model that creates good fleet schedules, especially during times of congestion at the anchorage (Chajakis, Welch and Murphy 1997, Chajakis 1997, Floudas, Lin and Chajakis 1999, Welch and Chajakis 1999b).

Simulation-based Capacity Planning

A lightering fleet typically operates within a limited geographical area that includes one or more refineries at a shallow-draught port. As the volume of crude oil arriving in the area to be refined changes, the lightering fleet must be reconfigured in size and composition in response. Higher-than-needed lightering capacity shortens the time that the crude oil spends en route to the refinery and consequently reduces needed crude inventory levels and tanker demurrage; but fleet utilization remains unprofitably low. On the other hand, a shortage in capacity has the opposite effects: higher fleet profitability but poor service.

There were no published works on fleet simulations embedding optimization, so we built our own. The capacity-planning tool we have built for a lightering fleet simulates the operation of the fleet in a miniature approximation of the system. A key strength of the tool is its ability to authentically capture every step of the lightering process in meaningful detail. The simulation logic is coded in blocks, as in a flow chart, and the movements of its elements are animated so that the user can watch the system in operation and make insightful observations. A most crucial part of the process is the assignment of lightering vessels to tankers, which an experienced scheduler does reasonably well, unaided by any decision support tool. Instead of trying to replicate a scheduler's arcane scheduling rules and mental heuristics, we coded an optimization routine called by the simulation every time a new tanker arrives at a lightering anchorage. The routine assigns vessels to queued tankers anew, so as to minimize the largest tanker service time. The simulation produces a service time graph over a period of a year or more, like that in Figure 1.

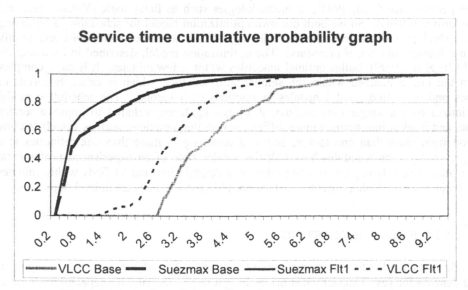

Figure 1. Comparison of simulated service times for two fleet scenarios

The simulation-based capacity-planning tool enables decision-makers to test several scenarios quickly and choose the optimal fleet composition for a service demand outlook. Taking certain vessels off the lightering fleet and having them serve other trades, sometimes replacing them with more appropriate vessels, can then eliminate excess capacity. Capacity shortages are cured by bringing to the fleet vessels from other trades, or by charter-ins of third-party vessels. A scheduler can study the output schedule of the tool and gain useful insights on how the optimization engine builds it, often realizing previously unexplored scheduling flexibilities. The tool motivated us to build a mathematical optimization model for scheduling, which incorporates as much as possible of a human scheduler's skill and experience.

Optimization-based scheduling

During times of congestion, when many tankers arrive at the lightering anchorage within a short period of time, it is difficult even for the most experienced scheduler to find manually the optimal combination of vessel-to-tanker assignments, timings and lightering volumes. The bibliography in ship scheduling is remarkably sparse; Ronen (1983, 1993) points out the fact. Brown, Graves and Ronen (1987), propose methods for scheduling crude oil tankers and Miller (1987) discusses a network flow-based MIP model for the scheduling of chemical tankers; both propose far more complex methodologies than we needed since the operation of both oceangoing tankers and chemical fleets are far harder than our own. In addition, we found articles describing the scheduling of distinct operations during a ship's itinerary, i.e., docking, loading and discharging (Suh and Yung, 1998, Kao and Lee, 1996), methods for optimizing a limited set of criteria, such as on-time performance (Vea, 1994), or methodologies such as fuzzy logic (Vukadinovic and Teodorovic (1994)). So we built our own optimization model for scheduling a lightering fleet, which provides a fleet scheduler with a good base schedule to work with and modify before implementation, if necessary. The optimization model, described in Floudas, Lin and Chajakis, (1999), builds optimal schedules within a few minutes. It is more complex than the one embedded within the simulation-based tool, which is called hundreds of times and must find good schedules in fractions of a second. The scheduling model optimizes over a longer time horizon; it adjusts lightering volumes to improve service time; and it takes into account more difficult scheduling practices, such as vessels loading crude from more than one tankers and/or discharging to more than one refineries in a single voyage. Its schedules have half the service time of an experienced professional scheduler. Even during severe congestion, our optimization model finds within minutes the optimal schedule that provides the best possible service times at minimal fleet costs.

FREIGHT RATE FORECASTING

The domestic market for marine petroleum transportation is subject to the law of supply of and demand for vessel capacity that drives freight rates. Demand for capacity has been in a long-term decline as oil companies realized the commodity nature of their products and have been shaping their distribution networks to require minimal transportation through mergers, acquisitions and product exchanges. Supply has been following demand and rates have been declining. However, the industry is headed for a period of freight rate uncertainly as 2004 is drawing closer. That is the date by which all petroleum carrying vessels in the US trade must be double-hulled by law and is expected to be preceded by an unusually large number of withdrawals of single-hulled vessels and introductions of newly-built or retrofitted equipment (Murphy 1995). We have built a model to forecast the US long-term freight rate trends. The model takes into account all known or anticipated changes in the US petroleum fleet and a forecast of transportation demand to generate freight rate forecasts as far out as a decade into the future. The methodology and its results are deemed too strategically important to reveal in a published article (Murphy 1999). But we should note that this is the first application of the methodology in forming corporate strategy and won an important distinction as a finalist in the Franz Edelman competition in 1998 (Mudrageda, Murphy and Welch 1998).

FLEET SIZE AND VESSEL MIX

The Oil Polution Act of 1990 (OPA-90) presents an opportunity for petroleum fleet operators despite its adverse effects on the short run. An operator of a clean oil fleet in Florida saw it as an opportunity to reevaluate their competitive position rather than as a threat. We are showing here how we went about helping the fleet operator make strategic fleet mix decisions in the face of a rapidly changing regulatory and market environment.

Section 27 of the Merchant Marine Act of 1920 is what is called the Jones Act, the domestic portion of which is known as the cabotage law. Together with OPA-90, they are the principal government policies affecting the domestic shipping market and determining the cost structure and profitability of shipping companies. To protect the domestic merchant marine for national policy reasons, the Jones Act requires vessels that can travel between two US ports to be built in a US shipyard, owned by a US corporation and manned by a US crew. Meeting those three requirements defines a US flag vessel. To reduce the size and number of oil spills due to accident, OPA-90 requires all vessels with a gross tonnage of over 500 that carry petroleum between US ports to be double hulled by the end of 2004, with a few exceptions. Single hulled vessels will be phased out according to a staggered plan based on their age (Murphy 1995).

In the short term, OPA-90 is certain to increase costs and cause erosion of profitability for US black and clean oil fleet operators. On the other hand, it presents an opportunity for them to reevaluate their fleet composition and position themselves strategically to better respond to the longer-term changing needs of the markets they serve. We will show how a Florida clean oil fleet operator goes about evaluating its fleet in the face of OPA-90.

Demand growth for oil products in Florida is so robust that despite the rise in imports, domestic product demand still grows steadily at about 2% a year. Conventional wisdom would point to larger vessels for moving increasing volumes of product from refineries along the Gulf Coast to Florida ports, as demand growth translates to increases in daily product consumption that forces petroleum companies to constantly reevaluate their Economic Order Quantities (EOQ), mostly resetting them upwards.

The fleet operator decided to respond to OPA-90 by double-hulling its existing single hulled vessels, taking them, one at a time, out of service for retrofitting during the summer months of off-peak demand. Double-hulling, provides an opportunity to independently increase a vessel's capacity by keeping it out of service a little longer, thus taking full advantage of the off-peak period. A vessel's capacity can be increased by adding a midsection and possibly installing a bigger engine to maintain current service speeds.

Instead of making a quick decision to increase capacity of their vessels together with double-hulling, they questioned conventional wisdom and are rather taking a systems view in evaluating their vessel mix. The fundamental question that they would like answered is: What is the number and capacity of vessels in our fleet that would enable us to profitably provide superior service in the Florida market under various scenarios of long-term demand growth?

Fleet size, mix and deployment had been well covered in the literature (see Everett, Hax, Lewinson and Nudds (1972), Koeningsberg and Meyers (1980), Lane, Heaver and Uyeno (1987), Jaramillo and Perakis (1991), Papadakis and Perakis (1989), Perakis and Jaramillo (1991), Perakis and Papadakis (1987a, 1987b), Rana and Vickson (1988,1991)), even for problems similar to ours (see Larson (1988), Larson, Minkoff and Gregory (1988)), or for tugboats only (Jaikumar and Solomon (1987), Schwartz (1968)). However, to capture all the elements specific to our problem and answer the question posed above as best as possible, we designed and implemented a new MIP model. The objective is to minimize the net present value of a stream of system costs. System costs consist of fleet and product inventory costs. Fleet costs include fuel, crew wages and the capital costs associated with double-hulling and with increasing vessel capacity and power. Inventory costs are computed both for product held at the distribution terminal tanks and in transit. The decision variables of the model specify which vessel, if any, will be double-hulled, lengthened and/or repowered, in what time period.

Being a deterministic, as opposed to stochastic, model the above gives answers using only static snapshots of future demand. Used in studies under many various scenarios of demand growth, it helps in the strategically very critical process of deciding on the multi-period sequence of steps to reconfigure the fleet.

PETROLEUM PRODUCTS DISTRIBUTION

Petroleum products are transported by pipeline, tank truck or marine vessel along the part of the supply chain downstream from the refinery. To lower consumer cost, a distribution system must be designed, planned and operated to be efficient in placing product volumes wherever they are most valuable. The first and foremost business issue that product fleet operators need to address is customer service, which has two dimensions: (i) meeting time windows for loading at the refinery, and (ii) minimizing product stockouts at the receiving terminals. The specific parameters that, in the end, determine customer satisfaction are not universal but depend on negotiated agreements between customer and fleet operator. The types of agreements between a fleet operator and a client petroleum company are:

(i)   Time Charter (TC): The client assumes complete control of a fleet vessel, so that no other client can use it during the contract period.

(ii)   Contract of Affreightment (COA): The fleet operator is only obligated to move a certain annual volume of product and provide a vessel when needed, on an agreed upon prior notice. The COA contract period could range from a couple of months to a year. A COA typically specifies, among others, number and frequency of product loadings and minimum advance notice to reserve a vessel.

(iii)   Spot Charter: The client charters a vessel for a single voyage. Since freight rates for spot charters are typically higher than same-time TC or COA rates, they present great revenue opportunities. So fleet operators try to fix as many of them as possible without disrupting the service to TC and COA customers.

In this section, we discuss how a Florida product fleet operator helps its customers make their product distribution system more efficient by integrating itself into their supply chain through the use of management science tools.

Simulation-based Capacity Planning

Florida's demand for petroleum products is satisfied by US refineries along the Gulf of Mexico Coast and imports mostly from the Caribbean Basin. Almost the entire product volume arrives by marine vessel. Product tankers load combinations of more than twenty distinct product types at the refineries and discharge at marine tank terminals, mainly concentrated around Tampa, Port Everglades and Jacksonville.

As for the case of lightering, the literature we could draw upon for oil product fleet capacity planning simulations with embedded optimization was nonexistent. Therefore, we developed a capacity planning model for the products distribution network across the Gulf of Mexico (Chajakis 1997). The model is a miniature, which can be easily adapted to any regional oil products network and uses simulation to mimic the network's operation. The real system is represented with as much accuracy as necessary for the scope of the model; superfluous detail is assumed away and sources of uncertainty, such as voyage times and product demand at the terminals, are approximated through stochastic distributions estimated through historical data. A small optimization model is called everytime that a vessel assignment needs to be fixed (Mudrageda and Chajakis 1999b).

The capacity-planning simulation model is used in testing various scenarios of fleet and contract mix, calculating critical figures such as:

- Equipment utilization by individual vessel as well as the whole fleet.
- Vessel and fleet revenue and profitability.
- On-time performance at the loading end.
- Average and variance of product inventory at the customers' terminals; useful in determining best levels for safety stock and working inventory.

The model assists the fleet operator in strategic and tactical decisions such as:

- Finding the optimal tradeoff between fleet utilization and customer service.
- Determining the optimal fleet size and composition for a given contract mix.
- Identifying the most profitable trades or routes in the system and forming strategies to gain market share in them.
- Gaining insights on how service contracts should be structured to best offset customer service and fleet profitability.

288

The use of graphical modeling software with animation allows the user to literally observe the system in operation and enables both upper and operational management to rapidly grasp the implications of each contract or policy decision.

Optimization-based Product Distribution Scheduling

The day-to-day allocation of vessels to satisfy customer service demands taxes a product fleet scheduler more than any aspect of her job. Scheduling difficulty depends on the fleet's contract portfolio. An entire fleet on Time Charter poses no problem: customers do the scheduling. It gets tough when Contracts of Affreightment dominate the portfolio as choices of vessel-to-customer-call assignments explode in number: the scheduler needs to match the fleet's short-term availability with the immediate demands of each customer's request for a product volume to be moved from a refinery to a terminal within certain time windows. On the other hand, the more the customers under COA the better the flexibility of the fleet to provide superb product inventory management and the higher its availability to take advantage of requests for Spot Charters, which present lucrative opportunities for extra revenue almost always at heftier profit margins than longer-term contracts.

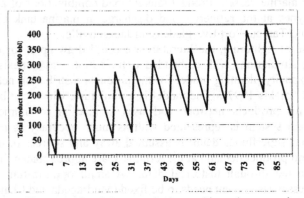

Figure 2. Pattern of inventory levels in a terminal served by a singe vessel on Time Charter.

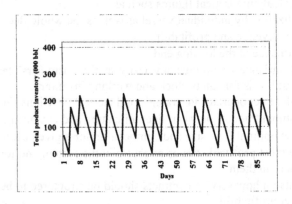

Figure 3. Pattern of inventory levels in a terminal served by 3 vessels on Contract of Affreightment

To demonstrate the superiority of COA over TC in product inventory management, let us consider the following example: A customer terminal has a total weekly product demand of 230,000 barrels, supplied entirely by a single refinery. The total voyage time, including loading, discharging, various delays and sailing both ways, averages seven days. If the customer chooses a TC on a single 250,000-barrel vessel, working product inventory levels at the terminal will follow the pattern of figure 3. Inventory accumulation results from the customer's trying to maximize time and capacity utilization of the vessel under Time Charter, the daily rate of which is perceived to be higher than inventory costs.

Suppose now that instead of the Time Charter, the customer chooses to sign a Contract of Affreightment with a three-vessel fleet operator. All vessels can complete the voyage in seven days, their capacities are 175,000, 205,000 and 250,000 barrels and they also serve other customers. Working inventory levels at the terminal will then look like in figure 4.

This pattern of working inventory levels results in lower inventory holding costs and creates an opportunity for the customer to lease out the excess terminal capacity.

Traditionally, fleet schedulers have been doing day-to-day vessel assignments relying on manual tools as well as their skill and experience. Meanwhile, Time Charters dominate their contract portfolio because creating good schedules for a COA fleet can be hard even for the most experienced scheduler since the complexity of the task rises enormously with the number of customers on COA and the number of vessels available to serve them.

As for lightering fleet scheduling, the literature for oil products fleet scheduling was spare, with a few notable exceptions (see Fisher and Rosenwein (1989), Psaraftis, Solomon, Magnanti and Kim (1990)). To capture all detail specific to our application, we developed an MIP product fleet scheduling model (Chajakis 1997, Chajakis and Murphy 1998, Chajakis 1999b, Welch and Chajakis 1999a), which takes as inputs customers' product demand and contract arrangements, vessels' characteristics and the region's geographical features to create forward one-month schedules. The model gives schedules only for TC and COA customers and creates suitable time windows to fit Spot Charters. We solve the model through a combination of branch-and-bound and heuristics. For a fleet of seven or eight vessels serving four or five customers in the Gulf of Mexico, all of who are on COA, the model takes less than five minutes on a Pentium II 300 MHz computer. Solution times drop dramatically when TCs increase in the contract portfolio.

CREW PLANNING

Given the worldwide labor shortage in the marine transportation industry, it is now more than ever important to attract, develop and retain qualified individuals for vessel crews. A shortage of crew members can cause a vessel to remain idle at the dock, missing revenue opportunities while depreciating as a costly asset. Balancing a fleet's crewing needs with the steep costs of a tight labor market requires sound forward planning. Petroleum vessels are crewed by professionals with specialized skills transferable across many vessels in the fleet, e.g., engineer, or tied to a specific geographical area, e.g., pilot. The crew planner must determine the right number of professionals of each specialty to hire, train to different specialties and promote, given the fleet's crewing demands and taking attrition into account. Training entails costs. Also, to reach the target for new hires in a tight market without incurring excessive labor costs, compensation levels must be set carefully.

There was little literature on crew scheduling for ships, e.g., harbor pilots (Wermus and Pope (1994)), and the works on airline crew or bus/truck operator scheduling were not capturing the specifics of our problem. So we built an MIP crew planning model that addresses a fleet's forecasted crewing needs for time periods of one to five years (see Mudrageda and Chajakis 1999a). Given compensation levels, training costs, historical attrition rates and demand forecasts for crew by specialty, the model suggests number of new hires per position versus training and promotion of existing staff from one position to the other. This model is still under development.

CONCLUSIONS

In the small case studies described in this article, we have demonstrated the role of management science in addressing business issues in marine petroleum logistics. The consistent use of computer-based models has given tangible benefits through a significant improvement in operations measurable by their impact on the bottom line. What is more, the process of their development yielded significant intangible value. While helping us develop these models, operations professionals came to understand their own system better, which in turn helped them initiate improvements well before the models were put to use. They gain further insights by using the models to continuously improve their jobs.

REFERENCES

Andrews, S.W., Murphy, F.H., Wang, X.P., Welch, S.E. (1996), "Modeling Crude Oil Lightering in Delaware Bay", *Interfaces*, November-December, 26/6, 68-78.

Brown, G.G., Graves, G.W., Ronen, D., "Scheduling ocean transportation of crude oil", *Management Science*, vol. 33, 335-346.

Chajakis, E.D., Welch, S.E., Andrews, S.W., Murphy, F.H. (1997), "Modeling Crude Oil Supply at Petroleum Refineries", Presentation at INFORMS Meeting, San Diego, California, May 4-7.

Chajakis, E.D., Welch, S.W., Murphy, F.H. (1997), "Optimizing Vessel Schedules for Tanker Lightering", Presentation at INFORMS Meeting, San Diego, California, May 4-7.

Chajakis, E.D. (1997), "Sophisticated Crude Transportation: Recent Advances in Petroleum Supply Modeling", *OR/MS Today*, December, 24/6, 30-34.

Chajakis, E.D. (1998), "Using Simulation to Analyze Lightering Operations", Presentation at INFORMS Meeting, Montreal, Canada, April 26-29.

Chajakis, E.D., Murphy, F.H. (1998), "Optimal Petroleum Product Delivery Scheduling", Presentation at INFORMS Meeting, Montreal, Canada, April 26-29.

Chajakis, E.D. (1999), "Optimising the Crude Supply of Refineries", *The Petroleum Economist*, February, 66/2, 21-22.

Chajakis, E.D. (1999), "Reflections on a Marine Vessel Affair: A Management Science Sea Story", *OR/MS Today*, August, 26/4, 32-39.

Everett, J.L., Hax, A.C., Lewinson, V.A., Nudds, D. (1972), "Optimization of a fleet of large tankers and bulkers: A linear programming approach", *Marine Technology*, October, 430-438.

Fisher, M.L., Rosenwein, M.B. (1989), "An interactive optimization system for bulk-cargo ship scheduling", *Naval Research Logistics*, volume 36, 27-42.

Floudas, C.A., Lin, X., Chajakis, E.D. (1999), "Optimal Continuous-Time Lightering Fleet Scheduling", Technical Report, Department of Chemical Engineering, Princeton University.

Jaikumar, R., Solomon, M.M. (1987), "The tug fleet size problem for barge line operations", *Transportation Science*, volume 21, 264-272.

Jaramillo, D.I., Perakis, A.N. (1991), "Fleet deployment optimization for liner shipping Part 2: Implementation and results", *Maritime Policy and Management*, volume 18, 235-262.

Kao, C., Lee, H.T. (1996), "Coordinated dock operations: integrating dock arrangement with ship discharging", *Computers in Industry*, May, 113-122.

Koeningsberg, E., Meyers, D.A. (1980), "An interacting cyclic queue model of fleet operations", *The Logistics and Transportation Review*, volume 16, 59-71.

Lane, D.E., Heaver, T.D., Uyeno, D. (1987), "Planning and scheduling for efficiency in liner shipping", *Maritime Policy and Management*, volume 14., 109-125.

Larson, R.C. (1988), "Transporting sludge to the 106-mile site: An inventory/routing model for fleet sizing and logistics system design", *Transportation Science*, volume 22, 186-198.

Larson, R.C., Minkoff, A., Gregory, P. (1988), "Fleet sizing and dispatching for the marine division of the New York City Department of Sanitation", in B.L. Golden and A.A. Assad (editors), *Vehicle Routing: Methods and Studies*, North-Holland, Amsterdam, 395-423.

Miller, D.M., (1987) "An Interactive, Computer-Aided Ship Scheduling System", *European Journal of Operational Research*, December, 363-379.

Mudrageda, M.V., Murphy, F.H., Welch, S.E. (1998), "Forecasting the Market for Jones Act Tankers", Edelman Presentation at INFORMS Meeting, Montreal, Canada, April 26-29.

Mudrageda, M.V., Chajakis, E.D., (1999), "Crew Planning for a Petroleum Products Marine Fleet", Presentation at INFORMS Meeting, Philadelphia, Pennsylvania, November 4-7.

Mudrageda, M.V., Chajakis, E.D., (1999), "Combining Optimization and Simulation in Marine Logistics Analysis", Presentation at INFORMS Meeting, Philadelphia, Pennsylvania, November 4-7.

Murphy, F.H. (1995), "Effect of US Maritime Administration Policies on the US Marine Transportation System", Working Paper, School of Management, Temple University.

Murphy, F.H. (1999), "Note: Developing Strategies for Maritrans' Business Units", *Interfaces*, January-February, 29/1, 131.

Papadakis, N.A., Perakis, A.N. (1989), "A nonlinear approach to the multiorigin, multidestination fleet deployment problem", *Naval Research Logistics*, volume 36, 515-528.

Perakis, A.N., Jaramillo, D.I. (1991), "Fleet deployment optimization for liner shipping. Part I: Background, problem formulation and solution approaches", *Maritime Policy and Management*, volume 18, 183-200.

Perakis, A.N., Papadakis, N.A. (1987) "Fleet deployment optimization models. Part I", *Maritime Policy and Management*, volume 14, 127-144.

Perakis, A.N., Papadakis, N.A. (1987) "Fleet deployment optimization models. Part II", *Maritime Policy and Management*, volume 14, 145-155.

Psaraftis, H.N., Solomon, M.M., Magnanti, T.L., Kim, T.U. (1990), "Routing and scheduling on a shoreline with release times", *Management Science*, volume 36, 212-223.

Rana, K., Vickson, R.G. (1988), "A model and solution algorithm for optimal routing of a time-chartered containership", *Transportation Science*, volume 22, 83-95.

Rana, K., Vickson, R.G. (1991), "Routing container ships using Lagrangean relaxation and decomposition", *Transportation Science*, volume 25, 201-214.

Ronen, D. (1983), "Cargo ships routing and scheduling: Survey of models and problems", *European Journal of Operational Research*, volume 12, 119-126.

Ronen, D. (1993), "Ship scheduling: The last decade", *European Journal of Operational Research*, December, 325-333.

Schwartz, N.L. (1968), "Discrete programs for moving known cargos from origins to destinations on time at minimum bargeline fleet cost", *Transportation Science*, volume 2, 134-145.

Suh, M.S., Lee, Y.J. (1998), "A hierarchical expert system for integrated scheduling of ship berthing, discharging and material transport", *Expert Systems*, November, 247-255.

Vea, Reynaldo B. (1994), "A method to optimize the on-time performance of containerships", *Marine Technology*, January, 52-65.

Vukadinovic, K., Teodorovic, D. (1994), "A fuzzy approach to the vessel dispatching problem", *European Journal of Operational Research*, July, 155-164.

Welch, S.E., Chajakis, E.D. (1999), "Integer Programming for Scheduling Petroleum Product Distribution", Presentation at INFORMS Meeting, Philadelphia, Pennsylvania, November 4-7.

Welch, S.E., Chajakis, E.D. (1999), "New Analytical Tools for Upstream Crude Logistics", Presentation at INFORMS Meeting, Philadelphia, Pennsylvania, November 4-7.

Wermus, M., Pope, J.A. (1994), "Scheduling Harbor Pilots", *Interfaces*, March-April, 44-52.

7. MULTI-CRITERIA DECISION ANALYSIS, AID & PRACTICE

DEALING WITH MISSING DATA IN ROUGH SET ANALYSIS OF MULTI-ATTRIBUTE AND MULTI-CRITERIA DECISION PROBLEMS

S. Greco[1], B. Matarazzo[1], R. Slowinski[2]

[1]Faculty of Economics
University of Catania, 95129 Catania, Italy

[2]Institute of Computing Science
Poznan University of Technology
60965 Poznan, Poland

Abstract: Rough sets methodology is a useful tool for analysis of decision problems
concerning a set of objects described in a data table by a set of condition attributes
and by a set of decision attributes. In practical applications, however, the data table
is often not complete because some data are missing. To deal with this case, we
propose an extension of the rough set methodology to the analysis of incomplete
data tables. The adaptation concerns both the classical rough set approach based on
the use of indiscernibility relations and the new rough set approach based on the use
of dominance relations. While the first approach deals with the multi-attribute
classification problem, the second approach deals with the multi-criteria sorting
problem. In the latter, condition attributes have preference-ordered scales, and thus
are called criteria, and the classes defined by the decision attributes are also
preference-ordered. The adapted relations of indiscernibility or dominance between
a pair of objects are considered as directional statements where a subject is
compared to a referent object. We require that the referent object has no missing
data. The two adapted rough set approaches boil down to the original approaches
when there are no missing data. The rules induced from the newly defined rough
approximations defined are either exact or approximate, depending whether they are
supported by consistent objects or not, and they are robust in a sense that each rule is
supported by at least one object with no missing data on the condition attributes or
criteria represented in the rule.

Keywords: Rough sets methodology, Missing data, Decision analysis, Multi-attribute
classification, Multi-criteria sorting, Decision rules.

S.H. Zanakis et al. (eds.), Decision Making: Recent Developments and Worldwide Applications, 295–316.
© 2000 Kluwer Academic Publishers.

INTRODUCTION

The rough sets philosophy introduced by Pawlak (1982) is based on the assumption that with every object of the universe there is associated a certain amount of information (data, knowledge), expressed by means of some attributes used for object description. It proved to be an excellent tool for analysis of decision problems (Pawlak and Slowinski, 1994) where the set of attributes is divided into disjoint sets of condition attributes and decision attributes describing objects in a data table.

The key idea of rough sets is approximation of knowledge expressed by decision attributes using knowledge expressed by condition attributes. The rough set approach answers several questions related to the approximation: (a) is the information contained in the data table consistent? (b) what are the non-redundant subsets of condition attributes ensuring the same quality of approximation as the whole set of condition attributes? (c) what are the condition attributes which cannot be eliminated from the approximation without decreasing the quality of approximation? (d) what minimal "*if ..., then ...*" decision rules can be induced from the approximations?

Some important characteristics of the rough set approach make of this a particularly interesting tool in a number of problems and concrete applications (Pawlak, 1991). With respect to the input information, it is possible to deal with both quantitative and qualitative data, and inconsistencies need not to be removed prior to the analysis. The rough set approach deals with inconsistencies by separation of certain and doubtful knowledge extracted from the data table. With reference to the output information, it is possible to acquire a posteriori information regarding the relevance of particular attributes or subsets of attributes to the quality of approximation considered in the problem at hand. Moreover, the final result in the form of "*if..., then...*" decision rules, using the most relevant attributes, is easy to interpret.

The original rough set approach is not able, however, to discover and process inconsistencies coming from consideration of *criteria*, i.e. condition attributes with preference-ordered scales (domains), like product quality, market share, debt ratio. Regular condition attributes, e.g. symptoms, colors, textural features, traditionally considered in the rough set methodology, are different from criteria because their scales are not preference-ordered (see, e.g., Pawlak, 1991; Pawlak and Slowinski, 1994). Consider, for example, two firms, *A* and *B*, evaluated for assessment of bankruptcy risk by a set of criteria including the "debt ratio" (total debt/total assets). If firm *A* has a low value while firm *B* has a high value of the debt ratio, and evaluations of these firms on other attributes are equal, then, from bankruptcy risk point of view, firm *A* dominates firm *B*. Suppose, however, that firm *A* has been assigned by a decision maker to a class of higher risk than firm *B*. This is obviously inconsistent with the dominance principle. Within the classical rough set approach, the two firms will be considered as just discernible and no inconsistency will be stated.

For this reason, Greco, Matarazzo and Slowinski (1998a, 1998b, 1999a) have proposed a new rough set approach that is able to deal with inconsistencies typical to consideration of criteria and preference-ordered decision classes. This innovation is mainly based on substitution of the indiscernibility relation by a dominance relation in the rough approximation of decision classes. An important consequence of this fact is a possibility of inferring from exemplary decisions the preference model in terms of decision rules being logical statements of the type "*if...*, *then...*". The separation of certain and doubtful knowledge about the decision maker's preferences is done by distinction of different kinds of decision rules, depending whether they are induced from lower approximations of decision classes or from the boundaries of these classes composed of inconsistent examples that do not observe the dominance principle. Such preference model is more general than the classical functional or relational model in multi-criteria decision making and it is more understandable for the users because of its natural syntax.

Both the classical rough set approach based on the use of indiscernibility relations and the new rough set approach based on the use of dominance relations suffer, however, from another deficiency: they require the data table to be complete, i.e. without *missing values* on condition attributes or criteria describing the objects.

To deal with the case of missing values in the data table, we propose an adaptation of the rough set methodology. The adaptation concerns both the classical rough set approach and the dominance-based rough set approach. While the first approach deals with *multi-attribute classification*, the second approach deals with *multi-criteria sorting*. Multi-attribute classification concerns an assignment of a set of objects to a set of pre-defined classes. The objects are described by a set of (regular) attributes and the classes are not necessarily ordered. Multi-criteria sorting concerns a set of objects evaluated by criteria, i.e. attributes with preference-ordered scales. In this problem, the classes are also preference-ordered.

The adapted relations of indiscernibility or dominance between a pair of objects are considered as directional statements where a subject is compared to a referent object. We require that the referent object has no missing values. The two adapted rough set approaches maintain all good characteristics of their original approaches. They also boil down to the original approaches when there are no missing values. The rules induced from the rough approximations defined according to the adapted relations verify some suitable properties: they are either exact or approximate, depending whether they are supported by consistent objects or not, and they are robust in a sense that each rule is supported by at least one object with no missing value on the condition attributes or criteria represented in the rule.

The paper extends the short version presented by the authors in (Greco, Matarazzo and Slowinski, 1999c). It is organized in the following way. In section 2, we present the extended rough sets methodology handling the missing values. It is composed of four paragraphs – first two are devoted to adaptation of the classical rough set approach based on the use of indiscernibility relations; the other two undertake the adaptation of the new rough set approach based on the use of dominance relations. In order to illustrate the concepts introduced in section 2, we present an illustrative example in section 3. Section 4 groups conclusions.

ROUGH APPROXIMATIONS DEFINED ON DATA TABLES WITH MISSING VALUES

For algorithmic reasons, the data set about objects is represented in the form of a data table. The rows of the table are labeled by *objects*, whereas columns are labeled by *attributes* and entries of the table are *attribute-values*, called *descriptors*.

Formally, by a *data table* we understand the 4-tuple S=<U,Q,V,f>, where U is a finite set of objects, Q is a finite set of attributes, $V = \bigcup_{q \in Q} V_q$ and V_q is a domain of the attribute q, and f: $U \times Q \rightarrow V$ is a total function such that $f(x,q) \in V_q \cup \{*\}$ for every $q \in Q$, $x \in U$, called an *information function* (Pawlak, 1991). The symbol "*" indicates that the value of an attribute for a given object is unknown (*missing*).

If set Q is divided into set C of *condition attributes* and set D of *decision attributes*, then such a data table is called *decision table*. If the domain (scale) of a condition attribute is ordered according to a decreasing or increasing preference, then it is a *criterion*. For condition attribute $q \in C$ being a criterion, S_q is an *outranking relation* (Roy, 1985) on U such that xS_qy means "x is at least as good as y with respect to criterion q". We suppose that S_q is a total preorder, i.e. a strongly complete and transitive binary relation, defined on U on the basis of evaluations $f(\cdot,q)$. The domains of "regular" condition attributes are not ordered.

We assume that the set D of decision attributes is a singleton $\{d\}$. Decision attribute d makes a partition of U into a finite number of classes $Cl=\{Cl_t, t \in T\}$, $T=\{1,...,n\}$, such that each $x \in U$ belongs to one and only one $Cl_t \in Cl$. The domain of d can be preference-ordered or not. In the former case, we suppose that the classes are ordered such that the higher is the class number the better is the class, i.e. for all $r,s \in T$, such that r>s, the objects from Cl_r are preferred (strictly or weakly) to the objects from Cl_s. More formally, if S is a *comprehensive outranking relation* on U, i.e. if for all $x,y \in U$, xSy means "x is at least as good as y", we suppose: $[x \in Cl_r, y \in Cl_s, r>s] \Rightarrow [xSy$ and *not* $ySx]$. These assumptions are typical for consideration of a *multi-criteria sorting problem*.

In the case of non-ordered classes and regular condition attributes, the corresponding problem is that of *multi-attribute classification*; it is considered by the classical rough set approach.

In the following paragraphs of this section we are considering separately the multi-attribute classification and the multi-criteria sorting with respect to the problem of missing values. The first idea of dealing with missing values in the rough set approach to the multi-attribute classification problem has been given in (Greco, Matarazzo, Slowinski and Zanakis 1999b).

Multi-attribute classification problem with missing values

For any two objects $x,y \in U$, we are considering a directional comparison of y to x; object y is called subject and object x, referent. We say that subject y is *indiscernible* with referent x with respect to condition attributes $P \subseteq C$ (denotation yI_Px) if for every $q \in P$ the following conditions are met:

- $f(x,q)\neq*$,

- $f(x,q)=f(y,q)$ or $f(y,q)=*$.

The above means that the referent object considered for indiscernibility with respect to P should have no missing values on attributes from set P.

The binary relation I_P is not necessarily reflexive because for some $x\in U$ there may exist $q\in P$ for which $f(x,q)=*$ and, therefore, we cannot state xI_Px. Moreover, I_P is also not necessarily symmetric because the statement yI_Px cannot be inverted if there exist $q\in P$ for which $f(y,q)=*$. However, I_P is transitive because for each $x,y,z\in U$, the statements xI_Py and yI_Pz imply xI_Pz. This is justified by the observations that object z can substitute object y in the statement xI_Py because yI_Pz and both y and z, as referent objects, have no missing values.

For each $P\subseteq C$ let us define a set of objects having no missing values with respect to P:

$$U_P=\{x\in U: f(x,q)\neq* \text{ for each } q\in P\}.$$

It is easy to see that the restriction of I_P to U_P (in other words, the binary relation $I_P\cap U_P\times U_P$ defined on U_P) is reflexive, symmetric and transitive, i.e. it is an equivalence binary relation.

For each $x\in U$ and for each $P\subseteq Q$ let $I_P(x)=\{y\in U: yI_Px\}$ denote the class of objects indiscernible with x. Given $X\subseteq U$ and $P\subseteq Q$, we define lower approximation of X with respect to P as

$$\underline{I}_P(X)=\{x\in U_P: I_P(x)\subseteq X\}. \tag{1}$$

Analogously, we define the upper approximation of X with respect to P as

$$\bar{I}_P(X)=\{x\in U_P: I_P(x)\cap X\neq\varnothing\}. \tag{2}$$

Let us observe that if $x\notin U_P$ then $I_P(x)=\varnothing$ and, therefore, we can also write

$$\bar{I}_P(X)=\{x\in U: I_P(x)\cap X\neq\varnothing\}.$$

Let $X_P=X\cap U_P$.

Theorem 1. (*Rough inclusion*) For each $X\in U$ and for each $P\subseteq C$:

$$\underline{I}_P(X)\subseteq X_P\subseteq \bar{I}_P(X).$$

Theorem 2. (*Complementarity*) For each $X\in U$ and for each $P\subseteq C$:

$$\underline{I}_P(X)=U_P - \bar{I}_P(U-X).$$

The P-*boundary* of X in S, denoted by $Bn_P(X)$, is

$$Bn_P(X)= \bar{I}_P(X) - \underline{I}_P(X).$$

$Bn_P(X)$ constitutes the "doubtful region" of X: according to knowledge expressed by P nothing can be said with certainty about membership of its elements in the set X.

The following concept will also be useful (Skowron and Grzymala-Busse, 1994). Given a partition $Cl=\{Cl_t, t\in T\}$, $T=\{1,...,n\}$, of U, the P-boundary with respect to $k>1$ classes $\{Cl_{t1},...,Cl_{tk}\}\subseteq\{Cl_1,...,Cl_n\}$ is defined as

$$Bd_P(\{Cl_{t1},...,Cl_{tk}\}) = \left(\bigcap_{t=t1,...,tk} Bn_P(Cl_t)\right)\cap\left(\bigcap_{t\neq t1,...,tk}(U-Bn_P(Cl_t))\right).$$

The objects from $Bd_P(\{Cl_{t1},...,Cl_{tk}\})$ can be assigned to one of the classes $Cl_{t1},...,Cl_{tk}$ but P provides not enough information to know exactly to what class.

Let us observe that a very useful property of lower approximation within classical rough sets theory is that if an object $x\in U$ belongs to the lower approximation with respect to $P\subseteq C$, then x belongs also to the lower approximation with respect to $R\subseteq C$ when $P\subseteq R$ (this is a kind of monotonicity property). However, definition (1) does not satisfy this property of lower approximation, because it is possible that $f(x,q)\neq*$ for all $q\in P$ but $f(x,q)=*$ for some $q\in R-P$. This is quite problematic with respect to definition of some key concepts of the rough sets theory, like quality of approximation, reduct and core.

Therefore, another definition of lower approximation should be considered to restore the concepts of quality of approximation, reduct and core in the case of missing values. Given $X\subseteq U$ and $P\subseteq Q$, this definition is the following:

$$\underline{I}_P^*(X)= \bigcup_{R\subseteq P} I_R(X). \tag{3}$$

$\underline{I}_P^*(X)$ will be called *cumulative* P-lower approximation of X because it includes all the objects belonging to all R-lower approximations of X, where $R\subseteq P$.

It can be shown that another type of indiscernibility relation, denoted by I_P^*, permits a direct definition of the cumulative P-lower approximation in a classic way. For each $x,y\in U$ and for each $P\subseteq Q$, $y\, I_P^*\, x$ means that $f(x,q)=f(y,q)$ or $f(x,q)=*$ and/or $f(y,q)=*$, for every $q\in P$. Let $I_P^*(x)=\{y\in U: y\, I_P^*\, x\}$ for each $x\in U$ and for each $P\subseteq Q$. I_P^* is reflexive and symmetric but not transitive (Kryszkiewicz, 1998). Let us observe that the restriction of I_P^* to U_P^* is reflexive, symmetric and transitive when $U_P^*=\{x\in U: f(x,q)\neq*$ for at least one $q\in P\}$.

Theorem 3. (*Definition (3) expressed in terms of I_P^**) $\underline{I}_P^*(X)=\{x\in U_P^*: I_P^*(x)\subseteq X\}$.

Using I_P^* we can give definition of the P-upper approximation of X, complementary to $\underline{I}_P^*(X)$:

$$\overline{I}_P^*(X)=\{x\in U_P^*: I_P^*(x)\cap X\neq\varnothing\}. \tag{4}$$

For each $X\subseteq U$, let $X_P^*=X\cap U_P^*$. Let us remark that $x\in U_P^*$ if and only if there exists $R\neq\varnothing$ such that $R\subseteq P$ and $x\in U_R$.

Theorem 4. (*Rough inclusion*) For each $X \subseteq U$ and for each $P \subseteq C$:

$$\underline{I}_P^*(X) \subseteq X_P^* \subseteq \overline{I}_P^*(X).$$

Theorem 5. (*Complementarity*) For each $X \subseteq U$ and for each $P \subseteq C$:

$$\underline{I}_P^*(X) = U_P^* - \overline{I}_P^*(U-X).$$

The P-boundary of X approximated with $\underline{I}_P^*$ is equal to

$$Bn_P^*(X) = \overline{I}_P^*(X) - \underline{I}_P^*(X).$$

Given a partition $Cl = \{Cl_t, t \in T\}$, $T = \{1,...,n\}$, of U, the P-boundary with respect to k>1 classes $\{Cl_{t1},...,Cl_{tk}\} \subseteq \{Cl_1,...,Cl_n\}$ is defined as

$$Bd_P^*(\{Cl_{t1},...,Cl_{tk}\}) = \left(\bigcap_{t=t1,...,tk} Bn_P^*(Cl_t) \right) \cap \left(\bigcap_{t \neq t1,...,tk} \left(U - Bn_P^*(Cl_t) \right) \right).$$

The objects from $Bd_P^*(\{Cl_{t1},...,Cl_{tk}\})$ can be assigned to one of the classes $Cl_{t1},...,Cl_{tk}$, however, P and all its subsets provide not enough information to know exactly to what class.

Theorem 6. (*Monotonicity of the accuracy of approximation*) For each $X \subseteq U$ and for each $P,R \subseteq C$, such that $P \subseteq R$, the following inclusion holds:

$$i) \quad \underline{I}_P^*(X) \subseteq \underline{I}_R^*(X).$$

Furthermore, if $U_P^* = U_R^*$, the following inclusion is also true

$$ii) \quad \overline{I}_P^*(X) \supseteq \overline{I}_R^*(X).$$

Due to Theorem 6, when augmenting a set of attributes P, we get a lower approximation of X that is at least of the same cardinality. Thus, we can restore for the case of missing values the following key concepts of the rough sets theory: accuracy and quality of approximation, reduct and core.

The *accuracy* of the approximation of $X \subseteq U$ by the attributes from P is the ratio:

$$\alpha_P(X) = \frac{\text{card}\left(\underline{I}_P^*(X) \right)}{\text{card}\left(\overline{I}_P^*(X) \right)}.$$

The *quality* of the approximation of $X \subseteq U$ by the attributes from P is the ratio:

$$\gamma_P(X) = \frac{card(\underline{I}_P^*(X))}{card(X)}.$$

According to Theorem 6, the accuracy and the quality are monotonic (non-decreasing) with respect to inclusion of new attributes to set P.

The quality $\gamma_P(X)$ represents the relative frequency of the objects correctly classified using the attributes from P. Moreover, $0 \leq \alpha_P(X) \leq \gamma_P(X) \leq 1$, $\gamma_P(X)=0$ iff $\alpha_P(X)=0$ and $\gamma_P(X)=1$ iff $\alpha_P(X)=1$.

The approximations of a subset $X \subseteq U$ can be extended to a classification, i.e. a partition $Cl = \{Cl_t, t \in T\}$, $T = \{1,...,n\}$, of U. By P-lower and P-upper approximation of Cl in S we mean sets $\underline{I}_P^*(Cl) = \{\underline{I}_P^*(Cl_1),...,\underline{I}_P^*(Cl_n)\}$ and $\bar{I}_P^*(Cl) = \{\bar{I}_P^*(Cl_1),...,\bar{I}_P^*(Cl_n)\}$, respectively. The coefficient

$$\gamma_P(Cl) = \frac{\sum_{t=1}^{n} card(\underline{I}_P^*(Cl_t))}{card(U)}$$

is called *quality of the approximation of classification* Cl by set of attributes P, or in short, *quality of classification*. It expresses the ratio of all P-correctly classified objects to all objects in the system.

Each minimal subset $P \subseteq C$ such that $\gamma_P(Cl) = \gamma_C(Cl)$ is called a *reduct* of S and denoted by $RED_{Cl}(C)$. Let us remark that a decision table can have more than one reduct. The intersection of all reducts is called the *core* and denoted by $CORE_{Cl}(C)$.

Decision rules for the multi-attribute classification problem with missing values

Using the rough approximations (1), (2) and (3), (4), it is possible to induce a generalized description of the information contained in the decision table in terms of *decision rules*. These are logical statements (implications) of the type "*if ..., then...*", where the antecedent (condition part) is a conjunction of elementary conditions concerning particular condition attributes and the consequence (decision part) is a disjunction of possible assignments to particular classes of a partition of U induced by decision attributes. Given a partition $Cl = \{Cl_t, t \in T\}$, $T = \{1,...,n\}$, of U, the syntax of a rule is the following:

"*if* $f(x,q_1) = r_{q1}$ *and* $f(x,q_2) = r_{q2}$ *and* ... $f(x,q_p) = r_{qp}$, *then* x is assigned to Cl_{t1} *or* Cl_{t2} *or* ... Cl_{tk}",

where $\{q_1,q_2,...,q_p\} \subseteq C$, $(r_{q1},r_{q2},...,r_{qp}) \in V_{q1} \times V_{q2} \times ... \times V_{qp}$ and $\{Cl_{t1},Cl_{t2},...,Cl_{tk}\} \subseteq \{Cl_1,Cl_2, ...,Cl_n\}$. If the consequence is univocal, i.e. $k=1$, then the rule is *exact*, otherwise it is *approximate* or *uncertain*.

Let us observe that for any $Cl_j \in \{Cl_1,Cl_2,...,Cl_n\}$ and $P \subseteq Q$, the definition (1) of P-lower approximation of Cl_t can be rewritten as

$$\underline{I}_P(Cl_t) = \{x \in U_P: \text{ for each } y \in U, \text{ if } yI_Px, \text{ then } y \in Cl_t\}. \qquad (1')$$

Thus the objects belonging to the lower approximation $\underline{I}_P(Cl_t)$ can be considered as a basis for induction of exact decision rules.

Therefore, the statement "*if* $f(x,q_1) = r_{q1}$ *and* $f(x,q_2) = r_{q2}$ *and* ... $f(x,q_p) = r_{qp}$, *then* x is assigned to Cl_t", is accepted as an exact decision rule iff there exists at least one $y \in \underline{I}_P(Cl_t)$, $P=\{q_1,...,q_p\}$, such that $f(y,q_1) = r_{q1}$ and $f(y,q_2) = r_{q2}$ and ... $f(y,q_p) = r_{qp}$.

Given $\{Cl_{t1},...,Cl_{tk}\}\subseteq\{Cl_1,Cl_2,...,Cl_n\}$ we can write

$$Bd_P(\{Cl_{t1},...,Cl_{tk}\}) =\{x\in U_P: \text{for each } y\in U, \text{ } if \text{ } yI_Px, then \text{ } y\in Cl_{t1} \text{ } or \text{ } ... \text{ } Cl_{tk}\}. \quad (2')$$

Thus, the objects belonging to the boundary $Bd_P(\{Cl_{t1},...,Cl_{tk}\})$ can be considered as a basis for induction of approximate decision rules.

An exact decision rule "*if* $f(x,q_1) = r_{q1}$ *and* $f(x,q_2) = r_{q2}$ *and* ... $f(x,q_p) = r_{qp}$, *then* x is assigned to Cl_t", is *minimal* iff there is not another rule "*if* $f(x,h_1) = \underline{r}_{h1}$ *and* $f(x,h_2) = \underline{r}_{h2}$ *and* ... $f(x,h_k) = \underline{r}_{hk}$, *then* x is assigned to Cl_t", such that $\{h_1,h_2,...,h_k\}\subseteq\{q_1,...,q_p\}$ and $\underline{r}_t=r_t$ for any $t\in\{h_1,h_2,...,h_k\}$.

An approximate decision rule "*if* $f(x,q_1) = r_{q1}$ *and* $f(x,q_2) = r_{q2}$ *and* ... $f(x,q_p) = r_{qp}$, *then* x is assigned to Cl_{t1} *or* Cl_{t2} *or* ... Cl_{tk} ", is *minimal* iff there is not another rule "*if* $f(x,h_1) = \underline{r}_{h1}$ *and* $f(x,h_2) = \underline{r}_{h2}$ *and* ... $f(x,h_k) = \underline{r}_{hk}$, *then* x is assigned to C_{t1} *or* Cl_{t2} *or* ... Cl_{tk}", such that $\{h_1,h_2,...,h_k\}\subseteq\{q_1,...,q_p\}$ and $\underline{r}_t=r_t$ for any $t\in\{h_1,h_2,...,h_k\}$.

Since each decision rule is an implication, a *minimal* decision rule represents such an implication that there is no other implication with an antecedent of at least the same weakness and a consequent of at least the same strength.

We say that $y\in U$ *supports* the exact decision rule "*if* $f(x,q_1) = r_{q1}$ *and* $f(x,q_2) = r_{q2}$ *and* ... $f(x,q_p) = r_{qp}$, *then* x is assigned to Cl_j", if $[f(y,q_1) = r_{q1}$ and/or $f(y,q_1) = *]$ and $[f(y,q_2) = r_{q2}$ and/or $f(y,q_2) = *]$ ... and $[f(y,q_p) = r_{qp}$ and/or $f(y,q_p) = *]$ and $y\in Cl_t$. Similarly, we say that $y\in U$ *supports* the approximate decision rule "*if* $f(x,q_1) = r_{q1}$ *and* $f(x,q_2) = r_{q2}$ *and* ... $f(x,q_p) = r_{qp}$, *then* x is assigned to Cl_{t1} *or* Cl_{t2} *or* ... Cl_{tk}", if $[f(y,q_1) = r_{q1}$ and/or $f(y,q_1) = *]$ and $[f(y,q_2) = r_{q2}$ and/or $f(y,q_2) = *]$ ... and $[f(y,q_p) = r_{qp}$ and/or $f(y,q_p) = *]$ and $y\in Bd_C^*(\{Cl_{t1},...,Cl_{tk}\})$.

A set of decision rules is *complete* if it fulfils the following conditions:

- each $x\in \underline{I}_C^*(Cl_t)$ supports at least one exact decision rule of the type "*if* $f(x,q_1)=r_{q1}$ *and* $f(x,q_2)=r_{q2}$ *and* ... $f(x,q_p)=r_{qp}$, *then* x is assigned to Cl_t", for each $Cl_t\in Cl$,

- each $x\in Bd_C^*(\{Cl_{t1},...,Cl_{tk}\})$ supports at least one approximate decision rule of the type "*if* $f(x,q_1)=r_{q1}$ *and* $f(x,q_2)=r_{q2}$ *and* ... $f(x,q_p)=r_{qp}$, *then* x is assigned to Cl_{t1} *or* Cl_{t2} *or* ... Cl_{tk}", for each $\{Cl_{t1},Cl_{t2},...,Cl_{tk}\}\subseteq\{Cl_1,Cl_2,...,Cl_n\}$.

We call *minimal* each set of minimal decision rules that is complete and non-redundant, i.e. exclusion of any rule from this set makes it non-complete.

Multi-criteria sorting problem with missing values

As was mentioned before, the notion of attribute differs from that of *criterion* because the domain (scale) of a criterion has to be ordered according to a decreasing or increasing preference, while the domain of the attribute does not have to be ordered. Formally, for each $q \in C$ being a criterion there exists an outranking relation (Roy, 1985) S_q on the set of actions U such that xS_qy means "x is at least as good as y with respect to criterion q". We suppose that S_q is a total preorder, i.e. a strongly complete and transitive binary relation defined on U on the basis of evaluations $f(\cdot,q)$. If domain V_q of criterion q is quantitative and for each $x,y \in U$, $f(x,q) \geq f(y,q)$ implies xS_qy, then V_q is a scale of preference of criterion q. If, however, for criterion q, V_q is not quantitative and/or $f(x,q) \geq f(y,q)$ does not imply xS_qy, then in order to define a scale of preference of criterion q one can choose a function $g_q : U \to \mathbf{R}$ such that for each $x,y \in U$, xS_qy if and only if $g_q(x) \geq g_q(y)$ (see, e.g., Roubens and Vincke, 1985); to this aim it is enough to order the objects of U from the worst to the best on criterion q and to assign to $g_q(x)$ consecutive numbers corresponding to the rank of x in this order, i.e. for z being the worst, $g_q(z)=1$, for w being the second worst, $g_q(w)=2$, and so on. Then, the domain of function $g_q(\cdot)$ becomes a scale of preference of criterion q and the domain V_q is recoded such that $f(x,q)=g_q(x)$ for every $x \in U$.

Also in this case, we are considering a directional comparison of subject y to referent x, for any two objects $x,y \in U$.

We say that subject y *dominates* referent x with respect to criteria $P \subseteq C$ (denotation $y \, D_P^+ \, x$) if for every criterion $q \in P$ the following conditions are met:

- $f(x,q) \neq *$,

- $f(y,q) \geq f(x,q)$ or $f(y,q) = *$.

The above means that the referent object considered for dominance D_P^+ should have no missing values on criteria from set P.

We say that subject y is *dominated* by referent x with respect to criteria $P \subseteq C$ (denotation $x \, D_P^- \, y$) if for every criterion $q \in P$ the following conditions are met:

- $f(x,q) \neq *$,

- $f(x,q) \geq f(y,q)$ or $f(y,q) = *$.

The above means that the referent object considered for dominance D_P^- should have no missing values on criteria from set P.

The binary relations D_P^+ and D_P^- are not necessarily reflexive because for some $x \in U$ there may exist $q \in P$ for which $f(x,q)=*$ and, therefore, we cannot state neither $x \, D_P^+ \, x$ nor $x \, D_P^- \, x$. However, D_P^+ and D_P^- are transitive because for each $x,y,z \in U$, the statements

1) $x D_P^+ y$ and $y D_P^+ z$ imply $x D_P^+ z$, and

2) $x D_P^- y$ and $y D_P^- z$ imply $x D_P^- z$.

Implication 1) is justified by the observations that object z can substitute object y in the statement $x D_P^+ y$ because $y D_P^+ z$ and both y and z, as referent objects, have no missing values. As to implication 2), object x can substitute object y in the statement $y D_P^- z$ because $x D_P^- y$ and both x and y, as referent objects, have no missing values.

For each $P \subseteq C$ we restore the definition of set U_P from paragraph 2.1. It is easy to see that the restrictions of D_P^+ and D_P^- to U_P (in other words, the binary relations $D_P^+ \cap U_P \times U_P$ and $D_P^- \cap U_P \times U_P$ defined on U_P) are reflexive and transitive, i.e. they are partial preorders.

The sets to be approximated are called *upward union* and *downward union* of preference-ordered classes, respectively:

$$Cl_t^{\geq} = \bigcup_{s \geq t} Cl_s, \quad Cl_t^{\leq} = \bigcup_{s \leq t} Cl_s, \quad t=1,...,n.$$

The statement $x \in Cl_t^{\geq}$ means "x belongs at least to class Cl_t", while $x \in Cl_t^{\leq}$ means "x belongs at most to class Cl_t".

Let us remark that $Cl_1^{\geq} = Cl_n^{\leq} = U$, $Cl_n^{\geq} = Cl_n$ and $Cl_1^{\leq} = Cl_1$. Furthermore, for t=2,...,n, we have:

$$Cl_t^{\geq} = U - Cl_{t-1}^{\leq} \quad \text{and} \quad Cl_{t-1}^{\leq} = U - Cl_t^{\geq}.$$

Given $P \subseteq C$ and $x \in U$, the "granules of knowledge" used for approximation are:

- a set of objects dominating x, called P-*dominating set*, $D_P^+(x) = \{y \in U: y D_P^+ x\}$,

- a set of objects dominated by x, called P-*dominated set*, $D_P^-(x) = \{y \in U: x D_P^- y\}$.

For any $P \subseteq C$ we say that $x \in U$ belongs to $Cl_t^{\geq}$ *without any ambiguity* if $x \in Cl_t^{\geq}$ and for all the objects $y \in U$ dominating x with respect to P, we have $y \in Cl_t^{\geq}$, i.e. $D_P^+(x) \subseteq Cl_t^{\geq}$. Furthermore, we say that $x \in U$ *could belong* to $Cl_t^{\geq}$ if there would exist at least one object $y \in Cl_t^{\geq}$ dominated by x with respect to P, i.e. $y \in D_P^-(x)$.

Thus, with respect to $P \subseteq C$, the set of all objects belonging to $Cl_t^{\geq}$ without any ambiguity constitutes the P-*lower approximation* of $Cl_t^{\geq}$, denoted by $\underline{P}(Cl_t^{\geq})$, and the set of all objects that could belong to $Cl_t^{\geq}$ constitutes the P-*upper approximation* of $Cl_t^{\geq}$, denoted by $\overline{P}(Cl_t^{\geq})$, for t=1,...,n:

$$\underline{P}(Cl_t^\geq) = \{x \in U_P : D_P^+(x) \subseteq Cl_t^\geq\}, \tag{5.1}$$

$$\overline{P}(Cl_t^\geq) = \{x \in U_P : D_P^-(x) \cap Cl_t^\geq \neq \varnothing\}. \tag{5.2}$$

Analogously, using $D_P^-(x)$, one can define P-*lower approximation* and P-*upper approximation* of $Cl_t^\leq$, for $t=1,...,n$:

$$\underline{P}(Cl_t^\leq) = \{x \in U_P : D_P^-(x) \subseteq Cl_t^\leq\}, \tag{6.1}$$

$$\overline{P}(Cl_t^\leq) = \{x \in U_P : D_P^+(x) \cap Cl_t^\leq \neq \varnothing\}. \tag{6.2}$$

Let $(Cl_t^\geq)_P = Cl_t^\geq \cap U_P$ and $(Cl_t^\leq)_P = Cl_t^\leq \cap U_P$, $t=1,...,n$.

Theorem 7. (*Rough inclusion*) For each $Cl_t^\geq$ and $Cl_t^\leq$, $t=1,...,n$, and for each $P \subseteq C$:

$$\underline{P}(Cl_t^\geq) \subseteq (Cl_t^\geq)_P \subseteq \overline{P}(Cl_t^\geq),$$

$$\underline{P}(Cl_t^\leq) \subseteq (Cl_t^\leq)_P \subseteq \overline{P}(Cl_t^\leq).$$

Theorem 8. (*Complementarity*) For each $Cl_t^\geq$, $t=2,...,n$, and $Cl_t^\leq$, $t=1,...,n-1$, and for each $P \subseteq C$:

$$\underline{P}(Cl_t^\geq) = U_P - \overline{P}(Cl_{t-1}^\leq),$$

$$\underline{P}(Cl_t^\leq) = U_P - \overline{P}(Cl_{t+1}^\geq).$$

The P-*boundaries* (P-doubtful regions) of $Cl_t^\geq$ and $Cl_t^\leq$ are defined as:

$$Bn_P(Cl_t^\geq) = \overline{P}(Cl_t^\geq) - \underline{P}(Cl_t^\geq), \quad Bn_P(Cl_t^\leq) = \overline{P}(Cl_t^\leq) - \underline{P}(Cl_t^\leq), \quad \text{for } t=1,...,n.$$

Due to complementarity of the rough approximations (Greco, Matarazzo and Slowinski, 1998b), the following property holds:

$$Bn_P(Cl_t^\geq) = Bn_P(Cl_{t-1}^\leq), \quad \text{for } t=2,...,n.$$

To preserve the monotonicity property of the lower approximation (see paragraph 2.1) it is necessary to use another definition of the approximation for a given $Cl_t^\geq$ and $Cl_t^\leq$, $t=1,...,n$, and for each $P \subseteq C$:

$$\underline{P}(Cl_t^\geq)^* = \bigcup_{R \subseteq P} \underline{R}(Cl_t^\geq), \tag{7.1}$$

$$\underline{P}(Cl_t^\leq)^* = \bigcup_{R \subseteq P} \underline{R}(Cl_t^\leq). \tag{7.2}$$

$\underline{P}(Cl_t^{\geq})^*$ and $\underline{P}(Cl_t^{\leq})^*$ will be called *cumulative* P-lower approximations of unions $Cl_t^{\geq}$ and $Cl_t^{\leq}$, t=1,...,n, because they include all the objects belonging to all R-lower approximations of $Cl_t^{\geq}$ and $Cl_t^{\leq}$, respectively, where R⊆P.

It can be shown that another type of dominance relation, denoted by D_P^*, permits a direct definition of the cumulative P-lower approximations in a classic way. For each x,y∈U and for each P⊆Q, y D_P^* x means that f(y,q)≥f(x,q) or f(x,q)=* and/or f(y,q)=*, for every q∈P.

Now, given P⊆C and x∈U, the "granules of knowledge" used for approximation are:

- a set of objects dominating x, called P-*dominating set*, $D_P^{+*}(x)=\{y\in U : y\,D_P^*\,x\}$,

- a set of objects dominated by x, called P-*dominated set*, $D_P^{-*}(x)=\{y\in U : x\,D_P^*\,y\}$.

D_P^* is reflexive but not transitive. Let us observe that the restriction of D_P^* to U_P^* is reflexive and transitive when $U_P^*=\{x\in U : f(x,q)\neq *$ for at least one q∈P$\}$.

Theorem 9. (*Definitions (7.1) and (7.2) expressed in terms of* D_P^*)

$$\underline{P}(Cl_t^{\geq})^*=\{x\in U_P^* : D_P^{+*}(x)\subseteq Cl_t^{\geq}\},$$

$$\underline{P}(Cl_t^{\leq})^*=\{x\in U_P^* : D_P^{-*}(x)\subseteq Cl_t^{\leq}\}.$$

Using D_P^* we can give definition of the P-upper approximations of $Cl_t^{\geq}$ and $Cl_t^{\leq}$, complementary to $\underline{P}(Cl_t^{\geq})^*$ and $\underline{P}(Cl_t^{\leq})^*$, respectively:

$$\overline{P}(Cl_t^{\geq})^*=\{x\in U_P^* : D_P^{-*}(x)\cap Cl_t^{\geq}\neq\emptyset\}, \tag{8.1}$$

$$\overline{P}(Cl_t^{\leq})^*=\{x\in U_P^* : D_P^{+*}(x)\cap Cl_t^{\leq}\neq\emptyset\}. \tag{8.2}$$

For each $Cl_t^{\geq}\subseteq U$ and $Cl_t^{\leq}\subseteq U$, let $(Cl_t^{\geq})^*=Cl_t^{\geq}\cap U_P^*$ and $(Cl_t^{\leq})^*=Cl_t^{\leq}\cap U_P^*$. Let us remark that x∈ U_P^* if and only if there exists R≠∅ such that R⊆P and x∈U_R.

Theorem 10. (*Rough inclusion*) For each $Cl_t^{\geq}$ and $Cl_t^{\leq}$, t=1,...,n, and for each P⊆C:

$$\underline{P}(Cl_t^{\geq})^*\subseteq(Cl_t^{\geq})^*\subseteq\overline{P}(Cl_t^{\geq})^*,$$

$$\underline{P}(Cl_t^{\leq})^*\subseteq(Cl_t^{\leq})^*\subseteq\overline{P}(Cl_t^{\leq})^*.$$

Theorem 11. (*Complementarity*) For each $Cl_t^{\geq}$, t=2,...,n, and $Cl_t^{\leq}$, t=1,...,n-1, and for each P⊆C:

$$\underline{P}(Cl_t^{\geq})^* = U_P^* - \overline{P}(Cl_{t-1}^{\leq})^*,$$

$$\underline{P}(Cl_t^{\leq})^* = U_P^* - \overline{P}(Cl_{t+1}^{\geq})^*.$$

The P-boundary of and $Cl_t^{\leq}$, t=1,...,n, approximated with D_P^* are equal, respectively, to

$$Bn_P^*(Cl_t^{\geq}) = \overline{P}(Cl_t^{\geq})^* - \underline{P}(Cl_t^{\geq})^*,$$

$$Bn_P^*(Cl_t^{\leq}) = \overline{P}(Cl_t^{\leq})^* - \underline{P}(Cl_t^{\leq})^*.$$

Theorem 12. (*Monotonicity of the accuracy of approximation*) For each $Cl_t^{\geq}$ and $Cl_t^{\leq}$, t=1,...,n, and for each P,R⊆C, such that P⊆R, the following inclusions hold:

$$\underline{P}(Cl_t^{\geq})^* \subseteq \underline{R}(Cl_t^{\geq})^*,$$

$$\underline{P}(Cl_t^{\leq})^* \subseteq \underline{R}(Cl_t^{\leq})^*.$$

Furthermore, if $U_P^* = U_R^*$, the following inclusions are also true

$$\overline{P}(Cl_t^{\geq})^* \supseteq \overline{R}(Cl_t^{\geq})^*$$

$$\overline{P}(Cl_t^{\leq})^* \supseteq \overline{R}(Cl_t^{\leq})^*.$$

Due to Theorem 12, when augmenting a set of attributes P, we get lower approximations of $Cl_t^{\geq}$ and $Cl_t^{\leq}$, t=1,...,n, that are at least of the same cardinality. Thus, we can restore for the case of missing values the following key concepts of the rough sets theory: accuracy and quality of approximation, reduct and core.

For every t∈T and for every P⊆C we define the *quality of approximation of partition* **Cl** by set of attributes P, or in short, *quality of sorting*:

$$\gamma_P(\mathbf{Cl}) = \frac{card\left(U - \left(\bigcup_{t \in T} Bn_P^*\left(Cl_t^{\leq}\right)\right)\right)}{card(U)} = \frac{card\left(U - \left(\bigcup_{t \in T} Bn_P^*\left(Cl_t^{\geq}\right)\right)\right)}{card(U)}.$$

The quality expresses the ratio of all P-correctly sorted objects to all objects in the decision table.

Each minimal subset P⊆C such that $\gamma_P(\mathbf{Cl}) = \gamma_C(\mathbf{Cl})$ is called a *reduct* of **Cl** and denoted by $RED_{\mathbf{Cl}}(C)$. Let us remark that a decision table can have more than one reduct. The intersection of all reducts is called the *core* and denoted by $CORE_{\mathbf{Cl}}(C)$.

Decision rules for multi-criteria sorting problem with missing values

Using the rough approximations (5.1), (5.2), (6.1), (6.2) and (7.1), (7.2), (8.1), (8.2), it is possible to induce a generalized description of the information contained in the decision table in terms of "*if ..., then...*" *decision rules.*

Given the preference-ordered classes of partition $\mathbf{Cl}=\{Cl_t, t\in T\}$, $T=\{1,...,n\}$, of U, the following three types of decision rules can be considered:

1) $D_\geq$-*decision rules* with the following syntax:

   if $f(x,q_1)\geq r_{q1}$ *and* $f(x,q_2)\geq r_{q2}$ *and* ...$f(x,q_p)\geq r_{qp}$, *then* $x\in Cl_t^\geq$,

   where $P=\{q_1,...,q_p\}\subseteq C$, $(r_{q1},...,r_{qp})\in V_{q1}\times V_{q2}\times...\times V_{qp}$ and $t\in T$;

2) $D_\leq$-*decision rules* with the following syntax:

   if $f(x,q_1)\leq r_{q1}$ *and* $f(x,q_2)\leq r_{q2}$ *and* ... $f(x,q_p)\leq r_{qp}$, *then* $x\in Cl_t^\leq$,

   where $P=\{q_1,...,q_p\}\subseteq C$, $(r_{q1},...,r_{qp})\in V_{q1}\times V_{q2}\times...\times V_{qp}$ and $t\in T$;

3) $D_{\geq\leq}$-*decision rules* with the following syntax:

   if $f(x,q_1)\geq r_{q1}$ *and* $f(x,q_2)\geq r_{q2}$ *and* ... $f(x,q_k)\geq r_{qk}$ *and* $f(x,q_{k+1})\leq r_{qk+1}$ *and* ... $f(x,q_p)\leq r_{qp}$, *then* $x\in Cl_s\cup Cl_{s+1}\cup...\cup Cl_t$,

   where $O'=\{q_1,...,q_k\}\subseteq C$, $O''=\{q_{k+1},...,q_p\}\subseteq C$, $P=O'\cup O''$, O' and O'' not necessarily disjoint, $(r_{q1},...,r_{qp})\in V_{q1}\times V_{q2}\times...\times V_{qp}$, s,t$\in T$ such that s<t.

As it is possible that $\{q_1,...,q_k\}\cap\{q_{k+1},...,q_p\}\neq\varnothing$, in the condition part of a $D_{\geq\leq}$-decision rule we can have "$f(x,q)\geq r_q$" and "$f(x,q)\leq r'_q$", where $r_q\leq r'_q$, for some $q\in C$. Moreover, if $r_q=r'_q$, the two conditions boil down to "$f(x,q)=r_q$".

Let us observe that for any $Cl_t^\geq$, t=2,...,n, and $P\subseteq Q$, the definition (5.1) of lower approximation of $Cl_t^\geq$ can be rewritten as

$$\underline{P}(Cl_t^\geq)=\{x\in U_P: \text{ for each } y\in U, \text{ if } y\, D_P^+\, x, \text{ then } y\in Cl_t^\geq\}.$$

Therefore, the statement "*if* $f(x,q_1)\geq r_{q1}$ *and* $f(x,q_2)\geq r_{q2}$ *and* ... $f(x,q_p)\geq r_{qp}$, *then* $x\in Cl_t^\geq$", is accepted as a $D_\geq$-decision rule iff there exists at least one $y\in\underline{P}(Cl_t^\geq)$, $P=\{q_1,...,q_p\}$, such that $f(y,q_1)=r_{q1}$ and $f(y,q_2)=r_{q2}$ and ... $f(y,q_p)=r_{qp}$.

Analogously, for any $Cl_t^\leq$, t=1,...,n-1, and $P\subseteq Q$, the definition (6.1) of lower approximation of $Cl_t^\leq$ can be rewritten as

$$\underline{P}(Cl_t^\leq)=\{x\in U_P: \text{ for each } y\in U, \text{ if } x\, D_P^-\, y, \text{ then } y\in Cl_t^\leq\}.$$

Therefore, the statement "*if* $f(x,q_1) \leq r_{q1}$ *and* $f(x,q_2) \leq r_{q2}$ *and* ... $f(x,q_p) \leq r_{qp}$, *then* $x \in Cl_t^{\leq}$", is accepted as a $D_{\leq}$-decision rule iff there exists at least one $y \in \underline{P}(Cl_t^{\leq})$, $P=\{q_1,...,q_p\}$, such that $f(y,q_1) = r_{q1}$ and $f(y,q_2) = r_{q2}$ and ... $f(y,q_p) = r_{qp}$.

With respect to approximate decision rules, let us observe that

1) for any $Cl_t^{\geq}$, $t=2,...,n$, and $P\subseteq Q$, the definition (5.2) of upper approximation of $Cl_t^{\geq}$ can be rewritten as

$$\overline{P}(Cl_t^{\geq})=\{x \in U_P: \text{for each } y \in U, \text{ if } x \, D_P^- \, y, \text{ then } y \text{ could belong to } Cl_t^{\geq}\},$$

2) for any $Cl_t^{\leq}$, $t=1,...,n-1$, and $P\subseteq Q$, the definition (6.2) of upper approximation of $Cl_t^{\leq}$ can be rewritten as

$$\overline{P}(Cl_t^{\leq})=\{x \in U_P: \text{for each } y \in U, \text{ if } y \, D_P^+ \, x, \text{ then } y \text{ could belong to } Cl_t^{\leq}\}.$$

On the basis of this observation, the statement "*if* $f(x,q_1)\geq r_{q1}$ *and* $f(x,q_2)\geq r_{q2}$ *and* ... $f(x,q_k)\geq r_{qk}$ *and* $f(x,q_{k+1})\leq r_{qk+1}$ *and* ... $f(x,q_p)\leq r_{qp}$, *then* $x \in Cl_s \cup Cl_{s+1} \cup ... \cup Cl_t$", is accepted as a $D_{\geq\leq}$-decision rule iff:

1) $y,z \in \overline{P}(Cl_t^{\geq}) \cap \overline{P}(Cl_s^{\leq})$, $s<t$,

2) $f(y,q_1)=r_{q1}$ and $f(y,q_2)=r_{q2}$ and ... $f(y,q_k)=r_{qk}$ and $f(z,q_{k+1})=r_{qk+1}$ and ... $f(z,q_p)= r_{qp}$,

3) for each $w \in U$, $[f(w,q_1)\geq r_{q1}$ or $f(w,q_1)=*]$ *and* $[f(w,q_2)\geq r_{q2}$ or $f(w,q_2)=*]$ *and* ... $[f(w,q_k)\geq r_{qk}$ or $f(w,q_2)=*]$ *and* $[f(w,q_{k+1})\leq r_{qk+1}$ or $f(w,q_{k+1})=*]$ *and* ... $[f(x,q_p)\leq r_{qp}$ or $f(w,q_{k+1})=*]$ implies $w \in Cl_s \cup Cl_{s+1} \cup ... \cup Cl_t$.

Since each decision rule is an implication, by a *minimal* decision rule we understand such an implication that there is no other implication with an antecedent of at least the same weakness and a consequent of at least the same strength.

We say that an object *supports* a rule if its evaluation by set C of criteria matches the condition part of the rule.

A set of decision rules is *complete* if it fulfils the following conditions:

- each $y \in \underline{C}(Cl_t^{\geq})^*$ supports at least one $D_{\geq}$-decision rule of the type "*if* $f(x,q_1)\geq r_{q1}$ *and* $f(x,q_2)\geq r_{q2}$ *and* ... $f(x,q_p)\geq r_{qp}$, *then* $x \in Cl_r^{\geq}$", with $r,t \in \{2,...,n\}$ and $r \geq t$,

- each $y \in \underline{C}(Cl_t^{\leq})^*$ supports at least one $D_{\leq}$-decision rule of the type "*if* $f(x,q_1)\leq r_{q1}$ *and* $f(x,q_2)\leq r_{q2}$ *and* ... $f(x,q_p)\leq r_{qp}$, *then* $x \in Cl_u^{\leq}$", with $u,t \in \{1,...,n-1\}$ and $u \leq t$,

- each $y \in \overline{C}(Cl_s^{\leq})^* \cap \overline{C}(Cl_t^{\geq})^*$ supports at least one $D_{\geq\leq}$-decision rule of the type "*if* $f(x,q_1)\geq r_{q1}$ *and* $f(x,q_2)\geq r_{q2}$ *and* ... $f(x,q_k)\geq r_{qk}$ *and* $f(x,q_{k+1})\leq r_{qk+1}$ *and* ... $f(x,q_p)\leq r_{qp}$, *then* $x \in Cl_v \cup Cl_{v+1} \cup ... \cup Cl_z$", with $s,t,v,z \in T$ and $v \leq s < t \leq z$.

Let us remark that application of any complete set of decision rules on the objects from the data table results in either exact or approximate reassignment of these objects to the classes Cl_t, $t \in T$. Let us explain this reassignment in more detail.

Given a complete set of rules, and an object $y \in U$, such that $y \notin Bn_C(Cl_s^{\leq})$ and $y \notin Bn_C(Cl_s^{\geq})$ for any $s \in T$, the following situations may occur:

- $y \in Cl_t$, $t=2,\ldots,n-1$; then there exists at least one $D_{\geq}$-decision rule whose consequent is $x \in Cl_t^{\geq}$, and at least one $D_{\leq}$-decision rule whose consequent is $x \in Cl_t^{\leq}$;

- $y \in Cl_1$; then there exists at least one $D_{\leq}$-decision rule whose consequent is $x \in Cl_1^{\leq}$;

- $y \in Cl_n$; then there exists at least one $D_{\geq}$-decision rule whose consequent is $x \in Cl_n^{\geq}$.

In all above situations, intersection of all unions (upward and downward) of classes suggested for assignment in the consequent of rules matching object y will result in (exact) reassignment of y to class Cl_t, $t \in T$.

Similarly, for each object $y \in \overline{C}(Cl_s^{\leq})^* \cap \overline{C}(Cl_t^{\geq})^*$, $s < t$, such that $y \notin \overline{C}(Cl_{s1}^{\leq})^* \cap \overline{C}(Cl_{t1}^{\geq})^*$, $s1 < [\leq]s$ and $t \leq [<]t1$, which means that y belongs exclusively to boundaries $Bn_C^*(Cl_v^{\geq})$, $v=s+1,\ldots,t$, and $Bn_C^*(Cl_z^{\leq})$, $z=s,\ldots,t-1$, there exists at least one $D_{\geq \leq}$-decision rule whose consequent is $x \in Cl_s \cup Cl_{s+1} \cup \ldots \cup Cl_t$. Thus, in result of application of the complete set of rules to object y, it will be reassigned (approximately) to classes $Cl_s \cup Cl_{s+1} \cup \ldots \cup Cl_t$.

We call *minimal* each set of minimal decision rules that is complete and non-redundant, i.e. exclusion of any rule from this set makes it non-complete.

ILLUSTRATIVE EXAMPLE

The illustrative example presented in this section will serve us to explain the concepts introduced in this paper. Let us consider the incomplete data table presented in Table 1, based on another example presented by Kryszkiewicz (1998).

Table 1. Car data table with missing values

Car	Price	Mileage	Size	Max-Speed	Decision
1	High	low	full	low	good
2	Low	*	full	low	poor
3	*	*	compact	low	poor
4	High	*	full	high	good
5	*	*	full	low	good
6	Low	low	compact	*	poor

The table describes set U composed of six cars, using four condition attributes (*price, mileage, size, max-speed*) and one decision attribute (*decision*). The decision attribute makes a dichotomic partition of set U into classes of "poor" (Cl_1) and "good" cars (Cl_2).

Let us consider first this example in the context of multi-attribute classification, where the domains (scales) of condition and decision attributes are not preference-ordered.

The following lower and upper approximations can be calculated from Table 1:

$\underline{I}_C$ (good) = {1}, $\underline{I}_C$ (poor) = $\varnothing$,

$\overline{I}_C$ (good) = {1}, $\overline{I}_C$ (poor) = $\varnothing$.

$\underline{I}_C^*$ (good) = {1,4}, $\underline{I}_C^*$ (poor) = {3,6},

$\overline{I}_C^*$ (good) = {1,2,4,5}, $\overline{I}_C^*$ (poor) = {2,3,5,6}.

The quality of approximation of the partition of U using attributes from C is equal to 0.67. There is only one reduct which is also the core; it is composed of the attributes *price* and *size*.

The following minimal exact rules can be induced from Table 1 (within parentheses there are objects supporting the corresponding decision rule):

1) *if* price is high *and* size is full, *then* car is good   (cars 1,4,5)

2) *if* size is compact, *then* car is poor   (cars 3,6)

It is also possible to induce the following minimal approximate rule from Table 1:

3) *if* price is low *and* size is full, *then* car is good *or* poor   (cars 2,5)

We claim that decision rules induced from an incomplete data table according to our approach are **robust** in the following sense: among objects supporting a given decision rule there is at least one object matching exactly all elementary conditions of the rule. This is due to the fact that each decision rule is induced using the indiscernibility relation I_P and, therefore, the basis of the rule is a referent object having no missing values on attributes from set P.

The robustness of decision rules is a distinctive feature of our approach in comparison with the approach proposed by Kryszkiewicz (1998). Her approach is based on the concept of a possible "completion" of an incomplete data table S=<U,Q,V,f>. The completion is understood as a complete data table S'=<U,Q,V,f'> obtained by substitution of each missing value "*" by some possible value from the domain of the corresponding attribute.

According to Kryszkiewicz's approach, a decision rule "*if* $f(x,q_1) = r_{q1}$ *and* $f(x,q_2)=r_{q2}$ *and* ... $f(x,q_p)=r_{qp}$, *then* x is assigned to Cl_t" is certain (exact) if for any possible completion of data table S the implication expressed by the rule is true. A certain decision rule is called optimal (minimal) if no elementary condition can be eliminated from the condition part of the rule.

Let us observe that some of the decision rules obtained using Kryszkiewicz's approach may not be robust, i.e. certain and founded on a real object present in the data table.

Consider for instance the following optimal and certain decision rule induced with this approach from Table 1:

4) *if* mileage is high *and* max-speed is high, *then* car is good   (car 4)

In Table 1 there is no object having a description matching exactly the condition part of this rule. In other words, there is no object characterized by high mileage and high max-speed. Therefore, rule 4) is not robust.

On the contrary, each of the rules generated using our approach is supported by at least one real object matching exactly the condition part of the corresponding decision rule and, therefore, they are robust. Precisely, rule 1) is founded on cars 1 and 4, rule 2) on cars 3 and 6, and rule 3) on car 2.

Let us consider now the above example in the context of the multi-criteria sorting, where attributes are criteria with preference-ordered scales and the decision classes are also preference-ordered. We shall apply the dominance-based rough set approach to the same Table 1.

As *price, mileage, size* and *max-speed* are criteria, then we have to precise that:

- with respect to *price*, "low" is better than "high",

- with respect to *mileage*, "high" is better than "low",

- with respect to *size*, "full" is better than "compact",

- with respect to *max-speed*, "high" is better than "low".

Moreover, with respect to *decision*, "good" is better than "poor".

Using the approach presented in paragraphs 2.3 and 2.4, we will approximate the downward and the upward unions of classes, i.e. the class of cars "at most poor" ($Cl_1^\leq$) and the class of cars "at least good" ($Cl_2^\geq$). Since only two classes are considered, these unions coincide with the class of "poor" cars (Cl_1) and with the class of "good" cars (Cl_2), respectively.

The C-lower approximations, the C-upper approximations and the C-boundaries of the classes of "good" and "poor" cars are equal, respectively, to:

$\underline{C}$ (good) = $\varnothing$, $\underline{C}$ (poor) = $\varnothing$,

$\overline{C}$ (good) = {1}, $\overline{C}$ (poor) = {1},

$\underline{C}$ (good)* = {4}, $\underline{C}$ (poor)* = {3,6},

$\overline{C}$ (good)* = {1,2,4,5}, $\overline{C}$ (poor)* = {1,2,3,5,6}.

Let us remark that car 1 belongs to C-lower approximation of the class of "good" cars when this approximation is calculated using the indiscernibility relation, however, it belongs to the boundary of "good" cars when this approximation is calculated using the dominance relation. The first remark is true because there is no "poor" car indiscernible with car 1. Observe, however, that car 2 has a comprehensive evaluation worse than car 1 ("poor" vs. "good"), nevertheless car 2 dominates car 1 because the *price* of car 2 is better than the *price* of car 1, the *size* and the *max speed* of the two cars are the same, and with respect to the *mileage* car 2 has a missing value. For this reason, car 1 and car 2 are inconsistent and thus they both belong to the C-boundary of the "good" class constructed using the dominance relation. The inconsistency between car 1 and car 2 cannot be detected using the classical rough set approach based on indiscernibility because these cars are discernible with respect to C.

The quality of sorting using criteria from C is equal to 0.5. There is only one reduct which is also the core; it is composed of the criteria *size* and *max-speed*.

The following minimal set of minimal decision rules can be obtained from the considered data table (within parentheses there are objects supporting the corresponding decision rule):

1) *if* size is (at most) compact, *then* car is (at most) poor   (cars 3,6)

2) *if* size is (at least) full *and* max-speed is (at least) high, *then* car is (at least) good   (car 4)

3) *if* size is (at least) full *and* max-speed is (at most) low, *then* car is poor or good
                                                                   (cars 1,2,5)

In the above example, for the sake of simplicity, we have considered only two preference ordered classes. Of course, a larger number of classes can be encountered in real problems. The number of classes does not affect, however, the way of handling the missing values by the extended rough set approach. For examples of the rough set approach to multi-criteria sorting problems with more than two classes and no missing values see, e.g., (Greco, Matarazzo and Slowinski, 1998a, 1998b, 1999a).

CONCLUSIONS

We adapted the rough sets methodology to the analysis of data sets with missing values. The adaptation concerns both the classical rough set approach based on the use of indiscernibility relations and the new rough set approach based on the use of dominance relations. While the first approach deals with multi-attribute classification problems, the second approach deals with multi-criteria sorting problems. The two adapted rough set approaches maintain all good characteristics of their original approaches. They also boil down to the original approaches when there are no missing values.

The rough sets methodology has several advantages in comparison with up to date methods of data analysis because:

1) it analyses only facts hidden in data without requiring additional information like probability or grade of membership,

2) it deals naturally with categorical attributes without transforming them into binary attributes,

3) it can discover inconsistencies in the data set and take them into account in final conclusions, while other methods have a tendency of eliminating inconsistencies prior to the analysis,

4) it supplies useful elements of knowledge contained in the data set, like reducts and core of attributes,

5) it prepares the ground for induction of decision rules expressing knowledge contained in the data set in a natural language of "*if...*, *then...*" statements.

The extensions proposed in this paper empower the rough sets methodology by enabling analysis of data sets with missing values. The case of missing values is very often met in practice and not many methods can deal satisfactorily with this problem. The way of handling the missing values in our approach seems faithful with respect to available data because the decision rules are robust in the sense of being founded on objects existing in the data set and not on hypothetical objects created by putting some possible values instead of the missing ones.

ACKNOWLEDGEMENT

The research of the first two authors has been supported by the Italian Ministry of University and Scientific Research (MURST). The third author wishes to acknowledge financial support from State Committee for Scientific Research (KBN).

REFERENCES

Greco, S., Matarazzo, B., Slowinski, R.: A new rough set approach to evaluation of bankruptcy risk. In: C.Zopounidis (ed.): *Operational Tools in the Management of Financial Risks*. Kluwer, Dordrecht, 1998a, pp.121-136

Greco, S., Matarazzo, B., Slowinski, R.: A new rough set approach to multicriteria and multiattribute classification. In: L.Polkowski, A.Skowron (eds.): *Rough sets and Current Trends in Computing (RSTCTC'98)*, Lecture Notes in Artificial Intelligence, vol.1424, Springer-Verlag, Berlin, 1998b, pp.60-67

Greco, S., Matarazzo, B., Slowinski, R.: The use of rough sets and fuzzy sets in MCDM. Chapter 14 in: T.Gal, T.Stewart, T.Hanne (eds.), *Advances in Multiple-Criteria Decision Making*, Kluwer Academic Publishers, Boston, 1999a, pp. 14.1-14.59

Greco, S., Matarazzo, B., Slowinski, R., Zanakis, S.: Rough set analysis of information tables with missing values. In: D.K.Despotis and C.Zopounidis (eds.), *Proc. 5th International Conference of the Decision Sciences Institute*, Athens, Greece, 4-7 July 1999b, pp. 1359-1362

Greco, S., Matarazzo, B., Slowinski, R.: Handling missing values in rough set analysis of multi-attribute and multi-criteria decision problems. In: N.Zhong, A.Skowron and S.Ohsuga (eds.), *New Directions in Rough Sets, Data Mining and Granular-Soft Computing Computing (RSFDGrC'99)*, Lecture Notes in Artificial Intelligence, vol.1711, Springer-Verlag, Berlin, 1999c, pp.146-157

Grzymala-Busse, J.W.: LERS - a system for learning from examples based on rough sets. In: R.Slowinski, (ed.) *Intelligent Decision Support. Handbook of Applications and Advances of the Rough Sets Theory*. Kluwer, Dordrecht, 1992, pp. 3-18

Kryszkiewicz, M.: Properties of incomplete information systems in the framework of rough sets. In: L.Polkowski, A.Skowron (eds.): *Rough Sets in Knowledge Discovery*. Vol.1, *Methodology and Applications*. Physica-Verlag, Heidelberg, 1998, pp. 422-450

316

Pawlak, Z.: Rough sets. *International Journal of Information & Computer Sciences* 11 (1982) 341-356

Pawlak, Z.: *Rough Sets. Theoretical Aspects of Reasoning about Data*. Kluwer, Dordrecht, 1991

Pawlak, Z., Slowinski, R.: Rough set approach to multi-attribute decision analysis. *European Journal of Operational Research* 72 (1994) 443-459

Roubens, M., Vincke, Ph.: *Preference Modelling*, Springer-Verlag, Berlin, 1985

Roy, B.: *Méthodologie Multicritère d'Aide à la Décision*. Economica, Paris, 1985

Skowron, A. and Grzymala-Busse, J.W.: From rough set theory to evidence theory. In: R.R.Yager, M.Fedrizzi and J.Kacprzyk (eds.): *Advances in the Dempster-Shafer Theory of Evidence*. John Wiley & Sons, Inc., New York, 1994, pp. 193-236

Slowinski, R. (ed.): *Intelligent Decision Support. Handbook of Applications and Advances of the Rough Sets Theory*. Kluwer Academic Publishers, Dordrecht, 1992

CARDINAL VALUE MEASUREMENT
WITH MACBETH

C. A. Bana e Costa[1], J.-C. Vansnick[2]

[1] Department of Operational Research,
London School of Economics and Political Science
Houghton Street, London WC2A 2AE, United Kingdom
and
Centre of Business Studies,
Instituto Superior Técnico, CEG-IST/SAEG
Av. Rovisco Pais - 1049-001 Lisbon, Portugal

[2] University of Mons-Hainaut, F.W.S.E.
Place du Parc, 20 - 7000 – Mons, Belgium

Abstract: Decision-making is above all a human activity in which value judgments about the attractiveness of options play a key role. The integration of technology and human decisions by means of the design and use of tools for the representation of value judgments that are simultaneously semantically meaningful, practically operational (user-friendly) and theoretically well founded is therefore an important research challenge. The MACBETH approach (Measuring Attractiveness by a Categorical Based Evaluation Technique) overviewed in this paper is a contribution in that direction. MACBETH is an approach designed for building a cardinal scale measuring the attractiveness of options, throughout a learning process supported by a visual interactive software. This is interesting for decision-making when one wants to measure by how much an option is better than another one. Moreover, cardinal preference information is required to meaningfully perform operations with numerical scales, such as comparison of average sums, as required by multi-attribute value theory.

Keywords: Cardinal value measurement, visual interactive decision analysis, multi-attribute modelling.

S.H. Zanakis et al. (eds.), Decision Making: Recent Developments and Worldwide Applications, 317–329.

INTRODUCTION

Decision-making in private and public organizations is above all a human activity in which value judgments of managers and other actors about the desirability or attractiveness of organizational decision opportunities and alternative courses of action play a crucial role. An important research challenge is therefore the integration of technology and human decisions by means of the design and use of decision support techniques and systems in view of answering to the key question: how to represent value judgments? It is also an opportunity to avoid the risk of decision science becoming simply a closed branch of pure mathematics. The existence of a theoretical base is a desirable but not sufficient condition for the legitimization of a decision-aid theory; it must be also subjected to practical validation. On the other hand, neither is visual appealing and user friendly "black-box" software based on theoretically weak technical procedures the right answer to the above question: it is a trap for managers and decision-makers in general. Decision-aiding tools are required to be simultaneously semantically meaningful, practically operational (user friendly) and theoretically well founded. The MACBETH approach presented in this paper is a contribution in that direction.

Assessment of value information is the first step towards the numerical representation of value judgments. A specific questioning procedure designed according to the particular paradigm adopted for preference modeling is used for that purpose. Bana e Costa and Vansnick [8] present several paradigms and questioning procedures that are useful for decision aid.

Let X be a finite set of stimuli, x and y any two elements of X, $\wp$ the property of (partial or overall) attractiveness and J the person who will express judgments about the attractiveness (for her or him) of the elements of X. The *classical paradigm (CP)* in preference modeling can be enunciated as: *Two (and only two) basic preference situations (distinct and exclusive) should be considered for the expression of value judgments: the situation of preference and the situation of indifference.* The *classical questioning procedure (CQP)* associated with *CP* is shown in table 1; J can choose one and only one of the possible answers indicated after each question.

The answers obtained with *CQP* allow the construction of two binary relations on X: a *strict preference relation (P)* defined by xPy if and only if J judged x more attractive than y, and an *indifference relation (I)* defined by xIy if and only if J did not judge any of the two stimuli more attractive than the other one (answer "no" to the first question). When P and I are transitive, the answers of J lead to a ranking of the elements of X (by order of relative attractiveness) and one says that J has given an ordinal information about the attractiveness of the elements of X.

Table 1. Classical Questioning Procedure (CQP)

$\forall x, y \in X:$		
Is one of the stimuli (x or y) more attractive than the other?	YES	NO
If YES, which stimuli (x or y) is more attractive than the other?	x	y

Assessing ordinal preference information is not too difficult but it is not enough in cases in which one needs to state not only that x is more attractive than y, but also by how much – that is, cardinal preference information must be assessed.

We say that J has given a cardinal information about the attractiveness of the elements of X when J has set the elements of X on a vertical axis in such a way that

1st) for all x, y in X, x is above y if and only if, for J, x is more attractive than y

2nd) the relative distances which appear on the axis between the elements of X represent the relative differences of attractiveness between these elements as J perceives them.

Cardinal preference information allows the construction of an interval scale[1] on X quantifying the attractiveness (for J) of the elements of X and it is required in order that mathematical operations other than the "min" and the "max" might be meaningfully performed. Unfortunately, the direct expression of cardinal value judgments is far from being an easy task because most people have not such a so rich information in mind. Therefore, we think that *direct scoring* of stimuli leads to unreliable and semantically meaningless information. Moreover, our experience as facilitators and analysts has shown us that these drawbacks are also difficult to avoid using assessment procedures based on (graphical) direct rating [11]. However, our basic conviction is that, by means of an adequate interactive process based on verbal judgments about differences of attractiveness between stimuli, it is possible to aid a person to progressively evolve from ordinal to cardinal preference information in view of constructing a *requisite* (in the sense of Phillips [15]) cardinal value model. The MACBETH software is a visual interactive system created to facilitate this process.

The basic ideas in MACBETH (Measuring Attractiveness by a Categorical Based Evaluation Technique) are:

✓ to adopt a straightforward questioning procedure (section 2) involving only two elements of X in each question and leading to a verbal (qualitative) judgmental answer; but to ask a significant number of such questions in order to make possible the testing of their compatibility (section 3) with the construction of a cardinal scale on X in a subsequent phase;

✓ in case of incompatibility (section 4), to search for its sources in order to stimulate J's reflection about her or his initial judgments and eventually revise some of them;

✓ in case of compatibility, to determine a first numerical scale on X (the MACBETH *scale*) representing J's verbal judgments, based on a simple principle (section 5);

✓ to facilitate J's perception of this first numerical scale, the reflection on it, and the evolution towards its progressive transformation into a cardinal scale, with the support of a visual interactive software (section 6).

This paper overviews and updates the key methodological and technical concepts and features developed to implement the MACBETH basic ideas in earlier papers ([4] to [8]).

---

[1] Scale unique upon a positive linear transformation:
$\phi(x) = \alpha.x + \beta$, α, $\beta \in R$ with $\alpha > 0$.

THE MACBETH QUESTIONING PROCEDURE

The *MACBETH questioning procedure (MQP)*, shown in table 2, starts with asking J for a *comparative* judgment between x and y, followed, in case of differentiation, by an *absolute* verbal judgment about the difference of attractiveness between them choosing one of six *semantic categories* (C_1 to C_6) from VERY WEAK to EXTREME. When x is judged more attractive than y (xPy), (x, y) is said to belong to the semantic category C_j, $j = 1, ..., 6 - (x, y) \in C_j$ – corresponding to J's perception of the difference of attractiveness between x and y, as shown in table 3. As a result of this interaction, J's verbal judgments can be presented by the analyst in a matrix format, as exemplified in figure 1 for a set of stimuli $X = \{x_1, x_2, x_3, x_4, x_5\}$ (when $x = y$ or x and y are judged indifferent, NO is inserted at the intersection of the row x and the column y, and vice-versa, and the pairs (x, y) and (y, x) are said to belong to category C_0).

Table 2. MACBETH Questioning Procedure (MQP)

$\forall x, y \in X :$

Is one of the stimuli (x or y) more attractive than the other? | YES | NO |

If YES, which stimuli (x or y) is more attractive than the other? | x | y |

For x and y such that x is more attractive than y, the difference of attractiveness between x and y is

| VERY WEAK | WEAK | MODERATE | STRONG | VERY STRONG | EXTREME |

Table 3. MACBETH semantic categories of difference of attractiveness (dif. att.)

$\forall x, y \in X$ such that x is more attractive than y :

$\quad (x, y) \in C_1$ if J judges the dif. att. between x and y as *very weak*

$\quad (x, y) \in C_2$ if J judges the dif. att. between x and y as *weak*

$\quad (x, y) \in C_3$ if J judges the dif. att. between x and y as *moderate*

$\quad (x, y) \in C_4$ if J judges the dif. att. between x and y as *strong*

$\quad (x, y) \in C_5$ if J judges the dif. att. between x and y as *very strong*

$\quad (x, y) \in C_6$ if J judges the dif. att. between x and y as *extreme*

	x_1	x_2	x_3	x_4	x_5
x_1	NO		STRONG		VERY WEAK
x_2	VERY WEAK	NO	VERY STRONG	NO	MODERATE
x_3			NO		
x_4	VERY WEAK	NO	VERY STRONG	NO	MODERATE
x_5			WEAK		NO

Figure 1. MACBETH matrix of verbal judgments of difference of attractiveness

THE CASE OF "COMPATIBILITY"

We say that J's judgments are *compatible* with the construction of a cardinal scale on X if they enable the derivation, without change but eventual tuning, of cardinal information about the attractiveness of the elements of X. The MACBETH matrix of judgments is then said to be <u>*consistent*</u>. Such a situation exists if and only if it is possible to associate a real number $n(x)$ to each element x of X satisfying the two following measurement conditions:

<u>Condition 1</u> (*ordinal condition*): For all x, y of X: $n(x) > n(y)$ if and only if J judged x more attractive than y. Mathematically:

$$\forall x, y \in X : n(x) > n(y) \Leftrightarrow xPy.$$

<u>Condition 2</u> (*semantic condition*): For all x, y, w and z of X such that J judged x more attractive than y and w more attractive than z: *if* it results from the judgments of J that the difference of attractiveness between x and y is greater than the difference of attractiveness between w and z, *then* $n(x) - n(y) > n(w) - n(z)$. Mathematically:

$$\forall k, k' \in \{1, 2, 3, 4, 5, 6\}, \forall x, y, w, z \in X \text{ with } (x, y) \in C_k \text{ and } (w, z) \in C_{k'}:$$
$$k \geq k' + 1 \Rightarrow n(x) - n(y) > n(w) - n(z).$$

Note that "then" ($\Rightarrow$) appears in Condition 2 instead of "if and only if" ($\Leftrightarrow$) because when (x, y) and (w, z) belong to the same category nothing can be deduced about the comparison of their differences of attractiveness.

THE CASE OF "INCOMPATIBILITY"

We say that J's judgments are *incompatible* with the construction of a cardinal scale on X if they do not enable the derivation, without changing at least one judgment before eventual tuning, of cardinal information about the attractiveness of the elements of X. The MACBETH approach distinguishes three types of incompatibility:

First type of incompatibility

J's judgments are such that it is not possible to associate a real number $n(x)$ to each element x of X satisfying the *ordinal condition* (Condition 1). That is, J's judgments do not allow to rank the elements of X by order of relative attractiveness.

Two examples of cases generating this type of incompatibility are:

♦ Example 1: J judged simultaneously x and y indifferent, y and z indifferent, and x more attractive than z *(I is not transitive)* – see figure 2(a);

♦ Example 2 : J judged simultaneously x more attractive than y, y more attractive than z, and z more attractive than x *(P is not transitive)* – see figure 2(b).

Second type of incompatibility

J's judgments are such that it is possible to associate a real number $n(x)$ to each element x of X satisfying the *ordinal condition,* but it is impossible to simultaneously satisfy the *ordinal* and *semantic conditions* (Conditions 1 and 2) due to at least one case of conflict between comparative and semantic judgments. Such case can happen for instance when J simultaneously judged that x is more attractive than y – implying $n(x) > n(y)$ by Condition 1 – and that, x and y being more attractive than z, the difference of attractiveness between y and z is greater than the difference of attractiveness between x and z – implying $n(y) - n(z) > n(x) - n(z)$ by Condition 2 - see figure 2(c).

322

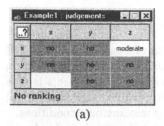

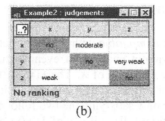

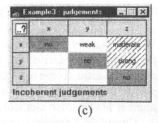

| (a) | (b) | (c) |

Figure 2. Examples of first and second type of incompatibility

Third type of incompatibility

J's judgments are such that it is possible to associate a real number $n(x)$ to each element x of X satisfying the *ordinal condition*, but it is impossible to satisfy simultaneously the *ordinal* and *semantic conditions* (Conditions 1 and 2) due to at least one case of conflict between semantic judgments (although no conflict exists between comparative and semantic judgments). The MACBETH matrix is then *semantically inconsistent*. A simple example is the judgmental situation of figure 3 involving four elements x, y, w and z of X: the semantic condition cannot be verified because one should have $n(x) - n(w) > n(y) - n(z)$ and $n(w) - n(z) > n(x) - n(y)$, which is impossible; indeed, summing up these two inequalities leads to $n(x) - n(z) > n(x) - n(z)$.

MACBETH distinguishes four *levels of semantic inconsistency*, each one linked with a specific *weakening of the semantic condition* (Condition 2):

First level – *J*'s judgments are such that it is possible to associate a real number $n(x)$ to each element x of X satisfying simultaneously the ordinal condition and the following weakening of the semantic condition:

$$\forall k, k' \in \{1, 2, 3, 4, 5, 6\}, \forall x, y, w, z \in X \text{ with } (x, y) \in C_k \text{ and } (w, z) \in C_{k'},$$
$$k = k' + 1 \Rightarrow n(x) - n(y) \geq n(w) - n(z)$$
$$\text{and}$$
$$k \geq k' + 2 \Rightarrow n(x) - n(y) > n(w) - n(z).$$

Second level – *J*'s judgments are such that it is possible to associate a real number $n(x)$ to each element x of X satisfying simultaneously the ordinal condition and the following weakening of the semantic condition:

$$\forall k, k' \in \{1, 2, 3, 4, 5, 6\}, \forall x, y, w, z \in X \text{ with } (x, y) \in C_k \text{ and } (w, z) \in C_{k'},$$
$$k \geq k' + 2 \Rightarrow n(x) - n(y) > n(w) - n(z).$$

	x	y	w	z
x	no	very weak	strong	v. strong
y		no	weak	moderate
w			no	weak
z				no

Semantic inconsistency (level 1)

Figure 3. Semantically inconsistent MACBETH matrix of judgments

Third level – J's judgments are such that it is possible to associate a real number $n(x)$ to each element x of X satisfying simultaneously the ordinal condition and the following weakening of the semantic condition:

$$\forall k, k' \in \{1, 2, 3, 4, 5, 6\}, \; \forall x, y, w, z \in X \text{ with } (x, y) \in C_k \text{ and } (w, z) \in C_{k'},$$
$$k = k' + 2 \Rightarrow n(x) - n(y) \geq n(w) - n(z).$$
$$\text{and}$$
$$k \geq k' + 3 \Rightarrow n(x) - n(y) > n(w) - n(z).$$

Fourth level – J's judgments are such that it is possible to associate a real number $n(x)$ to each element x of X satisfying simultaneously the ordinal condition and the following weakening of the semantic condition:

$$\forall k, k' \in \{1, 2, 3, 4, 5, 6\}, \; \forall x, y, w, z \in X \text{ with } (x, y) \in C_k \text{ and } (w, z) \in C_{k'},$$
$$k \geq k' + 3 \Rightarrow n(x) - n(y) > n(w) - n(z).$$

When the judgments of J are incompatible with the construction of a cardinal scale, the MACBETH software identifies the type of incompatibility and suggests how to bypass it (for more details see [8]). Figure 4 is a snapshot of a screen of the MACBETH software, showing the suggestions given by MACBETH in face of the semantically inconsistent matrix of judgments of figure 3. As can be seen, there exist four ways of bypassing the incompatibility problem: to move (x, y) or (y, z) one category "up", or to move (x, w) or (w, z) one category "down". Based on those suggestions, the analyst can launch an interactive learning discussion with the aim of helping J to reflect more deeply about her or his initial judgments and progressively revise them until compatibility is reached.

THE MACBETH SCALE

When the judgments of J are *consistent*, i.e. compatible with the construction of a cardinal scale, it is possible to associate a real number $n(x)$ to each element x of X satisfying the ordinal and semantic conditions (Conditions 1 and 2). In this situation, there exists an infinite number of scales $n: X \rightarrow R$ verifying these conditions. For example, for the matrix of judgments in figure 5, it is easy to verify directly that each of the scales $n^{(1)}$, $n^{(2)}$ and $n^{(3)}$ in table 4 satisfies the ordinal condition and table 5 shows that the semantic condition is satisfied.

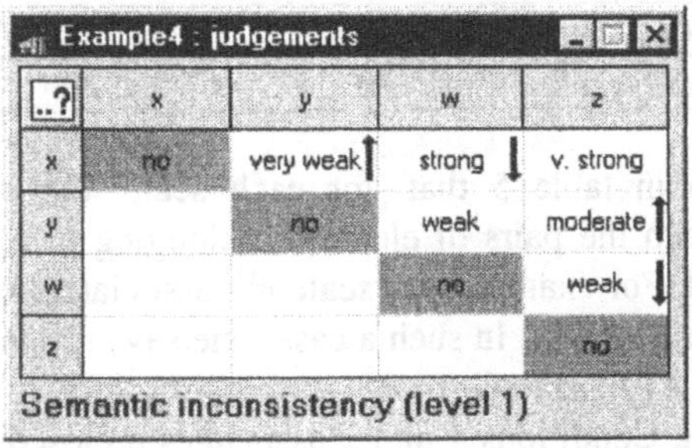

Figure 4. MACBETH suggestions to bypass incompatibility

	x_1	x_2	x_3	x_4	x_5
x_1	NO	MODERATE	VERY STRONG		WEAK
x_2		NO	MODERATE		
x_3			NO		
x_4	VERY WEAK	STRONG	EXTREME	NO	STRONG
x_5		VERY WEAK	STRONG		NO

Figure 5. Consistent MACBETH matrix of judgments

Table 4. Examples of scales verifying conditions 1 and 2 for the judgments in figure 5

	Scale $n^{(1)}$	Scale $n^{(2)}$	Scale $n^{(3)}$
x_4	25	20	25
x_1	20	18	19
x_5	14	10	10
x_2	12	9	7
x_3	5	0	-5

Table 5. Auxiliary table to verify Condition 2

MACBETH Semantic categories	Pairs of elements (x, y) of X	Numerical differences $n^{(1)}(x)-n^{(1)}(y)$	Numerical differences $n^{(2)}(x)-n^{(2)}(y)$	Numerical differences $n^{(3)}(x)-n^{(3)}(y)$
NO (C_0)	(x_1, x_1)	0	0	0
	(x_2, x_2)	0	0	0
	(x_3, x_3)	0	0	0
	(x_4, x_4)	0	0	0
	(x_5, x_5)	0	0	0
VERY WEAK (C_1)	(x_4, x_1)	5	2	6
	(x_5, x_2)	2	1	3
WEAK (C_2)	(x_1, x_5)	6	8	9
MODERATE (C_3)	(x_1, x_2)	8	9	12
	(x_2, x_3)	7	9	12
STRONG (C_4)	(x_4, x_2)	13	11	18
	(x_4, x_5)	11	10	15
	(x_5, x_3)	9	10	15
VERY STRONG (C_5)	(x_1, x_3)	15	18	24
EXTREME (C_6)	(x_4, x_3)	20	20	30

It can also be seen in table 5 that, for each scale, the corresponding numerical differences associated with the pairs of elements belonging to a same semantic category are not necessarily equal. For example, the scale $n^{(1)}$ associates the values 13, 11 and 9 to the pairs belonging to category C_4. In such a case, one says in MACBETH that the scale $n^{(1)}$ associates the interval $I_4 = [9,13]$ to C_4.

Every scale satisfying Conditions 1 and 2 associates a closed numerical interval I_j to each semantic category C_j that J has used (see figure 6).

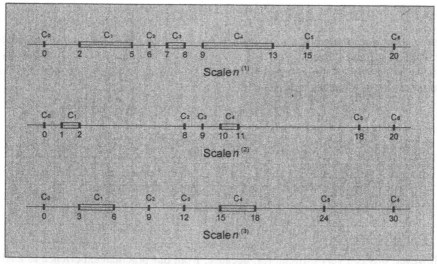

Figure 6. Intervals associated to categories for scales $n^{(1)}$, $n^{(2)}$ and $n^{(3)}$

Obviously, I_0 is always reduced to a point given Condition 1 and the precise definition of category C_0. However, the length of other intervals can be strictly positive. This is natural because of the qualitative nature of the terms VERY WEAK, WEAK, MODERATE, STRONG, VERY STRONG and EXTREME used in MACBETH to characterize the semantic categories C_1 to C_6.

Among all the scales satisfying the ordinal and semantic conditions, the first numerical scale proposed by MACBETH is obtained by linear programming and minimizes, when one takes as unity of measurement the minimal distance between intervals representing consecutive categories, the following objective function:

$D \equiv$ *[the average length of the intervals I_j] + [the average distance between intervals representing consecutive categories].*

This objective function is adopted for we consider that it is interesting:

1) to minimize the length of the intervals I_j that numerically represent the semantic categories C_j $(j = 1, ..., 6)$;
2) if possible, to equal the distances between intervals representing consecutive categories, by minimizing the average distance between intervals representing consecutive categories (taking into account that the unity is the minimal distance between intervals representing consecutive categories).

It is easy to verify from figure 6 that D equals 20/6 for the scales $n^{(1)}$ and $n^{(2)}$ and 10/6 for $n^{(3)}$, and it can be proved that *min* $D = 10/6$. Consequently, $n^{(3)}$ or any scale obtained from $n^{(3)}$ by a positive linear transformation $\alpha.n^{(3)} + \beta$ $(\alpha > 0)$ satisfy the ordinal and semantic conditions and minimizes D. Among them, the *MACBETH scale* is the particular scale such that the value of the least attractive element of X is equal to 0 and the minimal distance between intervals representing consecutive categories is 1. For the judgments in figure 5, the MACBETH scale is

$$n(x_4) = 10 \quad n(x_1) = 8 \quad n(x_5) = 5 \quad n(x_2) = 4 \quad n(x_3) = 0.$$

FROM THE MACBETH SCALE TO A CARDINAL SCALE

The preference information assessed from J by the MACBETH questioning procedure is richer than an ordinal information but is not a cardinal information and consequently the MACBETH scale is not an interval scale. As in all procedures for cardinal value measurement, one still needs to verify with J if:

$$\forall \ x, y, \ w, z \in X, \text{ with } n(x) > n(y) \text{ and } n(w) > n(z)$$

$$\frac{n(x) - n(y)}{n(w) - n(z)} = k \quad (k > 0)$$

$$\Leftrightarrow$$

the difference of attractiveness (for J) between x and y

is k times

the difference of attractiveness (for J) between w and z.

However, this is a very difficult test because, from our practical experience as analysts, it conflicts with the qualitative way how people usually reason.

MACBETH offers a path to attain the cardinal domain based on the visual support of the graphic display appearing in the main screen of the software (see example in figure 7).

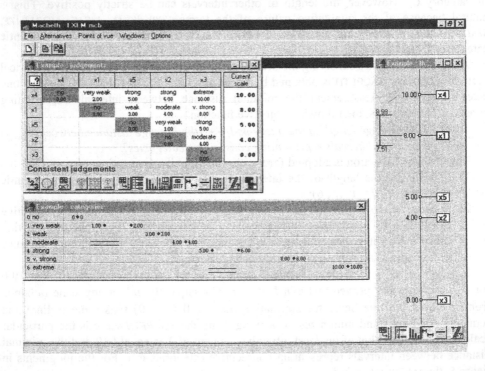

Figure 7. The MACBETH scale and its graphic display

J is confronted with the vertical axis appearing on the screen (see the right window in figure 7) and asked to appreciate the distances between the points representing the elements of *X*. *J* is then asked if she or he considers that the relative distances between these points adequately represent the relative differences of attractiveness that she or he perceives between the elements of *X*. When this is not the case, *J* can easily change these distances by dragging a point using the mouse. Moreover, once a point is selected, it appears bounded by two lines (see the right window in figure 7) defining the range within which *J* can freely move it without violating the ordinal and semantic conditions.

The path to cardinality used in MACBETH is appealing because the visual comparison of intervals is less abstract (and consequently less difficult for *J*) than to confirm the numerical value *k* of a ratio of differences.

A FEW OTHER FEATURES OF THE MACBETH SOFTWARE

The MACBETH software offers many practical and user-friendly features to facilitate the interaction with *J*. Three examples are:

- MACBETH can propose a numerical scale even in case of incompatibility. Of course, such a scale does not verify Conditions 1 and 2 simultaneously, but it always respects the ordinal condition and the weakest possible weakening of the semantic condition (see [8] for details).
- MACBETH offers the possibility of explicitly taking into account situations of hesitation in expressing semantic judgments. As exemplified in figure 8, when *J* is asked about the difference of attractiveness between two stimuli, *J* can answer with several consecutive categories. This is also useful for group cardinal preference modelling (see an application in [1]).

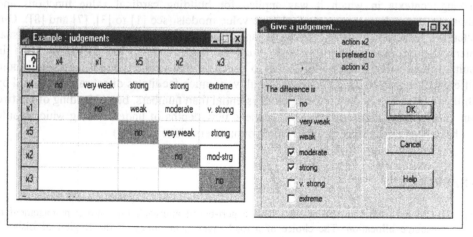

Figure 8. Dealing with judgmental hesitation

- The "large" number of judgements required (N.(N-1)/2, for a set of N stimuli) can be seen as "one of the drawbacks of pairwise comparison methods" [11]. Even though we do not share this criticism in general – indeed, judgmental redundancy is an important learning device – it is worthwhile to note that the MACBETH software also operates with incomplete matrixes of judgements (theoretically, the minimal number of judgments required to propose a numerical scale are the N-1 comparisons between consecutive rank-ordered stimuli). This feature is useful in situations of scarce time available for interactive questioning, but it should be noted that it reduces of course the reliability of testing judgmental compatibility with the construction of a cardinal scale.

CONCLUSION

Although based on sound underlying theory (see, for example, [13] and [16]) traditional approaches for cardinal value measurement require the decision-maker to answer very difficult judgmental questions and do not really offer any practical way for the verification of the reliability of the obtained preference information. The challenge to overcoming these weaknesses by developing a new constructive approach, at the same time theoretically well founded and practically operational, was the main motivation to the research that led to MACBETH:

✓   MACBETH involves only two stimuli in each question;
✓   MACBETH tests the consistency of the answers;
✓   MACBETH offers suggestions to bypass inconsistent situations;
✓   MACBETH provides the analyst with the means adequate for aiding the decision-maker to enter into the domain of cardinal measurement.

The MACBETH[2] software has proved to be useful in many public and private decision-making contexts in which it was applied for building cardinal value functions and assessing the scaling constants of additive value models (see [1] to [3], [7] and [8]). Our extensive experience using MACBETH and other powerful and user friendly visual interactive decision support systems (such as V.I.S.A. [12] and HIVIEW [10]) in multiattribute value frameworks, led as to conclude that explicit verbal jugdments about differences of attractiveness between stimuli very much facilitates direct rating. As said by Phillips [14]: "Words are essential, more essential than numbers, but a blending of the two can enable individuals and groups to achieve new depths of understanding which would not have been possible using either words or numbers alone." (p. 89)

REFERENCES

[1]   Bana e Costa, C.A. (to appear), "An expert-based approach for conflict management in resource allocation: The choice of a road investment policy in the Region of Lisbon", *Journal of Multi-Criteria Decision Analysis.*

---

[2]   A trial version can be download from: www.umh.ac.be/vansnick/macbeth.html.

[2]   Bana e Costa, C.A., Ensslin, L., Corrêa, E.C., Vansnick, J.C. (1999), "Decision Support Systems in action: integrated application in a multicriteria decision aid process", *European Journal of Operational Research*, 113, 2 (315 - 335).

[3]   Bana e Costa, C.A., Nunes da Silva, F., Vansnick, J.C. (to appear), "Conflict dissolution in the public sector: A case-study", *European Journal of Operational Research*.

[4]   Bana e Costa, C.A., Vansnick, J.C. (1994), "MACBETH – An interactive path towards the construction of cardinal value functions", *International Transactions in Operations Research*, 1, 4 (489 - 500).

[5]   Bana e Costa, C.A., Vansnick, J.C. (1995), "General overview of the MACBETH approach", in Pardalos, P.M., Siskos, Y., Zopounidis, C. (Eds.), *Advances in Multicriteria Analysis*, Kluwer Academic Publishers, Dordrecht (93 - 100).

[6]   Bana e Costa, C.A., Vansnick, J.C. (1997), "A theoretical framework for Measuring Attractiveness by a Categorical Based Evaluation Technique (MACBETH)", in Clímaco, J. (Ed.), *Multicriteria Analysis*, Springer Verlag, Berlin, 1995 (15 - 24).

[7]   Bana e Costa, C.A., Vansnick, J.C. (1997), "Applications of the MACBETH approach in the framework of an additive aggregation model", *Journal of Multi-Criteria Decision Analysis*, 6, 2 (107 - 114).

[8]   Bana e Costa, C.A., Vansnick, J.C. (1999), "The MACBETH approach: Basic ideas, software and an application", in Meskens. N., Roubens, M. (Eds.), *Advances in Decision Analysis*, Kluwer Academic Publishers, Dordrecht, (131 - 157).

[9]   Bana e Costa, C.A., Vansnick, J.C. (1999), "Preference relations and MCDM", in Gal, T., Stewart, T., Hanne, T. (Eds.), *Multicriteria Decision Making: Advances in MCDM Models, Algorithms, Theory and Applications*, Kluwer Academic Publishers, Norwell Mass. (4–1 - 4–23).

[10]   Barclay, S. (1987), *A User's Manual of HIVIEW*, Decision Analysis Unit, London School of Economics, London.

[11]   Belton, V. (1999), "Multi-Criteria Problem Structuring and Analysis in a Value Theory Framework", in Gal, T., Stewart, T., Hanne, T. (Eds.), *Multicriteria Decision Making: Advances in MCDM Models, Algorithms, Theory and Applications*, Kluwer Academic Publishers, Norwell Mass. (12–1 - 12–32).

[12]   Belton, V., Vickers, S.P. Vickers (1989), "V.I.S.A – VIM for MCDA", in Locket, A.G., Islei, G. (Eds.), *Improving Decision Making in Organizations*, Springer-Verlag, Heidelberg (287 - 304).

[13]   Keeney, R.L., Raiffa, H. (1976), *Decisions with Multiple Objectives: Preferences and Value-Tradeoffs*, Wiley, New York.

[14]   Phillips, L.D. (1989), "Decision Analysis in the 1990s", in Shahani, A., Stainton, R. (Eds.), *Tutorial Papers in Operational Research*, The Operational Research Society, Birmingham (73 - 90).

[15]   Phillips, L.D. (1984), "A theory of requisite decision models", *Acta Psychologica*, 56 (29 - 48).

[16]   Von Wintelfeldt, D., Edwards, W. (1986), *Decision Analysis and Behavioral Research*, Cambridge University Press, New York.

INFERRING A MULTICRITERIA PREFERENCE MODEL FOR RURAL DEVELOPMENT PROJECTS EVALUATION

E. Krassadaki, Y. Siskos
Technical University of Crete, DSS Laboratory,
73100 Chania, Greece

Abstract: The evaluation of proposals financed either from EU or National Funds is a complicated job for decision makers, which is usually based on qualitative and quantitative criteria. The aim of this paper is the structuring of a specific EU evaluation procedure by building a multi-criteria value system which is as consistent as possible with the judgmental policy of a European evaluator (preference disaggregation principle). The EU Initiative Leader II for Rural Development was used for this purpose. With the use of extrapolation techniques a final ranking of contributed projects can be achieved. The proposed methodology is illustrated by a real-world data set from Leader II Program consisting of four evaluation criteria (strategy, goal, reliability and quality) each of them being analysed by qualitative sub-criteria in order to evaluate the proposals. The UTASTAR disaggregation method assessed a marginal value function and the weight for every sub-criterion of this evaluation system.

Key words: Aggregation-disaggregation approach, multicriteria analysis, preference modeling, UTASTAR method, project evaluation

INTRODUCTION

The evaluation of EU programs, which is a recent issue at European level, requires the introduction of an appropriate methodology and the development of necessary decision-making tools. The process of EU Programs evaluation becomes more complicated due to the complexity of structures, the cultural and linguistic diversities, the need to obtain quick results, the major budgetary constraints etc.

Project evaluation is a problem of major managerial and academic interest which could be approached with several methodological tools (Worthen et al., 1996, Rossi et al., 1993, Posavac et al., 1996, Wholey et al., 1994). Zanakis et al. (1995) present an overview of

S.H. Zanakis et al. (eds.), Decision Making: Recent Developments and Worldwide Applications, 331–345.

methodologies already applied. Many of them point out the multicriteria character of the problem, where the alternative proposals are evaluated with multiple evaluation criteria in order to be ranked globally by means of an appropriate aggregation procedure. For details see Roy (1985), Roy and Bouyssou (1993), Goicoechea et al. (1982), Keeney (1992), Bana e Costa and Vansnick (1997), Pardalos et al. (1995), Gal et al. (1999).

Generally, a decision problem involves the examination of a set of potential alternatives over a set of criteria in order to reach a decision. The decision problems can be categorised in four problematics according to the objective of the decision: (i) selection of the most appropriate-best alternative, (ii) segmentation of the alternatives in predefined homogenous classes, (iii) ranking of the alternatives from the best to the worst, and (iv) description of the alternatives. Usually, the evaluation of submitted development or research proposals belong to the third of these problematics. Multicriteria decision aid (MCDA) methods constitute a significant and effective tool for decision support in ranking problems.

The basic goal of the paper is the structuring of a specific EU evaluation procedure by building a multicriteria value system which is as consistent as possible with the judgmental policy of a European evaluator (preference disaggregation principle). The EU Initiative Leader II for rural development framework was used for this purpose. The role of the decision maker was played by a Greek evaluator who was strongly involved in the evaluation procedure of the Leader II Program.

Using MCDA methods, the decision maker's (project evaluator, analyst etc.) preferences are incorporated in the decision analysis process through his/her cooperation. Hence, the obtained results represent in a consistent way the preferences and policy of the decision maker. To operationalise the experience, the UTA (UTilité Additive) method (Jacquet-Lagrèze and Siskos, 1982) and more specifically its improved version UTASTAR (Siskos and Yannacopoulos, 1985) as a preference disaggregation approach is proposed as the assessment tool of the evaluation model. For more applications on UTA methods see Baourakis, Matsatsinis and Siskos (1996) and Siskos and Assimakopoulos (1989).

The paper is organised as follows: Section 2 states briefly the problem dealing with the Leader's II evaluation procedure and provides with some definitions about the proposed preference model. Then, section 3 outlines the Leader's II evaluation system and section 4 presents the disaggregation approach applied. Finally, some concluding remarks were added in section 5.

PROBLEM STATEMENT AND NOTATION

MCDA is the theoretical background of the proposed model and especially Preference Aggregation-Disaggregation analysis. The last one is based on the principle that criteria aggregation leads to a decision while disaggregation of a decision points to the criteria involved in that decision. Leader II Initiative has been used in order to illustrate the implementation of the presented methodology. In this particular case the decision maker (project evaluator) wants to get acquainted with the evaluation sub-criteria and their relative importance and finally to proceed to the global evaluation process.

The National Committee of Leader II Initiative has announced the criteria, the sub-criteria and the criteria weights and therefore they are well known to the project evaluator. So the UTASTAR method focuses on the inference of sub-criteria weights and their marginal values for each criterion. This methodology points to the assessment of the value or utility of each proposal on each criterion and thus to the global evaluation of each proposal.

Let $A=\{a,b,c,\ldots\}$ be the set of proposals, which is evaluated on a consistent family of criteria and sub-criteria. For each criterion k is defined a consistent family of sub-criteria G_k, which fulfils the conditions of monotony, exhaustivity and non-redundancy (Roy, 1985). The sub-criteria are of ascending order and discrete type and they are defined by a real-valued function:

$g_{ik}: A \rightarrow R \,/\, \alpha \rightarrow g_{ik}(\alpha)$, where $g_{ik}(a)$ expresses the evaluation of proposal a on the i-th sub-criterion (k criterion). The preference conditions can be explicited as following:

$g_{ik}(\alpha) > g_{ik}(b) \Leftrightarrow \alpha$ proposal is preferred than b
$g_{ik}(\alpha) = g_{ik}(b) \Leftrightarrow \alpha$ proposal is indifferent to b

Then the proposed model has the following form:

$$\left.\begin{array}{l} U_{global} = \sum_{k=1}^{m} w_k U_k \\[3mm] \sum w_k = 1 \quad \text{and} \quad w_k \geq 0 \ \forall \ k \end{array}\right\} \quad (1)$$

where m is the number of criteria, w_k is the known weight of the k-th criterion and U_k is the global value on the k-th criterion, normalised between [0,1]. The assessment of the global value for each proposal for a particular criterion k is as follows:

$$\left.\begin{array}{l} U_k = \sum_{i=1}^{n_k} p_{ik} u_{ik}[g_{ik}(a)] \\[3mm] u_{ik}(g_{ik_*}) = 0 \\[2mm] u_{ik}(g_{ik}^{*}) = 1 \\[2mm] \sum_{i=1}^{n_k} p_{ik} = 1 \\[3mm] p_{ik} \geq 0 \end{array}\right\} \quad (2)$$

where:

n_k	: number of sub-criteria for k-th criterion.
p_{ik}	: the weight of the i-th sub-criterion of the k-th criterion.
$g_{ik}(\alpha)$	: evaluation of proposal α on i-th sub-criterion of the k-th criterion.

$u_{ik}[g_{ik}(\alpha)]$: normalised marginal value of proposal α on i-th sub-criterion (k criterion).

g_{ik*} : less preferred value on i-th sub-criterion of the k-th criterion.

g_{ik}^{*} : most preferred value on i-th sub-criterion of the k-th criterion.

Naturally, an additive value function as preference model is subject to some behavioural conditions, i.e. the mutual preferential independence between the criteria (Keeney, 1992). However this hypothesis is less restrictive in a disaggregation procedure because the aim of this procedure is to infer the preference model from behavioural data rather than supposing its existence a priori. Consequently, the quality of the model's assessment is judged here by the fitting index obtained by the inference procedure (see also Bana e Costa and Vansnick, 1997, for the case of MACBETH method).

THE LEADER II EVALUATION SYSTEM

Leader II is an Initiative that aims to encourage the undertaking of innovative actions by local agents, private individuals and organisations of local administration towards several directions, to help the diffusion of experiences and to contribute as much as possible to the integrated local development. The European Initiative Leader II offers the possibility to implement approaches of integrated development at a local level, often with an innovative character and aiming at the development of the rural area without necessarily rural activities. An action that is financed by Leader II is Rural Tourism, which aims at:

1. The development of an activity, complementary to the rural activities, that exploits existing possibilities and resources and provides a supplementary income to the rural population.
2. The upgrading of the quality and enrichment-differentiation of the total tourist product of the area.
3. The prolongation of the tourist period.
4. The enhancement and protection of the environment, natural and human, as a tourist resource.

Indicative activities that fall into the above framework are the creation of rural tourist lodgings and the investments for the exploitation and enhancement of Rural Tourism through the creation of kiosks, camps, restaurant and supplementary tourist facilities.

Leader II National Committee, which administrates all running regional projects, has established and circulated an evaluation table at regional level in order to help the project evaluators and enforce transparency. That table includes the criteria and their weights and sub-criteria for the evaluation process. Regional evaluators have to follow the proposed evaluation framework in order to rank proposals from best to worst.

The National Committee of Leader II Initiative has established a set of four predetermined qualitative criteria and a set of qualitative sub-criteria for each criterion (Development Organisation of Western Crete, 1997). The proposed budget for each proposal does not constitute a criterion since almost all projects are close to the upper limit. Thus, for strategy and goal criteria there are five sub-criteria respectively, for reliability criterion there are four sub-criteria and finally for quality criterion there are two sub-criteria. The hierarchical structure of criteria and their weights appear in Figure 1. Although the evaluation criteria and sub-criteria are known, there is still no analytical model allowing an automatic diagnosis for each proposal.

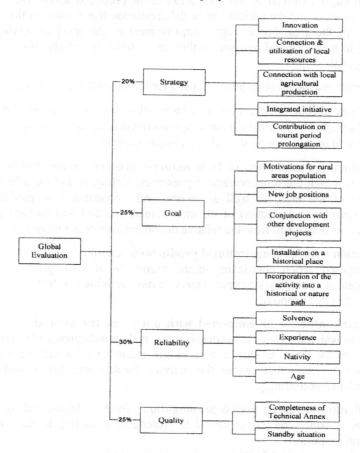

Figure 1. Hierarchical structure of criteria

An analytical presentation of the criteria and their sub-criteria is presented below, as they were described and defined by the National Committee for the Supervision of the Project, and they constitute by force the evaluation framework for the local evaluators of the submitted proposals. The tertiary qualitative scale by sub-criterion is also presented (the numerical scale from 1 to 3 does not operate through the model; its existence serves to indicate the preferential order of the scale: 3 preferred to 2 preferred to 1).

Strategy Criterion: This criterion measures how much a proposed project leads toward the satisfaction of the Leader II strategic goals, which is the development of less developed rural areas. Five sub-criteria are then set, which are:

g_{11} : **innovation,** determined by the innovation of the proposed action, the rendering of quality services and the enrichment or differentiation that ensues on the total tourist product of the area. For example: improvement of the level of services offered, turning to new forms of tourism, as they result from the relative documentation of the proposal.

A common evaluation scale has been used for the sub-criteria g_{11} to g_{41} that is:

Insufficient satisfaction of criterion (or/and without evidence/documentation) : 1
Partial satisfaction of criterion (Insufficient evidence/documentation) : 2
Satisfaction of criterion (with evidence/documentation) : 3

g_{21} : **connection and utilisation of local nature-tourist resources,** determined by the degree to which the proposed action preserves, highlights and exploits the cultural heritage of the area, as well as nature, and contributes in particular to the enhancement and protection of the environment (natural and human) as a tourist resource, as they result from the relative documentation of the proposal.

g_{31} : **connection with local agricultural production,** determined by the degree to which the proposed action contributes in the promotion of local products and in the development of activities complementary to rural activities, as they are substantiated in the submitted proposal.

g_{41} : **integrated initiative or connected with others on the area,** determined by the degree to which the proposed action is integrated or/and connected to other relevant actions in the area, so that it ensures the existence of a minimum quantity of provided services, that render the activity feasible and viable and which are substantiated accordingly.

g_{51} : **contribution to tourist period prolongation,** which is determined by the number of days in which the tourist period is prolonged, according to the submitted for approval proposal.
No prolongation or/and without evidence/documentation : 1
Up to 30 days with evidence/documentation : 2
More than 30 days with evidence/documentation : 3

Goal Criterion: It supplements to the strategy criterion. It includes five sub-criteria:

g_{12} : **motivations for population in rural areas,** determined by the retention of the population in the specific rural area and the revival of settlements, as results from relative documents included in the submitted action.
Insufficient satisfaction of criterion (or/and without evidence/documentation) : 1
Partial satisfaction of criterion (Insufficient evidence/documentation) : 2
Satisfaction of criterion (with evidence/documentation) : 3

g_{22} : **new job positions**, determined by the number of new job positions, included the self-employment positions of the investor/s as well as the part time positions, according to the submitted for approval proposal.

No new job position or/and untrustworthy evidence : 1
1 to 4 new job positions : 2
More than 4 new job positions : 3

g_{32} : **conjunction with other development projects**, determined by the degree to which the proposed action is connected to the results of the works of other projects and is substantiated in the proposal accordingly.

No satisfaction of the criterion : 1
Partial or indirect satisfaction of the criterion : 2
Direct satisfaction of the criterion : 3

g_{42} : **installation in a historical place**, determined by the degree to which the proposed action is scheduled to be installed in a qualified historical or traditional building and so through the proposed investment to carry out the restoration of the corresponding building.

Proposal without documentation, new building : 1
Restoration of a building with substantiated traditional, historical, cultural
and architectural value : 2
Restoration of a building qualified as preservable, with substantiated
traditional, historical, cultural and architectural value in a settlement
qualified as preservable : 3

g_{52} : **incorporation of the undertaken activity into a historical or nature path**, which is determined by the degree to which the proposed action is incorporated in a specific cultural or naturalist path, such as the legislated paths like E4 or those qualified as cultural paths by the Prefectural Councils or other agents. All the above must be substantiated accordingly in the proposal.

In no path : 1
In a path proposed by agents or by the investor, and accepted by the
Evaluation Committee : 2
In a legislated path (E4, Cultural Paths by Prefectural Councils) : 3

Reliability Criterion: It refers to the capacity and reliability of the investor/s. It is categorised in four sub-criteria:

g_{13} : **solvency**, determined by the degree to which the capitals are secured or available by the investor/s to cover their own participation through the relevant documentation.

Bad financial standing of the investor : 1
Modest financial standing of the investor (own capitals and loans) : 2
Satisfactory financial standing of the investor (own capitals) : 3

g_{23} : **experience**, refers to the experience of the investor/s as it is substantiated by the data from the resume, by certifications from employer/s, by revenue stamps, by certification for practice of profession, etc.

No specialisation or experience : 1

| Modest specialisation and experience | : 2 |
| High specialisation and experience | : 3 |

g_{33}: **nativity**, refers to the place of residence of the investor/s as it results from the submitted proposal.

Residence outside of the area of the project	: 1
Residence in the same Prefecture, outside of the Municipality or the Community of the investment	: 2
Residence inside the Municipality or the Community of the investment	: 3

g_{43}: **age**, refers to the age of the investor/s, as described in the resume. Since the aim of the Leader II is the development of rural areas, it is considered that the income of the young people has to be supported so that they stay in their villages; thus, the younger investors are promoted in the evaluation, as follows:

Over 50 years old	: 1
From 35 to 50 years old	: 2
Under 35 years old	: 3

Quality Criterion: It refers to the quality of the proposal as a set of factors like the thorough and correct completion of technical annex, the existence of contracts, etc. The criterion is analysed into two sub-criteria:

g_{14}: **completeness of technical annex**, which is determined by the degree of accuracy in the completion of the technical annex of the proposal (correct and thorough completion of the technical annex, authenticity of pre-estimated cost, accuracy of financial data and feasibility of schedule for the realisation of the work).

Insufficient completion	: 1
Partial completion	: 2
Thorough completion	: 3

g_{24}: **standby situation**, which is determined by the degree of existence of the necessary ratifications, permits and studies.

Non-existence of all the necessary ratifications, permits and studies	: 1
Existence of some ratifications, permits and studies	: 2
Existence of all the necessary ratifications, permits and studies	: 3

INFERRING A PREFERENCE MODEL

In order to proceed to the evaluation procedure the Greek project evaluator was asked to choose the proposals that would constitute the reference set, given that the proposals for evaluation was 150. Then, the evaluator was given four tables, similar to Table 1 except for the last column, that contained a small set of reference proposals he had chosen, and he was asked to mark them on the sub-criteria of the criteria, based on the tertiary scale of evaluation and rank them from best to worst.

The selection of the reference proposals has to take two issues into account (Siskos et al., 1999): (1) the set must cover all the evaluation scales of the criteria and (2) reference proposals have to be familiar to the decision maker. Another interesting exercise is the comparison of the inference results with other reference sets and different decision makers-evaluators.

For each criterion the decision maker, using the UTASTAR disaggregation model (Siskos and Yannacopoulos, 1985), provided a ranking for 15 selected reference proposals, from the set of 150. Then, analytical preference models (a set of weights and values) were derived for each sub-criterion, as consistent as possible with the initial ranking. The new ranking given by the model fits perfectly with the decision maker's judgement on all four criteria (Kendall's $\tau=1$). Consequently, an aggregated preference model, of the type (1), for proposals' evaluation was determined.

For the better understanding of the implementation of the method, we shall present the results of the method for one criterion. More specifically, for the first criterion of the Strategy, the marking given by the evaluator on the 15 selected reference proposals on the five sub-criteria and their initial ranking, are presented on Table 1, where the proposals appear as P1...P15. In this way, the project evaluator indirectly manifested his preferences, by arranging the proposals of the reference set from best to worst.

Table 1. Ranking for the 15 proposals of the Reference Set (Strategy Criterion)

Proposals	Sub-Criteria for Strategy Criterion					Ranking Order	Global Utility
	g_{11}	g_{21}	g_{31}	g_{41}	g_{51}		
P1	2	3	2	1	1	9	0,257
P2	2	3	2	2	2	7	0,386
P3	1	2	1	3	2	8	0,352
P4	1	1	2	1	1	14	0,062
P5	2	3	3	3	2	4	0,738
P6	3	3	3	3	2	2	0,805
P7	1	1	2	2	2	11	0,190
P8	3	3	2	2	2	6	0,452
P9	2	3	2	2	2	7	0,386
P10	2	2	3	3	3	3	0,771
P11	2	2	2	1	1	13	0,095
P12	3	3	2	3	3	1	0,838
P13	2	3	2	2	3	5	0,581
P14	1	1	1	2	2	12	0,129
P15	1	2	2	2	2	10	0,224

Thus, for the first criterion of Strategy and given the initial preferential ranking of the decision maker, the UTASTAR method assessed the value functions of the sub-criteria and the global utility of the proposals-alternatives (Figure 2). The value functions in this case express the value attached by the decision maker in the case of modest satisfaction on the sub-criteria. In the case of the substandard satisfaction of one sub-criterion the value attached by the decision maker is 0, while in the case of satisfaction the mark is 1, due to normalisation of the value functions. The global utility of each proposal, on the criterion of Strategy, appears in the last column of Table 1 and on the related graph of Figure 2 with their ranking. We note that the proposal P12 is the one with the greatest global utility, that is the one that is ranked first in relation to the others on this particular criterion, followed by P6, P10 etc, with the same initial ranking given by the evaluator.

Figure 2. Value Functions for Strategy Criterion Sub-Criteria. Ranking of the proposals.

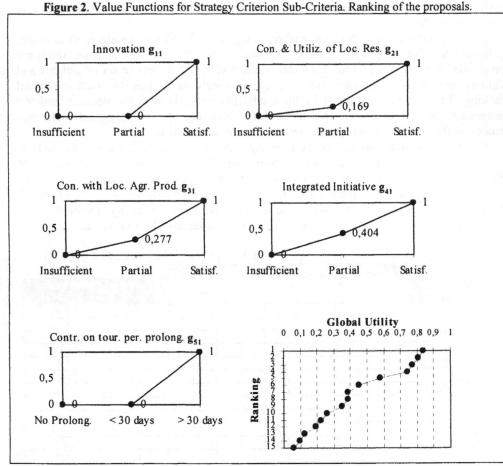

Figure 2, that refers to the criterion of Strategy, shows that according to the evaluator preferences the sub-criteria g_{11} (innovation) and g_{51} (contribution to tourist period prolongation) are marked on scale 0 or 1. This result indicates that according to the evaluator those particular sub-criteria could be marked simply on a scale of «yes-no» or «1-0». Thus, if a proposal for evaluation is judged that it moderately covers the sub-criterion of innovation, that is it suggests some actions that are not proved to be an innovation or the data for evaluation is not clearly substantiated, then it will be marked with 0. Similarly, the sub-criterion g_{51} will be marked with 0 if the decision maker considers that a proposal for evaluation does not decisively contribute to the prolongation of the tourist period for more than one month or there is no clear substantiation in the submitted proposal that proves the contribution of the specific action in the prolongation of the tourist period for more than one month. On the contrary, for the other sub-criteria g_{21}, g_{31} and g_{41} it seems that the decision maker is strict, since if for example a proposal for evaluation is judged, by the suggested actions, that it moderately covers the sub-criterion of connection with local natural and cultural resources of the region (sub-criterion g_{21}), then it will be marked with 0,169, which proves that the decision maker is demanding on that particular sub-criterion.

In addition to the estimation of the value functions the UTASTAR method assessed the weights of all sub-criteria. The weights of the sub-criteria of the first criterion, Strategy, are presented on Figure 3 and express the weight with which each sub-criterion participates in the formation of the global utility of each proposal. We note that the major weight for the decision maker lies with the sub-criterion g_{41} (integrated initiative or connected with others on the area) represented by 31,9%. The sub-criteria g_{21} and g_{51} have the same weight (19,5%), while the least weight lies with the sub-criterion of innovation: g_{11} represented by 6,7%.

Figure 3. Weights of Sub-Criteria for Strategy Criterion (p_{i1})

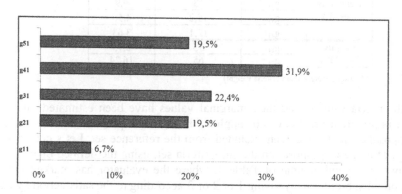

A similar procedure was held for the other three criteria, Goal, Reliability and Quality. Finally, the weights of sub-criteria set, as they were assessed by UTASTAR and as shown for the criterion of Strategy, are presented in Table 2 and they express the relative importance within each criterion. In order to provide comparable results among sub-criteria belonging to different criteria, we calculate the relative weight of each sub-criterion, which is the result of the multiplication of the criterion and sub-criterion weight. As it is shown in the last column of Table 2 the most important sub-criterion, concerning relative weight is g_{24}: standby situation (weight: 16,24%) and then follow g_{13}:solvency of the investor and g_{23}:experience of the investor with weights 11,91% and 9,9% respectively. The superiority of sub-criteria g_{24} and g_{13} is justified by the fact that the evaluator was interested in the immediate start of the works suggested by the investors, and by the financial state of the investors that demanded the realisation of the works without any time delays that would result from a request for bank loan. In the same sense the experience of the investor is of high interest for the evaluator. The sub-criteria with less importance for the evaluator are: the support of local work-force (g_{22}) and the proposed innovation of the projects (g_{11}), with weights 1,58% and 1,34% respectively.

Table 2. Weights of Sub-Criteria Set

Criteria	Sub-criteria	Weight (%) p_{ik}	Relative Weight * (%)
Strategy $w_1=20\%$	g_{11}	6,7	1,34
	g_{21}	19,5	3,9
	g_{31}	22,4	4,48
	g_{41}	31,9	6,38
	g_{51}	19,5	3,9
Goal $w_2=25\%$	g_{12}	18,3	4,58
	g_{22}	6,3	1,58
	g_{32}	21,4	5,35
	g_{42}	33	8,25
	g_{52}	21	5,25
Reliability $w_3=30\%$	g_{13}	39,7	11,91
	g_{23}	33	9,9
	g_{33}	15,2	4,56
	g_{43}	12,1	3,63
Quality $w_4=25\%$	g_{14}	35	8,75
	g_{24}	65	16,24

(* Criteria weight x sub-criteria weight)

As sub-criteria weights and their marginal values have been estimated, the proposed multicriteria preference model can be applied, through extrapolation, for the evaluation of those proposals, which have been excluded from the reference set. Let's consider that the evaluation of a «new» proposal on the sub-criteria set, using the defined qualitative scale, is as shown in second column of Table 3, where the evaluator has marked the specific proposal on all sub-criteria, by giving 1 or 2 or 3 according to the satisfaction by each sub-criterion. Then the marginal values for the sub-criteria set, (see third column in Table 3) are concluded from Table 4. (Table 4 presents the marginal values for the sub-criteria set, as they were assessed by UTASTAR according to the preferences of the decision maker on the reference set and as shown for the criterion of Strategy. All marginal values presented in Table 4 are in the range [0,1]. In Table 4, in order to present the marginal values of the sub-criteria set, we have used for reasons of simplification, a unified scale of satisfaction: Substandard-Medium-Satisfied). The global value, U_k, for each criterion k (see fourth column in Table 3) is then assessed by formula (2), where sub-criteria weights (p_{ik}) and their marginal values ($u_{ik}[g_{ik}(\alpha)]$) have been already calculated. For instance, for the first criterion of Strategy the global value is calculated: $U_1=(0,224 \times 0,277)+(0,319 \times 0,404)=0,191$, where the weights p_{ik} for all the criteria are presented in Table 2. Finally, the global value, U_{global}, of the «new» proposal is assessed by formula (1), as it is presented in the last column of Table 3. Thus, the $U_{global}=(0,20 \times 0,191)+(0,25 \times 0,33)+(0,30 \times 0,424)+(0,25 \times 0,7)=0,423$. Since the decision maker is interested in the ranking of the set of proposals for funding purposes, the model can support the decision maker's evaluation process in a systematic, effective and scientific way. The marking of the "new" proposal with 0,423, as shown in the last column in Table 3, allows the evaluator to rank it in relation to the proposals of the reference set and among the total of the proposals for evaluation. The specific ranking indicates to the evaluator the best submitted proposals from the total of 150, that are chosen to be subsidised by Leader II.

Table 3. Model Implementation - "new" proposal.

Evaluation on sub-criteria set		Marginal values of sub-criteria $u_{ik}[g_{ik}(\alpha)]$	Global values for the criteria (U_k)	Global value for the «new» proposal U_{global}
			U_1 *(Strategy criterion)*	
g_{11}	1	0		
g_{21}	1	0		
g_{31}	2	0,277	0,191	
g_{41}	2	0,404		
g_{51}	2	0		
			U_2 *(Goal criterion)*	
g_{12}	1	0		
g_{22}	1	0		
g_{32}	1	0	0,33	
g_{42}	3	1		0,423
g_{52}	1	0		
			U_3 *(Reliability criterion)*	
g_{13}	1	0		
g_{23}	2	0,636	0,424	
g_{33}	3	1		
g_{43}	2	0,512		
			U_4 *(Quality criterion)*	
g_{14}	2	0,714	0,7	
g_{24}	2	0,692		

Table 4. Marginal values for the Sub-Criteria Set

Sub-criteria	Qualitative Scale		
	Substandard (1)	Medium (2)	Satisfied (3)
g_{11}	0	0	1
g_{21}	0	0,169	1
g_{31}	0	0,277	1
g_{41}	0	0,404	1
g_{51}	0	0	1
g_{12}	0	0,32	1
g_{22}	0	0,435	1
g_{32}	0	0,313	1
g_{42}	0	0,648	1
g_{52}	0	1	1
g_{13}	0	0,383	1
g_{23}	0	0,636	1
g_{33}	0	0,381	1
g_{43}	0	0,512	1
g_{14}	0	0,714	1
g_{24}	0	0,692	1

CONCLUSION

This paper has examined the problem of Leader's II rural development projects evaluation, using a preference aggregation-disaggregation approach of MCDA. In structuring the evaluation model, a major role was played by the project evaluator. The relative importance of sub-criteria was assessed first, by dissagregation technique, and global evaluation for each proposal was then achieved by aggregation of the preferences.

This effort to evaluate the submitted proposals for financing by Leader II, was realised based on the restrictions of the National Committee for the Supervision of the programme. Nevertheless, the proposed model approached in a scientific way the procedure of the Global Evaluation of the proposals, avoiding empirical methods and proved that the difficult work of the evaluators can be supported by the Multi-Criteria Decision Aid theory. In this way the evaluator has expressed through the procedure his opinion and revealed his arguments in order to substantiate his decision for the ranking of the proposals from best to worst (initial ranking of the reference set) and has also ensured that the final ranking of the proposals is not a product of an arbitrary procedure of evaluation but it reflects his beliefs.

An interesting future approach of similar European projects would be the possibility to explore the criteria and sub-criteria of evaluation in the initial stage, that were now given, and the other possible restrictions that were dealt with in that particular case.

ACKNOWLEDGEMENTS

The authors would like to acknowledge three anonymous referees for their helpful comments and suggestions.

REFERENCES

Bana e Costa, C.A. and Vansnick, J.C., (1997), Applications of the MACBETH approach in the framework of an additive aggregation model, *Multi-Criteria Decision Analysis*, vol. 6, 2, pp. 107-114.

Baourakis, G., Matsatsinis, N.F., and Siskos, J., (1996), Agricultural product development using multidimensional and multicriteria analyses: The case of wine, *European Journal of Operational Research*, vol. 94, pp. 321-334.

Development Organization of Western Crete, (1997), European Initiative Leader II: Information pamphlet (in Greek).

Gal, T., Stewart, T., and Hanne, T., (1999), Multicriteria Decision Making, Advances in MCDM – Models, Algorithms, Theory and Applications, Kluwer Academic Publishers, Dordrecht.

Goicoechea, A., Hansen, D.R., and Duckstein, L., (1982), Multiobjective decision analysis with engineering and business applications, John Wiley and Sons, New York.

Jacquet-Lagrèze, E., and Siskos, J. (1982), Assessing a set of additive utility functions for multicriteria decision-making, the UTA method, *European Journal of Operational Research*, vol. 10, pp. 151-164.

Keeney, R., (1992), Value Focused Thinking: a path to Creative Decionmaking, Harvard University Press, Cambridge.

Pardalos, P., Siskos, Y., and Zopounidis, C., (1995), Advances in Multicriteria Analysis, Kluwer Academic Publishers, Dordrecht.

Posavac, E., and Carey, R., (1996), Program Evaluation: Methods and Case Studies, 5th Ed., Prentice Hall.

Rossi, P.H., and Freeman, H., (1993), Evaluation: A Systematic Approach, 5th Ed., Book News Inc.

Roy, B., (1985), Méthodologie Multicritère d'Aide à la Décision, Economica, Paris.

Roy, B., and Bouyssou, D., (1993), Aide Multicritère à la Décision: Méthods et Cas, Economica, Paris.

Siskos, J., and Assimakopoulos, N. (1989), Multicriteria highway planning: a case study, *Mathematical and Computer Modelling*, vol. 12, pp. 1401-1410.

Siskos, J., and Yannacopoulos, D. (1985), UTASTAR: An Ordinal Regression Method for building additive value functions, *Investigaçao Operational* vol. 5, pp. 39-53.

Siskos, Y., Spyridakos, A., and Yannacopoulos, D., (1999), Using artificial intelligence and visual techniques into Preference Disaggregation Analysis: The MIIDAS, *European Journal of Operational Research*, vol 113, pp. 281-299.

Wholey, J., Hatry, H., Newcomer, K., (1994), Handbook of Practical Program Evaluation, Jossey-Bass Publishers.

Worthen, B., Sanders, J., and Fitzpatrick, J., (1996), Program Evaluation: Alternative Approaches and Practical Guidelines, 2nd Ed., Addison-Wesley.

Zanakis, S., Mandakovic, T., Gupta, S., Sahay, S., and Hong, S., (1995), A Review of Program Evaluation and Fund Allocation Methods Within the Service and Government Sectors, *Socio-Economic Planning Science*, vol. 29, pp. 59-79.

AN ADAPTABLE FRAMEWORK FOR EDUCATIONAL SOFTWARE EVALUATION

I. Stamelos[1], I. Refanidis[1], P. Katsaros[1], A. Tsoukias[2], I. Vlahavas[1], A. Pombortsis[1]

[1]Dept. of Informatics
Aristotle University of Thessaloniki
Thessaloniki, 54006, Greece

[2]LAMSADE-CNRS
Univ.Paris-IX,Dauphine
Paris Cedex 16, France

Abstract: This paper proposes a framework for educational software evaluation based on the Multiple Criteria Decision Aid methodology. Evaluating educational software products is a twofold process: both the educational and the technical aspect of the evaluated products have to be considered. As far as the product educational effectiveness is concerned, we propose a set of attributes covering both the general educational features and the content of the product. From the technical point of view, a software attribute set based on the ISO/IEC 9126 standard has been chosen together with the accompanying measurement guidelines. Finally, an evaluation example involving three commercial educational software packages for mechanics is presented.

Key words: Software Evaluation, Educational Software, MCDA

INTRODUCTION

Evaluating software products is a particularly difficult process because many, often contradictory, attributes have to be taken into account. An important effort for defining a universally accepted model has been undertaken by the International Standard Organization (ISO), which has published the ISO/IEC 9126-1, 9126-2 and 9126-3 standards. ISO proposes six attributes, which characterize the quality of a software product: *functionality, reliability, usability, efficiency, maintainability* and *portability* (ISO/IEC, 1996). These attributes can be further analyzed in lower-level attributes.

S.H. Zanakis et al. (eds.), Decision Making: Recent Developments and Worldwide Applications, 347–360.

However, the ISO standards do not cope with software attributes that are appropriate for assessing product quality from a non-technical point of view. In the case of educational software it is generally accepted that it is very difficult to develop a predefined set of standards according to which the educational value of the software can be measured. The reason is that each educational software product does not necessarily serve the same learning objectives and the same target users (age, level of knowledge or skills). Therefore, the set of attributes to be chosen for assessing the educational value of a software product must clearly prescribe the evaluation context in each case.

This paper presents an adaptable evaluation framework for educational software products based on the Multicriteria Decision Aid methodology (MCDA) (Roy, 1996; Vincke, 1992), which is suitable for evaluation problems where many attributes must be taken into account. Since evaluating educational software is a twofold process, concerning both the technical and the educational aspect of the evaluated products, the proposed framework consists of two top-level attributes, one concerning the technical features of the evaluated products and one concerning the educational effectiveness of them. The ISO/IEC 9126 standard is chosen as the basis for evaluating the quality of a software product from the technical point of view, while an adaptable set of attributes is proposed for assessing the educational value of the product. A real example concerning the evaluation of three commercial educational software packages is presented. The overall evaluation model used in the example is illustrated and critical points are discussed

In the following section we present the principles of software evaluation using MCDA methodology. Next we present the attributes used for the technical aspect of the evaluation and subsequently we present the attributes selected for the educational aspect of the evaluation. We illustrate this framework with a real example and finally we conclude the paper and pose future directions.

MULTIPLE CRITERIA DECISION AID METHODOLOGY (MCDA)

An evaluation problem solved by MCDA can be modeled as a 7-ple $\{A,T,D,M,E,G,R\}$ where (Vincke, 1992):

- A is the set of alternatives under evaluation in the model
- T is the type of the evaluation
- D is the tree of the evaluation attributes
- M is the set of associated measures
- E is the set of scales associated to the attributes
- G is the set of attributes constructed in order to represent the user's preferences
- R is the preference aggregation procedure

In order to solve an evaluation problem, a specific procedure must be followed (Morisio and Tsoukias, 1997):

Step 1: *Definition of the evaluation set A:* The first step is to define exactly the set of possible choices. Usually there is a set A of alternatives to be evaluated and the best must be selected. The definition of A could be thought as first-level evaluation, because if some alternatives do not fulfill certain requirements, they may be rejected from this set.

Step 2: *Definition of the type T of the evaluation*: In this step we must define the type of the desired result. Some possible choices are the following:

- choice: partition the set of possible choices into a sub-set of best choices and a sub-set of not best ones.
- classification: partition the set of possible choices into a number of sub-sets, each one having a characterization such as good, bad, etc.
- ranking: rank the set of possible choices from the best choice to the worst one.
- description: provide a formal description of each choice, without any ranking.

Step 3: *Definition of the tree of evaluation attributes D*: In this step the attributes that will be taken into account during the evaluation and their hierarchy must be defined. Attributes that can be analyzed in sub-attributes are called compound attributes. Sub-attributes can also consist of sub-sub-attributes and so on. The attributes that can not be divided further are called *basic attributes*. An example of such an attribute hierarchy is shown in figure 1.

It should be noted that there exist mandatory independence conditions, such as the separability condition, and contingent independence conditions, depending on the aggregation procedure adopted.

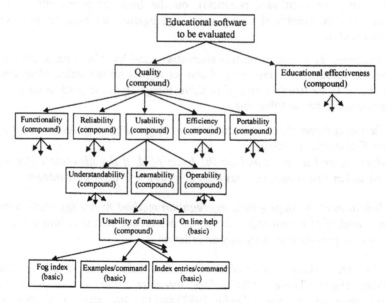

Figure 1. Example of an attribute hierarchy

Step 4: *Definition of the set of measurement methods M*: For every basic attribute d we must define a method M_d that will be used to assign values to it. There are two kinds of values, the *arithmetic values* (ratio, interval or absolute) and the *nominal values*. The first type of values are numbers, while the second type are verbal characterizations, such as 'red', 'yellow', 'good', 'bad', 'big', 'small', etc.

A problem with the definition of M_d is that d may not be measurable, because of its measurement being non-practical or impossible. In such cases an arbitrary value may be given, based upon expert judgment, introducing a subjectivity factor. Alternatively, d may be decomposed into a set of sub-attributes d_1, d_2, ... d_n, which are measurable. In this case the expression of arbitrary judgment is avoided, but subjectivity is involved in the decomposition.

Step 5: *Definition of the set of measurement scales E*: A scale e_d must be associated to every basic attribute d. For arithmetic attributes, the scale usually corresponds to the scale of the metric used, while for nominal attributes, e_d must be declared by the evaluator. Scales must be at least ordinal, implying that, within e_d, it must be clear which of any two values is the most preferred (in some cases there are different values with the same preference). For example, for d = 'operating system', e_d could be [UNIX, Windows NT, Windows-95, DOS, VMS] and a possible preference could be [UNIX = Windows NT > Windows-95 = VMS > DOS].

Step 6: *Definition of the set of Preference Structure Rules G*: For each attribute and for the measures attached to it, a rule or a set of rules have to be defined, with the ability to transform measures to preference structures. A preference structure compares two distinct alternatives (e.g. two software products), on the basis of a specific attribute. Basic preferences can be combined, using some aggregation method, to produce a global preference structure.

For example, let a_1 and a_2 be two alternatives and let d be a basic attribute. Let also $m_d(a_1)$ be the value of a_1 concerning d and let $m_d(a_2)$ be the value of a_2 concerning d. Suppose that d is measurable and of positive integer type. In such a case, a preference structure rule could be the following:

- *product a_1 is better than a_2 on the basis of d, if $m_d(a_1)$ is greater than $m_d(a_2)$ plus K, where K is a positive integer*
- *products a_1 and a_2 are equal on the basis of d, if the absolute difference between $m_d(a_1)$ and $m_d(a_2)$ is equal or less than K, where K is a positive integer*

Step 7: *Selection of the appropriate aggregation method R*: An aggregation method is an algorithm, capable of transforming the set of preference relations into a *prescription* for the evaluator. A prescription is usually an order on A.

The MCDA methodology consists of a set of different aggregation methods, which fall into three classes. These are the *multiple attribute utility methods* (Keeney and Raiffa, 1976), the *outranking methods* (Vincke, 1992) and the *interactive methods* (Vanderpooten and Vincke, 1989). The selection of an aggregation method depends on the following parameters (Vincke, 1992):

- The type of the problem
- The type of the set of possible choices (continuous or discrete)

- The type of measurement scales
- The kind of importance parameters (weights) associated to the attributes
- The type of dependency among the attributes (i.e. *isolability*, *preferential independence*)
- The kind of uncertainty present (if any)

Notice that the execution of the steps mentioned above is not straightforward. For example, it is allowed to define first D and then, or in parallel, define A, or even select R in the middle of the process.

ATTRIBUTES FOR EVALUATING THE TECHNICAL FEATURES OF EDUCATIONAL SOFTWARE

According to ISO 9126 the technical aspect of quality is decomposed into six sub-attributes and each one of them is further decomposed in sub-sub attributes. Quality is decomposed as follows:

- Functionality [suitability, accuracy, interoperability, compliance, security]
- Reliability [maturity, fault tolerance, recoverability]
- Usability [understandability, learnability, operability]
- Efficiency [time behavior, resource utilization]
- Maintainability [analyzability, changeability, stability, testability]
- Portability [adaptability, installability, conformance, replaceability]

ISO 9126 basically prescribes a general framework, which may be adapted to the characteristics of a specific evaluation problem. For specific types of educational software, some of the above attributes may be irrelevant. In the example presented in the next section, which concerns commercial multimedia software for personal use, maintainability and portability have been considered of no interest. In the following sub-sections, we discuss briefly the above attributes.

Functionality

Functionality is defined as the degree of existence of a set of functions that satisfy stated or implied needs and their properties. In the case of educational software these functions and properties may concern the coverage of one or more required subjects, the presence of experiments, various types of exercises e.t.c. It can be decomposed in five sub-attributes:

- *Suitability* is the degree of presence of a set of functions for specified tasks.
- *Accuracy* is the degree of provision of right or agreed results or effects.
- *Interoperability* is the degree to which the software is able to interact with specified systems (i.e. physical devices)
- *Compliance* is the degree to which the software adheres to application-related standards or conventions or regulations in laws and similar prescriptions.
- *Security* is the degree to which the software is able to prevent unauthorized access,

whether accidental or deliberative, to programs and data (i.e. login functions, encryption of personal data e.t.c.).

Reliability

Reliability is defined as the capability of the software to maintain its level of performance under stated conditions for a stated period of time. It can be decomposed in three sub-attributes:

- *Maturity* is the frequency of failure by faults in the software. In general, any fault due to software problems is unacceptable for educational software.
- *Fault tolerance* is the ability to maintain a specified level of performance in cases of software faults or of infringement of its specified interface.
- *Recoverability* is the capability of software to reestablish its level of performance and recover the data directly affected in case of a failure.

Usability

Usability is defined as the effort needed for the use by a stated or implied set of users. This attribute affects also the educational effectiveness of a software product, since if the product is hard to use, the attention of the trainee is mostly focused in the software itself, than in its educational content. Usability can be decomposed in three sub-attributes:

- *Understandability* is the user's effort for recognizing the underlain concept of the software. This effort could be decreased by the existence of demonstrations.
- *Learnability* is the user's effort for learning how to use the software.
- *Operability* is the user's effort for operation and operation control (e.g. mouse support, shortcuts e.t.c.).

Efficiency

Efficiency is the relationship between the level of performance of the software and the amount of resources used, under stated conditions. It can be decomposed in two sub-attributes.

- *Time behavior* is the software's response and processing times and throughput rates in performing its function.
- *Resource utilization* is the amount of resources and the duration of such use in performing the software's function.

Maintainability

Maintainability is defined as the effort needed to make specified modifications. It can be decomposed in four sub-attributes.

- *Analyzability* is the effort needed for diagnosis of inefficiencies or causes of failure or for identification of parts to be modified.
- *Changeability* is the effort needed for modification, fault removal or for

environmental change.
- *Stability* is the risk of unexpected effects of modifications.
- *Testability* is the effort needed for validating the modified software.

Portability

Portability is the ability of the software to be transferred from one environment to another. It can be decomposed in four sub-attributes:

- *Adaptability* is the software's opportunity for adaptation to different environments (e.g. other hardware/OS platforms).
- *Installability* is the effort needed to install the software in a specified environment.
- *Conformance* is the degree to which the software adheres to standards or conventions related to portability.
- *Replaceability* is the opportunity and effort of using the software in the place of specified older software.

ATTRIBUTES FOR EVALUATING THE EDUCATIONAL EFFECTIVENESS

In contrast with the technical aspect of the evaluation, there is no broadly accepted model for assessing the educational effectiveness of a software package. The reasons for this are mainly:

- It is very hard to describe the context of all possible educational software evaluation problems with a single attribute framework. For example, the evaluation carried out by a teacher or a trainer is a completely different problem compared to the evaluation process carried out by a decision-maker of an educational institution. In addition, factors that must be taken into account are the type of target users the evaluator has in mind while undertaking the evaluation and the way he or she intends to use the software (for example, to teach a specific topic, or to enhance students' understanding of a certain topic).
- There are several types of educational software products. According to Lockard et al. (1987) these types are: '*drill and practice*', '*tutorials*', '*simulations*', '*instructional games*' and '*problem solving*'. Each one of these software types may need different evaluation attributes.
- An educational software product may have such original characteristics that prevent the use of a predefined set of evaluation attributes.

In this work we tried to take into consideration all elements relevant to teachers, trainers, parents and users. The proposed set of attributes must be viewed as a general evaluation framework that in most cases should be adapted to the specific circumstances of an evaluation problem.

The proposed framework is based on the work presented in Severino (1998), which has been modified by removing the attributes related to the technical aspect of the evaluation and by extending in more detail the attributes related to the educational purposes of the evaluation. According to our approach the educational effectiveness attribute of a software product is decomposed in two sub-attributes, each one of them being further decomposed. The first two levels of this analysis are shown in table 1. In the following sub-sections we will discuss these attributes in more detail.

Table 1. Educational effectiveness decomposition

• educational features
- target users specification
- information for the topics addressed and the learning objectives
- instructional support materials
- adaptation to individual needs
- strategies for enhancing engagement, attention and memory
- usage of the product
- encouragement of critical thinking
- user performance assessment
• content
- quality of content
- appropriateness
- structure

Educational Features

– *Target users specification*: The software packaging or the accompanying reference materials must clearly inform about the approximate age of the target users and about the prerequisite level of knowledge or skills recommended for best use of the software.

– *Information for the topics addressed and the learning objectives*: It is very important that instructors and educators are provided with clear and comprehensive information concerning both the topics that the educational software deals with and the learning objectives that it aims to achieve. Obviously, the topics addressed by the software must be relevant to the set of learning objectives, so as to enable users to achieve them, and the learning objectives must be appropriate for the target users' age and competence. When the educational software is designed for classroom use to ensure that the software is a valuable educational resource, the topics covered and the learning objectives must be compatible with the education system of the country where the software is used.

– *Instructional support material*: Another aspect to take into account when evaluating the educational features of a particular piece of software is the quality of the instructional support material it provides, either in print and/or as printable files from disc or on-line resources. In fact, they can significantly help not only instructors but also users to focus the potentialities of the software, giving suggestions on the various teaching strategies instructors can adopt using it in the classroom, informing about how the program can be fitted into a larger framework of instruction etc.

- *Adaptation to individual needs*: This attribute is further decomposed in four sub-attributes:

  - *Feedback*: The software product provides feedback information that is not stereotyped, but appropriate for the situation and the users' performance.
  - *Possibility to follow different learning routes (exploratory learning environments)*: It is important that the software allows the users to follow different learning routes through the program.
  - *Differentiation of the level of difficulty in respect with the user's performance*
  - *Level of interactivity*

- *Strategies for enhancing engagement, attention and memory*: This attribute is decomposed further on in the following sub-attributes:

  - *User motivation*: User motivation is achieved when the software is able to:
    - Show to the users the usefulness of what they learn.
    - Set clear goals (e.g. number of questions that need to be completed without a mistake) and provide indication of how the user is proceeding periodically.
    - Encourage users to envision themselves in an imaginary context or event where they can use the information they are learning.
    - Inspire cognitive curiosity by giving partial information, elements of surprise, stimulating desire to know e.t.c.
    - Inspire sensory curiosity using sound, visual stimuli e.t.c.
    - Provide a level of user control, keeping always in mind that too much user control can be detrimental.

    Other characteristics related to user motivation are:
    - Confidence: provide reasonable opportunity to be successful.
    - Competition with other users (students)
    - Competition with the computer
    - Competition with the user him/herself
    - Competition with the clock
    - Adjunct reinforcement: Follow the successful completion of any activity with an activity that the user (student) finds enjoyable.

  - *Varied tasks & activities*: The diversity/motonony in the way performing various tasks.
  - *Retention of information*: Retention of information is encouraged when the difficulties are well distributed throughout the program, the topics are clearly connected and summaries of the main topics covered in each preceding section are provided.

- *Usage of educational software*: It is very important to consider the possible usage of the educational software as learning resource in the classroom or by a single user as self-instructional resource, whether it can be useful for the administration of tests, or can be used only for instructor-led tuition.

- *Encouragement of critical thinking*: The degree to which the program provides critical thinking and decision making activities that entail inductive or deductive reasoning and problem-solving skills must be taken onto account.
- *User's performance assessment*: For true and actual learning to take place, it is important that the educational software allows the users to constantly monitor and assess their learning progress.

Content

The *Content* of an educational software product is measured according to three sub-attributes:

- *Quality of content*: The quality of the content is analyzed in the following lower level attributes:
  - *Accuracy*: Measures the absence of inaccuracies in the content presented by the software.
  - *Clear formulation of the content so as to be easily understandable*
  - *Completeness*: Capability of the software in dealing with all the aspects of each topic.
  - *Up-to-date*

- *Appropriateness*: This attribute refers to the appropriateness of the reading level for the target users. Users should be able to understand the information presented, so it is essential to check if vocabulary, structure and sentence length are suitable for their level of knowledge, presenting an acceptable degree of difficulty.

- *Structure*: This attribute focuses on the organization of content, which should be logically structured and divided among the sections or modules, in order to help the user to progressively assimilate information.

A REAL WORLD EXAMPLE

This section presents an example in which three commercial educational software packages for personal use are compared. The packages concern mechanics for high schoolers and have been selected from the Greek market. We are not presenting the names of the evaluated products, since this would not increase the worthiness of the example, but we will refer to them with the terms *P1*, *P2* and *P3*.

In the following sub-sections we will present first the attributes used for the technical part of the evaluation, together with their weights, the measurement scales and the ratings of the evaluated products for the various basic attributes. Next we will present the attributes used for the educational part of the evaluation. Finally we will present the aggregation procedure and the way the final result was obtained.

It should be noted that the weights have been defined using the concept of "winning" coalition, that is the subset of criteria that enable to establish that a generic alternative X is better that a generic alternative Y. Once such subsets have been defined, the concordance threshold and the weights result from a constraining satisfaction problem.

Technical part of the evaluation

As mentioned before this part of the evaluation is based on the quality scheme of ISO 9126. Concerning *Functionality*, we removed attributes *Interoperability* and *Security*, since our specifications required neither capabilities for exchanging real experimental data with physical instruments nor user authentication. Moreover, we removed accuracy, since our packages do not perform computations that require high degree of accuracy. We have further decomposed *Suitability* in three sub-attributes: *Theory*, *Experiments* and *Exercises*. For *Theory* we used as a metric the number of *Subjects* covered by each package. For *Experiments* and *Exercises* we used as a metric the ratio of *Experiments/Subject* and *Exercises/Subject* of each package.

Concerning *Reliability*, we considered only its sub-attribute *Maturity*, which expresses the frequency of faults due to software problems. *Recoverability*, *Fault tolerance* and *Availability* have been considered irrelevant. We assigned an increased weight to *Reliability*, since for educational software this kind of faults is unacceptable.

Usability is decomposed in *Understandability*, *Learnability* and *Operability*. We analyzed *Learnability* in terms of *Usability of manual* and *Availability of help functions*. Finally we analyzed *Operability* in *Availability of installation program*, *Message clearness* and *Cancelability ratio*.

Concerning *Efficiency*, we considered both *Time behavior* and *Resource utilization*. In order to 'measure' the *Time behavior*, we used the subjective impression of the package's response times. Concerning resource utilization, we considered the requirements of the package in memory, disk space and CPU type and speed.

Finally, we considered *Maintainability* and *Portability* as being irrelevant for commercial multimedia software for personal use.

Table 2 presents all the attributes used for the technical part of the evaluation, together with their hierarchy, the measurement scales for the basic attributes, the weights assigned to the attributes and the values assigned to the three alternatives for the basic attributes. In case of arithmetic basic attributes, we define also a threshold, which represents the minimum difference that must exist between two alternatives, in order to consider the one superior to the other. In case of nominal basic attributes, specific procedures can be defined for assigning values to the alternatives, or expert judgement may be used.

Educational part of the evaluation

For the educational part of the evaluation we used all the attributes presented in the previous section. Table 3 gives the detail for the attributes used, their weights, the measurement scales and the values assigned to the three packages for the various basic attributes. In this case there are not arithmetic basic attributes, so no thresholds have been used.

Table 2. The sub-model for the technical part of the evaluation

	Attribute	Weight	Scale	Threshold	P1	P2	P3
1	Functionality	3					
1.1	Suitability	2					
1.1.1	Theory	4	Number of sections	2	14	15	13
1.1.2	Experiments	2	Experiments/Section	2	2.1	2.8	1.9
1.1.3	Exercises	2	Exercises/Section	3	4	8	5
1.2	Compliance	1	{high, average, low}		high	high	aver.
2	Reliability	9					
2.1	Maturity	1	{high, average, low}		high	high	high
3	Usability	5					
3.1	Understandability	2	{high, average, low}		high	high	high
3.2	Learnability	2					
3.2.1	Usability of manual	1	{high, average, low}		aver.	high	aver.
3.2.2	Help functions	2	{complete,partial,missing}		partial	compl	partial
3.3	Operability	1					
3.3.1	Installation program	1	{available, missing}		avail	avail	avail
3.3.2	Message clearness	2	{high, average, low}		high	high	high
3.3.3	Cancelability ratio	1	{complete, partial, missing}		miss	partial	miss
4	Efficiency	2					
4.1	Time behavior	1	{good, average, bad}		good	good	good
4.2	Resource utilization	1					
4.2.1	Memory	1	MB	16MB	8	8	8
4.2.2	Disk space	1	MB	10MB	17	15	21
4.2.3	CPU	1	Type/Speed	50 MHz	P100	486/33	486

Table 3. The sub-model for the educational part of the evaluation

	Attribute	Weight	Scale	P1	P2	P3
1	Educational Features	4				
1.1	Target users specification	0.5	fully > partially > missing	missing	partial	partial
1.2	Information for the topics	1	fully & consistent > fully but not consistent > partially > missing	partial	fully & consist.	fully & consist.
1.3	Instructional support material	0.5	complete > adequate > missing	missing	missing	missing
1.4	Adaptation to the individual needs	2				
1.4.1	Feedback	1	differentiated > stereotyped > missing	missing	differ.	missing
1.4.2	Different learning rules	1	possible > not possible	not	not	not
1.4.3	Differentiate the level of difficulty	1	possible > not possible	not	not	not
1.4.4	Level of interactivity	2	good > moderate > bad	moder.	moder.	moder.
1.5	Strategies for enhancing engagement	2				
1.5.1	User motivation	2	good > moderate > bad	bad	bad	bad
1.5.2	Varied tasks	2	varied > monotonous	monot.	monot.	monot.
1.5.3	Retention of information	1	good > moderate > bad	bad	bad	bad
1.6	Usage of educational software	1	many cases > one usage	one	many	many
1.7	Encouragement of critical thinking	2	existent > missing	missing	missing	missing
1.8	User's performance assessment	1	many types > one type > missing	one	many	one

Table 3. The sub-model for the educational part of the evaluation (continued)

	Attribute	Weight	Scale	P1	P2	P3
2	Content	6				
2.1	Quality of content	5				
2.1.1	Accuracy	1	accurate > inaccurate	accurat.	accurat.	accurat.
2.1.2	Clear formulation	2	clear > not clear	not	clear	not
2.1.3	Complete	1	complete > incomplete	incomp	compl.	incomp
2.1.4	Up-to-date	1	up-to-date > relatively old > old	to-date	to-date	to-date
2.2	Appropriateness	3	appropriate > not appropriate	approp.	approp.	approp.
2.3	Structure	2	modular > linear > unstructured	modul.	modul.	modul.

Aggregation phase

Having constructed the two evaluation sub-models, we have combined them into a single hierarchy, assigning weight value 4 to the technical sub-model and weight value 6 to the educational effectiveness one. Next we selected to use an aggregation method based on outranking relations, being motivated by the following two reasons:

- The type of available information, mainly as far as the evaluations are concerned (qualitative results, ordinal information, imprecise values), which we preferred to alter as less as possible.
- The will to have an easy and fast method in order to be able to make a clear idea of the problem in hand.

The method we selected was ELECTRE II (Roy and Bertier, 1973). This is an outranking MCDA method that provides a complete or partial ordering of equivalence classes from the best ones to the worst ones, considering also ties and incomparable classes. ELECTRE II calculates an ordering relation on all possible pairs of alternatives and uses an exploitation procedure to construct a preference relation among them, without providing any notion about their absolute distances. ELECTRE-II demands the definition of a concordance threshold, which in general indicates in what percentage of the attributes one alternative should outperform another (taking also into account the weights), in order that the former is considered superior to the latter. In our case, we set the concordance threshold to the value $c = 0.6$.

Since the computation of the ordering relations of ELECTRE is a hard process to be done manually, we used EPS (Vlahavas, 1999), an Expert System for Software Evaluation that supports evaluation with various MCDA methods. We entered the model together with the values assigned to the three alternatives, we selected ELECTRE-II (this was also the suggestion of the system) and the system extracted the final result. According to this, the three alternatives are ordered as:

$$P2 > P1 = P3$$

CONCLUSIONS AND FUTURE WORK

In this paper an adaptable framework for educational software evaluation is proposed, which takes into account both the technical and the educational aspect of this type of software products. For the technical part of the evaluation the ISO 9126 standard is adopted. For the educational part of the evaluation, it seems that it is not possible to define a single set of attributes appropriate for any problem. The attribute framework to be used depends on the type of target users the evaluator has in mind, on the way he or she intends to use the software and on the instructional strategy that has been chosen. Although a quite general set of attributes based on the ideas of Severino (1998) has been proposed, it seems to be more important to support the adaptation of the proposed set of attributes to the specific circumstances of an evaluation problem.

We have applied the framework in the comparison of three commercial educational software products for personal use. The evaluation has been performed with the Multiple Criteria Decision Aid methodology, which is suitable for evaluation problems where many attributes have to be taken into account. The evaluation process has been supported by ESSE, an Expert System for Software Evaluation, which embodies several MCDA methods, together with knowledge for various types of software evaluation problems.

In the future we will continue working on the proposed framework, applying it in a sufficiently large number of cases. Moreover, we plan to explore the applicability of more MCDA methods, such as other outranking and multiple attribute utility methods, some interactive methods, etc. Finally, we will explore the applicability of these methods to other categories of software evaluation problems, obtaining additional experience.

REFERENCES

ISO/IEC 9126-1, Information Technology - Software quality characteristics and sub-characteristics (1996).

Keeney R.L. and Raiffa H., Decision with multiple objectives, John Wiley, New York (1976).

Lockard J., Abrams P. and Many W., *Microcomputers for educators*, Little, Brown and Co., Boston (1987).

Morisio M. and Tsoukias A., IusWare, A methodology for the evaluation and selection of software products, *IEEE Proceedings on Software Engineering*, 144, 162-174 (1997).

Roy B. and Bertier P., La methode ELECTRE II - Une application au media planning, *in OR72*, M. Ross (ed.), North Holland, Amsterdam, 291-302 (1973).

Roy B., *Multicriteria Methodology for Decision Aiding*, Kluwer Academic, Dordrecht (1996).

Severino A.U., Educational Effectiveness Evaluation Criteria, *Emerging New Technologies in Education*, Symposium, Samos, Greece (1998).

Vanderpooten D. and Vincke P., Description and analysis of some representative interactive multicriteria procedures, Mathematical and computer modelling, no.12, (1989).

Vincke P., *Multicriteria decision aid*, Wiley, New York (1992).

Vlahavas I., Stamelos I., Refanidis I., Tsoukias A. (1998), *ESSE: An Expert System for Software Evaluation*, Knowledge Based Systems, Elsevier, 4 (12), 183-197 (1999).

ASSESSING COUNTRY RISK USING A MULTI–GROUP DISCRIMINATION METHOD: A COMPARATIVE ANALYSIS *

M. Doumpos[1], K. Pentaraki[1], C. Zopounidis[1†], C. Agorastos[2]

[1] Technical University of Crete, Dept. of Production Engineering and Management, Financial Engineering Laboratory, University Campus, 73100 Chania, Greece

[2] University of Macedonia, Dept. of Business Administration, Egnatia 156, P.O. Box 1591, 54006 Thessaloniki, Greece

Abstract: The recent economic and financial crises demonstrate the necessity to develop models that can be used by banks, international lending institutions, and institutional investors to determine the economic soundness, the creditworthiness, and the associated risk of countries worldwide. This paper explores the performance of a new approach in developing country risk assessment models. The proposed approach is based on the M.H.DIS multicriteria decision aid method (Multi-Group Hierarchical Discrimination). A sample consisting of 143 countries derived from the World Bank is used to estimate the performance of the method in classifying the countries into four groups. A jackknife procedure is employed for this purpose and a comparison with multiple discriminant analysis, logit and probit analysis is also performed. The results indicate the superiority of the M.H.DIS method compared to traditional discrimination techniques already applied in country risk assessment.

Key words: Country risk, Multicriteria analysis, Discrimination, Jackknife procedure, Comparison.

---

* A first draft of this paper was presented at the International Conference "Preparing the Manager of the 21st Century", Thessaloniki, Greece, December 16-18, 1999.
† Corresponding author: Fax: 30–821–69410, 37236, E–mail: kostas@ergasya.tuc.gr, kostas@cha.forthnet.gr

S.H. Zanakis et al. (eds.), Decision Making: Recent Developments and Worldwide Applications, 361–377.
© 2000 Kluwer Academic Publishers.

INTRODUCTION

The rapid growth of international lending of developing countries in the 1970s, the two oil crises in 1973 and 1979 together with the recessions in 1974–75, and the increasing number of debt reschedulings in the early 1980s led to an unstable and uncertain international economic, political, and social environment. International banks and credit institutions with massive loans to countries under development were confronted with the risk that these countries would fail to meet their debt-service obligations. This situation highlighted the importance of country risk assessment, and several attempts have been made, mainly by banking institutions, to establish efficient procedures for country risk evaluation.

Recently the world economy has slowly, but progressively, started to upturn. In the new globalized environment formed during the last decade, significant political and social transformations took place all over the world. These transformations have dramatically changed the world economic, political, and social environment. Within this new context, the evaluation of country risk preserves its significance in order to analyze the world economic environment, to prevent future recessions, and to contribute to the global economic as well as living standard improvement.

Several attempts have been made, mainly by banks, to establish efficient procedures for estimating country risk. These procedures were initially based on devising checklist systems which proved to be insufficient due to the difficulty in selecting the economic indicators and determining their relative importance (Saini and Bates, 1984). Since then, more sophisticated multivariate statistical techniques have been proposed, including discriminant analysis (Frank and Cline, 1971; Grinols, 1976; Saini and Bates, 1978; Taffler and Abassi, 1984; Somerville and Taffler, 1995), factor analysis (Mumpower, Livingston, and Lee, 1987), regression analysis and regression trees (Cosset and Roy, 1988 and 1991), cluster analysis (Mumpower, Livingston, and Lee, 1987), logit analysis (Feder and Just, 1977; Saini and Bates, 1978; Taffler and Abassi, 1984; Somerville and Taffler, 1995), and principal components analysis (Dhonte, 1975). Burton and Inoue (1983) review the use of country risk assessment methods, while Saini and Bates (1984) provide a comprehensive review and criticism of the application of such statistical and econometric techniques in country risk evaluation. Their criticism focuses on the exclusion of important social/political factors, the assumption of stable statistical relationships across countries, etc., and the overlooking of the dynamic nature of the world economy.

Recently, alternative non-parametric techniques, such as fuzzy logic (Levy and Yoon, 1995) and multicriteria decision aid, have also been applied in this field (Tang and Espinal, 1989; Oral et al., 1992; Cosset, Siskos, and Zopounidis, 1992; Cook and Hebner, 1993; Anastassiou and Zopounidis, 1997). A recent comprehensive review of country risk assessment methodologies with emphasis on multicriteria decision aid paradigm can be found in Zopounidis, Pentaraki, and Doumpos (1998).

The recent financial crises of 1997-1998 have demonstrated that despite the progress made after the crises of the 1970s, vulnerability is still evident in the global economic environment. Institutional investors and international organizations should consider the potential impacts of this economic/financial vulnerability and turmoil in their investment and financing decisions. Especially in the case of organizations such as the World Bank, the International Monetary Fund, the OECD, and the UN, who are responsible for monitoring the world economic and social environment, the development and use of reliable country risk assessment models is of major importance. Such models can be used as early warning systems of potential future economic and financial crises, and as tools supporting the specification of policy measures to prevent such crises both at the global and the regional level. Furthermore, country risk assessment models are of interest to institutional investors in measuring the risk of their foreign investments. Several organizations such as Moody's and Standard & Poor's regularly publish reports and ratings of foreign currency bonds issued by sovereign and sovereign-supported entities. These ratings follow a multi-group discrimination scheme and are very closely related to the country risk assessment problem. Investors worldwide use these ratings as a guide to their investment decisions.

These practical findings constitute the major motivation for the research presented in this paper. Following this methodological framework of multicriteria decision aid, this paper addresses the country risk assessment problem through a discrimination approach. On the basis of this approach, the objective is to develop discrimination models that can be used to support the country risk assessment process by classifying a set of countries into predefined groups according to the risk level of each country. The discrimination approach employed in this study, namely the M.H.DIS method, originates from the field of multicriteria decision aid (MCDA). The M.H.DIS method (Zopounidis and Doumpos, 2000) employs a hierarchical discrimination procedure to determine the group in which the countries under consideration belong. The method is applied to the country risk assessment problem in order to develop a model that classifies a sample of 143 countries into four groups according to their economic performance and creditworthiness. The data used are derived from the World Bank (World Bank, 1997) and refer to the year 1995 (Pentaraki, 1998). A comparison with three methods from the field of statistical and econometric analysis, i.e., multiple discriminant analysis (MDA), logit analysis (LA), and probit analysis (PA), is also performed to evaluate the relative discriminating performance of the M.H.DIS method as opposed to well-known statistical and econometric techniques. Numerous applications of these techniques have been conducted in financial decision making-problems (Altman et al., 1981), including country risk assessment (Saini and Bates, 1984). The comparison of the four methods concerns mainly the predictability of the developed discrimination models. Towards this perspective, 250 validation tests are conducted, using a jackknife procedure, in order to obtain an unbiased estimate of the performance of the four methods.

The rest of the paper is organized as follows. Section 2 outlines the main features of the M.H.DIS method. Section 3 is devoted to the comparison of the M.H.DIS method with MDA, LA, and PA through a series of validation tests regarding the country risk assessment problem. Finally, section 4 concludes the paper and summarizes the main findings of this research.

364

THE MULTI–GROUP HIERARCHICAL DISCRIMINATION METHOD (M.H.DIS)

M.H.DIS is a non-parametric discrimination approach based on multicriteria decision aid concepts and mathematical programming techniques. Its objective is to develop discrimination models classifying a set of objects into groups predefined in an ordinal way. The model development procedure employed in M.H.DIS is based on the well-known regression philosophy. Let $A=(a_1, a_2, ..., a_N)$ be a set of N countries used for model development purposes (training sample). The countries are described (evaluated) along with a set of m attributes $X=(x_1, x_2, ..., x_m)$ and they are classified into q groups defined in an ordinal way, such that $C_1 \succ C_2 \succ ... \succ C_q$ (C_1 is preferred to C_2, C_2 is preferred to C_3, etc.). In discriminating among the groups of countries, it is assumed that the decision maker's preferences are monotonic functions on the attributes' scale. This assumption implies that, as the performance of a country on an attribute x_i, that is negatively related to country risk, increases, the decision regarding the classification of this firm into a higher (better) group is more favorable to a decision regarding its classification into a lower (worse) one. A similar implication is also made for all attributes that are positively related to country risk.

The classification of the countries is performed progressively. Initially, in the first stage, the aim is to discriminate the countries belonging into group C_1 (low risk countries) from the countries of all the other groups. The countries classified into group C_1 (correctly or incorrectly) are excluded from further consideration. In a second stage the objective is to discriminate the countries of group C_2 from the countries of the lower groups C_3, C_4, ..., C_q. Once again, all countries classified in group C_2 (correctly or incorrectly) are excluded from further consideration. The same procedure continues in the next stages until all countries are classified into the predefined groups. The number of stages in this hierarchical discrimination procedure is $q-1$ (i.e., for two groups there will be only one stage; for three groups there will be two stages, etc.).

At each stage k of this process the discrimination of the groups is based on the development of a pair of additive utility functions of the attribute vector $X=(x_1, x_2, ..., x_m)$. These utility functions have the following form:[1]

$$U^k(X) = \sum_{i=1}^{m} p_i^k u_i^k(x_i) \text{ and } U^{-k}(X) = \sum_{i=1}^{m} p_i^{-k} u_i^{-k}(x_i),$$

The former utility function $U^k(X)$ characterizes the countries of group C_k, whereas the latter function $U^{-k}(X)$ characterizes the countries belonging into the groups C_{k+1}, C_{k+2}, ..., C_q. $u_i^k(x_i)$ and $u_i^{-k}(x_i)$ are the corresponding marginal (partial) utility functions of the attribute vector normalized between 0 and 1. The weighting parameters p_i^k and p_i^{-k} sum up to 1, i.e., $\sum p_i^k = 1$ and $\sum p_i^{-k} = 1$; they represent the significance

---

[1] These expressions are equivalent to $U^k(X) = \sum_{i=1}^{m} u_i^k(x_i)$ and $U^{-k}(X) = \sum_{i=1}^{m} u_i^{-k}(x_i)$ if $u_i^k(x_i)$ and $u_i^{-k}(x_i)$ are not normalized in the interval [0,1].

of each attribute in the corresponding utility function. If the global utility of a country according to the utility function $U^k(X)$ is higher than the global utility estimated according to the utility function $U^{-k}(X)$, then the firm is classified into group C_k. Otherwise, if the global utility of a country according to the utility function $U^{-k}(X)$ is higher than the global utility estimated according to the utility function $U^k(X)$, this indicates that the country belongs in one of the groups C_{k+1}, C_{k+2}, ..., C_q. In the next stages of the discrimination process, the specific classification of such a country will be determined. Figure 1 illustrates the hierarchical process employed for model development and discrimination in the M.H.DIS method.

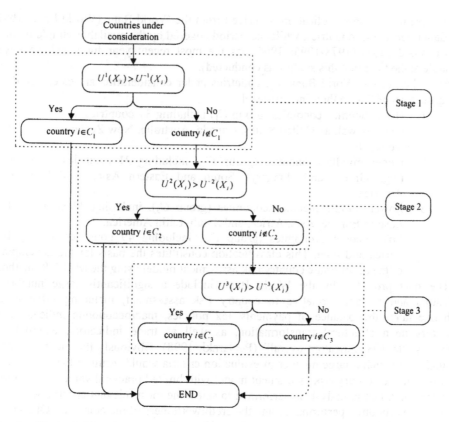

Figure 1. The Hierarchical Discrimination Procedure in the M.H.DIS Method

The estimation of the additive utility functions in M.H.DIS is accomplished through mathematical programming techniques. More specifically, at each stage k of the hierarchical discrimination process of figure 1, two linear programs and one mixed–integer program are solved to estimate optimally the two additive utility functions

$U^k(X)$ and $U^{-k}(X)$, both in terms of the total number of misclassifications and the "clarity" of the obtained classification. Details on the estimation procedure are given in the appendix. The M.H.DIS method has already been applied successfully in several fields of financial management, including portfolio selection, credit card evaluation, corporate mergers and acquisitions, credit risk assessment (Zopounidis and Doumpos, 2000), and financial distress prediction (Doumpos and Zopounidis, 2000).

APPLICATION TO COUNTRY RISK ASSESSMENT

Data set description

The sample used in this application is derived from the World Bank (World Bank, 1997). The data refer to 143 countries, while the period covered by the available sample involves almost two decades (1978-1995; 1995 was the most recent year for which data were available at the time that this study was conducted).

According to the World Bank, the countries under consideration are categorized into four groups according to their income level:

1. High–income economies (group C_1) including 31 countries, mostly European ones, as well as United States, Canada, Australia, New Zealand, Japan, Hong Kong, etc.
2. Upper–middle economies (group C_2), including 21 countries from Europe (e.g., Greece and Hungary), South and Eastern Asian, and Latin–South America.
3. Lower–middle income economies (group C_3), including 42 countries from Eastern Europe, Asia, Africa, and South–Latin America.
4. Low–income economies (group C_4), including 49 countries, mostly from Africa and Asia. This classification constitutes the basis for the development of the appropriate country risk assessment model using the M.H.DIS method.

The data provided by the World Bank include a significantly large number of indicators and variables relative to country risk assessment, including inflation and exchange rates, the balance of payments, tax policies, macroeconomic indicators, and indicators upon structural transformation, as well as trade indicators, external debt indicators, etc. (98 indicators overall) (Pentaraki, 1998). Obviously the incorporation in the analysis of such a large number of evaluation criteria would result in the development of an unrealistic country risk assessment model with limited practical value. To overcome this problem, a factor analysis is performed to select the most relevant criteria, which best describe the economic performance and the creditworthiness of the countries. Of course, it could be possible to override factor analysis if a country risk expert were available to determine the most significant country risk indicators, or if the decision maker had a clear view of the indicators that should be examined. Nevertheless, in any case the factor analysis results provide significant support with respect to data reduction through the identification of the indicators that best characterize economic performance and creditworthiness in the considered sample. Furthermore, country risk researchers commonly use factor analysis as a data reduction approach to handle the large volume of information that is available for country risk assessment purposes (Dhonte, 1975; Saini and Bates, 1984; Mumpower, Livingston, and Lee, 1987).

In this case study, factor analysis is performed using all of the available data on the study of 18 years (2574 observations, i.e. 143 countries for 18 years). The application of factor analysis resulted in the development of 20 factors that account for 72.65% of the total variance in the data (Pentaraki, 1998). The selection of the criteria is performed on the basis of their factor loadings. Initially, from each factor, the criterion with the higher factor loading is selected. Some of these criteria with factor loading lower than 0.7 are excluded from further analysis. Some others that do not contribute to discriminating the four groups of countries (e.g. population, working force, etc.) are replaced with criteria that in previous studies were found to be significant for country risk assessment (e.g. current account balance/GDP). Thus, on the basis of the factor analysis results (i.e., factor loadings) and the relevance of the considered criteria to country risk assessment as reported in the international literature (Saini and Bates, 1984, Cosset, Siskos, and Zopounidis, 1992, Oral et al., 1992), 12 evaluation criteria are finally selected (table 1).

Table 1. Initial Set of Country Risk Indicators

x_1	Current account balance/GDP
x_2	Export volume growth
x_3	Gross domestic investment/GDP
x_4	Import volume growth
x_5	Inflation (GDP deflator)
x_6	Net trade in goods and services
x_7	Present value of debt/exports of goods and services
x_8	Present value of debt/GNP
x_9	Total debt service/GNP
x_{10}	Income velocity of money (GDP/M2)
x_{11}	GNP growth
x_{12}	Gross international reserves in months of imports.

The significance in the differences between the group means of the 12 selected criteria is investigated through a one-way ANOVA test. The results presented in table 2 indicate that most criteria present statistically significant differences between the groups at the 5% significance level. There are three exceptions to this finding, involving the export volume growth (x_2), the import volume growth (x_4), and the net trade in goods and services (x_6). These three criteria are not considered during model development.

In order to investigate the performance of the M.H.DIS method and compare it with MDA, LA, and PA, several validation tests are conducted using the country risk data described above. The validation tests are performed using a jackknife approach (Theodossiou, 1993), in order to have, as much as possible, an unbiased estimate of the performance of the four methods used in this case study. Jackknife procedures allow the use of all available data in the estimation, resulting in a statistically more reliable model. The jackknife procedure is applied in six steps as follows: (1) randomly exclude one country from each of the four predefined groups, (2) estimate the four examined models using M.H.DIS, MDA, LA, and PA based on the sample without four countries identified in step 1, (3) use the models to compute the discriminant scores/probabilities for the four excluded countries, (4) reclassify the four excluded countries in one of the four groups, (5) repeat this procedure 250 times, (6) determine the percentage of times the excluded countries are misclassified. These percentages are unbiased estimates of the performance of all four examined methods. The subsequent sub–section discusses the results obtained through the M.H.DIS method over the conducted validation tests, and reports the comparison with MDA, LA, and PA.

Table 2. One–Way ANOVA Results

		Sum of Squares	df	Mean Square	F
x_1	Between Groups	2,126.39	3	708.80	22.808[*]
	Within Groups	4,319.63	139	31.08	
	Total	6,446.02	142		
x_2	Between Groups	1,236.49	3	412.16	0.92
	Within Groups	62,245.46	139	447.81	
	Total	63,481.95	142		
x_3	Between Groups	1,173.13	3	391.04	6.577[*]
	Within Groups	8,264.85	139	59.46	
	Total	9,437.98	142		
x_4	Between Groups	324.10	3	108.03	0.301
	Within Groups	49,826.86	139	358.47	
	Total	50,150.96	142		
x_5	Between Groups	9,257.78	3	3,085.93	4.483[*]
	Within Groups	95,688.63	139	688.41	
	Total	104,946.40	142		
x_6	Between Groups	851,304,453,990,242,000,000	3	283,768,151,330,080,000,000	1.819
	Within Groups	21,678,640,473,931,500,000,000	139	155,961,442,258,500,000,000	
	Total	22,529,944,927,921,800,000,000	142		
x_7	Between Groups	2,027,384.88	3	675,794.96	41.143[*]
	Within Groups	2,283,146.07	139	16,425.51	
	Total	4,310,530.95	142		
x_8	Between Groups	249,600.22	3	83,200.08	20.944[*]
	Within Groups	552,178.86	139	3,972.51	
	Total	801,779.09	142		
x_9	Between Groups	1,072.88	3	357.63	8.836[*]
	Within Groups	5,625.98	139	40.48	
	Total	6,698.86	142		
x_{10}	Between Groups	251.91	3	83.97	42.176[*]
	Within Groups	276.74	139	1.99	
	Total	528.65	142		
x_{11}	Between Groups	206.17	3	68.72	3.713[*]
	Within Groups	2,572.53	139	18.51	
	Total	2,778.70	142		
x_{12}	Between Groups	54.27	3	18.09	2.946[*]
	Within Groups	853.44	139	6.14	
	Total	907.70	142		

[*] *Significant at the 5% level.*

Presentation of results

The average classification results of M.H.DIS and the three statistical methods on the validation tests are presented in tables 3 and 4. All figures reported in these tables correspond to averages over all validation tests. The elements C_1–C_1, C_2–C_2, C_3–C_3, and C_4–C_4, represent average classification accuracy for each of the four groups, while all other elements correspond to average classification errors.

Table 3. Average Classification Results (Accuracy) for the Training Sample (139 Countries)

			Estimated classification				Overall accuracy
			C_1	C_2	C_3	C_4	
Actual classification	M.H.DIS	C_1	10.0000%	.0000%	.0000%	.0000%	97.6029%
		C_2	.0000%	98.3000%	1.7000%	.0000%	
		C_3	.0000%	2.5854%	97.3073%	0.1073%	
		C_4	.0000%	2.5417%	1.3917%	96.0667%	
	MDA	C_1	94.4000%	.0000%	5.6000%	.0000%	75.7871%
		C_2	14.8800%	23.9200%	44.7200%	9.0400%	
		C_3	7.1415%	4.8488%	78.7220%	9.2683%	
		C_4	.0000%	2.4000%	14.3417%	83.2583%	
	LA	C_1	90.9467%	8.4800%	.5733%	.0000%	69.9022%
		C_2	3.2267%	12.4000%	82.6400%	.1200%	
		C_3	6.9073%	8.3317%	67.4244%	17.3366%	
		C_4	.7000%	1.3333%	15.1417%	82.8250%	
	PA	C_1	88.6933%	11.2533%	.0533%	.0000%	69.0072%
		C_2	.2267%	14.1800%	85.4600%	.0200%	
		C_3	4.8000%	9.9512%	64.8878%	20.3610%	
		C_4	.0500%	1.9833%	14.9000%	83.0667%	

With regard to the training sample (table 3), the overall classification accuracy of M.H.DIS is significantly higher than the one of MDA, LA, and PA (97.60% for M.H.DIS vs. 75.79% for MDA, 69.90% for LA, and 69.01% for PA). Of course, higher model fit does not ensure higher generalizing ability, which is the ultimate objective in decision models developed through regression–based techniques. In that respect, the results on the validation tests are of particular interest towards the evaluation of the predictability of M.H.DIS and the other methods. The results presented in table 4 indicate that, in terms of the overall classification accuracy, M.H.DIS still performs better than the other methods, although the differences are smaller compared to the training sample. The average overall classification accuracy of the M.H.DIS method is 73.4% while the overall classification accuracy of MDA, LA, and PA is 64.6%, 62.5%, and 61.4%, respectively.

Table 5 presents the results of a t-test regarding the differences between the average classification accuracies of the considered methods. In the training sample, the differences between the average accuracy of M.H.DIS and the accuracy of all of the other methods are always significant at the 1% level. Most importantly, the performance of M.H.DIS in the validation sample is also significantly higher than the one of MDA, LA, and PA at the 1% significance level.

Table 4. Average Classification Results (Accuracy) for the Validation Sample (Jackknife Estimates. 250 Replications)

			Estimated classification				Overall accuracy
			C_1	C_2	C_3	C_4	
Actual classification	M.H.DIS	C_1	10.0000%	.0000%	.0000%	.0000%	73.4000%
		C_2	.0000%	52.4000%	30.4000%	17.2000%	
		C_3	.0000%	32.0000%	56.4000%	11.6000%	
		C_4	.0000%	5.2000%	1.0000%	84.0000%	
	MDA	C_1	94.0000%	.0000%	6.0000%	.0000%	64.6000%
		C_2	24.8000%	15.2000%	48.8000%	11.2000%	
		C_3	8.0000%	7.6000%	74.0000%	10.4000%	
		C_4	.0000%	7.6000%	17.2000%	75.2000%	
	LA	C_1	91.2000%	8.4000%	0.4000%	.0000%	62.5000%
		C_2	1.2000%	13.6000%	76.4000%	8.8000%	
		C_3	11.2000%	7.6000%	62.4000%	18.8000%	
		C_4	2.4000%	.0000%	14.8000%	82.8000%	
	PA	C_1	87.6000%	12.4000%	.0000%	.0000%	61.4000%
		C_2	.0000%	13.2000%	77.6000%	9.2000%	
		C_3	9.2000%	1.0000%	60.4000%	20.4000%	
		C_4	.4000%	2.0000%	13.2000%	84.4000%	

Table 5. Results of t–Test on the Differences in the Average Classification Accuracy of the Methods

	Training sample				Validation sample			
	M.H.DIS	MDA	LA	PA	M.H.DIS	MDA	LA	PA
M.H.DIS	–	275.92*	242.16*	316.49*	–	5.14*	6.18*	6.70*
MDA		–	44.42*	60.33*		–	1.23	1.85**
LA			–	6.41*			–	0.62
PA				–				–

*Significant at the 1% level.
**Significant at the 10% level.

In terms of the individual classification accuracies in the validation tests, M.H.DIS always correctly classifies all countries belonging to the high–income economy group (group C_1). Furthermore, there is no country belonging to the other groups that is classified incorrectly into the high–income economy group. MDA, LA, and PA also perform quite well in identifying high–income economies, although there are few cases of significant misclassification (i.e., of the form $C_1 \rightarrow C_3$). Similarly for the high–income economy group, M.H.DIS, MDA, LA, and PA also perform well in identifying countries of the low–income economy group. The average classification accuracy for this group is 84% for M.H.DIS, 75.2% for MDA, 82.8% for LA, and 84.4% for PA. MDA also performs efficiently in the lower–middle income economy group (classification accuracy 74%) as opposed to the 56.4% accuracy of the M.H.DIS method. LA and PA also outperform M.H.DIS with respect to the classification accuracy regarding lower-middle income economies. On the contrary, MDA, LA, and PA are unable to correctly classify upper-middle income economies. The corresponding classification accuracies of all three methods is lower than 20%, whereas M.H.DIS's accuracy exceeds 52%.

The average classification results for the training sample have almost the same characteristics as the ones obtained in the validation tests. M.H.DIS provides minor classification errors throughout the four groups. The rest of the methods also provide satisfactory results regarding their classification accuracies for high-income and low-income economies, but their performance in the two intermediate groups of countries is moderate for lower-middle income economies and quite low for upper-middle income economies.

CONCLUSIONS AND DISCUSSION

Country risk assessment has gained significant interest both in academic research and in the daily practice of financial and banking management. The aim of this study was to propose a methodological framework for evaluating the large number of alternatives that are usually encountered in country risk decision problems according to the level of risks that they entail. The result of this evaluation consists of a classification of the considered countries into predefined groups of risk, taking into consideration all of the pertinent country risk factors, both quantitative and qualitative ones. The developed classification model serves as a country risk assessment system that enables the decision makers to discriminate between countries of various risk levels. The decision-maker can base his actual financing and/or investment decisions upon this discrimination and his risk-aversion policy.

The methodological approach employed in this paper to develop country risk assessment models on the basis of a discrimination scheme was based on the M.H.DIS method. The M.H.DIS method constitutes a non-parametric approach in addressing discrimination problems, such as country risk assessment. The conducted comparison with MDA, LA, and PA has demonstrated that, except for the non-parametric nature of M.H.DIS that overrides the statistical restrictions of traditional approaches, the method is also able to provide high-discrimination performance.

The implications of the M.H.DIS method are not only restricted to financial risk assessment, but they also involve other financial risk management fields, including, among others, portfolio selection and management, credit risk assessment, and financial distress prediction. Of course, M.H.DIS is not the only non-parametric approach to address financial risk management problems. Actually, techniques such as artificial neural networks (ANN) and data envelopment analysis (DEA) have found several applications on this field (Trippi and Turban, 1996; Cooper, Seiford, and Tone, 1999). Both these methods follow a scoring approach similar to the one employed in M.H.DIS, leading to the estimation of a score for each alternative (country) that serves as a risk measurement evaluation index. Furthermore, numerous applications have been published on the use of ANN in addressing discrimination problems, such as the ones often encountered in financial risk management, while recently similar studies have also been conducted for DEA models (Sueyoshi, 1999). The connectives between M.H.DIS and these non-parametric techniques constitute an interesting future research direction towards the development of more reliable financial risk assessment models. Actually, ANN have already been used in the estimation of utility functions within the context of multicriteria decision aid (Malakooti and Zhou, 1994). Comparative studies among the methods would also be of interest to identify their relative strengths and weaknesses.

REFERENCES

Altman, E. I., Avery, R., Eisenbeis, R. and Stinkey, J. (1981), "Application of Classification Techniques in Business", *Banking and Finance*, JAI Press, Greenwich.

Anastassiou, T. and Zopounidis, C. (1997), "Country risk assessment: A multicriteria analysis approach.", *The Journal of Euro-Asian Management* 3/1, 51-73.

Burton, F. N. and Inoue, H. (1983), "Country risk evaluation methods: A survey of systems in use", *The Banker* 133, 41–43.

Cook, W. D. and Hebner, K. J. (1993), "A multicriteria approach to country risk evaluation: With an example employing Japanese data.", *International Review of Economics and Finance* 2/4, 327-348.

Cooper, W. W., Seiford, L. M. and Tone, K. (1999), *Data Envelopment Analysis-A Comprehensive Text with Models, Applications, References*, Kluwer Academic Publishers, Dordrecht.

Cosset, J. C. and Roy, J. (1988), "Expert judgments of political riskiness: An alternative approach", *Document de Travail* 88–12, Université Laval, Québec, Canada.

Cosset, J. C. and Roy, J. (1991), "The determinants of country risk ratings", *Journal of International Business Studies* (First Quarter), 135-142.

Cosset, J. C., Siskos, Y. and Zopounidis, C. (1992), "Evaluating country risk: A decision support approach", *Global Finance Journal* 3, 79–95.

Dhonte, P. (1975), "Describing external debt situations: A roll–over approach", *IMF Staff Papers* 22, 159–186.

Doumpos, M. and Zopounidis, C. (2000), "A multicriteria discrimination method for the prediction of financial distress: The case of Greece", *Multinational Finance Journal* (in press).

Frank, C. R. and Cline, W. R. (1971), "Measurement of debt servicing capacity: An application of discriminant analysis", *Journal of International Economics* 1, 327-344.

Feder, G. and Just, R. (1977), "A study of debt servicing capacity applying logit analysis", *Journal of Development Economics* 4, 25-38.

Grinols, E. (1976), "International debt rescheduling and discriminantion using financial variables", U.S. Treasury Department, Washington, D.C.

Levy J. B. and Yoon, E. (1995), "Modeling global market entry decision by fuzzy logic with an application to country risk assessment", *European Journal of Operational Research* 82, 53-78.

Malakooti, B. and Zhou Y. Q. (1994), "Feedforward artificial neural networks for solving discrete multiple criteria decision making problems", *Management Science* 40/11, 1542-1561.

Mousseau, V. and Slowinski, R. (1998), "Inferring an ELECTRE–TRI model from assignment examples", *Journal of Global Optimization* 12/2, 157–174.

Mumpower, J. L., Livingston, S. and Lee, T. J. (1987), "Expert judgments of political riskiness", *Journal of Forecasting* 6, 51-65.

Oral, M., Kettani, O., Cosset, J. C. and Daouas, M. (1992), "An estimation model for country risk rating", *International Journal of Forecasting* 8, 583–593.

Pentaraki, K. (1998), *Methodological Framework for the Analysis and Assessment of Counties' Creditworthiness*, Master's Thesis, Technical University of Crete, Chania, Greece (in Greek).

Saini, K. G. and Bates, P. S. (1978), "Statistical techniques for determining debt-capacity for developing countries: Analytical review of the literature and further empirical results", *Research Paper* no. 7818, Federal Reserve Bank of New York, New York.

Saini, K. G. and Bates P. S. (1984), "A survey of the quantitative approaches to country risk analysis", *Journal of Banking and Finance* 8, 341–356.

Somerville, R. A. and Taffler, R. J. (1995), "Banker judgement versus formal forecasting models: The case of country risk assessment", *Journal of Banking and Finance* 19, 281-297.

Taffler, R. J. and Abassi, B. (1984), "Country risk: A model for predicting debt servicing problems in developing countries", *Journal of Royal Statistical Society* 147/4, 541-568.

Tang, J.C. S. and Espinal, C. G. (1989), "A model to assess country risk", *Omega* 17/4, 363-367.

Theodossiou, P. (1993), "Predicting shifts in the mean of a multivariate time series process: An application in predicting business failures", *Journal of the American Statistical Association* 88/422, 441–449.

Trippi, R. R. and Turban, R. (1996), *Neural Networks in Finance and Investing*, Chicago, Irwin.

Sueyoshi, T. (1999), "DEA-discriminant analysis in the view of goal programming", *European Journal Of Operational Research* 115/3, 564-582.

World Bank (1997), *World Development Indicators*, World Bank Publications, New York.

Zopounidis, C. and Doumpos, M. (2000), "Building additive utilities for multi-group hierarchical discrimination: The M.H.DIS method", *Optimization Methods and Software* (in press).

Zopounidis, C., Pentaraki, K. and Doumpos, M. (1998), "A review of country risk assessment approaches: New empirical evidence", in C. Zopounidis and P. M. Pardalos (Eds)., *Managing in Uncertainty: Theory and Practice*, Kluwer Academic Publishers, Dordrecht, 5-22.

APPENDIX:

Mathematical programming formulations for the estimation of the utility functions in the M.H.DIS method

The mathematical programming formulations used in M.H.DIS during model development to optimally estimate the utility functions that best discriminate the considered groups of countries include two linear programs and a mixed–integer one. The solution to these problems at each stage k of the discrimination procedure described in section 2 has a twofold objective. First, minimize the total number of misclassifications through the development of a pair of utility functions that facilitate the discrimination between group C_k and the "lower" groups C_{k+1}, C_{k+2}, ..., C_q (henceforth denoted as $\sim C_k$). Secondly, to calibrate the developed utility functions in order to maximize the "clarity" of the classification. This objective is similar to the among–groups variance maximization in discriminant analysis. These two objectives are addressed through a lexicographic approach. First, the minimization of the total number of misclassifications is pursued and then the maximization of the "clarity" of the classification is sought.

The outcome of this procedure at stage k is a pair of additive utility functions U^k and $U^{\sim k}$ that accommodates these two objectives. The former characterizes the countries of group C_k, while the latter characterizes the countries belonging to the set of groups $\sim C_k$. Both utility functions are normalized between 0 and 1, while the marginal utilities of the country risk indicators x_i are monotone functions: If x_i is positively related to country risk, then $u_i^k(x_i)$ is a decreasing function and $u_i^{\sim k}(x_i)$ is an increasing one. Otherwise, if x_i is negatively related to country risk, then $u_i^k(x_i)$ is an increasing function and $u_i^{\sim k}(x_i)$ is a decreasing one. These properties (normalization and monotonicity) are incorporated as constraints to all mathematical programming formulations presented below.

Pursuing the first objective on the development of the two utility functions (i.e., minimization of the total number of misclassifications) requires the minimization of the following function:

$$EC = \sum_{i=1}^{N_k} I_{ki} + \sum_{i=1}^{N_{\sim k}} I_{\sim ki} \,, \tag{1}$$

where, I_{ki} and $I_{\sim ki}$ are 0-1 variables representing the classification status of each country belonging to groups C_k and $\sim C_k$, respectively (0 indicates correct classification, whereas 1 indicates misclassification). N_k represents the number of countries belonging to group C_k, whereas $N_{\sim k}$ represents the number of countries belonging to the set of groups $\sim C_k$. At this point it should be noted that, instead of the overall number of misclassifications, it is also possible to employ the overall misclassification cost as a more realistic measure of the quality of the obtained discrimination models (for an application to the two-group case, see Doumpos and Zopounidis, 2000). The overall misclassification cost is a function of the a priori group membership probabilities and the associated misclassification cost for each group. In the multi-group case, it is often difficult to define these parameters, especially in cases where the actual decision-maker is not available. Therefore, the application presented in this paper regarding the country risk assessment problem (section 3) is based on the use of the total number of misclassifications instead of the overall misclassification cost.

The development of a pair of utility functions that minimize the total number of misclassifications (1) (let EC_{min} denote the minimum total number of misclassifications) requires the use of mixed–integer programming techniques. However, solving mixed–integer programming formulations in cases where there are many integer variables is a computationally-intensive procedure. Even in cases of samples consisting of 50 countries (i.e., 50 integer variables), the development of the optimal classification rule could be a highly time–consuming process if there is a significant degree of group overlapping. To address this issue, M.H.DIS initially employs an alternate error function EC' that approximates the total number of misclassifications:

$$EC' = \sum_{i=1}^{N_k} e_{ki} + \sum_{i=1}^{N_{\sim k}} e_{\sim ki} \tag{2}$$

The error variables e_{ki} and $e_{\sim ki}$ are surrogates of the 0-1 error variables I_{ki} and $I_{\sim ki}$ in (1). Both of these classification errors are positive real numbers representing the magnitude of the violation of the classification rules employed during model development:

$$e_{ki} = \begin{cases} U^{\sim k}(X_i) - U^k(X_i), & \text{if } U^k(X_i) < U^{\sim k}(X_i) \\ 0, & \text{otherwise} \end{cases}$$

$$e_{\sim ki} = \begin{cases} U^k(X_i) - U^{\sim k}(X_i), & \text{if } U^{\sim k}(X_i) < U^k(X_i) \\ 0, & \text{otherwise} \end{cases} \tag{3}$$

The minimization of the function EC' is performed through the solution of the following mathematical programming problem:

LP1: Minimization of the overall classification error

$$\text{Min } EC' = \sum_{i=1}^{N_k} e_{ki} + \sum_{i=1}^{N_{\sim k}} e_{\sim ki}$$

Subject to:

$$U^k(X_i) - U^{\sim k}(X_i) + e_{ki} \geq s, \, i=1, 2, ..., N_k \tag{4}$$

$$U^{\sim k}(X_i) - U^k(X_i) + e_{\sim ki} \geq s, \, i=1, 2, ..., N_{\sim k} \tag{5}$$

$e_{ki} \geq 0, e_{\sim ki} \geq 0.$

LP1 is a simple linear programming problem that can be easily solved even for large data sets. In constraints (4)–(5), s is a small positive constant used to ensure the strict inequalities presented in definition (3) of the error variables e_{ki} and $e_{\sim ki}$.

Solving LP1 yields an initial pair of utility functions that minimizes the total classification error function EC' (let EC'_{min} denote the minimum total classification error obtained after solving LP1). If these utility functions correctly classify all countries, then all of the error variables e_{ki} and $e_{\sim ki}$ will be zero. Therefore, in such a case, $EC'_{min} = EC_{min} = 0$. However, this is not always the case. Usually, $EC'_{min} \neq 0$ and consequently $EC_{\min} \neq 0$. In such cases, bearing in mind the fact that EC' is an approximation of EC, it becomes apparent that the utility functions corresponding to $EC'_{\min}$ will not necessarily yield the minimum total number of misclassifications $EC_{\min}$. For example, consider that in a sample consisting of four countries classified into two groups (low-risk and high-risk), the utility functions obtained after solving LP1 lead to two misclassified countries i (low-risk country) and j (high-risk country) with the following classification errors: $e_{1i}=0.2$ and $e_{-1j}=0.1$. In this case, $EC'_{\min}=0.3$ and $EC=2$. However, an alternate solution that classifies country j correctly (i.e., $e_{-1j}=0$) but assigns a misclassification error to country i equal to 0.5 is clearly preferred. In this case, $EC'=0.5> EC'_{\min}$, but $EC_{\min}=1<EC$. Thus, it is worth exploring the possibility of finding an alternate pair of utility functions than the one developed through LP1 that yields a classification error $EC' \geq EC'_{\min}$, but provides a smaller number of misclassifications. In M.H.DIS, this possibility is explored through the solution of MIP.

MIP: Minimization of the overall misclassification cost

$$\text{Min } EC = \sum_{i=1}^{N_k^{\text{Mis}}} I_{ki} + \sum_{i=1}^{N_{-k}^{\text{Mis}}} I_{-ki}$$

Subject to:

$$\left. \begin{aligned} U^k(X_i)-U^{-k}(X_i) \geq s, \; i=1,2,...,N_k^{\text{cor}} \\ U^k(X_i)-U^{-k}(X_i) \geq s, \; i=1,2,...,N_{-k}^{\text{cor}} \end{aligned} \right\} \tag{6}$$

$$\left. \begin{aligned} U^k(X_i)-U^{-k}(X_i)+I_{ki} \geq s, \; i=1,2,...,N_k^{\text{mis}} \\ U^{-k}(X_i)-U^k(X_i)+I_{-ki} \geq s, \; i=1,2,...,N_{-k}^{\text{mis}} \end{aligned} \right\} \tag{7}$$

I_{ki}, I_{-ki} integers

Starting with the initial utility functions developed through LP1, MIP explores the possibility of modifying these utility functions so that the total number of misclassifications is minimized. This minimization is performed without changing the correct classifications obtained by LP1 (i.e., all countries correctly classified by the initial pair of utility functions are retained as correct classifications; cf. constraints (6)). Note that the 0-1 error variables I_{ki} and I_{-ki} are not associated with all countries, but only to the ones misclassified by LP1 (constraints (7)). The number of countries actually belonging to group C_k, which are misclassified by LP1, is denoted as N_k^{mis}, whereas N_{-k}^{mis} denotes the number of countries actually belonging to the set of groups $\sim C_k$, which are classified by LP1 into group C_k. Similarly, N_k^{cor} and N_{-k}^{cor} denote the number of the corresponding correct classifications obtained by LP1. All of these correct classifications are retained (constraints (6)). Since, in most cases, the number of countries misclassified by LP1 ($N_k^{\text{mis}} + N_{-k}^{\text{mis}}$) is a small part of the whole sample, the number of integer variables in MIP is small, thus facilitating its easy solution.

The pair of utility functions developed after initially solving LP1 and then MIP is optimal in terms of the total number of misclassifications. However, the ultimate purpose of the utility functions developed through M.H.DIS is prediction with respect to country risk assessment. Of course, it is difficult to ensure high predictability during model development. Utility functions that clearly distinguish the considered groups of countries, however, are expected to have higher predictability than utility functions that yield the same total number of misclassifications but achieve a "marginal" discrimination during model development. Traditional discriminant analysis addresses this issue through the maximization of the among–groups variance. In M.H.DIS, the measure employed to assess the distance between the countries belonging to the group C_k and the countries belonging to ~C_k, according to the developed discrimination model (utility functions) is the minimum difference d between the global utilities of the correctly classified countries identified after solving MIP ($d>0$).

$$d = \min\{d_1, d_2\},$$

where $d_1 = \min_{i=1,2,...,N_k^{cor'}}\{U^k(X_i) - U^{~k}(X_i)\}$ and $d_2 = \min_{i=1,2,...,N_{~k}^{cor'}}\{U^{~k}(X_i) - U^k(X_i)\}$

($N_k^{cor'}$ and $N_{~k}^{cor'}$ denote the number of countries belonging into groups C_k and ~C_k, respectively, which are classified correctly by MIP).

The maximization of d is achieved through the solution of the following linear programming formulation (LP2).

LP2: Maximization of the minimum distance

Max d
Subject to:

$$\left.\begin{array}{l} U^k(X_i) - U^{~k}(X_i) - d \geq s, \quad i = 1, 2, ..., N_k^{cor'} \\ U^{~k}(X_i) - U^k(X_i) - d \geq s, \quad i = 1, 2, ..., N_{~k}^{cor'} \end{array}\right\} \tag{8}$$

$$\left.\begin{array}{l} U^k(X_i) - U^{~k}(X_i) \leq 0, \quad i = 1, 2, ..., N_k^{mis'} \\ U^{~k}(X_i) - U^k(X_i) \leq 0, \quad i = 1, 2, ..., N_{~k}^{mis'} \end{array}\right\} \tag{9}$$

$$d \geq 0$$

LP2 begins with the utility functions obtained after solving MIP. $N_k^{mis'}$ and $N_{~k}^{mis'}$ denote the number of countries actually belonging to groups C_k and ~C_k, respectively, which are misclassified by MIP. LP2 seeks to modify the utility functions developed through MIP in order to maximize the distance measure d. All countries misclassified by the utility functions developed through MIP are retained as misclassified. Thus, the utility functions developed through LP2 do not affect the total number of misclassifications, since all correct classifications and misclassifications resulted after solving MIP are retained [constraints (8) and (9), respectively].

The pair of utility functions obtained after solving LP2 is the one used for country risk assessment purposes.

8. DECISION SUPPORT SYSTEMS AND INFORMATION TECHNOLOGY

RODOS: DECISION SUPPORT FOR NUCLEAR EMERGENCIES

J. Bartzis[1], J. Ehrhardt[2], S. French[3], J. Lochard[4],
M. Morrey[5], K.N. Papamichail[6], Kari Sinkko[7], A. Sohier[8]
[1]NSCR Democritos, Greece; [2]IKET, Forschungszentrum
Karlsruhe, Germany; [3]MBS, UK; [4]CEPN, France;
[5]NRPB, UK; [6]University of Manchester, UK;
[7]STUK, Finland; [8]SCK•CEN, Belgium.

Abstract: In the thirteen years that have elapsed since the Chernobyl accident, many studies and developments have been made with the aim of improving our response to any future accident. One project has been the development of a decision support system to aid emergency management. RODOS, a Real time Online Decision Support system for nuclear emergency management, has been built by a consortium of many institutes across Europe and the CIS. As it approaches (standby!) operational use, we face the task of tailoring the output to meet the specific needs of users and simultaneously opening up their minds to full potential of a modern decision support system (DSS). This paper reports a number of investigations into the decision support needs of the competent national safety authorities and reflects on the implications of RODOS for the emergency management process.

Keywords: Bayesian decision analysis; constraint satisfaction; decision support systems; emergency management; explanation systems; multi-attribute value and utility; RODOS;

INTRODUCTION

One of the lessons to be drawn from the Chernobyl accident was the importance of a coherent, harmonised and sensitive response to nuclear emergencies. Inconsistent responses from a variety of decision making bodies, regional, national and international – even if each is individually rational – confuses the public, leads to poor or ineffective implementation of countermeasures and raises the stress levels in the population, which can of itself cause health effects and increased morbidity [11]. A mechanism for achieving broad consistency of approach is the development and widespread installation of a common, comprehensive decision support system (DSS) for off-site emergency management. The RODOS system (Real time Online Decision Support) has been developed with this as its primary goal. Funded in part by the EU Framework R&D programmes, RODOS is being developed by a consortium of more 40 than EU, Eastern European and CIS Institutes.

The objectives of the RODOS project are:

S.H. Zanakis et al. (eds.), Decision Making: Recent Developments and Worldwide Applications, 381–395.

- to develop a comprehensive and integrated decision support system that is generally applicable across Europe;
- to provide a common platform or framework for incorporating the best features of existing DSS and future developments;
- to provide greater transparency in the decision process as one input to improving public understanding and acceptance of off-site emergency measures;
- to facilitate improved communication between countries of monitoring data, predictions of consequences, etc., in the event of any future accident;
- to promote, through the development and use of the system, a more coherent, consistent and harmonised response to any future accident that may affect Europe.

The RODOS system itself addresses the first, second and, in part, the third objectives; it also provides the platform and databases to act as hubs in an international network set up to facilitate data exchange. The project – together with the many interactions which it has catalysed between experts, organisations and government bodies throughout Europe – has in large measure addressed the third and fifth objectives.

Specifically, RODOS is designed to fulfil a number of roles, the more important of which are:

- a core DSS to be integrated into emergency arrangements at local, regional, national or supra-national levels;
- a stand alone interactive training tool for use, among other things, by those responsible for making decisions on off-site emergency management and their technical advisers at local, regional, national and supra-national levels;
- a more general interactive training and educational tool for radiation protection, nuclear safety and emergency planning personnel with professional interests in or responsibility for off-site emergency management;
- a demonstrator to provide governments and their agencies with a view of the state of the art in emergency management DSS;
- a research and development tool to explore the merits and limitations of new techniques or approaches before their more formal integration into operational decision support systems;
- a more effective means for communication and exchange between countries of information such as monitoring data and prognoses of accident consequences.

Its development has also contributed to the improvement of existing emergency management DSS's through the development and dissemination of improved stand-alone modules.

The roles for which RODOS is designed largely determine its potential users. These include those responsible at local, regional, national and supra-national levels for off-site emergency management and related training, for the operation of nuclear installations, for public information, or for communication and exchange of information (e.g., in accord with bilateral or international agreements); the research and development community concerned with improving decision support for off-site emergency management; and developers of decision support systems for the management of non-nuclear emergencies.

The system has been designed in a modular way so that its functionality can be tailored to each user's particular needs.

Background material on decision support for nuclear emergencies can be found in the conference proceedings [11], [12] and the references contained therein. Earlier descriptions of the RODOS system may be found in [2], [7]. This paper concentrates on aspects of the interaction between the users and the system. As we shall indicate, in the past these have not received as much attention as they deserve.

THE RANGE OF SUPPORT PROVIDED

RODOS is designed to support decision makers throughout all phases of a nuclear accident. The early versions of RODOS supported the decision making during the early stages of a release (2-3 days) for regions up to about 30km. from the plant. The current version extends the support to considerably longer ranges: indeed, the atmospheric dispersion chain can predict on European scales and the hydrological models can deal with river systems such as the Rhine basin. Countermeasures such as food bans running months and years into the future can be examined. By late 1999, the support will be truly comprehensive and for all time periods, supporting decision making at all ranges on countermeasures ranging from immediate evacuation through food bans and agricultural changes to permanent relocation.

RODOS needs to support a variety of DMs beginning with the plant or site managers and local emergency management teams who will have responsibility for countermeasures in the early hours of an accident. Their decision making is constrained by national and international intervention levels as well as many other pre-planned rules developed during emergency exercises. Their thinking will be primarily related to health and feasibility issues and have little to do with political, economic or social criteria. But later, when regional, national and international politicians become involved, the full range of criteria will become relevant. There will be little opportunity to deploy pre-planned countermeasure strategies, since specific aspects of the context will dominate the determination of appropriate countermeasures.

Of course, RODOS will not be 'driven' by the DMs themselves. Environmental scientists, meteorologists, public health, civil servants and other advisors will run modules and interpret the output in discussion with the DMs. Nonetheless, the graphical, tabular and numerical output should be understandable by the DMs; it is likely that it will be projected onto screens before them in a decision support room.

RODOS seeks to provide decision support at all levels ranging from largely descriptive reports to a detailed evaluation of the benefits and disadvantages of various countermeasure strategies and their ranking according to the societal preferences as perceived by the DMs: see Figure 1. Support at levels 0, 1 and 2 comprises the provision of information to DMs. Thus, data are organised within RODOS to provide maps of the predicted, possible and, later, actual spread of contamination and predictions of the effects of countermeasures. The system is able to perform 'what-if' calculations, allowing investigation of how the situation may develop. Level 3 support focuses on evaluation and thus explicitly seeks to model the DMs' judgements. It involves the use of techniques of prescriptive decision support based upon multi-attribute value and utility (MAV/U) models.

Level 0:	Acquisition, checking and presentation of radiological data, directly or with minimal analysis, to DMs, along with geographic and demographic information.
Level 1:	Analysis and prediction of the current and future radiological situation based upon monitoring and meteorological data and models.
Level 2:	Simulation of potential countermeasures, e.g. sheltering, evacuation, issue of iodine tablets, food bans, and relocation; determination of their feasibility and quantification of their benefits and disadvantages.
Level 3:	Evaluation and ranking of alternative countermeasure strategies in the face of uncertainty by balancing their respective benefits and disadvantages.

Figure 1. Levels of decision support provided by RODOS

Emergencies involve uncertainty. There are many unknowns, many sources of error: scale of the release, accuracy of radiation monitoring data, weather conditions, the reliability of expert judgement, the success in implementing countermeasures, and the accuracy of the many mathematical models used. During the progression of the accident many data sets will arrive from different sources and of varying accuracy. The design of RODOS addresses all issues relating to uncertainty and data assimilation in a coherent fashion[7]. Bayesian methods are to be used throughout in which all uncertainties are modelled using probabilistic methods and in ways that are compatible with the evaluation of the alternative countermeasures by means of MAV/U models: see Figure 2. This methodology separates scientific issues in understanding data and resolving uncertainty from issues of value judgement which belong to the realm of the political DMs: see [8]. By 1999 some uncertainty handling and data assimilation will be included in the modules, but work on this is ongoing both because of the need to develop the deterministic meteorological, environmental and health models first and because the task is a substantial one.

Among DSS's developed for use in the context of nuclear emergencies, RODOS is unique in its comprehensiveness, its approach to data assimilation and uncertainty handling and its ability to provide level 3 support.

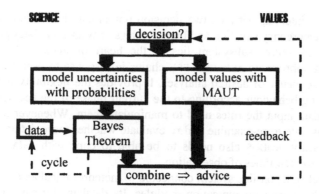

Figure 2. Bayesian methodology

THE RODOS SYSTEM

The conceptual architecture of RODOS consists of three types of subsystem:

- Analysing Subsystem (ASY) modules process incoming data and forecast the location and quantity of contamination including temporal variation.
- Countermeasure Subsystem (CSY) modules suggest possible countermeasures, check them for feasibility, and calculate their expected benefit in terms of a number of attributes (criteria).
- Evaluation Subsystem (ESY) modules rank countermeasure strategies according to their potential benefit and preference judgements provided by the DMs.

The development of ASY and CSY modules to predict, in a timely and computationally efficient manner, the spread of contamination, its likely effects and the scale of mitigation offered by possible countermeasures is a major scientific achievement of the RODOS project. Not only have new models been developed and old ones modified, but all have been integrated into a common system, sharing data and passing information seamlessly from one to another. For instance, the meteorological chain gathers together local and European scale weather forecasts, runs a local scale puff model to predict dispersion and deposition over a few tens of kilometres and then hands the task over to a long scale particle model to continue the predictions to hundreds and thousands of kilometres. Similarly, there are several hydrological models which combine together to predict dispersion through run-off, river and lake systems and shortly marine systems. Deposition data, either from prediction or from actual measurements on the ground can be fed into long term food chain and health models to predict long term population and livestock effects.

Each phase of a nuclear accident is distinct in countermeasures open to the DMs, the urgency with which they must be implemented and the forms, accuracy and quantity of data available. RODOS must recognise this temporal context in order to provide support during all phases. As time passes, RODOS will arrive at different decision points where it must select modules to form an ASY–CSY–ESY chain appropriate to the context of the decision. The time intervals between two decision points may be a matter of minutes or hours early in an emergency situation and longer – days or weeks – at later phases.

A sophisticated control subsystem lies at the heart of RODOS. This manipulates modules, building appropriate ASY–CSY–ESY chains in response to user requests or some pre-programmed sequence of desired analyses. It provides the flexibility within RODOS to change its operating behaviour according to the current phase of the accident. It monitors and controls all data input the rules used to manipulate them. Whenever RODOS receives data or input, it is able to re-examine and re-evaluate whether more detailed analyses are possible or necessary. RODOS also needs to be able to cope with data arriving out of sequence relative to their times of observation.

RODOS is a real-time, on-line system connected to meteorological and radiological data networks. Thus there are communication modules. Its database formats are defining the basis for designing data exchange on an European scale, with RODOS systems acting as hubs in the network.

Underpinning the whole user interface is a sophisticated geographic information system (GIS), which displays both demographic, topographic, economic and agricultural data along with contours of radiological data or predictions: see Figure 3. These displays seek to ensure that the output can be used and understood by the variety of users who may possess qualitatively different skills and perspectives.

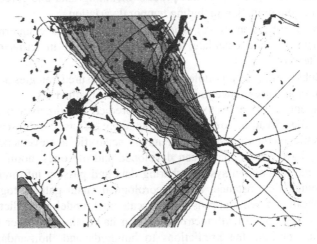

Figure 3. Part of the GIS showing the paths of two plumes, one the result of a second release some hours after the first after a change in wind direction.

RODOS operates in either a semi-automatic or an interactive mode. In the early phases of an emergency, monitoring data and expert judgement will be entered into the system. The system offers the facility to present all the relevant information for decision making automatically according to pre-agreed rules developed during exercises. Relying on interactive control would be inappropriate because of the urgency during the early hours of an accident. In later phases, operation will be more interactive and reflective, seeking value judgements from the DMs and indicating the consequences of these. At all stages there will be automatic checks on the quality of the models such that if the predictions depart significantly from incoming data, warnings will be issued to the user.

The modular design of RODOS recognises client-server design so that the system may be distributed across a network of computers. The interface has been built using standard X-windows for Unix, and the modules written in ANSI C, C++ or Fortran.

Further details of the system and the range of models employed in the ASY and CSY subsystems may be found in [2] and the references therein. We concentrate here on the ESY.

THE EVALUATION SUBSYSTEM

The first component of the ESY (Figure 4) is a knowledge-based system which we call coarse expert system [16] that generates feasible alternatives. In a nuclear emergency, there are several countermeasures such as evacuation, sheltering or food bans that can be applied to the areas around the nuclear plant. The number of alternative strategies i.e. combinations of countermeasures can be very large. However, not all of these strategies are worthy of further evaluation. Some strategies may be infeasible or do not follow some practicality rules. For example, there might be some temporal constraints that do not allow issuing iodine tablets to people who have already been evacuated. There are also some rules determined by international and national radiation protection bodies which strongly advice intervention in some specific circumstances. The knowledge-based system encodes these rules and constraints and discards those strategies that do not satisfy them.

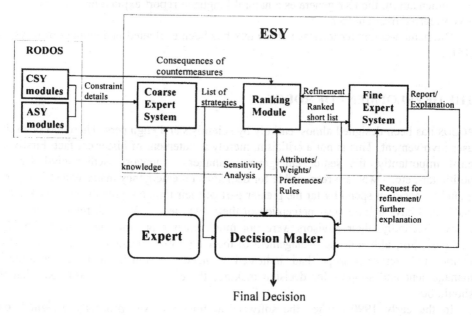

Figure 4. The ESY module

The second component of the ESY is a ranking module that evaluates and ranks the alternative strategies based on their consequences and the preferences of the DMs [3], [17]. A multi-attribute additive function is currently used for the ranking of the strategies. Other forms of utility functions that model the inherent uncertainties in a nuclear emergency are being considered. Several modules in RODOS assess the consequences of the strategies on the different attributes being considered; e.g. the EMERSIM, ECONOM and HEALTH modules [18] calculate the consequences of early-phase combinations of countermeasures such as evacuation, sheltering and issue of iodine tablets and the LCMT-FRODO [1] module estimates the effect of agricultural countermeasures such as disposal and process of food. Pareto plots are presented as well as sensitivity analysis graphs to illustrate the effect of the weight of an attribute in the ranking of the strategies.

The criteria and their associated attributes taken into account in the evaluation of strategies differ depending on the phase of the nuclear emergency. At the early phases of a nuclear emergency (hours and days after the radiation accident), the DMs are concerned with health effects, the public anxiety which would be caused by the incident and the measures taken, feasibility matters and to a lesser extent cost-related issues. At later phases (months and years after the accident), the DMs will have more time to spend on balancing both the short and long term health effects with the cost of the strategies.

The third component of the ESY is called fine expert system and it provides explanation facilities [14]. Previous studies [20] have shown that the advice of a decision support or expert system is very likely to be rejected if no explanation facilities are provided. In order to add transparency into the way that the alternative strategies are ranked and justify its recommendation, the ESY generates a natural language report explaining why one strategy was preferred over another.

The human-computer interface of the ESY has been evaluated in a number of ways: see [15].

THE DEVELOPMENT OF RODOS

RODOS has been designed almost entirely by scientists and engineers. There has been little user involvement. This is not a criticism, merely a statement of historical fact. Firstly and most importantly, the senior emergency managers – mayors, senior civil servants, politicians, etc. – who are responsible for decisions on emergency management in event of a nuclear accident spend by far the greater part of their time on quite different tasks. They had – and have – little clear perception of their own needs. We shall return to this point below. Secondly, their advisors were not much clearer on how the system should be designed. For, although the management of the Chernobyl Accident in the former Soviet Union and across Europe had indicated a need for much improved information management and support for decision making, there was little consensus on what this should be.

In the early 1990's when the software architecture was primarily designed, only scientists and engineers had a vision of what was technically possible. The growth in information and communication technologies at the time was such that much more detailed forecasting of the evolving situation was possible than was included in the then current emergency management processes. The emergency managers and their close advisors were unaware of what a system such as RODOS could offer and hence could not help in the detailed planning of interfaces and its integration into the emergency management process. Thus the RODOS system was designed by scientists and software engineers, at one remove from the emergency management process, with the intention of stimulating a vision of what was possible and so bringing about more constructive user involvement in the design of later versions.

In the intervening years a variety of modules have been developed for RODOS which enable it to predict and evaluate the consequences of a release, both before and after potential counter measures are taken, from the near to far range and from the short to the long term. This is a considerable accomplishment, and it is one on which we need to build as we take RODOS into operational use, tailoring it to the emergency management process.

EMERGENCY MANAGEMENT PROCESSES

The first point to appreciate is that there is no single agreed structure for the process of emergency management common to all countries and regions across Europe. The process, those involved and their responsibilities vary from country to country and, indeed, sometimes from region to region within country. In some countries there is a single national crisis centre, permanently staffed and responsible for managing any emergency, not just nuclear. In others there are national or regional crisis centres specifically focused on nuclear incidents. In others still, the process is much more devolved with many organisations playing a role. Nonetheless, there are common themes. The decisions which need to be supported are, by and large, the same.

When an accident threatens, plant managers will take engineering actions to avoid or reduce the risk of a release. The first decisions on protecting the public – and the first to be explicitly supported by RODOS – would be whether to take precautionary measures such as: issuing a warning, distribution of iodine tablets, and starting to evacuate some areas. If there is a release, decisions will be needed on advice to take iodine tablets, and on sheltering, and evacuation. The following days will see decisions on measures such as food bans, decontamination of livestock, agricultural produce and properties, and restrictions on business, leisure activities and access to the region. After several days or maybe weeks, there will be a need to consider longer term measures, e.g. permanent relocation (resettlement) and permanent changes to agricultural practice and local industry.

Here we focus myopically on the needs of DMs in relation to the support of *their* judgements and decision making. We do not directly address their informational requirements in relation to the outputs of dispersion models, ground contamination models, etc. RODOS seeks to provide judgemental support via Bayesian multi-attribute decision models: see [3], [8].

DECISION SUPPORT NEEDS IN THE MEDIUM AND LONG TERM

Given that most emergency exercises concern the decisions to be taken in the early phase, it is perhaps surprising that we have a much clearer idea of the needs of DMs in the medium and long term in relation to decontamination and clean up, changes in agricultural practice, relocation, etc. Although for these many of the issues are less structured than in the earlier phases, the time pressures are sufficiently less for decision models to be built or, at least, modified and tailored at the time. Uncertainty is less of an issue, because, although the health effects due to the radiation will be stochastic in the sense that we will not know *who* will get cancer, the uncertainty about *how many* will is much smaller. Moreover, we have a number of studies relating to the Chernobyl Accident [11], [13] and to carefully structured exercises [9] which show that multi-attribute value methods provide a powerful and effective form of modelling to help the DMs explore, understand and communicate the issues which drive their decision making. Indeed, some promote the use of these methods to enable various organisations and stakeholders to participate in these decisions. Thus for decision making in the later phases, we are relatively confident that the evaluation modules that we have designed and implemented are able to meet DM needs. Such is not so clearly the case for the early phase.

DECISION SUPPORT NEEDS IN THE THREAT AND EARLY TERM

In an attempt to understand better the needs of DMs in handling the early stages of a nuclear emergency we have run two series of exercises. In the first series held in 1994 to 1996, we ran five exercises: two in Germany, and one each in Belgium, France and the UK. The events were attended by the officials and their advisors who would be responsible for deciding upon and implementing emergency measures in their areas. The scenarios used focused on a threat of a release. There had been a failure in part of the reactor and the probability of a release was set at 10% (i.e. there was a 90% chance that engineering efforts would avert a release). To complicate matters the wind was swinging and the path of the plume could not be predicted with accuracy. We told the DMs that if the release *did* occur there was a 50:50 chance of the plume passing entirely over rural communities, who could easily be evacuated or over a densely populated city whose inhabitants could not be evacuated. See Figure 5. In each exercise, we created this scenario in the context of a real nuclear plant in the DMs' area.

The conclusions drawn from these five exercises were:
- The DMs generally found the presentation of data and predictions very useful: i.e. our level 0, 1 and 2 support was a success. Indeed, the interactive support simply provided by a geographic information system was novel and thought to be valuable in itself. 'What-if' analyses were used extensively. However, judgemental support (level 3) was not sought and the facilitators running the exercise were unable through discussion to convince the DMs otherwise. They felt able to make the decisions required of them without detailed modelling and exploration of their value judgements.

- In relation to the specific issue of building a multi-attribute model, no group were able to articulate an explicit set of criteria upon which they based their decision making. They did not find it natural to think in terms of the multi-attribute models. *Anticipated regret* seemed to be a major driver in their decision making. French *et al.* [5] propose event conditional modelling to address this issue.

- The introduction of uncertainty into an exercise was very discomforting to the DMs. None found the expression of this uncertainty in terms of probabilities useful. Generally, they adopted the heuristic of assuming that all the area at risk would be exposed: i.e. they effectively assumed a much larger and broader plume than would be formed by any possible release.

- Issues relating to the equity of treatment of different sub-populations were of considerable concern. Was it right to evacuate rural regions when it was quite infeasible to evacuate a highly populated urban region which was equally at risk in terms of individual dose? No consensus emerged on this issue. The matter is further discussed in [4].

- The issue of communicating with the public was discussed at length in all three exercises. All groups expressed concern that the communication of the risks should not raise stress levels unnecessarily. All felt need of advice on how to word press releases and other announcements so as to achieve their desired end. See [6] and [19] for discussion of some of the methods that might be employed.

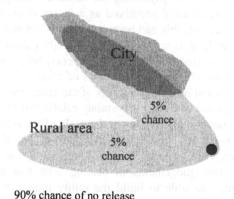

90% chance of no release

Figure 5. The situation during the threat phase of the first series of exercises

A distinctive point of these exercises was that we rehearsed a threat. This is contrary to practice in most practice exercises: a fact which concerns us. Resource constraints and the need to exercise as many aspects of the emergency arrangements as possible mean that most exercises assume the release of significant amounts of radioactivity. This does not accord with reality: most 'trips' at reactors do not lead to a release, but may set in motion the emergency management process. There is, thus, a distinct possibility that DMs are, through their training, being conditioned, albeit inadvertently, to believe the worst will happen. The implications for the future training and exercising of DMs warrant further analysis and evaluation. One means of overcoming such difficulties would be to involve DMs in more limited (and perhaps more frequent) table top exercises for which RODOS could readily provide the requisite input, analysis and evaluation in real (or artificial/contrived) timescales.

A second series of exercises have been run between 1997 and 1999. Some of the results are still being evaluated, but they have added greatly to our understanding of DM needs. These exercises were led by individuals and groups who had hitherto played no or little role in the design of RODOS. They are reported in [10] and a series of papers referred to therein. The scenario underlying these exercises was based on a LOCA accident followed by containment failure at nuclear power plant in Finland. All data were realistic, even though the chances of such an accident are estimated at less than 1 in 100 000 per reactor-year. An initial release of radionuclides was assumed, thus removing the issue to do with the *threat* of any release. This was done because it was felt that the first exercises had shown that uncertainty is so dominant an issue that other matters may be obscured: perhaps we had failed to build attribute trees because of the difficulty the DMs had in conceptualising the uncertainty relating to the threat.

After a number of iterations an attribute tree was built successfully: see Figure 6. It is interesting to note that this tree has a very similar structure to those developed in the Chernobyl studies and medium and long term exercises [9], [13]. One difficulty was in separating issues to do with social-psychological impacts from political ones. It is also interesting that economic costs were perceived as a factor in evaluating countermeasure strategies. In the earlier exercises this had been less clear. Cost was not perceived to be an issue in the early phase: at least is was not with one qualification. In one exercise it was noted during the threat phase, that if the accident happened funds would be made available from contingency provisions. If it did not, the costs of precautionary measures would fall on the already stretched normal operating budgets of the emergency services.

Although the scenario used excluded uncertainty relating to the threat, in a second run of the exercise there was uncertainty relating to the scale of the source term, i.e. how much was released. The tree used was modified from Figure 6, but shared the same generic structure. The facilitators were successful in building a multi-attribute utility model to reflect and support the DMs judgements in dealing with this uncertainty. However, because of the short time available to build the utility model, the facilitators were not confident that the DMs had a full understanding of its import. None the less, there is preliminary evidence here that once the threat issue is removed from the scenario, Bayesian multi-attribute decision analysis does offer a structure in which to analyse and support judgements.

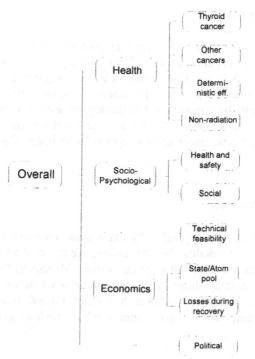

Figure 6. Final attribute tree built in the Finnish exercises

Again there was some evidence that the DMs faced up to uncertainty using conservative heuristics. They concentrated attention on the effects at the 95th percentile of the source term distribution: i.e. the worst case. While there is a *prime facie* case that such a conservative perspective provides the best protection for the public, it is not a foregone conclusion that it does. There are social and psychological costs, and potential health costs in addition to economic ones from implementing unnecessary countermeasures.

DESIGN OF THE PROCESS OF EMERGENCY MANAGEMENT

The advent of DSSs such as RODOS with their potential to support more detailed analyses and 'what-if' simulations mean that the emergency management structures in some countries or organisations might need revision to allow more interaction between technical experts and DMs. Indeed, it may be wise to reflect more widely on the structure of the process. As already noted, it varies from country to country and the differences in organisation are so great that we find it difficult to believe that all are equally effective. Some investigation and comparisons in order to develop international advice on the structure of the emergency management process would seem to be required.

CONCLUDING REMARKS

The design of RODOS has had to tread a difficult path between meeting the needs of users as they perceive them and opening up their minds to the possibilities that modern powerful DSSs provide. It is for others to judge whether we have negotiated this path successfully – so far. We recognise that for a variety of historic reasons, the early development of RODOS was influenced primarily by scientists and technologists. Recently, however, we have been able to investigate user needs more fully. What is clear is that there is much still to be done in shaping emergency management and its support to be better able to cope with nuclear accidents.

ACKNOWLEDGEMENTS

The RODOS system has been developed by many hundred individuals working in many institutions: see http:\\resy.fzk.de\rodos. As authors we report their work but do not claim it. Nonetheless, we take responsibility for any errors. Moreover, the views expressed are our own and not necessarily those of the project as a whole or any of the associated institutions. The development of RODOS has been funded from many sources, but particularly the EU Framework R&D programmes, all of which we gratefully acknowledge.

REFERENCES

[1] Brown , J., Smith, K.R., Mansfield, P. and Smith, J. (1997), Models for Decontamination, Relocation and Agricultural Countermeasures, Radiation Protection Dosimetry 73 (1-4), 75-79.

[2] Ehrhardt, J., Brown, J., French, S., Kelly, G. N., Mikkelsen, T. and Müller, H. (1997), RODOS: Decision-Making Support for Off-Site Emergency Management after Nuclear Accidents, Kerntechnik 62, 122-128.

[3] French, S. (1996), "Multi-attribute Decision Support in the Event of a Nuclear Accident," *Journal of Multi-Criteria Decision Analysis*, 5, 39-57.

[4] French, S., Halls, E. and Ranyard, D.C. (1997) "Equity and MCDA in the event of a Nuclear Accident". In Fandal, G. and Gal, T. (Eds) *Multiple Criteria Decision Making*. LNEMS 448, Springer Verlag, Berlin. 612-621

[5] French, S., Harrison, M.T. and Ranyard, D.C. (1997) 'Event conditional attribute modelling in decision making on a threatening nuclear accident.' In [8], 131-149]

[6] French, S. and Maule, J. (1999) 'Improving risk communication: scenario-based workshops'. In Bennett, P. and Calman, K. (Eds) *Risk Communication and Public Health*. Oxford University Press. 241-253.

[7] French, S., Papamichail, K.N., Ranyard, D.C. and Smith, J.Q. (1998), Design of a Decision Support System for Use in the Event of a Nuclear Emergency, in: F. Javier Giron and M. Lina Martinez (eds.), Applied Decision Analysis, Kluwer Academic Publishers, Boston, 2-18.

[8] French, S. and Smith, J.Q. (Eds) (1997) *Bayesian Analysis in Practice*. Edward Arnold, London.

[9] French, S., Walmod-Larsen, O. and Sinkko, K. (1993) "Decision conferencing on countermeasures after a large nuclear accident" Risφ-R-676(EN), Risφ National Laboratory, Roskilde, Denmark.

[10] Hämäläinen, R. P., Sinkko, K., Lindstedt, M., Ammann, M., and Salo, A. (1998) ' RODOS and decision conferencing on early phase protective actions in Finland' RODOS(WG7)-TN(98)-02, STUK, PO Box 14, FIN-00881, Helsinki, Finland.

[11] Karaoglou, A., Desmet, G., Kelly, G.N. and Menzel, H.G. (Eds) (1995) *The Radiological Consequences of the Chernobyl Accident*. EUR 16544 EN. CEC, Luxembourg.

[12] Kelly, G.N. and Baverstam, U. (Eds) (1997) 4th International Workshop on Real-time Computing of the Environmental Consequences of an Accidental Release from a Nuclear Installation, Aronsborg. Radiation Protection Dosimetry. 73.

[13] Lochard, J., Schneider, T. and French, S. (1992). "Summary Report of Decision Conferences held in the USSR, October-November 1990". EC Report EUR 14543 EN (ISBN 92-826-4631-9)

[14] Papamichail, K.N. (1998), Explaining and Justifying Decision Support Advice in Intuitive Terms, Proceedings of the 13th European Conference on Artificial Intelligence, 102-103, Brighton.

[15] Papmichail, K.N. (2000) PhD Thesis. The University of Manchester.

[16] Papamichail, K.N. and French, S. (1999), Generating Feasible Strategies in Nuclear Emergencies - A Constraint Satisfaction Problem, Journal of the Operational Research Society 50, 617-626.

[17] Papamichail, K.N. and French, S. (1999), Decision Support in Nuclear Emergencies, The Journal of Hazardous Materials. (in press)

[18] Päsler-Sauer, J. and Schichtel, T. (1997), The Simulation of Early Emergency Actions in RODOS, Radiation Protection Dosimetry 73 (1-4), 71-74.

[19] Sjöberg, L., Rundmo, T., Eränen, L. and Ekström, T. (1998) 'Countermeasures to the Chernobyl accident in the Nordic countries: public reactions.' Report 34, Centre for Risk Research, Stockholm School of Economics. (ISSN1101-9697)

[20] Teach, R.L. and Shortliffe, E.H. (1981), An Analysis of Physician Attitudes Regarding Computer-Based Clinical Consultation Systems, Computers and Biomedical Research 14, 542-558.

DSS FOR THE EVALUATION OF NATIONAL IT INFRASTRUCTURE INVESTMENTS: A STUDY OF CABLE TELEVISION IN GREECE

G.M. Giaglis[1], K.M. Manikas[2], V. Pergioudakis[2], G.I. Doukidis[2], P. Miliotis[2]

[1]Department of Information Systems and Computing
Uxbridge, Middlesex, UB8 3PH, United Kingdom

[2]Department of Informatics
Athens University of Economics and Business
76 Patission Street, Athens, 10434, Greece

Abstract: Although Decision Support Systems (DSS) have long been used for evaluating Information Technology (IT) *application* investments, not enough attention has yet been paid on IT *infrastructure* investments despite their unique characteristics and requirements. This paper reports on the development of a DSS for the evaluation of a national IT infrastructure investment, namely the introduction of a Cable Television network in Greece. We present the need for an automated tool to support such a complex decision making process and the architecture of the developed system. The DSS consolidates the knowledge elicited by an extensive market survey and the development of a mathematical model for estimating anticipated revenues from the investment. The DSS functional architecture is based on a case-specific Critical Success Factors framework that was developed to capture and structure the various aspects of the decision problem. The paper concludes with a discussion of the potential of DSS to support a rigorous holistic framework for IT infrastructure investments appraisal.

Key words: Decision Support Systems, Infrastructure Investment Evaluation, Cable Television

EVALUATING INVESTMENTS IN IT INFRASTRUCTURE

Information Technology (IT) investments have historically been notoriously difficult to evaluate and appraise before their introduction (ex ante evaluation) due to several reasons

S.H. Zanakis et al. (eds.), Decision Making: Recent Developments and Worldwide Applications, 397–412.
© 2000 *Kluwer Academic Publishers.*

(Ragowsky 1996, Strassman 1990, Parker et al 1988, Farbey et al 1993, Banker et al 1993):

a) The real benefits of such investments can only be estimated long after their installation and operation.

b) The benefits they deliver are intangible and usually take the form of strategic and competitive advantages that are inherently difficult to quantify and measure.

c) The impact of IT is indirect and therefore indistinguishable from several confounding factors (for example, people, processes, strategy, and the external environment).

These problems are further exacerbated when one leaves the sphere of the individual enterprise (that constitutes the fundamental unit of analysis in the vast majority of existing research in IT investment evaluation), and considers IT infrastructure investments. IT infrastructure can be defined as a set of shared, tangible resources that provide a foundation to enable present and future value-adding applications. The resources that constitute an IT infrastructure typically include platform technologies, network and telecommunication technologies, key data, and core data-processing applications (Duncan 1995).

In this paper we will be concerned with national IT infrastructure investments, i.e. projects undertaken by (or with the sponsorship of) national governments to develop nation-wide systems that can serve as foundations for facilitating business and/or residential value-adding IT applications. Such investments typically take the form of telecommunication networks and examples can be found in USA's National Information Infrastructure (Markoff 1993), France's Minitel videotex system (Cats-Baril and Jelassi 1994), and Singapore's Tradenet EDI system (King and Konsynski 1990).

The establishment of a national IT infrastructure has been argued to provide competitive advantages not only for the countries that develop it, but also for the companies that operate in these countries. However, the complexity and magnitude of a national IT infrastructure investment can make its *ex ante* appraisal problematic. Infrastructure investments are typically associated with indirect benefits (Brown 1994) that depend on the successful implementation of further investments (e.g. value-adding applications) made possible by the existence of the underlying infrastructure. Such indirect benefits are difficult to capture and quantify due to the increased complexity of the investment options and associated decisions, and the multiplicity of factors affecting investment payback in each case. For example, we can mention the additional impacts of government policy, (macro-) economic conditions, technological innovation, and critical user mass achievement that can significantly impact the success or failure of a national IT infrastructure investment.

Despite these distinct characteristics associated with infrastructure investments, previous research on their assessment has been very limited (for example, Cats-Baril and Jelassi 1994). Furthermore, such research has only been confined on the retrospective (*ex post*) evaluation of the investment success or failure factors, based usually on analyzing the political and economic environment of the countries that develop them. We are aware of no previous studies specifically concerned with the *ex ante* appraisal of national IT infrastructure investments.

However, due to the importance and sheer magnitude of these investments, the development of a sound and robust business case for development is of paramount importance. In the absence of a focused investment appraisal exercise, governments can find themselves wasting enormous amounts of public money in projects of little or no practical value.

In this paper we will be concerned with the evaluation of a proposed investment in a national broadband infrastructure network in Greece. The paper addresses the potential of computer-based Decision Support Systems (DSS) to support executives in evaluating infrastructure investments. In the following section we review existing cases of DSS use for investment evaluation and we argue for the need of a holistic approach when the evaluation concerns complex decision-making problems. We then proceed by setting the context of our case study in order to justify the choice of a DSS to support investment evaluation in the particular case. Next, we articulate the approach we followed for developing the system and present its architecture and characteristics. The paper concludes with a discussion of the potential of DSS to support a rigorous holistic framework for IT infrastructure investments appraisal.

DSS FOR IT INFRASTRUCTURE INVESTMENT EVALUATION: THE NEED FOR A HOLISTIC APPROACH

In the last two decades, there has been a growing amount of interest and research in the area of Decision Support Systems (DSS) as vehicles for supporting managers in their semi-structured or unstructured activities of decision-making (Eom and Lee 1990, Eom et al 1998, Doukidis et al 1989). DSS have been used to assist decision-makers in evaluating investments in many diverse application areas. However, a review of reported DSS environments for investment evaluation reveals that they typically focus on only one out of a number of factors that should be assessed when a complex infrastructure investment is evaluated. These factors can be classified into:

a) *Financial.* DSS in this area focus on the economic evaluation of alternative investment proposals. Examples include systems for financial risk assessment (Mareschal and Brans 1991, Siskos et al 1994), new product development funding (Kettelhut 1991), research and development projects selection (Stewart 1991), and small business financial planning (Chen 1989, Sterling and Stubblefield 1994).

b) *Commercial.* In this application area, DSS are typically used to support the alignment between an organization, its products, and the marketplace in which these products are sold. Application examples include DSS for industry analysis (Vickers 1992), product positioning (Belardo et al 1994), and corporate planning (Ramesh and Sekar 1988).

c) *Strategic.* In this application area, DSS are used to support strategic decision-making regarding proposed investments. Application examples include DSS for supporting executives in corporate strategy formulation (Islei et al 1989, Moormann and Lochte-Holygreven 1993, Quaddus et al 1992), planning corporate mergers and acquisitions (Dutta 1994), and evaluating strategy (Eden and Ackermann 1993).

d) *Technical*. This category of systems focuses on identifying the optimal equilibrium between performance, reliability, and cost factors within alternative technical investment options. Examples include DSS for designing fiber optic Wide Area Networks (Powell et al 1992), and evaluating different Local Area Network topologies (Liggett and Sullivan 1992).

We argue that a Decision Support System for infrastructure investments evaluation should be able to integrate these four categories of factors in order to be able to capture the complexity of the exercise and the diverse requirements of the investment stakeholders, sponsors, and users (including the government, the funding bodies, the business users, and the citizens). We will use the term '*holistic evaluation*' to refer to such an integrated approach to requirements capturing, investment proposal articulation, and evaluation process. The work reported in this paper aims at assessing the potential of DSS to support such a holistic financial, commercial, strategic, and technical appraisal of infrastructure investments. We illustrate this concept by documenting the development of a detailed and structural approach to the problem of evaluating an investment in a national broadband telecommunications network in Greece.

CABLE TELEVISION IN GREECE: ISSUES AND CONSIDERATIONS

OTE S.A. has traditionally been the state-owned, monopolistic provider of telephony and telecommunications services in Greece. During the last years, partly due to internal necessities and partly due to worldwide market trends, OTE is entering a new era of deregulation and free competition in the marketplace. In view of these changes, the organization has been assessing alternative avenues for diversification of its operations and opportunities for entering new markets.

One of the new markets that OTE is considering, not unlike many national telecommunication organizations (Johnson and Reed 1992), is the provision of Cable Television (CaTV) infrastructure services. The aim of OTE through this investment is to modernize its existing basic network infrastructure and to enter a completely new market, namely the provision of broadcasting services.

Due to its long-term dynamic presence in the telecommunications market in Greece, OTE presents a number of advantages over its potential future competitors. However, OTE has to transform these monopolistic advantages to competitive ones as soon as possible, in view of anticipated changes in the existing regulatory framework towards allowing free competition in the CaTV market (Constantelou 1993). Beyond the operational benefits that OTE is going to have from the development and exploitation of the infrastructure, there are certain long-term strategic goals that can be achieved (e.g. implementation of a necessary platform for the provision of advanced telecommunication services). The magnitude of the investment, the complexity and changing nature of the regulatory and market factors, as well as the inherent strategic nature of the project, all contribute towards the development of a fuzzy network of factors influencing and being influenced by any decision of OTE. In the light of the above, it was decided that the measurement of benefits from this investment, and hence the decision for implementation, should not be confined only to financial factors (cash flow) but should also include strategic (competitive advantages, positioning, corporate image building, etc.), commercial (customer satisfaction, new product/service introduction, etc.), and technical (network topologies, etc.) ones.

THE NEED FOR A DSS – RESEARCH APPROACH

To assist OTE executives in understanding the interactions between the various factors that influence the investment, it was decided that a holistic approach to investment evaluation was followed. To assist in structuring the process and formulating the problem parameters in a way that would prove beneficial to the whole organization, it was also suggested that a computer-based DSS should be developed to reflect and drive the evaluation process. The complexity, dynamism, and semi-structured definition of the problem, combined with the need for decision making support, all pointed to the appropriateness of a DSS to support the process (Bonczek et al 1981, Keen and Scott-Morton 1978, Thierauf 1982). In order to capture all contributing factors (financial, commercial, strategic, and technical ones) a five-phase research approach was followed (Figure 1):

   a) The user market was investigated by means of an extensive market survey of potential business and residential users throughout Greece. The aim was to establish a better understanding of the market opportunities and align OTE's strategic choices with the users' needs and expectations (*commercial picture*).

   b) A mathematical model was developed to estimate the expected penetration of CaTV in the Greek market within a time frame of five years. This model was used to calculate the anticipated revenues for OTE and facilitate a formal Cost-Benefit Analysis of the investment (*financial picture*).

   c) A Technical Analysis was carried out by OTE to determine the network development and maintenance costs, as well as the overall implications of a range of alternative technical options for network development (*technical picture*).

   d) A Critical Success Factors (CSF) framework was developed to explain the market dynamics and address the non-quantifiable issues that can affect the success of the proposed investment (strategic picture).

   e) Finally, a Decision Support System (DSS) was developed to incorporate the knowledge elicited during the previous stages in a holistic manner so as to provide a useful tool in the hands of OTE executives for assessing the proposed investment.

This paper documents the above process (with the exception of the technical analysis that presented no immediate research interest for our work) and the conclusions reached. We will start by briefly discussing the market survey, the mathematical model, and the CSF framework as tools for eliciting knowledge that was crucial for a holistic investment evaluation. We will then present the system that we developed to incorporate this knowledge into a useful decision-aiding tool.

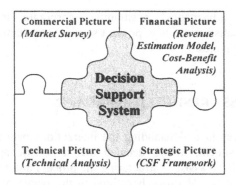

Figure 1. The Research Approach

THE MARKET SURVEY (COMMERCIAL PICTURE)

The objective of the survey was to evaluate the potential market for broadband communication and CaTV services in Greece. The survey was carried out in all Greek cities and towns with a population of more than 5,000 (a sample representing 20% of the total Greek territory, but accounting for 60% of the total population or 800,000 households). Data was collected via personal interviews with 2,000 households and was analyzed using various statistical analysis techniques such as descriptive analysis, chi-square tests and cluster analysis.

The survey yielded a significant amount of data that were used to identify important parameters relating to the potential of introducing CaTV and broadband telecommunications in Greece. Due to space limitations, only some example findings will be presented here. For example, Figure 2 illustrates the degree of interest expressed for CaTV in general, indicating that more than half of the sample (54.8%) showed a tentative interest in the new service, while Figure 3 presents the distribution of those respondents who expressed a tentative interest in CaTV with regard to the amount of money they were willing to pay for a basic CaTV service in terms of a monthly subscription.

Due to inevitable respondent bias, the above numbers cannot be taken at face value as representative of the actual expected penetration of CaTV in the Greek market over a short-term period. To identify the true potential of CaTV, cluster analysis was employed to relate the interest shown by respondents with their ability to adopt CaTV as shown by other questionnaire variables. Based on this analysis, a mathematical model was developed to estimate potential market penetration and anticipated revenues. This model will be presented in the next section.

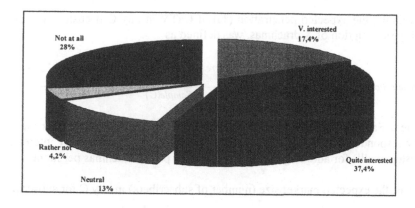

Figure 2. General Interest in CaTV

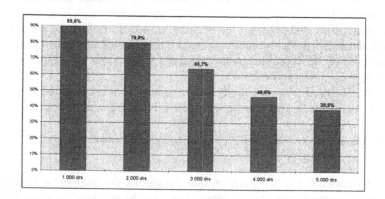

Figure 3. Intention to Adopt CaTV Depending on Monthly subscription

THE REVENUE ESTIMATION MODEL (FINANCIAL PICTURE)

This model constitutes an attempt at approaching the financial returns from an investment in CaTV based on the findings of the market survey. The revenues depend on a number of parameters, the most important being the range of services offered by the CaTV network and the monthly subscription (as these parameters both influence market demand). To allow for the identification of impacts of these variables on anticipated revenues we developed a parametric mathematical model that was later incorporated within the DSS. Due to space limitations, only a part of the model will be presented here.

In order to capture the true expected penetration of CaTV, the initial interest shown by the respondents had to be further scrutinized by correlating it to other variables.

Accordingly, the expected penetration (%) of CaTV in city C if customers have to pay a monthly subscription of X drachmas, was defined as

$$Penetration(C,X) = \frac{Interest(C,X,'very') + Interest(C,X,'quite') + \sum\limits_{y=X+1..Max(X)} Interest(C,y,'very')}{Sample(C)}$$

where Sample(C) is the sample size in city C and Interest(C,X,I) is the number of survey respondents in city C that showed interest I (ranging from 'very interested' to 'not interested at all') for adopting CaTV if they had to pay X drachmas per month.

Thus, the expected market size (number of subscribers) in city C for subscription X is:

$$Market(C,X) = Penetration(C,X) * Size(C)$$

where Size(C) is the number of households in city C (taken from population census data for each city).

Once penetration and potential market size have been estimated, we can proceed by identifying the anticipated revenues for a given time period. To accomplish this, market size data have to be combined with perceived time frame of adoption of CaTV as expressed by the survey respondents.

The total estimated revenues in city C if the investment is evaluated for a period of M months and we assume a steady subscription of X drachmas over this period, is:

$$Revenues(C,X,M) = X * Market(C,X) * \sum\limits_{Plan} [Months(M,Plan) * Adopt(C,Plan)]$$

where Months(C,Plan) is a function that transforms the qualitative Plan for adoption (ranging from 'Immediately' to 'In more than One Year') into an average quantitative figure representing the number of months of adoption, and Adopt(C,Plan) is the percentage of respondents in city C that plan to adopt CaTV in the Plan period.

Finally, if CaTV is to be introduced in a subset of the cities included in the survey, the total revenues anticipated in a time period of M months if we assume a steady subscription of X drachmas, are

$$Total Revenues(X,M) = \sum\limits_{Z} Revenues(Z,X,M)$$

where Z refers to the positive values of a vector v=[city1, city2, ..., cityk] where vi=0 if CaTV is not to be installed in city i, or vi=1 otherwise.

Figure 4 shows an example of applying the above model in a five-year evaluation of CaTV. Two scenarios are modeled (optimistic and pessimistic) and results are compared amongst five alternative assumptions regarding the monthly subscription fee. The results show that maximum revenues are achieved with a monthly subscription of 3,000 drachmas.

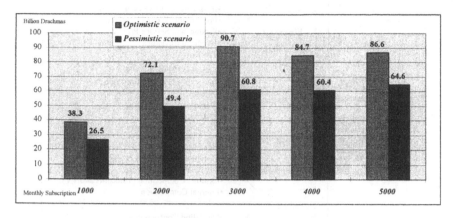

Figure 4. Expected CaTV revenues in a five-year plan

THE CRITICAL SUCCESS FACTORS FRAMEWORK (STRATEGIC PICTURE)

We have argued that a holistic approach is necessary to evaluate complex infrastructure investments. Although the market survey and the revenue estimation model (together with the technical analysis done by OTE) are powerful weapons for approaching the commercial, financial, and technical aspects of a potential investment in CaTV, they are by no means sufficient for capturing the complexity of the problem in its entirety. It was therefore deemed necessary to attempt an identification and classification of all four categories of factors affecting the investment (including strategic ones that were not captured before) within a robust framework of Critical Success Factors.

The use of Critical Success Factors (CSF) analysis has already been applied with success in cases of national IT investment evaluation. For example, Cats-Baril and Jelassi (1994) have applied a similar analysis for a retrospective evaluation of the factors that influenced the success of the French videotex system (Minitel). The following investigation follows the same line of enquiry, albeit applying it in a prospective context.

The framework consists of nineteen Critical Success Factors grouped into four categories representing different areas of influence (Figure 5). Some of the financial, commercial, and technical aspects are covered by the previously mentioned work, while some of the others, together with the strategic aspects, are of an inherently qualitative nature and therefore CSF analysis is the only means of investigating and incorporating them into a holistic investment evaluation.

Based on the CSF analysis, the aforementioned factors were transformed into a detailed set of direct and indirect cost and benefit factors that can be used for a detailed evaluation of the proposed investments. These factors were incorporated within the DSS that will be presented in the following section.

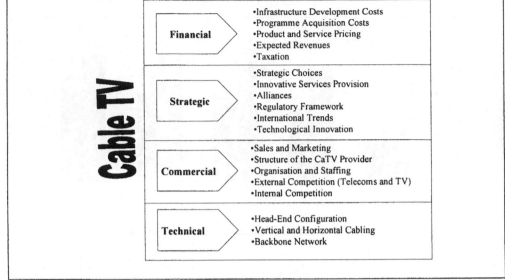

Figure 5. A Critical Success Factors framework for Cable Television

THE DECISION SUPPORT SYSTEM

The main requirement for DSS development was to build an automated tool that would help decision makers (mainly OTE executives) to share their specialized knowledge in different domains, gain a better understanding of the complexity of the problem as a whole, and be able to experiment with alternative courses of action before committing themselves to a particular investment proposal. Therefore, the developed tool should be sufficiently parameterized to support "what-if" analyses.

The DSS was developed using the SAS development environment (release 6.11) and it was used by the researchers and OTE executives for a 5-year evaluation of the investment. The system has been designed so that the user can examine alternative scenarios (different values of the input variables) and test the effects of these changes on the results of the investment evaluation (anticipated costs and benefits on a 5-year horizon). This feature of sensitivity analysis increases the usefulness of the system, as it allows the user to experiment with alternative scenarios and gain a better understanding of the influences of individual variables as well as their interactions on the investment payback. For example, the user can select the cities in which CaTV is to be introduced, the time frame for gradual network development, and the customer profiles of potential subscribers, and combine these into a formal Cost-Benefit Analysis (CBA) of the investment.

Some of the main features of the system are:

a) The system provides a global picture of the investment incorporating representation and evaluation of all identified influencing input and control variables.

b) The input variables are fully parametric. The system allows for experimentation with and examination of any number of alternative choices (scenario planning and what-if analysis).

c) The system includes a friendly graphical interface and context-sensitive on-line help, therefore increasing its ease-of-use and acceptability by the decision-makers.

One unique feature of the system is that the actual raw data gathered during the market survey, as well as the logic of the revenue estimation model, are incorporated within the DSS. This approach gives the ability to the system users to evaluate the investment based on the real anticipated market demand and reactions as the customers themselves identified them. For example, if the system user selects a particular value for the monthly subscription fee for the basic CaTV service, the system computes the anticipated penetration of CaTV and estimated total revenues, based on the market survey data for the particular subscription rate and the logic of the mathematical model. If the computed pattern is deemed inappropriate, the user can modify the pricing structure or the cities where CaTV will be introduced (or, indeed, any input variable) and see the implications of his actions on the final outcome. This interactive ability of the DSS can be greatly useful for teams of decision-makers that can use the system to test their ideas in real-time and obtain immediate feedback on the anticipated impacts of proposed changes.

The overall DSS architecture is illustrated in Figure 6. The system consists of three modular, interrelated sub-systems: the Market Survey Database (MSD), the Revenues Estimation Algorithm (REA), and the Report Generator (RG).

The Market Survey Database (MSD), as already mentioned, allows the decision-maker to make on-line use of the market survey data. Further to the raw questionnaire data, the MSD incorporates all the necessary demographic data required for analyzing the anticipated CaTV penetration for every city and town in Greece with a population of more than 2,000 people (it is not currently envisaged that CaTV services will be offered to smaller towns due to negative economies of scale).

The Revenues Estimation Algorithm (REA) takes the values assigned by the users on the input variables and applies the mathematical model on the data contained in the MSD. The output results that are generated are fed back to the user through the Report Generator (RG). This subsystem can produce numerical and graphical reports showing both aggregate results (i.e. related to the investment as a whole) as well as breakdowns of costs and benefits by selected town and cost/benefit category (as exemplified in the CSF framework). Emphasis has been given to the user-friendly interface and the use of diagrams and on-line help.

Figure 7 presents a selection of screen snapshots from the system. The first screen shows how the user can specify the cities where CaTV and broadband services are to be introduced and the time frame for provision. The second screen shows a subset of the criteria used for market size estimation (based on the survey results). The third screen shows an example of how the user can break down the estimated five-year penetration into annual projections, while the fourth screen shows an example of CaTV costs breakdown. By clicking on each button in this screen, the user can input all the necessary data for each cost category. The DSS will then combine them into detailed five-year costs, depending on the specified gradual network development plan.

408

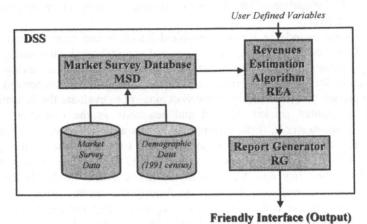

Figure 6. Architecture of the system

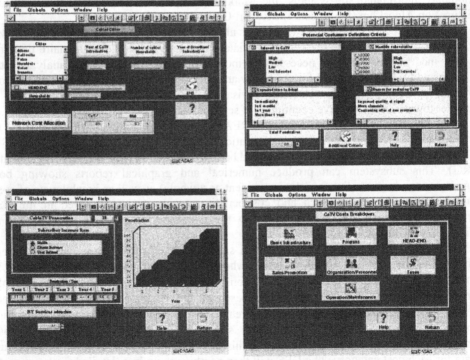

Figure 7. Sample DSS Screen Snapshots

Once all the input parameters affecting the investment costs and benefits have been specified, the DSS invokes the Revenue Estimation Algorithm to produce a five-year cost-benefit analysis of the investment. The user can modify any of the input variables and assess the impact of his actions on the anticipated investment payback in real-time. Output data are presented to the user in tabular and graphical form.

DISCUSSION AND CONCLUDING REMARKS

In this paper we presented a case study of a national IT infrastructure investment evaluation, we discussed some of the practical issues that arise, and we articulated an approach for addressing these issues. We argued that the complexity and magnitude of such investments call for a holistic approach towards their successful appraisal. Such an approach should encompass the financial, commercial, technical, and strategic facets of the investment. Finally, we presented the development of a decision aiding system that can support this holistic approach and be a useful tool for analysts and decision-makers alike.

It must be re-emphasized at this point that the objective of the paper was to make a case for the efficacy of DSS in supporting a holistic approach to infrastructure IT investment evaluation. As such, and due to space limitations, the level of detail in the description of the structure and functionality of the DSS, as well as of its constituent components, was kept to the degree necessary for conveying the paper's message effectively. In other words, our aim was to present a methodological account of a holistic approach to evaluation and argue for its need and generalizability, instead of exhaustively presenting any of the individual steps within the approach.

Although the work presented here was driven by the particular characteristics and requirements of the specific problem under investigation, there is no apparent reason to inhibit the generalization of the approach to be equally applicable in similar situations as well. In all cases where national IT infrastructure investment proposals are under careful scrutiny, governments (or other decision-makers) will need to investigate in detail the whole spectrum of factors that can contribute towards the successful or otherwise implementation of the proposals. Of course, the requirements of specific problems may necessitate that different weights are applied to each facet and/or may dictate that further facets are taken into consideration. Such facets may include the political, social, and regulatory environments, competitive and/or co-operative advantages, and others that are only partially addressed in the proposed approach.

In any case, a holistic approach to investment appraisal is beneficial as it can significantly reduce the risk of incorrect decisions that may result from incomplete or too narrowly focused investment appraisals (as the case seems to be with most extant approaches). Furthermore, a holistic approach facilitates group work and group decision-making as it necessarily brings domain experts together to co-operate in guiding the evaluation of individual facets and the development of various DSS parts. Such an interaction enables the sharing of knowledge and information, and can facilitate the establishment of a corporate-wide picture of the investment. The approach, combined with the structure-imposing nature of the decision support system, can also assist towards structuring the debate over an inherently complex and ill-defined problem.

Perhaps even more importantly, such a holistic approach can be applied throughout the life cycle of the investment. In other words, it can support not only the process of ex ante investment appraisal, but also the subsequent phases of infrastructure development (project management) and post-implementation evaluation (performance monitoring). For example, in the specific case study presented, OTE managers envisage that the approach and the DSS will continue to be used for the subsequent phases of the investment as well. The fully parametric features of the DSS allow its users to replace initial estimates (e.g. the market survey data) with actual investment information (e.g. actual implementation costs or market penetration information), as such information becomes available. As future uses of the DSS will be based on real data that will gradually replace the initial assumptions, the validity of the system and credibility of the results will be continuously improved.

Further work is needed to substantiate the validity of the approach in similar and different application settings. Broadband data communications and cable television were two completely new markets in Greece and therefore no previous case-specific experience was available to facilitate structured decision-making about the investments. The approach we advocate may be more suitable to such innovative application investments where evaluation cannot be safely based on codifying previous experience and existing patterns. Furthermore, the complexity of the approach may also render it more suitable for large investments, where the amount of resources required (time, expertise, and money) can impose a requirement for rigorous and detailed investment appraisal. To reduce the complexity of the approach, further research can be directed towards investigating the potential of developing archetype, re-usable DSS templates. Such templates will provide the basis for a structured and holistic approach to IT infrastructure evaluation and can be re-used in similar situations, thereby creating economies of scale and reducing the overall cost of the investment appraisal exercise.

REFERENCES

Banker, R.D., Kauffman, R.J. and Mahmood, M.A. (1993) *Strategic Information Technology management: perspectives on organizational growth and competitive advantage*, Idea Group Publishing.

Belardo, S., Duchessi, P. and Coleman, J.R. (1994) A Strategic Decision Support System at Orell Fussli, *Journal of Management Information Systems, 10, 4*, pp. 135-137.

Bonczek, R.H., Holsapple, C.W. and Whinston, A.B. (1981) *Foundations of Decision Support Systems*, Academic Press, NY.

Brown, A. (1994) Appraising Intangible Benefits from Information Technology Investment. In the *Proceedings of the First European Conference on IT Investment Evaluation*, Henley, England, September, pp. 187-199.

Cats-Baril, W.L. and Jelassi, T. (1994) The French Videotex System Minitel: A Successful Implementation of a National Information Technology Infrastructure, *MIS Quarterly, 18, 1*, pp. 1-20.

Chen, K.C. (1989) Developing Decision Support Systems for Small Business Management: A Case Study, *Journal of Small Business Management, 27, 3*, pp. 11-22.

Constantelou, N. (1993) Liberalizing Telecommunications Markets: Political Externalities in the Greek Case, *Telecommunications Policy, 17, 6*, pp. 431-445.

Doukidis, G.I., Land, F. and Miller, G. (1989) (Eds.) *Knowledge-Based Management Support Systems*, Ellis Horwood, Chichester.

Duncan, N.B. (1995) Capturing Flexibility of information Technology Infrastructure: A Study of Resource Characteristics and their Measures, *Journal of Management Information Systems, Fall, 12, 2*, pp. 37-55.

Dutta, S. (1994) Decision Support for Planning, *Decision Support Systems, 12, 4-5*, pp. 337-353.

Eden, C. and Ackermann, F. (1993) Evaluating Strategy: Its Role Within the Context of Strategic Control, *Journal of the Operational Research Society, 44, 9*, pp. 853-865.

Eom, S.B. and Lee, S.M. (1990) A Survey of Decision Support System Applications (1971-April 1988), *Interfaces, 20*, pp. 65-79.

Eom, S.B., Lee, S.M., Kim, E.B. and Somarajan, C. (1998) A Survey of Decision Support System Applications (1988-1994), *Journal of the Operational Research Society 49, 2*, pp. 109-120.

Farbey, B., Land, F. and Targett, D. (1993) *How to assess your IT investment: A study of methods and practice*, Butterworth-Heinmann, Oxford.

Islei, G., Lockett, G., Cox, B., Gisbourne, S. and Stratford, M. (1989) Modeling Strategic Decision Making and Performance Measurements at ICI Pharmaceuticals, *Interfaces, 21, 6*, pp. 4-22.

Johnson, L.L. and Reed, D.P. (1992) Telephone Company Entry into Cable Television, *Telecommunications Policy, 16, 2*, pp. 122-134.

Keen, P.G.W. and Scott-Morton, M.S. (1978) *Decision Support Systems: An Organisational Perspective*, Addison-Wesley, Reading, MA.

Kettelhut, M.C. (1991) Using a DSS to Incorporate Expert Opinion in Strategic Product Development Funding Decisions, *Information and Management, 20, 5*, pp. 363-371.

King, J. and Konsynski, B. (1990) *Singapore Tradenet: A Tale of One City*, Harvard Business School Case #9-191-009, Cambridge, MA.

Liggett, H.R. and Sullivan, W.G. (1992) Multi-attribute Evaluation of Local Area Network Topologies, *Engineering Economist, 37, 2*, pp. 91-114.

Mareschal, B. and Brans, J.P. (1991) Bankadviser: An Industrial Evaluation System, *European Journal of Operational Research, 54, 3*, pp. 318-324.

Markoff, J. (1993) Building the Electronic Superhighway, *The New York Times*, section 3, January 24, p.1.

Mooremann, J. and Lochte-Holtgreven, M. (1993) An Approach for an Integrated DSS for Strategic Planning, *Decision Support Systems, 10, 4*, pp. 401-411.

Parker, M.M., Benson, R.J. and Trainor, H.E. (1988) *Information Economics: linking business performance to Information Technology*, Prentice-Hall International.

Powell, P.L., Hall, M. and Klein, J.H. (1993) An Expert Decision Support System for Network Routeing: A Case Study, *Information and Software Technology, 34, 12*, pp. 771-778.

Quaddus, M.A., Atkinson, D.J. and Levy, M. (1992) An Application of Decision Conferencing to Strategic Planning for a Voluntary Organization, *Interfaces, 22, 6*, pp. 61-71.

Ragowsky, A., Athituv, N. and Neumann, S. (1996) Identify the Value and Importance of an Information System Application, *Information & Management, 31*, pp. 89-102.

Ramesh, R. and Sekar, C. (1988) An Integrated Framework for Decision Support in Corporate Planning, *Decision Support Systems, 4, 3*, pp. 365-375.

Siskos, Y., Zopounidis, C. and Pouliezos, A. (1994) An Integrated DSS for Financing Firms by an Industrial Development Bank in Greece, *Decision Support Systems, 12, 2*, pp. 151-168.

Stewart, T.J. (1991) A Multi-criteria Decision Support System for R&D Project Selection, *Journal of the Operational Research Society, 42, 1*, pp. 17-26.

Sterling, J.W. and Stubblefield, A. (1994) ADVIA: Planning and Decision Support for Smaller Business, *Planning Review, 22, 1*, pp. 50-54.

Strassman, P.A. (1990) *The business value of computers*, The Information Economics Press, New Canaan, Connecticut.

Thierauf, R.J. (1982) *Decision Support Systems for Effective Planning and Control: A Case Study Approach*, Prentice Hall, Englewood Cliffs, NJ.

Vickers, B. (1992) Using GDSS to Examine the Future European Automobile Industry, *Futures, 24, 8*, pp. 789-812.

GLOBAL IT OUTSOURCING DECISIONS: CONTRACT STRUCTURE, NEGOTIATIONS, AND GLOBAL DEAL TEAMS

S.T. Huhn, R.A Holloway, B.A. Potter, R.A. Berry

IBM Global Services
Global Business Development
44 South Broadway, MD 500
White Plains, NY 10601, USA

Abstract: For the last 10 years, IBM Global Services has been engaged in the negotiation and execution of national, multinational, and global contracts as a worldwide service provider for the information technology (IT) industry. While each engagement is unique in its own right, global engagements involving a customer located in more than one country present the most significant business challenges. Cross border communications, service delivery, and billing, as well as the legal and administrative concerns inherent to such deals, can entail staggering risks for both parties. Accordingly, successful engagements are contingent upon swift navigation of a highly intricate context of contending factors. Intensive familiarization with these factors has afforded a means for better anticipating their associated pitfalls and vagaries. This paper will explore the challenges of contract structuring, skill deployment, and communication methodology as they pertain to global IT outsourcing engagements. In the process, the paper will propose how global deal teams can be applied to engagements systematically to promote efficient decision-making and engender more valuable outcomes.

Key words: Global deal teams, Global IT outsourcing, Information technology, Outsourcing negotiation, Outsourcing contracts, Strategic IT outsourcing

ENVIRONMENT

Strategic outsourcing is the art of creating value through a strategic relationship with a customer by assuming responsibility for portions of the customer's IT environment,

S.H. Zanakis et al. (eds.), Decision Making: Recent Developments and Worldwide Applications, 413–424.

business processes, and operations.[1] Since Kodak brought the service to the corporate forefront by outsourcing major components of its information systems function in the early 1990's, the practice of IT outsourcing has gained tremendous momentum and acceptance. Industry analysts predict that the global market, which was only $86 billion in 1996, will grow to more than $137 billion by 2001. (DiRomualdo and Gurbaxani, 67).

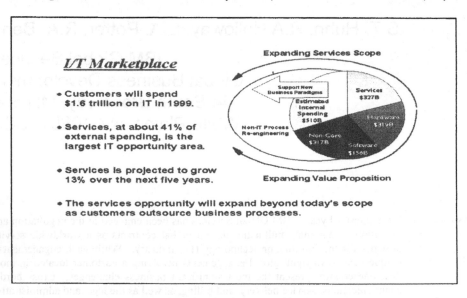

Figure 1. I/T Marketplace (Internal IBM Presentation)

Outsourcing decisions are sometimes reduced to evaluations of cost efficiency. For a given transaction, a company might generate two alternatives: perform and manage existing IT operations internally, or turn over the operations and ownership of assets to an outside vendor in order to achieve lower average costs through improved economies of scale. However, this reduction is not viable in the New Economy.[2] While restructuring balance sheets remains a primary concern, more and more companies are trying to find increased productivity and profitability on the Internet. In order to do so, companies need solutions that offer access to new skills, and in some cases fundamentally change the way they do business. Unlike traditional labor-based services engagements, these solutions use

---

[1] More specifically, strategic outsourcing agreements have traditionally been structured to address IT initiatives such as data center services, help desk services, and managed data network services. However, as business decisions continue to envelop IT decisions, companies are increasingly engaging service vendors to outsource their core business processes such as sourcing and procurement, customer relationship management, employee services, and application management.

[2] What is the difference between the Old Economy and the New Economy? "The key is whether the main product or service is information. If so, then the exponential gains in the speed of information processing ensure falling costs and enormous opportunities for growth. For example, financial services are in the New Economy because they are primarily an information business - no physical products or personal services change hands. By contrast, Old Economy industries produce tangible goods or personal services, which are less affected by information technology. Putting computers in the factory may cut costs and hold down inventory, but the cars or steel produced don't change very much. (Mandel 1999, 90-92).

an array of assets, including models, software, methods, tools, and other intellectual assets to drive down the time and cost of delivery; competitive advantage is derived from processes, knowledge, and innovative people. Value still rises and falls with cash flows, and cash flows still rise and fall on revenue. But revenue comes from intangible assets. This portends a dramatic shift in the relationship between customers and outsourcing vendors: to a business, a vendor is no longer just a vendor and a customer is no longer just a customer. They are either each other's teammates or someone else's teammates. And as businesses continue to redefine themselves, maintaining long-term relationships with valued teammates becomes an integral way to mitigate risk. For these reasons, the success of outsourcing engagements cannot be measured strictly in terms of cost efficiency, but must also reflect the extent to which they foster relationships capable of continuous change and responsiveness.

The most influential of the academic articles analyzing these conditions is "Strategic Intent for IT Outsourcing," by Anthony DiRomualdo and Vijay Gurbaxani. In this article, the authors demonstrate that optimal IT outsourcing decisions are induced by accurate evaluations of customer IT strategy. (DiRomualdo and Gurbaxani, 69), company's IT strategy, and in turn properly determine the character of the outsourcing relationship that is most conducive to the nurturing of that strategy. Their analysis of the selection of contracting partners is modelled in accordance with three strategic intents: IS Improvement- focusing on the reduction of cost and enhancing the efficiency of IT resources, Outsourcing for Business Impact- focusing on the improvement of IT's contribution to company performance within existing lines of business, and Commercial Exploitation- focusing on leveraging technology-related assets in the marketplace through the development and marketing of new technology-based products and services[3]. These intents entail different requirements with respect to performance measurement and evaluation scheme, the compensation scheme, the assignment of decision-making rights, and risk-and- reward schemes. To this end, the authors further demonstrate optimal outsourcing relationships depend upon the attainment of a harmony between strategy and contract For example, an agreement that offers incentives to a vendor to take a high level of precautions in order to minimize its own costs would likely be undesirable to a buyer that seeks to leverage that vendor in order to stimulate the development of new systems and applications. Developing and implementing new systems would demand management mechanisms that encourage and reward the vendor for undertaking the risks inherent to innovation. (DiRomualdo and Gurbaxani, 69) Thus, the authors affirm, "the literature often attributes failing to achieve the promised benefits of IT outsourcing to its intrinsic weaknesses.[4] Our research suggests that these poor outcomes are often due to failure to define clearly the intent and specific goals for outsourcing, to align the contract and relationship with strategic objectives, to make contracts flexible enough to adjust to

---

[3] These categories of strategic intent are cumulative, not mutually exclusive (i.e. a relationship focusing on business impact will generally hope to benefit from improvements in IS performance as well)

[4] See:

R. Hirscheim and M. Lacity, , "The Outsourcing Bandwagon," The Sloan Management Review, volume 34, Spring 1993, pp. 9-23

M. Lacity, L. Willcocks, and D. Feeny, "IT Ousourcing: Maximize Flexibility and Control," Harvard Business Review, volume 73, May-June 1995, pp. 84-93

M. Earl, "The Risks of IT Outsourcing," Sloan Management Review, volume 37, Spring 1996, pp. 26-32

changes in the business or technology, an to ensure that the vendor has the capabilities required to meet the objectives for outsourcing." (DiRomualdo and Gurbaxani, 69)

DiRomualdo and Gurbaxani correctly assert that as IT and business processes are becoming more intertwined and that as the market demands more and more industry-specific applications, the nature of outsourcing contracts should take on greater similarities to strategic alliances and even joint ventures. However, their arguments to these points implicitly assume that these conditions of harmony can apply in uniform to all parties, regardless of how they are organized or where they are located. In practice, these factors are crucial to the economic analysis of the preceding parts, and can distort the outsourcing decision if the optimal level of care is not taken by both parties.

GLOBAL ENGAGEMENT ISSUES

An engagement that includes more than one country yields a tangle of cultural, financial, legal, administrative, and technical implications that must be addressed. In the realm of legal issues, a permanent establishment may result if a service provider provides extended services, regularly enters into, or operates through an agent outside of its home country. This is significant because a permanent establishment can result in double taxation of profits, additional property or transaction taxes, and redundant tax administration costs. Further, where a service provider is receiving payment cross border, the service provider may also be subjected to withholding taxes and value-added taxes on payments for services.

Pricing methodologies used to accurately capture the value proposition become less flexible and predictable when the customer states the requirements for regionalized billing or the use of a specific currency in a specific country. Adjustments in pricing based upon exchange rate fluctuation and cost of living adjustments must also be addressed in these cases with proper delineation of risk responsibility.

In terms of technical and administrative concerns, the tools, processes, and management systems necessary to support national vertically aligned organizations must be coordinated for global execution. In order to guarantee the appropriate level of resource and skill required to perform and deliver services for customers internationally, service provider intercompany agreements between lead country and local country executives are used. Such agreements allocate cross border expense reimbursement for in-country employees while setting forth a functional guidance model to motivate management to use the resource effectively.

NEGOTIATE GLOBALLY - EXECUTE LOCALLY

The principle of negotiating globally while executing locally has been applied to address the structural challenges described above. The first half of the principle involves the negotiation of a master agreement between the lead customer party and the lead service provider party.[5] Upon execution by both parties, the terms contained in the master agreement apply globally. Such terms pertain to general legal and financial concerns such as intellectual property rights, confidential information, limitation of liability, and payment. The next step is for the lead parties to negotiate a separate country agreement. This country agreement is conceived as an addendum to the master contract and contains all country unique terms, including service delivery, country tax treatment, human resources, billing, and inflation. Together, the agreements provide a framework for terms and conditions applicable to the services that the lead customer party will receive, and the local service provider will provide, under the country agreement.[6]

The second half of the principle dictates that in each country where the service provider will deliver services to customer, the two parties will, before commencing services, enter into a country agreement. The local parties do not have any rights or obligations until the country agreement is signed. The country agreement incorporates the terms of the master agreement by reference and describes in detail the services that the local service provider will be responsible for delivering. Within this contract structure, an order of precedence governs such that in the event of a conflict, a term in the master agreement prevails over a term in an applicable country agreement. Moreover, any modification to the terms of the master agreement referenced in a country agreement is effective only for that particular country agreement. In practice, these structures apply to four different deal environments: (1) the customer and service provider lead country organizations make all decisions centrally with direction to their in-country counterparts to comply, (2) the customer and service provider organizations' decision making processes are decentralized, such that each in-country entity is not strongly encouraged to follow the lead country's direction, (3) the customer has a centralized decision making approach and the service provider is decentralized, and (4) the customer is decentralized while the service provider is centralized. Whereas the most efficient scenario is (1), scenario (2) presents the most formidable challenges to effective negotiations and global consistency.

ATYPICAL APPROACHES TO NONTRADITIONAL ISSUES

In trying to orchestrate these approaches across geographic, functional, cultural, and business boundaries, corporations must modernize "the hierarchy and bureaucratic control that were crucial to success in an age when change came slowly and markets were largely domestic" (Byrne 110, 1999). Companies of this era traditionally made decisions through escalation processes of upward appeal, under which any decision of consequence had to be made at the top or, at a minimum, be approved by enough other layers that the implementor of that decision was well-covered. In these models, project implementors operated carefully within accepted boundaries of individual accountability to pass along decisions in ways intended not to rankle the executives that they were beholden to, or not

---

[5] "Lead party" in this case refers to the person or entity that has the authority to represent, bind, and sign for its respective company in connection with all aspects of this Master Agreement
[6] "Local party in this case refers to the person or entity that has the authority to represent, bind, and sign for its respective company in connection with all aspects of the particular country agreement.

418

to leave them personally ensnarled in corporate politics. In static markets where the companies that owned the best product or the service won, such organizational models were effective. But in global outsourcing engagements, these models tend to obfuscate real issues and reduce highly nuanced decisions into meaningless generalities. Such inadequacies are exacerbated when within a gauntlet of decisions, everyone is empowered to say no to a proposal, while no single employee is empowered to say yes. Once a veto is lodged, it must work its way upward until, after weeks of meetings, it finally reaches a senior executive capable of resolution, and the answer flows back down through the chain of command. The upshot is that decisions are made by those furthest removed from the customer and least equipped make them.

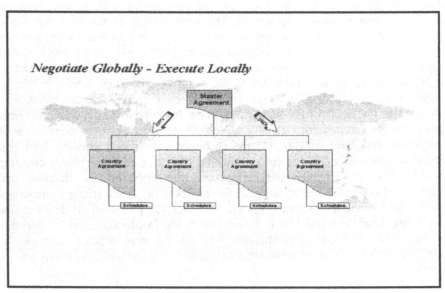

Figure 2. Global Contract Model (Internal IBM Presentation)

These lessons were learned firsthand by IBM as it entered the strategic outsourcing business in the early 1990s. In one particular case, a company identified here as "Company A" engaged a third-party consultant to solicit competitive bids on its behalf from candidates interested in managing its data center operations. Prior to a general announcement of its strategy to outsource, IBM had been sponsored by the chairman of Company A as the outsourcer of choice, and all responding vendors were told that the contract was expected to belong to IBM. Yet after two months of negotiations, Company A's deal team, consisting of fourteen cross-functional associates who were fully empowered to make the decision voted unanimously to award the business to an alternative vendor. Afterward, a loss review held with Company A provided dramatic insights. IBM's competitor had not only proven to be more flexible than IBM in its financial terms, but it had also been able to create more options for a heterogeneous technological environment which ran multiple vendor platforms. Meanwhile, the IBM team had been unable to quickly commit to positions on any of these issues. On several key terms, the IBM team could only offer its willingness to negotiate as it passed the decisions to its legal and financial communities. While Company A's cross-functional team structure allowed it to erase boundaries between its members and compress the time of each decision, IBM could not counter such liquid exchanges of information. Yet most fundamental to IBM's loss of this business was IBM's failure to understand Company A's decision-making model. IBM did not anticipate that the details uncovered during the negotiation would be used by a fully empowered customer deal team to redirect executive management's position on the deal, and negate IBM's prior relationship with the chairman.

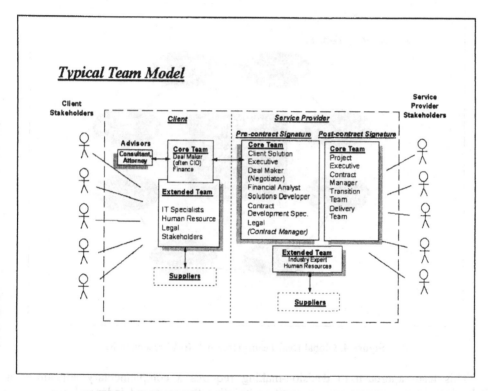

Figure 3. Typical Team Model (Internal IBM Presentation)

NONHIERARCHICAL, MULTI-DISCIPLINE PEER TEAMS AS DECISION MAKING BODIES

Wrenching revelations such as these have forced IBM to fundamentally rethink how it negotiates. The crucial task has become building cross-functional organizations that eradicate traditional barriers between practitioners and the "managers who police their decision-making" (Byrne 110, 1999). Tolerance for ambiguity and capacity to learn on the fly must be built into these engagement processes in which companies must act quickly and without perfect knowledge. Accordingly, IBM has established nonhierarchical, multi-discipline peer teams as decision-making bodies in global engagements. These core teams consist of extended technical, financial, HR, legal, negotiations capabilities and can be quickly assembled, deployed, refocused, and disbanded for each global deal. Clearly defined internal approval paths for each function have been established to enable members of the teams to achieve consensus on the front lines. The unwritten rule is that the team is both fully empowered with decision-making authority and fully accountable for understanding and validating the linkages of all customer deliverables.

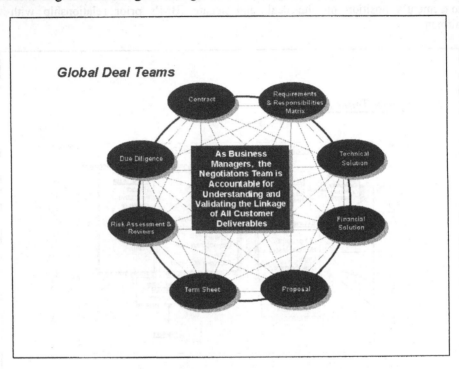

Figure 4. Global Deal Teams (Internal IBM Presentation)

This team approach to decision-making requires a complementary adjustment in behavior: team members must commit to building the trust and independence that are "necessary to move from individual accountability to mutual accountability" (Katzenbach and Smith 109, 1993). When employees chance personal exposure by engaging in the constructive conflict necessary to move forward, they foster decisions that are closer to the customer and therefore more responsive to the engagement. For each risk that they take, team members are accountable for getting "buy-in" from their constituents. In turn, the challenge for management is to encourage engagement teams to take the necessary risks to overcome constraints imposed by individual, functional, and hierarchical boundaries. Further, as deal teams create value through their innovation and risk-taking, the company needs to pay the team members in a way that motivates them to create more of that value. As repetitions are the key to building expertise and better judgment, it is essential to build a compensation and incentive system that rewards deal team members for confirmed participation on teams over many deals. Incentives that generate both a sense of ownership and a feeling of leverage over an engagement's performance can stimulate the creativity and velocity of decision-making that are critical (see Katzenbach and Smith, 1993).

ENGAGEMENT PROCESS

Companies rarely think systematically about their engagement process as a whole. Building a strong engagement capacity requires a coordinated approach to organizing and managing the process and the people. Application of nonhierarchical, multi-discipline peer teams as decision-making bodies to the methodology detailed in the figure below thus represents a radical change for large corporations:

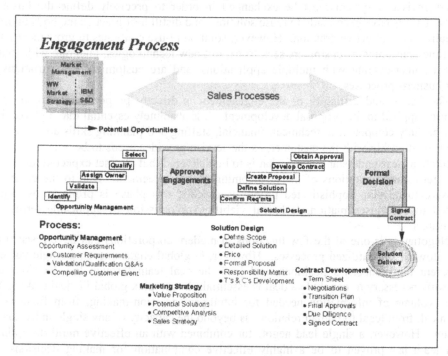

Figure 5. Engagement Process (Internal IBM Presentation)

Opportunity management is a service provider activity and is used to identify or respond to prospective customers that are interested in outsourcing their business processes or operations to a service vendor. Once identified, discussions may commence with a prospective customer to determine the customer's level of interest. If the parties decide to engage, the deal team is assembled and deployed.

In the solution design phase, the technical solution manager owns responsibility for developing a solution that integrates hardware, software, assets, and services to address the customer's business requirements. The solution must provide a complete, integrated capability, including business applications and technical infrastructure, which can be integrated within the existing customer environment. Typically, the architecture represents a large investment and is frequently of strategic importance to the growth and profitability of the customer's business. The customer must be confident that its chosen development partner brings the right breadth and depth of expertise to the project, understands very well the subject area represented, and has the ability to apply it in a way that markedly improves the chances of a successful outcome. Too many projects disappoint or fail to deliver not through any technical failure, but from an inability to completely and unambiguously define the requirements. To avoid such problems, the deal team works together with the customer during the solution design phase to establish joint financial, technical, and business assumptions. Visual expressions of architectural patterns, detailed walkthroughs of use case scenarios, and elaborations of the components of the envisaged system must be exchanged in order to precisely define the business needs. Efforts have been made to reuse solutions and distill best practice methods in order to realize more effective creation. However, solution re-use continues to grow more risky and time consuming as customers seek to exploit new technologies, integrate with legacy systems, inter-operate with multiple applications, and are customized for variations in their business processes.

The length and difficulty of the engagement is directly proportional to quality of resource applied to the proposal development. It is absolutely essential that a global deal team be fully competent in technical, financial, staffing and planning skills and possess a strong relationship with the customer, as the service provider needs to be able to not only articulate a clear understanding of what is to be delivered, but also set expectations for the basic terms and conditions of the forthcoming global agreement. Due to the enormous pressure to develop sophisticated proposals quickly, this phase is prone to oversights related to cost-misestimation, technical viability, or omission of applicable terms and conditions.

Negotiation is one of the few functions in modern corporations that have resisted the trend toward standardized processes. However, in global engagements, a single voice to represent the company's positions, and lead the deal team through the decisions and tradeoffs necessary to conclude a deal is essential. In complex global IT deal making, the sheer volume of information needed for intelligent decision-making, from financial to technical, from legal to human relations, is beyond the capacity of any single individual to master. However, a single lead negotiator combined with an effective multi-disciplinary deal team has proven to be a highly effective combination for making decisions and resolving conflicts in reaching deals between providers and customers. Thus, the efforts of global deal teams provide a broadly supportive infrastructure that guides negotiations and in turn produces better relationships. Rather than being a hindrance, this infrastructure yields creativity and value.

The critical first task in the negotiation is to define in clear, brief terms the basic tenants of the deal such as price, term, transition, scope, performance, and change. This is usually accomplished through creation of a term sheet, service matrix, letter of intent, or similar device. It is essential to understand at every point of the negotiation the major points of agreement and disagreement. While proposals are often ambiguous or incomplete on key issues, the term sheet must be explicit, and cannot be inconsistent with previous representations.

The next critical task is to create solutions that bridge differences. Negotiation sessions inevitably lead to discovery of fundamental mutual misunderstandings of key terms. The structural and business concerns in global engagements are too complex and interdependent for either party to expect otherwise. Once the contract structuring and technical issues are resolved as described above, the most pervasive differences stem from the definition of the value proposition. What set of costs are used to set price terms? What is the scope of services? Is growth built into the cost case? Which party bears the risk of the unforeseen? The answers to these questions can often be found in a range of options that is empirically definable. But as e-business opportunities proliferate, the value proposition needs to expand to incorporate new business paradigms and process re-engineering. The consequence is that delineation of the core drivers of value becomes a more arduous task. In an economy where intellectual capital produces greater returns than physical assets, relationships that foster the production of intellectual capital need to be more carefully considered by both parties.

These measures force parties to think more broadly and creatively about negotiations, both when strategies are initially established and as the bargaining unfolds. When negotiations become difficult, deal teams have to balance a host of considerations. The most common ramification in a global engagement is a pattern of negotiation formed by a succession of positions taken by each party. As more attention is paid to positions, less attention is devoted to addressing the underlying concerns of the parties. In contrast, "a principled negotiating method that focuses on basic interests, mutually satisfying options, and fair standards" typically result in more effective agreements and better long-term relationships between the parties (Fisher, Ury and Patton 14, 1991). The Harvard Negotiation Project has produced a substantial literature on methods to reaching such joint decisions with minimal transaction costs, and it is beyond the scope of this paper to explore them at length here. What is critical to understand, however, is that as companies grapple with such challenges in engagements, global deal team dynamics relating to focus, direction, size, skill, and mutual accountability promote the flexibility that is necessary to achieve consensus. In these situations, having people that can identify and build new options for mutual gain who are in the room for negotiation or available for consultation, can be the difference between success and failure. (see Fisher, Ury and Patton, 1991)

CONCLUSIONS

Decision analysis may be defined as the application of scientific methods to problems of choice and implementation. The analysis as it is usually practiced proceeds through the following steps: collecting and analyzing data bearing on the domain under scrutiny, understanding the relationships among variables, building a model that specifies these key relationships, and evaluating policies by testing them in the model and comparing their results through performance criteria reflecting specified objectives. How does this progression relate to the subject of this paper? The answer is that the application of nonhierarchical, multi-discipline peer teams as decision-making bodies in global IT engagements, which has been elaborated above, can provide a useful supplement to the standard methods associated with decision analysis. What the standard sequence of analysis generally omits is an explicit concern for the vagaries and shortfalls in performance that inevitably arise when fallible organizations, prone to characteristic structure and behavior of large corporations, attempt to translate a chosen performance objective into an operating reality. One aim of this paper has been to improve the comparisons that can be made of the challenges and risks inherent to global IT outsourcing engagements, and the success of organizations intended to address them. The other purpose has been to stimulate new ideas or entirely different systematic approaches to these problems.

In the old economy, businesses could master a few disciplines and use that knowledge to clobber their competitors. In the new economy, where markets are highly fluid, speed often trumps mass and whoever has the best relationships wins. Under such conditions, the ability to pull together skills and insight has become an IT service provider's most sustainable competitive advantage. In global engagements, deal teams must be able to identify the opportunities and problems as the arise, evaluate the options they have for moving forward, and quickly make the necessary tradeoffs and decisions about how to proceed. Knowing exactly what it takes to close deals is the essential trait of deal team members. This knowledge is based on preparation, negotiation capability, accurate understanding of mutual interests, and experience. Deal-making requires an intangible sense for the deal. Engagements are high-risk, high-reward affairs that demand people who are capable of anticipating nontraditional issues and forming atypical responses in a problem-solving mood.   Thus, as service providers come to terms with the fact that they doesn't own its most valuable assets but only rent them for a period of time each day, they are challenged to structure and approach engagements which leverage these assets in the most effective manner possible.

REFERENCES

Byrne, J. "The Search for the Young and Gifted: Why Talent Counts," BusinessWeek, 4 October 1999, 108-116.

DiRomualdo, A. and Gurbaxani, V. "Strategic Intent for IT Outsourcing," Sloan Management Review, Summer 1998, 67-80

Earl, M. "The Risks of IT Outsourcing," Sloan Management Review, volume 37, Spring 1996, 26-32

Fisher, R., Ury, W., and Patton B.. Getting to Yes: Negotiating Agreement Without Giving In. 2d ed. New York: Penguin Books, 1991.

Ghoshal, S., Bartlett, C., Moran, P.. "A New Manifesto for Mangement" Sloan Management Review, Spring 1999 Volume 40 Number 3 pages 9-20

Hirscheim, R. and Lacity, M., "The Outsourcing Bandwagon," The Sloan Management Review, volume 34, Spring 1993, 9-23

Katzenbach, J. R., and Smith, D. The Wisdom of Teams. Cambridge: Harvard Business School Press, 1993; HarperBusiness, 1994.

Lacity, M.C., and Hirschheim, R.. Information Systems Outsourcing. New York: John Wiley & Sons, 1993.

Lacity M., Willcocks, L., and Feeny, D., "IT Ousourcing: Maximize Flexibility and Control," Harvard Business Review, volume 73, May-June 1995, 84-93

Mandel, M. J. "The Prosperity Gap," BusinessWeek, 27 September, 1999, 90-102.

USING INTERNET MULTIMEDIA DATABASE INFORMATION SYSTEMS FOR DECISION SUPPORT IN CONSERVATION PLANNING

M. Angelides, M.C. Angelides

Department of Information Systems and Computing
Brunel University
Uxbridge, Middlesex UB8 3PH
United Kingdom

Abstract: This article shows how the efficiency and effectiveness of the current processes of conservation planning is increased through the implementation and use of Internet multimedia database information systems. This leads to new conservation planning processes that are not just automated but also do not succumb to the Quality of Service problems that current processes across Europe exhibit. Automating the processes for dealing with applications for listing and listed building consent, is in line with new national guidelines set in many European Union countries, including the United Kingdom, about modernising central and local government through the implementation and use of Internet multimedia database information systems.

Key words: Conservation Planning, Internet Multimedia Databases Information Systems, Decision Support

INTRODUCTION

The pressures on Local Planning Authorities (LPAs) in the UK to become more efficient in terms of reaching decisions quickly and accurately within constraints of procedure and time, together with a critical watch over their use of resources lead to the emergence of information technology in planning (Pickard 1996; Suddards and Hargreaves 1996; ACO 1997). Achieving the level of efficiency set by the central government requires constant feedback of standard information on patterns of trends and development in the community which could not be reasonably achieved without the use of information technology. In certain areas of planning neither the technology nor the information is yet available, either in quality or quantity, to achieve the efficiency levels expected because the vast majority of systems are

425

S.H. Zanakis et al. (eds.), Decision Making: Recent Developments and Worldwide Applications, 425–441.
© 2000 *Kluwer Academic Publishers.*

designed to deal largely with (a) relieving the administration burden relating to processing planning applications, (b) centralising information in one area, and (c) providing a tool for analysing information.

Most LPAs have strived to increase their information systems in the last two decades although not always in the right direction (Angelides 1999). The goal of centralised management information systems to meet the information needs of administration, case load officers and strategic management has never been fully achieved by any LPA. The barriers that existed between organisational and technological constraints meant that a single information system has not been able to serve all the information needs of an LPA simultaneously. As a result, the use of information systems in planning departments has been operational rather than managerial or executive.

The UK Government's White Paper on Modernising Government which announces (Garlick 1999a and 1999b) that both central and local government should be able to electronically conduct their procedures is set to change the entire planning process as we know it. By the year 2008, it states, all LPAs should be able to carry out their dealings electronically. This means that in eight years time the general public will be able to use the Internet to file planning applications and comment on others' applications, find out the planning history of a property and comment on development plans. The potential for public interfacing over the Internet would be immense. Presently only a few LPAs use the Internet. Capitalising on the potential of the Internet and information technology will improve the relationship between planning departments and the general public. The use of the Internet for public consultation through community participation in planning would be beneficial and it will provide an effective and efficient service. In any case, the government agenda is forcing LPAs to focus on their use of information technology since the White Paper puts information technology at the forefront of service delivery.

The paper also states that new media such as the Internet, interactive television and touchscreens could increase the choice of how citizens and businesses access public services (Angelides 1997). Banks, post offices, supermarkets and other private sector and voluntary organisations could provide access terminals outside the home for use by the public. However, there drawbacks. The submission of planning applications electronically would be workable for small household applications, but it would be difficult for major proposals because of the amount of information on those cases. Also allowing community participation in the planning process through the Internet will slow the consultation process. Problems of this nature have been experienced in the US who restricted Internet access to documents on which they wished to be consulted to chosen panels representing a cross-section of the local community and other interested parties.

Hewson (1999) argues that information management is poorly used in conservation planning. A conservation planning officer is faced with many problems when dealing with applications for listing and listed building consent (LBC) because these processes are largely paper-based and thus tedious, time-consuming and largely inefficient (Morton 1996a; Morton 1996b; ACO 1997; Angelides 1999). For example, if a member of the public makes a telephone enquiry on a listed building, it takes an officer a while to respond because the officer dealing with it would normally need to retrieve pictures of, and the files for, the listed building in question and may also have to consult separate survey maps for reference. Often, preparing a reply to an enquiry may require nationwide cross-referencing which takes days or even weeks to complete.

The efficiency and effectiveness of the current processes of conservation planning may be increased today through the implementation and use of Internet multimedia database information systems (Lermon 1996 and 1997; Dustdar and Angelides 1997; Dustdar and Huber 1998; Dustdar and Angelides 1999). This will lead to new conservation planning processes that are not just automated but also do not succumb to the Quality of Service problems that current processes across Europe exhibit. Automating the processes for dealing with applications for listing and LBC, is in line with new national guidelines set in European Union countries, including the UK, about modernising central and local government through the implementation and use of Internet information systems. The significance of using Internet multimedia database information systems to support these processes is to enable a conservation officer to assess applications for both listing a building and LBC swiftly and single-handedly either from the comfort of his own office or on-site by reference, through the Internet, to the multimedia database. The system will hold visual and textual descriptions of all the listed buildings in Europe indexed according to grade, architectural features, architect, etc. Although a vast undertaking to migrate from a paper-based to an automated process, this will ensure consistency and uniformity in content, practice and standards across Europe.

A conservation officer can use the system to retrieve the listing description of a building or of similar buildings across a country or across Europe, or of listed buildings across a country or across Europe designed by the same architect or of the same grade, etc. This would enable concurrent on-site assessment of a building through the Internet use of the system. Nationwide-referencing and Europewide-referencing will help reinforce the criteria against which a conservation planning decision is made which will in turn help enforcement control. This will result in the development of a European-level conservation planning process and strategy (de Figueiredo 1998).

A PROTOTYPE INTERNET MULTIMEDIA DATABASE INFORMATION SYSTEM FOR SUPPORTING PLANNING DECISIONS IN CONSERVATION

The Department of Culture, Media and Sport (DCMS) deals with listing requests and works in regions (DCMS 1997). London is one region. One officer deals with a request but his recommendations are verified by a senior executive officer. Anyone can make a request for listing such as LPAs, parish councils, amenity societies, public and private companies. There are no standard forms to complete. Individuals write in and provide as much information as possible. A listing request is then assessed. They are checked prior to being assessed if they are already listed, previously assessed and if any new evidence has arisen. If any of these are the case the request will not be assessed and the relevant LPA will be notified. If there is new evidence the DCMS will assess its urgency by contacting the LPA. The DCMS will contact English Heritage (EH) for them to assess the merits of the building. EH have 8 weeks to respond to the DCMS. If EH decide the building is not listable it will be directed back to DCMS. If listable an EH inspector considers the case and makes recommendations to the DCMS where a senior executive makes a decision. With controversial cases the Secretary of

State may make a decision. Once a decision has been made to list a building, this takes effect when it is signed for inclusion. The DCMS informs the LPA and owner/occupier of the listing. The listing is registered as a Land Charge by the LPA and LBC is required for any building works.

EH advices the DCMS on listing requests and LPAs on LBC applications (EH 1996a and 1996b). Two departments serve the above functions, one dealing with listing, the other with LBC applications. Both departments are divided in regional teams. One officer normally deals with individual cases but in some cases where it concerns a particular type or period of building, this is allocated to an inspector who has experience with buildings of that nature. Prior to recommendations being made, these may be discussed at team group or at the Advisory Committee before being directed to the DCMS and LPA. EH have 8 weeks to respond to the DCMS and this may be shortened if the building is threatened with demolition or a planning application is being considered. EH makes site visits for both requests and LBCs. Archivists and national amenity societies are consulted. With LBC applications EH have 28 days to make recommendations to the LPA.

The LPAs deal with LBC applications. Work is in area teams, that is in wards of the borough. Applications are allocated to a planning officer who seeks advice from a conservation officer. Requests for LBC have to be made on a standard form supported by photographs, plans, listing descriptions and what the consent is for, e.g. alteration, extension or demolition. The application is publicized on site and in local paper. Non-contentious grade II buildings are dealt by the LPA but other grades, i.e. I and II* and some II buildings are notified to EH for its comments. EH have 28 days to make their recommendations. EH may arrange a site visit with the relevant officer from the LPA. If the LPA intends to refuse the application then EH will not be notified. The LPA also notifies the national amenity societies and the (Royal Commission of Historic Monuments in England) RCHME for their comments. The LPA has to take into account any other comments made at the consultation stage and recommendations made by EH before making a decision whether to grant LBC. The LPA officer then forwards to the planning committee his recommendations and informs the applicant of the outcome.

The prototype is a multi-featured Internet-based Multimedia Database Information System that holds visual and textual descriptions of most Listed Buildings in the UK and was developed using user-driven rapid application prototyping. The prototype includes all the features that are necessary during decision making (screen 1): Architectural Dictionary, Architect's Dictionary, Listed Buildings Database, and Consultation Contacts. Since the system allows data interchange over the Internet an RCHME officer can use the system to retrieve archival material, an LPA can use it to retrieve the listing description of a similar building in another LPA, a resource library can use it to retrieve descriptions of all the buildings across the country designed by the same architect or an EH inspector can use it to assess on-site a building by reference to similar buildings across the country.

The Architectural Dictionary (screens 2-3) holds still and full-motion video, digital photographs, graphs and textual description of period architectural designs of buildings, e.g. a cut open front isometric view of a typical early 18th century terrace house with mansard (screens 4-8), of doors, e.g. Georgian, of windows, e.g. Victorian, of brick bonding, e.g. Flemish, of parapets, e.g. eaves, cornices, etc. The Architect's Dictionary (screens 9-10) holds all the architects whose buildings have been listed anywhere in the country. In this dictionary, all the listed buildings are indexed against their architect not the LPA in which they are in, thus a conservation officer can retrieve still and full-motion video, digital photographs and descriptions of listed buildings by an architect from across the country for perusal (screens 11-14) or for updating (screens 15-16), if the user has the authority to do so. The Listed Buildings Database (screen 17) is an A-Z multimedia database that holds all listed buildings across the country. Consultation Contacts (screen 46) includes details of all organisations that have a role to play in conservation planning.

The prototype using an indexing system can search (screen 18) for still and full-motion video, digital photographs, full textual description and Ordnance Survey map of a listed building. The indexing system uses a combination (screens 19-20) of Local Authority Reference Number, Ordnance Survey Reference Number, Planning Reference Number, Architect, age of building, date of listing, type of structure, type of building structure, style, use of structure and address to retrieve a building. If the officer omits some of this information then, the indexing system may result in retrieving more than one building (screens 21-24) that 'match' the description and the officer would then have to choose among what has been retrieved. He may re-search by providing more of, or all, the information required by the indexing system. The officer may retrieve a building simply by specifying the name of the architect, which invokes the Architect's Dictionary, and then by selecting from the catalogue of buildings listed against that architect, the building of his choice. There is help (Screen 25) if necessary. The officer may also search for a building by graphical browsing through an LPA's map (screen 26). First, he selects an LPA (screen 27), then a ward (screen 28-29) and then the building (screen 30-33).

The textual description includes its address, date of listing, group value, grade of listing, type of list schedule, type of structure, objects/structures within the curtilage, date when built, age of the building, style, the current use and what was originally built for, the architect, historical importance, condition of the building, whether it is in a conservation area, if it is a schedule monument, planning applications history including when granted and for what purpose and if any proposals were subject to appeals, type of appeal and outcome of decision, if the building is at risk, if the building is pending listing, maintenance and repair, architectural features, and the listing description.

The officer may add a new record in the database (screen 34) for a newly-listed building. The officer is presented with an empty record (screens 35-36) which he may then complete with the details of the newly-listed building (screen 37). As soon as the record is added in the database, it becomes immediately available for inspection (screens 38-45) or upgrading. This facility may be used to create records not only for newly-listed buildings but also for all the listed buildings in the country. This will involve both typing and scanning information in the database. In this way, the entire existing paper-based system can be migrated to the prototype. Undoubtably, migrating to the prototype is a vast undertaking, but once completed adding a new record to the system will become as routinely as in the current system. Both the Architectural and Architect's Dictionary can also be upgraded to include more architectural features and architects.

Dealing with Listed Building Consent applications using the prototype system

The prototype is not a planning applications processing system, therefore, planning applications made on the Internet are not processed by the system. On-line and paper applications are processed through an existing planning applications processing system in development control whose final outcome is then transferred into the prototype. Our research reveals that existing planning applications processing systems are not open, thus data transfer between them and the prototype has to be done manually. The white paper requires new planning applications processing systems and all other public systems to be open to enable automatic data sharing among them. The prototype is an open system.

As soon as the data has been transferred either currently manually or in the future automatically from the planning applications processing system to the prototype, the prototype will flag both the planning officer and the conservation officer in the relevant LPA, EH, the RCHME and the national amenities societies that a new application has been filed. All officers have access to the prototype and, therefore, when an application for LBC is filed, all officers can provide input *concurrently*. If the LBC application affects the exterior of a building then a notice is distributed electronically for inclusion in the local press. A notice also has to be displayed on-site. Future practice, may eliminate the need to advertise in the local papers and an advert on the LPA's web site may suffice. All officers using the prototype's indexing system can retrieve still and full-motion video and digital photographs of the building under consideration along with its Ordnance Survey map and textual description for their consideration (as in screens 17-33). The RCHME does not have to visit the site to create a visual record of the building, when the application is for partial or whole demolition, since the prototype includes still or full-motion video footage and digital photographs of it.

Perhaps the RCHME can assume another role if a system like the prototype is adopted, like maintaining and updating the video footage and digital photographs of buildings in the database. Although a vast undertaking when migrating from the paper-based system to the automated system, making one body responsible for capturing and storing video footage and digital photographs of listed buildings across the entire country will ensure consistency in content and capturing and storing standards. Of course, it would be more feasible and practical to suggest that each LPA should be made responsible for capturing their own video footage and digital photographs, nevertheless, this may result in inconsistencies in terms of video content and capturing and storing standards across the country which will be 'visible' when retrieving visual information from the database. EH does not have to act if the LPA officers indicate that the application is likely to be refused but If this is not likely then they may start considerations concurrently with the LPA.

Although an application has to be considered on its own merits, this has not always been the case. Both the LPA officers and the EH inspector usually consult the findings of similar cases. The LPA officers consult their files within their LPA and rarely outside their LPAs but with the prototype they can consult similar cases across the country at all times. The EH inspector, while on-site, neither has access to findings of similar cases nor can he consult his files as a result of an on-site finding. This may result either in several visits or prognosis of which cases are similar prior to the visit.

Once the LPA officer or the EH inspector has retrieved still and full-motion video, digital photographs, Ordnance Survey map and textual description of the building under consideration and he has considered the application on its own merits, he may then use the architect's dictionary in the prototype to retrieve similar buildings by the same architect (as in screens 9-14) in order to compare relevant features or see if LBC has been previously granted or if any were subject to an appeal on similar grounds and thereby assess the likelihood of enforcement control. Nationwide-referencing helps reinforce the criteria against which a decision is made which in turn helps enforcement control. An LPA officer or EH inspector may use the prototype's architectural dictionary (as in screens 2-8) to see if, for example, the interior of the building deviates from the traditional architectural design of that period if LBC is granted.

If the building is in a conservation area, he may use the LPA's conservation map (as in screens 26-33) to assess the effect of the changes on the surrounding area after the LBC is granted. The EH inspector may, while on-site, access the prototype and make decisions. Before final recommendation is made to the planning committee, comments received as a result of the notices are considered. If a decision is made to grant LBC then the record of the building in the prototype has to be updated (as in screens 15-16).

Dealing with listing requests using the prototype system

A listing request can be submitted through the prototype. Before submitting a listing request, the user may access the DCMS web site to retrieve information about 'what listing means' (screen 46), local and national archives to retrieve information about the building, the Architect's Dictionary to retrieve other but similar buildings by the same architect (as in screens 9-14) or the Architectural Dictionary to find its building design (as in screens 2-8) and what features according to that make it outstanding.

In addition, before a listing request is submitted, the user can check, by using the prototype's indexing system, if the building is already included in the database or deemed listed (as in screens 17-33). If it is already listed or it is deemed listed then it does not allow the user to submit a listing request. If it is not included in the database, the user may submit on-line video footage, digital photographs, Ordnance Survey map and textual description of the building in the same format as that of buildings already in the database. The user may request listing by creating a new record and submitting it for inclusion in the database (as in screens 34-45). However, unlike when a conservation officer uses this facility, the new record will not be automatically added in the database. This will be treated as a listing request and the process triggered.

The prototype will help the user in order to ensure that all information required has been provided and that if, and when, the building is approved for listing, there is no need to create a new record for the building but instead use the one created. The content may be subject to amendments to include information that can only be provided after it has been listed or to bring the description in line with all the other descriptions in the database. The building will be automatically given a 'listing pending' status with some fields left empty, e.g. date of listing, grade, etc. Once the request is submitted, the prototype will flag the conservation officer in the relevant LPA, the DCMS, and EH that a listing request has been filed. The

DCMS, EH and the LPA officers can assess the merits of the request concurrently. The prototype does not keep a record of unsuccessful listing requests and, thus, the DCMS officer has to check manually if it has been previously assessed for listing and what new evidence has emerged that warrants listing.

If new evidence has emerged, the EH inspector can assess the merits of listing a building on-site, in the same manner as with LBC applications. He can access archives on-line, similar buildings by the same architect (as in screens 9-14) that are already in the database, can determine the design of the building from designs in the architectural dictionary (as in screens 2-8), or can retrieve similar cases by using the indexing system (as in screens 17-33). If, according to the EH inspector, the building is listable, the DCMS will complete the record of the building in the database and amend the `listing pending' status. Once the `listing pending' status is amended, the prototype will flag the LPA officer and the RCHME that a new building has been newly-listed. The RCHME will proceed to capture video footage and digital photographs for inclusion in the building's record in the database and provide its input on the description of the building in the database. If the building is not listable, then the listing request is deleted. Only authorised officers can amend the prototype's database.

In addition, to the written documentation sent out by the LPA to notify all people involved, i.e. applicant(s), owner(s), occupier(s), of the outcome of the listing request, the LPA may post a notice on its web site informing users of a new listing. The listing description of the building along with video footage, digital photographs and its Ordnance Survey Map will be available (as in screens 39-45) for downloading on-line.

REFERENCES

Association of Conservation Officers (1997), "The Philosophy of Conservation: Reconstruction and Regeneration", *Context* 55/September, 8-13.

Angelides, M. (1999), *Enhancing Listing and listed building consent through automation*, MA Thesis, South Bank University, London.

Angelides, M.C. (1997), "Implementing the Internet for Business: A Global Marketing Opportunity", *International Journal of Information Management* 17/6, 405-419.

Department of Culture, Media and Sport (1997), "Planning and the Historic Environment-Notification and Directions by the Secretary of State", *Circular* 14/97.

Dustdar, S. and Angelides, M.C. (1997), "Organisational Impacts of Multimedia Information Systems", *Journal of Information Technology* 12/1, 33-43.

Dustdar, S. and Angelides, M.C. (1999), "Multimedia Information Systems", in: Furht, B. (Ed.), *Handbook of Internet and Multimedia Systems and Applications*, CRC Press/IEEE Press, Boca Raton, 311-337.

Dustdar, S. and Huber, R. (1998), "Group Decision Making on Urban Planning Using Desktop Multimedia Conferencing", *Multimedia Tools and Applications* 6/1, 33-46.

English Heritage (1996a), *Streamlining listed building consent procedures: A consultation paper.*

English Heritage (1996b), *Something worth keeping? Post-War Architecture in England.*

de Figueiredo, P. (1998), "LODIS - Local Distinctiveness Strategies to promote economic competitiveness", *Context* 60/December, 8-10.

Garlick, R. (1999a), "Take care on online future", *Planning* 9 April, 3.

Garlick, R. (1999b), "Untapped potential", *Planning* 9 April, 4.

Hewson, D. (1999), "Knowledge Management", *The Sunday Times* 25 April, 2-3.

Lermon, D. (1996), "The future is now", *Context* 51/September, 26-27.

Lermon, D. (1997), "The future is now: an update", *Context* 54/June, 25-26.

Morton, D. (1996a), "Building conservation: quantity or quality?", *Context* 51/September, 35-36.

Morton, D. (1996b), "Conservation, yesterday, today, & tomorrow", *Context* 52/December, 33-34.

Pickard, R.D. (1996), *Conservation in the Built Environment*, Longman, Singapore.

Suddards, R.W. and Hargreaves, J.M. (1996), *Listed Buildings*, Sweet & Maxwell, London.

434

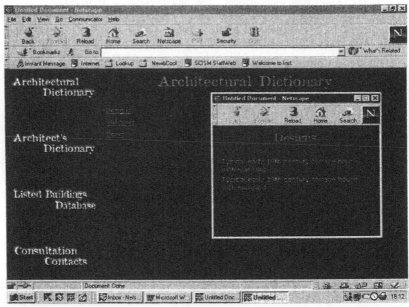

Screen 1

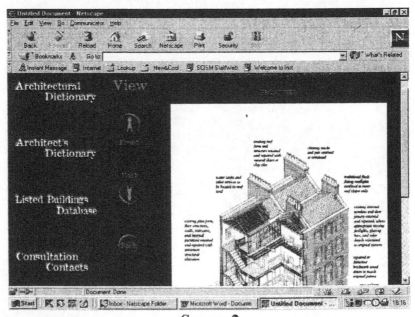

Screen 2

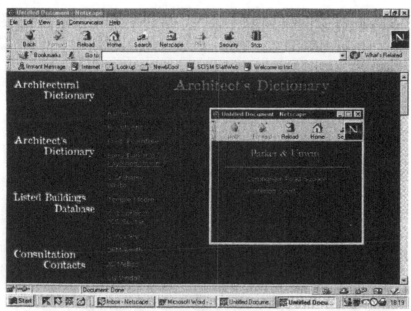

Screen 3

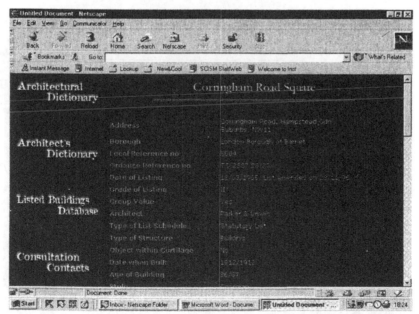

Screen 4

436

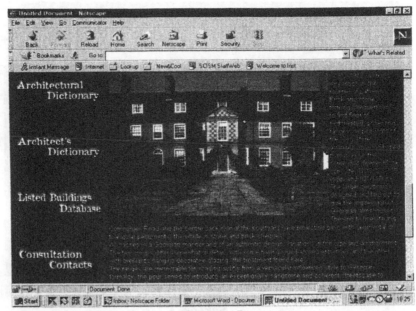

Screen 5

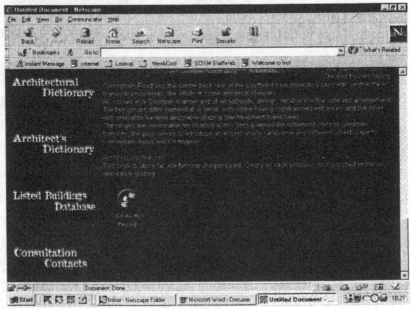

Screen 6

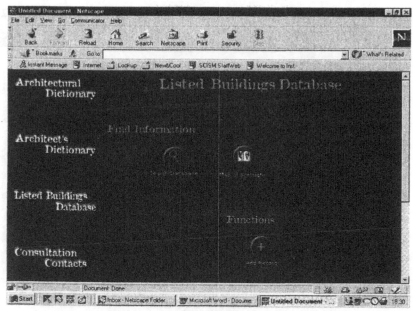

Screen 7

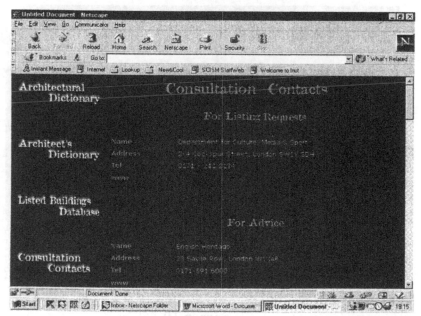

Screen 8

438

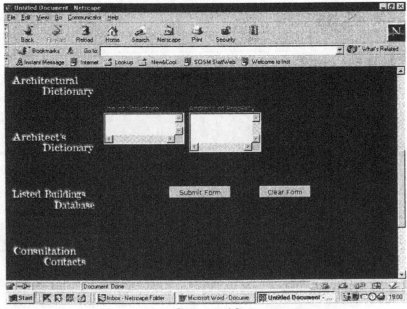

Screen 9

Screen 10

Screen 11

Screen 12

440

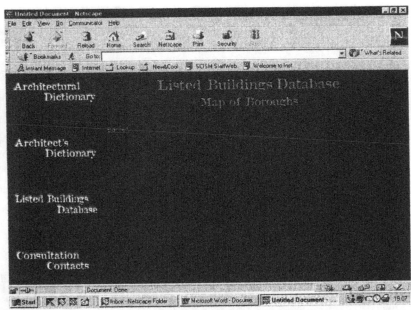

Screen 13

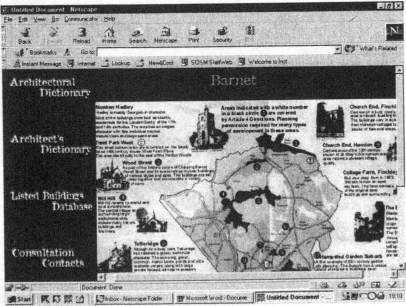

Screen 14

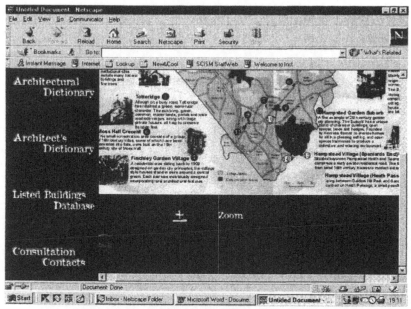

Screen 15

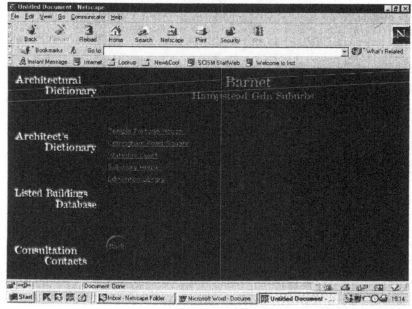

Screen 16

AN INTERACTIVE WORKLOAD AND RISK BALANCING MODEL AND DECISION SUPPORT SYSTEM FOR PROBATIONER ASSIGNMENT

J.R. Baker[1], A.C. Saydam[1], P.K. Lattimore[2]

[1] University of North Carolina-Charlotte
Belk College of Business Administration
IOM Department
Charlotte, NC 28223-0001, USA

[2] Research Triangle Institute
Research Triangle Park
P.O. Box 12194, NC 27709-2194, USA

Abstract: The purpose of probation is to protect public safety by deploying personnel to supervise individuals assigned to probation by the court. This paper presents a model for allocating probation officer resources that combines a statistical model for probationer risk classification and an integer, nonlinear multi-criteria programming resource allocation model for workload balancing. Data were obtained from the Florida Department of Corrections, which is implementing the model. The classification model identifies the expected likelihood of failure during discrete periods of supervision. These likelihoods are used to assign individuals to supervision levels. The proportion of probationers in each risk category is an input to the allocation model where decision variables are number of visits to probationers by type of visit and risk classification. Model constraints include performance characteristics, service time, public safety measures, and reduction in probationer failures. Officer contacts are allocated to minimize probationer failures and time and budget overruns.

Key words: decision support systems, risk classification, resource allocation, probation

443

S.H. Zanakis et al. (eds.), Decision Making: Recent Developments and Worldwide Applications, 443–456.
© 2000 *Kluwer Academic Publishers.*

INTRODUCTION

More than 3.4 million adults were on probation in the United States at the end of 1998, an increase of 28% since 1990 [Bonczar and Glaze 1999]. Most were on probation in lieu of serving time in prison or jail. Probation officers are responsible for supervising offenders sentenced to serve their punishment in the community. The purposes of supervision are to reduce the likelihood that probationers will commit new crimes and to assure that probationers comply with release conditions such as drug testing or payment of restitution. Probation agencies achieve these functions through surveillance, rehabilitation or some combination.

Level of supervision is established by classifying probationers—for example, to close, intensive, enhanced, or basic for 'regular' probation or to special caseloads such as drug offender probation or sex offender probation. Those assigned to higher classification levels are presumably riskier with respect to the threat they pose to public safety. Those assigned to higher levels are supervised more closely, with greater contact between the probation officer and the probationer through personal contacts in field, requirements for office visits, and so forth. Methods for classifying probationers range from assessments using risk instruments to calendar-driven systems in which probationers are assigned to the highest level and reassigned to lower levels following successful completion of specified periods.

Level of supervision depends on not only the number and "riskiness" of probationers but also on probation officer availability. In 1994, the average probation/parole officer caseload varied widely with average caseloads ranging from 33 to 400 and more than half of agencies reporting average caseloads larger than 100 [Maguire and Pastore 1996].

The relationship between level of supervision and probation outcome has proven difficult to establish. For example, a multi-site study of intensive supervision probation (ISP) showed those on ISP had higher failure rates for technical violations and similar rates for arrests for new crimes compared with those less closely monitored [Petersilia 1993; Turner et al. 1992]. Recently, Geerken and Hayes (1993, pp 552-3) reported a "great deal of inconsistency in the degree of failure observed across samples and jurisdictions...the range of failure rates is 12% to 65%." This range is ascribed to different definitions of failure (e.g., revocation, new arrest, reconviction), different lengths of follow-up, and differences in study populations. In discussing probationer failure and the effectiveness of probation, Petersilia (1993, p 67) noted "even if one accepts that recidivism is a useful measure of success, it is not clear which direction indicates success. If one believes that the major mission of community corrections is to protect the public—emphasizing the *surveillance* function—then perhaps *increasing* recidivism rates (for example, returns to prison) is a positive—not a negative—performance indicator. Even in the absence of conclusive evidence about the relationship between supervision and probation success, budget realities are likely to guarantee the continuation of two trends: Probation and other forms of community surveillance are likely to be the form of punishment assigned to *most* convicted criminals for the foreseeable future. Personnel and other resources for managing these populations will remain constrained. Thus, management and policy makers have a clear interest in assuring that those who pose the greatest public risk receive the highest levels of oversight.

This paper presents the results of a project conducted in cooperation with the Florida Department of Corrections (FLDC). The two-phase project has led to changes in the way that probation caseloads are assigned and supervised by probation officers. In the first phase, statistical models were estimated to identify risk of failure on probation (Lattimore and Linster 1996). In the second phase, the subject of this paper, a prototype decision support system (DSS) was developed to allocate probation officer resources to caseload supervision. The objectives of the model were to maximize public safety subject to resource constraints. The model was pilot tested in one judicial circuit and statewide implementation is currently underway.

FLORIDA PROBATION AND RISK CLASSIFICATION

The State of Florida has the third largest probation population in the United States—239,021 adults at the end of 1998 [Bonczar and Glaze 1999]. The Florida Department of Corrections (FLDC) supervises the majority of these cases with the remainder supervised by county agencies. Until recently, risk-level classification of probationers was "calendar based." All new probationers were classified as maximum. Reclassification to medium and minimum, followed three and six months of successful supervision, respectively. Supervision standards required one personal contact for medium- and minimum-level probationers and two personal contacts for maximum-level probationers each month. One collateral contact was required for maximum- and medium-level probationers; no collateral contact was required for minimum-level probationers. (Personal contacts are direct visits with the probationer—in either the probation office or elsewhere. Collateral contacts are verification of activities, for example, calls to an employer to verify employment.) Because of the size of caseloads, however, administrators admitted that for all practical purposes, all probationers were being supervised at the same level—about that of the medium standards.

In addition to caseload supervision activities, Florida probation officers also have investigative responsibilities, for example completing pre-sentence investigations. A workload study done in Florida in the 1980's recommended a probation officer-to-probationer caseload ratio of 1:68—the Department has never been staffed at that level, however. Currently, caseloads are about 1:90. The current political and fiscal climate is such that it is in the interest of the Department to allocate available officers so as to maximize the public safety "return to investment" of state resources. To this end, POWER—Probation Officer Workload Effectiveness Resource—was developed.

OVERVIEW OF POWER OPTIMIZATION MODEL

A DSS for probationer assignment was developed to assign probationer caseloads to probation officers taking into account the differential workload caused by risk classification. The DSS uses a linear approximation to the nonlinear goal programming formulation reported in Baker et al. (1998). The linear model is less flexible than the benchmark model, since some complex, nonlinear variable relationships that require interaction cannot be modeled, but it is much easier to solve and maintain. Further, the model formulation and solution procedure is supported through *Microsoft Excel*, a common spreadsheet software package. An *Excel* interface allows changes in the data inputs or acceptance of default inputs. A problem generator, written in *Visual Basic* and supported through *Excel*, is attached to the worksheet screen allowing generation of a new formulation for each administrative region. Once the inputs are provided by the user, the problem is generated and solved using a well-known linear programming solution package, *Lindo* (Linear and Integer Discrete Optimization). This interaction is transparent to the user and up to 75 different solutions can be generated, allowing for considerable sensitivity analysis. These solutions are available until purged in the reverse order in which they were run by clicking on the sequentially numbered "Report 75...Report 01" displayed at the bottom of the input screen.

POWER is designed to be a stand-alone software package—it is not linked to any database. The goal priorities are set differently than in traditional goal programming models. The priorities are set by selecting an integer between '00' and '99.' The scale is ordinal. A higher number corresponds to a higher priority but there is no real meaning to the interval between two priority scores. Assigning a goal a weight of '00' gives the goal no importance, deleting it from consideration in the solution. The numbers do not have to sum to any particular total. Assigning all goals the same weight implies that all goals are of equal importance. The priority ratings are assigned by the decision-maker; those used in this demonstration are arbitrary.

LINEAR MODEL FORMULATION

The purpose of the model is to provide an optimal assignment of probationer visits by type to probation officers while considering limited resources and the risk of probationer 'failure' due to re-arrest, technical violation, or absconding—in other words to maximize public safety subject to resource constraints. Public safety is indirectly measured by minimizing expected probationer failures among which re-arrests, as a proxy for new criminal activity, is typically assigned the highest priority. The most critical resource is probation officer time. The most important inputs affecting the allocation of these resources are the effectiveness of the contacts made by the probation officer, where effectiveness is measured in terms of the ability of these contacts to reduce failure. Generally, the effectiveness of a single contact is very small, implying that in order to substantially reduce the likelihood of failing a large number of calls must be made. Clearly, there are multiple objectives with varying degrees of importance in the problem and these objectives either are in conflict or compete for the same resources. To accommodate these objectives, the problem is formulated as a goal-programming model with weighted objectives. The objectives are:

1. Maximize public safety. This is measured by probation revocations for new arrests. The highest priority with respect to this objective is given to probationers

classified as 'close.' The remaining three risk classes—'intensive,' 'enhanced' and 'basic'--receive lesser priorities.

2. Set minimum contact standards for all risk classes.
3. Minimize the total number of absconders.
4. Minimize time and budget overruns.

The following subscript ranges will be used through the formulations:

$i = 1,3$ (Contact type: Field, Office, Collateral)
$j = 1,4$ (Probationer risk classification: Basic, Enhanced, Intensive, Close)
$k = 1, 3$ (Failure mode: Re-arrest, Abscond, Technical)

Define:

$c_{i,j}$ =   Number of contacts of type i to probationer type j per month
$lb_{i,j}$ =   minimum number (lower bound) of contact type i to probationer type j
$ub_{i,j}$ =   maximum number (upper bound) of contact type i to probationer type j
N_j =   total number of probationers of type j
$p_{j,k}$ =   mean probability of probationer type j failing by mode k
$\sigma_{j,k}$ =   standard deviation of failure for probationer type j by mode k
δ_i =   weighting factors for contact type i
$F_{j,k}$ =   expected number of failures of type k for probationer type j
F_j =   expected number of all failures for probationer type j
t_i =   average time in hours for contact type i
T_k =   average time in hours to process a failure of type k
H =   hours per month available for contacts per probation officer
NP =   number of probation officers in the circuit
TH =   total hours required for all services rendered by probation officers
THA = total hours available ($NP \times H$)

The constraints are formulated as follows:

$$lb_{i,j} \le c_{i,j} \le ub_{i,j} \quad \forall\, i, j \tag{1}$$

$$F_{j,k} + \sigma_{j,k} \sum_i \delta_i c_{i,j} = \overline{p}_{j,k} N_j \quad \forall j, k \tag{2}$$

$$TH = \sum_i t_i \sum_j c_{i,j} + \sum_k T_k \sum_j F_{j,k} \tag{3}$$

These first three constraints comprise the most significant part of the problem. Constraint (1) implements Circuit-based standards for minimum and maximum number of contacts allowed per probationer category. As this is a policy decision, these standards are lower- and upper-bounds on the decision variables ($c_{i,j}$).

The second constraint set defines the expected failures for every probationer clase ($j = 1, 4$) and failure mode ($k = 1, 3$). The right-hand-side of equation (2) is the expected number of failures. It should be noted that if no contacts are attempted ($c_{i,j} = 0$) then $F_{j,k} = p_{j,k}N_j$ which can be interpreted as the average worst case scenario (upper bound) for failures. Following the assumption that supervision of probationers has a positive impact, when $c_{i,j} > 0$ then $F_{j,k} < p_{j,k}N_j$. Therefore, $F_{j,k}$ can be used as goal (deviational) variables with the obvious, perhaps unachievable target, of zero.

Constraint (3) calculates the total number of officer hours needed for any prescribed number of contacts plus the time required for processing the expected number of failures. Given THA, constraint (4) below adds the 'overtime' and 'undertime' deviational variables to the formulation.

$$TH - overtime + undertime = THA \qquad (4)$$

Excluding the lower and upper bounds for the decision variables and constraint (3), there are thirteen (4 x 3 + 1) soft goal constraints in the formulation. Per the objectives, the top priority should be to minimize the re-arrests for 'close' probationers ($F_{1,1}$), followed by minimizing re-arrests for those classified as 'intensive' ($F_{2,1}$), 'enhanced' ($F_{3,1}$), and 'basic' ($F_{4,1}$).

The goal of reducing the total number of absconders can be formulated using the four variables ($F_{j,2}$), $j = 1, 4$, or via a new goal variable that is the sum of the absconders for all classes:

$$absconders = \sum_j F_{j,2} \qquad (5)$$

A general objective function for this goal-programming model can be expressed as:

$$Minimize \ \sum_n w_n g_n \qquad (6)$$

where w_n is the weight coefficient for the respective goal variable g_n for n goals. Table 1 summarizes the goals, corresponding deviational variables and the default linear weights.

Table 1. Model Goals

Goal Description	Priority	Weight	Variable	Target
Minimize rearrests for				
'close'	1	50	$F_{1,1}$	0
'intensive'	2	40	$F_{2,1}$	0
'enhanced'	3	20	$F_{3,1}$	0
'basic'	4	10	$F_{4,1}$	0
Minimize total number absconders	5	5	absconders	0
Minimize overtime	6	1	Overtime	0

Given the goals, the specific objective function for the model can be written as:

$$Minimize \ \sum_j w_j F_{j,1} + w_5 \cdot absconders + w_6 \cdot overtime \qquad (7)$$

Clearly, the decision maker determines the relative importance of each goal by assigning weights. This approach is preferable to a preemptive goal programming setup that is less flexible (Zeleny1982). Given that the goals are implemented by linear-weighted combination of deviational variables, the decision maker can effectively practice preemptive goal programming by assigning a relatively large weight to the variables that (s)he wants to obtain the optimal solution at the expense of other goals.

DATA FOR TAVARES CIRCUIT

Data for Tavares Circuit were used because Tavares was the first to implement the risk classification model and has been collecting contact data for the longest period. The approach and data requirements are standardized for this DSS, therefore, as other Circuits come on line, the appropriate information only need be developed. How often the data needs to be re-rerun depends on the volatility of the contact process or on changes in the system. Once every six months seems appropriate, although runs that are more frequent may be made. In this section, we review the risk classification data used in the model, describe how the contact effectiveness was determined, and report on the time probation officers spend doing contacts. The DSS results suggest that the measure of contact effectiveness may not be as critical to the solution as anticipated. Because the effectiveness of a single visit is very small, even relatively large differences in contact effectiveness have modest impact on the allocation decision.

Florida risk classification data

Classification and activity data were obtained from the FLDC for the period February 1 through October 31, 1997. The data required include classification frequencies for the four risk categories, parameter estimates on travel and contact time, average failure, and probability of failure by type. The data shown in Tables 2-9 provide the model inputs. Table 2 shows the minimum number of contacts, as set by agency policy. Table 3 provides information on average contact time that was derived from FLDC data.

Table 2. Minimum number of contacts required per month

Contact Type (k)	Type Case (j)			
	Basic	Enhanced	Intensive	Close
Field	0	0.5	1	2
Office	1	1	1	1
Collateral	1	1	1	1

Table 3. Contact time in minutes

Contact Type	Average Time	Average Time for Attempts/Visits	Attempts/Actual Visits
Field	8.63	6.07	0.255
Office	6.96	Not applicable	Not applicable
Collateral	5.96	Not applicable	Not applicable

Table 4 shows the probability of failing and the standard deviation of failure by type of probationer and type of failure. These data were generated by applying the risk classification models developed in Lattimore and Linster 1996 to the current probation population of Taveres. The average likelihood of failure by each mode was then determined for each classification category. (Certain probationers are assigned automatically to risk categories. For example, sex offenders and other violent offenders are automatically placed in 'close.' These 'overrides' were excluded from the calculations of failure risk.)

Table 4. Mean and standard deviation of risk of failure by category and class

Contact Type (k)	Type Case (j)			
	Basic	Enhanced	Intensive	Close
Abscond	0.0330 (0.0122)	0.0572 (0.0187)	0.0746 (0.0272)	0.1004 (0.0293)
Re-arrest	0.0221 (0.0113)	0.0518 (0.0230)	0.0993 (0.0512)	0.1744 (0.0734)
Technical	0.0247 (0.0114)	0.0544 (0.0197)	0.0854 (0.0225)	0.1106 (0.0362)
Total	0.0789 (0.2748)	0.1635 (0.3781)	0.2592 (0.0685)	0.3854 (0.9210)

The data in Table 4 show that Basic and Enhanced risk classes are more likely to fail by absconding than by re-arrest or a technical violation. Those under Intensive supervision are slightly more likely to fail by re-arrest than by the other modes. Close probationers are much more likely to be re-arrested than to fail by the other two modes. Overall, the higher risk classification of those under more stringent supervision is supported by their higher failure probabilities. For example, those under Close supervision have an almost 40 percent chance of failing during the six month period represented by these data.

Table 5 shows the expected impact of supervision on the various failure modes. These impacts are based on assigning probationers to the four risk classes and thus adjusting the levels of contacts over the 'average' level of supervision they were receiving prior to the implementation of the risk classification system. It was assumed that Intensive and Close probationers would receive increased levels of contacts, Enhanced cases would receive the same levels, and Basic would receive lower levels. The impacts of changes in supervision were established following extensive discussion with probation officials and officers. As can be seen, close supervision is expected to increase the likelihood of failure by a technical violation of probation due to the increased scrutiny of compliance with conditions of probation.

Table 5. Relative impact of changing supervision

Contact Effect on Failure Risk Relative to Medium*	Basic (minimum) cases should show	Enhanced (medium) cases should show	Intensive (maximum) cases should show	Close ('supermax)
Re-arrest	Increase	No change	Decrease	Decrease/unknown
Technical violation	Decrease	No change	Increase	Increase/unknown
Absconding	Increase	No change	Decrease	Unknown

*Medium is the assumed level of supervision for most probationers prior to implementation of classification using risk models

Table 6 shows the distribution of probationers over risk categories. The assignments were made by FLDC established cutpoints in the likelihood of failing by any mode. Specifically, those scoring between 0 and 0.12 were classified as Basic; between 0.121 and 0.249 as Enhanced, between 0.25 and 0.3 as Intensive, and between 0.31 and 1 as Close. Also shown are the system 'overrides' who score relatively low by the risk classification model—i.e., their likelihoods of failing are rather low—but who are assigned to Close supervision because of the nature of their offenses. ('Overrides' include violent offenders, including sex offenders.) As can be seen, using the risk classification cutpoints adopted by the FLDC, only 90 probationers were classified for Close supervision but an additional 606 are assigned to Close because of the override policy.

Table 6. Frequency of cases by model classification and 'overrides'

Assignment mode	Type Case (j)				
	Basic	Enhanced	Intensive	Close	Total
Risk classification model	1,727	1,644	312	90	3,773
Overrides*	450	140	16	0	606
Total	2,177	1,784	328	90	4,379

The number of probation officers in Tavares allocated to case management is 75. The travel cost per mile was $0.29 and the average travel distance in miles was 4 miles per trip. The average travel distance per probation officer was 92 miles per week or 1,280 per year. There were 'roughly' three attempted personal visits per completed visit.

Effectiveness of probation officer contacts

The risk classification model for differential supervision is premised on the assumption that riskier probationers need supervision that is more intensive. Balancing workload involves allocating supervisory resources in such a way as to effect the same outcome on a heterogeneous population of probationers. The basic tool of supervision is contact—between the probation officer and the probationer either in the probation office and the field or between the probation officer and others who can report on the probationer's progress (collateral contacts). The model is premised on the assumption that these contacts will have a measurable effect on failure. Intuitively, this seems reasonable but empirically these effects are not easily determined. In fact, attempting to determine the marginal impact of a single contact (Field, Office or Collateral) on a probationer of a particular classification (Basic, Enhanced, Intensive or Close) in terms of the probability of failure by mode (Re-arrest, Abscond, Technical) proved to be the most challenging aspect of this effort.

We attempted several approaches to this problem—empirical analyses, value function assessment, and ad hoc sensitivity analysis. The effectiveness of contacts is three-dimensional: marginal effect (absolute or 'true' effect), relative impact (effect conditional on risk class), and time-phased effect (effect conditional on multiple contacts). Ideally, we would like to determine, for example, that a field contact is δ-times as effective as an office visit of the same duration; that an office visit has δ-times the impact on an Intensive probationer as on an Enhanced probationer; or, that the effect of each subsequent visit of a particular type to a particular probationer shows diminishing returns. In other words, we would like to be able to establish the shape and parameters of the return to contacts function. However, the dynamics of the probationer/probation officer relationship are not well defined and the size of the effect may be inappropriately scaled for the sensitivity of the measures used. Specifically, it may not be possible to show that one office visit reduces technical failures when that effect may be smaller than the measurement error. Following extensive analysis of the data provided on contacts and failures for Tavares Circuit, we were forced to abandon, for the time being, use of an empirical approach for estimating effectiveness of contacts. There was too much variability in the data to have confidence in the results we produced. Value function assessment seemed a viable alternative but this, too, proved problematic largely due to the complexity of the domain. Probation officers agreed that contacts had an effect and could provide estimates of ranges of effectiveness. However, establishing first derivative information was not possible so this approach, too, was abandoned.

The approach we used, therefore, combined methods and was ad hoc in nature. Using in-depth interviews with probation officers, we were able to establish a set of underlying assumptions that could be used to better define the problem domain. We then used contact time as a proxy for relative effectiveness. For example, if an experienced officer spent twice as much time on an office visit as on a collateral contact, the office visit was viewed as (potentially) twice as effective as the collateral contact. This is an economic approach to estimating the effectiveness coefficients or weights. The assumption is that the marginal cost of an activity is equal to the marginal benefit. For the two types of in-person contacts, we need only assume that time in the field yields the same benefit as time in the office. It is less clear how time spent on collateral contacts should be valued relative to the in-person contacts. In the absence of any reason to judge collateral contacts as more or less valuable than the others, we assumed the value was the same. By normalizing, the relative value of each type of call can then be approximated by the average time spent on that type of contact. Development of these values and the results follow. The assumptions used were as follows:

1. There was no diminishing returns to contact effectiveness, i.e. the effect over repeated visits is linear.
2. The best a contact can accomplish in terms of effectiveness is to reduce the number of recidivists by 1.0—meaning every call saves a failure.
3. The absolute worst effect a contact can have is no effect. Here we assume that a contact cannot cause failure, i.e., the function over effectiveness is strictly non-negative.
4. There is a 'hard core' group of probationers who will fail regardless of the timing and type of intervention. This group was estimated based on discussions with experienced probation officers to be approximately 20% of the population.

Given these assumptions, the upper bound on effectiveness was 0.8. The average time spent per type of contact was identified at the 95th percentile for the FLDC data. These times were scaled and the weighted times were deflated by the maximum effectiveness bound of 0.8. The results of these calculations are shown in Table 7.

Table 7. Contact effectiveness

Contact Type	Average Time per Contact (minutes)	Scale to Collateral (smallest)	Effectiveness Calculation	Effectiveness Estimate
Field	26.96	26.96/10.06 = 2.68	0.8 (maximum)	0.8
Office	13.08	13.08/10.06 = 1.3	0.8/(2.68/1.3)	0.388
Collateral	10.06	10.06/10.06 = 1	0.8/(2.68/1.0)	0.298
Average	13.06			

Contact time

The number of work hours available per month was estimated to be 148 per officer. This number excludes vacation, required meetings, and other standard administrative tasks. This constraint was non-binding in our solutions. We then analyzed further the time officers were reporting as time spent on contacts in a new administrative reporting system established by the FLDC. The average time spent differed by type of contact with Collateral < Office < Field visit time. While the average time spent on each type of contact did not vary much by officers, more experienced staff were found to spend more time during Field and Office visits than less experienced staff.

In addition to contact time, staff must process failures. Paperwork must be completed and often time must be spent in court. Based on discussions with FLDC, we estimated that it would take 3, 2 and 3 hours of staff time to process failures due to arrest, absconding and technical violations, respectively.

RESULTS

The model was tested using a variety of values during development. We assumed 75 probation officers who could spend 60 hours per month on contacts. Goal weights were set as shown below. These weights suggest that the highest weight is given to minimizing the number of expected arrests for the most serious cases, i.e. those classified as 'close' or 'intensive'; equal, but less priority, is placed on expected arrests of 'enhanced' and 'basic' probationers; and minimal weight is given to reducing absconding or to minimizing overtime.

454

Relative Importance of goals	
Minimize "close" arrests	99
Minimize "intensive" arrests	99
Minimize "enhanced" arrests	50
Minimize "basic" arrests	50
Minimize "all absconders"	5
Minimize "overtime hours	1

Additionally, we assumed that the time required for each field contact is somewhat greater than that reported in the FLDC data. This time seemed insufficient and, based on discussions with officers about the total amount of time required to conduct a visit (travel time, time to complete reports, and so forth), we assumed that Field, Office and Collateral contacts require 0.75, 0.22 and 0.17 hours, respectively.

We ran the model under a wide variety of assumptions about goal priorities and found the results to be highly stable, primarily because of the constraint that was imposed by the contact minimums. The results for the model under the assumptions outlined above are shown in the first set of results in Table 8. What is shown is monthly number of contacts per probationer by contact type and risk level. The total hours allocated to each type of contact are also shown. As can be seen, the recommended contacts differ little from the minimum contact standards shown in Table 2. Only the number of office visits required of intensive and close cases (2.0 and 1.2, respectively, versus a minimum of 1) and of collateral contacts for intensive cases (1.2 versus 1.0) differ. This solution consumes 100 percent of available resources (3,716 contact hours and 808 hours to process failures) and reduces the number of expected arrests among intensive and close cases to zero, as shown in Table 9. Thus, the model generates a solution that satisfies the highest priority goals, with an expected number of arrests for the population of 68.7.

The second solution shown in Table 8 was generated when the minimum required contacts for the basic and intensive cases were set to zero. Such a scenario could reflect agency policy that wishes to focus resources on the cases viewed as most risky by placing a lower priority on arrests from these caseloads. Under this scenario, the model reallocates all of the resources previously assigned to basic cases among the other three risk levels. This solution also absorbs 100 percent of available resources (3,797 hours for contacts and 703 hours for processing failures) and yields 52.2 expected total arrests—a 24 percent reduction in arrests from the status quo solution without additional resources. This solution for the basic cases is not as farfetched as might be first thought—many jurisdictions have a probation status that requires no contact unless the probationer is rearrested.

The third solution was generated for the unconstrained case. Contact minimums were set to zero for all case types. Interestingly, the model's optimal solution was to devote all officer resources to office contacts—a solution that reduced the expected number of arrests by 63 percent (from 68.7 to 25.4 per month). Note that under this scenario, the officers would have more personal contacts with all cases than under either of the other scenarios. From a policy perspective, again, this solution may be viewed as unrealistic. Officers may feel that it is important to observe an individual in the home environment to better understand the risk posed. This solution may suggest that the number of field visits can be substantially reduced without increasing public risk.

Table 8. Model-generated monthly probationer contacts under different scenarios

Type Contact	Type Case				Total Hours
	Basic	Enhanced	Intensive	Close	
1. Status quo					
Field	0	0.5	1.0	2.0	1,895
Office	1.0	1.0	2.0	1.2	1,067
Collateral	1.0	1.0	1.2	1.0	755
2. No contacts required for basic & enhanced					
Field	0	0.6	0.5	2.0	1,938
Office	0	2.0	2.0	1.2	1,048
Collateral	0	2.0	2.5	1.0	811
3. No contact requirements					
Field	0	0	0	2.0	0
Office	1.7	5.8	5.0	6.1	4,033
Collateral	0	0	5	0	0

Table 9. Estimated number of monthly failures under different scenarios

Type Contact	Type Case				Total
	Basic	Enhanced	Intensive	Close	
1. Status quo					
Arrest	24.7	44.0	0.0	0.0	68.7
Abscond	42.4	60.6	6.8	21.4	131.1
Technical	29.2	54.2	13.0	17.0	113.3
2. No contacts required for basic & enhanced					
Arrest	38.2	14.0	0.0	0.0	52.2
Abscond	57.0	36.2	6.8	21.4	121.4
Technical	42.7	28.4	13.0	17.0	101.1
3. No contact requirements					
Arrest	25.4	0.0	0.0	0.0	25.4
Abscond	43.1	24.8	6.84	21.4	96.2
Technical	29.8	16.4	13.0	17.0	76.3

CONCLUSIONS

This paper recasts the benchmark, non-linear model presented in Baker *et al.*, 1998, as a linear model driven by DSS-POWER. The results use data from Tavares Circuit in Florida. POWER allocates contacts by type for a Circuit given a user-supplied priority scheme. The DSS runs off-line but is easily changed to reflect new information. The inputs must be obtained off-line from FLDC data. Using inputs on the number of probationers and the risk classifications of those probationers, the model can be easily adapted to other Circuits. In summary, the POWER DSS offers a user-friendly and flexible package for workload allocation in the probation environment.

The results obtained are consistent with the results of the earlier (benchmark) model and are reasonable for the inputs provided. The results also demonstrate that policymakers and probation management may have considerable flexibility in their assignment of a fixed resource to caseload management.

ACKNOWLEDGEMENTS

This work would not have been possible without the enthusiastic support of many probation and research staff at the Florida Department of Corrections. We acknowledge with gratitude Harry Dodd, Lana Arnold, Kristine Leininger, and Larry Hamilton for their insight and the data that allowed this work to proceed.

REFERENCES

Baker, J.R., A.C. Saydam and P.K. Lattimore (1998) "A nonlinear multiple criteria model base for the problem of balancing caseload risk in probation departments," *Computers and Industrial Engineering: An International Journal.*

Bonczar, T.P. and L.E. Glaze (1999) *Probation and Parole in the United States, 1998*, Bureau of Justice Statistics, U.S. Department of Justice, Washington, D.C.

Geerken, M.R. and H.D. Hayes (1993) "Probation and parole: Public risk and the future of incarceration alternatives," *Criminology* 31(4):549-564.

Lattimore, P.K. and R.L. Linster (1996) *Statistical Basis for a Management Information System/Model-Based Risk Classification System for Probationers,* National Institute of Justice, Washington, DC.

Maguire, K. and A.L. Pastore, eds. (1996) *Sourcebook of Criminal Justice Statistics 1995*, Bureau of Justice Statistics, U.S. Department of Justice, Washington, D.C.

Petersilia, J. (1993) "Measuring performance of community corrections" in *Performance Measures for the Criminal Justice System*, Bureau of Justice Statistics, U.S. Department of Justice, Washington, D.C., pages 61-84.

Turner, S., J. Petersilia and E.P. Deschenes (1992) "Evaluating intensive supervision probation/parole (ISP) for drug offenders," *Crime and Delinquency* 38(4):539-556.

Zeleny, M. (1982) *Multiple Criteria Decision Analysis*, Auerbach, Philadelphia.

9. HEALTH CARE PLANNING & HOSPITAL OPERATIONS

A GOAL PROGRAMMING SCHEME TO DETERMINE THE BUDGET ASSIGNMENT AMONG THE HOSPITALS OF A SANITARY SYSTEM

J.J. Martín[1], M.P. López del Amo[1],
R. Caballero[2], T. Gómez[2], J. Molina[2], F. Ruiz[2]

[1] Andalusian School of Public Health
Campus Universitario de Cartuja
Apdo. 2070, Granada, 18080, Spain

[2] University of Málaga
Department of Applied Economics
Campus El Ejido, Malaga, S/N 29071, Spain

Abstract: We develop a model in order to assign resources to public hospitals when the decision center has multiple objectives. This way, it will be possible to quantify the potential existing conflicts among the objectives of the decision center, and to determine the optimal activity vector for each one of the hospitals. The model is designed and applied for the special case of the Andalusian Health Service that is the decision center of the net of public hospitals in Andalusia (Spain). We identify the characteristics and priorities of the Central Services in terms of budget, optimum settings for action implementation, and risk transfer to the health care providers. First, a set of feasible actions is identified by using the so-called "technical-restrictions". Second, the problem identified is solved according to the alternative options identified in the multicriteria programming, by using pondered goals and lexicographic goals package

Key words: Goal Programming, Hospitals, Budget assignment.

S.H. Zanakis et al. (eds.), Decision Making: Recent Developments and Worldwide Applications, 459–474.
© 2000 Kluwer Academic Publishers.

INTRODUCTION

The Spanish National Health System shares with the rest of the European sanitary systems the necessity to make compatible the ethic principles of universality and equality in the access to sanitary services with the inherent requirements of the European Union.

In such Health System, reforms have been oriented in order to separate the financing and production functions, and in order to modify the juridical and organization aspects of the service offer. The separation of the purchase from the service provision has turned the contract into a central element in the reforming process and the innovations in the organizations of all the regional health systems (RHS) of the Spanish State. A critical feature of these reform strategies is the development of optimal financing models for the service purchasers.

The aim of this study is to develop a model in order to assign resources to public hospitals when the decision center has multiple objectives. This way, it will be possible to quantify the potential existing conflicts among the objectives of the decision center, and to determine the optimal activity vector for each one of the hospitals. The model is designed and applied for the special case of the Andalusian Health Service (SAS), that is the decision center of the net of public hospitals in Andalusia.

First, the result of the Health Economic literature on health provider financing is enunciated, with special emphasis on the main difficulties derived from the neoclassical microeconomic context in which they arise. Alternatingly, if it is assumed the limited rationality of the financer and buyer, and the existence of preferences functions, explicitly with several arguments or attributes that want to be satisfied simultaneously in a specific institutional environment, it is of enormous utility to explore the power of the multicriteria programming for the financing of hospital suppliers.

We go on to describe the powerful multicriteria techniques that operate within this theoretical framework, briefly describing the main theoretical works and empirical applications to date. Next, we propose a model, based on real experience, for the budgeting of the public network of district hospitals in the Andalusian Regional Health Service (ARHS). Finally, we present the results of our model, a discussion of these results and its main limitations.

FINANCING HEALTH PROVIDERS

An important part of the literature about optimal hospital financing contracts focuses on production incentives based on hospital cost heterogeneity; particularly, on information asymmetry related with management effort between the provider and the regulator (Newhouse, 1996, 1992).

In general, it is assumed that the regulator has only one objective to optimize – maximizing efficiency in hospital output, or maximizing the gross social benefit, for example, that it picks up some type of social specification of the good one, that he is benevolent and lacks self-interest.

The hospital is generally conceived as a self-interested agent, whose cost function includes a factor that cannot be observed by the regulator related to the management effort.

The literature identifies mixed payment systems (which simultaneously consider specific and standard costs for each hospital) as a basic element of the optimal contract between the regulator and the hospitals, although it does not define the appropriate mix and usually displays non-observable parameters (Newhouse, 1996, 1992). However formal, this literature can be not very specific and insufficient in dealing with the real decision context of a regulating agency.

The development and application of new instruments is required, in order to help the buyer in his decision making process, and to configure the contracts with the supplying centers. The buyers of the RHS (for example, the Andalusian Regional Health Service, ARHS), do not want to optimize a single objective, but they wish to satisfy some of them simultaneously in order to find the best possible solution.

At this point, multiple criteria techniques can be very useful to obtain the optimal parameters of the contracts, and to identify the potential contradictions in the objectives of the decision center.

MULTIPLE CRITERIA PROGRAMMING IN THE HEALTH SECTOR

When a decision involving multiple goals has to be taken, one of the most adequate multiple criteria schemes is Goal Programming. Besides, the previously mentioned scheme is appropriate for complex problems. Goal Programming, does not have a optimization philosophy: it can be included in the satisfying philosophy proposed by Simon (1955, 1957) which characterize the decisional contexts in complex organizations with incomplete information, scarce resources, multiple objectives and conflicts of interests, where it is not possible to maximize, but the decision maker tries that a series of goals become as close as possible to certain previously fixed satisfaction levels.

Since the middle of the seventies, a great number of works have appeared in the literature where both the theoretical and operative aspects of goal programming are developed, as well as applications of this scheme to very different areas. The literature review by Romero (1991, Chapter 8) picked up more than 350 references on goal programming; the work by Schniederjans (1995) is a reference guide to goal programming research available to date with over a thousand citations of goal programming books and citations.

In the sanitary context, there are several papers applicating multicriteria programming in national and international literature. Most of them focus on activity planning and internal resource allocation at the hospital level.

The first empirical application referred to in the literature is Lee (1973). He applies a lexicographic goal programming model to evaluate the priority structure (and its compatibility) for the objectives within the framework of yearly resource allocation. He formulates 2 models, along the same line. The first one of them takes into consideration as the main objective to ensure the availability of enough human resources: to offer an adequate service to the patient; to replace or acquire new equipment; to adequately raise salaries; to maintain worker to patient ratio; to adequately distribute professionals (by category) in the hospital; to reach adequate nurse to staff, nurse to professional, and professional to staff indexes. Also, to minimize costs and overcome the equilibrium point. The solution satisfies every objective except the cost minimization priority level.

Paints (1988) describes a situation where a mental health center must select the services that it wishes to offer, and to determine the staff in order to raise as much as possible the number of hours of public attention, and the occupation level of the staff. Riffai and Percenka (1989) illustrate how can goal programming be used to assign sanitary resources in situations of multiple objectives and competence. Blake (1997) uses goal programming in the Canadian sanitary context, in order to adjust the volume and quantity of activity that the sanitary suppliers must achieve within a budget constraint, taking into account the interests of the sanitary professionals about salaries and activity, and so as to avoid losses in the hospital. He considers 2 priority levels. First, feasibility for the hospital (meeting the budget) and for the medical doctors (desired salary). Second, that doctors engage in the activities they desire. Blake considers technical restrictions; upper and lower bounds for doctors' salaries, for each line of activity, and restrictions relative to capacity limits (operating room hours, and available beds).

Rodríguez Uría et al (1997) formulate a lexicographic goal programming model for the functioning of a surgery service (orthopedic surgery and traumatology) in a general hospital. They analyze the internal coherence of the objectives and whether it is possible to improve the service taking into account occupation, personnel availability and budget restrictions. The following objectives are considered: to insure there is enough personnel to provide satisfactory services to patients, to minimize costs, to reduce waiting lists and to improve the quality of the service. They conclude that with the present technical restrictions it is impossible to significantly reduce the waiting list. They suggest that in order to better achieve the objectives it is necessary to improve efficiency in resource use. Also, they suggest to raise surgical activity, to reduce consultations and hospitalizations.

Rodríguez Uría et al (1998) apply multiobjetive programming to schedule the work of two surgery services in a general hospital, in order to reduce the waiting list (both in numbers and in time) at the same time as costs are minimized. They study ophthalmology (cataracts) and traumatology (hallux valgus, knees and osteoarthritis). They consider as a restriction the time available in the operating rooms per month and per service, the monthly over-time cataract limits, and hallux valgus and knees in private clinics. They consider state equations that link a month's waiting list with the previous month's, admissions, hospital releases (non-operated patients) and the number of operations that were programmed, performed in over-time, and performed in private clinics.

The Goal Programming method is particularly attractive when applied within the sanitary sector context. Namely, it can help the decision center of the organization to establish the features of the contracts (or program contracts) which are signed with the supplying centers. More specifically, the decision center can understand the degree of feasibility to accomplish different potentially conflictive objectives. In this work, both weighted and lexicographic goal programming schemes will be used.

The first step in formulating a goal programming model consists in fixing the attributes that are relevant for the problem that is going to be solved. Once this is done, the aspiration level that corresponds to each attribute is determined, that is, the level of fulfillment the decision center wants to reach. Next, the attribute is connected with the aspiration level, by means of introducing the negative and positive deviation levels (respectively).

Solving the model consists in minimizing undesired deviation variables. Minimization can be done in several ways, but the most used are weighted goal programming and lexicographic goal programming.

In weighted goal programming, the weighted sum of the undesired deviation variables (normalized by level of aspiration) is minimized. Lexicographic goal programming means that the decision maker associates pre-emptive priorities to the different goals. That is, fulfilling the goals set for a certain priority Q_i is incommensurably preferred to fulfilling any other set of goals at a lower priority level Q_j ($Q_i>>>Q_j$). Fulfilling a goal with lower priority is not considered until the most feasible goal with a higher priority has been satisfied.

It is useful to compare the solutions obtained by weighted and lexicographic goal programming models. Most often the achievement function is larger in lexicographic models; this is a logical result, given that the first priority level has a higher level of goal realization.

Some theorists, like Harrald (1978), Zeleny (1982) and Debreu (1959) dismiss lexicographic goal programming on the grounds that it can be incompatible with the existence of a utility function on the part of the decision maker. In fact, lexicographic preferences are incompatible with the axiom of continuity of the indifference set, which in a lexicographic ordering is formed by a single point (Romero, 1993).

However, as Romero points out, preference continuity has not been empirically proven: "...it is only a debated and refutable axiom, necessary to axiom neoclassical consumer theory and to guarantee the existence of a competitive equilibrium" Romero, 1993: 93.

Romero (1993) refers to authors like Deaton & Muellbauer (1981), who give arguments in favor of the reasonableness of lexicographic preferences, although they discard them in order to preserve the neoclassical analysis.

Thus, Romero (1993) concludes that the lexicographic approach must not be abandoned for formal reasons, but applied if lexicographic preference structures are plausible.

FINANCING DISTRICT HOSPITALS OF THE ANDALUSIAN HEALTH SERVICE: A GOAL PROGRAMMING APPROACH

The decision center of the ARHS, must solve the problem of the budget assignment to district hospitals, as a central element of its strategy in order to elaborate the Program Contract.

The perspective that has been adopted does not explicitly include an analysis of the demand as an exogenous variable. This scheme is similar to the great majority of the revised literature. The complexity of the interrelation between supply and demand in sanitary systems is a common topic in Health Economy, due to the information asymmetries between the supplier (doctor) and the client (patient) (Arrow, 1963).

Nevertheless, the model which is described below implicitly incorporates the demand in different ways:

First, it is assumed that the characterization of the global purchase function carried out by the decision makers of the Andalusian Central Health Services takes the foreseeable demand of the hospitals into account. Second, the activity forecast that has been carried out by the hospitals can be considered as a proxy variable of the foreseeable demand, according to the doctors and the managers of each hospital. Finally, the designed model establishes structural stability conditions, in the sense that there is not a significant variation of the demand that really took place in the previous term (that is, at least a 70% of the historic activity must be carried out).

According to the SAS Strategic Plan and to the Program Contract of 1997, the attributes or arguments of the preference function which, potentially, can initially be considered are: $U = U(X_i, x_{ij}, g_j, G)$, where X_i is the global purchase function, expressed as the activity level per each production line considered, g_j is the founding required by each hospital to the decision center, x_{ij} is the activity prevision made by each hospital in each production line, and finally G is the global budget constraint of the decision center, established during the negotiation process with the fiscal authority. This utility function is plausible in the frame of a monopolist public founder.

The different attributes are expressed as a function of decision variables x_{ij}, which constitute the activities that the decision center finances for each hospital j and each line of activities i, decision maker defines a standard price for activity π_i. The elected standard price has been obtained by means of the application of Data Envelopment Analysis Charnes, Cooper and Rhodes (1978)[1].

X_i defines the objectives regarding the volume and type of activity desirable for the decision center. The specification of this purchase function depends on the purchase technologies which are available for the decision center, and on the objectives that he wants to be satisfied. The specification of the purchase function should take into account mainly the needs of the people, and not only the services presently provided and the waiting lists in the surgery, off patient and complementary tests activities.

Nevertheless, within the actual context of the RHS of the Spanish state, this is not possible, and most of the program contracts are oriented to raise the historical activity of each hospital, and to intensify the activity that, in principle, will help more to achieve a

---

[1] The average price of the efficient hospitals has been chosen obtained by means of the application of the following program:

Min $h_{j0}-\varepsilon(1_m S_m+1_s S_s)$
subject to:
$ZS-S_s=Y_{j0}$
$ZM+S_m=h_{j0}A_{j0}$
$z_j, s_i, s_r \geq 0, \forall j, i$ and r

Where (A_j, Y_j) are input-output vectors of each one of the n sanitary centers ($j= 1, ..., n$), $A_j = (a_{1j}, a_{2j},...a_{mj})$ and $Y_j = (y_{1j}, y_{2j},....y_{sj})$. M it is the matrix of the m considered inputs (of order $n*m$) corresponding to the n evaluated centers. S is the matrix of the used outputs (of order $n*s$) in the n observed centers. Z ($Z = z_1, z_2,....z_n$) is a vector of variable intensity that forms combinations of the observed vectors of inputs and outputs. S_m and S_r are the vectors in the slack variables in the relating restrictions to X and Y respectively, and and ε a number sufficiently small for not altering the good value of h_{j}.

significant reduction of the waiting lists, or the one that is induced by the professionals according to their preferences.

The preference function of the decision center is also characterized by an interest to attend the founding demands of the hospitals, as well as the prevision and activity composition that they carry out. In fact, this utility function reflects the interest of the decision center to attend, as much as possible, the objectives of the managers (more budget) and of the professionals (a kind of activity "mixture").

A drastic reduction of the resources for a hospital would be impossible, or, politically, very expensive to be assumed. On the other hand, the activity is, in a great part, defined by the professionals, and not controlled by the decision center.

The global budget constraint (G) is, with growing intensity, a priority to be satisfied by the decision center, in a context with increasing and continuous processes of fiscal consolidation. Normatively, all the RHS are obliged to respect this budget constraint. Nevertheless, the decision center does not have any incentive to save founds.

The formulation of the multiple objective problem contributes to analyze the feasible set and the specified objectives, and it constitutes the starting point for the analysis of a multicriteria problem.

Goal Programming models can be included among the methods with a priori information about objectives, weights and priorities. Decision makers provided us with preference information by comparing couples of attributes and goals. This information has been obtained through a semi structured interview with the Central Services of the SAS. They provide us with information about attributes, priorities, weights, bounds and undesired deviation variables. Two heads of the Subbureau of Attention Specialized and the Subbureau of Budgets of Central Services of SAS were interviewed. They reached an agreement about the consulted points. From this information, a goal programming problem is built, which solution constitutes the set of initial weights.

FORMULATION OF THE GOAL PROGRAMMING PROBLEM

The aim of our model will be to determine the value of each activity level in each hospital, in order to:

- Achieve certain global activity levels,
- Achieve certain activity levels for each hospital,
- Not to exceed the budget per hospital
- Not to exceed the global budget.

Our model has $r \cdot n$ variables, which represent each activity level in each hospital, that is:

x_{ij} is the level of activity i at hospital j, for $i = 1, \ldots, r$ and $j = 1, \ldots, n$, where r is the total number of activities, and n the number of hospitals.

Technical constraints:

a. The global level of each activity i must lay between two pre fixed values denoted by L_{x_i} and U_{x_i}:

$$L_{x_i} \le \sum_{j=1}^{n} x_{ij} \le U_{x_i} \qquad i = 1, \cdots, r$$

b. Each activity level in each hospital must be, at least, the 70% of the corresponding level in the previous year (h_{ij}): $x_{ij} \ge 0.7 h_{ij}$ $\qquad i = 1, \dots r \quad j = 1, \dots, n$

c. In each hospital, the total available hours of the surgery rooms (SH_j) cannot be exceeded. If we denote by SH_{x_i} the surgery room hours required for each intervention corresponding to activity i, then these constraints take the form:

$$\sum_{i=1}^{r} \left(x_{ij} \cdot SH_{x_i} \right) \le SH_j \quad j = 1, \dots, n$$

d. In each hospital, the total available days of stay of the patients (hospitalization) (S_j) cannot be exceeded. If we denote by S_{x_i} the mean number of days of stay required for each intervention corresponding to activity i, then these constraints take the form:

$$\sum_{i=1}^{r} \left(x_{ij} \cdot S_{x_i} \right) \le S_j, \; j = 1, \dots, n$$

e. In each hospital, the total available hours of the off-patient rooms (OH_j) cannot be exceeded. If we denote by OH the mean number of hours required for each off-patient appointment, and the variable corresponding to the off-patient activity in hospital j is x_{lj} then these constraints take the form:

$$x_{lj} \cdot OH \le OH_j \; j = 1, \dots, n$$

Goals:

1. The decision center wants to control the global level of each activity. Depending on the activity, the decision center may want to achieve, to exceed or to equal the target value X^*_i. So, the goals take the form:

$$\left[\sum_{j=1}^{n} x_{ij} \right] + n_i - p_i = X^*_i \quad i = 1, \cdots, r$$

In general, we will denote by $h_i(n_i, p_i)$ the achievement function corresponding to activity level i.

2. The decision center also wants to control each activity level at each hospital, and, as in the previous goal, depending on the activity, the decision center may want to achieve, to exceed or to equal the target value x^*_{ij}. So, the goals take the form:

$$x_{ij} + n_{r+(i \cdot j)} - p_{r+(i \cdot j)} = x^*_{ij} \quad i = 1, \cdots, r, \quad j = 1, \cdots, n$$

As in the previous case, the achievement functions will also be denoted by h.

3. The decision center does not want each hospital to exceed a budget assignment which equals the amount requested by the hospital (g_j). But the decision center decides that he wants to assign the 70% of the historical cost of the hospital (c_j) to pay a 70% of the activity levels of the previous year:

$$\left[\sum_{i=1}^{r} x_{ij} \pi_i \right] + n_{r+(n \cdot r)+j} - p_{r+(n \cdot r)+j} = g_j - 0.7 c_j + \left[\sum_{i=1}^{r} 0.7 h_{ij} \pi_i \right] \qquad j = 1, \dots, n$$

In this case, we wish to minimize the variables $p_{r+(n \cdot r)+j}$, $. j = 1, \dots, n$.

4. Finally, the decision center does not wish to exceed a global budget, which consists of a global quantity G, taking into account the same consideration as in the previous goal:

$$\left[\sum_{i=1}^{r} x_{ij}\pi_i\right] + n_{r+(n\cdot r)+n+1} - p_{r+(n\cdot r)+n+1} = g_j - 0.7c_j + \left[\sum_{i=1}^{r} 0.7h_{ij}\pi_i\right]$$

We want to minimize both positive and deviation variable $p_{r+(n\cdot r)+n+1} + n_{r+(n\cdot r)+n+1}$

Weights:

In total, the model has, as we have seen, $r+(r*n)+n+1$ goals. The decision maker may want to weight each goal (even to distinguish among the different hospitals or activity levels). The weight assigned to goal k will be denoted by W_k. It will be assumed that the weights are already normalized (for example, dividing them by the corresponding target value).

The decision centers emit value judgements or preferences for each of the established priority levels. They do pairwise comparisons of value judgements on the relative importance of criteria and alternatives that are displayed in matrix form. Each position shows how relatively more important is the criterion corresponding to the associated row with respect to the criterion of the associated column.

The Central Services decision makers agreed that the arguments of the purchase function should be, in order of preference: the global purchasing function of each line of activity, the predictions made by each hospital for each line of activity, funding required by each hospital and, finally, the global budget restriction of the RHS. In order to calculate the weights, they were asked to express their valuation of how much an argument must be considered relative to another in the purchase function (Table 1).

Table 1: Matrix of pairwise comparisons for the budget assignment criteria. Andalusian Regional Health Service District hospitals

	Global activity levels	Activity prevision made by each hospital	Founding required by each hospital	Global budget constraint
Global activity levels	1	2	5	7
Activity prevision made by each hospital	1/2	1	5	6
Founding required by each hospital	1/5	1/5	1	4.5
Global budget constraint	1/7	1/6	1/(4.5)	1

At first glance, we can see that the Central Services decision makers are primarily interested in activity levels, rather than in hospital fund demands. The set of weights consistent with the preferences of the decision center is obtained solving the following goal programming problem:

$$\text{Min } n_1+p_1+ n_2+p_2+ n_3+p_3+ n_4+p_4+ n_5+p_5+ n_6+p_6$$

W_1	$-a_{12}W_2$			$+n_1$	$-p_1$	$=0$
W_1		$-a_{13}W_3$		$+n_2$	$-p_2$	$=0$
W_1			$-a_{14}W_4$	$+n_3$	$-p_3$	$=0$
	W_2	$-a_{23}W_3$		$+n_4$	$-p_4$	$=0$
	W_2		$-a_{24}W_4$	$+n_5$	$-p_5$	$=0$
		W_3	$-a_{34}W_4$	$+n_6$	$-p_6$	$=0$
W_1	$+W_2$	$+W_3$	$+W_4$			$=1$

$$W \geq 0$$

Solving this goal programming problem yields the following results: certain global activity levels, 54%; achieve prevision activity levels made by each hospital: 27%; founding required by each hospital: 11%, and not to exceed the global budget: 8%. Another result obtained with the methodology is the relative importance of the different objectives included in each priority level.

In the same fashion, solving the goal programming problem that derives from the pairwise comparisons matrix yields the weights for each priority level, for each line of activity in the global purchase function, for each line of activity of each hospital, and for the funding demands of each hospital. Table 2 displays the weights for the first priority level.

Table 2: Weights for the global purchase function activities. Andalusian Regional Health Service District hospitals. 1997.

	Weight
Cataracts	7.5
Hernis	3.8
Colecystectomy	3.8
Varicose veins	1.3
Hip arthroplasty	7.5
Hallux valgus	1.3
RTU due to bladder tumour	3.8
Tonsils and adenoids	1.3
Other discharges	7.5
Consultations	7.5
Emergencies with inmediate discharge	7.5
Day surgery	1.5
TOTAL	54.3

In the second level, double priority is given to the activities of the hospitals whose incomes exceed expenditures given the efficient price as defined by the decision center (except for hip arthroplasty and RTU for bladder tumours). The pairwise comparison matrix for the 192 goals is formed by the comparison quadrants of the 12 lines of activity for the 16 hospitals. In this way, the activity for those hospitals with deficit and of arthroplasties and RTUs of those hospitals with a surplus have equal value: half of the rest of activities of the efficient hospitals. Of the 192 goals in this priority level, 40 have priority 0.2 and 152 have priority 0.1, summing 27% of the importance in this second level of priority.

In the third level, the same importance is given to not exceeding the demand for funds (0.7), which adds to 11% of the importance in this priority level.

These are the weights that are introduced in the multiple goal programming for assigning resources to hospitals. Additional information that was used includes SAS data about bounds and undesired deviation variables.

Weighted Goal Programming Model

As a result of the previously stated elements, the following weighted goal programming problem can be defined in order to solve the problem:

$$Min \sum_{k=1}^{r} W_k h_k(n_k, p_k) + \sum_{k=r+1}^{r+(n \cdot r)} W_k h_k(n_k, p_k) +$$

$$+ \sum_{k=r+(n \cdot r)+1}^{n+r+(n \cdot r)} W_k p_k + W_{n+r+(n \cdot r)+1}(n_{n+r+(n \cdot r)+1} + p_{n+r+(n \cdot r)+1})$$

subject to:

$$\left[\sum_{j=1}^{n} x_{ij}\right] + n_i - p_i = X^*_i \quad i = 1, \cdots, r$$

$$x_{ij} + n_{r+(i \cdot j)} - p_{r+(i \cdot j)} = x^*_{ij} \quad i = 1, \cdots, r, \quad j = 1, \cdots, n$$

$$\left[\sum_{i=1}^{r} x_{ij} \pi_i\right] + n_{r+(n \cdot r)+j} - p_{r+(n \cdot r)+j} = g_j - 0.7c_j + \left[\sum_{i=1}^{r} 0.7 h_{ij} \pi_i\right] \quad j = 1, ..., n$$

$$\left[\sum_{j=1}^{n}\left[\sum_{i=1}^{r} x_{ij} \pi_i\right]\right] + n_{n+r+(n \cdot r)+1} - p_{n+r+(n \cdot r)+1} = G - \sum_{j=1}^{n} 0.7 c_j + \sum_{j=1}^{n}\left[\sum_{i=1}^{r} 0.7 h_{ij} \pi_i\right]$$

$$L_{x_i} \le \sum_{j=1}^{n} x_{ij} \le U_{x_i} \quad i = 1, \cdots, r$$

$$x_{ij} \ge 0.7 h_{ij} \quad i = 1, ... r \quad j = 1, ..., n$$

$$\sum_{i=1}^{r}\left(x_{ij} \cdot SH_{x_i}\right) \le SH_j \quad j = 1, ..., n$$

$$\sum_{i=1}^{r}\left(x_{ij} \cdot S_{x_i}\right) \le S_j \quad j = 1, ..., n$$

$$x_{ij} \cdot OH \le OH_j \quad j = 1, ..., n$$

Lexicographic Goal Programming Model

Next, let us state a lexicographic goal Programming model, which implies the consideration of a different utility structure of the decision maker. As it is known, in this scheme, some goals are strictly preferred to other, so that only once the satisfaction of a goal placed in a high priority level is achieved, we intend to satisfy the goals placed on lower priority levels. The model, in our case, would be:

$$Lex \ min \left[\sum_{k=1}^{r} W_k h_k(n_k, p_k), \quad \sum_{k=r+1}^{r+(n^*r)} W_k h_k(n_k, p_k), \quad \sum_{k=r+(n^*r)+1}^{n+r+(n^*r)} W_k p_k, \quad n_{n+r+(n^*r)+1} + p_{n+r+(n^*r)+1} \right]$$

subject to the same constraints as the weighted goal programming model.

The set of goals with the highest priority are the ones corresponding to the global activity levels, next, the activity levels of the different hospitals are considered; in the third priority level, the budget goal for each hospital is placed and finally, the global budget goal is considered.

To place in the fourth and last priority level the achievement of the global budget does not necessarily reflect the preferences of the decision center. It is just a methodological strategy in order to determine the minimum necessary budget to verify the global production necessities of the SAS and the desired activity levels and founds of the hospitals.

In order to solve these problems, a computer package is used, written in FORTRAN 90 (Molina and Caballero, 1998), which uses the NAG subroutine library, mark 17, for the resolution of linear goal programming problems.

RESULTS AND DISCUSSION

The solution of the problem points out that the solution of our problem is satisfactory. The fulfillment function has a value of zero, both in the weighted and in the lexicographic goal programming models. However, the goals of the aspiration levels established by SAS Central Services are reached at the cost of strong deviations in the activity levels (Table 3) and strong budget deviations for each hospital relative to past expenditure (Table 4).

Note, for example, the strong increase that the solution proposes for hip arthroplasties in relation to the level of aspiration formulated by the ARHS Central Services (185%), which implies a 205% increment in the number of arthroplasties with respect to the previous year, 1996). This important deviation (or those deviations of other lines of activity), although significant in some cases (like the decrease from 19% to 17% with respect to the level of aspiration for varicose veins or hernias), does not mean that the desired goals have not been met. This is because the undesired deviation variable is the inverse (in these last two cases, positive)

Table 3. Weighted goal programming solutions for the global purchase function in the budget assignment to Andalusian Health Service hospitals. 1997

	Solution	% Δ Asp.	% Δ Act.
Cataracts	3496	2	12
Hernis	2836	-17	-5
Colecystectomy	1549	-9	-5
Varicose veins	369	-19	-4
Hip arthroplasty	4026	185	205
Hallux valgus	481	-13	-5
RTU due to bladder tumour	612	0	1
Tonsils and adenoids	1371	-11	-5
Other discharges	109403	-5	-1
Consultations	587308	-1	-1
Emergencies with inmediate discharge	564509	-6	-4
Day surgery	11650	0	8

% Δ Asp: % deviation from aspiration level.

% Δ Act.:% deviation from 1996 activity

Table 4. Weighted goal programming solutions for the budget assignment to Andalusian Health Service hospitals. 1997

HOSPITAL	Solution*	% Δ Asp.	% Δ Exp.
4	39085	0	0
2	43796	0	0
12	38570	0	0
5	27990	-5	-5
7	38368	-1	-1
6	37849	0	0
10	32423	0	0
1	40617	-16	-16
16	34722	0	0
3	40322	0	0
8	32463	0	0
15	20750	-17	-17
9	26159	0	5
14	39223	0	11
13	31401	-19	11
11	28876	-25	24

Data in hundred of thousands of pesetas.

% Δ Asp.: % deviations froma aspiration level.

% Δ Exp.:% deviations from 1996 expenditure

Although, as in the case of the global purchase function, the observed deviations do not show that the desired goals were not met, the results clearly point out that there are important variations with respect to the level of aspiration of the ARHS Central Services and with respect to hospital expenditure in the previous year. For example, for hospital 11 (25% decrease with respect to the aspiration level, although this hospital receives 24% more budget than it spent the previous year), hospital 13 (19% decrease with respect to the aspiration level, with an 11% increment over what it spent the previous year), hospital 15 (17% decrease with respect to the aspiration level), and hospital 1 (16% decrease with respect to the aspiration level).

What stands out is the fact that 10 out of the 16 hospitals reached the aspiration level. In 8 of them (hospitals 4, 2, 12, 6, 10, 16, 3 and 8), this level coincides with the previous years' expenditure, and in 2 of them (hospitals 9 and 14) this level implies an increase of 5% and 11% with respect to the previous year's expenditure.

The budget is adjusted in a way that it does not meet demands for funding in 6 cases, 4 of them (hospitals 5, 7, 1, and 15) whose expenditures exceed incomes given the efficient price as defined by the decision center–these hospitals demanded the same budget they had the previous year –and 2 of them (hospitals 11 and 13) whose incomes exceed expenditures given the efficient price. These last two hospitals asked for a budget corresponding to the efficient price; the solution cannot meet these demands by 19% and 25%.

Assuming lexicographic goals, the program solution yields the same levels of global activities expressed in Table 3. There are variations in the hospital budget assignation (priority 3), due to the higher priority given by the hospitals to accomplishing certain activity levels per type of activity.

Given that a satisfying solution has been obtained for the model, it is desirable to carry out a sensitivity analysis. Obviously, a satisfying solution would have been obtained despite the values given to the weights of the goals, unless the target values are changed. For this reason, a sensitivity analysis has been carried out on the target values of the model. Namely, the maximum possible improvement of the target values (in percentages) corresponding to the goals placed in the same priority level has been studied. That is, leaving the rest of the target values unchanged, the best improvement of the goals of each level so that there still exist satisfying solutions has been determined. As the goal placed in the fourth level is a two sided goal, both positive and negative deviations from the current target value have been considered. Besides, another analysis has been carried out to determine the maximum simultaneous improvement of all the target values of the model. The results obtained, displayed in Table 5, show that the model is stable, for changes of at least a 2% of the target values can be done on the goals of one level. On the basis of these data, a Goal Sequential Improvement algorithm has been carried out, as described in Caballero et al. (1998), in order to get a satisfying and efficient solution. Namely, the goals of the first level were improved a 1%, the ones of the second level a 2%, and the goals of the third level achieved their best possible value given the previous two new set of target values. The fourth level was left unchanged, because the original goal is a two sided one (see Table 5).

Table 5. Sensitivity analysis of the target values of the model.

Sensitivity Analysis					
	L1	L2	L3	L4+	L4-
Max. Imp.	2%	3%	2%	2%	5%
	Simultaneous (L4+)			Simultaneous (L4-)	
Max. Imp.	0,5%			1%	
G.S.I. SOLUTION					
		Solution		% Δ Asp.	% Δ Act.
Cataracts		3446		0	10
Hernis		3372		-1	13
Colecystectomy		1689		-1	4
Varicose veins		451		-1	17
Hip arthroplasty		1426		1	8
Hallux valgus		546		-1	8
RTU due to bladder tumour		618		1	2
Tonsils and adenoids		1528		-1	6
Other discharges		113850		-1	3
Consultations		589050		-1	-1
Emergencies with I.D.		594000		-1	1
Day surgery		11766		1	9

Further work will include new iterations with the regulator in order to adjust aspiration levels and restrictions.

Limitations of this model refer to the reliability of existing information systems, the static being of the model. It does not confront dynamic issues related to this topic. Another model aspect is that it drifts away from the standard orthodox economic approaches to financing. These usually maximize single objective utility functions.

REFERENCES

Arrow KJ (1963): *Elección social y valores individuales*. Madrid: I.E.F. [v.o.: (1974) *Social Choice and Individual Values*. New Haven & London: Yale U.P. (1ª ed.: John Wiley & Sons. New York, 1951)].

Blake J, Carter MW (1997). *A goal programming approach to strategic resource allocation in acute care hospitals*. In print.

Caballero R, Rey L and Ruiz F (1998). "Lexicographic Improvement of the Target Values in Convex Goal Programming". *European Journal of Operational Research*, 107: 644-655.

Charnes A, Cooper W, Rhodes E (1978). "Measuring the efficiency of decision making units". North Holland Publishing Company. *European Journal of Operational Research*, 2: 429-444.

Deaton A, Muellbauer J (1986). *Economics and consumer behaviour*. Cambridge University Press, Cambridge.

Debreu G (1959). *Theory of value –An axiomatic analysis of economic equilibrium*. John Wiley and Sons, New York.

Harrald J, Leotta J, Wallace WA, Wendell RE (1978). "A note on the limitations of goal programming as observed in resource allocation for marine environmental protection". *Naval Research Logistics Quarterly*, 25: 733-739.

Lee SM (1973). "An aggregative resource allocation model for hospital administration". *Socio-Economic Planning Sciences*, 7(4): 381-395.

Molina J, Caballero R (1998). *Resolución de problemas multicriterio de metas lexicográficas*. Departamento de Economía Aplicada (Matemáticas). Facultad de Económicas. Universidad de Málaga.

Newhouse JP (1992). *The basis of reimbursing health care providers*. Boston: Harvard University.

Newhouse JP (1996). "Reimbursing health plans and health providers: Efficiency in production versus selection". *Journal of Economic Literature*, 34: 1236-1265.

Numerical Algorithms Group (1995). *NAG FORTRAN library mark 17*. V. Oct 1995.

Panitz E (1988). *The services mix decision in not-for-profit organizations: A math programming approach to community mental health service mix selection*. PhD Dissertation, University of Kentucky.

Riffai AK, Percenka JO (1989). "An application of goal programming in healthcare planning". *International Journal of Production Management* 10, 28:37.

Rodríguez Uría MV, Arenas M, Lafuente E (1997). "Goal programming model for evaluating hospital service performance". In: Caballero R, Ruiz F and Steuer R (Eds.) *Advances in multiobjective and goal Programming*. Lecture Notes in Economics and Mathematical Systems, 455. Springer. pp. 57-65.

Rodríguez Uría MV, Arenas M, Bilbao A, Cerdá E (1998). "Management of surgical waiting lists in public hospitals". *Working Paper of the Instituto Complutense de Análisis Económico* (ICAE), 9817. Universidad Complutense. Madrid.

Romero C (1993). *Teoría de la decisión multicriterio: conceptos, técnicas y aplicaciones*. Alianza Editorial, Madrid.

Romero C (1991). *Handbook of critical issues in goal programming*. Pergamon Press, Oxford.

Schniederjans MJ (1995). *Goal programming. Methodology and applications*. Kluwer Academic Publishers, Boston/Dordrecht/London.

Simon HA (1955) "A behavioural model of rational choice". *Quarterly Journal of Economics*, 69: 99-118.

Simon HA (1957) *Models of man*. John Willey and Sons, New York.

Steuer RE (1986). *Multiple criteria optimization: Theory, computation, and application*. John Wiley and Sons, New York.

Zeleny M (1982). "The pros and cons of goal programming". *Computers & Operations Research*, 8: 357-359.

A SIMULATION MODEL TO EVALUATE THE INTERACTION BETWEEN ACUTE, REHABILITATION, LONG STAY CARE AND THE COMMUNITY

E. El-Darzi[1†], C. Vasilakis[1], T.J. Chaussalet[1], P.H. Millard[2]

[1] University of Westminster, Harrow School of Computer Science, Watford Road, Nothwick Park Harrow, HA1 3TP, United Kingdom

[2] St. George's Hospital Medical School Cranmer Terrace, London SW17 0RE, London, United Kingdom

Abstract: The flow of patients through geriatric hospitals has been previously described in terms of acute (short stay), rehabilitation (medium stay), and long stay states where the bed occupancy at a census point is modelled by a mixed exponential model using BOMPS (Bed Occupancy Modelling and Planning System). In this a patient is initially admitted to acute care. The majority of the patients are discharged within a few days into their own homes or through death. The rest are converted into medium stay patients where they could stay for a few months and thereafter either leave the system to support homes or die or move on to a long stay compartment where they could stay until they die. Patients released to the community from the acute and the rehabilitation compartments may be re-admitted into the geriatric department. The flow model forecasts the average length of stay as well as the average number of patients in each state, but there are certain limitations. In this paper we consider the problem as a queuing system to assess the flow of patients within a geriatric department and community homes, and to allow a greater understanding of bed requirements and effective utilisation of resources. Extensive sensitivity analysis is conducted to demonstrate the interaction between the different streams of flow inside a geriatric department and the different destinations of the patients after discharge.

Key words: Simulation Modelling, Queuing Systems, Bed Occupancy, Geriatric Medicine, Health Care Systems

---

[†] *Author for correspondence:* Dr. E. El-Darzi, email: eldarze@westminster.ac.uk

S.H. Zanakis et al. (eds.), Decision Making: Recent Developments and Worldwide Applications, 475–485.
© 2000 *Kluwer Academic Publishers.*

INTRODUCTION

Flow modelling is a different approach to the measurement and planning of health care resources. In previous work [El-Darzi et al.,1998] we used a simulation model to evaluate the flow of patients within the acute, rehabilitative and long-term compartments of a department of geriatric medicine. As in other situations where queues form, a key explanatory variable is the difficulty in servicing long-term patients. The analysis showed that simulation modelling has advantages because it demonstrates the fluctuations that can occur in occupancy and emptiness due to random variations in the number of people being serviced.

Key components of the simulation model were the concepts that patients arrive randomly and independently of each other, that length of stay in the three-compartments of acute, rehabilitative and long stay is exponentially distributed and that queues form (which 'block beds') when patients are identified as needing rehabilitation or long stay care and no beds 'server units' are available. Two models were executed, one with and one without resource constraints. In this paper we extend the model to include two community compartments, one representing those patients who are treated in acute wards and who return home well, another representing those who will need supportive care after discharge.

BACKGROUND TO THE METHODS

Flow modelling

Feldstein [1963] developed a behavioural theory of flow after he observed staff adjusting admissions rather than increasing discharges, the idea being the staff interact with resources to form streams of flow. Millard [1992a] further developed the behavioural theory as an explanation of observed changing annual admissions in his department of geriatric medicine. An observation that mixed exponential equations fit bed census data led to a mathematical solution, first to a two-compartment model of flow [Harrison and Millard, 1991] then to a three-compartment model of flow [Harrison, 1994].

Using task specific software bed usage behaviour can be generated from data collected in one-day censuses. The statistics concern the overall bed allocation and expected stay, the estimated daily admissions, the number of beds and average length of stay of short-stay, medium-stay and long-stay patients, the likelihood that a patient will be discharged from each compartment, and the conversion rates between the short stay, medium stay and long stay care [Wyatt, 1995; McClean and Millard, 1995]. Furthermore, because the model is based on a dynamic theory of flow, the outcome of different decisions can be pre-tested.

Although the model gives important insights into the process of care there are limitations in its usefulness as a decision making tool, due to the deterministic nature of the results. Work by Irvine and McClean [1994], McClean and Millard [1993b], Taylor et al. [1997] has further expanded the model to include community compartments and to estimate costs [McClean et al., 1998].

The geriatric department studied

The data used in this model are from a North London department of geriatric medicine [Mitchell et al., 1987]. Parry [1996] has applied to this census data the bed-census flow-rate methodology to evaluate the outcome of introducing a new style of in-patient management. The analysis indicated that a major explanatory factor for improvement in acute admissions was the enhancement of off-site rehabilitation.

THE SIMULATION MODELS

Discrete-event simulation models have been applied extensively for planning and managing health care departments [Davies, 1985b; Davies, 1985a; Davies, 1994; Davies and Davies, 1995; Crofts et al. 1997; Davies and Davies, 1997; Hudson et al., 1997], because this technique permits simulated patients to have attributes that influence their progress through the system [Davies and Davies, 1986]. Discrete-event simulations provide, in general, flexibility, robustness and accuracy. They can as easily deal with problems at a national level as with the problems and constraints of a single hospital unit.

As geriatric patients are referred to departments of geriatric medicine by their general practitioner randomly and independently of each other, their interarrival times can be considered to be independent, identically distributed variables (IID). Irvine and McClean [1994] have shown that the arrival behaviour of geriatric patients can be described by an exponential distribution. Thus, the number of patients arriving in the hospital follows a Poisson distribution. Although admission to a department of geriatric medicine is nearly always preceded by a stage of review, at this stage of model building the admission rate is considered to be the same as the arrival rate.

Although the numerical distribution of departure times in geriatric medicine is represented by a log-normal and exponential function [McClean and Millard, 1993a], the mathematical solution to the behavioural theory of flow [Harrison and Millard, 1991] gives an exponential survival time in each compartment. So the service times in each compartment for each patient are IID random variables that can be described by an exponential distribution.

The Unconstrained Model

The model contains five compartments (see figure 1) categorised as internal to the hospital and as external. The internal compartments are acute, rehabilitation and long stay. These compartments have been set according to the description of the flow model and their parameters (length of stay, conversion rates between the compartments) were set as in Parry [1996]. The external compartments are community (un-supportive) and community (supportive), the clinical reason being that rehabilitated patients are clinically more likely to need community support. The survival of these patients can be described by an exponential distribution [Taylor,1997]. The chance of dying in hospitals is around 20% [Millard, 1992b].

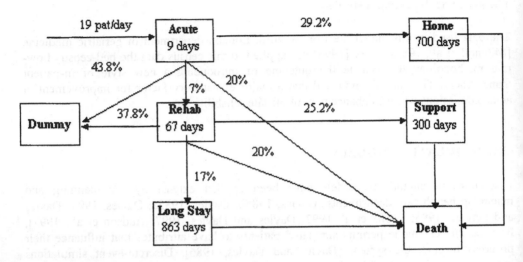

Figure 1. The 5-compartmental unconstrained model

The parameters of the model are:

- admission rate: 19 patients per day,
- average length of stay in the acute, rehabilitation and long stay: 9, 67 and 863 days respectively on exponential average,
- average length of stay in the community home and support homes: 700 and 300 days respectively on exponential average.
- conversion rate from acute to rehabilitation: 7%,
- conversion rate from acute to community homes: 29.2%
- conversion rate from rehabilitation to long stay: 17%.
- conversion rate from rehabilitation to support homes: 25.2%.
- death rate: 20% for both compartments

As may be seen in figure 1 a dummy node has also been added to the model. From empirical observations, and as has been confirmed by an analysis of data sets, around 60% of the incoming patients are former patient of the hospital. By introducing this node and by diverting 60% of the patients originally routed to the community and support homes, we avoid double counting the former patients in those two external compartments. However, these patients are counted in the internal compartments.

The patients enter the system through the acute compartment where they stay an exponential average of 9 days Then, 7% are converted into rehabilitation patients and 20% die. From the rest of the patients, 29.2% ($0.73 \times 0.4 = 0.292$) enter the community homes compartment where they will stay for 700 days before eventually dying; and 43.8% (0.73

× 0.6 = 0.438) leave the system through the dummy node and will not be part of the statistics. The patients in the rehabilitation compartment will stay an additional 67 days on exponential average and after that they leave the hospital at a rate of 83%. From those patients, 25.2% (0.63 × 0.4 = 0.252) will enter the support homes compartment where they will stay for 300 days before dying and 37.8% (0.63 × 0.6 = 0.378) will leave the system through the dummy node. The remaining 17% becomes long stay patients where, on average, they stay an additional 863 days. All long stay patients leave the system by death.

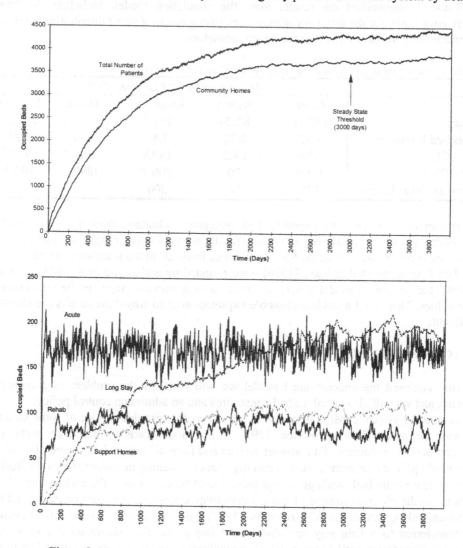

Figure 2. The warm-up period and the steady-state threshold of the system

The model was executed using the batch-means method, which is based on a single long run that was divided into 10 batches. Each batch represents 4000 days of steady state; the initial warming-up period was 5000 days. Data were collected after the model had reached steady state. Figure 2 shows that it takes more than 8 years (3000 days) for the system to reach steady state with its current configuration. This is because patients in the long stay, community home, and support home compartments accumulate gradually due to the high exponential average length of stay.

Table 1 summarises the results from the simulation model, including the 95% confidence limits for the mean occupancy rates (using the *student's t* distribution) and the estimates from the flow model for the same parameters.

Table 1. Simulation results from the 6 compartmental model (from 10 batches)

	Mean Number of Occupied Beds				
	Acute	Rehab	Long stay	Home	Support
Mean	170.91	88.74	195.3	3882.25	100.40
Standard Deviation	1.22	1.77	7.54	23.69	3.24
95% CL -	170	87.5	189.9	3865.3	98.1
95% CL +	171.8	90	200.7	3899.2	102.7
Flow-model estimates	175	94	204	-	-

It can be seen that the expected bed occupancy obtained from the flow model (BOMPS) and the unconstrained simulation model are very close, despite the fact that the flow model results are outside the 95% confidence intervals of the simulation model.

The figures reported in Parry [1996] were rounded up and as shown in El-Darzi et al. [1998], the simulation model is very sensitive to even minor changes in the conversion-rate values. This could provide a plausible explanation as to why these results are slightly different.

The Constrained Model

Having analysed the unconstrained model we will consider the problem as a queuing system, and we will also introduce bed constraints and an admission control policy.

A queuing system consists of one or more servers that provide service of some kind to arriving customers [Law and Kelton, 1991]. In our model, beds are the server units and patients are the customers. If a customer arrives and finds all servers busy, generally, he or she would join one or more queues. Similarly, patients waiting in queues within the health care system create bed blockage. In the behavioural theory of flow the beds occupied by patients in the different streams of acute, rehabilitative and long stay care are separated by decision-making thresholds [Millard, 1989]. For instance, if a rehabilitative patient cannot be transferred to a long stay unit that would imply that this patient must wait in the rehabilitation stream until a long stay bed is available. This, in a sense, is equivalent to an internal queue. If a patient arrives for admission and no acute beds are available then an external queue (the waiting list) is created. In reality, however, and especially in a geriatric medicine department, the incoming patient will be admitted by a different department, typically general medicine. Hence, in our model, if there are no available beds in the acute compartment the arriving patients will be rejected from the system.

The queue in the rehabilitation compartment represents bed blockage between the acute and the rehabilitation compartments, meaning that patients within the queue are still occupying beds in the first compartment. An occupied bed will again be available once a queued patient is allocated a bed in the second compartment. Accordingly, the second queue represents bed blockage between the rehabilitation and the long stay compartments.

The number of beds of each compartment was determined from the simulation results of the unconstrained model. The mean number of occupied beds was used and an assumption was made that the hospital operates under different levels of emptiness in each compartment. These levels were chosen as follows: 20% for the acute, 5% for the rehabilitation, and 1% for the long stay compartment and the number of beds were set at 214, 94, and 191 respectively. For example, the number of beds in the acute compartment was calculated as follows: $171 \div 0.8 \approx 214$ beds. These levels of emptiness were based on clinical judgement. In addition, the conversion rates were reduced to 6.5% from acute to rehabilitation and to 16.5% from rehabilitation to long stay. This reduction resulted in a more stable system. For a complete description of this model, refer to El-Darzi et al. [1998].

Furthermore, for a better approximation of the real-life system, it is assumed that 20% of the patients leaving the acute compartment enter the support homes compartment. After studying the system it became apparent that in a catchment area of the size of the hospital under study, there is a need for more places in homes than the figures the initial model suggested.

In table 2, a typical output from the constrained model is demonstrated with averages, standard deviations and 95% confidence intervals for the observed parameters. These include the percentage of emptiness in each compartment within the hospital and the percentage of patients for which admission was refused because the acute compartment was full. In addition, the figures of the two queues are reported for the rehabilitation and long stay compartments. These are the average number of patients in the queue, the average time spent (in days) and the maximum queue length. The last two columns report the average number of former patients in the two external compartments.

As a result of altering the percentage of patients entering the external compartments from the acute compartment (20% of the acute patients are now entering the supportive homes), we now have less people in the unsupportive compartment and more in the supportive one (3,110 and 427 respectively) as compared to the results of the unconstrained model (3,899 and 103) . These results are a very close approximation of the real life system.

Table 2 Results from the constrained model (10 batches)

	Acute		Rehab			
	% of patients refused admission	Avg % of emptiness	Avg. # of patients in the queue	Avg. time spent in the queue	Max queue length	Avg % of emptiness
Mean	0.3%	18.72%	3.52	2.48	43.9	10.54%
SD	0.4%	0.95%	2.5	1.8	19.14	1.91%
95% CL -	0%	18%	1.7	1.2	30.2	9.2%
95% CL +	0.6%	19.4%	5.3	3.8	57.6	11.9%

	Long stay				Home	Support
	Avg # of patients in the queue	Avg. time spent in the queue	Max queue length	Avg % of emptiness	Avg # in the compart-ment	Avg # in the compart-ment
Mean	1.54	7.62	18.1	7.1%	3,110	427
SD	1.29	6.47	9.76	2.51%	19.59	7.82
95% CL -	0.6	3	11.1	5.3%	3,096	422
95% CL +	2.5	12.3	25.1	8.9%	3,124	433

Sensitivity Analysis

This system runs under the assumption that 60% of the admitted patients are former patients. An extensive sensitivity analysis was carried out to evaluate the effect on the system by increasing the length of stay in the rehabilitation compartment by 5% and in the meantime reducing the percentage of former patients re-entering the system by 0%, 1%, 2%, 3%, 4% and 5%. There is a common belief among many geriatricians that an increase in the rehabilitation period could have a positive effect on the overall performance. The aim of the sensitivity analysis is to test this assumption.

As it can be seen from Table 3, the emptiness in the acute compartment can only be improved if the percentage of former patients re-entering the system is decreased by at least 2%. Also there are no major changes in the rehabilitation and long stay compartments. Nonetheless, a better utilisation of resources can be observed.

In conclusion, if we increase the length of stay by 5% and the percentage of former patients coming back is reduced then the system will be able to treat more patients in the long run.

Table 3 Results from the sensitivity analysis

	Acute		Rehab			Long stay			Home	Support
	% of pat. refused admission	Avg % of emptiness	Avg # of pat. in the queue	Avg. time spent in the queue	Avg % of emptiness	Avg # of patients in the queue	Avg. time spent in the queue	Avg % of emptiness	Avg # of patients in compartment	Avg # of patients in compartment
Initial										
Mean	0.3	19	3.52	2.48	10.54	1.54	7.62	7	3,110	427
SD	0.4	0.95	2.50	1.80	1.91	1.29	6.47	2.51	19.59	7.82
95 CL -	0.0	18.0	1.7	1.2	9.17	0.6	3.0	5.3	3,096	422
95 CL +	0.6	19.4	5.3	3.8	11.91	2.5	12.3	8.9	3,124	433
0%										
Mean	0.3	18	5.54	3.85	6.84	0.67	3.22	9	3,106	427
SD	0.5	1.90	4.32	3.00	1.81	1.20	5.66	3.20	18.56	4.62
95 CL -	0.0	16.5	2.4	1.7	5.55	-0.2	-0.8	6.9	3,092	424
95 CL +	0.7	19.2	8.6	6.0	8.13	1.5	7.3	11.5	3,119	431
1%										
Mean	0.3	18	5.61	3.91	7.28	1.07	5.22	9	3,173	436
SD	0.3	1.70	3.81	2.63	2.52	1.47	7.13	3.54	28.51	6.01
95 CL -	0.1	17.1	2.9	2.0	5.47	0.0	0.1	6.4	3,152	432
95 CL +	0.6	19.5	8.3	5.8	9.08	2.1	10.3	11.5	3,193	441
2%										
Mean	0.1	20	2.95	2.08	8.53	0.13	0.67	12	3,224	444
SD	0.1	0.81	1.47	1.02	1.52	0.20	0.98	1.67	21.43	4.60
95 CL -	0.0	19.3	1.9	1.3	7.44	0.0	0.0	10.5	3,209	441
95 CL +	0.2	20.4	4.0	2.8	9.62	0.3	1.4	12.9	3,240	447
3%										
Mean	0.2	20	3.56	2.50	8.89	0.49	2.38	11	3,301	455
SD	0.3	1.30	3.31	2.29	2.55	0.68	3.29	3.70	25.59	6.19
95 CL -	0.0	19.0	1.2	0.9	7.07	0.0	0.0	8.3	3,283	451
95 CL +	0.4	20.8	5.9	4.1	10.71	1.0	4.7	13.6	3,320	460
4%										
Mean	0.1	21	2.04	1.46	10.28	0.14	0.74	13	3,356	462
SD	0.2	0.69	1.70	1.23	1.79	0.36	1.85	3.65	20.83	6.65
95 CL -	0.0	20.7	0.8	0.6	9.00	-0.1	-0.6	10.6	3,342	457
95 CL +	0.2	21.7	3.3	2.3	11.56	0.4	2.1	15.9	3,371	467
5%										
Mean	0.1	21	2.52	1.80	9.72	0.84	4.14	9	3,416	469
SD	0.1	0.90	1.62	1.15	1.72	1.03	5.03	3.69	21.65	5.33
95 CL -	0.0	20.7	1.4	1.0	8.49	0.1	0.5	6.8	3,400	465
95 CL +	0.1	22.0	3.7	2.6	10.95	1.6	7.7	12.1	3,431	472

Technical Details

The models were built using the MicroSaint simulation package. MicroSaint is an icon-based, network simulation software package that lets the user build models to simulate real-life processes. The computer used was an IMB PC compatible with a 450 MHz Pentium III processor and 128 MB of RAM. The operating system was the Windows NT 4.0 . The average running time was approximately 1.5 hours for the single long run.

CONCLUSIONS

In this paper we used discrete-event simulation and flow-modelling techniques to evaluate the flow of patients within a geriatric department. Our results show that these models are viable tools to measure bed occupancy in a geriatric department. Where statistics are needed for community homes, the flow model could be used to generate the simulation model input parameters. The simulation model results have proved that by increasing the length of stay in the rehabilitation and in the meantime reducing the percentage of former patients entering the system the overall, performance will be improved in the long run.

As integrated services are becoming increasingly important, the need for models with the ability of incorporating these different services of care is becoming more urgent. The models described in this paper constitute one of the first attempts towards this target. Flow modelling is a well established methodology with sufficient scientific backing, and discrete-event simulation models can enhance its capabilities by including the stochastic nature of the real-life system and the extensive what-if scenarios.

REFERENCES

Crofts, P., Barlow, J. and Edwards, R. (1997) A CliniQueue Solution. *OR Insight* **10**, 22-27.

Davies, H.O. and Davies, R. (1995) Simulating health systems: modelling problems and software solutions. *European Journal of Operational Research* **87**, 35-44.

Davies, H.O. and Davies, R. (1997) A simulation model for planning services of renal patients in Europe. *Journal of Operational Reseach Society* **38**, 693-700.

Davies, R. (1985a) An interactive simulation in the Health Service. *Journal of Operational Reseach Society* **36**, 597-606.

Davies, R. (1985b) An assessment of models of a health system. *Journal of Operational Reseach Society* **36**, 679-687.

Davies, R. (1994) Simulation for planning services for patients with coronary artery disease. *European Journal of Operational Research* **71**, 323-332.

Davies, R. and Davies, T. (1986) Using simulation to plan health service resources: discussion paper. *Journal of the Royal Society of Medicine* **79**, 154-157.

El-Darzi, E., Vasilakis, C., Chaussalet, T., and Millard P (1998) A simulation modelling approach to evaluating length of stay, occupancy, emptiness and bed blocking in a hospital geriatric department. *Health Care Management Science* **1**, 143-149.

Feldstein, M.S. (1963) Operational research and efficiency in the Health Service. *Lancet* **i**, 491-493.

Harrison, G.W. (1994) Compartmental models of hospital patient occupancy patterns. In: Millard, P.H. and McClean, S.I. (Eds.) *Modelling hospital resource use: a different approach to the planning and control of health care systems*, pp. 53-61. London: Royal Society of Medicine

Harrison, G.W. and Millard, P.H. (1991) Balancing acute and long-term care: the mathematics of throughput in departments of geriatric medicine. *Meth. Inform. Med.* **30**, 221-228.

Hudson, P.E., Peel, V. and Rayner, A. (1997) Using computer simulation to plan Accident & Emergency services. *British Journal of Health Care Management* **3**,

Irvine, V. and McClean, S.I. (1994) Stochastic models for geriatric in-patient behaviour. *IMA J. Math. App. Med. Biol.* **11**, 207-216.

McClean, S.I. and Millard, P.H. (1993a) Patterns of length of stay after admission in geriatric medicine: an event history approach. *The Statistician* **42**, 263-274.

McClean, S.I. and Millard, P.H. (1993b) Modelling in-patient bed usage behaviour in a department of geriatric medicine. *Meth. Inform. Med.* **32**, 79-81.

McClean, S.I. and Millard, P.H. (1995) A decision support system for bed-occupancy management and planning hospitals. *IMA J. Math. App. Med. Biol.* **12**, 225-234.

McClean, S.I., McAlea, B. and Millard, P.H. (1998) Using a Markov reward model to estimate spend-down costs for a geriatric department. *Journal of Operational Reseach Society* **49**, 1021-1025.

Millard, P.H. (1992a) Throughput in a department of geriatric medicine: a problem of time, space and behaviour. *Health Trends* **24**, 20-24.

Millard, P.H. (1992b) Geriatric medicine: a new method of measuring bed usage and a theory for planning. MD Thesis, University of London

Millard, P.H. (1994) Current measures and their defects. In: Millard, P.H. and McClean, S.I. (Eds.) *Modelling hospital resource use: a different approach to the planning and control of health care systems*, pp. 29-37. London: Royal Society of Medicine]

Mitchell, J., Kafetz, K. and Rossiter, B. (1987) Benefits of effective hospital services for elderly people. *Br. Med. J.* **295**, 980-993.

Parry, A. (1996) An age-related service revisited. In: Millard, P.H. and McClean, S.I. (Eds.) *Go with the flow: a systems approach to healthcare planning*, pp. 127-130. London: Royal Society of Medicine Press Limited]

Taylor, G.J., McClean, S.I. and Millard, P.H. (1998) Continuous-time Markov model for geriatric patient behaviour. *Applied Stochastic Models and Data Analysis* **13**, 315-323.

Taylor, G.J. (1997) Geriatric flow rate modelling. [Faculty of Informatics]. University of Ulster. pp.1-204. Doctorate of Philosophy.

Wyatt, S. (1995) The occupancy management and planning system (BOMPS). *Lancet* **345** 243-244.

AUTHOR INDEX

Agorastos, C. 361
Alexouda, G. 131
Angelides, M. 425
Angelides, M.C. 425
Antunes, C.A. 251
Arcelus, F.J. 97
Baker, J.R. 443
Bana e Costa, C. A. 317
Baourakis, G. 115
Barrett, M.A. 65
Bartzis, J. 381
Berry, R.A. 413
Caballero, R. 459
Chajakis, E.D. 279
Chao-Fu, Chen 183
Chaussalet, T.J. 475
Chevalier, A. 157
Clewlow, L. 197
Clímaco, J. 251
Dhir, K.S. 49
Diakoulaki, D. 263
Doukidis, G.I. 397
Doumpos, M. 361
Drury, D.H. 3
Ehrhardt, J. 381
El-Darzi, E. 475
French, S. 381
Gefen, D. 17
Ghai, G.L. 143
Giaglis, G.M. 397
Gómez, T. 459
Greco, S. 295
Gupta, J.P. 183
Hodges, S. 197
Holloway, R.A. 413
Hort, L.K. 65
Huhn, S.T. 413
Iacopetta, J.-P. 157
Katsaros, P. 347
Krassadaki, E. 331
Kunsch, P.L. 157

Lamb, J.M. 31
Lassithiotaki, E. 115
Lattimore, P.K. 443
Lochard, J. 381
López del Amo, M.P. 459
Manikas, K.M. 397
Martín, J.J. 459
Matarazzo, B. 295
Matthew, D. 213
Mavrotas, G. 263
Miliotis, P. 397
Millard, P.H. 475
Molina, J. 459
Morrey, M. 381
Nasierowski, W. 97
Pactwa, T.E. 143
Pandey, I.M. 183
Papamichail, K.N. 381
Paparrizos, K. 131
Pardalos, P.M. 115
Pentaraki, K. 361
Pergioudakis, V. 397
Platt, W.H. 49
Pombortsis, A. 347
Potter, B.A. 413
Prakash, A.J. 143
Refanidis, I. 347
Ruiz, F. 459
Saydam, A.C. 443
Singh, H. 83
Sinkko, K. 381
Siskos, Y. 331
Skiadopoulos, G. 197
Slowinski, R. 295
Smart, C.R. 31
Smith, D.L. 213
Sohier, A. 381
Stamelos, I. 347
Theys, M. 157
Tsoukias, A. 347
Vansnick, J.-C. 317
Vasilakis, C. 475
Vlahavas, I. 347
Walczak, S. 173
Watts, G. 49

Wu, Y. 213
Yager, R.R. 233
Zopounidis, C. 361

Applied Optimization

1. D.-Z. Du and D.F. Hsu (eds.): *Combinatorial Network Theory.* 1996
ISBN 0-7923-3777-8

2. M.J. Panik: *Linear Programming: Mathematics, Theory and Algorithms.* 1996
ISBN 0-7923-3782-4

3. R.B. Kearfott and V. Kreinovich (eds.): *Applications of Interval Computations.* 1996
ISBN 0-7923-3847-2

4. N. Hritonenko and Y. Yatsenko: *Modeling and Optimimization of the Lifetime of Technology.* 1996
ISBN 0-7923-4014-0

5. T. Terlaky (ed.): *Interior Point Methods of Mathematical Programming.* 1996
ISBN 0-7923-4201-1

6. B. Jansen: *Interior Point Techniques in Optimization.* Complementarity, Sensitivity and Algorithms. 1997
ISBN 0-7923-4430-8

7. A. Migdalas, P.M. Pardalos and S. Storøy (eds.): *Parallel Computing in Optimization.* 1997
ISBN 0-7923-4583-5

8. F.A. Lootsma: *Fuzzy Logic for Planning and Decision Making.* 1997
ISBN 0-7923-4681-5

9. J.A. dos Santos Gromicho: *Quasiconvex Optimization and Location Theory.* 1998
ISBN 0-7923-4694-7

10. V. Kreinovich, A. Lakeyev, J. Rohn and P. Kahl: *Computational Complexity and Feasibility of Data Processing and Interval Computations.* 1998
ISBN 0-7923-4865-6

11. J. Gil-Aluja: *The Interactive Management of Human Resources in Uncertainty.* 1998
ISBN 0-7923-4886-9

12. C. Zopounidis and A.I. Dimitras: *Multicriteria Decision Aid Methods for the Prediction of Business Failure.* 1998
ISBN 0-7923-4900-8

13. F. Giannessi, S. Komlósi and T. Rapcsák (eds.): *New Trends in Mathematical Programming.* Homage to Steven Vajda. 1998
ISBN 0-7923-5036-7

14. Ya-xiang Yuan (ed.): *Advances in Nonlinear Programming.* Proceedings of the '96 International Conference on Nonlinear Programming. 1998
ISBN 0-7923-5053-7

15. W.W. Hager and P.M. Pardalos: *Optimal Control.* Theory, Algorithms, and Applications. 1998
ISBN 0-7923-5067-7

16. Gang Yu (ed.): *Industrial Applications of Combinatorial Optimization.* 1998
ISBN 0-7923-5073-1

17. D. Braha and O. Maimon (eds.): *A Mathematical Theory of Design: Foundations, Algorithms and Applications.* 1998
ISBN 0-7923-5079-0

Applied Optimization

18. O. Maimon, E. Khmelnitsky and K. Kogan: *Optimal Flow Control in Manufacturing.* Production Planning and Scheduling. 1998 ISBN 0-7923-5106-1

19. C. Zopounidis and P.M. Pardalos (eds.): *Managing in Uncertainty: Theory and Practice.* 1998 ISBN 0-7923-5110-X

20. A.S. Belenky: *Operations Research in Transportation Systems:* Ideas and Schemes of Optimization Methods for Strategic Planning and Operations Management. 1998 ISBN 0-7923-5157-6

21. J. Gil-Aluja: *Investment in Uncertainty.* 1999 ISBN 0-7923-5296-3

22. M. Fukushima and L. Qi (eds.): *Reformulation: Nonsmooth, Piecewise Smooth, Semismooth and Smooting Methods.* 1999 ISBN 0-7923-5320-X

23. M. Patriksson: *Nonlinear Programming and Variational Inequality Problems.* A Unified Approach. 1999 ISBN 0-7923-5455-9

24. R. De Leone, A. Murli, P.M. Pardalos and G. Toraldo (eds.): *High Performance Algorithms and Software in Nonlinear Optimization.* 1999 ISBN 0-7923-5483-4

25. A. Schöbel: *Locating Lines and Hyperplanes.* Theory and Algorithms. 1999 ISBN 0-7923-5559-8

26. R.B. Statnikov: *Multicriteria Design.* Optimization and Identification. 1999 ISBN 0-7923-5560-1

27. V. Tsurkov and A. Mironov: *Minimax under Transportation Constrains.* 1999 ISBN 0-7923-5609-8

28. V.I. Ivanov: *Model Development and Optimization.* 1999 ISBN 0-7923-5610-1

29. F.A. Lootsma: *Multi-Criteria Decision Analysis via Ratio and Difference Judgement.* 1999 ISBN 0-7923-5669-1

30. A. Eberhard, R. Hill, D. Ralph and B.M. Glover (eds.): *Progress in Optimization.* Contributions from Australasia. 1999 ISBN 0-7923-5733-7

31. T. Hürlimann: *Mathematical Modeling and Optimization.* An Essay for the Design of Computer-Based Modeling Tools. 1999 ISBN 0-7923-5927-5

32. J. Gil-Aluja: *Elements for a Theory of Decision in Uncertainty.* 1999 ISBN 0-7923-5987-9

33. H. Frenk, K. Roos, T. Terlaky and S. Zhang (eds.): *High Performance Optimization.* 1999 ISBN 0-7923-6013-3

34. N. Hritonenko and Y. Yatsenko: *Mathematical Modeling in Economics, Ecology and the Environment.* 1999 ISBN 0-7923-6015-X

35. J. Virant: *Design Considerations of Time in Fuzzy Systems.* 2000 ISBN 0-7923-6100-8

Applied Optimization

36. G. Di Pillo and F. Giannessi (eds.): *Nonlinear Optimization and Related Topics.* 2000
    ISBN 0-7923-6109-1
37. V. Tsurkov: *Hierarchical Optimization and Mathematical Physics.* 2000
    ISBN 0-7923-6175-X
38. C. Zopounidis and M. Doumpos: *Intelligent Decision Aiding Systems Based on Multiple Criteria for Financial Engineering.* 2000   ISBN 0-7923-6273-X
39. X. Yang, A.I. Mees, M. Fisher and L.Jennings (eds.): *Progress in Optimization.* Contributions from Australasia. 2000   ISBN 0-7923-6175-X
40. D. Butnariu and A.N. Iusem: *Totally Convex Functions for Fixed Points Computation and Infinite Dimensional Optimization.* 2000   ISBN 0-7923-6287-X
41. J. Mockus: *A Set of Examples of Global and Discrete Optimization.* Applications of Bayesian Heuristic Approach. 2000   ISBN 0-7923-6359-0
42. H. Neunzert and A.H. Siddiqi: *Topics in Industrial Mathematics.* Case Studies and Related Mathematical Methods. 2000   ISBN 0-7923-6417-1
43. K. Kogan and E. Khmelnitsky: *Scheduling: Control-Based Theory and Polynomial-Time Algorithms.* 2000   ISBN 0-7923-6486-4
44. E. Triantaphyllou: *Multi-Criteria Decision Making Methods.* A Comparative Study. 2000   ISBN 0-7923-6607-7
45. S.H. Zanakis, G. Doukidis and C. Zopounidis (eds.): *Decision Making: Recent Developments and Worldwide Applications.* 2000   ISBN 0-7923-6621-2

KLUWER ACADEMIC PUBLISHERS – DORDRECHT / BOSTON / LONDON